LETTER
NIGE

BY

ELIZABETH DEEKS

VOLUME TWO

FROM VINING CENTRE, AKURE
1972 - 1980

EDITED BY WINSTON FORDE

Published by New Generation Publishing in 2022

First Edition

ISBN

Paperback	978-1-80369-488-7
Hardback	978-1-80369-489-4
Ebook	978-1-80369-490-0

www.newgeneration-publishing.com

New Generation Publishing

Dedication

In memory of my parents, Spen and Cathie Deeks

Acknowledgements

I want to thank my mother who kept all the letters I wrote home for all the time I was working in Nigeria. I want to thank Winston, my nieces Sacha and Nicola and my 'bubble' friend Hilary who helped with all the typing of the letters. Hilary is my computer assistant for Volume 2. In addition, Katie Beardsworth who helped so much with maps. Thanks also to Winston Forde for continuing in his role as the editor. There would be no books without Winston. He has done more than half the work. It's 'our second book'.

Content

Prologue

The first volume of my 'Letters from Nigeria' was published in July 2021 and tells of the time between 1965 and 1970 when I was teaching in St Monica's Grammar School, Ondo. All my letters are written to my parents, Rev and Mrs. Spen and Cathie Deeks. I followed in their footsteps to go to Nigeria with the Church Mission Society. They were on the staff of St Andrew's College Oyo in the 1930's. My second volume contains letters written between 1972 and 1980 when I was in Akure on the staff of the Vining Centre, which is now called the Archbishop Vining College of Theology. As you will see, this became a new experience for me.

Introduction

Volume 1 of my Letters from Nigeria ended in December 1971 after I spent that year in England, working in Foxbury, the CMS house in Chislehurst, doing some Yoruba study at SOAS (the School of Oriental and African Studies) and helping my parents move from Enfield to Malvern where they eventually retired.

In January 1972 I returned to Nigeria to be the Women's Warden at the Vining Christian Leadership Centre in Akure. This was a challenging move because the job was completely different from teaching in a Secondary School like St Monica's Girls Grammar School in Ondo.

The women's work in Akure was part of the CMS history in Yorubaland where the education of women who were the wives of church workers or Christian teachers had begun at the end of the 18th century. There are letters in the Archive collection in Birmingham University written by women who went as missionaries with CMS, which I read when I worked in Crowther Hall in Birmingham. The early letters from Miss Caroline Cleggett Boyton relate to the women's training in Akure. She was born in 1867 and was a governess in Germany and England before she offered to go overseas with CMS in 1895. She sailed in October 1895 to be on the staff of the Lagos Girl's Seminary which had originally started with 16 pupils in 1869 when it was called the CMS Female Institution. That was even before CMS founded St Andrew's College Oyo as a teacher training College in 1896. It was the first educational establishment for girls in Lagos and there were 6 special places reserved for the daughters of clergy, catechists or school masters engaged in the service of CMS. These foundation members were educated free for 2 years but could stay for another year if they showed a desire to teach and agreed to work for CMS for 2 years.

The CMS Secretary of the Yoruba Mission who lived in the CMS House in Abeokuta at the time Miss Boyton came to Lagos was concerned for her welfare and said that she should not be left alone at the Lagos Seminary, so she was usually joined by a second woman missionary. After she spent 20 months in Lagos, she was unexpectedly asked to go to Sierra Leone to teach in the Annie Walsh Memorial School (AWMS) for the autumn term. The request came by telegram, and she sailed to Freetown on MV Accra in which I sailed to Nigeria in 1965.

Miss Boyton went on leave early in 1898 and she returned to Lagos in August and stayed there as a teacher and then as the Lady Principal until 1907. There were developments in the school and a new building was erected in the Mission grounds after the style of the AWMS in Freetown. The classes taught were reading, writing, arithmetic, and bible knowledge as well as what were called 'industrial subjects' – which were laundry, housework and sewing. A similar Centre for training women was set up in Ibadan where it was referred to as the Kudeti School and Miss Boyton was sent to be in charge there for the next 10 years. She did go on leave to England during that time by ship, but it was the time of the First World War, and some missionaries went to the Cameroons for their leave because going by ship was dangerous. Miss Wait had the terrible experience of her ship being torpedoed when she was returning to Nigeria in 1915 and although she was rescued after getting into a lifeboat…110 passengers and crew were lost on that day and some CMS missionaries perished at other times.

After Miss Boyton went on leave in 1916 it was suggested that she should start the training for the wives of church agents in the interior when she returned. Ado Ekiti was suggested as a suitable place, but it was impossible to find a suitable site there so Akure was chosen. When she returned from leave in November she went to Ilesha for a few weeks because it had not been possible to complete the arrangements for the beginning of the work in Akure but on December 11th she was sent to Zaria to keep another CMS missionary woman, Miss Paddan, company. (Miss Paddan is described as 'the lady of leisure' and Dr Walter Miller in Zaria expressed reservations about her suitability to be one of the CMS missionaries.) So, Miss Boyton stayed with her until she went on leave in May. Miss Boyton did go to Akure in 1917 and lived in the Akure Parsonage and started a preliminary class there for 6 girls. Lessons took place in a shed put up for the purpose in the Parsonage Garden. The Numbers were limited until new buildings were erected. Instruction was given in laundry work and sewing as well as in English

The site was pegged out for the new houses but in January 1918 there was a further delay because the cost of the buildings exceeded the estimates and there was £160 yet to be found. Miss Boyton wrote a report in January 1919 to say that the work had begun but had to be abandoned. So, nothing happened in Akure in 1918. Miss Boyton and a recruit, Miss J Mars were needed in Kudeti.

This was the rather shaky beginning of the Women's Training Centre (WTC). and Miss C Boyton and Miss J Mars began to work there in 1919. In the book – The Romance of the Black River – The story of the CMS Nigeria Mission written in 1931 by F. Deauville Walker, the girls training class in Akure is mentioned as "doing a very useful work for girls who want a thoroughly practical and non-literary education. Two European women are in charge, and it is the centre for girls' work in the whole Yoruba country. Girls come long distances for training. Such subjects as weaving, gardening, and farming are included in the curriculum. In connection with it, a nursery school has been started with the double purpose of saving babies' lives and of training girls in all that pertains to mothercraft" My mother visited the Training College in 1938 from Ado Ekiti and she says in her memoirs - "I stayed a weekend with Jessie Mars and Dinah Hart sometimes at Akure. It was run at that time as a Brides School for women who were marrying clergy or catechists. J and Diana were a great pair of CMS missionaries. J designed a cooking stove which was used all over Nigeria and called a Mars Stove." My mother signed her name in the Visitors Book and found it there when we later visited Akure in 1970.

In 1972 the name of the Centre had changed to the Vining Christian Leadership Centre. This change was in 1960 because it became a training Centre for male Catechists and their wives as well as some wives of men who were training for ordination in Emmanuel College, Ibadan. The first Principal of the Vining Centre was Rev Francis Foulkes who came with his wife Marjorie from CMS New Zealand. There were more developments and buildings of dormitories and classrooms on the compound. The founder women missionaries were remembered. One house for students was called Boyton House and another Mars House. Other CMS women missionaries who worked in WTC were well known as Gwen Hall who later worked in Bida and typed the whole Bible in Nupe when it was translated. Then a new dormitory was called Martin House after Ruth Martin who was the Mother's Union worker who I stayed with at the beginning of 1972 until I took over from Ethel Hime as Women's Warden.

The foundation of the Women's Training Centre by CMS women for training women was a lengthy and important part of the history of the church in Akure. I was disappointed that when there was a big 'Centenary Celebration' in 1917 that the women's work was hardly mentioned. Apart from the fact that there was nothing happening in Akure until 1919 according to the archives that I read. By 2017 the college had changed its name from Vining Christian Leadership Centre to Vining College of Theology to the Archbishop Vining College of Theology. I must say that I was disappointed and upset that the Events Brochure for the Centenary was full of large photographs of the men who had been on the staff of the College since there were men students in 1960 and some had become Bishops. Then there were important men who sent goodwill messages who thanked God for the work of the founding fathers. There is nothing about the founding women and the work of ATC from 1919 to 1960. That is 40 years out of the Centenary.

The only article that reflected on how the women's training benefitted a family was from Justice Anigbogu, a retired Judge from Nibo in Anambra State. He wrote: "We the children of Janet Ngozi Anigbogu, an old girl of the CMS Training Centre, Akure, 1944 – 1946, wish to Facilitate you on your centenary. The Anigbogu family of Nibo, proudly shares in the Christian and academic training conferred on our matriarch which training impacted on us, friends and relatives who met her. She was so proud of what she learnt at the CMS Training Centre, Akure that she preached and practised it faithfully all her life. We the 8 children, our spouses, children, grandchildren, benefitted immensely from her Christian experience to the glory of God.

At a time when it was not popular in Igboland to send girls to post primary schools, our maternal grandfather, late Pa Matthew Nwadiogbu of the St Faith's CMS Church, Awka, a devout Christian, defying protests from traditionalists, sent his daughter, Janet far away to the Training Centre in Akure for a 2-year programme, 1944-1946. Janet was confirmed in November 1946 by Bishop Akinyele and in December of the same year she married a young Godwin Anigbogu, a graduate of Dennis Memorial Grammar School, Onitsha by Rev Frank Drinkwater.

Mama always recounted with pleasure the hospitality of the Akure people and never forgot the ceremonies at the Palace of the Deji of Akure and the special ' akara balls' served on those royal Occasions.

Akure had such a positive influence on our mother that our grandfather deemed it right to send yet another daughter of his to Akure in 1954. Madam Joy Onyekuba (nee Nwadiogbu) proudly remembers the Principal Miss Smith, the Vice Principal, Miss Hall as well as an Igbo Teacher. We implore you as you move forward in this divine mission of producing priests, ignore the tasks of training young girls to be mothers and useful participators in the church and society. Akure did a good job of it in the past and our late mother Janet Ngozi Anigbogu and her sister Joy Onyekuba are proof. We believe that the 'Ministry of an Anglican Clergyman is incomplete without a wife, and a GOOD one at that.

May God bless and 'increase' the Archbishop Vining College of Theology as you stride forward in His name.

Hon. Justice Anigbogu. For the family.

Introduction to the People in this Book

Many of the people who are mentioned in Letters from Nigeria Volume 1 are present again in Volume 2. To introduce those people I worked with in Akure and those who I visited in 1972, I have written a list:

In Akure

1. Ethel Hime – Women's Warden at Vining Centre – CMS
2. Ruth Martin – Previous Women's Warden, Mother's Union Worker – CMS
3. Jane Pelly - Principal at Fiwasaiye Girl's Grammar School.
4. Sheila Davis – Vice Principal at Fiwasaiye.
5. The Eyesorun of Akure – The wife of the Deji (or King) of Akure.
6. Dr Sijuade – the Principal Medical of Akure State Hospital.

In Ondo

1. Inga Grosvalds – Principal of St Monica's Grammar School.
2. Grace Ohikhena - was on the staff of St Monica's – moved to Ibadan.

CMS People visited

1. Dr Anne Phillips – at Iyi Enu Hospital, Onitsha
2. Maureen Olphin – Headteacher in Oporoma
3. John and Anne Goodchild -in Umuahia.
4. Myrtle Hall in Lagos and later the School for Physically Handicapped children in Ondo State.
5. Ruth Howard- Principal of Anglican Girl's Grammar School, Ughelli.
6. Chris Cook - CMS Secretary in Lagos.

Family Friend.

Dr Yomi Bamgboye – Senior Surgeon at Ife University Hospital and his wife Kelu.

Arriving for Work in Vining Centre Akure

Vining Centre
21st January 1972

Dear Mother and Daddy,

I arrived safely in Lagos this morning after a rather long night flight getting off at Brussels and then stopping at Madrid around 2.00 am and Niamey around 6.30 in the morning. There was not much peace for sleeping.

Ethel was there to meet me and to accompany me round the freight sheds. After 2 hours (only!) I got my little bag out - no palaver - but they do write down the number and particulars of your case so many times.

This pink Marks & Spencer dress has been marvelous - it didn't crease in the plane at all.

I went to the Post Office, C.M.S bookshop and Leventis in the afternoon after a quick snooze.

Then I phoned Chief Ukpoma, Ewan's Papa, and he came around 5.00 pm in a gigantic Mercedes and took me home to meet his wife and her brother and the twins who were at home. A gorgeous Ikoyi set up with tele etc. They have asked me to come to stay with them sometime. It would be fun to have a 'Lagos' Weekend.

We have packed my 3 'loads 'into the Volkswagen bus and plan to travel up to Akure tomorrow, Saturday.

It was super to have you all at the airport AND John AND Ruth AND Stuart!!! Greetings to Ewan - from me and from her parents.

With much love
Elizabeth

Vining Centre
30th January 1972

Dear Ma and Daddy and Ruth (if still there),

Thank you both for the letters welcoming me back to Nigeria - from Daddy received in Lagos and from Ma received in Akure.

We came up to Akure last Saturday - taking most of the day at it for we stopped in Ibadan and had a snack in Kingsway and did some shopping. We stopped at Yomi and Kelu's to drink Fanta and I gave them that Worcester China dish for I thought that Kelu would appreciate it more than Jessie. They are all just the same - but Jide now talks in English sentences. Then we called in at St Monica's and I unloaded the recorders and saw Inga briefly to give her a present and letter from her mother. We also went to greet the new Bishop.

I started unpacking on Sunday morning after the Communion service at St David's Church and began to settle down to sharing the house with Ruth Martin. I think that it will work out happily - but it will be easier when Ethel and I have a car separately. This is the plan, but Chris Cook says we must wait until it comes through about mid-February.

I went to Ifon past Owo with Ruth on Monday to meet Mrs. Jegede who had written a letter to an M.U. branch in England saying that they were suffering from 'famine' after the war. The English M.U. were so concerned that they sent a food parcel and £6 to Ruth to give them. Ruth wanted to know why Mrs. Jegede had written this - knowing her to be a well-fed Yoruba mama! In fact, she just meant that there was 'famine' in the M.U. since members at Ifon were not attending the meetings regularly because there had been a lot of sickness last year and rising prices. She was very overwhelmed by the kindness of the English M.U. and only had to pay 9/- for the customs on the parcel.

I saw the Principal on Tuesday and the plan is that I shouldn't teach on the timetable here this term but go out visiting some Clergy in their Churches to learn what goes on and to spend time studying Yoruba. So, I have written to 3 Clergy so far and to Kelu to ask her if she would like to help me with Yoruba. She is at home most of the time so she would have time. Anyway, we'll see. I can do some Yoruba here too. The term here starts next Friday February 4th so now the compound is 'on holiday.' The reason for this is that some men were doing their G.C.E. up till 13th January.

Ethel and I went to Fiwasaiye on Thursday evening and joined the staff there - 2 Indians and an American Couple and the Oba's wife in a play reading of Oscar Wilde's - "Lady Wentworth's Fan." It was an enjoyable evening. There must have been about 20 of us altogether. Grace Webster came on Friday to stay the weekend and have a rest from Ado. We played Table Tennis on Saturday am. and in the afternoon went for a swim at the Agric - a very small pool right up on top of the rock - gorgeous place. We went with Jane Pelly and Ann Forgan from Fiwasaiye and met the Polish Doctor and his wife who live there, and the American couple called Tisdale who were at the play reading.

I borrowed Ruth's car for the day on Wednesday and went over to St Monica's. It was a Public Holiday so I had thought that there would not be schoolgirls around - but they were having lessons and keeping the holiday the next day. So, I saw everyone!

Susan the V.S.O girl is very pleasant and gets on well with Inga, I think. She has a motor bike and was going off to visit some other V.S.O.'s in Okitipupa.

It has been hot this week with temperatures almost 80F at night - and about 88F in the day. Yesterday we had the first hint of a storm and a little rain, so it was cooler. There are the remains of heavy harmattan, so we haven't seen Idanre yet at the back of the house.

Sadly, my hairdryer fused and now only blows cold air - after I had only used it for 10 minutes with the new "hat." So, my hair is a bit of a mess because I have not been able to put it in rollers and get it dry.

Also, there is some mystery about the record player which Angela left for me, with her wireless. The folks in the Guest House did not seem to have heard of it. So, I don't know what has happened. However, I expect it will turn up somewhere.

We have a staff meeting tomorrow morning which Ethel says may last 3 hours! Next Tuesday week 8th I may be going to Akoko to stay with Rev. Alegbeleye (the same name as the Panter's friend - but not the same man. He is at Ijero in Ekiti).

I hope that you are all well and that the week of Prayer for Christian Unity proved effective for the Nobles and the Cotterill's!

With love to you all - and greetings from Grace, Ethel, and Ruth

Elizabeth

Vining Centre
6th February 1972

Dear Ma and Daddy,

Thank you for your letter with news of soon after I left, and for the photographs. In fact, the photos got here first although you posted the letter 3 days earlier. The photos of you 2 are the better ones, I think! I thought that I would send 3 of them to C.M.S. The two of me outside the front door, and the one in the front garden with the pink frock on - and see what they can make of them.

I am not sure how Sunday is going to work out for letter writing at this place! We had Communion this morning from 9 - 11.30! Now it's 4.30 and the students are busy drumming and singing in the compound in practice for processing down the road to the Leper Settlement. We are to follow in 20 minutes time in the van and then we shall have an open-air Service.

We had our Staff meeting on Monday and then a very happy Supper in the Principal's House on Tuesday evening. It is a pity that you did not meet Cornelius Olowomeye the Principal when you were here. He is an extremely sincere man - very quietly spoken and kind and thoughtful. The men's warden Rev. Owadayo is a nice young clergyman who has just finished at the University. The Principal has 6 children and the Warden 3 with No. 4 coming up! The other member of staff is Mrs. Ademoye who is a clergy widow who really does most of the women's teaching - of things like Cookery.

I am going off to Arigidi Akoko tomorrow for a week's stay in a Nigerian Vicarage. I don't know if he was an old Andrian. No doubt the subject will come up!

I had a letter from Chris Cook this week with one bit of good news and one bad. The first is that he has ordered a new Volkswagen for me, so I am pleased that the alternative is the Renault 4L like Angela's. Maybe it has a bit more room for luggage, but I still prefer to drive the V.W. The other thing is that it seems that the carton which Angela left for me containing the radio and record player has disappeared and can't be traced. So, Chris is now investigating Insurance. Such a nuisance !

I went to Ado on Friday with Ruth who was going to a Finance Committee. I went mainly to see Sister Maura at the Catholic Girls School only to discover that she went home to Ireland last May!! So,

I had tea with another sister and came back to Akure with Ruth and Shelagh Jebb who came to us for the weekend.

Assuming that my car will be coming as expected I am planning a holiday with Grace and Ethel. We plan to go when term finishes here - April 21st. First to go to Oporoma to see Maureen Olphin - 1 week and then the second week to Iyi Enu to stay with Campbells and other folks there.

I hope to have another jaunt before that - going to Lagos for the car - with Ruth to Ibadan, stay with Grace and see Sola and have weekend at Ukpoma's and Sunday with Myrtle. It will be fun if it works out. I must do some Yoruba too!!

We have an Indian eye Specialist here in Akure and 2 Polish doctors, 1 Polish dentist and 2 Egyptian doctors. All these were at a Party that we went to on Saturday teatime to celebrate the 15th birthday of the Indian doctor's son. Masses of food in the cake line. I ate much too much and haven't lost any weight yet!

Ruth is just about to go off for 3 weeks to the Midwest - so we shall be away together. One student has already delivered a baby boy this term! It is certainly an added complication to teaching when you must contend with babies on backs! Mercifully there is a play group in the mornings for the toddlers. Students are allowed to bring 2 children under 6 years - that's the limit. Others must be left at home with Granny.

It's all very interesting and quite different from St Monica's.

Don't worry if letters are a bit erratic. I will write each Sunday, but I don't suppose there is any point in posting in Arigidi. It's away out past Owo. I think those photos have come in absolutely record time. You posted them in Malvern for the 4.30 post on Tuesday 1st February and I received them in Akure in the afternoon of the 4th of February! Extra-ordinarily quick.

I must think about getting things ready to go off tomorrow.

With much love to you all

Elizabeth

Staying with Pastors in Villages

The first place that I visited was a small town high up and surrounded by rocky hills called Arigidi. Canon Alegbeleye with whom I stayed is a saintly elderly pastor with five grown-up children. Each morning around 5.30 am he was up at the call of the church bell, in a 'nightcap' with a pullover under his Yoruba dress because he has bronchitis and feels the cold air of the high land. They had morning and evening prayers by the light of a tilly lamp in the church each day and afterwards the congregation of about 30-40 people would stand holding their own lamps or torches and sing and clap outside the church before dispersing to their homes, to go to the farm or the market in the morning and to go to bed at night.

They had a beautiful church compound with a church, a primary school, the pastor's two-storey house and a great structure which bristled with bamboo poles - the walls of the large new church which the people had been slowly building over the last four years. In Nigeria if you waited until you had saved up enough money to complete such a building project nothing would ever happen. So, people collect money and get the foundations laid, then in another year they start on the walls, and so on until the church gradually takes shape and gets a roof. After that it may be several more years before you can afford pews and altar, pulpit, and choir stalls. Only then may you think of luxuries like paint, windows and floor coverings or a harmonium. This new church in Arigidi had walls which reached roof level and 200 rows of concrete pillars where the two aisles would be on either side of the nave.

Vining Centre
12th February 1972

Dear Ma and Daddy,

I am here in Arigidi staying with Canon & Mrs. Alegbeleye. It is a typical 'Church 'compound with the old Church:

A bell tower, Church School and the Pastor's house - an "upstairs" and also - the great new Church, which has been in the process of being built for the last 4 years. It absolutely bristles with bamboo poles.

On the first evening that I was here there was a great storm with lashing rain and a high wind. Towards the end of the storm a soaking wet boy came in to report that the wall of the new Church had collapsed!!! So, when the rain abated, we all went to look - destruction - the two lines of pillars to make the two aisles - they and their bamboos had crashed sideways and bashed out the wall on one side. We then went to look at the old Church and saw that a whole section of the roof had been removed by the wind and blown across the compound about 10 yards.

Then people began to turn up to look at the damage - and of course to express their opinion about the waste of their money and if the Contractor had built it strong enough and if someone was making juju. Dear Canon Alegbeleye is a round-faced smiling man. He was very sad - but has a steady rock-like faith and he made them thank God that no-one was hurt or killed and thank God that the weaknesses in the structure had been revealed before it was too late - also he told them that it was not anyone's fault.

So, you can imagine that there was a good deal of coming and going with people coming to express their sympathy and then the Contractor coming and the Engineer who had been supervising the building.

I spend a good deal of time sitting in the 'parlour' upstairs watching the world go by, doing some embroidery, listening to Yoruba of which I hear very little and reading some Yoruba stories with the help of Segun the youngest Son who is 17. Yesterday I had to give a talk to the Clergy and Catechists' wives' group - in Yoruba! I read it and they seemed to understand what I said, so that was encouraging - but I still don't understand much of what they say.

One old St Andrews student was here the other day. He is Mr. Adeniran who is now the Principal of Victory College, Ikare. He said that mother cured him from some terrible attack of dysentery. He sends you both his greetings. He was in that Principals meeting at Ife of which we did not wait for the end.

Canon Alegbeleye here is an old boy of St Andrews himself - in the 1920's. He is a great character and so is she. There is a good deal of debate each day about what I want to eat - but we are managing with a few odd things like tinned peas floating in their green water, served with boiled yam. It's a lovely cool place because it is surrounded by hills, and I have slept better here than in Akure where I have been hot. This morning I was awakened around 5.30 by a voice shouting round the village with a bell - calling the Apostolic folk to prayer I imagine. I sleep on a pillow with 'Fidelity unto Death ' written right across it! They have a proper loo, clean too! The bath and basin are used for storing water, so you must manage with a bucket of cold water on the floor and let the water out by the hole in the wall!

Sunday

The services today so far have been 7.30 Communion with about 40 present and then 10.00 pm Morning Service lasting just about 1 1/2 hours and starting exactly at 10.00pm. All very orderly with a Sermon about Shadrach Meshach and Abednego being delivered from the furnace. Very lively preacher. I think he was saying that GOD would deliver them from the financial furnace that they were in, following the collapse of their new building!

After the service I was asked to speak to all the women in Church - about 100 I suppose. I read the same talk as yesterday - but by their blank faces they obviously neither heard much or understood much so Mrs. Alegbeleye translated my Yoruba and they all seemed very happy!

Then Mr. Adeniran and his wife and another teacher came to greet us here and so we all had lunch together - pounded yam, pepper stew, vegetable (green) and baked beans (for my benefit). It was very nice of them to come. They invited me to go and see them sometime after I have my own car.

I will be returning to Akure on Tuesday by public transport. It's about 60 miles or so. I hope it does not go too fast!! Then I may go to stay with Kelu at the end of the week if I hear from her to say that she can have me at that time.

Tuesday 15th February

Your letter posted on Sunday 6th arrived only today when I returned from Arigidi. Canon Alegbeleye insisted on sending his driver and car to bring me back here, so I did not come on public transport at all. It's country dancing and pancakes tonight at Jane Pelly's

With love to you both
Elizabeth

Vining Centre
19th February 1972

Dear Ma and Daddy,

I haven't heard from you yet - and there's not a lot of news this week since I last wrote, so I thought I would send a blue letter this time.

I have been here since Tuesday and am going to Ife tomorrow for a week or so. We had a pancake party with Scottish dancing on Tuesday evening at Jane Pelly's house. There were about16 people there - 4 Catholic brothers, an Indian doctor, and her son, the Eyesorun of Akure (wife of the Deji), an American Couple, another Nigerian, then Jane, Sheila, and Ann + Ethel and I. We did the Dashing White Sergeant and went wrong in the Waltz Country Dance and did an Eight-some Reel, so we were energetic.

On Wednesday we had 3 services here. Litany in the morning. The Communion Service at mid-day and Evensong at night.

On Thursday I went and watched a couple of lessons with the women. One on Childcare and how to put a baby in a Cot and how to bath it. The other was how to scrub floors without getting the whole place swimming in muddy water. The women are a bit tough, noisy, and clueless but it's better when you get to know them a bit as individuals.

I was in Ondo on Friday morning because the Principal had to go to see the Bishop. So, I went and found Titi in Ondo High School. She is not very happy teaching there, but she was not allowed to transfer to another School - quite right too. Too many teachers pop into Schools for one term at a time.

One of the Catholic brothers - called Martin Walsh, came here on Friday afternoon and brought me a whole Set of Notes and the Tape that goes with it - a Course that they use for learning Yoruba. It looks good but is on a Cassette type tape which I don't have. In fact, I am a bit stuck without a tape recorder now. Chris Cook was going to send me one but so far it has not appeared.

Yesterday I was at the Provincial Athletics here in Akure.. There was a priceless Announcer who kept telling athletes to 'Wake up! Try harder and you will win'. I met 4 St Monica's girls there - but none of them qualified to go to Ibadan next week. At the end there was almost a 'fight 'because the boys in the outside lane in the Relay were crowded by Spectators and were furious.

With much love to you both

Elizabeth

Vining Centre

26th February 1972

Dear Ma and Daddy,

I expect that there will be a letter waiting for me from you when I get back to Akure. I am now staying with Kelu and Yomi & Co in Ife. I am sitting on their front veranda looking out towards Ife. Ebun is bashing a table tennis ball against the wall with a book. Kunle is walking around with a stick following the 2 dogs. Jide is solemnly eating his omelette and bread at the table. Yomi has gone to the hospital and Kelu has just emerged from bed. It is 08.45 am.

It is good to see them all again - but it is not in fact working out to be an ideal place for Yoruba learning. The 2 youngest children only speak English and the rest do so naturally in English. However, Kelu has made some effort to talk in Yoruba every now and then and visitors come who talk in Yoruba. The main snag is that both Yomi and Kelu are so busy with their minds on other things. Yomi is planning to set up a private Clinic in the town. How he is going to have the time to do that as well as the Hospital work, I don't know - but most doctors do this to gain some extra money. They have rented rooms in a building and Kelu is planning to open a Medicine Stores and Cosmetics Shop below Yomi's Clinic which will be upstairs. So, planning for this is the focus of attention. Then in addition they now have about 120 chickens in a battery at the side of the house and this produces 80 - 90 eggs a day. These eggs must be sold in the town through various women. We went to Mrs. Ojo's Shop the other day and sold her 4 doz. eggs. She has a Cloth Shop and does knitting with knitting machines. The finished products looked very good. You will remember when we went to visit Prof. Ojo that his wife was out in her shop. I think it is a compulsive thing for all Yoruba women to trade if they are not teaching or nursing. I suppose it is really because they don't have the housework to do at home.

Kelu has a new Igbo boy now who seems very hardworking to me, but Kelu is very critical, and the poor boy gets shouted at a good deal. In fact, Kelu's ability to 'shout 'seems to have increased. There are constant eruptions in the kitchen. I am even afraid of going in there and doing something wrong! It's partly I think that she is not feeling very well because she is tired out after travelling 3 times to and fro to Ibadan in the last week. But also, she seems to have become very critical and disgruntled with life in Nigeria.

The extraordinary thing is that she is so fussy about cleanliness in some things - like the white top of the Cooker must be as clean as a whistle but the black Gas rings are left sticky and uncleaned! Masses of flies are attacked viciously with the flit gun and slaughtered daily, but she happily spits over the front veranda into the garden! I suppose that we are all strange mixtures.

I came from Akure to Ilesha last Monday with the Picard's from Emmanuel College, Ibadan. Then I got a very comfortable public transport from Ilesha. On Tuesday Kelu and I drove Yomi's car to Ibadan for repairs and came back by public transport. On Wednesday we dealt with eggs and the market. On Thursday we went to a school Sports in the afternoon and sweated under a tarpaulin. Then on Friday I stayed at home while Yomi and Kelu went to Ibadan to fetch the car.

My plan for the next 3 weeks is now fixed. I will go back to Akure probably on Wednesday this week. Then on 7th March I shall be going to stay with Grace in Ibadan. Then 9th – 11th with the Ukpoma's in Lagos. Sunday 12th with Myrtle and Monday 13th – 20th to Ilaro to stay with Foluso and Comfort Akinbamijo. He is the Superintendent of Ilaru District Church Council. He is an Ondo man - the one who I gave the grey Volkswagen to. He was previously on the staff of Lagos Cathedral and is a Canon.

After that I will be back in Akure for Easter and then the first term will be almost done.

Happy Birthday Daddy on 4th March. I hope to be able to get a card of some sort tomorrow, but the bookshops are so busy selling books to schools at the beginning of the year that they don't even have postcards now.

Also, I have left my English Cheque book in Akure so I can't send any money now. Yomi and Kelu and Co. all send their love.

With love from

Elizabeth

Vining Centre
12th March 1972

Dear Ma and Daddy,

You nearly got a phone call from me on Friday night because the Ukpomas were going to book a call! I don't know what I should have said - and probably we shouldn't have heard each other clearly. Also, I thought you might think that something was the matter if you heard me on the phone! Anyway, the whole problem was solved because the Nigerian Post & Telephone people have some technical hitch and there are no International Phone calls this weekend.

The Ukpomas have all been extremely kind. Their house is large and spacious with T.V. and air conditioning. They are in fact more "English " in their habits than Bamgboye's. They have a lovely separate dining room where you eat cornflakes and bacon, egg & tomato - toast & marmalade for breakfast - and very little pepper in the food. We went into Lagos this morning and Dora (Mrs.) collected her wig which had been washed and then we bought some cloth and later returned to Ikoyi to go and shop in the supermarket where I saw Lychees in tins!!

This afternoon I went out and had a meal at the Federal Palace Hotel with Olu and Marie Ogunlami. We went to town and had 'everything '- prawn cocktail, veal, ice cream and Rose wine. It was good to see them again and to meet their 5 children.

I came to Lagos from Ibadan on Thursday in a Greyhound bus and spent that night at the Guest House. I discovered from Chris Cook that my car has arrived in Lagos and is in the yard belonging to M & K but that it has not yet been released because the Customs people have run out of the forms or certificates to say that the customs is paid, and they are waiting for the Government Press to print some more. So, I must go to Ilaro on public transport and then come back to Lagos next week again. I hope that it is ready by then.

I stayed with Grace in Ibadan. She was very kind. Tokunbo has grown very much since I last saw her. Tunde is now in Form 1 in Secondary School - in the Baptist School in Oyo. While I was in Ibadan, I went with Ruth Martin to see Bishop & Mrs. Okunsanya. He has lost a lot of weight, but people say he looks much better now than he did last year. They sent greetings to you.

I went to U. I. to see Shola, but I couldn't find her in her room - so I went and greeted Richard instead. I have not yet been able to contact Folarin. It will be easier when I have my own transport.

Now today, after Church, I am hoping to go and stay with Myrtle for the night. It will be good to see her and Pat again.

We went to a real Ikoyi party last night with all sorts of gorgeous lace clothes and flowing robes etc. It was to celebrate the Christening of two children aged about 6 & 4. I think that it was just an excuse for the parents to ask all their friends round and to entertain them to a great feast with coloured lights decorating the whole garden.

Really if you live in Ikoyi you hardly live in "Nigeria" at all. It's good to have a bit of both.

With much love from

Elizabeth

Visiting the Akinbamijo's in Ilaro

Vining Centre
19th March 1972

Dear Ma and Daddy,

I received your letter describing the Concert at Windsor. It was forwarded to me from Akure to Ilaro where I have been staying for the past week. I have had a very happy week here in the home of Foluso and Comfort Akinbamijo. They have been very kind and it is an extremely easy house to stay in - but I am not sure if I have learnt any more Yoruba - or anything especially useful about Church life. I shall be glad when I get settled down into the teaching at the Vining Centre.

I have not been able to get the Volkswagen out of Lagos yet. They are still waiting for the customs forms to be printed. I went for the day on Friday to Lagos because Foluso had a meeting. I had hoped to collect the car. However, they have arranged that I should borrow a Humber that belonged to Donald Mason. It is in Ibadan, and I am to go and collect it there tomorrow and use it until the Volkswagen is ready.

During my time in Lagos, I borrowed Margaret Ingram's car and went to the Federal Palace Hotel pool and had a swim and a sun bathe. Then I did a little shopping in Leventis and returned to the Guest House to find Inga and Susanne there. We had a great long talk about the results which have just come out, and other related St Monica's topics. Then in the evening I went and stayed the night with Myrtle and Pat and returned to Ilaro on Saturday morning.

While I have been here there have been 2 notable services that I have attended. On Wednesday afternoon at 3 Comfort, Foluso and I went to a Funeral in a village about 7 miles from here. It was a tiny Church with tatty streamers dangling about and the ceiling collapsing because white ants had devoured most of the timbers. You could smell the body if you got too near the coffin! It was all rather pathetic.

The other service was yesterday when one of the chiefs in Ilaro celebrated his 60th birthday. They had a service which lasted 2 hours in the morning. The street outside the church was lined with schoolboys belonging to a House named after him in a local school. Then 2 Obas came in large cars with trumpeters leaning out of the windows blowing their trumpets. There was a crowd of men and women all dressed in their best for the occasion.

On Thursday evening I went out for supper to Ron Howarth's house. He is the Chaplain of Egbado College here in Ilaro. I also met 2 very pleasant V.S.O. folk - a married couple. He teaches Physics and she teaches Domestic Science subjects.

Wednesday - Akure

I returned here last night after an eventful couple of days travelling. It started on Monday morning at 05.00 am when I was squashed into the back of a van with about 2 ''of sitting space. Just as I was getting a painful cramp in one leg and really beginning to think that I couldn't bear it any longer, the woman next to me got out with her bag of gari and the pressure was released. But about 5 minutes later another even bigger woman got on and sat half <u>on</u> me and half on my neighbour! However, it was only about 30 miles from Ilaro to Abeokuta in this fashion. After that people got out and I was 'called 'to the front seat. So, then I was very comfortable, and we continued without event to Ibadan, but just before we got into the town there was a puncture, so we all got out and I took a taxi from there with another woman. I went to the Fowler's and collected the Humber which is big and grand and drives very steadily on the road but consumes a gallon of petrol for each 20 miles, so it is not exactly economical.

I saw Shola in the afternoon at the University and later I went with Grace to see Jose Aighbohai and her new baby girl. Then I stayed the night with Grace and returned to Akure via Ife and Ondo. Kelu was at home suffering from delayed shock after somersaulting in her old Renault with all the children in it, just outside the Staff School at the University. Mercifully no-one was badly hurt. Ebun had a cut in his arm which had to be stitched and the others were bumped about. Anyway, it was enough to put Kelu off driving that car again.

I had lunch in Ondo with Inga, Susanne and Joseph and then saw Janet and family, Bola, and Mr. Ademodi (old student of St Andrew's) before returning to Akure. Students here are hoping to do the Dramatised Service for Palm Sunday on the Wednesday in Holy week and so I spent yesterday evening with Ethel in the Chapel practicing the service.

There were 2 letters waiting for me when I arrived back here, so I now feel more up to date with home news. It sounds as though you are going to have plenty of visitors during the next few months. I hope that you have a happy Easter time together with Pat, John and the 3 children. By the way, you forgot to write down Lewis ' birthday. Have you any ideas of what Stuart would like from me for his 21st birthday? Or is there any large item that you would like a contribution for?

Papa Ukpoma is going to England sometime in April, I think. Maybe he will come to Malvern then and you will be able to see him.

My link vicar in Notting Hill has found one lady who lives within walking (just) distance of Park Royal who would give Dr Kumuyi Bed and Breakfast: so, I hope he gets on O.K. Maybe he will find something through the hospital - I have heard nothing from him, but it was amazing really that I wrote to Mr. Richardson. I know that he had been around that way - but he said that his previous Parish went up to the boundary of Park Royal and so he had contacted his successor in that Parish!

I have got a Map of Nigeria produced by Esso in 1960. It's a bit out of date about some roads but I think that it will be a help to you to see where I am at different times. I have marked Oporoma. Ethel, Grace, and I are planning to go there to see Maureen from May 2nd - 7th. It seems that the best way to go is to travel down the River Niger from Onitsha. So, it will all be rather an adventure.

I may go to Ado and to Okeigbo (on Ondo-Ife Road) before then.

I hope this letter reaches you by Easter time. It's a bit late.

With much love to you all,

Elizabeth.

Map of Nigeria

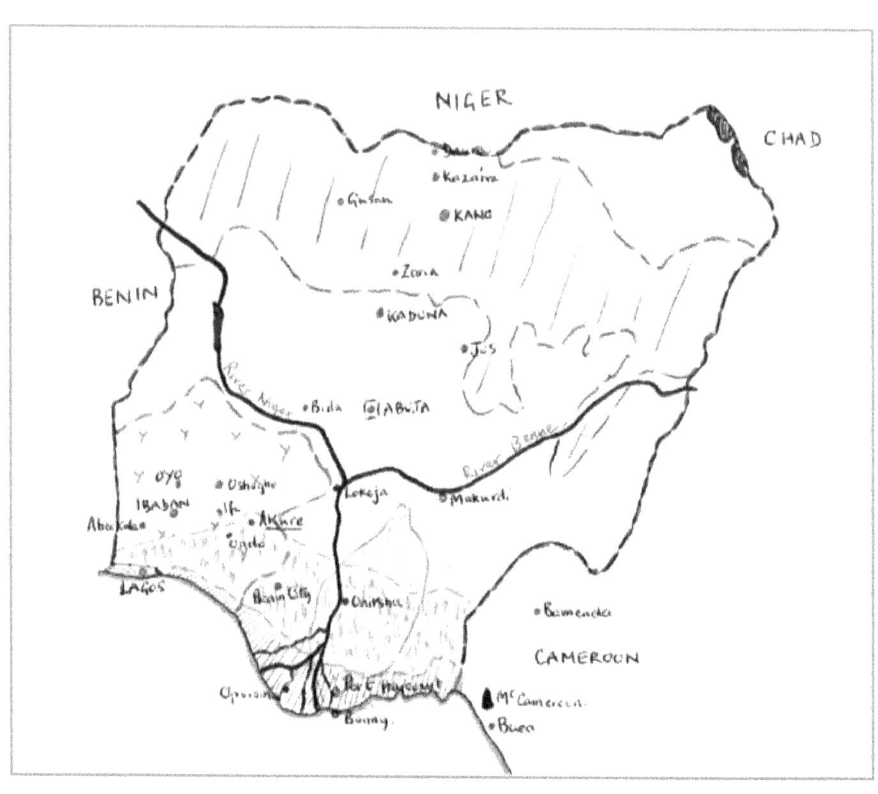

Key

Mangroves - shading along the coast.
Rain Forest - pale green area in the south.
Main Language areas - HAUSA in North - blue stripes
- YORUBA in South West - green Y's
- IGBO in South East - pink spots.

Vining Centre
28th March 1972

Dear All,

I have been here in Akure over Palm Sunday weekend and will still be here over Easter. Ruth is going to Bida to see Gwen, with Joan Stephenson from Ilesha. It will be interesting to join the activities here. We have been practising each day for the Dramatised service tomorrow evening and tonight and I am to take the evening service. I expect on Easter Sunday that students will be up about 5a.m dancing and singing round the town.

We seem to have had a postal dispute over pay in Western Nigeria. Certainly, the post office workers in Akure have been either 'on strike' or 'go slow.' Nothing is very clear to the public except that letters are either erratic or non-existent. So, I am hoping to send this with Martin - the Catholic Father at Aquinas College who lent me Yoruba tapes. He is going on leave and says he will be in London on Thursday. So, he is going to be laden with our various 'posts.'

I went to 2 classes yesterday morning. The first in how to deal with babies having convulsions. The students demonstrated how not to do it and how to do it. The first was very funny with the baby getting its toes toasted on the fire and its nose tickled with a feather rubbed in native medicine.!

The second class was how to serve tea and sandwiches to an English visitor. The thing which caused the most interest was how you can remove a tomato skin by putting it in boiling water!! Ruth is busy trying to sort out the Centre Accounts for the last 6 months. This is no ordinary task because it seems that neither the principal nor the Clerk do things methodically - some amounts are not entered, others are entered wrongly, and the principal doesn't keep the Cash in the Safe so you can never check it. Crazy upside-down system and I think just now the principal is realising that it is not to his advantage if the money is not exactly accounted for because he will be asked to refund the difference. It is like sorting out the books written by two Mrs. Nobles each as confused as the other!

Thank you for the photos and the Easter Card. I like the picture of a Sailor especially. I hope that Stuart, Sasha, and Lewis can get out on the 'hills 'without getting their cars blown too much this time. I should think that the ridge will be crowded on Easter Monday if Boxing Day is anything to go by. I shall be thinking of you all. I may go out to Idanre on either Saturday or Monday and visit the Akinbadewa's - or take a picnic to the swimming pond on the rocks at the Agric.

I hope that you all have a Very Happy Easter, and that the services are joyful.

With love

Elizabeth

Vining Centre
Easter Sunday
2nd April 1972

Dear All,

Because of the 'go slow 'in post here I have only just received your letters of 21st March and 17th March. And this was only because Ethel went and begged the sorting officer man in her best Yoruba. Anyway, it's good to hear all your news and to know of new experiences in Malvern. Daddy's Conference at Cropthorne sounds most stimulating. I am sure it will all help in your contacts with folk in the Parish at Powick.

I haven't yet been able to contact Folarin at U.I. I wrote a letter to him but don't know yet if it reached him. Shola is expecting her baby in September, but she is doing her finals in May. So, it is well planned in fact. You do seem to be having plenty of visitors. It will be interesting to have Chrissie's comments on the new set-up. I should think she would approve of Malvern!

Grace, Ethel, and I are not going on our holiday till 24th April. Then we are hoping to spend one week with Ken and Pearl & Co at Iyi Enu, followed by a week at Oporoma and then when we come back from there, we are going to see Jenny Carey at Owerri for a few days and return via Jane Backhouse at Ekpoma.

Today the students were up by 4 am drumming and dancing and singing in the town. Then we had Communion at 7 am. On Good Friday afternoon we also went out on an Open-Air Witness - going round the town - singing and dancing and then stopping for a talk at different places collecting a small crowd on each occasion. I went for part of that but both Ethel and I stayed in bed this morning! We are going to Fiwasaiye to lunch with Sheila, Jane, and Ann and tomorrow I am planning to go with Ann to Idanre to see Pat Akinbadewa. She is expecting No. 4 and hoping to go home to Guernsey for it. I hope she gets home. It will be her first time in 5 years.

We start driving on the right side of the road today instead of the left. We had a 'practice 'on Wednesday for 2 hours. They had police or soldiers out at every single junction along the main street and many cars and bicycles turned out just for the fun of it!

Ruth is away over Easter. She has gone to Bida to see Gwen Hall. But Ethel is very good company, and we have most meals in one or other of our 2 houses. This is nice because I don't really enjoy eating on my own, especially surrounded by Stephen the Steward and the shiny brass bell you are supposed to ring between courses!

Rev. Owadayo's wife is now on Maternity leave so she has been helping me with some Yoruba in the mornings this past week. Progress is slow.

The roses are out here! Pink ones and red ones

With love

Elizabeth

Vining Centre
9th April 1972

Dear Ma and Daddy,

Thank you for your letter of 29th March which I received when I returned from Ado via Akure yesterday. I am now in Okeigbo - 9 miles from Ondo on the Ife Road.

I had a most interesting time in Ado last week. I stayed with Sam and Deborah Adebusuyi. He is the Ekiti Diocesan Youth Chaplain as well as the Vicar of one parish in Ado. They were both in Manchester last year and so he was often telling tales of his experiences in Manchester. In one parish the Vicar's wife was obviously rather starchy and didn't have a clue about Nigeria. In the next parish his vicar was a bachelor and apparently a 'jolly good fellow' called Fred.

He and his wife were very welcoming, and we all sat down to table together with the children who were already six, and another expected within the next month. I ate so much it wasn't true and I have regained the weight that I thought I had lost. Deborah asked me how I liked eggs for breakfast - boiled or fried or omelette? So, I said that I liked anyone! - so, for breakfast the next day I had 3 fried eggs on bread fried in egg, a great lot of omelette and about 6 pieces of bread fried in egg … ALL placed in front of me. I made some inroads into it and shared the rest out. I had already taken eko - like thin porridge and corn flakes before we got to the eggs!!!

Rev. Adebusuyi took me round a whole lot of villages around Ado to meet the pastors or catechists there. It was very interesting to have the chance to meet a number in a short time. I also met the Bishop of Ado, Bishop Adetiloye who is the youngest of the Nigerian Bishops, and he is introducing a lot of new ideas into his Diocese. Then we had tea with the provost and his wife. He is called Rev. Famewo and was taught by N.S.D at St Andrew's Oyo. He was very upset to know that he missed you both when we went and snooped around his office in Ado.

Another person I met was Archdeacon Alegbeleye who the Panters know. He was very welcoming and friendly. He is in Ijero which is a small town, but the Archdeacon's house is built right up on the hill looking over the whole town. It has a beautiful view right over all the rooftops.

During the time I was in Adebusuyi's house several of the women came to greet me, or they sent their children... but the funny thing was that whenever they came, they carried a pineapple. By the time I was ready to go we had received over 20!! We ate some and I brought the rest back to Akure and distributed them around the compound. There were also eggs and oranges to bring home. Really the people are so very generous.

I returned to Akure on Saturday morning with Millicent Wood from Abiye Hospital. She is an older woman who had done a 2-year C.M.S Associate business. The Batts from Ibadan were also in Ado, so I met them for the first time. They seem a very pleasant couple, with one little girl aged about 6 years. He is a Social Worker, so he is trying to do some sort of social work under the Bishop of Ibadan.

I then came on to Okeigbo via Ondo in the afternoon. I saw Janet and Bose taking a stroll along the main road - but didn't see anyone else. Inga was at the principals' Conference in Ibadan.

It sounds as though you will have had a very busy Easter. Perhaps it's just as well that John and family only came for a few days after all. Please let me know any ideas for Stuart's 21st birthday.

It is interesting how Yoruba houses vary so much - and again vary tremendously from the Ikoyi set up. Adebusuyi's place was overall very orderly and to have all the children at the table was unusual. More often the children must eat 'below stairs' with

Grandma - as they are just given a plate to get on with it and get any old place to eat theirs. Then some people spend their time hollering at the 'servants' - or extra children but others seem to manage without that and make a more peaceful atmosphere.

Greet all friends in Malvern. It's time I wrote a quick letter again.

With much love from

Elizabeth

Visit the Fabuluje's in Okeigbo

Vining Centre
16th April 1972

Dear Ma and Daddy,

The post here is not good at all now. I haven't had any letters for over 10 days - either from inside Nigeria or overseas. I don't know if the post office has gone back on strike without telling us or if they are just in a muddle. I hope that they are not dumping letters in the Lagoon!

I had a very interesting week at the Fabuluje's - they had to manage without electricity or decent running water and their pit latrine was not to be recommended. In fact, at night, I went in the field behind the house under the stars and with clear air around! Mrs. Fabuluje was very friendly and delighted to have her first European visitor. But the household was run in a very Nigerian type of fashion. She called her husband 'the Master 'and the children just ate what they liked when they liked without sitting down together at mealtimes. The baby was generally nappy-less with inevitable results and goats sometimes were walking in the house.

I went visiting some of the Women's Guild members - mostly very ancient ladies in 1930 (or before) type houses. I was quite embarrassed because most of them gave me 1/- presented in a tin plate. Mrs. F told me that she was sorry we didn't have time to go to more houses because when she and her husband first came there and went visiting the members they came back with, £11.14.0! Not the British style of Parish visiting!! I came_back here with 2 dozen eggs, 1 bottle of groundnut oil, 2 ducks which I am expected to breed (i.e., male and female), 1 pencil, 10/- from old ladies and £6.11.0 in cash from other sources. It was a bit overwhelming because I did nothing but give them the pleasure of entertaining me.

I saw Bola in Ondo and greeted his new baby which is gigantic and looks very well fed. Bola entertained me to supper in his house. He is being transferred from Ondo Forestry Office to a project near Ijebu-Ode so it will probably be a good long time before I can see him again.

Please pray for Titi. I had hoped to see her last week, but she disappeared, and no-one knew whether she had gone to Ibadan or to

Ilesha - but her mother and other relatives are very worried about her because they feel she is behaving so strangely that she ought to see a psychiatrist.

With love to you all

Elizabeth

Vining Centre
22nd April 1972

Dear Ma and Daddy,

On Wednesday I received 17 letters all at once, two of them from you. I don't know what the reason is, but someone in the post office seems to be holding our letters back and we didn't get any until the principal went and "begged" the Postmaster. Very odd and very annoying. I hope that my letters have been getting to you.

It sounds as though you have had an extremely busy time over Easter. I am very glad that you had such a happy time with Stuart. I can't quite imagine Ruth going to Yemen of all places! Yes, I heard from Angela that she is going to see Ron Diss I think, after discussing C.M.S with John Harwood. I don't think she has got to the stage of "offering" - rather than exploring the possibilities. I see that you will be at Lee Abbey just now so you will be more up to date than I am on this subject.

I had a letter from Dr Kumuyi amongst my 17 this week, saying that he has moved to Central Middlesex and is in a Hall for Medical students for a month, but the housekeeper says he will have to go after that. So, he is still looking for somewhere to live. His present address is Horace Joules Hall, Central Middlesex Hospital, N.W. 10 in case you have any more ideas. The lady who offered him bed and breakfast, who was contacted through one of my link vicars, 'changed her mind' he says.

We had the end of term here this week, and the Commissioning of the 17 outgoing Catechists and about 12 women. Then on Thursday and Friday I was in Ado for the Ekiti Synod meetings. This was most interesting because the Bishop of Ekiti is the youngest bishop and certainly the most progressive and active in the West of Nigeria. Most Synods spend ages reading reports, but he has changed all that and has the reports all printed and then Committees meet and discuss what is to be done in the future and that is discussed. It was very orderly with Chief Ogunlade as the Secretary (Principal of

Christ's School) Provost Famewo sitting on the right of the bishop (old student of N.S.D) and Chief Akomolafe on the left of the Bishop as the Registrar of the Diocese (He was asking when you were coming again because we missed seeing him when you were last here in 1970!) There were other old Andrians, one Canon Awosusi came and wrote down your present address. Prof Ojo was the Chairman of their Finance Committee - but he wasn't there. Anyway, I felt that I knew 'the tops'!

The bishop gave his presidential address - and it took 2 hours to read! He gave a rather too long extract from Reader's Digest about clergy poverty in England with the aim of convincing the Ekiti people that they need to invest money wisely to prepare for increases in the rise of the cost of living and the need to increase clergy salaries. He was also talking about building a guest house at Ikogosi and the idea of having a clergy (& others) retreat and holiday place - like Lee Abbey on a very small scale.

I brought Grace back with me to Akure. Ethel is not feeling very well - has diarrhoea but will be O.K by tomorrow when we set off, I should think. Anyway, we are going to a hospital.

Yesterday, Saturday I spent most of the morning stamping around the market buying food for my ducks and a big bowl so that they can have a basin of water to play in - and they do, and they make it filthy almost immediately. We have made a wire netting enclosure for them and so we shall wait and see if there are any ducklings. If not Ma & Pa will get eaten for Christmas.

I had a letter from Folarin, so I now know where to find him at U.I. Also, Dr Olasimbo wrote a note with a friend. I've not seen him yet. Then yesterday John Fabuyi popped in to say hello. You will remember it was at his house that we ate snails!

I hope that you have a super birthday Ma. We shall be going to see Jenny Carey on that day. I think I gave you the holiday dates before:

April 24th - May 1st Iyi Enu
May 1st - 7th Oporoma
May 8th - 11th Owerri

then back to Akure. But don't rely on the post getting to any of these places in a hurry.

With much love
Elizabeth

Vining Centre
30th April 1972

Dear Ma & Daddy,

Thank you for your letter which reached me here at Iyi Enu as you'd hoped. Pearl, Ken and Toyin are all well and in high spirits. They send you, their love. They have now moved into the two- storey house next door to the house where they were before. They have made a fine tarred road with concrete ditches right down the centre of the compound and there is now a group of 5 good staff houses all nicely painted at the lower end of the compound. It is amazing what a lot has been done since we were there before in 1970. They are in the middle of the building of a new out-patients block near the road. In Onitsha too there are lots of changes. Fine new houses have appeared all over the place and the road out of Iyi Enu is completely newly tarred. The Cathedral is painted, and new pews made, so that it looks gorgeous - we went there this morning for a very beautiful service.

It has been a very happy holiday so far and everything has worked out well. We have seen several folks that you will remember. We went to Asaba on Wednesday and saw Arch. Echenen who is now in Asaba and had coffee there. Then on to the Girls School where we had lunch with Mary Eldridge who is running the school while Mandy is on leave. She is now in her new house. In the afternoon we went up to R.T.C. We saw Gabriel and he asked about his photograph - Can we send him a print? He would be very happy. The house at the top of the hill now looks super. It is being used as a guest house and has a new roof and everything re-made so that it is a good house again. The R.T.C is now functioning again as a 'farm 'with crops being grown and palm oil collected etc., also poultry. They have over 200 labourers working there. Some of the Army have gone, but some are still there.

We spent Friday going to Enugu where there is hardly any evidence of war damage at all. On route we stopped in Awka and visited the carving Co-operative which is now functioning again.

We all bought things. I bought a small table which is carved on top and on the sides for £3.3.0. Grace bought a bread board and Ethel 2 tables and a tray. She plans to take her purchases home when she leaves. Her plan at present is to leave Vining Centre after the second term (June - Aug). She will then go to Lagos and take over running the Guest House from Margaret Ingram when she leaves in October. So, Ethel will be there for 6 months till she leaves Nigeria next March.

The only snag about Enugu was that we didn't take our swimming things and we discovered that there was a gorgeous pool at the Presidential Hotel.

On Saturday we went with Pearl and Toyin to Okigwi via the Oji River. It is a glorious road right across the most beautiful countryside with hills - it looked like China in places with terracing and the roads climbed up super hairpin bends. We went to see Chris and Eta Jones. Their place is 4 miles off the road along a real bush track. When you get there, it is glorious - a bungalow up on a hill surrounded by hilly agricultural land. It was most interesting to see them and to hear a little about their Co-operative Farm Settlement place. The only snag was that we had a puncture in Awka en route, so we had to wait for 1 1/2 hours in a lorry park while some local mechanics changed the wheel and then vulcanised the tyre using the primitive method of clamping an old piece of rubber to your inner tube to make a patch and then 'cooking 'it by burning methylated spirit in the top of the clamp. We were very fortunate to be in Awka when the puncture happened because we were able to sit in a line in a shack in the lorry park and drink coffee out of our flasks while the tyre was being mended.

We have seen several people while we have stayed here. Tricia Davies, Jean Wright, and Doreen Wren were passing through going back to Kaduna. Elizabeth Edmonds and Mary Bunting are opposite, and Bessie Parker is next to them although we haven't seen much of her because she has German measles. She is Australian C.M.S and came from Tanzania. We had lunch today with Ann and John Philips (Patrick Philips 'brother). I stayed with them before in Kabba. Jenny Carey came to Onitsha also the other day and we saw her. She is going on leave this weekend together with Bishop Nwankiti so unfortunately, we shall miss them when we go to Owerri. However, her house is ready for us, and the Kirkpatrick's will be there. Then Maureen Olphin has shown up here so we shall be able to all travel together on Tuesday when we set sail down the Niger. It will be good to have someone who knows the ropes. She is 'out 'from Oporoma because she went to Port Harcourt to make a report at the Ministry of Education because the principal was only seen in the school for 3 weeks during the whole term!! It takes only 24 hours to get to Oporoma but on the way back it takes about 36 hours because of the current of the river.

When we come back from Oporoma we hope to go and see Ann Travis at Umuahia, from Owerri. After a rather difficult start there it sounds as though things have improved a bit now and they have a few sensible doctors.

With much love to you all

Elizabeth

Sailing down the River Niger

8th May 1972

Dear Ma & Daddy,

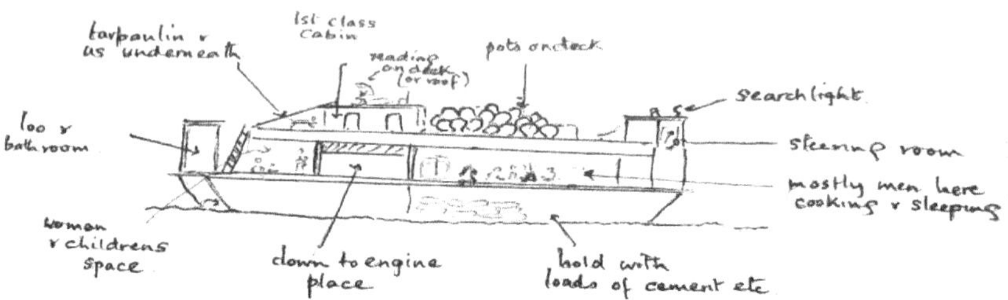

Grace, Ethel, and I have had a most interesting week going down to see Maureen Olphin at Oporoma. It has been quite an adventure.

On Monday, before we set sail on Tuesday, we went with Ken and Toyin to explore the caves at Obonike near Iyi Enu. We had to scramble down a steep slope and then we went into part of the cave system on hands and knees and then walked up a riverbed. Ethel and Toyin opted out when bats flew in our faces but then Ken, Grace and I went on a bit longer till I felt it was oppressively hot and my specs were steaming up. We didn't in fact go in very far.

On Tuesday morning we went down to the waterside to embark and join our boat.

The beds inside the 'first class 'cabin were already occupied so we asked the crew to fix us a tarpaulin on the upper deck and so we were able to stack our cases, put up our camp beds and cook under a tent. The first part of the journey, on Tuesday afternoon, was extremely hot. We sat in the sunshine with our umbrellas to shade us, and Ethel in her white straw hat imagined herself as Mary Slessor sailing into the unknown! It was good to have Maureen on board with us because she knew the ropes already and was a great help.

Just after dark a storm blew up and the wind whistled around our tarpaulin and the rain swept underneath it, so we had to make a quick exit into the cabin. It was hilarious really because we had so many bits and pieces and we bundled them all in through the window onto one man's bed. Then we sat inside and waited till the rain went off.

When the rain stopped, we moved out again with our camp beds and all four of us slept in a row under the tarpaulin. It rained a bit during the night and dripped through onto my feet, but overall was well. Maureen and I were on the outside and so we were chilly because of a draught. Ethel and Grace were in the centre and were hot. We chugged and chugged all night. Every now and then there was a thump, and the bells rang, and the engine was put into reverse - we had bumped into a sand bank. Then we stopped through the night at the riverbank and unloaded bags of cement or other things and people struggled up and down the very steep and slippery bank in the dark.

The journey proceeded throughout Wednesday. It was cloudier and so pleasant to sit on deck. One man 'slept off' and fell in! He was picked up by a small boat and returned - very angry because people were saying 'Papa, you drink too much!'

Now on Sunday afternoon we are all three sitting inside the 1st class cabin on the returning boat. It has been raining most of the afternoon and now I am sitting on a box in my cardigan and mac for it's quite cold. Half an hour ago I was sitting on my top bunk (wooden boards and straw mattress) with my umbrella over my feet and Grace was on hers with her umbrella over her head. The rain was dripping through the roof in a lot of places! Now the crew members are busy above us patching up with extra pieces of tarpaulin.

It was most interesting to visit Oporoma after hearing so much about it. It is a very beautiful place with a long line of thatched roofed houses down the main street and then the school and health centre at the end of the town. George Banbury lives in one of the ordinary village houses with everything - his bed, cooking pot on floor, carpenter's bench - all in the one room. He is a strange mixture of a person and really lives a very 'higgledy piggledy 'life. He teaches part time in the school and then is trying to start some farming in the swamp land. It is very muddy and swampy land with quite tall trees that must be felled before anything can be done.

Maureen seems to manage the situation there very well, but I think that they are constantly short of staff, and all material goods, including food must be "brought in" so life is not without its problems. On the other hand, it is very peaceful - some people have never even seen a car. It was real "Africa."

You can't buy meat or vegetables (except onions) nor yams nor oranges in Oporoma. Most of the children eat bread or cassava and health is not a very strong point. There is a Norwegian doctor at the health Centre now. In fact, he spends most of his time travelling around the villages in a boat. But this means that he can only visit places every 2 weeks or more. While we were there, he was having a course to train helpers in many of the villages. The idea is that these people should sort out the sick people and then make sure that those ones see the doctor on his visit.

On Monday afternoon we shall be going to Owerri for 2 days and then we must face the Asaba - Benin road en route for home. We are going to spend 2 nights in the Forestry rest house near Benin. I hope that the car manages the road. It has rained heavily so you can imagine exactly what it is like.!!

With love to you both
Elizabeth

Vining Centre
14th May 1972

Dear Ma and Daddy,

It was good to receive your 2 letters on my arrival back from the Midwest yesterday. I am sorry to hear that Daddy gets so exhausted that he missed part of the Lee Abbey week - but glad to hear that he recovered quickly. I am sure that Ruth would be happy to see you both.

We got back to Akure very happily without any mishaps - a notable achievement on the roads of the Midwest. Ken and Pearl got stuck in a hole the week before and spent 2 hours in the mud before they were dug out! Since I wrote last Sunday on the boat, we did a good deal of travelling. We went on Monday afternoon to Owerri where we had planned to stay with Jenny Carey and see Bishop Nwankiti. In their absence we stayed in Jenny's house and were looked after beautifully by Mary and Robert Kirkpatrick. They have been in Nigeria for 20 years and lost everything in the War. They were in Enugu before where she was the Principal of Queen's School Enugu - the only Government Girls School for the East in the pre-war days. (Now all the schools in the East Central State are under Government.) They are from Northern Ireland and although now C.M.S are very 'Colonial' in many ways - carpet on floor and sherry before Supper - but they were extremely interesting to talk to. He is the Diocesan Missioner for Owerri Diocese, and this means that he is now training Catechists and one Ordinand on a part time course basis, because the training centre at Awka is no more. He also organises retreats and they hope to have more of these in their Centre at (I can't remember name of place! This is a compound in the bush with accommodation for 24 and dining arrangements for 60.)

From Owerri we went to Umuahia for a day and saw Ann Travis and Albert Clothier. Ann has a job in the hospital. At first the sisters and nurses didn't really want a European Matron - but they seem to have got over that hurdle. On the other hand, there are colossal problems facing the hospital - no grant to pay salaries. I think the State owes them £60,000 for some such. Then they are to re-open their training schools for General and Midder, but they have no qualified Sister Tutor for Midwifery and no equipment. Physically the hospital hasn't suffered a lot of damage to wards etc. - but a lot of equipment like sterilisers etc. have been lost. They have a very good Surgeon - a Nigerian who is S.M.O and 2 other doctors but they could do with 3 more. Ann really needs someone there to support her.

Albert Clothier is now at Trinity College Umuahia. He is doing some teaching- Accounts and Library work and seemed quite settled - still smoking like a chimney.

We broke our journey on the way back in the Midwest. We went to a very beautiful forestry rest house about 20 miles from Sapele. Maybe on your map? - At Sapoba. You can swim there in the river which is deep and clear. We also went out in a canoe with an old Baba and were able to enjoy more of the river.

On our return to Akure we met Ruth Martin and the news of her mother's death. It had been a shock to her because the letter telling her that she was sick in hospital came after the cable that she had died. All the Nigerian staff and the folk at Fiwasaiye had rallied around with sympathy and help. She couldn't go home for the funeral because she didn't get the cable till afterwards. Anyway, Bishop Martin has said that he can manage during the summer and is taking the opportunity to stay with relations and friends. Then in September Ruth is going to go home for 6 - 9 months to help her father sort out things in the house and to decide where he should go to live on his own. So, it looks as though I shall be on my own in the compound at the Vining Centre after September. Ethel will be going to the Guest House in Lagos sometime around then.

I have come to Ado with Grace - to bring her back and stay one night before returning to Akure. We still have 3 weeks of holiday left before term starts.

With much love to you all

Elizabeth

P.S. Can you tell Barnard's Green Bank that my address is Vining Centre, Box 3, Akure and not St Monica's, Ondo. I don't know how the mistake has come about.

Vining Centre
22nd May 1972

Dear Ma and Daddy,

We returned to Akure last Monday and then I spent Tuesday and Wednesday mornings with Ethel trying to plan our teaching for the new term which starts on June 2nd. I have plenty to do in the next few weeks before then to prepare lessons in English, Health, New Testament etc.

On Thursday I came to Ibadan to buy some books and uniform material for the Vining Centre. I am staying with Grace Ohikhena. Her husband is away in Dakar at a Conference on Educational planning, so Grace is on her own for the next 6 weeks.

I have been able to see several people while here in Ibadan. Finals Exams start today at the University, so I went to greet Shola and Richard. Shola's doctor thinks she may be having twins. She is feeling well. Richard has applied for jobs with the Federal Civil Service so he may be sent to a school in the North - or anywhere in the country. I also went and found Folarin in his Hall of Residence. He seems to be a quite cheerful undergraduate and is enjoying Nigeria. He is glad that he came. He said that he would like to come and stay sometime during the holidays in Akure. I also saw Dr Olasimbo and he came here to Grace's house last night and chatted for about 1 1/2 hours. Grace hadn't seen him since leaving St Monica's, so it was quite an ex-Ondo reunion. He is busy on Preventive Medicine measures and visiting schools and Clinics in the Ibadan area.

Yesterday Grace and I went to the morning service at Emmanuel College. It was a Methodist type of Communion service - much like Series 2. Don Pickard and John Nightingale did the Sermon between them - like a discussion. They had planned it well and it made a lively change. Afterwards we had coffee with the Pickard's, Fowlers, and Joy Fletcher. The Gardeners are packing up to be going from Ibadan at the end of June; and so too are the Fowlers so the number of C.M.S folk in Ibadan will then be drastically reduced.

I had my hair cut on Saturday - and am going to have it shampooed and set this morning. I couldn't have done it on Saturday because the electricity went off in that section of Ibadan.

I expect I shall get a letter from you when I return to Akure this afternoon. I hope to stop in Ife en route and hear their news there.

With much love to you all

Elizabeth

Vining Centre
28th May 1972

Dear Ma and Daddy,

I have just been to Fiwasaiye School to attend their morning service. I told the story of the 3 trees and played 'Worthy is the Lamb' from the Messiah. They seemed to listen well - but I didn't hold their attention throughout I didn't feel. Perhaps I talked too fast for Yoruba school- girls.

This week has been one of preparation for the term which starts next Friday. It is rather nice to have the opportunity to start all over again with planning subjects and lessons. And not to feel that things are going to be overwhelming - at least in the first term when Ethel is still here.

The Board of Governors was on Tuesday. It was rather a rough time for Cornelius, the Principal, because the Accounts are in a certain state of 'muddle', and he was hauled over the coals. It is not entirely his fault except that he doesn't deal with checking the transactions until long after the event and the clerk is vague and careless and doesn't get the Cash book written up till about 3 months later. Then Ruth has the job of checking it all and writing the Ledgers. It is all a very stupid system. Anyway, they have a committee next week to go into it all - and so Ruth has been hard at it trying to get everything clear before that. They ought really to sack the Clerk for he hasn't a clue, but he is from the same town as the Archdeacon!

We had a play reading of Blithe Spirit on Wednesday at St Peters. Then on Friday night we had a party at Mrs. Tisdale's (Americans) in honour of the Eyesorun (wife of Deji) whose birthday was on Sat. There were heaps of food of different sorts because most people brought a contribution. On that night we went to the Palace for a rather select 'Ladies Party '- about 10 of us: One Scottish Grail member from Ibadan, 2 Nigerian Catholics, Jane, Sheila, Ann, Ethel, Ruth, and me. We ate up the remainder of the food from the day before. It was Eyesorun's own birthday party. She really is a Treasure. I think she did her own nursing training at Simpsons.

White air mail paper is out of the shops now. I hope that you are all well. I got your letter of the 11th on Mon 22nd. No headaches here. Praise the Lord.

With love

Elizabeth

PS - I have sent off 2 lots of slides. I hope you get them.

Vining Centre
4th June 1972

Dear Ma and Daddy,

It was good to get both your letters this week - telling of the visit to London to Stuart's 'modern' noises concert. It sounds as though you are both really settled-in in Malvern with plenty to do with all the meetings and music gatherings as well as people all round who you can help with their problems.

This week has been one of preparations for the new term, and now the students have arrived to start. I went to Ondo on Tuesday and stayed a night with Inga and borrowed some books on English Language Teaching from her. The new women look pleasant, but we don't know yet how much English they have. I have been cutting out dresses for their uniform - they sew it themselves. Most of them are 32" - 34" busts but one is 42" with 48" hips and 6 months pregnant so I am not sure how to make her a dress. I have cut it out in newspaper and am now going to try that before I cut the material.

We had the Finance Committee today on Friday and everything was laid out on the table. It was a miracle how everyone was so tactful so as not to hurt the principal's feelings over his inefficiency and yet they were able to bring out all the main things. We hope that from now on we can have more up to date account writing.

Ruth has been a bit down this week - not sleeping well and has headaches sometimes. It's basically 'the change 'I think. She had a period in Jan and now has it again and pain .... so maybe it's just as well for her that she will be having a spell at home this year. She is planning to go either in August or September.

We have a visitor this week - a man who works in the 'Islam in Africa' Project. He has come to talk to our students each day about the relationship of Islam and Christianity. Some of their 'campaigns ' to Moslem areas and meeting with Imams sound most encouraging. He is an extremely good speaker and has told us all sorts of interesting information about Islam, as well as how Christians can witness effectively to them.

Tues. June 6th.

I received your letter of 29th May today - including the letter from Stuart. You have had a full house with Geoff and Marguerita and Co. Yes, please send the slides - I would like to see them even if I send them back perhaps with Ruth when she goes home.

No, I am not teaching in Yoruba - English mostly for teaching - some translation, but you need Yoruba to tell them what to do in needlework.

Ruth has 2 sisters and a brother all in England, so her father has been staying with relatives during the Summer - but Ruth wants to be home for the Winter.

With lots of love

Elizabeth

Vining Centre
11th June 1972

Dear Ma and Daddy,

I have already answered your letter which came on Tuesday. Since then, I have received the Woman & Home for March and a few Church Times. I read in the Manchester Guardian Weekly (at Jane Pelly's) that Marion Turner was feared missing in Burundi but had been found safe and sound on her mission station. I wonder what the story behind that remark is. It all sounds a bit dodgy in Burundi now.

It has been rather an odd first week of term. I have only taught one lesson of the New Testament and one of Needlework!! The reason has been mainly that each morning we have had a 2-hour session on Islam. Then on Friday, in addition to that, we all went to the Mosque to watch the Friday prayers. There are a good number of Moslems in Akure - all going to the Mosque, washing their feet, and then praying in Arabic. We met the Chief Imam afterwards and they took us into the Mosque and showed us around.

Ruth has gone off on her travels for 10 days, so I have the house to myself. I seem to have picked up some tummy bug which gave me stomachache and burping gas the day before yesterday. It is better today.

There is not a lot to report. I am beginning to get into the routine of things here - but I am not sure if I shall survive the boredom of evensong every day. The morning prayers are not so bad - they are shorter and more varied - with some lessons but I find daily evensong terrible. Also, although I agree that our men ought to know how to read the Prayer Book, I also think that there should be more space for Services which they have thought out themselves and for free prayer - we have none of that, which I think is a pity. Anyway, we shall have to see if some alterations can be brought in slowly.

I am writing to Skiddy to see if she would like to send me the Manchester Guardian Weekly. I find that a copy of the Geographical Magazine comes to the Centre - free from the British Council so don't think of sending that anymore. I had a nice letter from Auntie Kath this week - and all the activities of her children and grandchildren. I can't get air letter paper now - so I hope you don't mind blue air letters for a bit.

With love

Elizabeth

Vining Centre
19th June 1972

Dear Ma and Daddy,

A nice long letter earlier in the week. Maybe the next one will arrive tomorrow. I have had a long weekend and no chance to sit down and write letters. Gillian Martin who is at Ughelli teaching Maths and Geography came for the weekend. It was her Half Term, so she came on Friday and left today (Mon). It rained on Sat. a.m. so we just went to the town and round to Fiwasaiye to see Ann Forgan.

Then yesterday after Communion we went and climbed right up to the Radio mast at Idanre. My muscles ache today! It was a beautiful clear sunny day and not too hot, so we had a splendid view of the hills all around. They have built a new Rest House halfway up - but it is not furnished or 'opened' yet. It looks like a gorgeous place to go and stay for a weekend.

After our climbing we went to see the Akinbadewa's. Pat is going home for 4 months leaving next Sunday and taking the 3 children with her. She is expecting No. 4 in September.

Marjorie Cockburn came on Sunday afternoon. She is having her local leave here with Ruth. Ruth arrived back from her travels around Okenne and Kabba yesterday afternoon.

I had a complete teaching week last week - and am getting into it more now, although we only have 5 lessons each morning compared with 8 in Gram. Sch. and some days I only have one or two! I had one lesson on flower arranging in Church. Next week it will be 'polishing 'the pews and the brass (if any). There are 50 men - in 3 years and about 20 women. The men have either been to Sec. Mod. School before or Primary - and then some have worked as Church Agents before they came here. A few have had some time in Grammar Sch. They are the ones who are most likely to go on to Emmanuel College, Ibadan.

It's nice to have a Woman and Home every now and then - but I shouldn't buy it specially for me. Ruth gets Women's Realm from some lady. The College gets the Geographical Magazine, and it comes to me. It's a gift of the British Council. I get the Church Times regularly from the Bennetts and I have written to Skiddy to ask if she would like to send me the Man. Guardian Weekly (airmail). You remember she said she wanted to give me something up to £15.

Poor Ruth! Two pairs of sandals have been chewed by white ants when she was away. Stephen forgot to clean the bottom of a cupboard. And her cock died one morning before I could get it to the Vet! However, I have managed to stop the goats from eating the roses and other plants, so we are not doing badly. We were invaded today for Cholera injections, so all men, women and children are suffering from sore arms.

With much love to all

Elizabeth

Vining Centre

25th June1972

Dear Ma and Daddy,

Thank you for your long letter all about the Retreat at Cropthorne. I hope that you got my letter last week because I fear that I must have forgotten to put on the 3d stamp.

I have been getting into the routine of the Centre this week. We have had a clear week of teaching and it was my turn to go to the Women's Guild meeting at the Leper Settlement on Tuesday. Four of our women take the meeting each time and Victoria Olowomeye, the Principal's wife and I went with them this week. I should think it's just like women's meetings in the 1930's!

On Friday we had 2 visitors - 2 Catholic Sisters (Nigerians) in training - one Igbo girl and one Urhobo. They were very nice girls and very interested to see everything that we do in the Centre with the women. They are the most 'Christian' young women I have met for a long time - really these orders do something for people. I am sure that there is a genuine feeling towards more cooperation and understanding between Catholics and Protestants in this country - certainly from the Catholic side. But the Principal here made me mad by querying these 2 girls coming here - saying that they must be coming to spy out our Secrets!! Really! Especially when the Catholics already have much more superior training places and things like a Weaving Centre for women in Ekiti. We can learn so much more from them.

Marjorie Cockburn has been here this week staying with us for her local leave. She likes breakfast in bed, reading books and resting. They have gone off to Ilesha for the weekend and Ruth will be back on Monday.

I have had another go of Pruritus this week - most irritating but have now some ointments and I hope it goes quickly. Ethel has had a similar thing for the past month. I don't know if it's catching because mine arrived after I went to her loo once. Ethel has been offered a job of teaching in St Hilda's, Ootacamund where Celia Rance was. She is thinking about it, but the matter is really in the hands of C.M.S. She wants to continue as a missionary. If she goes there, you'd better not tell this to the Priory folk. At present it is only an idea.

Ruth's roses are blooming beautifully now. There is a red one and a pink one just outside my window. I have been doing some more typing this week with a Pitman's book of Exercises. It is very useful to be able to type notes or exercises for the lessons and it's not worth duplicating for English for example, because there are only 6 students. I am going to Sunday Sch. this morning with Ethel. The students are trekking off in the drizzle in their white suits or black cassocks and their umbrellas up.

I haven't heard from Angela about her C.M.S Interviews. I wonder what happened? I wish we could have the 'Greetings of Peace 'in our Communion here. I find 1666 awful especially when the Sermon is long, and the Hymns from A & M drag like nobody's business. It's better when they have Yoruba Lyrics - but even so we are stuck like glue to the Prayer Book in all our Services. I am glad you have Doreen and her guitar - and Drama Do's at the Priory.

With much love to you all

Elizabeth

Vining Centre
2nd July 1972

Dear Ma and Daddy,

Thank you for the letter this week. I can imagine that John and Pat's news of going to New Zealand and the selling of Jimmy must have been 2 big upsets. I am sorry that you got no more than £50 for the car. New Zealand does seem the other end of the earth - and probably we shall not see them all for ages and ages - but I should think the advantages for them are great. I imagine Auckland as a beautiful place, and I should think that life in New Zealand is a good deal more interesting than Carpenter's Park. Also, that John will really enjoy working in a university set up - rather than the old "board." Maybe if they are away from home, they will begin to want to write letters!! Let's hope so anyway.

There is nothing to report here this week. I received one box of slides - but none of Iyi Enu so I imagine you still have those. I'll send them back with Ruth on Aug 22nd. I am glad that she is going then - for her sake. In fact, it might be better if she went sooner. She hasn't been sleeping well and really isn't her usual self.

Jane Pelly looks terribly tired now. She was expecting 4 new graduates from the State Board in Ibadan yesterday and none of them have shown up. It is miserable to be a principal when you are not allowed to choose your own staff and those 'sent' don't even appear! I really think Jane may go home or elsewhere at the end of her present tour.

Yesterday morning, Sat. I spent up Idanre hills with our men's Boys Brigade. I took Mrs. Owadayo, the Men's Warden's wife and we all trekked up the mountain with Rev. Jayeioba the local Pastor as well. He has 21 churches, 2 pastors, a few catechists, and no car so he finds his 'Parish 'quite difficult to visit. Anyway, some places are 20 miles along unmotorable roads.

It's the wet season setting in now. Last night in Chapel we had a swarm of flying ants - all over us in the Service. It was rather a hoot because Ethel asked one student to put out the lights at the back. Then with one accord the ants swarmed around the poor fellow who was preaching the Sermon!! So, the lights went on again and we all suffered together.

I had a letter from Dr Kumuyi this week saying that he is still in the Medical Students Hall or Hostel and can be there till July. I guess he is hoping to beg to stay longer. When did Mrs. Ballinger say she had a friend of Nicholas till?

I am sending this to St Julian's and hope that it reaches you there. I hope that you have a super restful time and meet lots of interesting people.

I am preaching a Sermon on 'Seek Peace and pursue it 'tonight. I want to talk about the Reconciliation in Sudan after 17 years of Civil War and the situation in Burundi which seems to be getting worse. I hope that dear Marion is O.K.

I hear from Ruth that Angela is accepted by C.M.S but have heard nothing from Angela about her future.

We have Half Term on 15 - 16th and I hope to go to Ado and then Ijero - Ekiti to stay with Archdeacon Alegbeleye for the W/E. That's the one that the Panters know.

With much love,

Elizabeth

Vining Centre
9th July 1972

Dear Ma and Daddy,

A super long letter this week. I have received the slides. What a lot of postage you had to pay. Isn't it possible to send slides 2nd Class Air Mail at a cheaper rate? Perhaps in future I should ask Kodak to send them here - and then they will pay the postage. Is it O.K if I send the photos back with Ruth on Aug 22nd or do you want them sooner? I am a bit disappointed with the darkness of faces in some photos. I think I didn't let in enough light with this new camera. Anyway, it gives some idea of the Creek holiday and the four of the Children's Home are fair. I took the ones of the children brushing their teeth and going to bed with the flash so that's encouraging.

I do hope that you are enjoying St Julians this week and that you have a real rest. I have my half term next weekend. I am going to spend it at Ado with Grace. Archdeacon Alegbeleye has another Archdeacon visiting him that W/E, so I have put off my visit to Ijeru for 2 weeks.

It has been a quiet week. I was at Fiwasaiye for supper on Friday and Ann and Jane came here last night. I bought a bottle of Cider! Thursday was the most eventful day for I went 4 times to the hospital. Twice in the morning was to get 13 children vaccinated with Triple Vaccine - and twice in the afternoon with a man student who cut the top off his index finger on his right hand. It was horrid! There was this nasty 'piece 'like a minute pig's trotter with nail, flesh and skin completely severed off by a piece of wire. It couldn't be replaced - although we carried it carefully to the hospital in a piece of lint! Then the students in the Dispensary had put cotton wool directly onto the bleeding piece of finger - so I got that off and replaced it with lint before we went to the doctor. They gave him a pethidine injection but, in the evening, it had worn off and the pain was so great that we went back, and he was admitted for the night. Anyway, he is back now and is very cheerful and it's no longer so painful.

From this you will gather that I have now taken over the dispensary from Ethel.... and I am busy sorting out the dosage of different things for children and babies.

I think 20 mins grace is much too avant-garde for Vining Centre now. Could you send me copies of Series II or III? Matins and Evensong and Communion. The booklets are quite small. We are still in 1666 here - sometimes we advance to 1928! Ethel at least enjoyed my Evensong last week! I had Bach from Salisbury Cathedral to begin with and took the theme of 'Seek Peace and Pursue it 'from the Epistle of the day and then followed the idea of the Collect of 5th Sunday after Trinity. I told them about the peace resolutions in Sudan (with a map on the black board) and explained how prayer is needed for Peace in Burundi. I used Max Warren in the Church Times and recent reports of Clergy killed in Burundi. We also included the tune from the Messiah - Glory to God in the Highest....and on Earth Peace Goodwill to men.

Ruth is very depressed and not sleeping well - taking Phenobarb most nights. I hope she manages the next 6 weeks. It might well have been easier for her if she had gone home earlier. She is away this weekend in the Creek area near Okitipupa South of Ondo. I am very thankful that I am sleeping extremely well and feel better than I did most of last year at home. No mouth Ulcer either - thanks to Marmite I reckon!

With love

Elizabeth

Vining Centre
16th July 1972

Dear Ma and Daddy,

You have had a busy time before getting to St Julians. I should think that you needed your breakfast in bed!! I do hope that you are now feeling rested. I am jealous of you going to Wimbledon. I would have liked to have seen Yvonne Goolagong against Chrissie Evert in the Semi-Finals match.

I am at Ado for the weekend - staying with Grace. In fact, today, Sunday, is the first day I have really felt relaxed and enjoying myself on holiday. The reason for this is that I was up half the night (about

2 hrs.') on Wed. night because Ruth had rigours. She hasn't been sleeping well and got depressed over the Accounts books on Wed. So, Malaria took over. Only hot drinks and bottles and blankets were necessary in the night, but it meant I was tired on Thursday. I thought that I would be able to sleep it off on Fri. and I did have breakfast in bed, but Grace and I spent the afternoon looking for the relative of one midwife who had taken herself off to Lagos without any by-your-leave. Then Grace chatted on and on in the evening and yesterday, Sat. she was 'off' in the afternoon, so we went to the hot springs and although it was restful, I didn't sleep in the afternoon. Anyway, this morning after a good night I had breakfast and then went back to bed and slept till 10.30 a.m.... so now I feel fine again. Ruth is here with Marjorie and seems much better and more rested.

Grace is in good form and sends her love. Her sister and cousin are coming out for a 3-week holiday at the beginning of August. So, she is busy planning for their visit. Dr Matthai the Indian doctor is coming back to Ado after 3 months leave so everyone is happy about that. He and his wife are exceptionally nice people.

We have a lot of children with coughs at the Vining Centre.... possibly whooping Cough in some cases. So, we have had small classes in the past week because we have sent the Mums of the 'coughers' to their houses to look after their children there. Much to most of their annoyance "Why should we be punished" they say, "when we didn't bring the cough to the compound?"

Dr Olasimbo suddenly phoned up on Wed evening and then came over with his cousin and wife for about 15 mins. He was staying just one night in Akure while going to a Court Case in Ondo on Saturday. It was nice of him to call.

We had a play reading on Tues. night at the Palace - about 8 of us were there - we read a play about telling the truth...... and how when the truth comes out in a group of people it sometimes causes quite painful embarrassing situations.

Grace is busy cleaning rice and picking stones out of it - I ought to go and give her a hand - and do the washing up. Some Zionists are singing and drumming over the back of the bush. We have just listened to a Service from Westminster Abbey celebrating the 100th Anniversary of Trinity College of Music. Good organ... rather a lot of references to "benefactors". Cardinal Heenan was the preacher.

Greetings to the Panters and other friends in Malvern. I don't know what I shall do on Link visits to St George's - with Mass and the lot.

With much love
Elizabeth

Vining Centre
23rd July 1972

Dear Ma and Daddy,

Before I forget - when you send out my circular letter can you change the address of the following: Mrs. Mary Tribe - now at 45, Broom Hall Drive, Ushaw Moor, Durham, UK.

I am glad to hear that you had such a super time at St. J. I haven't had the letter or books sent by Ewan yet - but I am not very surprised. Post is very erratic within the country. I expect that it will come. In fact, I have just written to the Ekpoma's to ask if I can stay there a couple of nights when I go down to Lagos with Ruth on Aug 21st.

It has been an uneventful week - one trip to the hospital with one baby whose foolish mother didn't tell me till her child had been stooling all day - about 6 pm. He is a baby of 4 months, so I didn't dare to treat him here. I was furious with her stupidity - she said she thought it would go off!! Anyway, he is better now - and so too are most of the children with coughs.

This morning after Communion, peace and quiet was shattered by the noise of some bust up between the 3 wives of the College driver Ezekiel. He only has <u>one</u> room! And I think one wife lives in town, but she had come to visit. I don't know what it was all about - but to have 3 wives and one room anyway is bound to lead to complications. My mind boggles!

I am glad it's hot with you - it's cool to cold here- my white cardigan is dirty - for overuse and I can't find a good day for drying it because there is so little sunshine.

I have toothache today which is rather a blow because the nearest dentist I would trust is at Ife. My duck has laid 2 eggs and I am waiting to see what happens next. I gather ducks are not very good mothers - but it would be fun to have a line of yellow ducklings.

I am taking the women to Ado on Thursday this week to look over the Textile Factory and to visit the hospital (Ile Abiye) specially to look at how they treat the children in the Children's Ward.

Ruth is away for the weekend. I hope that she doesn't return too exhausted. Ethel has had a couple of days rest with a sore throat and cold, so she is coming here for lunch. I have made a mousse and at last it is successful!! With the electric beater. Can you check that Greta Williamson, Foxbury is on my circular list?

John Fabuyi popped in this week. He is expecting to be transferred from Adeyemi College soon. He said he would come again for a chat before he goes. The Archdeacon's wife here is the sister of an old Andrian! She in fact is a bit of a washout and thinks mostly of her Cloth Shop and is always putting off M.U. meetings!!

With much love

Elizabeth

Vining Centre
30th July 1972

Dear Daddy and Ma,

I have had 2 letters this week - a long amusing screed written in the garden and the one sent via Ewan containing 2 nice handkerchiefs and a 'What-sit 'for covering the milk. Thank you!

This past week has been a busy one. I've been to Ibadan and therefore was able to buy some writing paper. By the way your letter with 6 pages and the newspaper cutting about Bp. Martin weighed more than 1/2 oz on our Scales here. I didn't have to pay anything, but they might send such by sea which would be a nuisance.

I think that I said last week that I had toothache, and that I wanted to avoid going to the Polish lady here in Akure. So, I arranged to go to Ife and see the Egyptian dentist who is now there. He used to be in Akure before and had filled my teeth when I was in Ondo. Then on Tuesday I had a letter from the C.M.S Office in Lagos asking me to go to Ibadan on Thursday with the car, to meet a Clergyman, Rev. Ude from Umuahia who was interested in buying the car. So, I decided to go on from Ife to Ibadan and stay Wed. night there and return to Akure on Thursday. This was possible because all the women were going to Ado that day and Ethel offered to go in my place.

So, I had 2 days off in the middle of the week and I was able to collect my new passport in Ibadan. It is valid till 1982! I was also able to visit some of my friends en route! I had breakfast with Inga and Susanne and coffee with Kelu and lunch with Jose in Ibadan. I also saw Grace and Titus in Ibadan and John Fabuyi in Ondo on the return journey. I stayed in Ibadan with Jose Aighbohai. Her husband Sam is working in the Midwest now, so she is very lonely and miserable on her own in Ibadan with the children. Sam is trying to get a job in Ibadan, but he missed several jobs or heard of the interviews too late to get there. They don't want to move to the Midwest because of the lack of Schools for the children and Jose has a good job in Ibadan. Sam had thought that he might be better off in the Midwest in the Civil Service because he is a Midwesterner and felt that there was no prospect as a teacher in Ibadan because all promotions go to Yorubas first - but now he has decided that he is not cut out for a Civil Servant and is trying to get a job in the University or in a Book Publishing Firm.

Kelu has had yet another spell without a 'boy', so she has had to do her own housework and neglect the 'Shop.' Therefore, obviously it wasn't doing well. She has just got another Igbo boy to work in the house for her. If she didn't shout at them, they might last longer! I don't know what she pays them, but I don't suppose it is much.

The dentist gave me a temporary filling in my tooth, so I must go back again next Wednesday. I only have one lesson on Wed. so it's possible to go. The car deal in Ibadan was a wild goose chase. The man had no intention of buying such a large car for £500, the price fixed by John Fowler.

Ruth and Ethel are away this weekend, so I am on my own on the Compound. Ruth was not feeling very well so Ethel offered to go with her to share the driving. Ruth would have been better to see a Gynae doctor when she was at home last year - and to be taking some medicine to help with the Menopause 'Dumps' which is part of her trouble - apart from her mother's death.

I am sure Bishop Martin would love to see you. He is at 'Woollton' Middle Littleton. But you had better not say anything about Ruth's 'blues' since I don't know how much she has told him. She will be home on Aug. 22nd.

I was supposed to be going to Ijero this weekend but am now going next weekend when they have a Choir Festival there. Instead, yesterday I went to a Funeral near Owo with Canon and Mrs. Olowomeye (Principal here) and Rev. Owadayo. It was the funeral of Rev. Fabuluje's mother. I stayed with them in Okeigbo. Inga was there and several others from Ondo Cathedral Congregation. It was a packed Church with hundreds milling around outside as well. It was a very joyful Service except that Fabuluje, and his brothers and his wife all looked completely worn out with the arrangements to entertain so many people - and to keep awake half the night for the 'Waking.'

I was amused to see their little girl in a new hat - yellow plastic looking like 'straw 'with a ribbon. She had it on back-to-front and the price tab was dangling down her neck at the back!!

Jane and Ann came here this morning for Communion and stayed for breakfast. I am going there for lunch.

My duck has laid 8 eggs but shows no sign of sitting on them. I hope they don't all die. The weather is cold now. I am even using a blanket in the afternoon when I have my rest.

Your garden sounds good. I will have to think about mine when I move house.

Our Oba's wife is a Nigerian. She was a nurse who trained in Queen Charlotte's before her husband became Oba. He was a lawyer. She does a tremendous lot of work with women's affairs in Akure and is a great Christian Witness.

I will try to post this today. Your letter of 23rd arrived on Saturday morning which is much more satisfactory than when they take 10 days.

With much love to you both,

Elizabeth

The Work of the Women's Warden

Vining Centre
July 1972

It is time that I wrote to you to tell you something of life here in the Vining Centre. I have now started teaching the women and I am beginning to find out the 'ins and outs' of the place.

The Centre was started here in 1960, as a training centre for catechists and their wives. Now there are 54 men and 19 women in training, with five members of staff. The men do a three-year course, and their wives can join them for the last year. This means that most of the women are the wives of the third-year students, but some others are the wives of ordinands who are in Ibadan at Emmanuel College. Consequently, in the various houses, we have a mixture of unmarried men, men without their wives, men with their wives and small children and wives with children but without their husbands because they are in Ibadan. The women here are allowed to bring two children under six years to stay with them, so we have about 30 children and babies to cope with.

All this needs to be understood before you can picture the set up. When you imagine my class of 20 women, you need to bear in mind that a couple may be feeding their babies during the lesson, half the class are in various stages of pregnancy, about six speak no English and one speaks neither English nor Yoruba so she can understand only if everything is translated for her by the one other woman who only speaks a little of her language. The new women this term range from three who have been to Modern School to two who have never been to school at all and so are struggling to learn to read and write. It requires a good deal of ingenuity to keep them all interested, or even awake!

In case you are wondering what happens to the 30 children during lessons, we have a 'nursery', so called; in fact, it means that the children are minded by a clergyman's wife in a garage! They have some basic equipment like stools, blackboards, and chalk, a slide, and a few old toys, but really, they are just 'managing'. It is by no means ideal, but it does make lessons possible for their mothers.

To give you an idea of my activities I will spell out the main items on my timetable for this week: -

English .... I have a class every day with seven women who can speak some English.

- Health ....I spent most of this week's lesson explaining why it is wrong and indeed dangerous to think that all white tablets with ICI written on them are for malaria!
- New Testament ...... We are studying the Sermon on the Mount now - the mote and the beam has a very relevant message for a group of women living in daily contact with each other.
- Group bible study .... Each week I write an outline and get it duplicated for our study. We have been reading the Epistle of James and following themes with parallels in the Sermon on the Mount.
- Care of churches .... I demonstrated how to make furniture polish out of soap, candle wax and kerosene! In fact, my effort was a semi-failure because I didn't make it hot enough.
- Needlework .... The new students are making their uniform dresses and the others are knitting jackets for their children; but remember that none of them can read the knitting pattern and some have never used a sewing machine before.
- Cross bearer .... We have a system of cards each with seven questions on them to test their knowledge of the Bible and the Prayer Book, so we spend one period a week testing what they have learnt.

These classes are all in the mornings. On Tuesday afternoon I went with a group of women to the Women's Guild meeting at the local settlement for leprosy patients. On Friday afternoon there are preparation classes for the Sunday schools and on Sunday morning this is followed up by going to see what happens in the Sunday schools. Next Sunday I am taking our evening service and each day I listen to one of the men students rehearsing before taking our daily morning or evening prayers.

I have yet to take on the college dispensary (every morning and in all emergencies - deliveries, chicken pox, malaria and vaccinations are all included!), the Old Testament lessons and house-craft lessons as well as the correspondence and over-all responsibility for the women's training. Ethel Hime, from whom I am taking over, is doing these jobs at present. She is leaving at the end of this term (August 18) and is going to be in the CMS Guest House in Lagos until she returns to England next year. So, as from September I shall oversee the women's work and shall be doing the teaching with the help of Mrs. Ademoye, our Yoruba matron, who takes cookery and childcare classes in Yoruba for those who have no English.

You will be glad to know that I am feeling fit and well now and I am not overworked. I have time to sit and knit, to feed my two ducks, to read 'Crime and Punishment' and to climb Idanre Hills. But I should be glad of your continuing prayers as I get more things to do, so that I should continue to find the way of 'balance' between creative relaxation and work. This morning I read the following in a book called 'The Secret of Inward Peace'. It said: "Today the world's supreme need is more men and women more able to stand the strain of modern life and to deal efficiently with its challenges without becoming hard or nervous or irritable. And the reason why so many are found inadequate to the needs of today is fundamentally that they lack that inward peace which a relationship to God alone can give." It is easy to agree with this or even to preach about it, but it is not so easy to put into practice.

May the Lord of peace himself always give you peace, wherever you may be.

With my sincere greetings,
Elizabeth Deeks.

Vining Centre
5th August 1972

Dear Ma and Daddy,

I am just now in the house of Archdeacon and Mrs Alegbeleye in Ijero - Ekiti. Mrs. Alegbeleye is sitting in the backyard poking sticks under a large pot with chicken inside. The sticks are damp so there's more smoke than flame. It is 5 to one but by the state of the chicken I should imagine they keep Bamgboye hours for meals!

Anyway, they are extremely welcoming and keep thanking me for coming! It seems to me it should be the other way round. This afternoon's 'entertainment 'is the funeral of an ex-Oba at Owo! The bishop is coming, and they have borrowed chairs from here although the village is 18 miles away - so it sounds as though it will be a big do! A funeral 2 Saturday's running is a bit much really - but I thought that I'd better get part of my letter written to you now while I wait for lunch.

It has been a busy week again. Wednesday was a hey-day. I went to the dentist again in Ife - and so had breakfast with Inga and coffee with Yomi. Then after I had a rest in the afternoon Ruth Howard and Mary Griffin turned up - to stay!! It was a wee bit awkward because I was coming to Ijero for the W/E and Marjorie Cockburn was coming for a quiet rest with Ruth. Ethel is busy with end of term exams etc. Anyway, we fixed them with beds in Ethel's and they ate in ours. Then Titi turned up - to stay the night! Then Dr Olasimbo phoned and said he would come round. So, Ruth was swamped with 4 of my visitors all at once!!! However, it was great to see them all, but I shall be glad to have my own house from the point of view of visitors.

Then on Friday Ruth Howard and Mary decided to come to Ado to stay a night with Grace. I phoned Grace to say expect the 3 of us. They left Akure at 4 p.m. I was just setting off at 5 p.m. when Grace came driving Marjorie in the hospital car. She said, "Where is my sister and cousin?' They were supposed to be in Akure in Sheila Davis' very ancient Citroen. So, I decided to leave my car in Akure and go with Grace. When we got to Ado, we found her sister and cousin who had been to Akure but couldn't find the Vining Centre but there was no sign of Ruth and Mary! And Grace had not asked for supper for them because Marjorie had said that she would persuade Ruth and Mary to stay in Akure to see her. It's all very confusing! So, we asked Geoffrey to make supper for 6 instead of 4 and he did... both Ruth and Mary didn't turn up till around 9 p.m. - and they had already had supper at the bishop's!

Anyway, all this meant that I brought the ancient Citroen to Ijero. It just managed it, and I hope it gets back to Ado tomorrow. I don't think I have ever driven such a doubtful car! It makes a lot of noise. It gets hot. It jerks in 1st gear; it hasn't got much power for going up hills and it hasn't got much in the way of brakes for going down them!

I slept on a camp bed at Grace's last night without a mosquito net. It was not a good night. We were late to bed in the first place, and I couldn't "get off" to sleep. Then there were mosquitoes pinging all around my head - so I covered my head with the blanket - and then it got hot...... of course!

Sun. a.m.

It was a great 'funeral' yesterday. Absolutely masses of people and all sorts of gorgeous clothes. We stayed for an hour or so afterwards and sat on a wooden bench and ate meat, peppery stew, pounded yam and drank Coca-Cola. Then we came back here and had more pounded yam and pepper stew!! I slept well, but found it very difficult to wake up this morning - and hope that I don't sleep through the Choir Anniversary which we have at 10 a.m. Mrs. Alegbeleye asked if I would like 'tea' at 6.30 a.m. this morning - and I said 'yes' but I forgot to specify which sort of 'tea' - and so Bournvita was served (because I chose that last night I suppose). It certainly doesn't help to wake you up in the morning!!

I will be returning to Akure this afternoon - provided the Citroen manages the roads. I gather that a tree is down on the way that I came so I will have to go back through Iddo and Ifarki. It is only 2 miles longer.

I forgot my towel at Grace's - so I haven't had a bath this morning. I have also forgotten my petticoat so I am wondering if I can wear my Dacron dress without it. Snags!!

1.20 p.m.

The Choir Anniversary lasted 3 hours and 15 mins! and they collected £36. The songs were very lively - mostly with drums or rattles in the background. It was drawn out by the fact that if someone liked a particular song, they paid 5/- (or something) for an encore!!

Tues. evening.

Sorry this letter hasn't reached the post-box yet. Life has been somewhat non-stop since Sunday. The Citroen did not make it!! It went 9 miles to Aramoko and conked out... long story really but the gist of it was that I went to the local Vicar (who I'd met), and he helped me to get advice - no garages or phones in the place. I left the Citroen in Aramoko for Sunday night and went on to Ado by public transport, stayed with Grace and phoned Ruth in Akure and arranged for Sunday our very obliging mechanic to drive my car to Ado early on Mon a.m. He arrived by 7.30 a.m. We went to Aramoko, and he tinkered for about an hour and got it going enough to bring back to Akure for treatment.

Then I taught health, then lunch, then 2 service rehearsals, then 10 mins rest, then I took Ruth and Mary (my somewhat neglected visitors) up to Idanre. We climbed to the radio mast. Then returned to have a bath and then supper and Scottish dancing at Jane Pelly's.

Today there were exams in the morning and a Women's Guild meeting in the afternoon. I received your letter of 31st July with news of Ilka etc. and the Circular Letter in the same post. In fact, Tuesdays are good days for post. They always seem to produce more than on other days.

It looks as though Jacqui Henry will come here for about a month - Sept. > Oct. both for local leave and then to see what we do in the Vining Centre. Then one Mothers Union lady called Mrs. Threadgold is going to come and stay for a bit towards the end of Oct. That's the one that Jane Backhouse's message was all about.

I also had a letter from Richard today - He is working for the Federal Government in Sokoto, after getting his degree (3rd class). So, it doesn't look as though I shall be seeing anything of him. He couldn't be much further away.

We have exams now - I must get on with preparing mine. I am a bit behind hand because of the activities of the weekend and the visit of Ruth and Mary.

Ruth Howard and I are discussing going to spend Christmas with Maureen Olphin.

With much love to you both,
Elizabeth

Vining Centre
14th August 1972

Dear Daddy and Ma,

I am afraid it will have to be a 'shorty 'this week. The end of term has been a busy one, especially yesterday when Grace and her sister and cousin came, and I took them all up to Idanre and cooked lunch and breakfast (no great effort really!) But Ruth was in bed all day, so she had to have her meals on trays. The reason for this was that unfortunately on Saturday night she fell on the step at Ann's House and hit the bottom of her back. It is still extremely painful when she moves at all - so we are spending the morning today endeavoring to see a doctor and get it X-rayed, if necessary, in Akure hospital. I hope that it will be alright for her to fly next week - and that we can cope with the packing up between us this week. She is still not sleeping well - and the pain from the back does not help that very much.

N.B. I have asked Ruth to leave me her B.R.F notes for Sept. - Dec. because I have none this year. Please can you send one copy to her by Sept. 1st - "Woollton", School Lane, Middle Littleton, Nr. Evesham.

We had a super walk in Idanre yesterday. On Sat. I went to Ife again to the dentist. Yomi and Kelu were going off to Lagos for the W/E to collect Ayo and Yinka from school.

I have sold the Humber car for £475. It is a bit sad really because it is a super car and I think they will just spoil it and use it for a taxi.

Later. In fact, there is now another complication about the car because the Ekiti Diocesan Accountant also offered £475, and they want it kept "in the Mission."

We managed to see the Surgeon this morning and the opinion is that nothing is fractured - but it is jolly painful. We couldn't get an X-ray because the Electricity went off!! Anyway, I think she will be O.K to fly - but they say it may be very painful for up to 2 weeks.

After this hospital morning - I spent about 40 mins in the evening trying to persuade one of our women that she should have a D & C. She was refusing. I think she thought that she wouldn't be able to become pregnant again. I failed to convince her - but Cornelius and Victoria have been to see her in the hospital again this evening and she has said that she will have it. Victoria had her last child after having D & C before so that convinced her.

I got to Lagos on Monday and then will be staying with Ukpomas for a couple of days - then with Olasimbo's in Ijebu then Grace in Ibadan. Then move house.

With much love

Elizabeth

Vining Centre
20th August 1972

Dear Ma and Daddy,

Thank you for your letters, with all the news of Malvern. It is super to have so much gorgeous countryside within easy reach of you there. Symonds Yat sounds like a very beautiful place.

The term here has ended this week, and I managed to get my exams marked in between visits to the hospital with Ruth. The Polish Surgeon examined her back and said that he thought that nothing was fractured but he wanted X-rays done. In fact, they also are inconclusive. Anyway, Ruth has had this week in bed and really it has been a blessing in disguise because she is so much better in herself - sleeping better overall, and not so depressed. We set off tomorrow for Lagos, and I hope that we have a smooth journey.

I am sending 3 boxes of slides with Ruth (or Ewan). I have not packed them into a proper parcel because I thought that you could either phone her and ask her to post them if you are in a hurry - or collect them when you meet, which I hope you will do in the not-too-distant future.

Also, Ruth has a slide with me on which I have asked her to get made into a colour photo - for you. She may have to get 3 copies… in which case perhaps one could go to John and Pat and one to Ruth. But I haven't given her any money. Can you pay the necessary and I will refund you?

I seem to have lost Mother's letter this week. You mentioned Alison Layland - yes, she was at St Louis Ondo for 2 years. She was always rather a withdrawn person - desperately wrapped up in her family - and rather difficult to get to know. She may well be much happier in a Malvern School.

I have been round Ethel's house with her today to have a look at furniture and furnishings etc. I shall be doing some shopping in Lagos and Ibadan. I need all sorts of things - curtains, saucepans, ironing board (probably) baking tins, buckets, washing up basin etc. etc. I will also get a radio and record player, I hope while I am in Lagos, because C.M.S folk can get discounts in one Electrical Shop there.

We are taking the Humber car to Lagos because it runs so much more smoothly than a Volkswagen. Then when I come back it is to be sold to Ekiti Diocesan Accountant and I shall then use Ruth's

Volkswagen. Since it is a 'Mothers Union" car they send a grant for its upkeep, so I only must pay for petrol. This works out much cheaper than the C.M.S arrangement of paying for your mileage. So 'up the Mothers Union'!

Mon. evening

We had a very smooth journey down from Akure and arrived here in Lagos around 3.30 p.m. to spend the night at the Guest House before Ruth goes tomorrow on the plane. She will post this letter for me at home.

I phoned Ewan and I will go there tomorrow to see them. She says brightly on the phone - we will go to Dahomey! on Thurs. - then I am supposed to come back on Friday to go to Dr Olasimbo's. I can't see that it will be worthwhile to spend one day in Lagos going around offices dealing with Immigration papers and Visas to spend only one day in Dahomey!! Anyway, we shall see. I don't think that Nigerians must get the same papers that a European must, so it is much less trouble for them.

Lagos traffic is very bad mannered! The movement of cars seems to have improved since 'Right Hand Drive '- but along the main road where they have made 2 lanes each way it its hair raising because cars overtake on the right - on the inside lane and change lanes just as they fancy.

I will be moving house on Sept. 1st. It will be fun to have a place of my own again - but I shall miss sharing the house with Ruth as far as meals are concerned. Anyway, the Fowlers are coming to stay on Sept. 4th and Jacqui Henry comes around Sept. 13th for a month. Then the M.U lady for a week - so I shall not really be lonely.

With much love

Elizabeth

Vining Centre

26th August 1972

Dear Ma and Daddy,

I am now in Ijebu-Ode staying in the home of Dr Olasimbo. We went today to a 50th Birthday party of a Consultant Gynaecologist from Adeoyo Hospital in Ibadan. They had a Thanksgiving Service in the Church and then ate at the 'Mansion 'house in the village. It was a great show of brocade and lace and there must have been about 100 doctors there. It is not the "shortage" of doctors but the distribution of doctors in this country which is the real trouble. There are loads of doctors in Ibadan and Lagos, but it is just about impossible to shift them up-country.

I took Ruth to the airport on Tuesday morning and then went back to Lagos. I had a flat tyre underneath Eko Bridge where you are not supposed to stop - like on a motorway. However, I did stop, and 2 fellows helped me to change the tyre before a breakdown truck arrived to tow me off. They have a lookout tower and from there they spy out any breakdowns and send their fellows to tick you off!

Anyway, I survived, but I was glad to get to the peace and quiet of the Ukpoma's house. All the Ukpoma family were at home, so it was nice to meet them all together. The two oldest daughters were doing a holiday job in the N.B.C and so they kept going off to do "programmes." They all went together to Dahomey on Thursday afternoon. I decided not to go with them because it would have meant changing my arrangements for this weekend and spending a morning in Lagos offices trying to get Visa and other permits to cross the border. I was a bit sad when I saw them pack their tennis rackets into the car - but since then I am sure that it was the right decision.

I saw several ex-St Monica's folk in Lagos. Shola is there with her sister. She is now working in the Federal Training School teaching French to the bi-lingual Secretaries. She is expecting twins!

Foluke (the girl who came shopping with us) is now working in the Co-operative Bank just near the Cathedral in Lagos. So, I saw her there and she took me to the Nigerian Ports Authority office which is on the other side of Bishop's Court where 2 more St Monica's girls are working. Then 2 of them took me to find Jessie's house in Surulere. So, I met her husband. She is just the same - full of giggles. She is expecting a baby later this year.

Then I went and stayed the night with Myrtle. She had just come back to Lagos from a holiday in the North. She and Gwen went to Jos together. She is much thinner but looks very tired. She is still having trouble with her period, despite the D & C earlier this year. On Friday morning Myrtle came with me to the Pan Electrics warehouse in Ebute Metta to help me buy a radio and a turntable. I had thought that I would buy them separately, but we found a super combined radio and stereo record player in a cabinet on legs. It cost £75. But Pan Electrics gives C.M.S folk 20% discount. So, I only had to pay £60 for it and since this was the amount that I had decided to spend I was delighted. If I had bought them separately it would have cost £40+ and £20+ and this thing looks so much nicer. Also, it will work from batteries as well as mains - just 6 torch batteries!

Then on Friday afternoon I came on to Ijebu - Ode to stay with Dr and Mrs. Olasimbo. On Sat. a.m. I went to visit Jumoke Lajubutu in her School at Ijebu-Igbo. Then I have also seen Bola Asafa and his family. He lives in an upstairs flat in the most extraordinary great enormous house painted pink and green with a red light like a lighthouse on the roof.

I go on to Ibadan today to spend 2 nights with Grace and then I hope to do some shopping in Ibadan on Mon and Tues and then go on to Ife on Tuesday afternoon and spend the night with Yomi and Kelu. Go to the dentist on Wed a.m. and then return to Akure in the afternoon. Then I just have Thursday to tidy up before moving over to Ethel's house on Friday.

I must write to Pat and John before they go. It is not so long now. I hope that they can sell their house without too much trouble.

I expect there will be letters from home waiting for me when I get back to Akure. I always look forward to post when I have been away. Thank you very much for the books which you sent via Ewan. I haven't sent anything back with her - I couldn't find anything that I wanted to send. Lagos prices for curios are stupid. I hope that you get the slides that I sent by Ruth.

With much love

Elizabeth

Moving into my own house

Vining Centre
3rd September 1972

Dear Daddy and Ma,

I seem to have 3 of your letters here to answer from Aug 15th and 27th. It is good to keep up to date with all your news. I am always pleased when your letter gets here by Saturday. I am glad to hear that Geoff and Marguerita and Co all enjoyed Lee Abbey and that everyone seems to approve of Trevor. I am glad that you had such a happy time with Sheila Tam. I have her Chinese lantern on my bookcase in my new sitting room. All the Nigerians think it must be made of gold!

The main activity of this week, after I arrived back in Akure on Wednesday via Ife and Ondo - has been moving house. We did this on Thursday, and it was quite a do, but really very easy because we had about 8 men and boys to carry everything to and fro. It has been great fun unpacking all my various things and I discovered that I had kept more things than I remembered from Ondo, especially in the Kitchen line. I seem to have everything that I need, except a cheese grater! which I can get without difficulty in Ibadan.

Ethels' house is very convenient with all mod cons. especially a decent gas stove and a new electric fridge which gets so cold that today a bottle of water turned into ice and the bottle broke and the water dripped all over the place. The only snag of the Kitchen are those wretched little ants which get into everything. Today I made a casserole in the oven for lunch with Ethel and a sponge which Jane and Ann came and ate at teatime. Both were good.

I should like the cookery book called "Better Cookery" by Aileen King, Publisher - Mills & Boon. I think it cost about 30/-. It is the one Greta recommended at Foxbury. This is an idea for a birthday. I wonder if you could send anything via this Mrs. Streatfield. The other thing I suggest is a tray cloth. You know those 3 little plastic containers that I bought in the Jumble Sale at St George's for 6d. I think they are in 'my 'cupboard? Perhaps Mrs. Streatfield could bring those.

Castlemorton Common seems very popular with you for picnics. Unless you wrote twice about the same picnic.

I am sure that you will have enjoyed having John and Co to stay - but it is a bit hard to say goodbye to them all.... until you go and retire in New Zealand of course! I hope you don't do that, by the way. I can't do my Link visits in New Zealand!!

My new record player and radio are working well. I have been listening to the Magic Flute today and enjoying it even more than before because I can remember the different events as seen in the Academy.

My ducks still haven't hatched out any eggs. They can't all be duds - but it seems to take a very long time. I shall not be surprised if the mother gives up sitting.

I still have the Humber car because the Ekiti Diocesan Accountant who was going to buy it phoned to say that the Diocese couldn't loan him the money after all because all their cash for cars is going on a big new car for the bishop and that car has arrived so must be paid for. So, it is not sold after all. Anyway, John Fowler is coming tomorrow, and the sale is really his affair. I thought I had sold it too easily!

It's Ethel's birthday on Wednesday so we are having Ann and Jane and the Eyesorun to supper. The Eyesorun is the Oba's wife who I have mentioned before. We may go out for the day on Wednesday, probably to Ado.

Fiwasaiye has started back at school again. Really, we have gorgeous long holidays and although there are several things to be done in them you can plan things as you like. We start the term again on October 1st. There is supposed to be a 'Mission' for the last 10 days of the holiday, but goodness knows what is happening about it. The provost said we were not to go to Ilaje area after all (near Okitipupa) because there is a new Superintendent there - and it seems they say that they 'can't afford us' in Owo district - I can't see what great expense it will make for them, but that's the excuse I hear.

Autumn must be beginning at home. I'll try to take some pictures of my nice new house. I haven't bought any curtains or cushion covers at all. All the ones from Ondo fit!

With much love,

Elizabeth

Vining Centre
10th September 1972

Dear Daddy and Ma,

The post has not obliged by producing your letter yet this week. I expect it will come on Monday. I now have the charge of the typewriter that belongs to the Women's Warden in the Centre, so I am trying to use it as much as possible to practice before the new term starts at the end of the month. I can do it without looking but I must concentrate very hard and as you will see I still make a few mistakes.

The only 'Event' of this last week was Ethel's birthday which was on Wednesday. I made a fruit cake for the first time in my new oven and was happy to find that it came out all right and everyone seemed to enjoy it. In the evening we had a small dinner party in Ethel's house with Ann and Jane and the Eyesorun (the wife of the Oba). Then on Thursday Ethel and I went out with a picnic lunch to Idanre. We went to Olofin Grammar School and saw Francis there. He directed us to find the way up onto one of the rocks. We scrambled up and found a place with a gorgeous view. We had a lovely picnic until it started to rain, and we had to come down. There has been a lot of rain this past week and everything is damp. It is difficult to find a time when it is dry enough to put the clothes out to dry.

My ducklings have hatched out at last, but I am not sure if I couldn't have done something to help more of them to have hatched out. There were 12 eggs and 6 of them hatched. One died of these. But it seemed to me that there were babies inside the other eggs, but the mother didn't continue sitting on them after the first lot had hatched. Now I have 5 small yellow ducklings to keep an eye on. They never taught us at Foxbury how to look after ducks!

I am planning to go to Ibadan on Wednesday this week to do some shopping for the beginning of term and to meet Jacqui Henry who is coming up from Lagos on Friday. I shall go by Ife to get my last filling polished. Then we shall only have two more weeks before the beginning of the term. We were supposed to be going on a Mission in the last week of the holiday but that has completely fallen through this time because the churches that we thought we would go to have said that they can't afford to have us at this time of year! The cocoa farmers are waiting for their cocoa money so everything tends to come to a standstill. Even the Centre may well be in queer street at the beginning of the term because so far none of the 5 supporting dioceses have been able to pay us their termly grant.

John Taylor has let rip about pollution in his last newsletter hasn't he? It is certainly a sad world that we live in. I suppose that most of the young men who are members of the 'Black September' gang have been brought up in the Arab refugee camps.

This compound really is like a farmyard. I keep having to go outside to shout at the goats or sheep who will come and eat up all my bushes. Then yesterday I saw that a pair of pigs that often come visiting from the town have had piglets and there are 7 little ones! Just now there are some chickens scratching around under the trees. I haven't yet done anything much about my garden. I have started a few pots on the veranda, and I think that I shall concentrate on them. There is a lot of Pride of Barbados all around the house. I think that when Ethel has gone, I shall have some of it dug out, because there is not much room for anything else.

My new record player is working well, and I am getting a great deal of enjoyment out of it. I can get B.B.C clearly on the radio, but it is not very good for music. I tried to listen to part of the proms last night, but it was not very successful. Mary Skidmore is now kindly sending me the Manchester Guardian Weekly by air, so I can keep in touch with news in the world much better than I did before.

It is amazing how much you can get into an air letter form if you type it! And I could have spaced it closer together.

With much love to you both

Elizabeth

Vining Centre

17th September 1972

Dear Ma and Daddy,

I received your letter on Monday, telling of your hectic week with John and Pat, the Marvels and then Pat Withers affairs. Eku ise o! There's not much "retirement" in Malvern as far as I can see. I am glad that you have met up with Alison. She needs friendly understanding, I am sure. We always found her "difficult to get to know" in Ondo. She is not very good at making conversation. I am very sorry to hear about Mrs. Bebbington's death and that Doris Ayton was in hospital. She will be very upset by it all.

I hope that you may have seen Bishop Martin and Ruth by now. How is she, I wonder? I hope that she is more cheerful and sleeping better at home.

I can get records here, but I am sending you a list of my records (practice in typing!!) I should be glad to have a record of one of these modern gospel groups singing - especially if there are words included. But don't worry unless you have a willing carrier.

I have been to Ibadan this week, from Wed. - Friday. It was a very happy journey except that the windscreen smashed. It was the first time that I had driven Ruth's car any distance. However, it didn't take long to get a new one in Ibadan. Rev. Owadayo came with me, so I had company on the road. We seem to take all day to get there - stopping at Inga's, Ife hospital and Yomi and Kelu's for lunch (about 2.30!) and then picking the glass out of the windscreen.

I stayed with Jose and Sam was there too, so she was very happy. Also, he has at last got a job in Ibadan with Oxford Univ. Press so their time of being separated is about over. I am very glad for them.

I spent a good deal of time in bookshops getting books for the beginning of term. Then on Friday I met Jacqui and brought her back here via Ilesha where we collected the medicines from Joan Stevenson. Jacqui is tired after all her travelling around - but she can have a break here and a time to relax. Already today she is feeling better. I hope to get her to help me to make some visual aids and models for the beginning of term.

We went to visit Dr and Mrs. Perzina yesterday afternoon. You can walk from here - about 1 1/2 miles. They are so very friendly and welcoming. He is the Polish Surgeon who examined Ruth when she fell. His wife is called Barbara and she is a Dentist but also an Asst. Professor in a Polish University specialising in Orthodontology and treating children with cleft palates. She makes her own cottage cheese - so I want to start some too.

I shall be thinking of you as you go to see Pat and John off on the 27th. I am sure that it will open a whole new world for them all and be much more interesting than Carpenter's Park. But it will be sad to say goodbye to them all.

Angela should be going to Crowther Hall soon. I hope that she will be able to come over and visit you from B'ham. Is Janice Hobday on leave? News of Uganda is not very encouraging especially if they start a 'blame the British' campaign.

I expect I will get your letter tomorrow. St George's Mag. is full of 'Father this and that 'isn't it? On the other hand, they seem to have had some splendid do's. I wonder what the regular services are like - much more important really.

With much love

Elizabeth

P.S. Please thank one Mrs. Jean Simpson for her very nice letter. She is a member of Free Church Malvern Link and wrote me a letter after my last Link letter.

P.P.S. I hear today that Ruth's father has had a coronary and is to stay in bed resting for a month. Poor Ruth! She is to have a D & C sometime soon to fix up her own troubles. I hope that she is strong enough to cope with looking after her father - perhaps she will be better with something definite to do. Maybe you have already heard of this new development? I hope that you will be able to see them.

Vining Centre

23rd September 1972

Dear Ma and Daddy,

Thank you both for your letters this week. I am glad that you were able to go and see Bishop Martin and Ruth. Also, that you like the photograph that Ruth took of me. I am glad to hear that Bishop Martin isn't so seriously sick and hope that he does get well again quickly for Ruth may have to stay home for a much longer time.

I have Jacqui Henry here this week. She is on holiday but also wanting to see what we do in the Vining Centre. We went together to Oshogbo on Wednesday after staying Tues. night in Ilesha with Joan Stevenson. Joan is always very bright and full of talk. She had recently been to Lake Chad. They went for just 10 days - 4 days getting there and back and 2 days in Maiduguri and going to see the Lake.

We had a very pleasant day in Oshogbo while the car was serviced in M and K. We wandered all down the long main street greeting the shop keepers and eating akara, which was freshly cooked at the roadside. We also went into their small Museum and looked at some of the old masks and head dresses etc. which they had there - and at the paintings done by local artists. Then there is a Shrine down by the Oshun River which has been "developed" as a kind of centre for modern sculpture in clay. Did we go there together? I can't remember. Certainly, since I was last there a lot more peculiar-shaped clay model things have been produced.

Today (Sat) we have come over to Ado. Grace was supposed to be 'off 'for the day after 11 a.m. but she tells us when we arrive that she is 'on 'after all. All the others - Marjorie and Shelagh have gone to Ilesha for the Opening of their New Building. We got there much earlier than we had expected because we went to a naming ceremony at Iju, about 15 miles from Akure on the Ado Road. That began around 7 a.m. and was finished about 8.30 so we got here soon after 9.a.m. We are staying the night here and returning to Akure tomorrow so we shall be able to see something of Grace tomorrow.

Then I shall have a week of hard work before me for the last week of the holidays. There is a good deal of preparation yet to be done before the students come back on Friday. Our 3rd Nigerian member of staff Rev. Jaiyeoba is complaining very much about his accommodation. The church where he is for part-time have put him in the 2 rooms which were previously used by the Catechist. It is upstairs in a large and rowdy house with about 40 other people - some Ogun worshippers some Aladura members. He is very upset because he feels that the Archdeacon and the Bishop have insulted him by putting him in such a shabby house. So, he is asking the bishop to transfer him if he doesn't get any better accommodation. This will be a great pity for us because he hasn't yet taught anything, and we do so badly need a third member of staff for the men.

Ethel is making her final arrangements about going down to Lagos, on Oct. 16th. We are going to give her a "tail" - with beads on around the handle, for her farewell gift.

I am busy with "Lists" - rooms, cooking, flowers, timetable etc. I must get down to my lesson preparation.

With much love

Elizabeth

Teaching in Vining Centre

There will be 17 women next term, and three of these will be newcomers. One, Mrs. Ajiboye is the mother of baby twins so she will have a job to concentrate on classwork as well as two babies. A second, Mrs. Aderibole, didn't come last term because she had a miscarriage and is still under the doctor so she may well find it difficult to get up at 4am when it is her turn to cook the breakfast! The third newcomer is an ordinand's wife who has already spent two years in the Akure Training Centre (as this place used to be called when only women trained here) in the 1950's and she spent one year travelling around villages with the CMS missionary here at that time. So, she is coming for one term only to prepare herself to be a pastor's wife. She will need a good portion of humility in order not to be feeling that some of our classes are, for her, a waste of time.

One problem which the centre has faced for some time is a shortage of staff for the men's teaching. There are three years of men (17 per class) preparing for GCE in four subjects and studying to be catechists. The principal, Canon Cornelius Olowomeye and the men's warden, the Rev. Matthew Owadayo are the only two permanent full-time members of staff. They can't possibly manage to teach all the subjects in all three classes and so in 1969 the Board of Governors agreed that a third permanent member of staff should be appointed. But there was no-one available and so it was agreed to 'manage temporarily' by employing an HSC teacher (someone who has done 'A' - level). This temporary arrangement has continued until this year and has proven unsatisfactory because the teachers come and go and, they do not help with all the extra-curricular activities of the centre.

So, strong representations were made to the bishop to appoint a third clergyman to teach the men. Much to our delight this was done, and on August 1 the Rev. J. Jaiyeoba who has just finished a diploma course in Bristol was asked to come to Akure, to teach here during the week and to be the pastor of a small church in the town. They were to provide the accommodation. Unfortunately, this part of the plan was not given all the attention that it might have been, and he was put in the rented house previously used by the catechist. This accommodation is just two rooms - 'a room and a parlour' (i.e., one bedroom and a sitting room) upstairs in a double storey house with about 40 other noisy inhabitants. They must share the kitchen, wash houses and latrine out in the backyard with the other inhabitants. They have four children and although most of them are usually away at boarding school there is hardly room for them in two rooms. As you can imagine this is all very difficult, especially for a senior clergyman who has previously had a vicarage to himself and who has just returned from three years in the UK. He is very angry and feels 'insulted' by the Bishop and Archdeacon that they should 'punish' him by putting him in such a house. We must pray that some other accommodation can be organised before he becomes so frustrated that he insists on a transfer, and we lose our new teacher.

I feel bad about this accommodation difficulty because I have just moved into the women's warden's house. It is a very nice little bungalow built about three years ago with Lino tiling on the floor, a fridge which freezes and a gas cooker that regulates, as well as a shower over the bath and a spare room for visitors. In fact, it has everything that I need, and I am doubly fortunate because all the furnishings that I kept in my trunks when I left Ondo fit in the new house here and so I have not had to buy any new curtains or cushion covers. I have enjoyed unpacking and settling into a place of my own again. I have bought a new record player and a radio (these were stolen when I was at home last year) and so I can hear the world news clearly and enjoy Mozart and others in the evenings. I thank God for all his gifts, but I have so much, and many others have so little.

Vining Centre
1st October 1972

Dear Daddy and Ma,

I have 2 letters this week - arriving on Tuesday and then Saturday - I am glad that Stuart and Jutka have been to stay with you and that you liked her very much. It will be good to have Ruth with you now - especially after saying goodbye to Pat and John and Co. I thought of you all last Wednesday, and I hope that they got off without difficulty.

We have started the new term this weekend - so all the students are back (or sick and therefore late!) We just have one new woman so far, although we were expecting 3. We nearly didn't start at all because there was no money. All the Diocese's have failed to pay us their Grants - but we have managed to loan from Akure District Church Council, enough to pay our food supplies. The Govt. ought to be paying the cocoa farmers soon - and then money will start to circulate again.

Inga is going home on leave in 2 weeks' time - I saw her yesterday; struggling with her budget - everyone is in the same boat at this time of year. Jacqui is still here. I took her to Ondo yesterday and I am afraid she was bored stiff in a 2 1/4-hour long service in Yoruba to confer a Church "Chieftaincy" on 2 elders. They had Sermon and Litany and a special song +welcome address + Communion Service all combined. Jacqui hasn't been well this week - malaria and diarrhoea … so, she spent a couple of days in bed and is only just now feeling better.

Sad news about my ducklings - ALL have died!! Like 10 little nigger boys - 2 drowned, one disappeared to the bush, others I think got pneumonia. So, I must start again.

I hope that John and Pat have managed to sell their house otherwise how will they manage to buy another one in N.Z? Far less beach chalets and 2nd cars!?

I didn't know that Ewan wasn't going back to Ellerslie. Some 'grannie' of theirs died in Benin - and according to the Notice in Daily Times the Oba sent the traditional cloth for the burial because she was a 'Princess.' I should think the funeral was quite a do. Yesterday there was a Chief's funeral in Ondo. The procession with the coffin went from U.C.H Ibadan to Ado to lie in state and for Service conducted by Bp. of Ekiti. Then to Ondo Cathedral for service conducted by Bp. of Ibadan and now today there is a 3rd service conducted by Bp. of Ondo! So, he ought to get there!

Angela will have started at Crowther Hall by now. I think Janice must be at home - Ruth said something about it in her letter some time ago. Shola has twin girls!! We go to the Leper Settlement today for their open-air Service. Next Sunday I am taking the Service at Fiwasaiye (Oct. 8th) Jacqui and Ethel are going to the Creeks - to 'Aiyetoro the Holy City.'

With much love,
Elizabeth

Vining Centre
8th October 1972

Dear Ma and Daddy,

It was good to get your letter earlier in the week telling of John and Pat's departure to N.Z. It seems that our family get-togethers are often at Heathrow airport! I am sorry that I wasn't there to complete the gathering.

We have started the new term. I was exhausted by Friday! The teaching timetable is not very heavy - although since all the lessons are 'new 'there is a good deal of preparation. But things like 'needlework 'take up a lot of time, because the women are both helpless and demanding attention. The first week is the worst - getting them all started on new things - deciding what they want to make and getting them cut out. I gave 5 of them 5 yards of material to cut into 5 pieces to make tablecloths with. It was like a market in minutes. The last piece was only 35" long and no-one would take it!!! Also, on Friday we have the Sunday School Preparation classes - so those had to be organised - the men sorted out for their different Sunday Schools and the lessons for the term chosen.

Then one small girl cut her head open on a stone - not a big cut - but a lot of blood and a hysterical mother. Last night one baby wouldn't sleep but cried… so I was woken at 3.15 a.m. to diagnose …. probably worms or eaten too much. I gave 1/4 Aspirin in water and the baby slept off!! But I can't say that I did - at least not properly.

However, all is well - and I usually get a decent rest in the afternoons. I have started growing things in pots. I will take a photo when they have grown a bit. Ethel and Jacqui have gone to Ayetoro, the Holy City of the Apostles, for the weekend. I think that they will enjoy it. We are expecting them back tomorrow. Tokunbo my Steward (Ethel's before) is working very hard. He makes superb bread, and this week has made v.good egg custard and ice-cream and chocolate sauce. Gorgeous.

There is still no money from the Diocese, so Cornelius is 'running up and down' as they say, making sure that when the bishops have any spare cash we don't get forgotten.

If you come across any coloured pictures of Palestine - in magazines etc you might send me them with the Woman's Home. I am teaching about background to the New Testament - but have few pictures e.g., of Jerusalem, Bethlehem - houses - people etc. Or drawings of the Temple, a Synagogue or Tabernacle.

I am going to take the service at Fiwasaiye this afternoon. I am glad that you were able to come to Akure in 1970 and so have met people like Jane Pelly and Ethel.

It is getting hotter here - but with sudden storms to cool the air. I expect you are wrapped up in your Winter clothes.

With much love

Elizabeth

P.S. I must fill in Income Tax Forms here. Could you find out the amount of Interest that I received from Jan 20th to Mar 31st, 1972?

Vining Centre
15th October 1972

Dear Ma and Daddy,

I think that the workers in our Post office have been having a private Strike this week. Post has been almost non-existent. However, I expect that they will wake up and we shall get it all in a bundle.

We have had classes in full swing in the past week. Jacqui went to the Midwest on Thursday to stay for a few days with Jane Backhouse. She and Ethel had an interesting time last weekend at Aiyetoro. The only snag was that I think that they got out into the wrong guest house and there was a party of noisy school children with them. Also, there was very little water so having a bath was no joy.

Ethel goes this coming week (Oct 18th) to Ibadan for a week before going on to Lagos. Jacqui goes on Tuesday to Lagos with John Fowler who will be here on Mon. night/ Tuesday for our Board of Governors meeting. Today (Sun) we are having a Valedictory Service for Ethel followed by a Send-Off by the students in the hall. We are giving her a beaded tail with her name on it.

Yesterday, Saturday was the opening of the new Library and Staff Room block, and a Dormitory at Fiwasaiye. It was opened by the Deji of Akure and the Eyesorun. Jane gave me her cinecamera to work so I went around taking pictures. Goodness knows what it will look like because I have never taken a cine film before. In the evening the schoolgirls did part of Julius Caesar. So long as you forgot it was Shakespeare it was O.K. All the supposedly tragic bits became rather a hoot - and it was difficult to hear their words. One of our women is in hospital - with 'fever plus'?

She is pregnant so maybe that has something to do with it. Most of the women seem to be pregnant this term - or to have children under a year. We are hoping to have a session on Family Planning this term - but it is a bit late as far as most of them are concerned.

Tokunbo my steward is celebrating his birthday today - so we are in for a noisy afternoon I suspect. He has hired a record player! He has a wife and 3 children and is to be confirmed on Tuesday by the Bishop. So tomorrow he is going to have his marriage blessed. It is a native law and custom marriage.

The plants in my pots are beginning to grow and I have some tomatoes that we have just planted out. I hope that you are all well.

With much love

Elizabeth

Vining Centre

22nd October 1972

Dear Ma and Daddy,

Post seems erratic now. I am not receiving yours till about 10 days after you post it.

Ethel went away on Wednesday morning taking the Humber with her - so now I only have <u>one</u> car to keep on the road - much better. We had the Board of Gov's Tuesday. Archdeacon Banjo was there since he is now the Principal of Emanuel College Ibadan. Did I tell you this before? It seems a strange appointment when he had already retired, and one would have thought that they needed a much younger man for that job. Then on the same day I met another old Andrian called Rev. Fapolumide. He asked to be remembered. We must have passed his house in 1970 because he lives on the road between Akure and Ado.

At the Board it was decided that the 'year 'here should start in January in future. This means that our present 3rd year students will leave in December - and their wives will go with them so 15 out of our present 17 women students will be leaving all at once. So, we shall have to start recruiting quickly to fill up the places. Now I have 9 New ones coming.

One student delivered a baby boy this week - on Thursday. It was unexpected as far as I was concerned because I hadn't realised that

that student was due so soon. And neither she nor her husband had prepared anything for the new baby!! So suddenly we had to go shopping. They hadn't even got S.T.s, Olive oil, nappies, or a razor blade - as required by the hospital. Part of the trouble was that they had no money to buy them - but partly I felt it was just thoughtlessness for they have 2 other children and they had left all the old nappies and baby clothes at home.

Mrs. Threadgold comes here on Friday 27th and goes to Benin on Monday 30th. I am going to take her to Ifon, past Owo and hand her over to Jane Blackhouse there.

I had a letter from John. They seem to be settling in very quickly. I think that New Zealand is a nice place. What a pity that the May Panter didn't enjoy the guitar music. I doubt if she would approve of our lyrics with drumming and dancing and even clapping that go with it in our Chapel! In fact, I can think of quite a lot of things she wouldn't't approve of in this place! Babies puddle in the classroom……. even on the table!!! How you get over the importance of basic cleanliness to Yoruba women - I don't know.

The enclosed picture is Ethel's farewell last weekend.

With much love
Elizabeth

Vining Centre
29th October 1972

Dear Ma and Daddy,

Mrs. Treadgold is here with me this weekend - so it has been busy. She came on Friday evening, and we had supper together. Then on Saturday we went round the Compound to visit the women in their houses and I discovered that the one-week-old baby was very jaundiced and had a large 'haematoma' on the head - so we took it to the hospital for a check-up. They saw a doctor who prescribed phenobarbital and an injection of paraldehyde. Mrs. Treadgold and I went into town and looked round part of the Oba's palace and she bought some writing paper etc. She is a very 'lively' person - and very nice indeed - but much nicer when she relaxes and doesn't talk loudly.

We went to Idanre in the afternoon on Sat and visited the Vicar there and his wife. Then we came back for the evening Service, and I was called out to take the same baby again to hospital. It was admitted. Then she went on to Ann's for supper. After the morning Communion Service, the father came to say that the baby had died in the night. I don't really know what the matter was unless it was chronically anaemic or had some infection. Very sad. The parents were very controlled, but weeping. The students made a box, and they buried the baby in St David's churchyard.

We went to the Leper Settlement this morning and greeted the folk there. Mrs. T. had never seen anything like our Leper Settlement - and it is ghastly. One poor man is very sick there - with tetanus I think.... but they won't admit a leper into the hospital, and it seems that they don't get any medicine except for their leprosy pills. I fear he will die soon - but I will go and tell them in the health Office in the morning tomorrow.

Rev. Jaiyeoba our new teacher, has been transferred because no solution was found to his housing problems. So, we are rather back to square one!

I am going to Ifon with Mrs. T. tomorrow and will meet Jane Backhouse there - I hope it all goes according to plan. This evening we had a session of plays in the hall in honour of our guest. It was great fun and went off very happily with men dressed as women in the men's play and vice versa in the women's play. All a great laugh.

I am very sorry about your parcels not getting to Nottingham in time. They say they are sending them on. So, I shall be hoping around Christmas. But she bought me a super box of chocs from you - and a very lovely lace Nottingham tablecloth. So that's very nice - but I am doubtful about posting records .... anyway. I think it will be too late to stop now if her husband has sent them.

Lots of love

Elizabeth

Vining Centre
5th November 1972

Dear Daddy and Ma,

I received 2 letters from you on Monday, posted at home on Oct. 17th and 23rd. Now, on Tuesday the post office here has been on Strike and Mon and Tues next week are Public Holidays for the end of Ramadan, so I am not likely to get any 'birthday cards 'till well after the event. I am sending this letter down to Lagos tomorrow so maybe it will reach you a bit quicker.

You sound as though there is not much 'let up 'at St Mary's and in the Malvern circuit of meetings. You'd better come here for a holiday! Although, in fact it is a bit hot. The harmattan dust has started to come extra-ordinarily early this year and it is suddenly dry and hot in the daytime but cool at night.

I took Mrs. Treadgold to Ifon, 20 miles past Owo, on Monday afternoon and met Jane Backhouse there in the house of Canon Jegede. We were given coffee and boiled eggs. They were soft boiled.... and we didn't quite realise it. Mrs. Treadgold dropped hers on the floor!! It was good to see Jane again. She is coming over here on Nov. 17th with Jean Lawrence. Then Jane will stay the night before returning to Ekpoma. I must go to Ekpoma for a weekend sometime and see what Jane is doing there. She is sending her Catechist's wife here next January. I gather she isn't literate so I can see that she will need a lot of help.

We have lost Rev. Jaiyeola unfortunately for the men students who are doing their G.C.E. in January. He and his wife went and begged the bishop to transfer them to a Parish, on account of the lack of housing in Akure. It is a great pity, and very disappointing. He had returned from U.K., and it was understandable that he didn't like the house, but it seemed that he had no notion of 'service 'at all - and that he could help the students here. I think training catechists is not a very in-Job. It is certainly not popular with the clergy. They would much prefer the Church posts, in Parishes. I think it its partly the fellowship of a whole lot of parishioners around them and Church members to come and greet you etc. etc. Life here on the staff is by comparison a very lonely affair. Also, in this case it seems to me that Cornelius and Rev. Jaiyeola didn't really "hit it off" and neither was very anxious to work with the other.

I am very glad that you had such a happy visit to Freddie. It is certainly much more encouraging if he can be looking forward to getting out of prison in a few years' time.

That train trip to London for £1.35 is a great bargain, isn't it? I am glad that you were able to see Stuart and Jutka as well as Ruth and Trevor. Angela must be kept very busy at Crowther Hall - for she hasn't had time to write any letter to me since she got there (maybe it's lost in the postal Strike now).

This week has been very unusual here. I went to bed early on Mon. and Tuesday nights since I was quite tired after having Mrs.

Threadgold. She was very nice and very appreciative and interested in all we are doing here… but the tempo of talking is faster at home and things are much slower here.

The Polish doctor and his wife Dr and Mrs. Perzina are very nice to go and visit. She has not been very well, but they are always very welcoming. I hope to invite them to come on Wed. evening for a small 'Birthday Party.'

On Thursday I went to St Peter's the Catholic Training College where Mrs. Adinlewa the wife of the Principal of the Anglican Boys School was speaking to the students about Leprosy. I was the 'supporter' and helped her to answer questions.

On Saturday I went to the Sunday School Open Day at St David's Church. It was quite a do with 'Opening Glee 'and about 6 different plays. I stayed for 3 plays and "Donations" and then came home (about 1 1/2 hrs).

Ann came to supper last night, and I am going to Fiwasaiye for lunch tomorrow. Next Sat 10th - 12th we have our Half Term holiday, so I am planning to go to Ibadan and stay with Brenda and Joe Batt and see Grace and family.

I had a letter last week from Mr. Ukpoma, Ewan's daddy. He says that he has a holiday in December sometime and that they may all come and stay a few days in Akure!! If Dora and himself, 6 children and 2 drivers come I can see that I may have problems with accommodating them!!

Give my love to Alison. It is true that Ann is leaving here next year - and Jane and Sheila are talking about 'last tour '- but for Sheila anyway that won't be till 1974.

We have now changed here to having the beginning of the year in Jan - ending in Dec with a 3-month holiday in July - Sept. I am thinking that it may be better for me to come home in 1973 during that time and have 3 - 4 months rather than waiting till 1974 July by which time, I would be due 6 months leave. On the other hand, I am so fit now that I can't really justify a shorter tour again. It's just that it will fit in better here.

With much love,
Elizabeth

Vining Centre
13th November 1972

Dear Ma and Daddy,

We have had a Postal Strike and then Half Term holiday weekend, so I haven't received any letters from you for some time. I am going back to Akure today, after a very happy weekend in Ibadan, so I hope to find some posts when I get there.

I had a very happy birthday on Wednesday, except for the fact that there was no post outside Akure. I was busy most of the day preparing for the evening. I had 15 people in for a Celebration. It went very happily - our staff, the 3 from Fiwasaiye, Dr and Mrs. Kohli (Indians) and their son Raj, Dr and Mrs. Perzina, and the Eyesorun. We had a good feast of chicken, sausages, jollof savoury rice, tomato in yoghourt, beans and moin moin with fruit salad and trifle and lemon mousse to follow!! They are all very kind, these folk in Akure. The Eyesorun gave me 2 stuffed lizards, then I was given a necklace, bracelet, and earrings from Kashmir - coloured stones set on a chain. Some serviettes from Poland and a tablecloth and serviettes to match made by Ann at Fiwasaiye. Ethel sent a towel - all very useful. Then we all enjoyed the box of chocolates that Mrs. T. brought in lieu of your parcels.

On Thursday afternoon I went to Ibadan for our Half Term and stayed for 3 nights with the Batts at Ibadan Grammar School. I did the usual shopping in Kingsway and U.I. bookshop and visited friends - Grace, Titi now at U.I. again, Jose and Sam, Bishop, and Mrs. Okunsanya. On Friday afternoon I went to the pool with the Batts. Saturday, I spent most of the day at Grace's. On Sunday I went with the Batts to the War Memorial Remembrance Day Service in Ibadan. Gen. Gowon read the lesson. He was in Ibadan with President Senghor of Senegal who is on a State Visit to Nigeria. Everything was done with great pomp and ceremony. They had the lot - Last Post Reveille, Guns Salute, March past (or round the clock tower) brass band, red carpet, laying of wreaths and an enormous grey Rolls Royce - in which the 2 Heads of State sat up at the back and waved to the crowds. The only snag was that although all of us in the enclosure stood solemnly for 2 mins of silence - all the folks behind the barriers in the streets around hadn't got the message so there was by no means silence!!

Then I came on to Ife for lunch. Yomi and Kelu both send their love to you. Yomi has now accepted the job at Ife University Medical Dept. although it means a fair drop in Salary and giving up the private Practice. I am not sure that Kelu is convinced it's a good idea. It is possible that Yomi may go to the UK on Study leave later next year.

I then came on to Ondo and stayed the night with Suzanne, the V.S.O. now here. Janet and Bose came yesterday evening for supper. Janet is as fat as ever. The school seems to be well staffed, now. It is rather strange to come back here. I know so many of the girls 'faces - but I have forgotten most of their names.

Later this morning I shall complete the journey to Akure, then we have 5 more weeks of term.

With much love

Elizabeth

Vining Centre

18th November 1972

Dear Ma and Daddy,

Thank you for your letter, Daddy this week. I couldn't think why you were writing in such minute detail about everything - until I got to the end and realised that you were being the substitute for Ma with a black eye and stitches in her head. I am very sorry to hear about that. I hope that by the time this letter reaches you she will be feeling much better and that it doesn't leave a permanent scar.

We have our 'Harvest 'here today. It's the great do of the year. You decorate the Church with palm branches and banana trees with yams in the window and a trussed chicken on the chancel steps - the Choir practices several anthems and then you have an almighty thanksgiving service with everyone called out to dance up and down the aisle and put money in a basket at the front. I would enjoy it better if it were shorter……. ours lasted from 10 a.m. till after 1.30 today. By then I had both a headache and a backache, so I made a quick exit for home and my bed. But the rest of the compound and the various visitors continued to eat Jollof rice and then to have a 'Bazaar' - to sell the yams and other produce. They were still at it at 3.30 when I got up from my rest and went off to Ado with Ann Forgan. I have just come back after a very pleasant outing except that all the Abiye folk had gone off to a Confirmation at Christ's School, so we saw no-one and came back again! The reason for going was that Jean Lawrence left her bedroom slippers in my bedroom when she had a rest on Friday afternoon. It was good to see her, although her visit was very short. Jane Backhouse stayed the night here before going back to the Midwest.

Thank you for your card and good wishes and the cheque for my birthday. They all showed up this week Tuesday after our postal Strike, and after I returned from Ibadan. I also heard during this week from John, Ruth, Stu, Angela, and Marylou.

The men in the photo wearing forage caps as you say, are all in their Boys Brigade officer's uniform. The 3rd year students have cassocks the 2nd years are in navy suits and B.B caps, the 1st years in white Uniform and B.B caps. All carefully planned for the photograph!

You certainly sound as though you have found some super haunts in the Wye Valley area. I am looking forward to seeing them all on my next spell of leave - which may well be Aug. 73 so that I shall be at home for just over 3 months during the time of the proposed long holiday here. It is not fixed yet, but I have written to Chris Cook about the possibility.

I am sending your cheque back in this letter - I hope you don't mind - I should prefer it to be paid into the Barnard's Green A/C. I seem to have enough money here. I will treat myself to something to the tune of £2.

We finish term in 4 weeks' time so there is going to be plenty to do in the next few weeks - with Exams, reports, and commissioning of all the 3rd year students.

Hoping to hear good news about your eye Ma.

With love

Elizabeth

Vining Centre
25th November 1972

Dear Ma and Daddy,

It is good to hear that Ma is better in the letter of 14th Nov. and that everyone spoiled you with flowers, shortbread, and sago pudding during the time you were laid up. The C.M.S. Conference sounded good. I had a letter from Angela for my birthday. She says everyone is a bit pessimistic about her returning to the West. But it seems to me if her application got into the right hands in the Govt. that they would fix her with a job. They are still extremely short of Maths Graduates both in schools and in the Teacher Training College. But unfortunately, the Chairman of the State Board in Ibadan has just been killed in a motor crash at Shagamu.

This past week has been busy, and quite tiring. It's hot. The driver and the clerk are both off sick so that makes extra work. I hope that the clerk reappears next week as I can see that I shall be busy typing exam papers.

On Thursday night at 12.30 a.m. I took one student to the hospital in the last stages of labour …… literally…. She was lucky not to produce it in my car - and there is not enough space in a Volkswagen! Anyway, we got there - she hopped out……. squeaking "it's coming' "o ti de o '! She ran to the delivery room. They shut the door, and the next thing we heard was the baby's cry! So, after about 15 mins the husband and I visited her in bed. Quick work.

On Friday evening it was Sheila Davis 'birthday party, so we had a very pleasant evening there at Fiwasaiye. Gillian Martin the Y.S.A from Ughelli is here this W/E with about 15 of her schoolgirls on a Geographical visit. She took them up to Idanre on Friday, and yesterday they went to the waterfall near Ilesha. Today I have said that I will go with them to the hot springs at Ikogosi. Then Ann is coming for supper, after she takes our evening service. Yesterday was the 'Harvest 'at the Leper Settlement. Ann and I went to it…but came away before they had started their bazaar. They had about 6 Chairmen and Chair Ladies. Each of these gives a donation - about £2 or so and then they hand round a tin plate and call out "Support" and the people put in their money to 'support 'the Chairman and then you read out the amount collected. It takes ages.

Please thank Mrs. Munns for her letter, which I received this week. I haven't written a 'Circular 'for Christmas yet. I hope that I may find time to do it soon or it will be a New Year Issue.

I have just read 'John Macnab", by John Buchan. Have you ever read it? It is very amusing. About a cabinet minister, a Banker and an Attorney-General who become stuck in a rut and so cure themselves by going poaching for deer and salmon in the highlands of Scotland.

Jesse has a baby boy by the way. I don't know if Angela knows.

With much love

Elizabeth

Vining Centre
3rd December 1972

Dear Ma and Daddy,

Thank you for your letter this week. I am glad that you took a couple of evenings off during your busy week - you can't go to all the meetings in Malvern - it's too much ... and you will only get exhausted if you go around chasing your own tail.

We have had quite 'a week 'here this week. We had premature twins on our hands. One died. It was sad, but just as well really because she was such a tiny thing - only 2lbs 4 oz - and very undernourished. The second one, a boy is bigger - 4lbs 10 oz and we have that one here. It was discharged at aged 36 hours so we all hope and pray that it will do O.K. So far it is O.K. but I am a bit afraid that the mother will do something stupid, out of ignorance… and I'm not exactly an expert on prem babies!

Then I discovered that one small boy had a bad sore on his leg and we sent it to the doctor who said it was starting to go gangrenous. Presumably because the fellows in the dispensary were using mucky dressings. So, we had to sort that out.

Then at 4 a.m. on Friday morning I was woken up to go and see what the matter was with the principal. He was all in a jitter. He had woken in the night and felt 'giddy 'and light, so he drank iced water and poured iced water over his head so that I think he was suffering from shock and a great panic. Anyway, he went to the hospital and was given Phenobarbital. The next day he went to the Doctor for a complete checkup - and was told to rest for a week. So please pray for the end of our term. We finish on Dec. 15th. But Owadayo is going to mark School Cert. papers as from 11th so will miss the last week - so if Cornelius is sickly then there is only Mama Ademoye and I to keep an eye on everything. In fact, the men are pretty good at organising themselves, but it is going to be a busy end of term because 17 men (one Class) and 15 (of the 17) women are all leaving.

Grace is here this weekend. They are busy at Ado - and now have the "Ewi of Ado" (the Oba) in one of the houses - being "specialled" through bronchial pneumonia - all hush hush so that he should not be swamped with visitors.

We have our exams next week. So far, we have done the practical exam. From Mon - Thursday the women do their other exams.

I have written a Christmas letter – almost - and hope to get it off to you. I am sorry I am always late in the day with these letters. If it doesn't get out till the New year it won't matter. Don't make yourself sick addressing envelopes.

I shall be thinking of you especially in your 'talks 'with May and Noel.

With much love,
Elizabeth

Christmas Letter – December 1972

This letter comes to you with my greetings for a Very Happy Christmas and my prayers for you as you move into the New year of 1973.

One is not likely to miss the Christmas message of the miracle of "New birth" here at the Vining Centre. On Thursday last week I was awakened just after midnight with the information "Mrs. Ibitoye is preparing to put to bed." So, I took her in the Volkswagen to the hospital. She was obviously in the last stage of labour and was very fortunate not to have her baby in my car. When we reached the hospital, she got out and ran to the delivery room squeaking out "o ti de o!" "o ti de o!" (It's coming, its coming!) The door closed and about 2 minutes later we heard the cry of the newborn child.

On Saturday morning the mother and baby were discharged, both fit and well. There are not enough beds in the Maternity Ward and in our Akure hospital for the mothers to stay more than one night after a normal delivery. Anyway no one wants to stay more than one night because it costs 2/6d a night and 3/- for food each day. Here in Nigeria everything is much closer to the "no room at the Inn" situation.

We had a second delivery this week on Monday. This time it was Mrs. Eyitemi, our most illiterate wife, who comes from the Midwest State. She is a poor, skinny and sickly-looking woman with big round eyes in a drawn face. She gave birth to twins, a boy of 4lbs 10oz and a girl of 2lbs 4oz. I have never seen such a wizened wee thing as this second minute infant. She only lived for 30 hours. The nurse said they were slightly premature but that the main trouble was malnutrition during the pregnancy. On Wednesday I went to collect, first the tiny body for burial and then later the mother and the surviving baby boy, who although less than 5lbs in weight was discharged from the hospital on the second day of his life. Now we are busy caring for the mother and the child here on the compound. My contribution now is simply a glass of milk a day. This couple do not have enough money even to afford that! The £1/13/6d which was the hospital bill had to be loaned to the father until he has started work as a Catechist.

At Christmas we remember that GOD has given us 'life'. How easily it can be snuffed out. How much it needs to be carefully nurtured so that it grows strong enough to stand on it's own in the world. We have been reading the book of Ephesians in our Bible Studies here this term and following the theme discussed by Watchman Nee, the Chinese pastor, in his book "Sit, Walk, Stand." First, we must "sit", or completely relax and rely on GOD's strength entirely, as a baby relies on its mother. Secondly, we must learn to "Walk" step by step with GOD in our daily lives. Then we shall be able to "Stand" firm as the soldier described in Ephesians Chapter 6. The "standing firm" here in the Vining Centre means not getting rattled when called in the night for those who are sick or delivering their babies. It means not giving up repeating again and again that the dispensary materials must be clean, or the children will get infected sores. It is having patience when the women quarrel at the tops of their voices about the division of the food in the dining hall.

I shall not be spending Christmas in Akure this year, for I am going "down the Creeks." I, together with 3 other friends, am going to stay with Maureen Olphin who is with C.M.S. and is the Vice-Principal of the Southern Ijaw Secondary School in Oporoma. This is right down in the delta of the river Niger. Most of the year you must travel for 2 days in a boat to get there, but now in the dry season you can get to Yenagoa by road and then take a boat for the last 25 miles. It is a very undeveloped part of Nigeria where life is very slow, and most people live with just the necessities. I will write and let you know how we celebrate Christmas there.

With my very best wishes

Elizabeth

Vining Centre

9th December 1972

Dear Ma and Daddy,

It was good to get your letter on Wed. this last week - but I am sorry to hear of your frustrations with Noel and May (especially the latter). I suppose that there are frustrations everywhere. As here - the Principal will not get a move on and decide things. So many things are left vague and unplanned until the 11th hour. Like the first day of next term! He still hasn't decided! Far less the other dates for the terms next year.

Then now in the last week of term the cooks have decided to celebrate (yet again!) the funeral of the cook's mother - so lo and behold this means that both our cooks get the whole week off and the women must do all the cooking - i.e., meals 3x a day plus 2 'Feasts' - especially meals for our Carol Service and Commissioning Visitors. And to add to that Owadayo is going off to Enugu to mark W.A.S.C. Exams. Anyway, there are no classes - obviously if everyone is cooking… so, there will be stacks of time for me to get the various cupboards and stores in order and to complete my end of term reports.

We had exams last week and I have finished the marking… not a very arduous task. There is no gas. Rather a nuisance for I wanted to bake a Christmas cake. Maybe I can borrow a cylinder for the event. I am down to a rather smelly kerosene stove.

I am going to Ibadan on Friday with Grace - returning on Sunday. Then off on Tues. 19th to go to Oporoma for Christmas. I should be back here around the 28th or 29th. And then I think that the Herrington's may come to stay here in the New Year. They are coming to Nigeria for a holiday and want to come to Akure, for Bones used to be here - a good time ago.

I meant to do a lot today! But I borrowed a Georgette Heyer from Ann - called 'Venetia '- so not much was achieved. Anyway, Jane and Ann and Sheila are coming to supper so I must do some cooking for that. I am planning to make a Chinese Sweet and Sour type thing with rice and pineapple and pork luncheon meat!! Goodness knows what it will be like.

Glad that you are getting off to Broadstone. Don't take on too much over Christmas. It's a pity that we can't relax in the Creeks together - paddling our canoes with the brollies up.

With love

Elizabeth

Vining Centre
14th December 1972

Dear Ma and Daddy,

I hope that this reaches you by Christmas Day. It comes with much love. I shall be thinking of you at St Mary's and in Malvern on that day.

Thank you for the super Calendar of British Scenery - and for your card and the circular letter that came today. It reads very well. It is a pity that you had to fall after such a great effort.

Perhaps, it's just as well that I'm going to the Creeks for Christmas - the town noises are very clear here. Tonight, there is a loud juju band just over the back. I expect it will go on all night - or at least till about 4 a.m. Then there is Bingo at the Club, and I can hear the voice of the 'Caller '- over the jingling of the dance band.

Yemi is here now - she has all manner of things to get for her Grade 2 Training College course - especially for the Needlework exams - so she is busy on the borrowing.

I am going to Ibadan tomorrow with Grace Webster to stay with Grace Ohikhena for a couple of nights. I hope to get some sleep done - to see the Herrington's and decide about their coming to Akure, then come back on Sunday.

Today I made 3 fruit cakes - one for Grace, one for Kelu and one for us in the Creeks. They are small but smell good.

On Tuesday I am going to Benin and will be staying with Mrs. Oviasu. Eunice's sister's husband has died - Great funeral in Benin last Sunday. Don't do too much.

With love

Elizabeth

Vining Centre
16th December 1972

Dear Ma and Daddy

With luck this letter may reach you by Christmas Day because I hope to post it in Ibadan. I am staying here with Grace and going to the S.C.M. Seminar on 'Education for Living.'

We reached the end of term on Thursday morning- much to my surprise because I thought it was going to finish on Friday morning, but Cornelius suddenly changed his mind! We had 'Carols' on Tuesday night, and this included 2 plays. One short one by the children and the second called 'A Short Play' by the students. This was by no means short and was the most incredible Christmas play I have ever seen. A man took the part of Mary and gave a very realistic show of labour pains! They had a whole lot of 'odd bods 'going to Bethlehem to pay their taxes - very amusing … and ended up with soldiers in uniform with machetes and knives going to Bethlehem to kill the children under 2 years. The whole Carol Service lasted about 2 1/2 hours.

On Wednesday we had our Commissioning Service in the afternoon at 4. The Provost of Ondo came and took the Service. I was "at it" from morning to night from Mon - Wed. nonstop - writing reports, inscribing in books and on Certificates, clearing up, checking Lists of equipment, collecting keys, doing the flowers in the Chapel etc. At the same time there was a Community Development Workshop going on in the town - aiming at bringing together the Government Community Development workers and workers in Voluntary Agencies. 3 of our students went as representatives of the Vining Centre and they found it very useful. I was at one lecture given by an official from Ibadan. He was speaking about Literacy and was extremely good - especially in challenging the Church workers to live out their faith in practical ways - helping the people in the villages to read and write - and being concerned with their health and their food supplies - all these things are part of our Christian Mission to the Community...... there is too much getting into the pulpit and preaching things that are not meeting the people's real problems.

Greetings from Grace and Co. here.

I am off to Benin on Tuesday and will stay with Mrs. Oviasu who came with Eunice to Enfield - and has a pharmaceutical factory in Benin.

Have a very happy Christmas time.

With much love,

Elizabeth

Christmas in Oporoma

Vining Centre
Boxing Day 1972

Dear Ma and Daddy,

I am afraid that you will have to wait some time before you get this letter. Communication either for people or for letters in and out of Oporoma is slow, and unreliable, especially over the holiday.

I was in Ibadan the last time I wrote. Then I returned to Akure on Sunday night. That evening we had a very pleasant party at the Palace, to say 'farewell 'to Mrs. Adinlewa the wife of the Principal of the Boys Anglican School, who is going to transfer to Ikare. Then there was Monday when I did some baking - mince-pies and shortbread, sorted Christmas presents and cards and visited folk in Akure.

On Tuesday Ann and I set off in the morning and drove to Jane Backhouse 'place at Ekpoma. It is a lovely drive from Ifon across a very beautiful open heathland type of country. Unfortunately, Jane was out when we got to her house - she had gone to a meeting. So, we had our picnic in her sitting room and went on to Benin. There, we had a swim in a tiny swimming pool at the Motel before going to the house of Mrs. Oviasu. You will remember that was the lady who came to Enfield with Eunice. She entertained us royally on duck and rice the first evening and then duck, roast potatoes, cabbage, and peas on the second day for lunch. She is extremely nice - and gave us the main air-conditioned bedroom which was a great treat. In the evening she took us round to visit Mrs. Osula who is Eunice's sister. Her husband died about 3 weeks ago - of cancer of the bladder. Apparently, he was in U.C.H Ibadan but they thought that London doctors might be able to do better so the wife flew him to London only to be told that it was hopeless and so they returned, and he died the next day. Everyone was very thankful that he hadn't died in England because the expense of transporting a corpse by air is great. He was a big Chief in Benin so there were great goings on at his funeral.

Anyway, I was glad to meet Eunice's sister - she seemed quite different from Eunice and a good deal older - but perhaps that was because she was still in deep mourning - dressed all in navy. The sickening thing is that her house is exactly next door to the Catering Rest House in Benin where we had lunch for 17/6d each, with the footballers. If we had known, we could easily have called to greet her.

On Wednesday morning we had a terrible time because there was no petrol in Benin. Eventually we found one place with a queue of cars and an even longer queue of fighting pushing youths with cans to be filled. We bought a gallon can - and Ann waited in that queue while I scouted around elsewhere and discovered an ESSO Station where petrol had just arrived. There was chaos - and constant arguments as to who should be served first - the car owners or the can queue. After 3 hours standing in the sun - they served me with a full tank and a four-gallon spare can - but I have never known such confusion. At times 2 men would get hold of the petrol pipe and be pulling it in opposite directions. One man got squirted all down his shirt front and the owner of the garage kept shouting - "turn off the supply..." 'which they did every now and then to let the pushing, shoving and shouting mob calm down. Even when a couple of policemen turned up and there could have been some order enforced, we were disappointed because they joined the pushers and got their can filled by jumping the queue!!

We proceeded by an improved (since 1970) but still 'bad in patches 'road to Onitsha and were welcomed as usual by Pearl, Ken and Toyin. They are all well. Elizabeth Edmunds and Bessie Parker gave us such depressing reports of the road to Yenagoa that we didn't bother to make an early start on Thurs. morning because we thought that there would be no chance of getting the boat by 1 p.m. In fact, this was not so - the road had improved since they were there, and we reached Yenagoa in 5 hours from Onitsha. Since we didn't leave Onitsha till 10 a.m. it was obvious that the 1 p.m. boat would have gone - and it had. So, we stayed the night in the Sec. School dormitory in Yenagoa. We were kindly looked after by the Vice Principal there who laid on rice and fish stew, and water to wash in etc.

Thus, we didn't get to Oporoma till Friday. The schools boat came for us, so we didn't have to wait for public transport.... but nevertheless, the waiting first for the boat, then for the clerk to go to the Treasury and then the chug-chug journey (3 1/2 hrs.) through the creeks and rivers occupied the whole day. We got here at about 4 p.m.

Maureen is well, and we have had a very happy Christmas all together. There are 6 of us - Ruth Howard, Jill Metcalf, Ann, Maureen, me, and Kay Williamson who is from Ibadan University. She is a Linguist and has been studying the languages of the 'Rivers' area and writing reading books for primary schools. She is going off tomorrow to launch a new reading book in Northern Ijaw. We spent Christmas Eve going through the 'town' with a group of young people from the Church who did a simple Nativity play with Carols interspersed. It was quite a short effort, but we repeated it 7 times in all the 7 'quarters' of the town. I should think that we carried most of the children with us, so they saw it 7 times over. It went on from around 7 p.m. till 10.30 so by then we were feeling hoarse and tired. It's a pity that I didn't have any flash for the camera to take a picture of the rows of wide-eyed brown bodied children, and the church agent sitting beside an Aladdin lamp on a table with a tray on it - to collect the people's donations. This matter rather made a 'disturbante' because the people had decided to have a competitive collection - so if £2.10s.0d was given in the first quarter then the next wanted to 'top' it. The last quarter won with £11 or so. So, the Catechist and Church Agent were quite pleased because then they can take their arrears in Salary.

(Pause…to spray 'off 'on my legs.) On Christmas Day, we went to the morning Service at 10 a.m. There were about 100 children present and around 30 adults, so it wasn't exactly peaceful. I don't think that May would have coped at all!

Then we had 'Santa Claus 'and opened our Christmas parcels to each other. We had Salmon and Salad for lunch and made our Christmas dinner by candlelight in the evening. We had chicken, sausage and stuffing, peas, new potatoes, and mushrooms in sauce, followed by Christmas pudding and brandy butter!! Very English and very nice too.

Boxing day morning was spent doing a puzzle and reading books. Really it has been a delightfully lazy time. It's just a pity that the humidity is almost 100% here. You don't feel like doing anything else apart from sit or sleep, or eat, or 'stroll.' Also, Ruth and Jill both got some tummy bugs - possibly from the Yenagoa fish stew - and so they were not able to enjoy the goodies at first.

27th Dec.

I wonder what has happened to Angela. I hear that she has left Crowther Hall. Ann and I are still here - although the other 3 have gone this morning. The boat was not big enough to contain us all and our loads - so we are waiting until tomorrow. We hope to manage to get to Onitsha in the day and then get back to Akure on Friday.

I have the Herrington's coming to stay next week - and it will be nice to be in Akure for the New year. Also, it will be good to see what the post brings over Christmas. We are becoming decimal here as from Jan. 3rd. So, in future we shall be working in Naira and Kobo. The one Naira will be 10/- in value. Then there are to be 100 Kobo to a Naira … so, it is not as difficult as New P because 1/- = 10 Kobo and so instead of having 12 pence in a 'shilling 'value now there will be 10 and so I think 1/2d will be ignored.

I expect that there will be a certain amount of confusion - but not as much as in the Secondary Schools where the principals are playing "all change." I don't know what Inga will do at St Monica's. She is to stay there - but both Janet Olowoyo and Mrs. Ariyo have been told that they must go and teach in Primary Schools because they are not Graduates. It is madness really - because they are really the pillars of the school…and they will both be impossible to replace especially as they are teaching Yoruba, B.K and Needlework up to School Cert. level - and they are not likely to produce Graduates for any of these subjects.

I am glad that I am not in the schools now. They are tending very much to run them like a Civil Service - which in this country means to agree to transfer your job at a moment's notice without any thought that you might have an opinion on the matter and that if you are transferred it will affect your wife and family.

We have got silver stars up at all the doorways here. Like the ones I made with Stuart and Sacha last year. I wonder how they are all getting on in New Zealand.

I hope that you got my Christmas presents via Mr. Barnet - and that you had a very happy time.

29th - we came from Oporama yesterday - so I hope to get this posted today in Onitsha before the New Year holidays.

Greetings from many - Ken and Pearl, Maureen, Jenny Carey, Elizabeth Edmunds.

With love

Elizabeth

Vining Centre
31st December 1972

Dear Ma and Daddy,

I hope that you didn't have to wait too long for my letter, posted in Onitsha. The whole time between Christmas and the New Year seems to be a holiday and the shortage of petrol is getting worse. Here in Akure petrol has gone onto the black market as far as I can see. You must pay more per gallon and pay the Manager of the Petrol Station before he will give you any. So, transport costs are rising very quickly. It now costs £1.50 to go to Ibadan whereas before it cost 12/6d.

Ann and I arrived back in Akure safely on Friday afternoon - after about 6 hours driving. We went to see Jenny Carey at Owerri on our way to Onitsha, on Thursday. She seemed well, but I think she works very hard and keeps rigidly to the days of holiday that are laid down by C.M.S. We met Mandy Dees at Jenny's place. She told us that Archdeacon Echenin has been 'demoted' from being Archdeacon by the Bishop. It seems to me that the Bishop of Benin is a bit round the bend. He has been acting very strangely - ex-communicating Jane Backhouse's Archdeacon at Ekpoma, and several keen Christians in Benin who were accused of 'forming' their own Church with Pentecostalist leanings. The case of Arch. Echenin is a great tragedy. The incredible thing was that it was since the Asaba C.G.S. girls didn't have a certain book that the bishop had written, at their Confirmation Service. So, the Bishop refused to Confirm them - and sent them out in the middle of the Service! Arch. Echenin protested, and the bishop turned on him and shouted at him - also in the middle of the Church. The next day the bishop wrote a letter to say that Charles Echenin was to be demoted - to the Superintendent of the District with a drop in Salary etc......and that all the furniture that belonged to the Archdeacon of Asaba would be removed from his house!! We went to call on the Echenins at Asaba but unfortunately, they were out - so we didn't see them.

Yesterday, Saturday I had a lazy day here. Ann came for the evening, and I went to visit the Perzyna's in the afternoon. She was in a bit of a state - because her husband is wanting to renew his contract here in Nigeria whereas she has got to go home to return to her job in Poland.... so, they will have to be divided.

Today I was supposed to be going to Rev. Owadayo's father's Memorial Service - but I decided at the last moment not to go. It was going to be a 3-hour journey in the College van to get there - and 3 hours back again. I have had enough of driving in the last few days... anyway, I don't enjoy these long services and great gatherings of expensively dressed people getting themselves in debt...just to keep up with the Joneses. So, I went back to bed and slept till 10 a.m. My ducks are laying eggs again! Happy New Year! We decided to wait until 11 p.m. and see the British New year in!!

With love

Elizabeth

Vining Centre

7th January 1973

Dear Ma and Daddy,

It was good to have your letter telling of the Christmas festivities at home and in St Mary's.

I have Mr. and Mrs. Herrington here this weekend – and I am taking them back to Ibadan tomorrow. They are very well and enjoying being back in Nigeria – but it has been very hot this week. I haven't had any gas yet, so food has not been very inspiring, with just a kerosene stove – and now today, Sunday, when Tokunbo is off duty, they have turned off the hot water!! However, we are managing.

They are both writing their diaries this morning and discussing the spelling of the names of the people that they have met. Mr. Herrington came to Nigeria in 1929! We discovered that he taught our Archdeacon here in 1937 at Moor Plantation.

Yesterday I took them to Ado – with several stops for photographs of rocks etc and we had lunch with Grace and Marjorie. The Richardsons have had their first baby – Andrew. He was born on Boxing Day. We went to their house in Christ School.

On Wednesday, I went to Ondo and stayed the night with Janet and Bose Olowoyo. It was good to see them all again. Inga returned that day – so, I saw her too on her return to Ondo. She has got plenty of problems to face at the beginning of the term. I think I told you that Mrs. Ariyo and Janet have both been asked to teach in primary schools. They have both been made headmistresses! Although neither of them have ever taught primary school children before. It seems to me a great waste of good, useful people in the secondary schools.

Thank you very much for the 2 hankies in your last letter. I haven't seen anything of the famous parcels yet – but I have not given up hope. I am glad that the shortbread arrived, and the small tools. I wonder if Stuart got a box of chocolates. I can't remember if I sent them to Malvern or Offord Road. As for Ruth! I haven't heard a squeak from her, not even a card. I heard from John about their new house etc… and had a nice card from Stuart… and many other cards and letters.

It is very hot here. Well over 90°F but today there is a breeze so that is better.

With much love,
Elizabeth.

Vining Centre
13th January 1973

Dear Ma and Daddy,

There is no letter yet this week – and now we have yet another public holiday so things like post sieze up. This time it is a Moslem Festival. I have just received the November Woman and Home so that's a nice diversion. Thank you.

I took the Herrington's to Ibadan via Ilesha last Monday. We had a picnic lunch with Joan Stephenson and then went on to see Richard Childerstone in Ibadan for we had to deliver a kitten to him from Sheila Davis. Richard is now in Ibadan teaching in a private school belonging to Mrs. Ogunlesi the sister of Bp. Okusanya. He is not very happy there particularly because although he is supposed to be the Chaplain of the school which has a lot of 'Apostolic 'connections and Mrs. Ogunlesi quite often invites 'prophets 'to come and take services and Richard is not keen on all the 'Hallelujahs'!

I had a busy time in Ibadan and managed to get all the shopping done that I intended in 2 days. I stayed with Grace but had supper out with Jose and Sam who have moved to a new and larger house – and I had lunch out with the Herringtons in the flat that they have been loaned at the University. They had also invited Kay Williamson who was at Maureen's with us for Christmas. It was good to see her again, to know her house, and to have another possible place in Ibadan.

On Wednesday I started coming back – I called on Kelu and co briefly and went on to stay the night with Joan in Ilesha before taking Ruth's car to be serviced in Oshogbo on Thursday. It wasn't a long job and I sat and read Daphne du Maurier while they did it. I was back in Ilesha in time for lunch.

I got gas in Ibadan and so now the kitchen is back to normal. The Batts were supposed to be here for the weekend but they haven't come because Brenda's father died suddenly and so she has gone home. However, Marjorie Cockburn is coming here on Monday to rest for a few days so I shall not be devoid of company.

This weekend the Anglican Youth Fellowship of Nigeria have their National Conference here in Akure. All their plans and organisation for it have been put a bit out of joint because they had hoped to use Oyemekan School in the absence of the pupils – but all the students are there – and so they are having to distribute their 400 or so delegates all round town and arrange cooking of food outside the school – and then bringing it in for each meal. General chaos ensues and the few stalwart helpers are running round in circles. We have some delegates in our dormitories – and Mama Ademoye and our 2 cooks are making breakfast each morning. I find it a bit miserable in that for such an event men do all the organising – and a European woman is not much use in a Yoruba kitchen. Anyway, I am not a "member" and only a visitor – but they could save themselves a lot of panic stricken running to and fro if they did a bit more advanced planning in detail it seems to me.

Term starts on Friday. I hope that you are all well.

With much love,

Elizabeth

Vining Centre
20th January 1973

Dear Ma and Daddy,

Thank you for your letter of January 7th received last Wednesday. Our Post Office is still slow to post – I think that it is a combination of lack of petrol and a multitude of Public Holidays. Every weekend since Christmas has had a Public Holiday on the Monday – first the New Year, then a Moslem Festival and now tomorrow there is a special holiday to celebrate Nigeria coming second to Egypt in the All-Africa Games!!

We have started our term – the women are only 11 but they all arrived by Friday. We will start work with them on Monday. Jane Backhouse came on Friday bringing one Catechist's wife from her area of Midwest. She is a rather timid person, and unfortunately this term we only have 2 without their husbands – so they will need special thought and care. This Mrs. Elabor doesn't have anyone else who can talk her own language… and her English is small.

The Men's Interviewing, as I thought, was a bit of a shambles – but I had not reckoned on being involved in it… and it was so slow it wasn't true. We spent 2 ½ hours and only got through six men!!! Over 50% have not shown up yet, because they haven't got their letters presumably… The whole thing was a slight waste of time anyway.

Marjorie Cockburn has been here since Monday – having a good rest and staying in bed til about 11am. She is storing energy for her last few months at Ado. Jane Pelly went to the Wesley Guild on Monday for a check-up because she was feeling very low and getting all tensed up. She is to stay there for 2 weeks and take Librium and Largactlil. I hope that she can relax enough to cope with the rest of the term at Fiwasaiye. You will be glad to know that I am sleeping well!

I am sorry that you had such a lot of foggy driving over the New Year… and that Mr. Barbour has died. It is good that you were able to stay with the Sweetings.

There is a lot to report this week – I won at Scrabble on Tuesday night – have made progress with my knitting – our Clerk is sick – and the Driver has been given his holiday now just when we all need him! Our staff meeting took three hours. Cornelius is very slow… and nothing is planned before the event. It can be very annoying. Sheila and Ann are coming for lunch – I am going to fry chicken… and make blackberry mousse… I hope!! I had a nice letter from Mrs. Sainsbury, this week in answer to my circular letter. I don't see your parcels yet – but haven't given up hope – they may still come. Yes, I did get the small book by Air – very useful. Thank you.

With much love,

Elizabeth

Vining Centre
29th January 1973

Dear Ma and Daddy,

Thank you for your letter this week, and my letter included. I am glad that you had the chance to hear the tape recording at the Martin's house. It will be good to have Ruth back here at the beginning of April. We need her to help to keep Cornelius in order. This week we had a bit of 'do'. The women always go out to Women's Guild meetings on Tuesdays and usually the driver drives them in the van, but this week he is on holiday. There is a student who drives the bus often called Asojo, so I asked him to drive and then I went to Cornelius to ask if that would be OK and at first, he was asleep and then he was out – so I found the key and gave it to the student. He took the women and Mama Ademoye to the Leper Settlement and returned after Cornelius, Owadayo and I were in Chapel. Cornelius went out of Chapel and without consulting any of us he told Asojo that he was suspended for 2 weeks for using the bus without his permission. Then in a great rage he went off to tell the Archdeacon what he had done. You can imagine that when we came out of chapel and found the student saying he was to be suspended – I was upset because I had asked him to go and Owadayo was furious because he is the 'Men's Warden 'and felt strongly that Cornelius had no business to suspend the man without consulting him. And really Cornelius was very stupid to suspend like that when he never checked up the circumstances.

Anyway, when he had cooled down and I explained that I had sent Asojo, and Owadayo had been to the Archdeacon and the Archdeacon had phoned Cornelius he decided to climb down, and the student was pardoned.

Today I was woken at 5.30am by an Urhobo student and his wife, who has just come here. "My wife has a pain in her stomach"‹ "What sort of pain?" says I. "She always has this type of pain before she sees her "time" (i.e. period). At 5.30am!! I gave her a bit of my mind – and then 2 Aspirin. Really, they are the limit.

Tell Ruth that I haven't yet received 'The Living Bible – 'but thank you all the same. I will write to her – but I have seen no letter from her since my birthday – nor even a Christmas card – so I was rather narked… but maybe its altogether with 'The Living Bible'.

It is very nice of Mrs. Harris to send £2. I think the best thing to do is to put it in my bank account in Barnard's Green. There is no point in spending half of it on transfer charges. We only get about 16/- for an English £1 here now. So, I can put the money aside here and use it for the next crisis. I have written Mrs. Harris to thank you.

I had a letter from Dr Kumuyi this week saying that he has been all over the country at different hospitals and is now in Edinburgh for 5 months. He is staying in a Guest House of some sort in Minto Street. Edinburgh 9. I wonder where that is? Are Hamish and Colin in Edinburgh still? I don't even know what they are doing. It's a pity that Mary Tribe has moved because she is a friendly hospitable type. I may write to Auntie Marjorie – but I can't imagine Dr Kumuyi enjoying a visit to Auntie Chrissie I'm afraid!!

Our latest difficulty here is that there is no water. There has been no rain for a good long time – so suddenly all the water is finished. I have some in my bath, and it seems to run in the taps at night some days. We have a couple of rainwater tanks on the compound so we can use those but if 'no water 'continues for long we shall be in a pickle – and so will the schools – and even more so the hospital.

Grace Webster is probably coming to stay next weekend, for part of her holiday. That will be fun.

Jane Pelly is now back from the Wesley Guild – and seems much better. I went to see her there on Wednesday, but she still looked tired.

Dr and Mrs. Perzina came to supper on Saturday night, and we had a very enjoyable evening – playing records. They gave me Tchaikovsky's Piano Concerto – super.

The bishop has asked if Ruth or I could represent Ondo Diocese at the MU Central Council in July in London. Obviously, Ruth can't when she is just back. The Diocese can't afford the fare for the 4 days meeting. So, I <u>may</u> come at the beginning of July!! But don't spread this about – it may not come off – I have written to Chris Cook. He hasn't yet confirmed that I should come in 1973 rather than '74 so I had better not count my leave before it happens!

I hope that you are well – and not too cold over there?!

Bola blew in yesterday. It was good to see him again. I must go to Ondo sometime and see how they are getting on there. I had a letter from Gemma telling of Ewan's coming. I hope that she paid for her call to Benin!! Ewan and Gemma having a great natter together!!

With much love,

Elizabeth

Vining Centre
4th February 1973

Dear Ma and Daddy,

Thank you both for your long, interesting letters this week. It is always good to see them and to keep up with your doings.

We seemed to miss out on the week of Prayer for Christian Unity. I think that it was kept in the town, and there were joint meetings and a collection of clothes which were taken to the Leper Settlement. I didn't get to know anything about it here – partly I suppose because we have been so occupied with the beginning of term. We have the same problem as you in relationships. Cornelius is still busy taking decisions on his own without consulting Owadayo, the Men's Warden. This week he sent all the 2nd year students away to bring some money which they owed on some jerseys. So Owadayo discovers that all his 2nd year students have gone away, without his knowledge!! This meant that we were a bit short because the 1st year only started arriving on Friday.

Our greatest trouble this week is lack of water. Suddenly Akure is completely without water in the taps. No previous instructions were given about the economy, so everyone is taken by surprise. So now we send people to the hospital and the doctor prescribes 'Mist Aspirin 'or something – but the Dispensary can't supply – no water! If you go to the Lab for a test you are asked to bring a bucket of water! In fact, we are quite fortunate here because there is water in a large water tank on the compound, and yesterday we had a tanker which filled 2 other smaller tanks. But others are not so well off. Jane Pelly has very little water on her school compound – and the tanker hasn't reached her yet. It seems that they only have one tanker for the whole town! And if it stops in the street then there is a fight for the water.

I have Grace staying here this weekend – as part of her holiday. She sends her love to you both. She is lively as usual, although has had plenty on her plate recently. Her cook Geoffrey collapsed and became unconscious last Sunday. She drove him to Wesley Guild Ilesha, but he died shortly after admittance. So that was a great upset.

More transfers this week in the hospital. The Matron has gone to Abeokuta and the Medical Officer has been asked to man the ship at Ikare. He had only been here since November having returned from America. He found working in Akure frustrating – so what he will think of Ikare I don't know.

My knitting is finished today. I have made 2 pink jackets for Shola's twins. I hope that they are big enough – and that it will be cold enough in the wet season.

You ask about our petrol shortage. They say that one of the reasons for the shortage was that so much was used in Lagos for transport involved in the All-Africa Games held in Lagos. Anyway, it's better now.

They say that this is the first time that the river Owena has failed to supply Ondo and Akure. Part of the reason is that it has been a very long time since we had rain – but also, they have now started a new water scheme at Igbara – Oke and taken the water from the same River Owena – further up! So, the water doesn't get to our waterworks!

We have some English men working here in Akure with the GEC. They are putting up radio transmitting stations and working on the Telecommunications network. Ann and I went to greet them on Thursday evening. Two we met are long-haired fellows who have worked all over the world on different projects. The third one is called Sid – a typical middle-aged Londoner engineering type. They have their own private water tanker, so they are not short of water – and have promised to help us out if we completely run out.

On Monday night I had a hospital adventure because Tokunbo (my cook) brought his baby to me at 10.30pm breathing like a steam engine – obviously with bronchial pneumonia. So, we took her to the hospital, and she was admitted with her mother. They all said it was 'serious' – and she was put onto crystalline penicillin – but there is none in the hospital. So Tokunbo and I had to drive up and down the streets of Akure looking for a Chemist shop which was open. There was none – obviously at 11pm. So, we returned to the hospital – and they arranged a swap whereby we used someone else's medicine and then promised to go and buy our own in the morning. Anyway, by the next day Toyin the baby had responded well, and the breathing was much better. She was kept in 3 days and is now home again.

It is over 90° here in the afternoons – and sometimes still 80°F when you go to bed around 10pm. You can survive the heat if there is plenty of water. Without water it becomes more of a problem. Still, I can't complain – I have stacks of water available compared to most folk in this town. We just pray that there may not be an outbreak of cholera or dysentery… and that it will rain before too long.

With much love to you all,

Elizabeth

Vining Centre
11th February 1973

Dear Ma and Daddy,

The post has missed your letter out this week – I expect that they will find it next week. Today I have 3 visitors. Grace from Ado, Sue Davies from Bida and a retired teacher called Dorothy Browning from Shaftesbury near Salisbury. She is a tiny little, slightly hunchbacked lady who has been staying in Zaria since early December. She is travelling towards the East on her own on public transport… without having ever been in Nigeria before. She is an incredible little lady – a keen supporter of CMS and SPG in her village. Sue and Grace both send their greetings to you.

Our main news here is still lack of water and lack of rain. The student men are going out each morning and head loading water in buckets. There is a well in the Army barracks next door. It is all a game. Some people are up all night getting water from springs and streams because there are such crowds and queues in the daytime.

It looks as though I shall be coming home at the beginning of July – to go to the MU Central Council 3-6th. What a laugh! I don't know if I should come home first – or fly to Heathrow on Monday 2nd July and go straight to the meetings and then come home afterwards. I will have to see how it works out.

We have the Magic Flute blaring here – gorgeous. Sue is drying her hair in the bedroom with the hair drier. Miss Browning is sitting outside in a basket chair. The women students are in the kitchen. The men are off at Sunday Schools and preaching engagements.

It was funny in the middle of the night last night. It was hot and I got out of bed and went to the fridge to get a drink of water. I put the light on. A few minutes later the phone rang – it was Cornelius from over the other side phoning to find out if I was all right!! Grace and Sue were awake and had a good laugh at my voice calling out 'Hullo… No. I am all right… it's just a bit hot!!'

I had a letter from the Bennetts. He has put his notice in as organist, I gather. They seem to be going up and up at St Georges. I wonder how I shall get on as their Link Missionary this time. I also heard from Auntie Kath and Auntie Ruby this week. All their grandchildren seem to be doing great things.

I often think of you all at home – it will be good to see you so soon.

With much love, Elizabeth

Vining Centre
18th February 1973

Dear Ma and Daddy,

Thank you for your letter of February 5th. Castlemorton Common seems to be a very popular hide-out.

Our main concern this week has again been ‘water’. We now send the bus out to a village 8 miles away where there is a tap. They go out with oil drums and other containers and bring back drinking water. Most of the washing water must be head loaded from local streams or from the army camp next-door.

I escaped from the compound on Saturday morning and went with Inga and Susanne to the hot springs at Ikogosi. There is plenty of water there – the swimming pool is full, and the warm river is running as usual. We had a great time – swimming, then washing ourselves, our hair, and our cars in the river below the pool. We stayed the night in one of the ‘Cabins ’at the Baptist Camp. Then on Sunday I went on to Ondo and had lunch with Inga and greeted Janet and Bose there. Janet was ‘resting ’She seems to be getting on alright as the Head of a Primary School, but it seems that they are expected to run these Primary Schools with no money for repairs or equipment and you are expected to have over 40 children in the 1st 2 classes! Ghastly.

On Sunday evening I went for supper with Ann Forgan. Brother Fred showed his slides of going across the Sahara Desert and Jane showed some of her visit to America.

You will be happy to know that the parcel of books that you sent in October to Mrs. Treadgold has arrived today. Thank you very much for the 2 bibles and the Cookery book. The pictures in the New World bible will be very useful.

You will have Ruth with you this week. I hope that you have a happy time together. Also, on Daddy’s birthday – for which I send special greetings in a separate envelope.

Our 2nd and 3rd year students have gone off to Ekiti today to take part in a Mission to the Diocese of Ekiti. So, we only have the 1st year men, and the woman and children on the Compound. We may go and join the others for an Open-Air Service in Ikerre next Sunday. Then we have Half Term. I am thinking of going to Lagos to see Ethel… and to visit Shola and her twins. That’s the weekend of March 2nd. I just might try to phone for Daddy’s birthday – so don’t be alarmed, but I don’t promise at all – it may be impossible. Anyway, it looks as though I shall be coming at the beginning of July. We had better wait until I get dates from CMS for deputation before we plan holidays. Scotland would suit me fine. I am trying to get some reply from Angela as to what she is doing in the summer. Dr and Mrs. Perzina have invited me to go and see them in Poland. It would be fun if it were possible.

With much love to you both,

Elizabeth.

PS Hurrah! It looks like rain!!

Vining Centre
19th February 1973

Dear All,

It certainly did rain!! I went to chapel at 6pm and the sky was black. It was obviously brewing, but I have never experienced such a storm. Perhaps we have been praying too hard!

We were in the chapel, which has a wide overhang on the roof but no windows on the sides. The rain drove right in – and the students kept shifting their places. The first-year student who tried to read the Bible and pray at the front lost his voice. The lights went out. The bush lamps were lit, but the wind blew them out. So, we ended promptly, and all stood together in the only dry place – up beside the altar. The wind was terrific – and the lashing rain combined with lightning and thunder was awe-inspiring.

Thump! And a tree was down over the drive – uprooted.

Then the rain ceased, and we went out to discover the electricity wires down all over the compound – several trees and branches scattered all over the place… but no damage to buildings mercifully. The telephone was off, so I went out to ask ECN to disconnect our electricity. There was chaos in the town with trees and wires down and in one place I saw some roofing pan hanging on the telephone wire like washing on a line.

In my own house Tokunbo had shut the windows – louvre type – but despite that the rain had got in and flooded all over the floor to the living room and in the spare bedroom. That's how your letter got so speckled with rain.

Incredible business. But good in that the temperature has promptly dropped by 10° at least and its now a cool 76°F. And the water tank at the back of Ruth's house is ¾ full of water. Our drought has ended with a bang!

With love,

Elizabeth

Vining Centre
25th February 1973

Dear Daddy and Ma,

Thank you for your letter of 16th February. I have now heard from CMS confirming that I should come home at the beginning of July, until towards the end of September. They also ask me to keep July 14th-28th and September 1st-8th free for Links and Deputations so that only leaves August for holidays. I am still interested in Scotland, and Iona, but maybe only a week there so that there is time to see friends and folk like Geoff and Marguerita. Could Angela be included in Iona do you think? I would like to spend part of August with her. If she came to Iona with us, then we could stay longer. Maybe you can get in touch with her directly. Her address is 48, The Avenue, Yeovil, Somerset.

I have started reading New Dimensions in Preparation for the Central Council meetings!! I will need to find out the opinions in Ondo Diocese before I set sail as their 'representatives'.

After our storm last Monday everyone on the compound became very concerned about cutting down trees that were near the houses in case, we should have another storm. So, on Tuesday we employed a wood cutter with an electric saw who said that he knew the job perfectly! We all stood and watched while he cut a tree near my house. Lo and behold it fell towards the house with a great thump and the top branches hit the roof and broke some of the asbestos sheets and the timbers at the end!!! So, we all decided to try a different woodcutter for cutting the other trees on the compound. Mercifully he knew the job and about 6 trees are now sprawled around the place without any further mishap.

I spent Thursday and Friday in bed. I had a cold about 2 weeks ago and a cough developed. Then on Tuesday and Wednesday I felt a bit 'off'. On Thursday morning I woke up and felt giddy and was sick and distinctly disinclined to eat or get up… so I didn't. In the afternoon I went to see the doctor who said he thought it was some chest infection or virus, or some such and since then I have been taking antibiotics – and staying in the house. Anyway, I feel better, although I don't think it has completely cleared off. The doctor has just returned from 7 years in the UK. He knows the Malvern Hills because he was in Worcester for a period and he and his wife both spent time training in Edinburgh. He is a Specialist Physician.

Dr and Mrs. Perzina the Polish surgeon and his wife are leaving Akure tomorrow. I shall miss them very much because their house has been a regular visiting place for coffee or ice-cream in the afternoons.

I am sorry to hear all your ups and downs with May and Noel. It seems a bit daft to have a Stewardship Campaign without the support of the main laymen of the Parish. Only they can put the idea over to others – the clergy can't do that.

Temperatures here are still well in the 90°s by day and don't fall much below 80° at night – so I was very happy yesterday to receive a gift of a super fan from the Herringtons. It was very kind of them – and came at just the right time. So now I can sit happily with the air blowing about. I even went to bed with it on last night.

I am hoping to go to Lagos next weekend for our Half Term. I think I told you that I hope to see Shola and her new twins and to stay with Ethel at the Guesthouse. It looks as though I shall just miss Chris Cook because he is going to the Midwest with Beatrice Waddington, I think. She is coming back anyway at the end of this month.

I heard from Ruth this week – on a card that she had found and liked. It seems to be a whole row of hopeful ladies sitting on the shelf! There is not a man in sight. It is called St Valentine's Day. Rather near the bone I thought!!

I still haven't seen or heard of the £3 Bible. I think that I shall have to call a stop to the postage of Bibles! You know that you have now given me 2 copies of the New English bible (one big and one smaller)! Then the New World bible as well; and I already have one RSV, one Philips, one NEB New Testament, and Good News for modern man and 2 Yoruba bibles – because the staff and students gave me a second one for my birthday.

On re-reading your letter about holidays I see that you are to have your holiday for a month before 18th August. That's a bit tricky. CMS won't want me for Links, or Deputation in August I don't suppose – so it is probably best for me to spend the last 2 weeks of July doing Links and have August free. Therefore, in the 1st 2 weeks of August we shall be free together – for Iona? (Or from Monday July 30th-

Friday August 17th is almost 3 weeks.) I don't mind about Bishops-court or the Abbey. Where are the comfortable beds? Maybe there are more people to meet in the Abbey? I don't really need my own company and time to read and write letters. I have plenty of that here. The trouble is that now one feels too hot to bother to use the time.

Do you think that I should fly on June 29th and have the weekend at home? Or fly to London on July 2nd and come home after the MU Central whatnot? Chris Cook suggests the former. Maybe that's better. It looks as though there is going to be a good deal of popping up and down the railway. The MU ends on July 6th I think, and CMS Missionary's Day is on the 10th. Probably it will be better to come home first – and have a weekend to talk before the MU. Jolly dee!

With much love,

Elizabeth

Vining Centre
4th March 1973

Dear Ma and Daddy,

I am now on my half term weekend in Lagos – visiting Ethel at the Marina and Shola in Ikeja. I came down here on Friday, travelling via Ibadan. It was a long day's driving – and hot and dirty as well – the situation not being improved by our having a puncture before Ibadan and then meeting difficulty in getting the new tyre that I bought fitted onto the wheel. I was glad that I had taken the precaution of bringing 2 students with me because they helped in all these events. So, we reached Shola's place about 5pm – and I had a bath, in a whole bath of water! Gorgeous, after our long experience without any running water in Akure.

In the evening Shola and I went out to the University to watch 2 short plays done by 2 English actors who are on tour in Nigeria. It was very cleverly done and well-acted. The first play was called 'The Dumb Waiter' and the second 'Dock Brief'. We got home about 11pm – and I had rather a hot night – but didn't sleep too badly. Then on Saturday we set out to go to the airport to say goodbye to Mr. Awokoya, of St Andrew's fame – an uncle of Shola's – but we were turned back for 'security reasons'… Gowon was arriving from a State Visit to Mali. So, we went to Kingsway and played with her dear fat twin girls. Then in the afternoon I came here to the Marina and had supper with Ethel and 2 Professors, one from Ife and one from Ibadan universities. One is from Troon and the wife of the other from Edinburgh. After supper Shola and Funsho came and took me to the Federal Palace Hotel where we had chicken sandwiches and Fanta Ginger Ale. There was a band playing and the place was full of people – very pleasant atmosphere, so it's been a very happy visit in Lagos.

I have completely recovered from my 'bug', and I have been back on the beat full time during the past week. Ann has had a cold and a bad throat and Marjorie Cockburn has measles!! So really, I have nothing to complain about. Ethel seems well – although she hates Lagos and finds it dirty and noisy. There is a boat over in the harbour which has been belching black smoke for the past 2 days so that doesn't help. I saw Kelu on Friday. They have no water AND no electricity, so she is thoroughly fed up. They are supposed to be moving onto the University campus but so far there is no house available for them, so they are still where they were before.

I hope that you are all well. I am thinking of you very much since it is Daddy's birthday. The Scots Professor told me that the phone was very clear, so I tried it – but I am sorry we were unfortunate and didn't hear well till the end. Disappointing but not very costly.

With love,

Elizabeth.

Vining Centre
10th March 1973

Dear Ma and Daddy,

It was a bit sickening to get back to Akure last Monday to hear that Jane Pelly phoned her parents last Sunday from Akure! and that she heard perfectly well what they were saying. So, I was very disappointed. I think it is better to stick to letters, but I don't know if it's your strikes or what but the letters are coming very erratically.

It has been a full week here, occupied a good deal with collecting water. The van goes daily or twice a day to the nearest tap, which is sometimes 8 miles away, sometimes that is dry, and you must go nearly 20 miles and then queue up for your turn. We have a muddy pond on our ground which we use for washing – but we get the tap water for drinking and cooking. We want to avoid cholera at all costs

On Friday, at last I played tennis!! Event. I discovered that Terry, who is a radio expert with GEC, wanted to play so we went to the courts and joined some Nigerian men who play there regularly. They were better than us, but still it was fun. Except that I now have blisters on my toes.

On Thursday afternoon we had the great drama of a small piece of the bush behind my house catching fire and with a high dry wind it was a bit dangerous – so we called the fire engine. This took time because, of all stupid things they are not on the phone… so by the time they came there was nothing much to do – our students had already cleared a stretch of ground and stopped the fire moving near to the houses. But notwithstanding the firemen had to show their paces so with helmets on their heads, boots on their feet and long hose pipes they proceeded to pour Water on the trees and bushes that were smouldering or still flaming. It would have been useful to have poured the water from their tanker into our buckets.

On Friday evening Bola came and stayed the night. He has had a lot of trouble with fires in his forestry areas. Some people have lost complete cocoa plantations, which is serious because it is their livelihood, and it takes 4 years for the cocoa to produce again. Bola sends greetings to you. You will remember that he sent that giant photo album. We went to Owo on Saturday to greet a friend of his who has just been promoted. So, I went with them to various 'eating-houses' and 'places for drinks'. A bit hauf Daddy would have thoroughly enjoyed himself. Then he stayed with his friend, and I stayed with Joan Steward at St Catherines. It was good to meet some people with different lines of interest – different from the usual run of Church and Education and the Hospital. We now have 6 Egyptian doctors in Akure, I hope that they are hard-working ones.

Today, Sunday – Ann, Jane and Sheila all came to lunch here, and I am going to them for supper, after chapel. Ann has been very tired and depressed during the last week, so we have all been trying to cheer her up.

I had a letter from Stuart this week – and your letter Ma saying how upset you are at their sharing the flat in Offord Road. I can understand how you feel about it all – but I don't think that you should torture yourselves with the idea that you have failed somehow. You have faithfully brought up all of us – and done a good job of it. Whatever choices the children make we still all have the basic stability of loving caring parents – and that counts for so much these days. Maybe living here in Nigeria and seeing some of the incredible muddles that there are in family life – the number of men who live far from their wives and children – the 'girlfriends' of married men – the promiscuity among students – even in schools. All manner of things which make people become hard and cynical and uncaring. So, it seems to me that a loving, caring loyal relationship between a fellow and one girlfriend has the seeds of good in it, and may well work out happily in the end. You said that you liked Jutka and that she was good for Stuart. It is good that they came together for Christmas to Malvern. Stuart is not hiding some nasty hussy and keeping you in the dark.

Don't think that I don't understand your distress about the flat arrangement. I do… but at the same time, I think we should pray that God will help us all to see His positive will for the future of the relationship. God still loves Stuart, even in the new set up… and this Jutka too. Hang on – and I think that you will see some rays of light. I hope anyway by the time you get this that your voice will have returned. Thank God that Ruth is happily engaged.

I got your second parcel last week – I don't think I told you in my letter from Lagos. So that's good – except that the Nigerian customs are real 'crooks' and get their pound of flesh. The most incredible thing to me – and rather a joke really was that the Tupperware containers which I bought in a Jumble sale for 6d – I had to pay 63 Kobo to claim them!! (That's 6/3d). Anyway, I was very happy to have these things and have been listening to the records. Unfortunately, the 'Gospel' is a bit warped – but you can hear most of it. The GEC fellows liked the 'Light' song… which was something. One of them, Jim, is incredibly 'anti' – anti-religion, anti-Akure, anti-Nigerian and very bitter – he never stops talking and gets quite narked if someone else holds the floor. He is divorced from his wife.

Its time I went to bed. It's hot – so I have Herrington's fan going in the bedroom at night these days.

With lots of love to you both,

Elizabeth.

PS Is your phone number Malvern 4043? Because that was another reason for complications about the phone call. I wasn't positive of the number!

Vining Centre
18th March 1973

Dear Ma and Daddy,

Thank you for your letters this week. I have been thinking of you often, particularly in your concern for Stuart. We had our first Lent Fellowship meeting here on Tuesday and we read Mark 14, 1-11 and contrasted the 2 people – Mary who gave her love completely to Jesus, and Judas who was blinded by selfishness. It was a very thought-provoking discussion. We shall be meeting again next Tuesday at St Peters, the Catholic Training College. It is good to have this chance of contact with other denominations, especially Catholics.

I spent Wednesday going to and fro 'to the hospital with one of our women who had broken a bone in her foot the week before – and she had removed the plaster! Because she said it was too painful. The doctor was very decent and put on a new plaster for her.

I played tennis again on Friday. On Saturday Sheila and I went up to Ado to say Goodbye to Marjorie. We arrived there right in the middle of her official farewell by the Board of Governors. So, we stayed for the service, the speeches, and the Presentations. Anyway, it was good to be part of it all – but we hardly had any chance to speak to Marjorie at all. Marjorie has been sick for the past 3 weeks – she has measles – she looked weak still and was rather het up about all the Farewells. The Ewi of Ekiti was there and he made a speech saying that throughout the history of the Hospital it had been saved many times from the crisis of closing by different European women. So, I thought of Mummy in 1938. Marjorie certainly has had her share of holding the fort there – particularly in 1969 when they had no doctor.

I am taking our evening service here today. We have our Board of Governors on Tuesday. We hope Ethel will come for the day to say goodbye to folk. Ruth comes on April 6th, when we start our 3 weeks holiday.

With much love to you both,

Elizabeth.

PS I don't know yet about times on 29th June but go ahead with Peterhouse plans.

Vining Centre
24th March 1973

Dear Ma and Daddy,

Thank you for your letters this week. I am glad that you were able to have a long talk with Stuart about his set up. Why doesn't he marry her?

I was a bit astonished this week when Cornelius said to me "Has the Bishop said anything to you". 'No' I replied. "I hear that they decided at the West African synod that they would send <u>one</u> delegate for the whole Province of West Africa – the wife of the archbishop probably – to the MU Conference"!! No one has yet told me this officially… but it looks as though, after all, I shall not be going to the conference. So don't worry about where I am going to stay in London. I may stay here another week and finish off the end of term – or I may keep the same date as planned and go to the CMS Conference at Rhyll. We shall just have to wait and see.

Concerning the holidays. Maybe it is best for you two to take your holiday in June as you say – and have a good rest. It is very good of you to think of my using the car for deputation and links. The dates for those may be slightly amended because I have said that I would like to go on the missionaries retreat at Foxbury in the last week of July – since Iona has fallen through. As you say there are plenty of gorgeous places to go and visit from Malvern. Could you go to a Travel Agent for me and try to find out about the possibility of getting to Poznan, in Poland – by bus, or by train. Ann Forgan says that there is something called Europa bus. But I need to know details of price, time it takes, and arrangements that you must make about accommodation en route… before I can decide whether to continue with the Polish idea. Also, please discover details of Visas needed, where obtained etc. – and if you need a 'letter of invitation'– if you are going to stay with friends in Poland.

Can you also investigate the possibility of going to Poland via Amsterdam, Pforzheim (Germany) and Czechoslovakia. Presumably you can do this by car (Ann just might have a car) – but can you also go by railway or bus. Doesn't Daddy have cousins in Amsterdam? Presumably you can go up the Rhine to Pforzheim. Then across Munich-Prague-Poznan.

What are the alternative routes and prices for taking a car across the Channel?

We had quite a busy week here. The Bishop of Lagos came on Monday night and stayed the night before the Board of Governors which was on Tuesday. That meant that all our 12 women and Mama Ademoye, Victoria (Cornelius' wife), and Owadayo's wife spent the morning stirring pots – to supply food for 7 members of the Board!!

On Wednesday I had 2 of the GEC fellows round for supper. We planned to play tennis on Thursday, but it rained.

On Tuesday evening we had a very good Lent Fellowship at St Peter's, led by Brother Fred. Next week it's to be at the Noviciate led by Sister Martinian.We have had rain 3 times during the last week – but still no sign of water in the taps. There was quite a storm on Thursday and one of our electricity poles blew down – so we had no electricity on Friday or Saturday. The liver that was in my fridge went bad – horrid pong

Monday morning. Hurrah!! There is water in the taps. What a good thing. We have exams at the end of this week – then the following week is the last week of term, and I shall be going down to Lagos to meet Ruth on April 6th. It will be good to have her back. Ethel and Marjorie both go at the end of this week. I have yet to decide what to do over Easter. I may go to Ibadan for part of the time and see Grace. There is only 3 weeks so it's not so long anyway, but it will be my last break before coming home (apart from weekends of course).

I hope that your cough is gone now Ma.

With much love,

Elizabeth.

PS I hope you get a 'something 'on April 1st.

Vining Centre
1st April 1973

Dear Ma and Daddy,

The post hasn't obliged this week! – but I have had a letter from Ruth with plenty of news of her mail order system. She is a hoot. We are now facing the end of term affairs here in the VC. I have been composing my exams in Yoruba and trying to mark them. The actual exam is not restful either because you must take the illiterate women individually and see what they have to say for themselves. I have 7 women doing English and I have divided them so that I have set them 3 different exams in English!! Quite a game.

I played tennis again – on Saturday – with Terry and a VSO girl and another GEC fellow – from Ilorin. In fact, Saturday was quite a day! There were 2 parties in the evening – one at Dr Kohlis – and Tokunbo made the jollof rice for that – the second was at the GEC House – my basket chairs went to that. I went to both! One after the other – from 7.30-11.30. I discovered that one of the Egyptian doctors who I thought was a Moslem (as most are) is not – but an Orthodox Coptic Christian. He's fasting for Lent – completely vegetarian – no milk, eggs, meat, or fish. So, I hope that he will come to our Lent Fellowship this week. He also wants to play tennis.

Our water in the taps was rather a short-lived joy, it's now 'off' again so I have some water stored in my bath, and that's it. This means that I went to the GEC House and had a bath there – they have running Hot and Cold! – because they have their own tanker. It's 94° again!

I go to Lagos on Friday to meet Ruth off the plane. Sheila Davis and I will be going down together in her car. Then I will bring back my own new Volkswagen which Chris Cook says is already in Lagos. That's good news!

Ann Forgan is going to come home for 2 weeks over Easter – I think. So, I may think of some things for her to bring back. This may be the last letter to get to you by Easter. If so, I hope that it is a time of great joy and that you don't get too tired. I haven't written to Stuart yet – but still hope to, sometime. Also, must write to John and Pat. I have written to Poland to ask if they will be at home in August. Ann Forgan is talking of going to Czechoslovakia in the second half of August so I hope we can fix something together then. Where are you hoping to go to in June?

With much love,

Elizabeth

Vining Centre
7th April 1973

Dear Ma and Daddy,

I am in Lagos, having met Ruth last night. I hope that this letter will get to you quickly. Thank you very much for the book and the chocolate – Gorgeous! I am afraid that you may not get anything from me for Easter – but I will be home in not so long, and I hope the orange tree does well.

I have just been given a new car by Chris Cook – so I am rather excited. It is a 1300 VW – brand new. White outside and dark red upholstery. It is left hand drive. So now I am going to drive it back to Akure, with Ruth. I came down with Sheila Davis yesterday – and we went to have supper with Shola in Ikeja. She is well and her twins are lovely.

I may go to Yomi and Kelu for Easter, if they are in Ife during that time. We have a 3-week holiday, so it will soon pass, and I need to go to Ibadan and buy stuff for the new term. I will stay a few days with Grace then. It has been a busy week, with the end of term – finishing marking exams, doing the reports etc. We had a very good Lent Fellowship on Tuesday. The last one is this week, at the Catholic Seminary. The Egyptian doctor, Dr Salama who is a 'Coptic' came, and I think was happy to meet other Christian folk.

Maureen Olphin was here at the Guest House. Surprise! Surprise! She is just on her way home. Then also Myrtle and Pat were here to greet us last night, so it was quite a reunion. Thank you for the information about Poland. I think I will write straight to Regent's Street and see what they have to say. I may be down in Lagos next weekend because Ann Forgan is going home for 2 weeks for an interview. She may fly from Ibadan, but if not, I promised to bring her to Lagos. Then I will see Myrtle & co.

With much love,

Elizabeth.

Vining Centre
12th April 1973

Dear Ma and Daddy,

I expect that you received my short blue air letter from Lagos last week. With any luck this one will reach you even more quickly because I am sending it with Ann. She is going home for an Interview – for 2 weeks. The fares are paid by the British Government, except for £20. I am taking her down to Lagos tomorrow, Friday, in my new Volkswagen. Then I hope to stay over this weekend with Myrtle and return via Ibadan and Ife, staying with Grace and Yomi and Kelu.

We had a good journey back from Lagos with Ruth last Saturday, but I was tired on Sunday and Monday. Ruth is in good spirits but unfortunately on Monday she clicked her back again by pushing the seat of her car forward. So, she is having to rest yet again. It is a bit of a test of faith for her because she is wondering how she is going to manage her travelling if the back is troublesome.

On Tuesday we had our Lent Fellowship at the Sacred Heart Seminary. The subject was Christ's sufferings – so it was very relevant for Ruth. They have been very good discussions this year. Some of our Catholic folk put things in a new and vital way. It is very stimulating and quite a revelation to me. My friend, Dr Salama couldn't come to the Fellowship because he was too exhausted after a busy day operating. So, I went to see him after the meeting and we had a long and very interesting discussion. He is a very thoughtful and deeply committed Christian. He likes quiet places, and mountains and table tennis so we have much in common. Please pray for our friendship that it may be a relationship of joy and peace that we may each help and support the other… whatever the outcome in the long run. I was there again yesterday and sampled his bean cakes, fruit salad and halawa. All very intriguing.

I hope that you have a very happy Easter season. I shall be enjoying your chocolates. I am glad that you can get away just after Easter, and I hope that you will be able to have a completely restful time.

Marjorie Cockburn hasn't retired! She is going home and hopes to work in a place like St Christopher's Hospice. She and Ethel are on the boat together and they should be in Southampton today.

I have written a letter to the Polish Tourist office asking them to send me information directly about travel to Poland.

Fri 13th.

We are now with Myrtle and Pat in Surulere. They both are well and send their love to you. We had a good journey down from Akure – via Ilesha (Joan Stephenson), Ife – (Mama Scott and Kelu) and Ibadan – (Grace). So, I was able to fix up beds for the journey back. The programme now reads – stay here till Monday, go to Grace in Ibadan Mon-Thurs. Yomi and Kelu on Good Friday, with them to Ibadan on Easter Saturday for Chris Groves wedding and Kelu's brother's birthday. Return to Ife on Sunday and back to Akure either Sun or Mon. Then I have a week to prepare for the new term starting on April 27th. Oh! Also, on Wed we shall go to a British Cocktail party at the British High Commission in Ibadan.

I hope that you have a happy week in Malvern. I shall be thinking of you. I hope some flowers will appear for Easter.

With love, Elizabeth.

Vining Centre
23rd April 1973

Dear Ma and Daddy,

Thank you for your blue letter. I am thinking of you today as you sit in your Herefordshire cottage. I do hope that you both have a restful time there. I have had a full week coming from Lagos via Ibadan and Grace and then Ife and Yomi and Kelu. I travelled from Lagos via Ijebu–Ode and found both Bola and John Fabuyi in their offices. So, they took me, and another forester out to lunch in the Catering Rest House. Nigerians are so hospitable – entertaining friends can always be included in office hours!!

I stayed with Grace in Ibadan and did a fair bit of shopping for books etc. for the coming term. She has not been very well (gynae) but is now having treatment at UCH. She is always happy to have visitors, and to get the chance to go and see some of her own friends. Without being able to drive it becomes very lonely for her on her own – and Titus is often out in the evenings.

The children have grown enormously. I took them all to the swimming pool one afternoon and they enjoyed it. The only snag was that my purse was stolen while I was by the pool. There were very few people around and I left the purse beside our bags on the ground. The thief could have only been one boy who came and played on the swings. I went and reported to the reception desk but there wasn't much they could do – then a boy came and said that he had seen a fellow walking down the hill – so I jumped in the car to chase him. It was only when I got to the bottom of the hill to the busy main road that I realised I only had my bathing costume on and no shoes. So even if we had seen the thief I couldn't have got out and given chase in bare feet and a bathing costume!!! Fortunately, the purse didn't have much money in it – but it did have my front door key – so that's a nuisance.

On Wednesday evening we (Ruth, Jane P, Sheila and her friend and I) all went to the British High Commissioners Cocktail party. It was a very formal affair – all standing around on the grass with floodlights in the trees – but really there was very little chance of meeting anyone that you didn't already know. Quite fun, but rather a washout as a social function.

On Thursday I went on to Ife, in time to join them in the evening communion service in their Methodist Church. It was a lovely service and I understood most of what the minister said in his sermon (in Yoruba) (unusual!). Then on Good Friday we all went again to the service (about 20 minutes late I suppose – Kelu doesn't change!) I was not so fortunate and didn't hear the sermon hardly at all – it was an older man who spoke quickly and not very distinctly. Then in the afternoon we went for an open-air service attended by all the different churches in Ife – a complete shambles in my opinion – mobs of children with groups of very sweaty choristers in complete disarray pushing their way through the town to the assembling place. Then when everyone eventually arrived – as I say already hot and bothered – all they did was chat! I don't think anyone heard a word of the short service which was shouted out at the top of the Archdeacon's lungs to a great crowd who didn't listen to a word!

On Saturday we set out in the car to Ibadan to go to Chris Grove's wedding in St Annes (we were about 30 minutes late but since the service lasted about 1hr 45mins it didn't matter much). It was a very beautiful marriage service with very carefully thought out wording and gorgeous singing. Afterwards there was a very grand and proper reception with some exceptionally good speeches. It finished around 2pm. Then we went on to Kelu's brother's house and joined them in the Thanksgiving Service at 4pm. This was taken by Bishop Okunsanya. It was for her brother's 50th birthday and was followed by another reception and more speeches. Kelu changed into a different fancy lace rig-out – she already had worn white lace in the car and changed once for Chris Grove's wedding. We then all drove home in the dark – back to Ife. It was quite a tiring day.

On Easter Sunday morning we all went to the Methodist Church service. I wished afterwards that I had gone off to the English service at the University because firstly it wasn't communion and secondly it was spoiled in my opinion by having 'Thanksgivings' after the main service. This meant that they called everyone out to the front in groups and then took money from them. The worst of it is that they extend the business so by thinking up so many 'groups' i.e. (1) Babies (2) Small children (3) Primary children (4) Secondary school children (5) University (6) Youth club members (7) Young women (8) Young men (9) Visitors (10) Members of the church from Lagos (11) from Ibadan and elsewhere (12) Older women – some society (13) Older men (14) The choir….!!! It seemed to take ages.

Then I came back here in the evening via Ondo, where I saw Inga. I was bothered with diarrhoea on Sunday so when I came back, I went to see Dr Kohli (Indian woman doctor) and got some medicine. So, I was better by Monday, and Dr Kohli came at teatime. Ruth returned in the evening from Oka where she and Jane and co went for Easter – to a non-catering rest house. I went and ate bean cakes with Dr Salama this evening from 6.30-8.30 or so. He is overworked but seems to be managing. The gynaecologist has broken his hand, so Nabil is doing all the work of the surgeon and the gynae ops. So, tonight is Caesar and one other thing and 2 accident cases to cope with, when he has already worked from 8am until 3.30pm without a break!

I don't know how our friendship will develop – my hopes are not very high at the present... but we enjoy each other's company. It's a pity that he is so tied to the phone, and Akure because it would be much easier if we could go and do something together like climbing Idanre or visiting friends – but he says he can't until this other fellow's hand is out of plaster in one month's time. Anyway, we will see. I don't really know anything about Egyptians so it's a new experience.

I am sending this letter to Lagos with Sheila's friend tomorrow so I hope that you will get it quite quickly.

With much love to you both,

Elizabeth.

Vining Centre
28th April 1973

Dear Ma and Daddy,

I am in Ado this morning, having spent the night with Grace. We went to the Communion service in the Cathedral at 7.30. Greetings from Provost Famewo! He took the service and seemed fit and well now after a major stomach operation. Grace is in very good form and sends her love to you both. She is acting Matron until Tuesday when the new Matron arrives. She seems to have been enjoying herself being in Charge. The nurses held a Concert last Friday and it was very popular. It was to raise some money to help to clear the Hospital's debt of £4,000. At the Synod last week, the financial straits of the Hospital were brought out and there were spontaneous donations produced on the spot. I think about £100 was collected there and then. Grace said it was like a miracle; she was very thrilled by it all.

At the moment I am 'waiting'. Waiting for Dr Salama! He brought me to Ado last night – because he had gone to keep the night with his Coptic friends at Iyin-Ekiti. In their Church calendar today is Easter Day so they had a special Easter celebration last night at Midnight. So, I am waiting for him to come and pick me up to go back to Akure this morning. I seem to have spent a lot of time this last week waiting for the same Dr! Yesterday evening was very funny. He phoned at 5pm and we planned to go – but he wanted to go to check up at the hospital first. Next phone call was at 6pm! He'd got to do an emergency Caesar. So, we didn't get away until getting on for 8pm and Grace had just about given up when we arrived after 9… The situation at Akure Hospital is ridiculous now. Nabil is the surgeon. There is another fellow who is supposed to do the gynae as well. Several days last week he was operating from 8am till 4 or 5 in the afternoon and then again in the evenings as well as calls in the night. It is a killing business. He gets very exhausted – but seems to be able to manage remarkably well on very little sleep. He doesn't have much time to go visiting friends. Anyway, he is worth waiting for!

Term started at the Vining Centre on Friday – there are 5 new students but so far only 4 have shown up. We have 6 students who are soldiers, and they are to come and live on the Compound this term. So, we are re-roofing some rooms next to the classroom to make an extension to the dormitories. But in typical Nigerian style the roof has been removed – and they promised to have it ready by Friday… but now it's going to be Tuesday! – next week. So, I had to turn around and fix up some temporary arrangements for 10 students sleeping accommodation for the next few days. Fortunately, they are all very obliging and are prepared to 'manage' camping out in the 'parlours' in some of the other dormitories. Then another confusion! It seems that Cornelius made a muddle about telling the soldiers whether they could bring their wives or not. They seem to have the impression that they were to bring them – and their children! – but Cornelius says he didn't say so and anyway they have never 'applied to me' and, we haven't enough space for them now. All very difficult.

Ruth is busy trying to get things organised so that she can start travelling again – and talking of weekend training courses for the women etc. Did I tell you that they had an accident when coming back from Ibadan? It was Ruth's car that was smashed a bit at the front – bumper and wings and head lights – but it was Jane Pelly driving and

Sheila's retired teacher friend who was on a visit who got a cut in her forehead that needed one stitch. Anyway, it might have been a lot worse.

Our post seems to have gone defunct again this week. No letters have appeared for me from overseas, at all. I am glad that you have received the stainless-steel dishes. I thought they looked rather good in 'Women and Home', and I adore corn-on-the-cob. Ann Forgan is back, and she has brought the ones she ordered with her – so I have seen them. They look nice.

Tuesday. This letter seems to have got stuck and not posted. Sorry. I still haven't heard anything from you since your letter of April 10th. I don't know what they are doing in the Akure Post Office.

They have whooping cough at the Leper Settlement – and one 3-year-old died on Monday. I was there when the news came so it was all rather miserable. So today we distributed tinned milk and glucose to all the children, and I hope tomorrow to get them some cough mixture. There are about 25 children all of whom seem to be coughing and 8 of them are vomiting and coughing. It is a great shame – because the local Health Office who are supposed to be in charge really seem to do very little for them there.

I went yesterday evening to Dr Salama's house and ate chicken and a strange Egyptian soup made of chicken stock and green spinach like vegetables. Nice. There was a second Egyptian doctor there too who is living at the Catering Rest House where he is very bored with the repetitive food. He is an older man – a widower I think who has only come to Nigeria this year. His English is not very easy to understand.

Nabil and I are good friends – but you can cancel any ideas of any 'future' in the friendship because I discovered that he is already engaged to a girl in Cairo! So, I have had to do a bit of demolition of 'castles in the sky'! However, please still pray that we may strengthen each other as Christians and that I may be able to help him to find ways of relaxing in the odd moments when he is not standing over the operating table at the hospital. He has promised to let me watch a Caesar... that would be interesting.

Ann is back from her 2 weeks in England. Unfortunately, she has a cold so she is a bit 'low' – and she still can't throw off her depressions about teaching – particularly the senior girls who she maintains don't listen to her lessons and don't really want to work. She has accepted the job of teaching Geography at Chorleywood

College which is a Secondary School for the Blind. The classes will be small so she thinks she will manage better. Ann and Ruth both came for supper this evening. The electricity failed. There are masses of mosquitoes this evening. I suppose it is because the rain has started. There are also a whole lot of black moths on the ceiling. It's like a plague.

One of our new students, I discovered, has yet to learn the alphabet. I am teaching her to write her own name. She is going to stay with us for 5 terms. It's just as well because she is going to need it. She is Urhobo so she has no Yoruba and just a little pidgin. The other new women are English speaking Yorubas.

Thank you for the gen about Poland. The bus that gets there in 2 days sounds like the thing to me. I wish Angela would reply – maybe the Post Office has her letter too. Anyway, I doubt if I can fix it up before I come home. It's only 8 weeks you know. It doesn't seem quite possible to me. I am sure I don't deserve any leave yet. I hope that you are all well.

With much love to you both,

Elizabeth.

Vining Centre
6th May 1973

Dear Ma and Daddy,

Thank you for your letter of Easter Monday, received last week. I am glad that you were able to get away for a break after Easter, and so recover a bit from your weariness, and be able to relax in the countryside. I haven't got the letter that you sent via Ann Forgan, yet. I think that she went to stay with Sheila's parents for a few days before she flew back to Lagos.

I am very sorry, but I haven't got anything into the post in time for your birthday Ma. I should have done it last Sunday… but going to Ado put me out as far as letter writing is concerned – and during the week I rarely settle down to it. So, I hope that you are not too disappointed on May 9th. I would try to phone but I am afraid that it may not be clear again and that would be too miserable. Anyway, I shall be thinking of you very much on Wednesday.

This past week has been a busy one and ended up with a flourish on Friday night with a new baby so there was a trip to the hospital between 12 midnight and 1am. It is a nice baby boy, born to Mrs. Arotiowa.

Ruth and Jane Pelly have had a bit of trouble going to the police to report their accident to fill up the Insurance form. They hadn't reported it immediately after the event so of course when they went the Police said they would charge them with delaying to report damage to their car!! In fact, they haven't been charged and all may be well, but the Police here are really to be avoided at all costs.

Ruth had her birthday on Friday, and we had a very happy party in her house – 3 from Fiwasaiye, our own staff and the Eyesorun. We finished up by listening to the end of the Messiah –the Hallelujah Chorus part and then we had prayers together.

I have been to the Leper Settlement this week several times – particularly because they have whooping cough and when I went there on Monday a child had died of it. I was very upset and went to Fiwasaiye to tell them. Jane gave me 20 Naira and so I went and distributed milk, glucose, and cough mixture. When I went again on Saturday, they said that all those who were coughing and vomiting before had now improved. I gave them all a bottle of chloramphenicol syrup each. So that was good, but I dare say they will be coughing for a few weeks to come.

I played tennis with Terry yesterday – and had supper with them on Thursday evening. They had brought some ham – about 3-4lbs in Ibadan so they said that they wanted help in eating it up! I helped. They asked me to go swimming in Ife today. Perhaps I should have gone… but I decided that I ought to stay here, to write some letters, have lunch with Fiwasaiye folk – and just to be in the compound because I was away last Sunday.

Dr Salama came for supper here last night. Tokunbo cut his finger, so I took him to the hospital for ATS and dressing. So, he served supper to the Doctor with a large white bandage around his finger. Nabil and I listened to the Geleneau Psalms together which was super. But please continue to pray for this friendship that all may be under God's control.

With much love to you both.

Elizabeth.

Vining Centre
13th May 1973

Dear Ma and Daddy,

I received your letter written before Easter and sent to Mrs. Forgan. So, I hadn't realised before now how 'down' you were – not sleeping etc. I hope that you have found renewed strength from your holiday and that you are able to find renewed strength each day to face the problems of the Parish. The words of the hymn 'Peace Perfect Peace' have been in my mind very much since Easter – especially the verses: "Peace, perfect peace, with loved ones far away? In Jesus keeping we are safe, and they". And "Peace, perfect peace, our future all unknown? Jesus, we know, and he is on the throne".

But it is not always straightforward to find this peace. I have been struggling to find it as I try to demolish the castles in the air that I had started to build around Dr Salama. It is not easy to reverse the process of 'falling in love'! Please pray that I may have the will power to direct my thoughts to other things and try to forget what might have been! In fact, it is not so tragic. I can't imagine myself learning Arabic in a hurry and overall, I don't 'like' Egyptians or feel drawn to their ways of living – from the few I have seen here. So don't be worried too much. On the other hand, I want you to share my disappointment in prayer… because it is very real now.

We have had quite a busy week here – and it has been frustrating too. I think I told you of our problem about the soldiers who Cornelius told to bring their wives – but then he told me that they weren't bringing them – so they brought them and there were no rooms prepared. Anyway, this week we decided to make a solution to the deadlock by admitting the wives as students and turning things inside out to give them rooms on the compound. So, I interviewed them and discovered that one is Hausa and completely illiterate, one is Ibo and only 14, but already pregnant! One is Ijaw and doesn't want to come yet, one is Yoruba and Modern III and the last is Efik! Since then, the Hausa woman has withdrawn so we have 3 new students. It's a bit of a do when we are already starting the 3rd week of the term, but there it is. Last night I took our second pregnant woman to the hospital at 3 am. She has not 'delivered' yet – but is waiting in labour. We had the naming ceremony for the first delivery on Saturday.

Yesterday, we went to Ikogosi – the hot springs, and had a picnic lunch and came back about 7.30. Grace was here for her weekend off.

She stayed at Fiwasaiye with Jane so Ann and I and Grace went together. There were a lot of friends there – Inga and Susanne from Ondo with 30 St Monica's Form 5 girls – Brother Fred and another Catholic missionary – and Jim and Terry of the GEC. So, it was quite a crowd. Susanne, Terry and another VSO and I all played tennis together for a short time.

In the evening we had a play reading at Dr Kohli's house. We read a play called Crammer of Canterbury by Charles Williams. It was in verse – and very difficult to understand. I find his prose difficult – and this was almost impossible... so I didn't really enjoy it much. However, next time we plan to read something lighter.

I am writing to Chris Cook about the time for coming home. Now I think it may be best to plan to fly on Monday July 2nd, but I shall have to confirm this with them in Lagos. I hope that doesn't mean that it's too long for you to be away from Malvern. It will be better in the end.

Shelagh Jebb is here this weekend, staying with Ruth. They have the new Matron now at Ado, so they are busy settling in there.

Chris Groves' husband used to be the Principal of Government College Ibadan. He is called Derek Bullock. They have been close friends for years and everyone, including Chris I think, wonders why he never proposed before!!

8pm. O ti bimo! It's a baby girl. So, I have just phoned the husband at Immanuel College, Ibadan. That's the woman I took to the hospital last night.

Terry came round after the evening service at 5. We went and drank 'Sprite' at the club and had a talk about finding a purpose in life. He is from a Catholic family in Liverpool I gather and doesn't have any faith – certainly not in the Catholic church. I am not very good at assembling my thoughts in such a discussion. His world of radio towers is so different from ours here in the Vining Centre. Anyway, he is seeking to find what it is all about. Jim, the engineer with GEC is probably leaving Akure next week because their contract has finished so I had the 2 of them, and Ruth to supper on Friday and I killed one of my ducks. It was jolly good too. So now I must plan what to do with the other 2 ducks before I come on leave.

It sounds as though one of the soldiers has a radio which is going to blare in the house at the back of mine. I can see a lot of problems arising from their arrival. Their whole attitude is so different from our 'simple' students.

I hope that you had a good birthday Ma. I am sorry that I was late with my good wishes – I think that I have said that before.

I do hope that as the weather gets warmer that you will both get extra strength and that you will keep well.

With love,

Elizabeth

Vining Centre
20th May 1973

Dear Ma and Daddy,

Thank you for the 2 letters received this week and written about the time of Ma's birthday – both mentioning the red, white, and blue dress, which sounds very nice. By the time that you get this letter you will be preparing to go for your holiday in Wales. I hope that you have good weather and a super time there. I seem to have had a very busy week here especially since Wednesday when I went to Idanre with Terry and the Bulgarian doctor who has recently come to Akure. We climbed up to the Radio Station and sat and looked at the view for about an hour. It was superb. Then I came back and had supper with Ruth.

We had a Red Cross Committee on Wednesday afternoon and continued to discuss the plans for Recruiting Blood Donors in Akure.

On Thursday afternoon one of the Committee came here to discuss the Campaign and brought a husband with him who was looking for a pint of blood for his wife who was being operated on for a Caesarean. So, I went and gave a pint of blood and ended up with a gigantic bruise on my arm which I have been trying to disguise since then so that it doesn't put our students off from donating!

On Thursday evening we had a staff meeting which lasted till 10.25 pm. On Friday I invited Dr Kohli and her son Rajan for supper, and Ann came round for coffee. There had also been an invitation to go round to GEC House. I had to refuse that – but I discovered later that I had missed a feast of prawns! On Saturday, Susanne came over from Ondo. In fact, that was another mix-up because Terry had invited her to go to Ibadan with him – but they missed on the road somehow, and she came here instead. So, she stayed the night with me and went away this morning. I then went to Fiwasaiye and had lunch with them there. Ruth has been away this weekend taking a training course for women up in Kwara State. She is back this evening and coming for supper. Ann and I went to a service of Dedication of the new school bus at the Commercial School.

Our 3 soldiers wives have now moved onto the compound, and they seem to be settling in well. They have all started on the cutting out of their dresses. The rest of the women are busy knitting "soxes" as they call them i.e., booties.

I am very glad to hear that you are both feeling so much better. Your holiday in Wales will set you up well. Congratulations Ma on getting elected to going on the Home Committee. I assume that is the Home Committee for members under the new set up. It will be fun to get up to London to meet all your old mates again twice a year. I haven't heard from Chris Cook yet about the dates of flight home – I am still planning for July 2nd.

With much love to you both.

Elizabeth.

Vining Centre
28th May 1973

Dear Ma and Daddy,

Thank you for your letter. I hope that this one reaches you before you go to Welshpool. I will send the next one there. It looks as though I shall be coming home on July 2nd, arriving at Heathrow in the afternoon so you can plan around that, and I will let you know the time and flight number later, when I hear it from Chris Cook.

Just at this very moment I feel that I need to go back to bed! I feel half asleep… mainly after a busy week and a hectic weekend. Also, I felt the effect of my period this week more than usual – I think because of the blood donation last week. Susanne came to stay on Friday night – so we played tennis on Friday evening. Then we had a play reading at Fiwasaiye – but we also celebrated the Eyesorun's birthday and so I cooked 2 sponge flans and some flapjacks – that was before tennis! Then on Saturday morning I did an inspection of the houses here, visited the Leper Settlement with Susanne and then we all had a meal at the GEC house of prawn curry. It was to say Goodbye to Jim of the GEC. There were about a dozen of us there. Jane, Sheila,

Ann, Ruth, Brother Fred, Mick (Catholic teacher), the Bulgarian doctor. Susanne and I and Jim, Terry, and Brian – all of GEC.

In the afternoon Terry and Brian challenged Susanne and I to tennis – and we won! Then I went to the SU Monthly Prayer meeting at the Agricultural College and spoke to them. The subject was given to me – 'Facing the World'. So, I spoke about the book of Ephesians taking the ideas of sit, walk, stand – the book by Watchman Nee. It was a happy and worthwhile prayer meeting. That finished just after 9pm and I then went on to join Jim, Terry, Brian, and Susanne and some of the Post and Telephone workers at a farewell drinks party. We came home just after 11pm.

Then on Sunday, after Communion at 7am, Susanne and I were asked to play a return match – and we beat them again… thoroughly! So, the business is not finished!! Susanne will have to come from Ondo again. I had lunch yesterday with Ruth and Joan Stephenson who was staying the weekend. Then I took our Evening Service – and we had a speaker from the hospital about Blood Donation – because we hope that our men will go and donate blood into the Blood Bank on a regular basis. Then I had supper at Fiwasaiye. Ruth's back has been playing up again – so we arranged to go and see Dr Kohli this morning.

So, my week has been a bit like yours in Malvern! One thing after another! Enjoyable but tiring. Don't worry about Dr Salama. He rarely comes here – he is too busy. I see him about once a week. He was in Ibadan most of last week so hasn't been around. He told me himself that he was engaged.

I hope that you have a lovely holiday. I ought to write a Link letter to tell people that I am coming home this summer. I hope the coming week will have more breathing space in it!

With much love.

Elizabeth.

Vining Centre
3rd June 1973

Dear Ma and Daddy,

I shall be thinking of you this week as you go on your holiday. It's not long till I come home now! We have Half Term next weekend and I hope to go and see folk in Ibadan and Ife and Ondo.

It has been a good week overall – and I am not so tired as I was last weekend… but it has not been entirely uneventful. One of my women has a horrid breast abscess which has now been lanced. Revolting. So, I have been hopping up and down the road to the hospital on her behalf and getting her sorted out with Lactogen and Milton and baby bottles.

Ruth's back was troublesome earlicr in the week, so we organised the making of boards for her bed. Then she went to the hospital and had an x-ray of her spine. She came back very depressed by what the Bulgarian doctor there had said. In fact, she was already depressed so she only listened to the worst bits of what he said. So please pray for Ruth – she is very 'up and down 'and needs a lot of love and understanding, at this time in her life.

Susanne came yesterday with Inga. We went together to the opening of a new Tennis Court at the Messiah Sec. Mod. School. Then we came away and enjoyed a game of tennis together afterwards. Terry also came… I beat them both… because my service was going well. Dr Salama came here briefly later in the evening, and we went together to GEC house to see if Terry could help in the fixing up of my tape-recorder.

Ann is going by ship next Thursday. She has packed her big loads and taken them to Lagos… but she is in a bit of a state of depression and exhaustion now. I hope that she can recover when she gets home. We have planned to go to Poland for a week from August 8th-17th and then on to Czechoslovakia where she has friends from 17th-25th. That's the idea anyway. We will try to book by bus to go – but may come back another way. I have heard from the Perzinas and they are happy to have us both to stay. I have asked Angela to come to Malvern sometime between July 31st and August 8th.

Sunday night. I have just had a very happy supper party with Ann, Jane, Sheila, and Ruth. We had roast duck, apple sauce, carrots, roast potatoes with ice cream and loganberries or raspberries from tins. We had tomato juice to drink beforehand and cider with the meal. It was very good cider! It came from Herefordshire. Ruth has had a grand weekend and her back has not been troublesome at all – she was in a very buoyant mood – but Ann is 'sick' with depression. I hope that she will be OK.

Have a lovely holiday. I hope the weather is good and you can get out and enjoy some sunshine.

With love,

Elizabeth.

Vining Centre
11th June 1973

Dear Ma and Daddy,

I hope that you can rest on your holiday. I have just had Half Term weekend and so I have been able to get away and have a breather and so prepare myself for the next 3 weeks when as far as I can see a lot of things will have to be fitted in.

I went to Ibadan on Thursday. I was feeling tired because I had the first cholera jab in the morning and my arm was quite sore. I stayed with Jose this time and had meals with Richard Childerstone, Grace and John and Janet Nightingale. Then on Saturday afternoon I went on to Ife and stayed with Yomi and Kelu. Kunle was sick in bed with diarrhoea and a high temperature.

On Sunday Susanne came from Ondo on her bike and we swam – then had lunch with the Bamgboyes. Then Terry and Brian turned up from Ibadan, so we swam again and played tennis. Brian didn't play for he still has stitches in his leg. Then we went to Ondo, and all had supper together at Inga's house – with the addition of a Dr Dodds (PHD type of Dr!) who teaches English at Adeyemi College. He is rather an odd fellow, aged about 50 – but he plays the piano very well... and we listened to him and Susanne play duets and then recorder and piano pieces. It was very good.

Ann has now left Akure. The Aureol went on Friday. Jane and Sheila took Ann to Lagos. We had a farewell party at Fiwasaiye on Tuesday. I made 4 fruit flans – a la Foxbury on Saturday mornings! Much appreciated.

Ruth got Malaria on Thursday morning so was tired on her course over the weekend – but she seems to have managed it – and her back is not troubling her as before. I will try and find out the flight number for July 2nd and confirm that it will be the 10.30am plane from Lagos to Heathrow.

I meant to write a letter to my pals saying that I am coming home – but it hasn't got done – perhaps just as well because I am not going to have over much spare time for visiting folk.

With much love

Elizabeth.

Vining Centre
15th June 1973

Dear Ma and Daddy,

No letter from you this week. I expect it's the fault of the Post Office. This will probably be the last letter that you will get before I come home. It hardly seems possible that it's so soon. I have not heard from Chris Cook concerning the flight number and exact time of arrival at Heathrow, but I have written and asked him to let you know at Westwick House. I am looking forward to seeing you both on July 2nd. I hope that its warm! You might bring a pair of tights for I think that the ones I have here are laddered.

We have had one child with measles this week – admitted in the hospital. It looks as though others may get it – unfortunately, the vaccine has finished in the Health Office – as the man concerned is 'on tour'.

The Bishop came and visited us this last Wednesday, so the men students cut grass all day on Tuesday and the women made buttonholes on their dresses in a great rush. Then all the students 'marched past' the bishop! It was rather a joke as far as the women were concerned. Mama Adeyeye aged 53 and about as fat as Julie Okusanya was at the front and the back 5 women marched along with babies tied to their backs… some of the babies with very surprised faces!

The Ilera-de Land Rover had an accident this last week. All the people in it were OK but the Land Rover is spoilt. I am planning to go to Ado this afternoon and see Grace and greet Shelagh and Co.

Dr Salama was here this morning taping The Sound of Music and the Gelineau Psalms from my record player onto his tape-recorder. We went together halfway up to Idanre on Friday afternoon.

Ruth is better from her back trouble. She is away in Ondo this weekend. Jane is probably leaving Akure in August.

Looking forward to seeing you.

With love,

Elizabeth.

Visit to Poland and Czechoslovakia

Dr Perzina was the surgeon in Akure hospital and he and his wife, Barbara, invited Ann Forgan, the maths teacher at Fiwasiaye, and me to visit them in Poland after they had returned home. So, we set off on August 8th and travelled with the Anglo-Polish Friendship bus which Stuart had discovered for me. I think it only cost £16 to go from London to Poznan. We crossed the channel and spent a night in a hostel in Ostend and then by road right across Germany from West to East. There was a lengthy wait at the Iron Curtain where we looked out of the window to see soldiers with guns in towers looking down on us and where soldiers came into the bus to search passenger's luggage. Fortunately, they didn't look in our bags. Ann was anxious about that because she had brought some bibles with her.

The Perzina's welcomed us to their home, and we enjoyed interesting meals with them and visits in Poznan and learnt a good deal about the history and suffering in Poland during the Second World War. After a week we took an overnight train over the mountains to Prague in Czechoslovakia to stay with Ann's Czech penfriend. That was another amazing experience as we visited many of the well-known sites - St Vitus Cathedral, Prague Castle, Charles Bridge, the amazing astronomical clock, the Jewish Ghetto, and the Old Jewish Cemetery.

Vining Centre
30th September 1973

Dear Ma and Daddy,

I arrived back safely in Akure on Wednesday evening. The journey was a smooth one except for the security check at Geneva airport. I was searched twice and everything in my hand luggage disturbed and turned out. The reason why I had to go through it twice was that I was sent by mistake to the wrong waiting room and so then had to go on to another place and there was a thorough check when you went into each waiting lounge.

The snag of course was that I had so much stuff in my handbag so that when everything was removed it wouldn't go back in again!

At Lagos I had no trouble at all in the Customs and Ezekiel our Vining Centre driver was there to meet me. Then we went to Myrtles for the night and came up to Akure on Wednesday, via Ibadan and Ondo.

On arrival here I had supper with Ruth. She is better in some ways in that she is sleeping now with the tablets that Elisabeth Edmunds has given her. But she is still very easily upset and depressed. She is away now for the weekend in Ekiti, visiting the Parish of old students.

Dr Salama brought my record player back – I gave it to him to 'mind' because he doesn't have one – and so I was able to give him the famous tablets! They are not for his mother even! They are for some uncle in Egypt. Anyway, he was grateful for them – but I don't know if he wants to order some more and get them sent by air. If he does, I'll let you know, and send the money.

I hope that you had a good time at Stuart's and the CMS Committees Ma. I am looking forward to hearing all about them. I shall continue to pray for the situation at St Mary's/Christ Church.

With much love,

Elizabeth

Vining Centre
30th September 1973

Dear Ma and Daddy,

I am now back in my house looking out onto the veranda wall with its line of plants in pots. Tokunbo has done very well and has kept them all watered. I have 3 gorgeous African violets which are flourishing and lots of other ferns and busy lizzies. My record player is singing out Brahms. We have just had the first Communion Service of the term, and all the students are back apart from the soldiers and their wives. They tend to be a law unto themselves. I have had to fix the rooms so that they can be fitted in – with I gather, 3 new wives coming. One is the gentleman from the SE State who had the troublesome 14-year-old pregnant Ibo girl before. According to Cornelius, Mama, and the other students he is intending to bring another wife this term… a new one that is. It makes life rather confusing.

I have written a blue air mail as well as this letter, because I have no 18k stamp for this, and it is a public holiday tomorrow so the Post

Office will not be open so I thought that the blue air mail might reach you more quickly.

There is plenty to do here, with the room lists, duty lists, rotas etc. for the new term. As well as the orders for medicines etc. to be dealt with I started it all on Thursday afternoon, and Friday morning too. Jane Backhouse came on Friday afternoon and stayed the night. She brought Mr. Elabor, the student from her area of the Mid-west. Jane was wanting to talk out all her problems about working under the Bishop in Benin diocese. Much worse than the Panters! The bishop had called her in front of a committee of senior diocesan officials and told her that she was not being loyal to him and was working against him because she had taken part in the SU Christian Leadership Conference in Benin without asking his permission. SU and all its works are supposed to be heretical. So, Jane was hauled over the coals, and told to go away and write a letter to the bishop answering the question "Miss Backhouse, are you for us or against us?" So, we helped her to write a reply to the bishop.

On Saturday morning we had the first assembly, and I had more things to sort out. Then I went and had lunch with Sheila and met the new Irish VSO at Fiwasaiye, called Sandra. Sheila seems to be getting on OK at the school, and things are not getting on top of her.

Then in the afternoon I discovered that the GEC fellows were in Akure and having trouble with the handing over of their house to the landlord. It was a great long palaver about the removal of the air conditioners from the house. They belonged to GEC, so they were removing them, but the landlord was making a great noise about the condition of the house, especially that they were not going to repair the windows properly where the air conditioners were put. Anyway, it was a long rigmarole and he had taken them to the police to report that they were not leaving his house in good order. Then he had locked their rooms with the air conditioner and their clothes inside and said he would keep them until they had made completely new windows. They all got very heated and abusive about it. I went to the Eyesorun to greet her at teatime and told her of the troubles. She called the landlord and then we went to the house altogether to try to make a peaceful arrangement. We thought that we succeeded but in fact as soon as we left the landlord apparently went quite mad and very abusive to Brian and Terry… but in the end, they reached some agreement.

I came back for evening Chapel at 7 and it was only after I got back that I found a note from Mick, the fellow at the Seminary, asking me to join him, Terry and Brian and Hilary, the other VSO for supper. So, I went round there, along a very muddy rutted road and we all spent the evening together. It just wasn't Terry's Day because as he had driven into the Seminary in his Land rover he had skidded in the mud and got his wheels stuck in the ditch, in about 1ft 6" thick mud.

Cornelius is well and has received his consignment from Whippels without being asked to pay any customs. So, he is very pleased. Our new men's warden has been appointed, and he is expected next Thursday October 4th. He is Rev. Adeoba from Lokoja. Sorry, I forgot to get this letter posted on Tuesday. Now it is Thursday, so it will be some time before you get it. Ruth is better now than when I left in June.

I hope that all is well with you. I am looking forward to hearing your news.

With much love.

Elizabeth

Vining Centre
7th October 1973

Dear Ma and Daddy,

I received your letter Ma, yesterday. I hope that you were able to rest on your retreat. I am sure that you needed a rest after all your travelling to and fro. As you get on in the 'sixties 'you will both have to rest content with doing less than you were able to do before. It's a bit the same problem as we have here in Nigeria. Because of the heat you just must attempt less and rest more.

I was going round in circles last weekend trying to prepare for the beginning of term. This weekend things are more sorted out and I feel that I am getting back into the work here. There is still plenty to do, but it is easier in the framework of a routine of classes etc.

I went up to Idanre to see Pat on Monday afternoon. Her house is still in a muddle, but she seems steadier in the whole situation. Yesterday I went with Sheila Davis and the VSO at Fiwasaiye, Sandra, to Ado to visit Grace. Then we travelled on to a place about 25 miles from Ado called Ode Ekiti to visit a VSO couple who are there. It is right out in the bush. When we got there, we discovered that they had gone out to Ikole. So, we came back. It was good to see

Grace. She is looking well, although she has plenty to do. They are one sister short and so she is staying on till after Christmas.

Most of our students are back, except for 3 of the soldiers. We were expecting 5 out of 6 of them with their wives. The one who wasn't supposed to come was the illiterate Hausa woman. But on Saturday night who should turn up but that one! It remains to be seen if she stays on. If she does, I am not sure how we shall set about teaching her.

We had our Leper Settlement Committee on Thursday. We are starting to build a new kitchen area and latrines. Then there is an idea for the sponsoring of a physiotherapist for working in the new Gov't Clinic.

We have our new men's Warden this week. He has arrived from Lokoja with his wife and family. He seems a very pleasant smiley man. I hope that he will be able to work well with Cornelius. We have our Open-Air Service at the Leper Settlement this afternoon. Then I have asked Sheila, Sandra, Hilary (VSOs) and Ruth for supper. I am going to have lunch with Dr Salama and his mother and a dentist and his family who are friends of Grace's from Ado. I haven't yet got organised to play tennis yet, but the prospects are hopeful because Hilary is keen. But the rains haven't finished yet so there is often rain around 5pm when we would play tennis.

Ruth has had a very encouraging weekend this weekend. She came back very stimulated – but it is a tiring business.

With much love to you both.

Elizabeth.

Vining Centre
15th October 1973

Dear Ma and Daddy,

I received Daddy's letter from the Convent this week. I have just returned this morning from Ikogosi (the hot springs). We spent last night there staying in one of the Guest Chalets. It was a lovely change. 'We 'was Grace who came to stay the weekend with me, and Inga who was thinking of going there on her own so we arranged to go all together. Grace and I went and had a picnic lunch and then a swim and a game of Table Tennis in the afternoon. Dr Salama and his mother and another Egyptian Doctor who is at Okitipupa also came for a swim, so we all enjoyed the hot water together. Then it started to rain and thunder and lightning, so we stayed in the hot water with the cold rain coming down on our heads and afterwards went back to the chalet and had some hot coffee to combat the general dampness. Inga was in good form, as she always is when away from the school – but we had a good long discussion about St Monica's and coping with the whole situation of working here in Nigeria and how you 'sink 'if you take everything too seriously. I felt that she was much more settled in her work than I have known her for a long time, and I hope that we shall be able to repeat the visit to Ikogosi. Even, I would like to take a group of the women there and stay with them and the children overnight. We shall have to see if it can be arranged.

Ruth is back from her weekend. This weekend and last one has been very encouraging for her because the clergy have really co-operated and seen the point of having training courses such as she has been doing. So, she came back last weekend very elated about it all and then had a great down on Monday and Tuesday. I wondered if she would make it on Friday morning when she was preparing to go off on the next weekend. But she just made it and now has come back and seems to be in good spirits. I pray that we may be able to help her to cope on Mondays which she wants to take as her 'day off' but Sheila and I are both busy… it is particularly unfortunate that I am most occupied on Mondays so that I can't have time to be relaxing with her.

Tomorrow, in addition to the normal activities we have a naming ceremony at 2pm so it will be a full day. The baby was born last Monday morning – a gorgeous girl. I was especially happy about it because the father really behaved as I think a Christian father should behave at the birth of a new baby. He obviously adored the new infant and held her so gently and treated his wife with real care and feeling. They are a very united couple, and it is encouraging.

We had a play reading on Friday night at Sheila's house – the Kohlis (Dr s), Dr and Mrs. Sijuade, some Fiwasaiye staff, Sandra, the VSO and the Eyesorun were the main members, and it was a very happy evening.

Thursday evening was the usual staff meeting. It was good to have the new men's warden with us. I think that he is going to get on well with Cornelius. The staff meeting was from 8pm till 10.20! At least yours are in the mornings!! We spent quite a lot of the time at the end discussing the Centre clerk who Cornelius has sacked this week. He has been unsatisfactory in many ways for a long time – not least his habit of going round the drinking bars in town both late at night and during working hours. He has been warned countless times – and gradually Cornelius has become convinced that we should find another one. Anyway, the crisis came this week when the clerk was apparently abusive to Cornelius. It is a pity that it should blow up just now because the clerk's wife and 2-year-old son are still sitting in the hospital waiting for Akin's burns on his bottom to heal up.

Our men students are going on an Evangelistic campaign this week in St Luke's Church which is a less popular church in the town with a small apathetic congregation. They are going to go each morning at 5 for prayer meeting and sermon! And then each evening again for preaching and visiting in the Parish.

Dr Salama and the other Egyptian doctors may be called home to Egypt because of the War. He was in the military hospital in Cairo before he came here so may easily be chosen to go. I will miss him, and his mother. Both are so very hospitable. There are apparently 600 Egyptian doctors in Nigeria – 'on loan'. It won't be much fun here in the hospitals if many of them are withdrawn. It's a terrible war, and it doesn't look much as though there will be a quick solution this time.

I hope all is well with you. I shall be looking forward to your letters.

With much love.

Elizabeth.

Vining Centre
21st October 1973

Dear Ma and Daddy,

Your letter of 15th October arrived yesterday so things are looking up this week! It is good to hear of all your doings over the Harvest period. I like the idea of sharing the Harvest bread together. Our Harvest jamboree is yet to come – late Nov-Dec I think. I was the preacher at the Communion Service this morning… a bit of a hoot really because I was chosen since Cornelius' Uncle in Law has died so they have all gone off to dance through the night for that. Then the new Men's Warden has had fever this week, so he has been sickly. I was therefore deemed the fittest!! But in fact, I have had a filthy cold, collected I think at the hot springs last weekend. It resulted in a cough, catarrh, and a temperature of 100°F – so really, I wasn't very fit either!! Anyway, I haven't felt so bad, and the sermon went off OK.

It has been quite a busy week for entertaining. Sandra and Hilary, the 2 VSOs, came here for supper on Tuesday. Then we played tennis with Mike on Thursday went to Sandra's for supper with Sheila. On Saturday night we were all at Dr Salama's house for chicken and meat roasted out of doors. Sheila, Ruth, and Sandra were here today for lunch and Brian, Mike and Hilary are coming for supper tonight. Mrs. Salama came to see the Vining Centre on Tuesday and I thought that she would come again on Friday to show our women how to crochet but somehow communications broke down. She doesn't always hear what you say in English and yet gives the impression that she has heard. She does beautiful crochet.

Next weekend it looks as though Ruth, Sheila and I will go to Iyi Enu. Ruth wants to go to see Elizabeth Edmunds as this is her only free weekend. Sheila is too tired to drive all that way, so I offered to go with them. It will be good to see Ken and Pearl again, and other folks in Onitsha and Asaba. Apparently, the new road from Benin to Asaba is now made so that it is like the Ife-Ondo Road, so that's a great help.

I like our new men's warden. He is an older man who I think will get on easily with Cornelius. The students have been going off each morning this week at 5.30am and again at 5.30pm to lead an Evangelistic week in St Luke's parish. They were so exhausted by Saturday that the day was deemed rest day and all the men were told to stay on their beds!

I have been asked to go onto the Board of Governors of St John/Mary Teacher Training College at Owo. I have agreed, although really, I don't know what I shall have to say on a Training College Board!

Tokunbo has just learnt to make a very delicious Orange and Raisin loaf out of the Be-Ro Cookery book. It is nice and moist, and I think will keep well… except that it looks as though it will get eaten up rather quickly.

I must get round to writing to Ruth and Stuart – also Ethel in Sudan and Angela and others. I seem to have got a bit out of joint for letters. What with being away last weekend and again next weekend. It doesn't look as though there is any more time here than at home!!

With much love to you both. Thank you for your prayers.

Elizabeth.

Vining Centre
29th October 1973

Dear Ma and Daddy,

We have had Public Holiday for the end of Ramadan so post has been held up. We went to Iyi Enu with Ruth on Friday and both Sheila and I were able to discuss the whole situation with Elisabeth Edmunds and I think it was altogether a good thing. Ruth has certainly been much happier today and back to her normal busy self. We hope that with the help of the drugs, and by taking time to care for her when she is low, that she will come through this period of depressions.

We saw lots of friends in the East. Elisabeth is a very understanding person. There is a new Sister Tutor there instead of Bessy. She is Maire Pearson who is transferred from East Africa. She has only been there 3 weeks. I pray that she settles down happily for I thought that she wasn't finding it easy. Ken and Pearl are well, and Pearl is now able to take a positive line on the Children's House. She says that she is encouraged by many understanding letters from folk at home… because she felt that all the MU folk would think that she had let them down. She has been able to find good Christian homes for most of the children except for one who is a bit backward, and he is still a real problem. They all send their love to you.

We also saw Beatrice Waddington briefly and Mary Eldridge at Asaba. Then Chris Cook was staying with the Campbells, and we took Jane Backhouse back to Ekpoma from Onitsha. Ruth Howard and Mary Griffin were there in Ekpoma, so we saw them too. So, it was quite a gathering of the clans! Ruth and Mary have invited me to go with them to the Cameroons at Christmas time to climb Mount Cameroon!! We'll see! It's 13,000 feet high you know. Anyway, I am going to see if Inga is interested in going to the Cameroons too and we may all go together.

Although it has been Public Holiday here, we have had classes today. We have our Half Term on the weekend of November 10th. I hope to have a birthday party on November 8th and then go off to Ibadan the next day. I am thinking of having candles outside on the 'lawn' so that I can have a few more people than will fit into my little sitting room.

I hope that you are all well at home. I expect there will be a letter tomorrow, but I will send this to the post in the morning. Love to Ruth if she is at home. I must write to her separately. Going away at the weekends is not good for letter writing.

Greetings from all here.

With much love.

Elizabeth.

Vining Centre
4th November 1973

Dear Ma and Daddy,

I received Mother's welcome letter written on September 17th this week. Very nice too. I wonder where it's been. It's funny what happens to post. Some of the postcards which I sent from Czechoslovakia only reached here about 2 weeks ago so several people were thanking me for cards which I thought would have reached them ages ago. On the other hand, the books that I sent at the end of September have already come… but I don't see the famous parcel yet.

Ruth has been much better this past week, and not nearly so depressed as during the previous few weeks. It may be that Elisabeth Edmunds change of the dosage is doing the trick and really helping her. I hope so. She still gets tense before she goes off on a weekend visit but overall, she is much more cheerful and busy making clothes and so on. It is more encouraging when there are more times of 'up'. Then it is easier to ride the 'downs'.

I am going to have a birthday party this week and have invited about 30 people. I hope that it doesn't rain for there isn't room inside my house for 30 and I hope to use the garden outside. Tonight, the students are going to do a dramatized version of Jonah. It will be interesting to see how they spit him out of the whale! Last night Terry and Mike came round for supper and stayed till about 11.30pm! Terry is at last going off to the East. I expected that he would be going there before I got back in September.

On Friday evening we had a play reading at the Palace. We read 2 Yoruba plays and it was a very enjoyable evening. There were only about 8 of us there but it was good. Dr and Mrs. Kohli and Raj their son were there and the 2 sons of Dr Velev the Bulgarian. They have just arrived in Akure and are proposing to join the VIth form at the Anglican Grammar School – Oyemekan. They seemed very nice quiet youths. Then Sandra, the VSO at Fiwasaiye went with me and a French Graduate who is the Nigerian Youth Corps member at

Fiwasaiye. There was also a production of Midsummer Night's Dream on, the same night at Oyemekan Grammar School. It seems to often happen in Akure that for ages nothing is 'on' and then suddenly 2 things are on at the same time.

I got Mrs. Salama to come here on Wednesday to show the women some crochet patters. She is an excellent crocheter. She was going to come again on Friday morning but started baking bread instead and so called off at the last minute. They have gone away this weekend, so I haven't seen either Dr S or her. They have gone down to Okitipupa to visit another Doctor there and taken Hilary the 2nd VSO in Akure with them. She has gone to visit Brian who is in Okitipupa. I know it is stupid, but I still feel 'hurt 'and upset when Dr Salama goes off enjoying himself, and I am not included. Still, I expect I shall get over it in time. But it is amazing how easily you can hurt a close friend just by a little thoughtlessness.

If you go to New Zealand in 1976 you had better see if you can be routed via Lagos! Rather unlikely I should think – but a good idea. I am glad to hear that Ruth has fixed a date for her exit from Lee Abbey. Does that mean that they have found a new cook? I must get round to writing to her and to Stuart. Has Ruth fixed a wedding date yet? Is Stuart still planning to go to California for Christmas?

I have seen the film about the Bp of Birmingham before. I remember it well.

The new Warden is turning out to be a bit of a mixed blessing. He gets on OK with Cornelius – but he gets on so well that Mama Ademoye doesn't like him a bit! She says he's just a 'Yes man' and toadies up to the principal all the time. She lives next door to the Men's Warden so it is important that the two should get on… but he doesn't greet her as the old Men's Warden did! Then today one woman came to me to tell me that she didn't like what was going on in the Women's Dormitory – one of the soldiers's wives (whose husband has gone on a course in Kaduna) was apparently seen meeting the Men's Warden in the dark at night!! What truth there is in this gossip I don't know but I don't like the sound of it, and I don't see that I can warn the Men's Warden not to visit the Women's Dormitory!!

Another piece of gossip upset me this week which was to hear that Dr Sijuade the senior doctor is going to take a 2nd wife – and that its Tokunbo's sister! If it's true it is a crazy mixed-up business and I feel very sorry for Mrs. Sijuade. Tokunbo told me that his sister is going to be married in church in Owo to Dr Sijuade's brother from Lagos. But now I hear that that is all a cooked-up tale, and he has no such brother. He himself is going to marry the girl. She was married before, but that marriage broke up – and he has his wife living with him… so how they set about getting married in church! I can't think. Maybe it's all a story. I hope so, but I fear not. Things that go on in Nigeria are quite incredible.

I think that I told you that we have Half Term next weekend – so I will be going to Ibadan. I expect to stay with Grace, and then I will visit Yomi and Kelu on the return journey on Sunday. Jumoke Lajubutu may come here to stay sometime this week. She is now married, and her husband has gone to London to study so she is hoping to go to the golden city too and to further her education too. Anyway, it will be good to see her again.

Thank you for your continuing love and prayers.

With much love.

Elizabeth.

PS I seem to have got the old intermittent rash back – like the one I had in 1970. It may be a reaction to something – but I suppose it could be Filaria. But I will have tests before I start on Banocide again. It's just very itchy about twice a day now.

Vining Centre
11th November 1973

Dear Ma and Daddy,

Thank you for your cards and good wishes for my birthday. As you see the pen is still in good shape and I am using it often – so I am thinking of you at home at the same time. I had a lovely birthday party on Thursday. I held it on my lawn in front of the house, and we put candles on bamboo posts to light up the place – together with an electric bulb set up in the tree. I had about 30 people, so it was quite a big do! We killed 3 cocks and had a duck and had snails as well. Janet and Inga came over from Ondo and stayed overnight so that was very nice. Then Jumoke came and stayed a couple of days, so she was at the party too.

Then the following morning I came to Ibadan with Sandra and Jumoke, and I have spent this Half Term weekend with Grace. I dropped in on Yomi and Kelu in Ife. They were a bit disgruntled and down the drain… Jide was sick with fever, Yomi had been operating round the clock. Kelu was complaining that I had neither written to them when I was on leave nor brought the 6 pairs of pants which she said she had asked for! So, it wasn't much of a welcome really. I had planned to go and stay with them tonight, but they are off to Lagos. I will have to go and see them in Ife one weekend.

So, we came to Ibadan – and Grace had 2 tickets for an invitation football match at Liberty Stadium between University of Ibadan and University of Ghana. It was by floodlight – and very enjoyable. It is the 25th Anniversary Celebrations of the University. So, there are a lot of activities going on there this week – plays and music and exhibitions and so on. Most of them are happening next week so there isn't much chance to go – but we went to the Exhibition in the morning… and got hot walking around.

In the afternoon Sandra and I took Tokunbo and Akin to Premier Hotel to swim… and there we met another VSO – a friend of Sandra's who offered her a lift back to Akure today… so that was good – and then who else should be staying in the hotel in a 5th floor suite… but Mr. and Mrs. Ukpoma!! So, I went up and had a drink with them and heard all about their holiday in Rome – etc. Then he had gone to Norway and Sweden and then USA for 12 days!!

Today, Sunday, Grace and I went to the Communion service at Immanuel College. Afterwards we had a drink with John and Janet Nightingale and then I went to look up the Owadayo's (our Men's Warden before). He was away taking a service at the other end of Ibadan, so I had to return in the afternoon to see him, and I saw the Picards at the same time and then we went later to see Jose Aigbokhai.

Monday. Jumoke came early in Ibadan, and we set off to Oshogbo to get the car serviced. It seemed that when we got there, they might not agree to do it within the day – but they have agreed to have it ready by the afternoon. So Jumoke and I are now sitting in the Catering Rest House for the rest of the day – reading books and writing letters. Jumoke is now married and is going to follow her husband to London where he is on a Commonwealth Scholarship at Imperial College. She hopes to go in December. Maybe they will come to Malvern sometime.

It has been good to get away from Akure for a weekend. Ruth has had a bad week.

With much love.

Elizabeth

Vining Centre
21st November 1973

Dear Ma and Daddy,

I am afraid that there will have been a long gap before you get this letter, because the last one I wrote in Ibadan and this past weekend I didn't get a letter written at all. I have just received your letters of 10th, 13th, and 16th all in the same post. Thank you. I was especially interested to hear news of Jane Pelly, and I am looking forward to hearing more about Marion Turner's engagement.

We seem to have been busy over the past weekend. At the end of last week there were sports – the finals of the Grier Cup in this area. I was at that 2 afternoons. Ruth was away Sat/Sun and I had meals with Sandra and Hilary and met another VSO girl – Janet who is at Ikare. Ruth and I went to Dr and Mrs. Kohlis for supper on Tuesday and I had Ruth, Sheila, Sandra, and Hilary here yesterday because it was Sheila's birthday. We listened to most of the Magic Flute. We had fried prawns first then chicken and orange sauce with roast potatoes, peas and corn and apple pie and ice cream to follow.

On Saturday I took an old man from the Leper Settlement to the hospital to see Dr Kohli the eye specialist. He needs specs, and so she has tested him for them. She has also given us some old frames, so we only need to buy the new lens. The Kohlis are good to the Leper Settlement. They have given £10 towards a feast there – and so Vining Women are going to prepare it for them.

On Tuesday this week a second of our soldiers celebrated his 'marriage'. Or rather he was married in Church. The service was at 10am and the reception followed here from about 10.30-3pm. Although it seems odd at first, I think that it is a good idea that these folk should be legally married before they go out as Christian workers – and if they have seriously gone through the Church marriage as well as the Registry procedures then I think it may mean more to them and make them take monogamy seriously.

Sheila is having a party on Saturday, so I have been trying to make a long skirt. It seems successful so far – I hope it will be ready in time.

Next week is the National Census week here in Nigeria. Everyone is to be counted... it's quite a task here.

Last weekend the women had an almighty palaver about the 'ogi' –the corn porridge that they make for breakfast. And last Saturday evening our ex-clerk came to abuse the Men's Warden and then they fought, and the Men's Warden beat the clerk thoroughly!

There is terrible drought in Northern Nigeria and there is a national campaign to collect money to send there for food supplies etc. They are starting to collect here in Akure.

I am preaching the sermon and taking the evening service at Fiwasaiye on Sunday. I may talk to them about a glass of water!

How are you getting on with the threatened petrol rationing? And strikes this winter?

Our term here finishes on December 13th, so we have exams and all the end of term activities like Carols and the Commissioning service to fit in before that. Then I don't know how the plan to go to the Cameroons will work out. We shall just have to see. Our term at the Vining Centre doesn't start again until February 1st (Fixed by E. Deeks!) so we do much better than the schools who only get 3 weeks holiday.

With much love and prayers

Elizabeth.

Vining Centre
28th November 1973

Dear Ma and Daddy,

I only posted my last week's letter on Wednesday or Thursday so there is not a lot to report on since then. I was interested to read your comments on Jane Pelly at the CMS Birmingham Conference. Ruth has been much better this week – much more cheerful and generally able to cope with things. Sheila had her birthday party on Saturday night, so we were all at that. On Saturday morning the Leper Settlement celebrated their Harvest, so our students went to help them by drumming and singing. Ruth and I went for about an hour and then came away. It started at 10.30am and finished around 4.30 in the afternoon… that is the Harvest followed by a 'Bazaar 'which I think is run a bit like an auction.

Today, Sunday is Dr (Mrs.) Kohli's birthday, so Ruth and I went to greet her in the morning. Her husband was away in Ilorin. At lunch time she and I went to the Salama's for lunch together with 5 other Egyptian doctors. They all talked Arabic, so it was good that Dr Kohli and I were together. So, I brought her back to her house and it was only then that she discovered that she had brought out the wrong key and she couldn't get into the house. So, she came back with me and waited till her husband returned from Ilorin.

I took the service at Fiwasaiye this evening – and I talked about 'a glass of water'. I felt that the schoolgirls were with me. There is very serious drought in the Northern region of Nigeria and every day now the Daily Times has headlines giving a different aspect of the drought – and then lists of those who have donated money to help the situation. We have very heavy harmattan here already – the air is dry and dusty, and the nights are cold – so it must be much more severe in the North.

We have all the end of term and the end of year events before us – exams, reports, accounts, writing of Certificates etc. So, the next few weeks are going to be busy.

I have received a parcel of paper backs from you today and the 1928 prayer books – and a Calendar of Warwickshire and Worcestershire life… so I am doing very well. My own parcel of clothes etc. has never turned up. Maddening. Maybe they have taken it as 'secondhand clothes 'so have stopped it in Lagos. Secondhand clothes are a prohibited import!

Ruth is not so well last night and today – just generally in the doldrums because everyone else is so busy and she has nothing that <u>must</u> be done – so feels 'unneeded'. However, she is not so weepy as she was a few weeks back. She is going to Bida for Christmas with Gwen and Myrtle. Jolly nice. Goodness knows where I shall be for Christmas.

We have the Census this week – so everyone is being counted. You have indelible ink stamped on your thumb when you have been 'done 'so that no-one can be counted twice… I rather think the error may be the other way and some people will get left out. The counting is to go on for a week.

Thank you for the Bible Study pamphlets enclosed with the 1928 Prayer Books.

With lots of love to you both.

Elizabeth.

Vining Centre
2nd December 1973

Dear Ma and Daddy

Thank you for your letter received this week and also for the parcel of books and the Calendar of Worcestershire and Warwickshire. All very welcome. I am sorry to hear that Ruth and Stuart have both been ill. I must write to them. I am afraid that general letter writing has gone by the board recently. I haven't done anything about writing people for Christmas either. Maybe I will write a circular letter in the New Year.

We had a 'harvest' service this morning at the Vining Centre. I sat through the 3-hour service and then came to Fiwasaiye to have lunch with Sheila and Sandra. There was going to be 'lunch' followed by 'Bazaar' at the Vining Centre this afternoon – so I have happily missed that. Yesterday (Sat) I went to see Inga in Ondo. She was in good form, and I stayed the night with her returning this morning before the Harvest at 10 am. I went to discuss what we are going to do in the Christmas holidays with Inga because it looks as though it will not be sensible to go to the Cameroons after all. Inga has had a lot of big bills on her car, and she says that she can't afford it - and I don't really have the money either. So, we are hoping to go to Lagos for a few days – to stay in the Guest House and have a swim and to see some of our old students like Jesse and Shola and their families. Then Inga may invite Jose to come to Ondo and I will join them there. Failing that Inga will come to Akure, and we may go to Grace at Ado. Anyway, we shall see.

The other reason is that I don't really want to travel very far away and do a lot of long-distance driving – because this week I had a blood test in Akure and filaria has been <u>seen</u> in my blood! A great triumph. At long last it is definite. So, I must take another course of Banocide. I will start this week when we have finished our exams. I don't feel bad but have intermittent swellings on my arm, hand, or foot and then the old allergic type of rash which comes sometimes in the mornings. It is very itchy when it does come, and it came last Wednesday morning when I was eating my breakfast, so I went up to see Dr Kohli and he told me to come to the lab later in the morning. So, I did, and had the blood test. He looked at it under the microscope and said it was negative, but then on Thursday I got a message to say that the second smear test which he hadn't looked at on Wed was positive. There were 2 dead filaria or microfilaria in his picture! So, he was pleased to have found something for often you don't catch them, and I was pleased to have it proved that these symptoms are due to filaria and not just some allergy. Apparently when the creatures die and disintegrate in your blood, they produce some toxins which give you this allergic rash.

Tuesday am.

We are now in the middle of our exams. It is quite a tiring business to get the papers written and typed and then marked. And it is not so restful as in Secondary School because you can't sit down and mark one set while the next exam is going on because you must have the women doing the exam orally one by one and then there are the small ' pikin' to cope with too.

Wed. am

This letter is taking time to get off the ground. I'm waiting for patients in the Dispensary. The women in the Dining Room next door are having a shouting match so I suppose that is why they are not coming to the Dispensary in time. We finish the exams today – then the marking and reports and writing of Certificates have yet to be done before Sunday 9th when we have our Commissioning Service.

Ruth has stomachache. Last night she didn't sleep hardly at all despite Mogadon – but mainly because of the pain in her stomach. I don't really know what it is, but she has gone to Ado today to stay with Grace for a few days so the is good because she can rest as well as have medical attention close at hand.

We shall be having our Carol service and Christmas play next week on Monday, I think. Before that we are going to cook a feast for the folk at the Leper Settlement. Dr Kohli has given N20 for this. The women will be busy over the end of term.

I will be writing again before Christmas to let you know where I shall be then. I am going for 10 days travelling with Ruth in mid-Jan to Bassa which is the missionary area on the other side of the Niger river from Lokoja.

I hope that you are all well. I am hoping to play tennis today with Sandra, Hilary, and Mike.

With love,

Elizabeth

Vining Centre
11th December 1973

Dear Ma and Daddy,

Thank you for letters received this week telling of plans for Christmas holidays by Stuart and plans for Ruth's wedding. It is a pity that the air fare is so much because it would be lovely to be home for both Christmas and the wedding. You will be busy making all the arrangements. It is probably just as well that it's not at Christ Church because it's such a big place it is difficult to make it homely. A smaller village church will be much nicer. I hope that all the arrangements go smoothly so that you are not having to rush up and down the roads to Pilsdon too much. Is Ruth going to be at home for Christmas? And then going to Pilsdon after the wedding, or what? January is not the most comfortable month to be married in. What are you going to wear? I must write to Ruth.

I am sorry that Stuart was not well again and hope that he feels better before going to California. I have tried to make a tape recording of our doings over the past weekend – the last weekend of the term at the Vining Centre – I hope that it will reach you safely – either before or just after Christmas – so I won't also write down a report of the weekend. Perhaps you could get someone with a cassette tape recorder to record parts of Ruth's wedding and reception speeches – and send them back to me in due course.

I am now at St Monica's – I came over here yesterday to see their Christmas play. They did some scenes from 'A man called Jesus' by JB Philips. It was not the Christmas story – but scenes from the New Testament – Calling of the disciples. The man who came through the roof – the healing at the Pool of Bethesda etc. It was beautifully done with extremely good crowd scenes – but unfortunately, some boys came from St Joseph's and displaced girls from their former seats so that they had to stand at the back – and then there was a lot of noise, and it was difficult to hear well.

Inga and I are planning to go down to Lagos next week. We have rooms in the Guest House booked and we hope to be able to see Shola and Jesse and other old girls in Lagos. Jumoke is travelling to England on the 22nd December. I will give her your address so that she can contact you. Her husband sounds very sensible from the letter he wrote to me – but looks a bit of a lad from the photograph she gave me of their wedding.

I am going back to Akure later this morning – and then hope to play tennis with Hilary, Sandra, and Mike in the afternoon. Tomorrow we are all going to have supper at Hilary's house. I hope to go and see some folks here in Ondo this morning. I haven't seen them since I came back this time for I haven't had the chance to be in Ondo since the term started. I hope to see the provost, and Chief Akinkugbe and Janet the nurse who took us to the club.

I have started taking the course of Banocide and so far, have no ill-effects except that I feel sleepy in the morning from the Antihistamine tablets that you must take alongside the Banocide. Anyway, I hope to be through by Christmas. Elisabeth Edmunds may come on Sunday this week to stay the night en route for Ibadan where she has a conference. She will probably take Ruth with her and then Ruth will go on to Bida with Myrtle and Pat to stay with Gwen.

Ruth went to Ado last week with Grace and wasn't very well. She has become anaemic 65% and I think this was a cause of her feeling low so now she is on Iron tablets etc and is feeling much better. I hope that she can really pull up over Christmas so that the next 6 months are not a drag.

I have at least got round to some dressmaking. I cut out one dress this week and am now in the process of sewing it up. I certainly need some new dresses. My old ones are becoming very tatty.

On arrival back to Akure I hear that it has been announced that there will be no water supply to the town for two weeks because of road works. That's a right nuisance. I think that I am going to start using the students pit latrine down the compound. Anyway, I am going to be in Lagos next week for those few days – and I expect Grace will be OK in Ado for they have a good reservoir there. I will write again from Lagos. Maybe you will get it quickly.

Thank you for all the books that you sent for Christmas – and I owe you about £2 for those Prayer Books. Was there anything else?

I hope to write a 'New Year 'letter! I don't know if it will be ready for Christmas.

With much love to you both.

Elizabeth.

Vining Centre
14th December 1973

Dear Ma and Daddy,

There doesn't seem to be much to say this week – because my last letter didn't get off till Wednesday. On Thursday I didn't feel well and so didn't do much. I thought at first that the reason was because I had increased the dose of Banocide that day – but I realised about midday that I must have had a touch of Malaria as well. So, when I took Nivaquin everything improved. I made a new dress and top to go with my long skirt and I made some Christmas cards, because the cards in the shops in Akure are ghastly as well as being very expensive.

Sheila and Sandra and Ruth went off to Ibadan and then the North yesterday. Grace came here in the afternoon and gave me some shopping to do in Lagos so I think that it is certain that I shall go there for Christmas Day. I am going off tomorrow, Monday, to spend the night with Inga before we go to Lagos on Tuesday so I will post this letter and your card then. Hilary is going to be in Lagos too – she is going to say goodbye to Terry and Brian – the GEC fellows who used to be in Akure. They are going home on the 22nd. I hope that you get the tape that I sent. I registered it and sent it by airmail so it should be OK.

Wednesday: I am now in the Guest House in Lagos after a good drive down yesterday. The noise is fantastic – from the traffic hooting on the Marina to thousands of bats which have taken up residence in the trees nearby and chatter day and night.

We are going to do some shopping this morning – I hope to buy some Christmas cards for local people… and try to get some Polaroid sunspecs. I lost mine when I went to Ibadan at half term.

The Cathedral Choir here were singing Carols last night – I suppose it was a Choir Practice. They were singing soon after 7 and still at it at 11pm.

It is hot in Lagos – as usual, so I expect we shall escape to the beach in the afternoon. We hope to see Shola and Jesse and Jumoke… but hope that they will come here so that we don't need to go looking for them!

Have a very happy Christmas.

With love

Elizabeth.

Vining Centre
14th December 1973

Dear Ma and Daddy,

I don't know which of my various postings will get to you first. The newspapers don't give a very hopeful picture of rapid transport facilities at home now. I hope that you don't have to spend Christmas wrapped up in bed with hot water bottles – or have the services all by candlelight.

I am sending this card with the 2 GEC fellows who were in Akure before. They are going home on the 22nd. Inga and I hope to see them in Lagos sometime this week.

It looks as though we are going to have a petrol shortage here which is a bit silly when Nigeria is exporting oil to Western Europe. Nevertheless, several petrol stations are out of stock. I hope that it doesn't become as serious as last year.

As I said in my other letter I will probably go to Ado for Christmas Eve and Christmas Day and be with Ruth Howard and Mary and Grace there.

Anyway, I hope that you have a happy Christmas with the folk at St Mary's.

With love and prayers.

Elizabeth

Vining Centre
30th December 1973

Dear Ma and Daddy,

Thank you very much for your letters of good wishes for Christmas. I was thinking of you all at home as we had the morning Communion Service in the hospital at Ile Abiye. I am looking forward to hearing in due course all about your Christmas, but I expect I shall have to wait for some time because letter sorting grinds to a halt here at the least excuse and of course 2 days were holiday last week and then we have New Year's Day as a public holiday. That's on Tuesday – but there is a Moslem festival too and so 2 more public holidays on Thursday and Friday! So, we shall have a 2-day working week for the first week of 1974… without any strikes.

My writing is a bit odd because I am writing this letter while sitting in bed. There is a nasty 'flu virus jumping around Nigeria now, and I got it – or it got me… but fortunately, not until after I had already had a most enjoyable Christmas at Ado. So, I have been 3 days in bed and today the 4th day I am trying out my legs but still find it more relaxing to be in bed.

I think that my last letter was sent from Lagos when I was down there with Inga. We came back to Ondo on the Friday, and I stayed that night with Inga before returning here on the Saturday morning. Then I made 3 cakes in the afternoon. One round Christmas cake and 2 oblong fruit cakes. The latter were to give to Mama Ademoye and the Olowomeye's for Christmas. The Christmas cake was to take to Ado… somehow it sunk in the middle, which was a pity, but people seemed to enjoy it alright.

I went to Ado on Sunday afternoon. In the morning I took Tokunbo and a friend and his sister to Idanre to visit the Akinbadewas. The next 3 days were full of very pleasant activities – Carol Service in the hospital, Carol Service in the Cathedral, Communion, Carols in the wards and Nativity play by the PTS at the outpatient's block – as well as turkey and plum pudding on Christmas evening and on Boxing Day night. The swimming pool at the textile factory in Ado had been repainted and filled with water so we all enjoyed swimming there twice. Both Ruth and I had brought puzzles, so we did 2 of those which was nice.

We were a very happy group – 9 in all and in the evenings, we sang carols or Youth Praise songs accompanied by Mary on her guitar. The 9 people were Ruth and Mary from Ughelli, Grace and Shelagh from Ado and 2 couples working in Ode-Ekiti about 30 miles from Ado. They were the Eptons and the Hicks. The Eptons are a delightful young VSO couple – both keen Christians. The Hicks had only been in the country for 1 week and so were rather strained and not very relaxed yet. They were older, 35+ I should think and had only been married since May and went about holding hands all the time, so it was difficult to get to know them as individuals.

On Boxing Day, I went for lunch to the Egyptian doctor's at Ikerre. They are called Zakari and are a delightful couple with children aged 5 and 3. They are also Coptic Christians, and they are good friends of the Salama's. Dr Salama, his mother, and another Dr Hanna came later in the afternoon, so I saw them for a little while before returning to Ado to have tea with Grace and the others in the house of Dr Ketab and his wife. He is also an Egyptian, a dentist at Ado. They are Catholics.

On Christmas Day we heard the news that the Deji of Akure died on Sunday evening. He was only 48 and had a sudden heart attack and died straight away. It was a terrible shock to everyone and made the Christmas celebrations in Akure reduced to nil. The Eyesorun has been in a state of shock since then and is under sedation. I went to see her on Thursday morning but was told that she was sleeping. I was just starting my own fever/flu then, so I just left a note and came back to bed. It means that there is no market in Akure for a week, all the shops are shut, the town is completely quiet at night, and no-one is supposed to go out on foot after 7pm. The Deji is buried secretly by the Chiefs… it was probably on Christmas Day.

Monday 31st. Tomorrow is New Year's Day. A happy New Year to you all. It's not long till Ruth's wedding day. I hope that all goes well for that. I am much better – no temperature and feeling normal with just a bit of a cough left. I finish my course of Banocide tomorrow so that's another good thing. Tokunbo has had the same 'flu and he was off sick all last week as well, but he is on his legs today and starting to work a little again.

Anyway, I hope that you are fit and still managing the electricity and petrol restrictions without too much trouble.

With much love from,

Elizabeth.

Vining Centre
7th January 1974

Dear Ma and Daddy,

I was very glad to hear that my tape recording reached you on the Sunday before Christmas - and that you were able to enjoy it with Sheila Tam's tape recorder. I am looking forward to hearing your reply after Ruth and Trevor's wedding. I shall be thinking of you all, especially on that day.

I am now in Ibadan staying in Grace's house. There is a Yoruba comedy on the Tele, so I am better writing a letter. I came here yesterday via Janet's house in Ondo where I had lunch. I called on Yomi and Kelu, but they were not at home.

We had a quiet and uneventful week last week. Sheila had malaria so Ruth went round to Fiwasaiye to look after her for a few days. I recovered from my flu and gradually felt like doing things again. I finished my course in Banocide. Then on Tuesday, as I wrote my circular letter, we had a bit of an upset because Yinka, Tokunbo's 3-year-old daughter, died very quickly of viral pneumonia. I had to keep the body in my spare room until the students had formed some old boxes into a rough coffin and then the body was buried in the bush.

Oh! I know what I did was very interesting. On Thursday evening I went and watched Dr. Salama do a Caesar. I have talked about doing this for some time, but the opportunity didn't arise. However, I went. Really, I am surprised that I am alive at all! It was a bit like a lucky dip - put in your hand and pull out the baby! - this one was a girl, and she was alive but looked a bit doubtful at first - and had to have oxygen blown in her nose. Altogether rather a messy business! I would like to watch an operation in England. I would imagine that the whole thing would be more obviously sterile and a good deal less informal.

I had lunch today with Brenda and Joe Batt - and I will go there again tomorrow after I do the rest of my shopping. Then I went to see Rev. and Mrs. Owadayo. He was our former Men's Warden and is now doing postgraduate Theology at University of Ibadan.

Titi came to see me last week .... in a bit of a state. She says she can't teach anymore and is going to stay with her cousins in Lagos. She is not really fit to be teaching children now anyway .... but she won't go to any doctor or psychiatrist happily, so she is very difficult to help.

I am going to Bassa on the other side of the Niger on Friday. I am to be Ruth's driver and projectionist for the next ten days after that. It will be quite an adventure. Guess what!! My parcel has arrived in Akure. I will go and claim it when I get back. I must pay £3.50 or so for it - but too bad. I am glad to have it. We had rain last night in Ibadan so today everyone is complaining of cold!

With much love

Elizabeth

Lokoja
13th January 1974

Dear Ma and Daddy,

I am very sorry to hear via Ruth that Ma was not well just after Christmas - and that it was like a mild hepatitis. I hope that you will be able to relax over the arrangements for Ruth's wedding. It sounds as though she will have the cooking etc. in hand. I shall be very interested to hear exactly which relations etc. show up. I wonder if Angela will be there?

I am now in Lokoja with Ruth. We had meetings with the women on Friday and through Saturday - but today is for resting before we cross over the Niger tomorrow by ferry to do two more courses for women at Bassa Komo and then at Akabe. There is very heavy Harmattan now. Aeroplanes are not even landing at Kano. This makes it very cold at night, so it was particularly good that my parcel arrived last week and now I have my sweater and windjammer. That red dress that I bought in Ledbury market fits round the hips! But don't think I am wasting away - far from it .... I have just reduced to 11½ stone!!

I got most of the shopping done in Ibadan on Monday, Tuesday and Wednesday and then returned to Akure for Wednesday and Thursday nights. Elisabeth Edmunds and Marie Pearson from Iyi Enu came on Thursday and stayed the night. It was especially good because Ruth had a very bad stomach pain on Thursday evening and Elisabeth was able to cope with it. Ruth seems to get constipated with her medicines, and then takes a laxative to get right again and Elisabeth thought that maybe the laxative had something in it that reacted with her other medicines to give her terrible wind and pain. Anyway, she is better.

I am the driver and projectionist - but then I just sit and listen for most of the rest of the time. I have been enjoying reading Brian Hessian's book "Determined to live". It is very inspiring reading. The part about prayer is especially striking. I shall be with you all in prayer next Saturday when you rejoice together at the marriage of Trevor and Ruth. I am sure it will be a great day. I thank God that they have been drawn together to share together in love, and to support and help each other through life. We need others and only become 'whole' persons as we give and take in deep personal relationships. I thank God that He has given me many different friends through which I can learn this. Maybe this is His way for me. Only He knows what is best. I had a helpful discussion on this with my friend Dr. Salama. He was saying how he waited so long before he found the right wife - and encouraging me to trust God to find a husband for me .... or to think that it is better to be unmarried than to be married to the wrong fellow.

My love to Ruth and Trevor - and to you both. We must trust God that he will guide them into the future together.

With much love

Elizabeth

Vining Centre
23rd January 1974

Dear Ma and Daddy,

I am writing this quickly today so that you will know that I am O.K. We got back from Lokoja and Bassa yesterday after 'a week' of interesting new places as well as coping with Ruth in a state of ill-health, which really was rather like the book of Job .... one thing follows another. I will write more fully on airmail paper. Anyway, we survived! and we met some delightful people. I like the Nupe people. They are much less sophisticated and noisy than the Yorubas!

When we got back yesterday, I found two letters both written in the early part of January and describing your plans for Ruth's wedding. I shall look forward to the next letter telling me how it all went. I was thinking of you very much on Saturday. In the evening we had a 'Social' - the women on the course had prepared plays from the Bible and songs. I was the "Chairlady" so in my "Opening Remarks" I told them that I was happy to be the Chairlady for a special reason - that it was my sister's wedding day! So, they all said that the evening's entertainment should be in honour of Ruth and Trevor! So that was good .... and it was a very joyful occasion. The earlier part of Saturday was not such fun because Ruth developed a chest infection and a fearful sore throat, so we had to arrange that she went to the doctor 25 miles away while the pastor's wife and I took the meetings for her. So, I was kept busy telling the women how to clean their churches and polish their brass and silver if any - and not to use Vim on silver chalices!!

We got back tired yesterday evening .... only to be met with the information that Elisabeth Edmunds has arranged for Ruth to go to

Benin for some tests and X-rays - today or tomorrow! Neither of us could face it today .... but we hope to go there tomorrow. It's just as well that our term doesn't start here till February 1st!

Glad to hear that you are better Ma, and that you are getting a week off.

With much love,

Elizabeth

Visit to Bassa with Ruth Martin

Vining Centre
24th January 1974

Dear Ma and Daddy,

I think that you will have received a blue air-letter from me written yesterday. Ruth and I returned from Bassa on Tuesday night to meet a letter from Elisabeth Edmunds asking Ruth to go to see a Doctor in Benin on Wednesday or Thursday. We couldn't face travelling again on Wednesday, so we came today, Thursday. But I really want to tell you about our journey into Bassa land.

On Monday morning we crossed over the Niger from Lokoja to Shintaku. It is a big ferry that can hold about ten lorries - but it was almost empty, so we had plenty of room and were able to park in the shade in the middle of the boat. Eunice Adeosun came with us so the V.W. was well full to bursting point with three of us, our loads and bedding, boxes of books, the kerosene lamp and projector and screen for the film strip meetings - not to mention a gigantic sack of clothing which the Eyesorun had sent with us for the people in Bassa.

From Shintaku we went first to Oguma which I don't think you will find on your map. The main road goes to Dekina. It's a good road but about five miles before Dekina we turned left and drove for 8 miles or so along a very sandy and pot-holed road to Oguma. There we were met by the Ondo Diocesan Missioner, Rev. Oni and Mr. and Mrs. Aibe. (Mrs. Aibe is the woman in the pink dress on my slide). Rev. Oni is a Yoruba sent by Ondo Diocese. Two and a half years ago his wife was drowned in the river Benue after a canoe capsized. He was left with seven children ranging from a teenage son to an eighteen-month-old baby, Alaba. So, he has a problem on hand, especially as they are the only Yoruba family in the village. He is now looking for a new wife - and Mrs. Adeosun has been asked to help to look for somebody sensible. It will have to be a remarkable woman to take on seven children - and go and live in Oguma!! But he is greatly respected there .... particularly for not running away when his wife drowned, and Ruth remarked that there is a tremendous change in the church members in the past two years since she was there before.

Most of the women, wives of evangelists and others at Oguma are illiterate so the church agents and evangelists were asked to come too. Some of them came from 15 miles on their bicycles, and they were the people who benefited most from this course. Because there were three different language groups, everything took a good long time. We started in English or Yoruba and then everything was translated into Bassa-Nge, Bassa-Komo and Isoko. So, a 15-minute talk took an hour to say! It didn't help that the first day was market day, so all the women were occupied and although the meeting was supposed to start in the morning at 8.30 nothing much happened till about 10am.

The bed was a bit lumpy, and Ruth's back was troublesome for a day, and she got a touch of fever, but she coped very well and with much more patience than I would have had.

Then on Thursday morning we went to Akabe about 30miles away - nearer to Shintaku but off the main road. We stayed with Canon and Mrs. Kato. They were delightful. He was the clergyman who went to Mary Skidmore's parish for his 1 year of experience. Akabe is his hometown (village). I think there were 3 houses with tin roofs - the rest grass .... apart from church, school, clergy houses etc. Most people were cooking in clay pots .... and I don't suppose there would be more than a dozen or so beds in the place. What he made of Acomb I can't think!

Ruth was not well most of the time at Akabe. First diarrhoea (we all had a bit because I think the children were refilling the water bottles with unboiled water). Second, she fell and twisted her ankle, so she stayed in bed, and I took over the film strip meeting. Third - sore throat, cough, temperature i.e., the flu that has been going around here. So, we arranged for her to go to Dekina to see a doctor and Mrs. Kato and I took the meetings. It was wonderful that on a Saturday afternoon they should find a doctor - but they did, and she was given Penicillin capsules (Penbritten). But she was in bed half Saturday and Sunday. We hoped to travel home on Monday, but the ferry was under repair, so we had to wait till Tuesday. This wasn't so bad because Ruth was able to stay in bed on Monday too. I had great fun cooking scrambled egg and white sauce and soup over 3 stones outside. I even did Scotch pancakes!

So, you can imagine that it wasn't a very welcome surprise when we got back on Tuesday night to Akure – tired, to say the least .... to receive letters from Elizabeth Edmunds to say that she had arranged for Ruth to have tests on Wednesday or Thursday!

Anyway, we went on Thursday and saw Dr. Strauss from Arbroath. He is an old gentleman with a white beard - a real Scots character - he has been in Nigeria since August - and is an extremely thorough gentleman. I sat in on Ruth giving her 'history' and it was incredible all the details he wanted to know. It was like a detective on a trail.

The main snag is that Ruth has been having diarrhoea or constipation and nothing much in between for several months. It may be caused by the medicines that she is taking. Dr. Strauss examined her very thoroughly and took stool and blood tests and he says he has a hunch that there is nothing seriously wrong with her digestive track. (Ruth had an odd diarrhoea - indigestion - dizzy - heartburn and air in stomach 'do' when Elizabeth Edmunds was here .... this is what made Elizabeth go to this consultant I think).

As I say Dr. Strauss is not to be put off until he has investigated all. So, he wants to be 100% sure that nothing is the matter by giving her barium enema and then a barium meal and so X-raying her 'gut' as he so nicely calls it. Poor Ruth feels a bit of a guinea pig - for possibly no good reason. And it all takes time. At first, he suggested that we did all the tests in a line - and it would take about one week from last Thursday because they don't X-ray on Fridays. So, we decided to return to Akure on Friday and go back to Benin today ready for the enema tomorrow. Then he says since there is no urgency that she can wait till later in February for the 'meal'. So, we shall get to know the Akure - Benin road quite well!!

One consolation is that if this Scots detective finds nothing - I think there isn't anything to find! I have had a cough since I had the flu, and it came back again when we went to Benin. He noticed it at once and promised to go over my chest on Monday! - and maybe check with an X-ray for good measure. And I was only the driver taking the patient to see him!! Anyway, he is very kind and puts us up in his house and feeds us on roast chicken, and muesli for breakfast.

Thank you for your letters. The next one should tell me about the events of the 19th.

With much love

Elizabeth

Vining Centre
3rd February 1974

Dear Ma and Daddy,

I was delighted to receive your tape last Tuesday (January 29th). I was just setting out for a farewell party in honour of an American couple who have been at the School of Agric. So, after the party I borrowed Dr. Salama's cassette recorder and sat up in bed between 11 -12 to enjoy listening to you all. It is a very good way of communicating - especially when your voice gets more relaxed and natural. It was good to hear news of John and Pat as well, and if they can get a tape recorder too, we shall be well away. Somehow halfway through your voices became blurred. I think the reason will be that if you are recording with one of these small machines you need to turn the volume off when you record and then turn it up when you play back. It's easy to forget to turn it off again when you want to record more. The only other snag was that I was convinced that Ruth and Trevor's wedding was on the second side .... but it went on and on and I kept waiting for the wedding and wondering how it was going to fit into such a small piece of tape!! Then it stopped! and I concluded that there must be a second tape to come .... so, I am looking forward to that.

It was good too to hear all the news of the wedding. It sounds as though it was a very happy affair. Were Joe and Mollie or Rod and Olive there? I had a very enthusiastic letter from Lynette. She obviously enjoyed every minute of it and thoroughly approved of Trevor and Jutka.

I went with Ruth to Benin last Sunday and she had her barium enema on Monday. It wasn't much fun because they pump the stuff in - then pump in air so that you get blown up like a balloon inside and Ruth said she thought she was going to burst. The only consolation is that apparently, they relay the X-ray onto a sort of tele screen and so Ruth said that when she lay on one side on the X-ray table, she could see the picture of her inside on the tele!

Anyway, she was groggy and weak for the rest of Monday and on into Tuesday and Wednesday; but recovered by Thursday ready to go off on the next weekend. She is convinced that it's all a wild goose chase, and it looks as though it may well be - but Elizabeth Edmunds will then be content that she hasn't missed anything.

The set up at Pilsdon sounds very interesting. I wonder how long Ruth and Trevor will stay there? It sounds as though it might be a very absorbing Community once you get involved in it - at the same time it is very demanding to deal with folks who are depressed or have great problems to cope with.

I am glad that you were able to have a good rest at Barbara's. We started our term on Friday - we seem to be very overpopulated with men students.

With love

Elizabeth

Vining Centre
10th February 1974

Dear Ma and Daddy,

Thank you for your letter this week .... but I am sorry to hear that Daddy is having trouble with his urine. On the other hand, if it has been going on for some time maybe it's just as well to get into the hands of the doctor. Perhaps it's prostate trouble or something? I wonder if you will be able to see your inside when they do the X-rays? It makes it more interesting. I am glad that you met Dr. Sinclair and that you had so many old Edinburgh memories. I remember that Dr. Sinclair was very kind when I went to see him with Dr. Kumuyi.

I received the cake this week. Thank you very much indeed - jolly good cake. I am looking forward to receiving the tape of the wedding. I don't have a cassette recorder of my own. Dr. Salama has two, so I usually borrow one of his. The V.S. O's also have small ones - Phillips I think - but they are less good I find than his which is a Sony - but all these cassette recorders are interchangeable as far as I can see. People who have had the small Phillips have said that the motors run out after a time.

I am glad to hear that my slides have turned up. I have another film now to be processed - but I think that I will send it to France because it is apparently quicker there.

We have had the first week of the new year here. I have 13 new students and 4 old ones. It has been quite a busy week, but it is good to get back into the swing of it - and once lists and things are made then things can tick over more smoothly. One baby of about a month old is a bit of a worry. It doesn't grow! and looks very puny and weak. Maybe the mother doesn't have enough milk, maybe they have used some native medicine. Anyway, after a lot of to-ing and fro-ing they have at last got to Dr. Sijuade and are getting treated carefully. Another new student, the wife of a clergyman in Lagos Diocese, went to Dr. Kohli on Friday for an eye test and she apparently had advanced glaucoma - so she may go blind - and it is unlikely that she will be able to do much reading here. This is a pity because she has never been to school and the whole point of coming here was to become literate.

On Friday evening we had an extra-ordinarily eventful evening. I invited Dr. Kohli and Mrs. Kohli and Rajan (17-year-old son) and Ruth and Dr. Salama for supper. All came and we had just finished the first course of antelope, roast potatoes, mushrooms, tomatoes, and dodo when Hilary (V.S.O.) came in a flap carrying a spare tyre. She and Sheila had been to Ibadan and had two punctures just outside Akure, so Sheila waited in the car and Hilary wanted to get the tyre mended. So, she borrowed my car to go to the garage. We ate our sweet. Then Dr. S and Rajan went to sit in the garage and Hilary came to eat some food. After a bit Ruth decided, she should go to Fiwasaiye to tell Sandra not to worry about Sheila's non-arrival. So, she exited and later came back. Then after about one hour Dr. Kohli and Hilary went to see what was going on in the garage. They discovered that Dr. S and Rajan had gone 5 minutes before - so we cooked food ready for Sheila. Then the two men came back - but Sheila had gone straight home so that Sandra shouldn't worry (now about 10pm!). So, then I went to get Sheila to come and eat her food and to get Hilary's key and bag. She came back with me. Later, after 11pm, we all dispersed. Dr. Kohli took Hilary home, Dr. Salama went to the hospital for an operation, and I took Sheila to Fiwasaiye. So, all in all we have a very happy evening shuttling to and fro in our motor cars!

This week - on Wednesday I started my evening classes with the men students. I have been asked to take a class once each week in 'General Knowledge' with special geographical emphasis. It is really to stretch their brains a bit so that they know that the earth turns and not the sun, that they know that Jerusalem is an actual town and not a Biblical myth and that they have heard that there are 800 million Chinese living under a Communistic regime .... and such like. Anyway, the first one went well, and I hope that we shall be able to have some stimulating discussions.

Ruth is here this week - and much better in all respects. Shelagh Jebb is down from Ado for the weekend, so she is staying with Ruth.

My cough has completely gone, you will be glad to hear .... I had an X-ray in Benin, and the result was dull .... "No abnormality seen".

What are slim Jim glasses? It looks as though Trevor and Ruth have masses of containers for drinking but no plates or knives and forks which really are rather vital.

Benin is 100 miles, but you can drive it in 2½ hours so it's not too bad.

I am going to talk about going to the moon in this week's 'lecture' .... so, I have been swotting up all about the Apollo missions etc.

Water is off and on - but nothing like the problems of last year. Even though we had a little rain last night, it is hopeful that the dry season will be normal this time.

I read the book about Paul Brand "Ten Fingers for God " this week - and found it really fascinating. Have you read it? We are going to the Leper Settlement this afternoon for our beginning of term Open Air Service.

My love to you both - and hope to hear good news of Daddy's tests in the next letter. Please thank Mrs. Harris for sending £1.

With love,

Elizabeth

Vining Centre
14th February 1974

Dear Mummy and Daddy,

I received your letter today - saying that Daddy is to have 'a cauliflower' removed from his bladder - and that it has already happened .... because it's today. I shall be thinking of you especially in the next 4 days as you wait for the result of the biopsy. I hope that it is benign. Dr. Salama tells me that most of them are! So, I am hopeful. Anyway, we can only wait and see.

I am sorry to be so far away when this kind of thing happens .... because everything is a week out of date before it gets here. I am glad that Stuart was able to come home and be with you for a few days. In some ways it is worse to be at home wondering what is happening than to be in the hospital where even if it's serious everything is very interesting going on around - and you feel thoroughly spoilt.

We are going to Benin again on Tuesday next week. Ruth will be having her barium meal - so she will be on the starvation and then X-rays lark. How funny that Aline Chapman should know Dr. Strauss. He is an interesting character. Perhaps Aline can tell me why he doesn't have his wife with him - and why he talks about his 'ex-wife'. He has a son who has recently had a coronary.

Daddy will still be in hospital when you get this - if he must stay in 6 weeks. I was reading our favourite hymn at the staff meeting last night - "Peace Perfect Peace" - it is applicable here especially this week when it seems to have been one thing after another without much time to spare. But it is also applicable when you are confined to a hospital bed - or waiting at home for the next visiting time .... and one thought chases another in your head. So that I pray that you both may find 'Peace' during this time of anxiety. Also, no doubt you will make new friends. It's good to have met Dr. Sinclair - but there will be others in the hospital and folk in the parish who come out of their shell to share this trouble with you both. I thank God for my friends.

With much love and prayer

Elizabeth

Vining Centre
17th February 1974

Dear Ma and Daddy,

I think that you will have received the letter that I wrote on Friday (15th). By the time you get it and this one you will have the result of Daddies operation. I shall be waiting for your next letter to see how everything is, but it will probably be the following week before I hear the result.

On Friday evening I started 4 men students on G.C.E. geography. This is an experiment to see if I can help some of the brighter fellows to get an extra subject at G.C.E. I don't intend to 'teach' them but rather to give them work on their own - test it and give them assignments to do. We shall see how it goes.

I went to Dr. Kohli's in the afternoon, and they gave me a whole pile of books that they were throwing out .... they were all Rajan's G.C.E. textbooks for Geography! - and they have already given me his globe before. So, it was marvellous because then I could hand out some books to the men in the evening

I am also doing my evening lecture each Monday with the men students. Last Monday we went to the Moon - very exciting! This coming Monday I am going to talk about the sun and its influence on the Earth - particularly the changing seasons of the year .... and why they see the sun at midnight North of the Arctic Circle, and such like.

Yesterday, Saturday, I went to Ado Ekiti with Sheila and Joan. Hilary and Sandra were there staying for the weekend. In fact, they had made a bed up for me to stay the night - but I decided it was stupid for us to travel in 2 cars and so it was better to go with the others and come back together. We didn't in fact get off till around 12 and so we had lunch on arrival - then a sleep - a swim and did a jigsaw before returning for supper. It was a nice break.

This morning I went to play a game of table-tennis with Raj Kohli - I promised that I would play last week and didn't - so today we went to the Catering Rest House and played 5 games. I won - 3-2 but it was good fun because it was close. Then I came back here and did some letter writing and preparation for classes next week .... and returned to Dr. Kohlis for a very nice Indian lunch of potato chapattis, meat, yoghurt and lentils with plums and custard afterwards.

Ruth is back this afternoon from Kabba. She seems well. We shall be going off to Benin on Tuesday. I shall enjoy telling Dr. Strauss that we have a mutual friend in Aline Chapman.

Sheila is coming to preach the sermon here tonight at our evening service. I am to give the Lent Talks at Fiwasaiye this year, so I am trying to think of something to talk to them about. We hope to have the Lent Fellowship meetings this year again. On Wednesday Ruth and Sheila and I went to 'Mass' at St. Louis School. It was a special Mass arranged by the sisters at St. Louis for the Deji who died. Eyesorun asked us to go with her. It was a lovely service with pure singing .... very beautiful. I was amazed how the Catholic Mass is so <u>very</u> like the Series 2 and 3 services. I think that one day there will be a real breakthrough and a return to worship together with the Catholic Church .... but the Vining Centre isn't really in the running because we are still in 1662!

Daddy is now on the prayer list in our Chapel here, and so he is mentioned by name twice daily at Morning and Evening prayers. The students send you their greetings and love. No doubt we shall still be praying when Daddy is already home and better - but not to worry.

I had a very interesting letter last week from Dougan Hayes. He had received my letter of January telling of the death of the Deji and he went and looked up an old diary of 1933 and quoted it to me - of how he attended the laying of the foundation stone of St. David's Church Akure and the old Deji was there with his trumpeters and courtiers and that he put a bottle of gin? under the foundation stone! I also heard from Miss Pickstone. I must try and answer both.

I shall look forward to seeing the slides. I have another set to send. I may send them to France and not to the U.K. Yemi Paul is getting married on March 2nd in Ondo. She brought her future husband to meet me last week. I promised to take photos for her. Guess who says she will come through Akure next Monday? Gabi!! Now married to a Papuan and spending one month in Nigeria. What a hoot!

I hope Daddy is better by the time this reaches you - that the worries are past - and the whole upset has brought you both closer together - and closer to our Lord.

With my love and prayers

Elizabeth

Vining Centre
10th March 1974

Dear Ma and Daddy,

No letters this week at all - mouldy! But I don't suppose that it's your fault .... much more likely the post. I received a questionnaire the other day from London University .... sent to the School of African and Oriental Studies - then Foxbury, then C.M.S. It was posted in January 1972!

We had our first Lent Fellowship on Tuesday. It was a good meeting - on the Introduction to 'School for Prayer' by Arch. Antony Bloom. We were about 15 people - Catholics and Protestants. Then on Wednesday at 8.15 I took the Fiwasaiye Lent meeting - on 'Don't worry about anything at all - but pray about everything'. I wasn't as well prepared as the first week - and it was very hot and that put me off. However, they listened well. This coming week I must take the Lent Service here at Vining Centre and the Fiwasaiye one. So, I think I am doing my 'extra' for Lent this time!!

Prices are rising here - very rapidly. The latest thing is flour. It used to cost 45K a bag. Now it has doubled to over 1 naira

(100K). So, the price of a loaf of bread has also doubled. I think the inflation is worldwide. Groundnut oil seems to increase by about 2K a week!! However, we are very thankful this year to have water - it is intermittent and comes and goes, but the rains have begun a bit and it is nothing like as bad as last year .... here anyway. I think the North is bad. Jane is having a job up at Kazaure near Kano. She is coming down to Akure for Easter - so that will be good.

On Friday evening .... my only free evening during the week, now .... Hilary had some of us for supper .... i.e., Sandra, Mike, Dr. and Mrs. Kohli and Rajan, Dr. Salama and I. It was an enjoyable evening. On Saturday Sandra and I went to Ado to the dentist and to see Shelagh Jebb. We also went on Tuesday - I wanted to check my teeth - nothing - Sandra wanted to have some fillings done. We just dropped by to take some medicines to Ile Abiye .... and went to Shelagh's house. She was in bed .... I breezed in and said, "What's the matter with you?" She replied cheerfully "I have just had a mastectomy this morning!" She was just recovering from the anaesthetic. I had no idea. Nor had she. She had only discovered a week before that the doctor thought it should be removed.

Anyway, we went to see her again on Saturday .... she was already sitting in a chair knitting. I think she should have stayed in bed for a week! and enjoyed herself.

We went swimming in the Textile pool. Hilary was there too and the dentist and his wife and children. All a nice relaxing day. The Eyesorun, Sheila and Richard Childerstone came for supper last night - and 2 V.S.O.'s and Sandra and Mike came for lunch today. Ruth is back from her weekend at Ikare.

I hope that you are well after your time at St. Julians.

With much love
Elizabeth

Vining Centre
22nd March 1974

Dear Ma and Daddy,

Thank you very much for your letter talking about the strides forward in house hunting plans. I think that the bungalow sounds the thing. Ruth always says how much of a blessing her parents found being in a bungalow, because if anyone gets sick you have no stairs.

The lounge is big enough and one bedroom a fair size. The view of the Malvern hills and the river at the bottom of the garden sound glorious.

I can't think that I shall ever want that big bed and cupboard again. I would suggest that you get rid of them completely - if you get any money for them, you could buy a reasonably sized trunk and put my junk in it - i.e., winter clothes etc. You could use one of the bedrooms for a small "study" couldn't you? If the place is only five minutes from St. Mary's, then overflow visitors can still be billeted in the parish with friends, can't they?

The hut behind, with windows, could be used for storage of small items - and as you say you could put visitors there.

It's a pity that I can't come home this summer to sort you out!

Anyway, my vote is for the bungalow. How is it heated?

With love

Elizabeth

Vining Centre
31st March 1974

Dear Ma and Daddy,

I received Daddies letter this week telling of how Dr. Sinclair is keeping him in order and not allowing him to do too much. That seems very sensible. It is easy to struggle to do things after an operation when you really should relax and wait for your strength to return. I think that Shelagh Jebb at Ado is not very good at that. She was quite determined to be back at work two weeks after her mastectomy and then was disappointed when she couldn't manage it .... and according to Gwen Hall has more pain now than she did at first.

Thank you very much indeed for your gift of the book of meditations. I started reading them today - beginning with 'Joy'. It is true that there are many things to rejoice about. I am sitting this morning in Inga's house in Ondo. I was supposed to come here to see her last weekend, but it didn't work out. Next weekend Mandy Dees is coming to Akure and the following one is Easter, when Inga is going to Ibadan - so I decided to come here yesterday when Dr. Salama offered me a lift. He has gone with some other Egyptian friends to Ife and Ogbomoso. I hope that he will come back today to give me a lift back to Akure - but he is not very reliable at times.

We had a busy week with our usual Lenten activities on Tuesday and Wednesday. I got a group of our students to mime part of Pilgrim's Progress while I did a commentary - prepared by Rosemary Stephens. It took quite a lot of preparation and we practised on Sunday, Monday, Tuesday, and Wednesday and then did it in Fiwasaiye on Wednesday evening. It was called "At the Foot of the Cross" - with the main theme being the falling of the burden of sin, at the Cross. I think the girls got the message although at first, they thought that the miming was rather strange and amusing.

After Wednesday - the last Lent talk at Fiwasaiye I began to feel that a burden of Services had fallen off my back! It is just as well really because now I can concentrate on the end of term activities and the Exams which come up at the beginning of Holy Week. I am still doing my Monday night lecture - this past week I did "Rain" (why we get seasonal rain in Nigeria - and storms at the beginning of wet season) and "No Rain" - i.e., problems of drought. There is still plenty to say about that.

Inga and I have just been to see the new Ondo Cathedral. It is a light and open plan with the altar standing under the dome and the choir behind - with people in balconies on the right and left. The building is beautiful but inside in my opinion they have wasted money unnecessarily on "marble". The pulpit, the communion rail, the font, two reading desks and the bishop's seat are all in pale grey marble. These marble things were given by different big families in Ondo and must have cost the earth. It was all imported from Italy. Such a pity when they could have had some beautiful wood carving. Then they have a bright red carpet in the Chancel which is not properly laid and curls up at the edges - and the padded chairs all around are a crimson red that just does not "go". The other thing that I thought was a bit shabby was that the brass which they had brought from the old Cathedral was not properly polished.

I went over to see Yemi and her husband at mid-day. They seem to be happily installed in their new home.

Last night Inga and I went out for supper with the Whittals. They are C.M.S. Associates at Adeyemi College. He teaches Physics there and she teaches B.K. and General Science here at St. Monica's. They were entertaining 2 English gentlemen for supper - one was a Professor at Durham University, and the other was a senior English master at the Upper Latymer School, Hammersmith. Both were just in Nigeria for 2 weeks advising the West African School Certificate A-level examiners on how to set about marking. It made a change to meet some Englishmen. We have none in Akure. Mike is Irish. He and I played tennis twice last week - on Monday and Friday. I won on Monday, but he got his own back on Friday!

Tuesday morning:

I received your letter yesterday Ma, telling of the Mothering Sunday services. I was <u>very</u> sorry to hear that Christine had a miscarriage. Still, they have time to try again.

Yesterday I had to come from Ondo in the school bus because Dr. Salama didn't show up! He was very apologetic when he did come - there was a storm and trees across the road, so they had to sleep the night in Ilesha.

I am glad to hear that Daddy is steadily getting stronger - but you mustn't overdo it over Easter. I hope that you have a very happy Easter time. I shall be here throughout - because we shall still be in term time at the Vining Centre. Our term starts again on May 10th. Jacky Henry is hoping to come to stay on Easter Monday or thereabouts.

I didn't hear before that Vi Phinn had died - or did I? £50 will be useful for something - what are you going to do with it? (If you get it).

The Committee of St. Mary's seemed to have their ideas a bit mixed - Is Playgroup reckoned to be 'secular' while Brownies is 'spiritual'? Or what? It seems to me that they should be on precisely the same basis as far as paying for the Hall is concerned.

I must try and write to John and Pat - it is ages since I wrote or heard from them.

We have our last Lent Fellowship tonight. The title is "Managing Time" - so it will be very relevant. Today I feel that we shall soon be at the end of term, and I feel ready for it - it must be because the schools are finishing this coming Wednesday - we have 2½ weeks still to go!

It seems like a very long time since I was on leave. I can't believe that it was only 6 months ago.

With much love to you both.

Elizabeth

Vining Centre
9th April 1974

Dear Ma and Daddy,

This will be a shorter letter - I expect that you will get it after Easter. I hope that you have a very happy time in St. Mary's over the Easter Festivities. It looks as though we shall be well occupied here. Good Friday reads - 8.30am Matins and Play; 12 - 3 Meditation on the 7 words from the Cross; 5pm Open Air Procession of Witness. Sunday, we have Communion at 9am and I have been asked to give the address!! So, I hope that I get some inspiration from that.

We have exams for the 1st 3 days of Holy Week - so I have been busy at the weekend typing and planning. I haven't in fact finished - there are 2 more exams to set for Wednesday.

We have had a lot of visitors this weekend. Mandy Dees was supposed to come, but she never showed up. Instead, I had Inga and a nurse from Ondo Catholic Hospital. They stayed Saturday night. Then we had 2 English couples on Saturday from Ode - the 2 who we spent Christmas with at Ado, Bob and Alicia Epton are V.S.O.'s and they came to lunch with me and Sandra. They are a lovely young Christian couple.

On Tuesday Gill Cotterill who is a friend of Angela's - a law lecturer at Zaria (she used to be at Ife - we stayed in her flat when we evacuated from Ondo) -she came to Akure with an Indian law lecturer, and they stayed the night.

Then Jane Pelly has been here for the weekend, staying with Shelagh - so we have invited her to meals - Saturday night at Ruth's and Sunday night at Sheila's. She is going off to Ibadan and Lagos today.

Hilary went to Ibadan on Friday - and is supposed to be having her operation - or whatever they decide to do - next Thursday. Sheila Jebb has heard the result of her biopsy - no malignancy - so perhaps she didn't need to have the whole breast removed after all. Ruth was not well last weekend - and on Monday and Tuesday - but she seems to be better now. She is sorting out her belongings and getting rid of things that she doesn't want so that she can get everything packed up in time to go home in mid-May. I think her proposed date is now Saturday 25th May. I hope that her father is not too unwell with his congestion. It is a pity that he couldn't come to St. Mary's for your mothering Sunday Service.

I hope that you are both well now; and that you find patience to listen to Noel and May and yet don't get ruffled by them.

With much love

Elizabeth

Vining Centre
15th April 1974

Dear Ma and Daddy,

It is Easter Monday - I have been thinking of you all at home, very much over the past weekend. I do hope that you had an Easter of great Joy. I had a very happy weekend - with several visitors coming and going. Jane Pelly has been staying for the weekend - and so has Joan Steward. Both stayed with Sheila at Fiwasaiye.

We had some very good services during Holy Week. Cornelius spoke each evening about the book of James - then we had Communion on Thursday and on Friday morning my group of men did the mime of Pilgrims Progress again. We then had a 12 - 3 service on the 7 words from the Cross. Rev. Adeoba took it very well - except for that Ruth and I thought there was not enough time for meditation - but we decided that the students didn't mind. I read again parts of "In Debt to Christ" by Douglas Webster. I find it a very helpful book.

On Saturday morning there was an Official Memorial Thanksgiving Service for the Deji. It was a great occasion with all sorts of important people present. Last Wednesday the people of Akure created a 'Regent' until they sort out their decisions about appointing a new Deji. They choose the eldest Daughter of the Deji - who is Eyesorun's eldest daughter - now doing A-level at the International School, Ibadan. It is a bit much for a schoolgirl and the Eyesorun is not happy about it - but it is "tradition". We all hope that they will get a move on and choose a new Deji, quickly.

On Saturday Busola (the Regent), an old girl of Fiwasaiye - was all decked out in the Deji's clothes with man's dress and ornaments and a yellow crown with feathers poking out the top. She was carried on an open couch with a large umbrella waving above her. The service that we had was inter-denominational .... including Moslems!

On Saturday evening I prepared my sermon for Sunday morning - when I talked about Emmanuel - 'God is with us' and the 2 fellows on the road to Emmaus. Then I went and did a jig saw at Fiwasaiye till 12 midnight. When I came back Ruth came because she was depressed and weepy - and I tried to help her - till about 12.45. I then read a Woman and Home story (thank you for January - March magazines .... good relaxation material during the past week). I suppose I slept at about 1.30. Then I woke up when the students started singing their Easter morning hymns - at 4am. They went off to the town to sing for a couple of hours. I didn't go too!

One of the children 'Olu', has been in hospital since Saturday afternoon. It is the third time this term that he went into convulsions. This time he probably has chickenpox. So, I spent a good deal of time on Saturday afternoon getting him to Dr. Sijuade and then to the hospital. His father is at Immanuel College Ibadan - he came on Sunday and took over the duties of hopping up and down the road to the hospital. Olu started to have terrible diarrhoea on Sunday am .... and there was no water in the hospital so I had to take a 4 gallon can along to help in washing the sheets.

We now have just a couple more days to the end of term and I need to write my reports, finish my exam marking, write the certificates .... etc..... etc.

Jacqui Henny and a V.S.O. called Sue are here for Monday and Tuesday nights.

We are also planning a college farewell for Ruth who is now going to go home on 11th May instead of 25th. We all feel that this is the right date from this end. She can be ready to go then and there is no good reason to stay 2 weeks more. Also, her father has not been so well recently, and it seems better for her to go as soon as possible from his point of view. She is still on Valium and Tryptizol .... antidepressants/tranquilisers and I think the sooner she settles down to a peaceful routine at home the sooner she will be able to come off them. The only snag is that she is not allowed to drive - so she can't be driving her father around.

Anyway, this May 11th scheme means that I can go with her down to Lagos on May 9th and then come back here to start the new term on 10th. I can help her during our 3 weeks holiday with the packing up.

We went to the Akinbadewa's new house on the way to Idanre - for our Easter picnic. The house isn't yet finished, but the view is superb, and it will be very nice sometime.

I want to get this letter off so that Jane Pelly can post it in Lagos.

With much love

Elizabeth

Vining Centre
21st April 1974

Dear Ma and Daddy,

Thank you for your last letter, which was written on the road to Swansea. Since then, you will have had Stuart and Jutka to stay. I hope that you had an enjoyable time together. I am glad that they are now engaged and have a ring. Surely, they said something about it during their stay at Easter!

We finished the term here on Wednesday - with a flourish. We had a Service of Commissioning for 4 women who have left: 3 Immanuel College wives and one other. We combined the Commissioning Service with a 'Farewell' for Ruth. She decided to go home on May 11th on Monday so we had to organise everything quickly on Tuesday because the students will not be here again until after she has gone down to Lagos. We had the Commissioning first and then Ruth was asked to come out and kneel before the Archdeacon for special prayers. It was a very appropriate farewell service. Afterwards we had refreshments in the Hall and some speeches and then dancing by the students.

I should suggest that Mrs. Filsel sends you a cheque for the £10 and put it in my bank account and then I will take out the equivalent amount here. It is very generous of her. She must have been working hard.

On Friday morning I spent a very successful morning with Ruth - helping her to do her packing into the trunk and the boxes that are to go by sea. We finished it all off in 1½ hours!! So that was a great triumph. Ruth had been busy for the previous couple of days - sorting out her things and deciding what to take so it was just a case of the actual packing on Friday morning. She is not taking home crockery or household gear - because most of what she uses doesn't belong to her - and her father has a whole household of equipment at home so there is no point in transporting her rather old and shabby stuff from here.

I played tennis in the afternoon with Mike - and I won .... so, it was my turn to be broadcasting what a good game we had, while Mike said nothing!

Yesterday, Saturday, Ruth and I went to Ado to see Shelagh Jebb. She is much better now. Ruth took a good deal of useful equipment to Shelagh - for distribution around her clinics -

some children's clothes and cot blankets that they will use there in the hospital. The new Indian doctor - Dr. Thomas and his wife, also a doctor, have now arrived and seem to have settled down very quickly. They are even turning Marjorie's old house into a male ward so that they can do some operations - like hernias, for men and so make the hospital more financially stable.

In the evening Sandra and Sheila and Ruth come for supper. They start term again tomorrow - the schools just have 2 weeks holiday. It is a pity really that we are beginning our holidays when everyone else is finishing theirs.

There are a few arrangements being made for Ruth's farewell in the next 3 weeks. The Board of Governors is meeting on Friday, and they are going to name a house after Ruth - "Martin House" and give her a ram's tail and a photograph album with an 'address' in it. Yours truly has been asked to inscribe the address which has been written by Provost Akintemi of Ondo. I haven't seen it yet - and hope to goodness that it is not too long because it will be a big job.

I have just read a delightful book by Rummer Godden called "An Episode of Sparrows". I wonder if you have read it. It is worth reading.

I am hoping to stay here in Akure for most of my holiday - 3 weeks. I hope to get "sorted" as far as letters and so on are concerned - and to have time to read and organise my plant pots - as well as help Ruth in her final weeks of farewells. I may go to Ibadan briefly sometime and go to get my car serviced in Oshogbo. I shall have Anne Harris in the summer holidays so I shall do plenty of travelling then. I do hope that she won't have trouble with her visa.

It must be getting warmer at home now with the spring advancing. We are all green here with rains started - but still there is not so much rain .... and my front garden is invaded by 'locusts' - of a green sort. They are extra-ordinary - and the whole ground 'jumps' when you walk over the grass where they are busy eating, or rudely mating in public.

I hope that you will be able to get out to Castlemorton Common and see the lambs.

With much love
Elizabeth

Vining Centre
26th April 1974

Dear Ma and Daddy,

Thank you very much for your letter written on Easter Monday. I hope that by now you will have received the simnel cake from Belfast and enjoyed eating it. I also hope that Daddy's pulled thigh muscle is better. I have had back-ache the past couple of days - but it seems to have eased after Sheila rubbed it for me yesterday. I think it started on Wednesday when I spent most of the day writing out the provost's speech in Ruth's farewell album and then sticking in the photographs. On Friday we had the Board of Governors meeting when Ruth was presented with a beaded tail plus the album, and she was asked to unveil the notice which is eventually to be used to name the new dormitory that we hope will be built this year for families.

This week has been a good holiday week. I have been reading quite a lot. Then I have been going to Fiwasaiye - on Thursday and Friday to help to revise with Form V. Mrs. Wilde, their geography teacher is off sick for 2 weeks so I said that I would help them in some revision of world geography. I am enjoying it.

The flowering trees are all coming out beautifully now. I have a glorious pink cassia tree outside my bedroom window and then plenty of Pride of Barbados and orange bougainvillea. It is very colourful.

This coming week is going to be full of farewells for Ruth - Monday at St. Louis Convent, Wednesday at Dr. Kohli's and Friday at Sheila's house. I am hoping to fit in a visit to Oshogbo to get my car serviced - and I may possibly go on to Ibadan on Tuesday night. I don't want to travel about too much - partly so that I can keep Ruth company here, and partly so that I can save up for our holiday journey to the North which I am planning for August. But I ought really to go and see Grace in Ibadan and Kelu in Ife.

It is very hot today - maybe it will rain again soon.

Sunday evening:

Good! It is raining and so the air is cooling down. Maybe I shall be able to get on. One becomes very lethargic when it is hot and sticky. Now I feel much clearer headed and should be able to do some of the things that I planned to do during my holiday period. Ruth is back from her last weekend visit - so she is now on the last lap. It seems that Bp Martin has not been very well in the last month or so -

and that he has aged a good deal. I expect that he will be happier when he can be settled in his own home with Ruth to look after him.

It will be interesting to see what happens next in Portugal. I wonder what Uncle Joe has to say about it.

Looking forward to seeing John's slides and tape when you have finished with them.

With much love to you both

Elizabeth

Vining Centre
5th May 1974

Dear Ma and Daddy,

It was good to hear from you this week and to hear of Stuart and Jutka's happy stay with you in Malvern. I am sorry to hear that May Panter is in an even more difficult mood than usual. They do always seem to be unfortunate in the weather when they go on holiday. Why do they have to go "touring" when they generate a tense atmosphere between them in a car at the best of times? If they sat down to relax and enjoy themselves in one place, they wouldn't notice the weather.

I had an enjoyable few days "holiday" last week in Oshogbo. I stayed with Gordon and Daphne Evans from Tuesday - Friday. They used to be at Adeyemi College in Ondo. It was a surprise holiday and not intended but a good thing, nevertheless. I went to Oshogbo on Tuesday to get my car 'lubricated', but it had a funny noise in reverse gear which I asked them to check. The result was that they took the engine and the gear box out on Tuesday/Wednesday - put it together again on Thursday and discovered that it still made the same noise - so took it all to pieces again on Friday and didn't get it organised for the road till Saturday morning! So, I was very happy when Daphne asked me to stay Tuesday night and extended the invitation till Thursday night. On Thursday Gordon was going to a Ministry of Education meeting in Ibadan so I went too (in his air-conditioned Toyota). On Friday I had to be in Akure for a farewell party for Ruth - so Daphne loaned me her ancient Cortina and I came to Akure in that and took it back to Oshogbo on Saturday morning.

Today, Sunday, Sheila came for lunch and for breakfast and I am going to her for supper at Fiwasaiye. I have just played a very hot game of tennis with Mike. Last night I played my first game of bridge! It was a great mystery to me, but everyone else seemed to know what they were doing.

We had a very happy farewell party for Ruth on Friday evening - at Sheila's house. On Monday we went to St. Louis Convent and had supper outside on the lawn. I missed the party that the Kohli's gave on Wednesday - then this coming week Dr. Salama is giving a farewell party on Tuesday. Ruth and I go to Lagos on Thursday.

I don't have any BRF this year. Can you send me some?

Today is really the last day of my holiday for I had better start preparing for the new term tomorrow. Mrs. Wilde, the geography teacher at Fiwasaiye, is off sick so I have been helping her to do some revision with Class V. They have their School Certificate Exams soon. I have enjoyed my teaching. The schoolgirls are keen and a bit brighter than our women!

With much love to you both

Elizabeth

Vining Centre
(Actually - Lagos)
10th May 1974

Dear Ma and Daddy,

I brought Ruth down to Lagos yesterday - a long drive from Akure - with the usual chaos at the end of the line, along the Ikorodu road. Lagos traffic does not seem to improve. I went walking along the Marina to Kingsway and got hot!

Now I am sitting in the Guest House, drinking coffee with Ruth before going back to Akure in the bus (Vining Centre Bus). I didn't work things very well because this means that I don't have a chance to visit friends in Lagos. I will manage better when Ann comes in July. I hope she can come.

I will write properly from Akure but thought you might like a note via Ruth. She is in good form, and I think now 'ready' to be going home. I hope that her father doesn't do too much in preparation and so make himself ill. It sounds as though he hasn't really been well since the beginning of the year so will be glad to have Ruth back at home.

I hope that C.M.S. Medical Department let Ruth just relax and get well again at home.

I hope that you are both O.K. - Don't hang on at St. Mary's too long. It's not worth it, when you could retire, a little sooner if the way opened. Although if Stuart is thinking of getting married in 1975 maybe 1975 is a good time to think about it.

Each day is a new day, in which we can rejoice .... and serve others.

With my love

Elizabeth

Vining Centre
12th May 1974

Dear Ma and Daddy,

Thank you for your letters and the photos of Ruth's wedding. Everyone looks very cheerful. I like the one particularly of Ruth and Trevor outside the church.

I am very interested to hear that you are making investigations about retiring places. I think that it seems a wise move, and as you say if it all falls through now then you can stay on a bit longer at St. Mary's. It does seem to me best to make the move while you can still enjoy retirement - before you become too exhausted.

I expect you will have got my letter written in Lagos. Ruth's leaving meant several farewell parties and I gained about half a stone! But on arriving back from Lagos I had diarrhoea and so have reduced a bit. We had a very tiring return journey in the Vining Centre van. It rattled terribly. There were several showers of rain, so the road was wet in places - and it is badly eroded at the sides which doesn't help driving. In one place we skidded and turned right round, landing in the ditch facing the opposite direction!! We were quickly pushed out and continued our way.

The new term is just starting at the Vining Centre. There are 5 new women replacing the 4 who left. We shall see tomorrow how they begin to settle in. I spent most of yesterday in and out of bed. I think I had a touch of fever - and was tired after the journey to Lagos. Anyway, I feel better today - and had lunch with Sheila and am going to Sandra's for supper. I shall miss Ruth here on the compound, so it is good that I have Sheila and Sandra and Hilary still around.

The flowering trees on the compound are beautiful at this time of the year. I have a pink cassia outside my bedroom window. It is worth being in bed a bit to look at it.

You did very well in the Lent Project.

I am sorry to hear that Daddy is having pains in the legs, and hope that Dr. Sinclair can help to find some solution.

On the journey back from Lagos on Friday I called on Bola - you remember he sent the wooden album. His wife has recently had a second daughter. She is teaching in Ijebu where he now works in the forestry office. I also called on Inga who is still battling at St. Monica's. She has been having serious trouble with her car. It has been in the workshop in Mandilas, Ibadan, for two weeks now and they want N300 to repair it!! Terrible, because the car is only just over 1 year old. My car seems to be running OK since its repairs.

Thank you for your letters and your prayers. I hope that you had a good birthday Ma. I expect that I shall hear about it in the next letter.

With my love

Elizabeth

Vining Centre
19th May 1974

Dear Ma and Daddy,

We have now had the first week of the new term. Not entirely uneventful either. One student found a spitting cobra disturbing the turkeys that he is breeding in his back kitchen. It spat in his eye before he could kill it. So great panic! I took him to Dr. Kohli who treated his eye promptly and then we went to the hospital for snake serum etc. He seems to be OK.

On Wednesday evening Mama Ademoye and Rev Adeoba, the men's warden had such an almighty row that Cornelius cancelled the staff meeting on Thursday, while he negotiated - and to allow the smoke to settle!! They seem to have settled everything .... but I was amused at Mama's remark after Communion this morning - which lasted about 1¾ hours - "Only God can save us" she said - from Adeoba's long and waffly sermons!!! I was inclined to agree.

Yesterday, Bob and Alicia Epton who are the V.S.O. couple who were with us at Christmas at Ado came for the weekend in Akure. They stayed with Sandra and the 4 of us went to Idanre in the morning. We climbed up to the radio masts - then they all came back here for lunch. In the afternoon I went out with Sheila - to Ado to see Shelagh Jebb and Sister Martinian from the St. Louis Noviciate. She was sick this week with gastric malaria, so it was a gorgeous day out!

This morning we all met for elevenses on the Agric Rocks - Sheila, Bob, Alicia, Sandra, and Hilary and Yemi (Sheila's neighbour). It was a lovely hot bright sunny day. I am going to have lunch with Dr. Salama and his friend Dr. Hanna, an Egyptian doctor from Okitipupa. Dr. Salama is leaving Akure at the end of this month to go to Ghana to prepare for his Primary F.R.C.S. Exams. Then he is going home to Cairo to be married in July. We shall all miss him in Akure.

This evening, I shall be having supper with Sheila and 3 of the Catholic brothers - Brother Tom - the Principal of St. Peter Teacher Training College - Bro. Alfonse - a very old retired Canadian brother - maybe you met him - he used to be in Ondo and Brother Anselm, a Nigerian brother. This event is after our usual beginning of term Open Air Service at the Leper Settlement. So, it's quite a busy Sunday. I am supposed to be talking to our students tomorrow about "something". I had thought that I would talk to them about Portugal - their coup and the effects that this has on Mozambique, Guinea - Bissau and Angola .... but this needs quite a lot of preparation. I may choose a simpler topic this week and prepare properly for next week.

I cut out 4 dresses for the 4 incoming women on Friday - that's a good thing done - but I must get round to cutting out some for myself. I keep putting it off, and some of my dresses are becoming tatty.

With much love

Elizabeth

Ebun's Story Begins

Vining Centre
May 26th, 1974

Dear Ma and Daddy,

I think that you will have received my letter written earlier this week commenting on the bungalow/house question. I am looking forward to hearing how things are progressing.

I received 2 Women and Home magazines this week and in the very same post George Appleton's book of meditations. I think you asked me to let you know which arrived first. I haven't yet seen the tape or slides of New Zealand. Perhaps they haven't left your end yet.

It hasn't been a very eventful week. I showed slides and film strips to the men on Monday night - partly to show them how the projector works and partly for the pictures. I showed the strip of Myrtle's school in Lagos, which they found interesting. Then on Friday night we had a great treat .... the sisters at St. Louis had got hold of the film "The Sound of Music" and they showed it outside on the wall of a building. It was very successful - but it was strange watching the film with a lot of Nigerian school boys. I remember the first time I saw it was when Daddy took me to cheer me up when I was grieving about Richard, and we saw it in Tottenham Court Road. Rather a different set-up.

I had a letter this week from Kelu. She is missing Yomi, and I feel bad that I have not been to see her. I haven't been to Ibadan since Christmas with my own transport. Anyway, I hope to go one weekend soon. She is talking about going to the U.S.A. to see Yomi in July and maybe coming to London, and possibly getting out to Malvern to see you.

I have just been to the Leper Settlement where one man has been very sick. He was taken to a doctor by Sister Martinian of St. Louis, but he really needs careful after care - whereas he is lying on a wooden bed in a dark room at the Settlement.

Sandra and Hilary have been trying to help a young woman who was sitting in the ditch near Fiwasaiye school last week. I think that she was thrown out of the town because she is supposed to be a witch. Hilary and I are going to go to the hospital with one of our women to give her some clean clothes and to try to see that she is washed.

Later! It was quite a performance - you've no idea 2 Europeans and one Vining woman carrying one dotty lady, with matted hair to the washroom - cutting the hair, washing her from top to toe - sitting her on the bed pan where she made loud grunting noises .... etc. I guess that we shall have to repeat the performance today because she doesn't ask for a bed pan! or the nurses don't give her. Not very nice. I think that she will have to be transferred to the mental hospital at Abeokuta. She keeps people awake at night in the wards - singing and shouting - but she is not mental. She speaks Yoruba and some English and answers questions lucidly. She has one foot with a terrible sore on it - and a knee that looks as though it has guinea worm in it.

I hope all's well with you - at least you are not likely to have guinea worm!

With much love to you both
Elizabeth

Vining Centre
2nd June 1974

Dear Ma and Daddy,

Thank you for your last letter - written outside the Hospital in Worcester and including the notice about the bungalow. Who is next door? Semi-detached can be noisy - but we survived at Queen's Park. I don't remember being disturbed by the neighbours. Anyway, I hope that plans go ahead. I am sorry to hear about the truss and the hernia again. But it will be a lot less trouble than if the table tennis ball had been cancerous!

You seem to be very busy with preparing your services - I have been thinking of you at St. Mary's today as you start the Family Service. I hope that it started well.

We have spent quite a lot of time this last week worrying about our crazy woman - Ebun who we got into the hospital. In the end, after a lot of coming and going Dr. Kohli wrote a letter to refer her to Aro Mental Hospital at Abeokuta, and the hospital sent an ambulance and a nurse. <u>But</u> they wouldn't take her in because she had no relative with her!! So, they brought her back. On Saturday morning Sheila and I went to see her and found her bright and perky - but obviously a bit round the bend - and saying amusing things .... the snag was that about 20-30 people were all standing around - gawping - and the nurses were nearly standing on their heads trying to drive the crowds of spectators away. In the end Dr. Kohli had to call the police to keep order in the hospital. So, Sandra and I went to the Eyesorun and asked her where we could take her. She suggested that the only place is an "Herbal Healing Home" run by some Jehovah's Witness people that specialises in down and outs and crazy people. So, we went there and found a clean and tidy compound with we thought a peaceful atmosphere - they keep pigeons and rabbits - but I shouldn't be surprised if their methods of "treating" the patients aren't straight out of 19th Century looney bins + 'native doctor' methods. Some of the patients have a band of iron round one leg and it's fixed to a plank of wood!! We shall see. But there doesn't seem to be much choice. None of us can really cope with a looney girl who can't use the loo .... apart from the fact that other Nigerians would be unlikely to accept her on the compound. It is said that she was turned out of her village in Ekiti because she was a witch who was accused of causing the death of several people. If she went back to her village, they say she would be stoned to death. It seems to be either the J. Ws or the road. And the J.W. place has the reputation of helping people and several people have been completely cured - after their treatment and prayers and so on. But they want 300 Naira!! All really very difficult - and boils down to the fact that there is no adequate care for mentally sick in this country yet.

Dr. Salama has gone off today - going to Accra for his refresher course and exams. Rajan Kohli helped him to pack this morning. I have never known such chaos in my whole life. He must be lbs overweight and was proposing to take 2 large suitcases, 2 large handbags and I think one box - by AIR!! I have never known anyone so impulsively generous, but so completely disorganised and unplanned. I hope someone has organised his wedding for him. He was so exhausted in the end - having been up all night for the last two nights with accidents and so on that we had to send a driver to take him to Lagos in case he fell asleep on the road!!

Love

Elizabeth

Vining Centre
10th June 1974

Dear Ma and Daddy,

It was good to get both your letters this week and the interesting article on Ruth's place. I am glad that things are going ahead with the retiring plans. It is great news that John is prepared to pay the rent. That will be a help. I am sorry that I can't offer to do the same - but sorrier that I can't be there to help in the move. However, it shouldn't be such an upheaval as the move from Enfield to Malvern. If Ruth and Stu, clear out some of their junk then there is only mine and your own!! It looks as though you will move at the beginning of September.

I am very sorry to hear of Phil Spurgeon dying so suddenly. What a shock! I will try and write to Jose.

Yomi went to U.S.A. for a year I think - to do more research type work in connection with his post in the University. I hope to see Kelu during our half term break - 20th to 22nd June.

I wonder if you could send with Ann - 4 pairs of Mark's pants. The last lot are OK .... called Combed Cotton to fit 40-42" hips. Yes, dress size is 38". That's a nice idea. I still haven't got round to making up some of the material that I brought back with me - and some of my old dresses are really falling apart.

This week we have had more high jinks with our Ebun. Hilary and I took her to the Hospital to have her foot dressed. She was in a demanding mood .... "Buy butter" .... "Buy sardine" .... "Buy me a stove" .... etc. She didn't seem to have sobered down much in the healing establishment. The other folks were complaining that she disturbed them with her singing and shouting. But worse was to come. The next time we went they told us that she had eaten the heads off 2 chickens!!! They were very annoyed - not surprising! Now she has killed 2 more and they are asking that we should remove her! But where to?? Sheila and I will try and see Dr. Sijuade to see if he can help us get her into Aro, the mental hospital.

Sandra hasn't been very well. She saw a doctor in Ibadan last week and was given heavy antibiotics. She managed to teach while taking them, which was perhaps a mistake. Tuesday night and Wednesday night she stayed here and rested for the 2 days - but she still wasn't right, so we sent her back to the doctor on Friday. She was admitted in the Catholic hospital there. So, Hilary and I went to see her yesterday. We met a very watery Sandra - sitting in bed 'being observed' in a private room with air conditioners at N10 a night. She was upset by the loneliness, the money, and the fact that she wasn't having any tests done till Monday. So, we tried to cheer her up and encourage her to wait and see because it would be waste if they discovered something useful. Then we went to see Joe and Brenda Batt and they promised to go and see Sandra today.

One new baby boy arrived this morning - all very quick and very little trouble. The father is an older student, and he is delighted.

The Whittals who are C.M.S. Associates at Adeyemi College Ondo, were over here today to take the morning service at Fiwasaiye. We all had lunch together at Sheila's house. I have said that I will take the service next week at Fiwasaiye. We did so much service taking during Lent - that I am feeling unemployed in that respect this term.

I hope that you are well. It's wet here, and stormy at night. You must be getting warmer.

With love

Elizabeth

Vining Centre
16th June 1974

Dear Ma and Daddy,

No letter this week, but I hear from Ruth that she has been to see you and that you didn't get the bungalow. What a shame! She mentions some 'house'. I wonder which one that is.

I have just had a rather frustrating Sunday. I had a cold on Friday and a slight sore throat this morning, so I didn't really feel like doing much. However, I was to take the Evening Service at Fiwasaiye tonight, so I spent most of the morning planning the service - and looking up Mother Theresa of Calcutta because I wanted to speak to the girls about the needs for social services in Nigeria - especially thinking of the saga of our friend Ebun. Then we had a naming ceremony at 4pm. So, the service at Fiwasaiye was at 6pm. I started with some prayers and the first hymn and then the heavens opened, and it poured with rain. No one could hear a word, so I had to stop, and we sang for a whole hour! So, my throat is now sore and my voice hoarse and I never gave my sermon!!

On Wednesday Sheila and I went to Ilu Omoba in Ekiti to find the relations of Ebun, the crazy lady who is now in the stocks at the local looney-bin. It was an incredible visit. All the neighbours and the pastor came out and told their tale - and they had plenty to say.

Ebun did Primary IV and then went to Lagos as a house maid. She married a soldier from the next village. She was perfectly normal .... but then "her character changed" they said. She was the only remaining child of her mother - and was said to have caused the death of all the other children - what's more she had boasted of the fact herself. She had also caused the death of one pregnant nurse in Ado and one Adeyemi College student who died in a road accident. She said she ate someone's heart! So, she was clearly a witch. They had locked her in and as far as we could tell starved her till she was in a coma. They thought she was dead and dug her grave. After 4 days of coma, they prepared to bury her - but she woke up!! So, she was a witch - they drove her out of their village 4 months ago and they certainly didn't want her back. She had a baby boy which the husband had removed and given into the care of his mother before it could walk. Tragic tale. Even the vicar supported chucking her out of the village - he gave us a long lecture on how mental sickness was one thing and curable, but this case was different. Once you had this 'power' within you - that Ebun has, then there is no hope.

I went on Saturday morning to Ondo to the naming ceremony of Yemi Paul's baby daughter. Inga was there - I will be going to Ibadan next weekend to see Grace. Sandra is out of hospital. It was discovered that she has mild diabetes.

With much love to you both

Elizabeth

Vining Centre

23rd June 1974

Dear Ma and Daddy,

I am writing this from Kelu's house in Ife. It is our half term and I have had a very pleasant break - although it's not particularly restful moving about from house to house. It's Jide's birthday party today so Kelu is busy cooking. We made cakes last night and this morning it is chicken and rice in the pots. Her house boy (yet another) is still dim and slow, and Kelu has plenty to say on the subject! She is leaving Ife this Thursday and then flying to London sometime next week with the 3 older children. I have given her our address and telephone number for she hopes that she will be able to get in touch with you. She is even talking of hiring a car and driving to Malvern. That will be fun!

I spent yesterday and Friday in Ibadan with Grace and family. Grace Webster arrived by air in the morning - so she and I went into Ibadan to the shops. She has got an idea that she should do medicine - and is proposing to stay only 3 months - return to UK in September and then start doing A-levels!! Then it will be 7 years before she is qualified. It seems a long time - and it's going to be difficult to explain to the folks at Ado that she is only back for 3 months! But she seems certain that God wants her to try all the doors in the medical direction. I don't know. Maybe she is right. If nothing else, it will get her across the age of 40 feeling that she was doing something useful! I shall miss her out here - everyone seems to be leaving Nigeria - or going to the Northern region.

One of our women disgraced herself last week. She beat her 7-year-old daughter with a stick and lashed her over the forehead so that there were marks on it. The next morning there was a nurse in the school, and she sent for the mother - who then further disgraced the Vining Centre by not even being repentant!! So, she had to 'scrub' on Thursday. She comes from somewhere down in the creeks near Okitipupa, and I should think they make them tough down there. She has certainly got a lot to learn about being a pastor's wife.

It is now 2pm. We went to the Methodist Church - 10.15 till 12. Then we have been cooking since. It is ready - but the visitors who are supposed to come for lunch haven't arrived. Two girls who are photographers have been sitting waiting since 12.30. Jide is lying on the floor reading a Babar book.

Have I commented on the house in Malvern link? It sounds OK - especially if you can see the hills from my bedroom - and it has a private garden. It is true that we should probably be happier with a little more space than the bungalow which you saw.

I am doing my Monday lectures to the men on 'Israel' now. I have done one about the "people of Israel" in the Bible - Promised Land etc. Now I want to do something about Judaism and about persecutions of the Jews and Zionism and the setting up of the State of Israel - leading up to the Middle East war situation.

Letter finishes here see explanation in next letter.

Vining Centre
24th June 1974

Dear Ma and Daddy,

I am a clot! I wrote a whole letter to you when I was at Kelu's yesterday - and then I left it lying in her sitting room - not quite finished. She may see it and send it to you. She is leaving Ife this coming Thursday and going to fly to London next week with the 3 older children. She talks of phoning you or coming to see you in Malvern. It will be nice for you to meet the children again.

I spent Thursday and Friday in Ibadan staying with Grace. We went to the University on Friday afternoon to watch some tribal dancing put on in the School of African Studies - but unfortunately at 5pm it rained and drenched all the seats that were outside. Then the rain stopped, and the seats were wiped. We all took our seats and watched the dancing for about 5 minutes. Then it rained again harder than before, and the event was declared 'a wash out'.

Grace Webster arrived in Ibadan on Saturday morning. She has a great idea that she is going to try to do medicine. She has just come back but proposes to return to the UK in September to embark on A-levels. It is going to be difficult to explain to them at Ado that she will only be staying for less than 3 months!

I am at Inga's today and have spent most of the morning reading about Israel. I am doing a series of talks to our men students on the background to the Israeli-Arab conflict in the Middle East. There is certainly plenty to read. Now the problem is sorting out the information so that our students can understand the main points.

I enjoy my Monday lectures, but I seem to have got in a bit of a rut with the women's classes. It is only a one-year course, so I am already repeating lessons that I have done in 1972 and 1973. It is easy to repeat - but rather dull.

Tuesday: Back in Akure. Sheila has a streaming cold, so she has gone to bed. It was good to get back to my little house after being away for the weekend. It is good to have a change of scene - but good to be home again, and to find your regular letter waiting.

Yes, I should think Iona in 1975 will be fine. I should be home early July - end of September as before. Maybe August for holidays.

I am so glad that the Family Service seems to be cottoning on. That's great. What a pity that May and Noel can't be a bit more positive in their opinions and statements. I am glad they're not here!

With much love to you both

Elizabeth

Vining Centre

29th June 1974

Dear Ma and Daddy,

Thank you, Daddy, for your letter this week. I am so glad that your Family Services are proving to be popular. That's very encouraging isn't it. We had a very good Communion Service this morning when Cornelius talked about 'Healing' in the Anglican Church and how Christ still has the power to heal.

Inga is here this week - so that's very nice. She came yesterday and we went for a picnic on the rocks at Agric and then we walked all-round the place. It is especially good there because the land is divided into fields, as at home, and there are shady lanes to walk along between the fields.

In the evening she wanted to phone home to speak to Joseph in Newcastle who has just finished his exams. I think we managed the whole operation in about 40 mins. It is like magic!! We have an old St. Monica's girl working in the International Telephone Exchange in Lagos - so it is good. Sandra phoned to Northern Ireland on Friday evening and talked to all her family. Her sister was married yesterday. So, I may try it again sometime. It is especially good if I can sit in my sitting room here and speak to you at home.

I discovered that my car was going on only 3 cylinders. I wondered why it had no power. Now it is fine. Rather the same thing happened to me this week. Tuesday - Thursday were 3-cylinder days. Then I came to life again on Friday. I don't know whether I had underground malaria or what. Anyway, now I am fine.

I am glad that you enjoyed Dudley Zoo. It sounds as though you had a very good outing.

We are preparing to say goodbye to Mike and Hilary and Sheila and the Kohlis. I hope to have a barbecue for the V.S.O. crew on Friday - and some of their friends. Then we may have another farewell party to say goodbye to Sheila. She is going on 3 months leave. Her parents live next door to the Church where Derek Blundell is now in Brixham or Tulse Hill.

Inga and I are going to Mrs. Kohli's for lunch today. I think she has invited some other Indian friends so it will be interesting to meet some new people. Apparently, there is a new Water Engineer in Akure - a man and his wife - from Ceylon - now called Sri Lanka. I shall be interested to meet them.

I hope to go to Oshogbo on Wednesday with Hilary and Jo (V.S.O.'s) to buy the cloth for Ruth - and then I will send it with Sheila. 70 miles is quite a way to go for a few pieces of cloth, but Jo hasn't been to Oshogbo and is very keen, so I thought we should go while we have the chance.

Bother! Isn't that just like it. We can phone England from my home - but I just thought I would ring Grace Webster .... no chance .... Ado line is bad!! I hear today from one of the Indians in Ondo that there has been a lot of upset at Ile Abiye and that the new doctor and his wife from India have left there for the time being and gone to Wesley Guild. I was wanting to commiserate with Grace, because I am sure that she knew nothing about it when she arrived last week.

We had a lovely Indian lunch. Now it is raining again. It is cold enough for a sweater and I am wondering about tights!

With much love to you both

Elizabeth

Vining Centre
5th July 1974

Dear Ma and Daddy,

Thank you, Daddy, for your letter this week. We have made some progress with 'Our Ebun' at last. Sheila has been working hard to persuade Dr. Sijuade to write a letter to the Aro Mental Hospital where a friend of his is a psychiatrist. He wrote the letter - so yesterday Sheila took Ebun out of the Jehovah's Witness 'home' at 6am - drove with Hilary and one of our women - to Abeokuta - got her admitted and drove back! It is 170 miles to Abeokuta from Akure, so it was quite a marathon. Anyway, we hope she may improve with some proper treatment - but we will still have to face the problem of what she should do when she is discharged and where she should go.

In the meantime, I was here entertaining Shelagh Jebb who was down from Ado - and Sandra and Eugene (the Chinese V.S.O.). They came to lunch, but it rained all afternoon and early evening - so they stayed on to tea and supper and then we played scrabble in the evening.

On Friday Sandra and I arranged a barbecue supper for Hilary and Mike who are leaving. It was very enjoyable. We were 8, and we sat out on my verandah on low stools roasting first corn and then meat on skewers on charcoal braziers. The cooking and the eating occupied most of the evening.

On Wednesday I took Hilary and Jo (V.S.O.'s) to Oshogbo to see the shrines. Did we go there? The section which they are modelling in clay now is growing every time you go - they have now done an incredibly intricate 'elephant' figure. After looking at the shrines we went to see the Evans - and then to buy cloth for Ruth (that was my main reason for going) - but there were only 2 pieces for sale and Jo and Hilary bought them before I realised that that was all - anyway I wanted 4 pieces. So, I got <u>none</u>!! However, I have now asked Cornelius to see what he can do - he has gone to Oshogbo this weekend. I want to send it with Sheila who goes on leave a week from today. Maybe if she goes to stay with Ruth Martin sometime, she may come over and see you. I would like you to meet her. She is a great buddy.

Today Sunday I went to preach at the Salvation Army, I occupied 40 minutes - everything was translated line by line. By the time I was finished with my sermon and saying Hallelujah many times I was quite hoarse!

Ile Abiye is in trouble. Matron and Indian doctors have come to blows and the Manager seems to have managed to mismanage the Accounts. They need a lot of prayer.

With love

Elizabeth

Vining Centre
14th July 1974

Dear Ma and Daddy,

Thank you for letters this week; and for your concern and prayers for our friend Ebun. We shall just have to wait and see what they say in Aro and try to help her when she comes out.

I am glad that you were able to see Bp Martin and Ruth again. Thank you for sending the slides to Ann. I shall look forward to seeing them in due course. It is not long till she comes. I hope that it stops raining before then - both from the point of view of travelling on the roads and so that she may see the sun and enjoy the expected heat of the Tropics. I am now using 3 blankets on my bed. My white cardigan is grubby and doesn't get washed because it always seems to be raining and so it's not good for drying - I am now wearing my blue sweater - and I have started knitting a new cardigan, with a pattern full of holes. Goodness knows when it will be finished.

I look forward to receiving your tape too - and I will send it on to John and Pat. I will find a recorder somewhere, don't worry.

Grace Webster has been here this weekend from Ado. They had a Board of Governors meeting in Ado on Friday and seem to have sorted some of their troubles. The Manager has been asked to go - there had been an inquiry into the Accounts and Management etc. and he had been discovered to have seriously 'mismanaged' the office to his own financial advantage. The Matron was given a warning that if there were any more clashes with the doctor she would also have to depart. So, the doctors are returning tomorrow from Ilesha. Grace feels that she must stay on for a year because of the situation and then think about her proposed medical course. I think she is having doubts about it all, but it certainly seems clear that she should stay at Ado just now.

Sheila has gone today - and Sandra has gone with her to Ibadan for her diabetic check-up. So, I have no close buddies in Akure for the next few days. However, we have exams on Wednesday, Thursday, and Friday so I have plenty to do with preparation for that.

We had a party on Friday evening to say goodbye to Sheila, so I was busy with that. Also, I have been trying to help Sheila write her reports - then Grace came for the weekend as I said and so I am a bit behind with Vining work.

This afternoon I took Grace back up to Ado and came back between 7 and 8 pm - and it poured with rain.

I seem to have got some minor eye infection - so I went to Dr. Kohli the Eye Specialist, and she recommended some drops. So far, they don't seem to have cleared it. It is nothing very alarming - just irritating and a bit of pus in the mornings - but it is annoying. A few of our children had eye troubles this term. Maybe I picked up something from them. Anyway, I will go and see Dr. Kohli again.

I preached the Communion sermon this morning - and talked about God's abundant blessings to us - referring to the multitude of fishes which broke the net and they had to use 2 boats to carry them home.

I also taught our students the chorus – 'Give me oil in my lamp,' and the Hymn 'Lord Jesus Christ' from Youth Praise. I think that they enjoyed them - but they got one note in the second line of 'Lord Jesus Christ' wrong.

All my women are knitting - sweaters or socks so I am required to interpret the pattern and to pick up the stitches often. Some of them have worked hard at it and learnt well. Some are useless.

I am enclosing a cheque for £50 which is to be spent please on something you need when you move into the new house. Maybe it can go towards the cooker - or something else .... or if you like use it for petrol for picnics!

With much love and prayer
Elizabeth

Vining Centre
23rd July 1974

Dear Ma and Daddy,

Thank you for your letter saying that you have sent off tapes and so on with Anne. Sorry to hear about Sailor. If he is so decrepit, might it not be better to have him put down? But I suppose if his kidneys are better, and he is getting fatter you will want to keep him. I am not very surprised that Kelu didn't make it. It was a nice idea.

We have now finished the term - in a bit of a flurry as usual. The two men staff must go to the Ondo Diocesan Synod tomorrow, Wednesday, and we were going to tell the students to go then - I thought! But they went yesterday instead - except for the women who went this morning. I was thoroughly put out because I hadn't got my reports finished - since we only finished our exams on Friday. Also, I have some sort of conjunctivitis in my right eye - not bad, but annoying. Anyway, I went to Dr. Kohli and now have drops and Penicillin eye ointment at night - but she put in that eye drop that makes your pupil become enlarged and so the vision in my right eye is blurred .... and it's not easy getting used to working with one eye. She says she will do it for a week, then see what's what.

It's a bit sickening because I want to read and knit and sew and all these things are tiring. However, I can drive OK - and am going to

Lagos on Friday to meet Anne off the 'plane. Then Myrtle is coming here for a few days with a friend from a Link Parish. Then on August 5th Sandra, Anne and I will be going to the North for 2 weeks.

Did I tell you that the Evans from Oshogbo are moving to Akure? He is to be the Principal Inspector of Education here. So, Daphne and the 3 children will be here in August. Then she will go home for a time anyway.

I have finished my 4 talks on Israel to our men. I think that they found it interesting. Certainly, I found it interesting finding out all the facts. There is an S.C.M. Conference here in the first few days of August. I am billed to talk about "Modern Israel" so I think I could do it - having just read up all about it. It sounds a bit like their Conferences often are - rather unorganised. The S.C.M. are having a project to plant trees near Jane Pelly's school at Kazaire. It will be interesting to go up there and see what they have done - also to see how the 'drought' areas are.

I miss Sheila Davis here, but it is good to have Sandra. We see each other most days. But she is on a policy of late to rise and early to bed .... because of her diabetes. I think she is feeling better this week - but she is easily tired.

I hope all is well with you. I am glad that someone <u>wants</u> the big cupboard!

With much love to you both

Elizabeth

Vining Centre

25th July 1974

Dear Ma and Daddy,

I had your usual newsy epistle on Tuesday. It is always good to hear what you are doing. Our women students went away on Tuesday morning. We had our visitor from Ibadan on Monday - but she didn't stay very long. We all made polite noises - showed her our new building and made a petition for money for furniture.

I had quite an adventurous week after that with doctors. I went to spend the night with Grace at Ado on Tuesday - and then had my Annual Medical at Ile Abiye on Wednesday. The 2 Indian doctors are now back from Ilesha - but the Matron is on leave for a month so it is not tested as to whether they will be able to work together or not. Anyway, they discovered nothing in my various specimens - but

I think that I had a touch of malaria because I stayed in bed most of the day except for the actual medical test and the lab tests.

Then on Thursday I went again to Dr. Kohli about my eye. She had tried different antibiotic eye drops and it hadn't improved so she was a bit doubtful as what to do next. Then she had the bright idea to syringe my tear ducts!! I didn't know you could do such a thing - but after giving cocaine drops presumably to keep the eye still then you poke a thin wire like tube into the tear duct - and the water comes down your throat!!! Rather unpleasant really - but it seems to have done the trick. Dr. Kohli said my duct was blocked and certainly the eye now feels much better. Directly after that I went to the health Office to get a smallpox injection and a cholera jab. So, then I drove to Ibadan with a stiff arm.

Now I am at the Batts in Ibadan - staying here this morning and driving to Lagos this afternoon - to meet Anne off the plane tonight. I hope to spend the evening at Shola's house in Ikeja. I feel a bit groggy this morning - I think it is just a reaction to the cholera jab. I hope to go by Abeokuta and see what has happened to Ebun in the mental hospital. I hope to goodness they don't want to discharge her - or I shall be in the soup.

Saturday a.m. 27th July:

I met Anne last night - very good to get your letter and super box of chocs. Anne hasn't opened her case yet, so I haven't seen what else she has brought. They confiscated her 3 apples at the Airport! Her plane was 2 hours late - so it didn't arrive till after 12 midnight. We arrived here at the Marina at 2am! It is cool so I don't think that we shall be too exhausted. I was fortunate to have Shola at Ikeja last night because I spent the evening with her - and went back there for coffee when I discovered that the plane was late.

All is well here - looking forward to a month's holiday and travel!! The road to Ibadan is closed so you must go a longer way round. I saw Ebun yesterday. She is not discharged yet - but responding to treatment.

With much love

Elizabeth

P.S. There has been an interesting development after the death of the Deji at the end of December 1973. The Akure people have not yet settled who should be the new Deji, so a 'Regent' has been appointed and they have kept strictly to tradition and chosen the first daughter of the Deji. This is a girl of about 18, called Busola. She is in the Lower VIth in the International School, Ibadan, but she has been removed from school and installed in Akure. She is called 'Kabiyesi' (Yoruba for Your Majesty), and everyone prostrates before her, as they would to her father. She is dressed completely in men's clothes and with the aid of advisers she takes quite a lot of decisions about town problems.

On occasions Busola is dressed in a coral beaded crown with feathers poking out of the top, and she is driven through the town in a Mercedes with a trumpeter trumpeting out of the window. On very special occasions she is carried in a kind of open cart, decorated with brightly coloured cloths, with a giant umbrella twirling above her head. It is quite an experience for a schoolgirl! Her mother, the Eyesorun, is just hoping and praying that the Chiefs in the town will get on with choosing the new Deji so that Busola can get on with her H.S.C. (A-level) exams.

Vining Centre
4th August 1974

Dear Ma and Daddy,

This is a bumper week. I have had the whole family in Akure! We listened to your tape with both of you on it as well as Ruth and Trevor and Stuart and Jutka's Highbury Special. We have enjoyed that particularly here because it brings back so many bits and pieces of English life - Anne and Sandra enjoyed it and then Myrtle as well - she is here for the weekend. I have added a little bit - you didn't leave me much room! I just about had time to say hello.

Then I also want to thank you for all the lovely presents that you sent with Anne. We didn't unpack her suitcase until we got up here. The 2 dresses fit exactly, and I have worn them already. I have also played the records and enjoyed them immensely. The pants are also most welcome.

This weekend Myrtle is here with a friend teaching at Norwich T.T.C. who was taught by Faith Dew etc.!!! Yesterday we went to Ado Ekiti and saw Shelagh Jebb and Grace - and Mary Hill - Geoffrey's daughter who is at Ile Abiye for a month. Anne and Barbara were busy taking slides of all the local sights. I have told

Anne that you would welcome her for a weekend so that she can show her slides of her visit. She has taken plenty.

Anne is enjoying herself in Akure I think. We went to the Eyesorun's new house last night and she gave us a delicious supper. It was partly a house-warming party, partly to say goodbye to the Kohli's, and partly to welcome Dr. Salama and his wife back to Akure. They arrived here on Wednesday. She is a sweet person - very neat, with beautiful big brown eyes and an attractive soft speaking voice. We took her to the town on Friday morning and went all together to visit the palace. There we were greeted by the regent - Busola. She is a poppet and it's all a bit of a hoot. Her father's old wives come and greet her as though she was their husband - kneel, heads on floor and thank her for providing for their welfare. They hope that a new Deji will be installed by the end of August so that she will be free. They have a place for her to do A-levels at St. Michael's Limpsfield!!

Today we went to the Leper Settlement and the Agric in the afternoon. The folk at the Leper Settlement gave us a tremendous welcome, and our photographers were in great demand. Then this evening we showed the filmstrip 'With love to Lagos' to an S.C.M. group - meeting for a bible study conference at Fiwasaiye. There are only about a dozen youngsters at the Conference, but we told them about the Leper Settlement and about Myrtle's school. They seemed very interested.

Journey to the North with Anne Harris

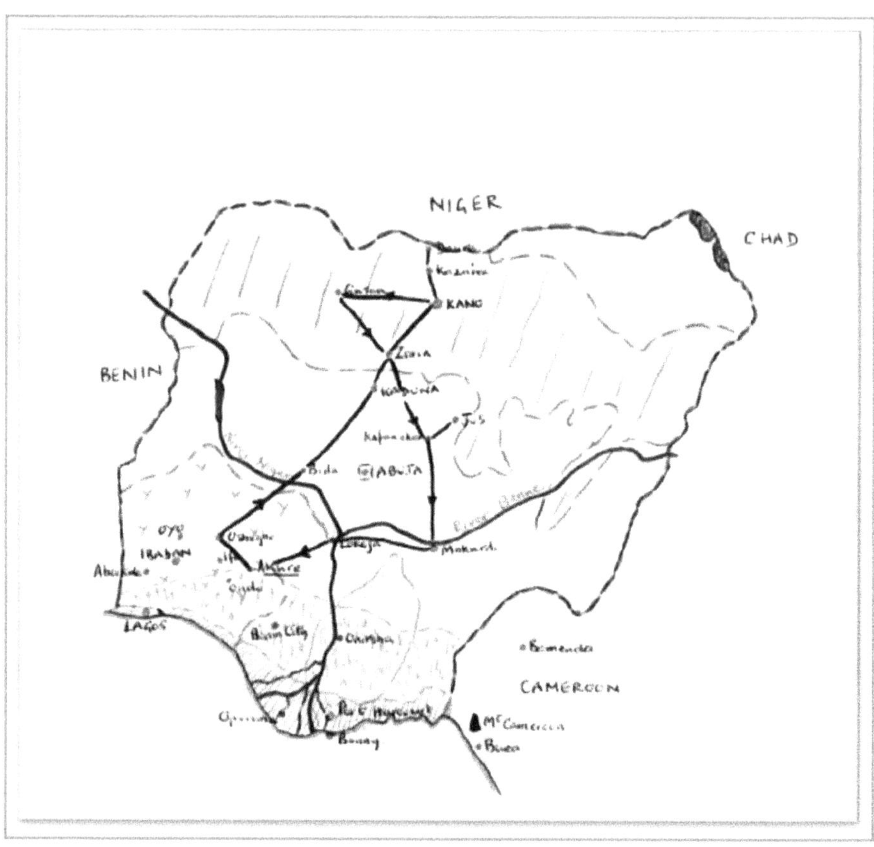

Tomorrow we are travelling off to the North - going Bida - Kaduna (Atkinsons) - Kazaire (Jane Pelly) - Kano (Bill Palmer and wife) - Gusau (Richard! and his family) - Zaria (Marguerite Batchelor) - Kafanchan (Jacky Henry) - Makurdi - Akabe near Lokoja – (Skiddy's friends) - Akure on 19th. We hope!! There is a petrol shortage so we may get held up en route. But I expect it will turn out OK.

Wednesday a.m. in Kaduna

Dear Ma and Daddy,

In bed (7am) at the Atkinson's - they have orange sheets! Mike is not here. He is in Kano on a course, but Rhona and the children are here, and it has been super to meet again and catch up on news. Mike was at Leicester in the Education Department and then I used to stay with them at Igbobi College, Lagos.

We have done 2 long days of driving but managed to see the shrine at Oshogbo and the craft workers in Bida en route. The glass blowing was new to me and quite incredible. They have a clay furnace in the middle of the hut and long metal sticks with melting glass at the end which they fashion into beads or bracelets etc. One boy works the bellows all the time so there is a beating, thumping noise going on.

We met the Bida brand of mosquitoes and the Bida heat last night - but today we are enjoying Kaduna cool - and the Atkinson's have the most superb house with a great big garden - VERY British Council! .... but very nice.

We go to Jane today - so I thought that I would post this in Kano.

With much love to you all

Elizabeth

9th August 1974

Dear Ma and Daddy,

We are now at Jane Pelly's at Kazaire. Today we went to Daura, which if you look at your map is on the border of Niger - almost! Both Daura and Kazaire are very ‘desert-like' towns - rather biblical in atmosphere with donkeys used everywhere for carrying the loads and women drawing water out of wells, and even water holes in the dry sand and then carrying the pots home on their heads. The flies are horrible - they are all about - and get on everything - hands, legs, face etc. - very nasty. Then during the 2 days that we have been here it has been blazing hot - but just now there is a thundery storm, and it is raining so everything should be a bit cooler tonight.

The rains this year have been good so there are crops of millet and guinea corn everywhere - but the soil is very sandy, and you can see that without rain it's a dead loss.

We haven't seen any camels yet - disappointing! We are going to Kano tomorrow so maybe we shall be lucky there.

Jane has got a great open "site" on which to build her school. She has got a big job in hand. I think you could survive here if you got rigged up with air conditioning, plenty of ice in the fridge and wiring on the windows to keep the flies out. Now there is an electric generator in the town which goes from 6pm to 6am and only sometimes in the afternoon. This is a bit sickening if it is baking hot in the afternoon and you can't have the fan on.

Kazaire is a very interesting town and today we went to the market - which was fascinating. It was quite different from the market in Akure. Jane took us to visit the Emir of Kazaire - a big fat man with a pink turban - and a white robe. He let us look round the old palace - thick, thick walls and dark passages inside with the 3 wives and 10 concubines of the previous Emir in their quarters at the back. In one dark passage there were hundreds of bats hanging in the roof.

Tomorrow we are going to Kano, and then on Sunday we shall go to see Richard and his family in Gusau. It will be interesting to meet his wife and children and to see how they are coping with life in the North. Then we go on to Zaria, and Jacky Henry at Kafanchan.

I shall look forward to hearing your news when I return to Akure.

With much love

Elizabeth

18th August 1974

Dear Ma and Daddy,

I am again at Akabe staying with Canon and Mrs. Kato. These are the people who I stayed with when I came with Ruth in January. I thought that it would be a nice place to bring Anne and Sandra to experience a Nigerian clergyman's home and to go to a village Church Service. At the same time, it is good to have a rest day at the end of our travels. It has been a long trip with a lot of driving - but it has been well worthwhile. I think that we have seen as much of Nigeria as would be possible within 2 weeks.

We were at Kafanchan on Tuesday and Wednesday staying with Jacky Henry. Barbara Norrice (who was taught by Faith Dew) was staying with her, so we were quite a full house. It poured with rain during the night while we were there - and on the following morning so that turned the streets of Kafanchan into mud. I had a slow puncture, so I was very anxious to get to the mechanic to get it fixed before it went completely flat, and we had to change it in 6" of mud. In fact, all was well, the mechanic fixed it overnight and we haven't had any trouble since. In the afternoon Jacky took us to a village market in the Land Rover. It was along a laterite road which was muddy, and it was a very 'village' market - with Fulani women selling milk and butter and most of the produce lying higgle di piggly di on the ground with women squatting all about. There were very few market stalls.

Then we went to a village house with Jacky, to visit one of the women leaders in her compound. We sat in a tiny house on stools and 4 women came in and welcomed us with a song. Afterwards we went back to Kafanchan and those in the back of the Land Rover took interesting photos such as a boy carrying a pig home from the market over his shoulders!

On Thursday we went on to Jos. It is a great blessing that now all the main roads in the North are tarmacked so there is no worry about travelling in the wet season. The only thing is that the distances are still long. We had a very enjoyable 24 hours in Jos. The plateau country is very beautiful. We found Myrtle and Gwen and their niece Carol having a picnic in the hills behind Jos. It was incredible how we came across them. We knew vaguely where they were staying and went in that direction. Then we explored up a steep winding road among the rocks after we had a picnic lunch - and who should we see but Myrtle and Co. relaxing after their picnic! So, we went back to their very nice Lutheran Guest House and had tea with them there.

Then we went on and stayed the night with Jane Sutton who used to be the Scripture Union travelling secretary in the West. She is working with S.U.M. in Jos and has a lovely house and beautiful garden (Sutton's Seeds!). She has a dog, a cat, a parrot, 2 rabbits and a potto!! The latter sleeps in the daytime and lives in the bathroom at night. It is rather like a bear with big round eyes and a stubby tail. It has very human looking hands and feet and loves to swing on the rail to hold the clothes in the cupboard and then peep at you from behind the curtain. Jane's work with the S.U.M. will finish this year and then she may take on the job as State Horticulturist for Benne-Plateau State. This will suit her down to the ground I should think, and she will still have time to be involved with Christian work among students.

After Jos we travelled down to Makurdi and stayed a night in the house of a V.S.O. at the Government school there. Then the next day we continued to Akabe and spent Saturday and Sunday night with Canon and Mrs. Kato. They were very kind to us and looked after us beautifully. The church women came and presented us with a mat each. It was a lovely ending to our holiday. Then on Monday morning we took the ferry over the River Niger to Lokoja and reached Akure by 3.30 in the afternoon.

When I got home, I received 3 letters with news from home - and some other post. So, it was good to be back too. I am sorry to hear that Daddy must have 2 trusses to keep his hernia in. What a pest for him. I am sure that it is good that you are retiring - and I am glad to hear that Stuart can come and help with the move. I would suggest that you would be best to 'let go' of the Family Service and retire properly - although it seems hard to do so when you are so nearby.

I wonder if Jumoke Lajubutu - now Daramola, has written to you to ask if she and her husband can stay with you? If she does- please let her come and entertain her free of any charges and send me the bill if necessary. Richard and his wife entertained us so well in Gusau - and in fact brought a lot of extra tinned foods etc. that we didn't eat in the short time that we stayed there. They had another family staying with them, so they organised us to have a whole house where we cooked our own food. Then in the evening they took us out to the 'club' in Gusau - a nice country type club where we enjoyed a game of table tennis together. One of Richard's closest friends had just been posted to Oyemekun Grammar School, the Anglican boys' school here in Akure. I have not seen him yet. He was the fellow whose wedding I went to in the registry office in Oshogbo.

Then today I had a note from John Fabuyi who used to be at Adeyemi College - you remember his wife gave us snails for supper! He has just been made Sole Administrator for the State School's board of Akure/Akoko/and Owo divisions. That oversees the teachers etc. in the Primary Schools around. So that's rather a hoot.

I am going with Anne to Ibadan tomorrow and then Lagos - and hope to bring Grace back to Akure with me on Sunday or Monday. I will send this letter with Anne to post it for then it will get to you as quickly as if I had posted it here earlier this week.

With much love to you both. Anne is bringing you 2 pouffes - very suitable for retirement, I think. I hope they will do in the new house. She is also bringing one piece of cloth for Ruth's curtains -

and a small Christmas present for Ruth and Trevor and Stuart and Jutka. I have labelled them so that I think it will be clear. Perhaps you could keep them and distribute at Christmas time. Then I have also given the New Zealand tape to return it to you. She would like to come and show you her slides sometime in October. So, you will see that I am not fading away! - nor am I 15 stone!

My knitting is getting on. I have finished the back and started one front - but progress has not been very rapid on our holiday. Maybe I shall have time to sit down and knit when Grace is here.

With my love

Elizabeth

Vining Centre
26th August 1974

Dear Ma and Daddy,

By the time that you get this letter you will have retired! I hope that the moving of house is not too exhausting and that you can soon get your feet up on the pouffes that I sent with Anne. I shall be thinking of you especially next weekend when Daddy gives his farewell sermons at Christ Church and St. Mary's.

I took Anne to Lagos on Friday. We spent the evening with Sola and enjoyed her twins and the baby. Then on Saturday morning I returned to Ibadan and called at Abeokuta on the way to find out what has happened to Ebun. There I learnt that she has been 'discharged'! and was waiting for someone to come and pick her up. I couldn't take her then because I had a full carload from Ibadan, so I said that I would go and fetch her next Monday. That means that we have a week in which to decide what we should do with her at this end.

So, then I came on to Ibadan and stayed the night with Grace - and brought her and the 3 children on Sunday to Ondo and then leaving the children there I came on to Akure with Grace. She is wanting a good rest, so she is going to stay until Friday with me.

Dr. Kohlis' go this week - I think on Wednesday - so I am going to have their cat. It is a lovely fluffy gingery cat - rather elite! I hope it remains that way in my house.

Dr. Salama's wife Marcelle has gone back to Cairo today. He is going to Edinburgh to work for the F.R.C.S. - probably leaving next week. I shall miss them all very much. But Gordon Evans is now here - and there are bound to be new people coming to the hospital.

Tokunbo had the naming ceremony for his new baby girl yesterday - so his wife is preparing pounded yam for our lunch today. Then we shall have our share in the celebrations.

When do you move? When shall I start writing to 64, Church Road? Grace sends her love to you. You wouldn't recognise her children now because they are all so big. Anne has taken photos of everything and everyone - so you will have a real jamboree when she brings them to show you.

With much love
Elizabeth

Vining Centre
31st August 1974

Dear Ma and Daddy,

I am thinking of you today as you give the farewell sermons in St. Mary's and Christ Church. It will not be easy to say goodbye to so many friends, but I am sure that God will give you both the strength, and you will know what best to say to help people. It is good that you will not be moving too far away so that you can still enjoy visiting and being visited by the many friends you have made in Malvern in the last 3 years.

I am sorry to hear that you have mislaid the list of addresses for the duplicated letter. No, I don't have a duplicate - but I can copy most of them out of my address book. Let me know if you don't find it. Don't worry anyway. I sent a copy to C.M.S. Deputations department (I think!) and so they will send it to the Link Parishes. Other friends can wait till you have moved house comfortably!

Sister Martinian at St. Louis Noviciate here in Akure has agreed to have Ebun for the first 2 weeks after her discharge from Abeokuta so that's a great help. She has about 8 Nigerian sisters there in training and they will help Ebun - and while she is there, we can get a better idea of how she is responding to treatment and so decide how best to help her next. She may be well enough to help in the school kitchen at Fiwasaiye. We shall have to see. I am going to Abeokuta tomorrow to collect Ebun. Sandra is coming with me to Ibadan; but I may leave her there to go and see her doctor and go down to Abeokuta myself.

I am sorry to hear that Dahosa has left home. I haven't seen Folarin since he first came to U.I. Grace said that she would try to look him up sometime in the University. She was here until Friday morning, and we enjoyed a week of peace and quiet together. I think I had a touch of malaria at the beginning of the week and Grace was very tired, so we did a lot of sleeping.

The Kohli's left on Wednesday morning - and now I have their cat. She spends most of the time sitting and sleeping inside my cupboard and comes out to look beautiful every now and then. On Thursday Grace and I and Sandra went up to Idanre and had a very pleasant lunch with the Akinbadewa's. The road is terrible to get there but I was very glad that we made the effort. The children are much more settled now and behave quietly and politely. The Akinbadewa's are proposing to move into their new house in the next few weeks - even though the floors are not yet cemented! I think that it will be chaos.

I am sorry to hear that Harvey Cantrell has died. Mamie will have a lot of adjusting to do to continue living on her own. I have tried to write to her - but I am not very good at sympathy letters.

With much love to you both

Elizabeth

Vining Centre

9th September 1974

Dear Ma and Daddy,

I am looking forward to hearing how the move went and how you are settling into your new house. I hope all is well. I am sure that Stuart was a great help in getting things organised.

I forget whether I wrote last Sunday or on Tuesday? i.e., before fetching Ebun at Abeokuta, or after? On Sunday night we had a puncture at Grace's house and discovered that Sheila had no proper tools in her car. So, we had to go begging around Bodija about 9pm at night asking people if they could loan us a wheel spanner. Then we went on and slept the night with a clergyman and his wife - the Adebamiwas who are now living in that great mighty house beside the almighty church at St. Peters - Aremo where we went to greet Archdeacon Banjo.

On Monday morning, after getting the puncture mended, I went to St. Louis Convent to meet Sister Martinian. Then we went together to Abeokuta to fetch Ebun, and to visit Vero who is the girl who the St. Louis' sisters here in Akure picked off the road in much the same way as we collected Ebun. Ebun seems to have responded to treatment remarkably quickly. Vero has been much slower and seemed to be in a daze. Anyway, we brought Ebun back to Akure and the sisters at the Noviciate have been looking after her. She is quite transformed from before. She is clean and tidy - has her room very neat - she can use the toilet - and wants to help with sweeping and cooking etc. She is still on drugs, her hands are a bit shaky at times, and she sleeps a lot. But it is all very encouraging - but makes you think about the tragedy of others in this country who are mentally sick and turned out of their homes and just exist on the roadsides. They are talking of having psychiatric units in the local hospitals. It will be grand if they can do so, but I should think that it will be some time to come.

I have found it a bit lonely this week here on the compound by myself (except that Cornelius and Mama and so on are around) - Sandra is busy at Fiwasaiye preparing for the beginning of the new term. However, I have got some good sorting out of letters and so on done and have almost finished a dress I was making - and started reading "Cancer Ward". I was trying to listen to the Prom on Wednesday evening, but I think there must have been a thunderstorm in the way. Anyway, I turned it off - and then Doug Evans came. He had also been listening to the Prom and turned it off because of the same atmospherics.

There are 2 new Canadian volunteers who have just come to Akure - Bob and Dennis. Bob is married and his wife is in Ilesha where he has been up till now. They seem nice boys. Dennis is wanting to play tennis so that's good. We all met together at Sandra's on Saturday evening, and I have invited them here on Tuesday.

Dr. Salama has been here over the weekend, so I went there on Saturday afternoon and again on Sunday to try to help him to get on with his packing up. He has masses of papers and letters to sort out - and finds it very difficult to get down to it. Anyway, I think we made some progress even if it was only emptying drawers and transferring the muddle to the surface! He is off today to Lagos to finish his money transactions. Then he will be going to Edinburgh next Monday or Tuesday. I have given him Auntie Kath's address, and

Auntie Marjorie's in case they can help him and his friend Dr. Hanna with any bright ideas of places to stay.

I am glad that Jumoke phoned you, I hope that she may be able to come to Malvern sometime. I think that I said before - if she does come - please do not ask her to pay for hospitality - because Richard was so over-generous to us when we went to the North. I would be most embarrassed if we didn't reciprocate in the same way, in her case.

You seem to have had a good concert while cleaning up. I had Paganini's Violin Concerto, 100 best tunes and the Sound of King's College Cambridge when I was tidying the other day. It certainly makes the whole business much more enjoyable.

Guess what!! I had a letter from Di this week - and she is going to be married in October. She sounds very happy about it. She will probably move to live in Maidstone. He is in the same office as she is and is called David Aspinall. He was married before, but it didn't work out happily and he has been divorced for some time. Anyway, I am very happy for Di. I think she will make him a very good wife because she is steadily always the same.

I also heard from Kelu. They are planning to return to Nigeria at the end of September.

With much love to you both

Elizabeth.

Vining Centre

15th September 1974

Dear Ma and Daddy,

I hope that you will have received my annual letter copy. I sent it yesterday with Dr. Salama. At last - and in a great flurry, he has left Akure, and gone off to Edinburgh to do post-graduate work. I gave him our home address in case he is ever in the Midlands - but I doubt it - it is a long way from Edinburgh. I spent most of yesterday trying to help him with the final clear up of his house.

Today I am going, with Ebun to Ibadan and then Abeokuta. I hope all goes well. Plans are moving ahead that she should move over to Fiwasaiye and help there with washing plates etc. in the kitchen. I hope that all works out well. Everything rather depends on the co-operation of the Matron.

I have had a quiet week and have been reading "Cancer Ward" and finishing another stole and doing some more knitting. I am glad that you like the pouffes and that the move was OK. You will find it quite difficult to adjust to being "retired", but it is nice that you are near enough to your friends in Malvern to be able to have them round to visit. The Church people were very generous to give you a percolator and a pen and £63 plus flowers etc. and other cheques.

There are 2 weeks left of our holidays and I have said that I will go to Fiwasaiye and help with their B.K. in Form I during this 2nd week. In fact, I shall have plenty to do here as the time moves towards the beginning of term.

I am to go to Ado next Sunday - to take the evening service there. So, I will have the chance to see Grace and Shelagh and find out how they are. Sheila Davis returns around October 12th, I think. It will be good to have her back. Her address is 55, Trinity Rise, London. SW2 2QP - but I can't think of anything that I am needing here now.

Sandra is coming round for lunch. Did I tell you that we have 2 new C.V.S.O. boys in town now? But I miss the Kohli's and Salama's.

With much love and prayers

Elizabeth.

Vining Centre

22nd September 1974

Dear Ma and Daddy,

No news from you since Daddy's letter of September. I expect that you are enjoying settling into the new abode. I had a letter from Ruth this week and she said that there had been some very blustery weather with quite a lot of high winds and storms. Maybe you are sheltered by the Malvern Hills. Ruth also said that she met the new Vicar for the Priory - and that it is Bill and Elizabeth Richards from Nairobi. That's very interesting - I met them at Foxbury in 1971 - a very lively young couple. I should think they will do well at the Priory

I went to Aro last Monday with Ebun - I think I may have told you that. She is still at the Noviciate, but we have brought her a mattress and she may move over to Fiwasaiye this week.

I taught some lessons in B.K. in Fiwasaiye on Tuesday and Wednesday and enjoyed it very much. I like teaching Class I. Then on Tuesday evening I had a very itchy leg which I felt was like the filaria I had last year so I went and discussed it with Sijuade, and the fact that my eye's still irritated. He suggested that I went to Oshogbo about the eyes and Ilesha for a blood test for the ?filaria. This I did on Friday in record time. I left Akure about 7.30am - reached Oshogbo 9.30. Saw the Eye Specialist - went to Ilesha by 10.45 saw Doctor, had lab test, got results and returned to Akure before 1pm. The results of these efforts is that I am advised to go to Ibadan and get my spectacles changed and although the blood test was inconclusive, I was advised to take Banocide for 2 weeks. Now, of course, the itching has gone off!!!

On Thursday we interviewed new students for Vining 1975 and I gave them a dictation which I then had to mark - not so easy because some of them made 50 - 60 mistakes.

On Saturday Sandra and I came to Ado. Sandra wanted a stool test to prove that worms that she had were no longer. We stopped in Ikerre en route and met a new V.S.O. there called Roy. He had nasty pink feet - allergic rash .... so, we picked him up in the car and brought him to Ado too. Then we came here and had a picnic in Shelagh Jebb's house and went on in the afternoon to Ode Ekiti which is where the Epton's and the Hicks live (we all spent Christmas together here in Ado). We had a very pleasant evening in Ode - and stayed the night.

Sue Hicks is expecting her first baby this week and she is going to come here to Ile Abiye to have it. No electricity or running water in Ode. It will not be all picnic with a newly born baby.

This morning Sandra and I came back to Ado and had lunch with Shelagh Jebb. Then Sandra went back to Akure, and I stayed on to give the talk at the evening service. They have been having a 'Mission' with a lot of high-powered speakers all this last week - so I was afraid I would be a bit of a letdown. I talked about Ebun .... and I think that they all 'felt' for her and will join us in prayer.

Tomorrow I am going to Ibadan - I will get my eyes tested and do some Vining Centre shopping - and probably return to Akure on Wednesday. Term begins on Friday - so I will not be jobless anymore.

With much love to you both

Elizabeth

Vining Centre
29th September 1974

Dear Ma and Daddy,

Your long screed from Harpenden came this week - so I feel up to date with your news. By now you will be back in Malvern Link and glad that you like the pouffes. What is your phone number? If ever I want to use it. Yes, I think if you take a small photo and send the rest to me - and the film too. If it's before October 10th you could send it to Miss Sheila Davis, 55 Trinity Rise, Tulse Hill, London. SW2 2QP. She is coming back sometime between 10th - 15th October.

We moved Ebun to Fiwasaiye on Friday and she had a hero's welcome from the schoolgirls. She is sleeping with one of the cooks. The only snag is that so far (only Saturday and Sunday) she hasn't offered to do anything. We hope that she will do some work like sweeping or washing plates in the kitchen. She seems rather happy just to sleep and eat! Maybe she was a bit spoilt at the Noviciate. But we don't feel that it is good for her progress if she doesn't do anything useful. However, it is good that the Matron there has accepted her and is ready to help her.

I forget exactly where I got to in the saga about my eyes and the filaria last week. On Monday I went to Ibadan and got new specs in U.T.C. The optician there is a Ghanaian who has just come to Ibadan after working for 15 years or so in Hull in Yorkshire. He was very talkative - all about getting his children admitted into a school in Nigeria. I should think he talked for 30 minutes before he did anything about the eyes!! The specs cost N42 which was a bit steep. They insisted that my old frames were <u>too</u> old for new lenses and then the new lenses are thicker and according to the technician there the lightweight frames would fall down my nose so there wasn't much choice in the end. The result is that my eyes feel better overall, but it has taken some time to get used to the new lenses - especially for reading. I seem to have become immune to any effects of Banocide - and I am taking 6 a day now without any ill-effects.

Term started on Friday evening. The students are back and so there is suddenly plenty to do. Today our Morning Communion Service started at 9am and ended around 11am!! Then Sandra and I went to Ado for lunch - specially to greet Sue Hicks from Ode whose baby arrived on Thursday night. They haven't given him a name yet. The nurses call him Hick-y-Hicks because he seems to hiccough a lot! After returning I went to the Leper Settlement for the usual 1st Sunday open air service.

I hope that you get the copy of my annual letter. Dr. Salama took it to post it in London on his way to Edinburgh. I think he will remember to post it.

I am reading a very interesting historical novel about Mozart. It is called 'Sacred or Profane' and is by David Weiss. It gives a very clear picture of Mozart's father taking the small prodigy round to play to all the Kings and Queens of Europe - so far, I haven't got past age 12.

I was interested to hear that you met Skiddy at St Julian's She wrote and told me! - and said that you wore your red dress Ma!

How are Ruth and Trevor? I haven't heard from them for a long time. I must write. Did they get the cloth that I sent via Ann, or Sheila I wonder...?

I hope all goes well with Dad's exam. I see the election is on October 10th.

With much love

Elizabeth

Vining Centre
5th October 1974

Dear Ma and Daddy,

Thank you for your letter this week Daddy and your thoughts about loneliness. I am glad that you are enjoying 'Windows of Heaven' I have always found it most helpful and inspiring. I have not been lonely this past week - because term has started, so there is plenty to do. I am still taking Banocide - and I am sure it makes me forgetful, and woolly headed but it doesn't make me feel physically sick. But maybe it weakens your resistance because yesterday I came out with a streaming cold, and I spent half the day in bed.

Tuesday was Independence Day and therefore a Public Holiday. We all went to the local stadium and watched the school children - and students - and soldiers - and army marching round. It was all very orderly and well organised. General Gowon made a speech over the radio about the plans for the country. He says that it will not be possible to return to civilian rule in 1976, because the country is not ready. He also says that they are going to modernise the Army and double the Police Force. The country is fortunate to have oil and so plenty of money - this means a great potential for real 'development'. We just pray that the benefits filter down to the ordinary man in the street and don't get deposited in Swiss banks. At present, the ordinary fellow is only seeing rising prices in the market.

Sandra and Dennis and Bob and I went for a picnic lunch on Tuesday - to the Agric Rocks.

Doug Evans and Sandra came last night, and we had supper together. Then around 10.30pm Joan Steward from Owo came through en route back to Owo. She has just returned from leave. Sheila comes next week Monday.

Ebun is still at Fiwasaiye. I went with 2 of our women to visit her on Tuesday afternoon. She is fit and well and likes to 'play' with the girls in the dormitories. She seems to have made a few friends among them and has got her hair tied etc. The only snag is that we thought that she could do some work in the school kitchen with the cooks there. They have accepted her very well BUT she doesn't seem anxious to work and now says that she will not work till Miss Davis comes back. But it would be a lot better for her progress if she joined the other women in some of the chores.

I hope that the results of your renal X-ray and bladder investigation were OK. It is amazing what they can do isn't it?

One of our students was bitten by a snake this week so he spent one night in the hospital after having about 6 different injections - snake serum and A.T.S. and so on. He was OK. On Friday someone at the hospital needed blood .... so, I took 3 men along as volunteers. They needed O+ so their blood was not required.

How is Sailor? My cat, Sundri, is gorgeous - and no trouble at all. I must take her picture so that you can see her.

Myrtle and Pat want to come for a few days holiday October 17 - 21 or so. That will be very nice. I may go down to Ughelli next weekend with Shelagh Jebb and Grace Webster - but they are going on Saturday and returning on Sunday, and it's a long drive down there and back - and I have been invited to a 'Profession' at the Noviciate which I would like to go to.

Much love to you both
Elizabeth

Vining Centre
14th October 1974

Dear Ma and Daddy,

Thank you for your letters. I shall be interested to get your next one telling of the result of Daddy's X-ray. I hope all was well.

I had a letter from Ruth Martin saying that she had not passed her driving test - and sounding a bit glum about job possibilities. She needs a lot of prayer and help I feel. I am sorry to hear that she doesn't feel able to help with C.M.S. things locally. It is not easy to settle down if you have nothing definite to do. It is a bit the same with retiring from a busy life. I hope that Anne can come with her slides, and that you all enjoy looking at Nigeria together.

I have had a very interesting weekend. On Friday night I got a bug in my ear - one with legs. It kept me awake for about 1 hour while I tried to get it out, but it wouldn't budge. On Saturday am I was woken by Shelagh Jebb en route for Ughelli - she thought I was going too, but I had decided not to. So, she took one of our students with her for company. While we were waiting for him to have a bath and take his food Shelagh tried to get at my insect with some tweezers but couldn't get it. Then I did my inspection of the women's house and finished about 10am. I then discovered that I had a flat tyre - so we started to change it but on getting the spare out of the boot discovered that it was completely airless. So, I got the College van and the driver, and we drove to the Garage and left the 2 tyres to be mended. About 10.30 I reached the hospital - got a card - jumped the outpatients' queue and got the doctor's signature and went to the O.P.D. Treatment Room and got my ear syringed! The bug came out! It was then 10.50 .... returned to the Vining Centre and changed and went in the bus to the other end of town to St. Louis. I got there about 10 past 11 but they hadn't yet started. It was the service of 'First Profession' for one of the sisters "Julianalo". It was a lovely service with beautiful pure singing by the choir. They had the Gelineau Psalm 42 - "My soul is thirsting for the Lord" and at the end sang "How great thou art" as everyone processed out. Really church disunity is a bit nutty. I noticed that at the altar the bishop folded the purificatory and other cloths precisely as we do - in 3 sections. I had just been teaching our women how to set it out the day before!

After the service we went to the Noviciate for lunch and talked to Brother Arthur who Daddy talked with in Ondo in 1970.

Then I went to Ife .... my tyres being now fixed and stayed the night with Professor and Mrs. Rodgers from Belfast. He is now a Professor in the Ife Medical School and a C.M.S. Member. He worked before with Sydney McCan, in Belfast. He is now 66 - so "retired" but taken on this job in Nigeria. I should think he is a very gifted Surgeon, as well as a good administrator - and a fine Christian. He will be Yomi's boss when Yomi comes back from America. Kelu came back last Tuesday. She didn't enjoy her couple of days in London at all - she said it was wet and cold and windy and they had no telephone in the house where she stayed so she couldn't even phone her friends.

Sandra was staying with the Rodgers too so on Sunday morning we went all together to the morning service. There must have been about 700 students there and the Service was in the American Baptist Style with a Billy Graham type appeal at the end. Several people said that this was a bit 'much' every week and I would agree - but it was encouraging to see so many students present.

Sorry Ruth fell off her horse. I must go to Oshogbo again and get her cloth. I should like to read Max Warren's book. Would you like it for Christmas? Sheila comes today, Monday.

With much love to you both

Elizabeth

Vining Centre

20th October 1974

Dear Ma and Daddy,

Thank you for your letters, both in the post, and via Sheila. We went to New Zealand again the other night and saw the 3 slides that you sent of the children. I have just heard that John and Pat have received the tape so now I shall venture to put the slides in the post.

I am happy to hear that Daddy isn't asked to go again for a check for 3 months. I hope that there is no more trouble, and that some solution is found to the stiff legs.

I have had Myrtle and Pat here this week for the Half Term Holiday. It has been lovely to have them, and I think that they enjoyed being with us in Akure. The week has been quite eventful. On Wednesday morning we had a short service of prayer and thanksgiving taken by the Archdeacon to mark the roofing of Martin House. It was billed for 7.30 but didn't begin until nearly 8am because it just poured with rain and everything that was prepared outside had to be suddenly moved inside. Anyway, all Yorubas take rain to be a sign of God's blessing on the event, so it was not regarded as a calamity at all.

On Thursday Myrtle and I went to the funeral rites in the house of the mother of the late Deji - that is Eyesorun's mother-in-law. It was a bit disappointing in that we saw nothing of what went on in the back yard - only heard shouting and wailing, gunfire and trumpeting. We were firmly sat inside the house while this went on.

We had supper on Friday evening at Sheila's and on Saturday with the brothers at St. Peter's .... and on Friday afternoon we had a picnic on the rocks at the Agric.

I had a letter from Ruth Martin saying that she had been transferred to a psychiatrist in Evesham who she didn't take to. I am sorry that she has told Philip Rees that she doesn't want to take part in C.M.S. in the Diocese. Maybe she just means 'speaking at meetings'. I can understand that - if you are not feeling well the idea of being a speaker can be ghastly and Ruth doesn't enjoy it at the best of times. But I should have thought that she would be very glad to have fellowship with C.M.S. folk in the area - and that this would help her.

Your new garden with grapes, quinces and figs sounds super.

I hope that you enjoyed the Sudan Thanksgiving Service on Tuesday. I shall be thinking of you all over the weekend of 25th August as you look at the slides of our holiday to the North. It seems to me you are still having plenty of visitors if Lynette and Carlo are coming 21st - 25th.

Myrtle said that she could do with a bottle of sherry to start her on contemplative prayer! She sends her love to you. She should be home on leave next April.

I went to see Doug Evans this morning and found him frustrated with his job in the Ministry of Education. They make decisions so late in the Headquarters that those in the local offices must just do as they are told and are not able to plan anything in advance.

I have a lovely picture of Worcester Cathedral over the river on my October calendar. It's the one you sent me last year for Christmas.

Thank you for whatever you have sent via Sheila for my birthday. She has hidden them away! Sundri sends greetings to Sailor. She likes best to sit and sleep.

With much love

Elizabeth

Vining Centre
27th October 1974

Dear Ma and Daddy,

I was thinking of you especially last night - when I imagine that you were busy looking at Anne's slides of our Northern holiday. I tried to put an international phone call through to surprise you all in the middle of the showing - but it didn't come through before 11pm so I cancelled it. I had a house full of folk too. Ruth Howard and Mary Griffin and an Indian member of staff are here for their Half Term Holiday from Ughelli. The Eyesorun was here to supper too, and Sheila Davis and Doug Evans, so we were quite a party.

Ruth and Mary turned up on Friday evening just as Sandra and I were going off to Ondo to stay the night with Inga to watch some films that she has from British Council. They were superb films. The first was 'The D.N.A. story' - about the discovery in the 1950's in Cambridge of the Double Helix. We have both just read a book about this - and the writer of the book and all the people in the book were speaking on the film so it was very exciting. Then she had another film of the setting up of the Abuja pottery in N. Nigeria. A beautiful colour film with a lot of lovely photographs of Nigerian life. Produced in 1973. And then we looked at the film of the Desert Sands again - also super.

Ruth and Mary and I are now talking of planning to go to the Cameroons at Christmas. We are going ahead with all the visa and other arrangements .... but we don't yet know where we are going to stay. You don't have any cronies in the Cameroons, do you?? Whether we climb up Mt. Cameroon or not remains to be seen. I will need to start and play some tennis I think if I am to make it up 13 000 feet.

Doug Evans tells me that the Harborn's are now in Athens!! He is working on some project in the Persian Gulf. They have a spacious flat on the hills outside Athens. Perhaps I will stop off there when I come home next year - if they are still there.

Today Cornelius and Adeoba have both been away - in Ibadan - at the Consecration of the new Bishops of Ilesha and Offa (Kwara State).

I went tonight to take the service at Fiwasaiye. We had a special thanksgiving for Ebun - she came out to the front, and we had a long prayer in Yoruba led by one of my women. I talked about 'Surprises' and how Miracles are like God's surprises! I started by saying that I was very surprised to find my blue plastic washing up bowl turned upside down in the middle of my kitchen floor with the electric kettle on top of it when I came in for lunch at Fiwasaiye today! And more surprised to find a live chicken underneath!! Eyesorun must have left it - she said she would send a chicken to help to entertain my visitors! She really is a dear.

Hope that you are well - and enjoying some surprises in retirement.

With love

Elizabeth

Vining Centre
2nd November 1974

Dear Ma and Daddy,

Thank you for your letters of October 20th with news of your visit to the Sudan Association Thanksgiving and visit to Stuart. I am looking forward to your next letter telling of Anne's visit, and what you thought of her slides. Thank you also for the quotations from Windows of Heaven.

Thank you too for the lovely birthday card and the nice Irish Blessing inside. I don't think that I am going to have a "Party" this year - certainly not on my Birthday - because it is our Half Term. We have our Leper Settlement Committee on Thursday afternoon. Then I may ask a few friends round in the evening. On Friday I will go to Ibadan and hope to stay with the Batts. Sandra will probably come with me because she hasn't been able to see her doctor this weekend. Then Sheila and Joan both have birthdays a couple of weeks later than mine so I think that I shall join them in a joint party - we all have the same friends anyway.

I have had a very happy week - nothing remarkable has happened. I have just felt fit and well and enjoyed what I was doing. We had some people from the hospital on Monday night talking about blood donation. The questions were rather a hoot. One of our students got up and asked, "Is it true that 'Dr. Haemaels' mixture is made of human blood? (It is an Iron Tonic). If it is true, why can't we use it instead of blood transfusion"!!

On Tuesday I went to the Leper Settlement with Mrs. Sijuade, the doctor's wife. She had never been there before. Then I also visited the Army Commander's wife, Mrs. Bale, who is rather lonely. She comes from Jos and her husband has been in Ibadan most of the 3 months that they have been in Akure.

On Wednesday I asked the 2 Ceylonese Water Engineers to supper .... about time too. The senior one, Mr. Sambasivam, is married with teenage children at home and his wife is in Ceylon. She may come after Christmas - but he is very lonely I think and doesn't know many people in Akure. He would like to play 'bridge' - so I have asked Brother Tom to invite him to one of their bridge gatherings.

On Thursday Janet Olowoyo came from Ondo - to stay the night and do a Yoruba A-level exam on Friday morning. She was hoping to stay over the weekend and study to prepare for the rest of the Yoruba and BK papers next week. But she must transfer schools and has asked to hand over her present one on Saturday and take on the new one on Monday!

On Friday Sheila and Sandra went to Ibadan with Ebun. Sister Martinian and Mildred came here for supper. On Saturday I went round to see Tom and Alphonse and had tea with them. Then I went to see Doug Evans in the evening before going round to greet Sheila and Sandra on their return from Ibadan. Today Sandra and I went to Eugene Chang's and had Chinese lunch. In between all these friends I have done the usual things at Vining Centre!! I hope that you are both well.

With love

Elizabeth

Vining Centre

9th November 1974

Dear Ma and Daddy,

I am so glad to hear that you had such a good weekend with Anne. I hope Daddy didn't sleep through the slides! Anne really has entered C.M.S. life, and has great enthusiasm for Nigeria, hasn't she?

THANK YOU for all the lovely things that arrived on my Birthday, via Sheila. The 2 new nightdresses have gone into use immediately. I am starting on the blue one and enjoy wearing it. It is very "shorty". Thank you too for the book on Worcestershire. I haven't started reading it, but it looks very interesting. We had a birthday 'gathering' in my house on Thursday evening - Sheila, Sandra and another V.S.O. and Mama Ademoye and Rev. Adeoba, on our staff. Cornelius and Victoria were to come too but Cornelius had just arrived from Ibadan and was dead beat, and Victoria had lost the key to her clothes cupboard and felt she couldn't come in her "kitchen dress". So, we sent their food over for them.

It was all a bit of a game on Thursday because I had no steward, no gas in the morning, no water in the taps, and no electricity in the evening!! The reason why I had no Tokunbo was because just as I was getting into the bath on Wednesday evening there was a commotion outside, and I rushed out to discover that Tokunbo was bitten by a snake in the bush. He had gone there hunting and didn't realise that he was bitten at first so carried on. Then he began to feel ill and decided that the pain on his head that he thought was a scratch by a thorn must be a snake bite so then he came home. Janet Olowoyo was staying with me, and she and I took him to the hospital where he vomited and vomited and vomited. They put him on a drip and gave him snake serum, but he was still groggy next morning, so they kept him in. He was OK on Friday morning, when I left to come to Ibadan.

Also, on Thursday I did a demonstration to the women of how to cook eggs for breakfast. Just as I was about to start in the classroom the gas failed. So, I had to bring the women to crowd into my tiny kitchen while I 'demonstrated' with the kerosene stove - including burning your finger with the hot fat!!

In the afternoon of the same day, we had the Leper Settlement Committee - and it was a great occasion because we had it at Dr. Sijuade's house and Chief Akinola - the Leprosy Officer came to the meeting for the first time since I have been in Akure. It was a great pity that the Eyesorun wasn't there. But it is super because it really means that there is now the possibility of co-operation between the Leprosy Office and the Medical Authorities at the hospital, and the voluntary agency people who want to care for the welfare of the Lepers.

When I went to the meeting the 2 chickens for supper were still walking round the compound! The meeting was at 4.30, and I had asked 7 for supper at 7.30. I had asked 3 of the women to make 'jollof' and I was hoping that Kadri, Sheila's steward, would come and help to kill the chickens. Anyway - the meeting didn't finish till 6.30 and when I got home, I discovered the jollof ready and Kadri and Michel (Sandra's steward) had everything ready in my kitchen. Wasn't that super!!

Sheila gave me a lovely record - Mozart's Flute Concerto and we played that - and opened parcels from you folk at home. It was all very nice and homely. On November 23rd Joan Steward and Sheila and I are having a joint party - at Fiwasaiye. We are inviting between 30 and 40 people.

On Friday morning Sister Martinian came round with a card and a nice cake of Morny's soap. Wasn't that sweet of her? Then Sandra and I came together to Ibadan. We stopped in Ondo to see Inga; and then came on to stay with Joe and Brenda Batt. Sandra went to have her check up at the hospital on Saturday morning, and then went back to Akure. I have been having a delightful Half Term Holiday. We went swimming with a picnic lunch on Saturday at the Premier Hotel - and again had a dip on Sunday after the Church Service at All Saints. On Friday evening Christine and Joseph Adebamiwa came for supper. They are the Nigerian couple we stayed with once - now at St. Peter's Aremo - the 'Giant Church'. Then on Saturday we had the Archbishop for supper!! Mrs. Scott is in U.C.H. for tests and treatment - so I went there and fetched the archbishop and brought him to the Batts. He came to Nigeria for the Consecration of the 2 new Bishops of Ilesha and Kwara and now is having to stay on extra time for his wife's tests. He is staying in the Institute of Church and Society and is a bit at a loose end - so Joe Batt had asked him to come for a meal. He is a very nice very relaxed person - slightly overwhelmed with the size of the Province of West Africa, I guess.

I have seen some of my usual cronies while in Ibadan - and missed seeing others. Grace Ohikhena has now got a place in the University of Ibadan doing a diploma in Religious Studies for 2 years. She is very happy to have a break from teaching .... but I don't know how she will get on with Greek!

John and Janet Nightingale have gone down with hepatitis. This is a bit unfortunate - but they don't seem to have got it very badly - except Janet has had a good deal of nausea and vomiting and hasn't been able to eat anything. Their little boy David is being looked after most of the time by Jan Picard - who already has 2 of her own - so now she has her hands full.

I went off looking for Titi yesterday afternoon and found her school down a very bumpy road - but met her absence.

I heard from Louise for my birthday. Incredible how some people are so good about Birthdays!

It is now Monday morning - and I will go shopping this morning - go to see Grace at the University - and maybe the Nightingales if I have the time - then I will have lunch here with the Batts before setting off back to Akure. Inga should be staying the night with me .... she is going to Akure today for a Board of Governors meeting at Fiwasaiye.

I have a slightly sore back and shoulder - from the sun at the pool yesterday. Maybe it will peel.

Did I mention last week that I will probably be free to come home around June 15th - and stay at home till end of September? It is not so long now.

Thank you again for all the Birthday Gifts - showing your love and caring.

With much love
Elizabeth

Vining Centre
17th November 1974

Dear Ma and Daddy,

Thank you for your letters. It is good to be thinking about holidays! I am going ahead with plans for Cameroon. Shelagh Jebb has given us the address of 2 hospitals run by the Presbyterian's - one at Bamenda and one at Kumba so I have written those to try to get accommodation. I have heard from Buea with some information about accommodation and guide and carriers in Buea.

Concerning next summer, I think I said that I would be home mid-June till September ending. I suggest that we go to Scotland after 9th August - maybe straight on from London. It sounds fine to plan 1 week in Iona and then stay in Joppa for a time coinciding with the festival. I will write to Helen to find out if they are planning on Raasay .... also, to Meg Wilkes to see if she will be around Edinburgh at that time. I don't think a companion is a necessity - unless maybe Anne was very keen to go to Iona. It would be nicer to have a holiday "together" - we didn't do so in 1973 - Anne will probably want to do something with her mother - since she was here this year.

I am very glad that you have had the chance to hear the 3 Ugandan evangelists. It is exciting how many things are happening in the worldwide Church just now which are like the Acts of the Apostles all over again. I have just read this week "9 o'clock in the morning" - by Dennis Bennett. It is his personal story of how he was baptised in the Spirit in Los Angeles in 1960 - and all the amazing things that have happened since then. Then I am also reading Michael Harper's "As it was in the beginning" - both very interesting. I hear that this last week in Ibadan there was a special workshop on "Healing" led by Catholic, Anglican, Methodist and other members of the charismatic movement.

I took the sermon this morning in Communion, and we had a very moving service. Cornelius followed up the idea of my sermon and took it right through the service. I spoke about Eph 4 v3 in Living Bible - "Try always to be led along together by the Holy Spirit". Then we sang from the Youth Praise 'I want to walk with Jesus Christ'. It has a very catchy tune and our students really seemed to enjoy singing it, and the words are very meaningful.

Did you see in the Church Times that the new Archbishop of Cape Town is a charismatic?

I am glad that you were able to send Di a wedding present .... because I didn't send anything. Do you know her address? I got a piece of cake - it tasted pretty good to me .... perhaps it was the humidity here.

Please can you send me a copy of my circular - and if you haven't sent it yet - hold on .... I may be able to adapt it for Christmas - and include a Christmas card .... if they are printed in time - of Martin House. But I should be glad if you can send it off to C.M.S. then it can be used as a Link letter as it stands .... but stupidly I have no copy of it here so I can't remember exactly what I put. You don't seem to be bored in retirement!!

With much love to you both

Elizabeth.

Vining Centre

24th November 1974

Dear Ma and Daddy,

Thank you for your letter of 18th received on Saturday. Yesterday was a bit hectic, and I hardly had time to read my post. One letter will interest you. I heard from C.M.S. Publicity Department that they want to write the story of Ebun in the January "Yes"!! They are assuming that the 'Sheila' in the story is Shelagh Jebb!! I have written back directly to say that it is nothing of the sort. I hope they get my letter before printing it because it's an unfortunate blunder since the main responsibility for Ebun has fallen on Sheila Davis. Anyway, we shall see what they put.

Yesterday we had our joint Birthday Party - at Fiwasaiye. We invited about 30 people .... Grace and Dr. and Mrs. Thomas from Ado, Inga from Ondo and Patrick and Cynthia Whittle, Eyesorun, Sandra and Janet and Eugene – V.S.O.'s. Bob and Dennis - C.U.S.O.'s. The Ceylon Water Engineers, Doug Evans. Sobukunola, Brother Tom and Alfonse, Sisters Mildred, Martinian and Macnoase, Father Wheelan. It was a very happy occasion .... rather many expatriates - but a lot of variety of people. I spent the morning shopping and then cooking sponges for our sweet and doing stuffed eggs and so on. Then in the afternoon there was a sports meeting.

Inga and the Thomas's stayed the night with me. My cistern overflowed in the night, so Inga and I were up about 6.30am brushing the water out!!

Today I have been to the school of Agriculture Evening Service. I preached a slightly extended version of last week's sermon. It is a very S.U. Service, very informal, but full of enthusiasm. I am asked to go again next Friday for their End of the Month Prayer Meeting - and talk to them again.

You had better wait before fixing Iona in July because of Deputation. I think it would be better mid-August - followed by the festival time. It's too bad if it rains. I had a post card from Mary Harborn the other day inviting me to come and visit them in Greece - Athens on my way home next year. I am going to find out how much extra it would cost. It used not to be much extra to stop places en route.

I am glad that Ruth was able to come and bring Nancy with her. Yes, I have read Gussie Lyward's book. Inga has just been reading another book about the same type of school. She has promised to loan me it to read.

Janet Olowoyo was here from Monday - Thursday when she was doing her A-level exams. It was nice to have her company. Eyesorun may come tomorrow to speak to our women. I have a new friend - Mrs. Bali, the wife of the Army Commandant! She comes from Jos. She is coming to tea tomorrow. The next few weeks are going to be busy with the end of term.

Much love to you both

Elizabeth

P.S. We had 2 babies arriving this week - on the same day!!! 10am and 10pm!

Vining Centre
30th November 1974

Dear Mummy and Daddy,

Thank you for the long newsy letter of last Sunday and the Max Warren book. Super. But I hope that you have got one for yourselves as well. I am glad that Daddy has been corresponding with Anne because she wrote to me, and I wasn't able to reply directly as I would have liked because I was up to my ears here. Also, I have had a cold and now a cough so only really did the compulsory things this last week. Now I feel much better. Dr. Thomas at Ado gave me some antibiotics to try and drive the cough off more quickly.

Thank you for all your efforts concerning my letter. I should think you had better write a happy Christmas on the bottom of it. Yes, I think it is a very good idea to use Mrs. Sainsbury's £10 for Newsletter Postage. Please send me Freddie's new address at Maidstone so that I can send him a Christmas Card.

I am very happy to hear that Stuart has such a good line on a house in Hackney. Super that he has 3 rooms upstairs .... I need somewhere to stay in London now that Di has moved. Perhaps I should give him a bed for a wedding present - for the guest room!

I went to Ado on Friday evening and stayed the night with Grace. She is in very good form. On Saturday morning we went to Ikerre together to the 'Launching' of the Ekiti Diocesan Technical Industries. It is a place where they are going to train boys in metal work and woodwork etc. There is a Dutchman there starting the place off. All very impressive - and all the big Ekiti men there donating N100 or N50 or some churches N200 or N400. I should be interested to know how much they were able to collect in the end.

Then I came back in the afternoon and went to speak to the End of the Month Prayer Meeting at the Agric. College. I spoke for almost an hour - including playing some records - Let there be Light in the Land and parts from Godspell. They enjoyed this so much .... and the Clarkabad song by the Glory-landers ...that some of them want to come and tape them. The whole meeting went on for about 2½ hours.

Today we had our Harvest here at the Vining Centre. I only stayed for half of it - the service. It began at 10am and finished by 1.40pm. Then I escaped to have lunch at Fiwasaiye - when I came back at 4, they were still auctioning yams .... I think it finished about 5.15, but I am afraid my stamina is not that long! My student Dispenser came to say that he had run out of Aspirin!

On Thursday we had the Board of Governors meeting. Rev. Faji who is the new Administrator in the C.M.S. Office in Lagos came. It was good to see him and to get to know him a little. He seems a very pleasant gentleman.

The coming week is going to be very busy as far as I can see. We have exams. I have the Certificates to write. There are stoles to finish .... mainly making of fringes - it is quite a job to make them from thread. I must buy some when I am next at home. Next weekend we have Carols on Saturday, Ordinations in Ondo on Sunday, and Commissioning Service here on Monday. Then we finish on Tuesday 10th. You sound as though you are busy too. Who is going to be with you for Christmas?

With much love

Elizabeth

Vining Centre
10th December 1974

Dear Ma and Daddy,

Thank you both for your letters received in the past week. Your visit to Birmingham sounds very thrilling. It is good to be retired and to have the chance to go and visit so many folks around Malvern. I am now reading a book called Catholic Pentecostals which tells about the beginning of the charismatic movement in the Catholic Church in U.S.A. It certainly seems to be a movement here in Catholic circles .... not a lot of evidence in the Anglican Church in Nigeria .... because sadly the charismatic minded in Benin Diocese for example were all excommunicated or frowned on.

We have had a very busy end of term here. I have been writing Certificates etc. The Commissioning Service was on Monday. It all went off well. On Sunday we went to Ondo for the Ordination of 10 fellows. It was a very lovely service - the first that I had been to in the Cathedral. There was great jubilation here in welcoming our newly ordained student - the first to be ordained while still at the Vining Centre.

We had our 'Carols' on Saturday afternoon - rather dreary affair this year - and not improved by the fact that there was a wrong announcement about the time and so everyone was late .... and there was a nasty row about it between the men staff and the senior student at the beginning. Fiwasaiye service was on Sunday evening - the singing there was good. Then on Tuesday evening we went to St. Louis, the Catholic girls school. Their singing was the best - but very "correct" - not very spontaneous I felt.

We are still on for the Cameroons - and have one night fixed at a Presbyterian Hospital. I haven't heard from others yet. But I think that we will still go even if the accommodation is doubtful. We will carry camp beds with us and take food supplies.

Yesterday a painter from Ondo came asking for work so I suggested that he painted my kitchen. He bought paint and got an old ladder and started .... crash bang! He fell off the ladder and a whole pot of emulsion paint was spattered over the floor - cupboards, fridge, and stove etc. etc. So, then operation scrub! Most of it has come off .... except for the concrete floor which is patchy. Tokunbo was not amused.

Concerning my letter - thank you for getting it duplicated. I am writing Christmas Cards which I will send to you via Inga if she goes home for Christmas as she says. I suggest you put the letter in with them where relevant and keep the envelopes that you have addressed till another time - if you haven't sent them off already.

With love

Elizabeth

Vining Centre

15th December 1974

Dear Ma and Daddy,

I am now at Myrtles, having spent a very happy weekend in Ibadan visiting friends, while staying at the Batts. I expect that you will be wondering what on earth has happened to my 'cards' .... and I am wondering if you have already sent off the letters, or if you are still waiting. The thing is that I discovered last week that Inga is going home for Christmas, and she promised to take my cards and post them to you BUT then I missed her in Ondo on Saturday so I haven't been able to give them to her - unless I can get her at the airport when she goes on Wednesday. It was a good idea anyway.

I have already started reading the "Crowded Canvas" and am enjoying it very much indeed. I am enclosing a cheque for £5 for your own copy. I hope that you will both enjoy it as much as I am.

We are planning to set off for the Cameroons next Monday. So far, we don’t know where we shall be for Christmas Day, but it should be somewhere in the Bamenda area. Then on Boxing Day night we shall be at Kumba and the next 3 nights at Buea or climbing the mountain. Then one night possibly at Victoria before returning to Iyi Enu Hospital for New Year's Eve. We shall be 4 - Ruth Howard, Mary Griffin, and Thankanma their Indian teacher. I am not sure how it will all work out because Thankanma doesn't want to climb. Sue Davis is not coming after all. She is only just back from leave and apparently had never intended to come. I don't know how Mary got the idea that she was going to come with us at all.

I have spent the past week getting a bit straighter after the end of term. We went to the carol service at St. Louis on Tuesday and then the Christmas play at Fiwasaiye on Wednesday evening. On Thursday we had carol singing with Sheila. Doug Evans is now transferred to Ibadan from the New Year, so he won't be in Akure anymore. They say that there are going to be a lot more transfers of Principals in the New Year - so I hope that Sheila is not moved.

I shall be thinking of you at Christmas time. It would be nice to be with you on that day - but we shall just have to look forward to next summer holidays. That will be super. I am glad that Stuart and Jutka will be able to be with you.

I was fortunate when I got to Ibadan on Saturday because I arrived just in time for a children's Christmas party at the Batts. They had the house all beautifully decorated with a casuarina tree - and fairy lights, a nice crib and Happy Christmas written in 6 or 7 languages written in different types of letters all around the walls. They had it in English, Yoruba, French, German, Spanish, Russian and N.T. Greek! Then we had very nice eats including mince pies .... so, it was a real prelude to Christmas. I have made 2 cakes - one for us to take to the Cameroons, and the other one for Jane and Sheila and Joan who will probably be in Akure. I don't suppose that we shall have turkey or plum pudding - more likely to be tinned ham - but that will be nice.

It is very relaxing to be with Myrtle and Pat - but it is much hotter here in Lagos than in Akure. There I have been sleeping with 3 blankets at night, because of the harmattan. I have borrowed a big Norwegian sweater from Joe Batt so I may not be frozen in the Cameroons.

With love

Elizabeth

19th December 1974

Dear Ma and Daddy,

I have now sent my cards through the post from Lagos so there is no point in your waiting for anything before sending the letters off. Sorry for the delay. Inga went this morning, but I didn't in fact see her again - and I posted the letters yesterday morning.

Myrtle and Pat and I are going to Lagos Cathedral tonight for the Lagos Choral Society Carols. I think it will be good. We are going to the Guest House for supper first.

Tomorrow I will drive back up to Akure via Ibadan. I have been shopping here - but really prices are very off putting. However, I have bought some nice Christmas paper and some Swiss Chocolate and apples. I will distribute this up country!

Thursday:

The Concert was gorgeous. Beatrice Waddington was at the Guest House - on her way home. Sheila, Myrtle, Pat, and I are talking of arranging a retreat together over the Easter weekend.

Have a very Happy Christmas. You may get this letter before the other one.

With love

Elizabeth

To Mount Cameroon

Note: I spent Christmas Day in Bamenda in the Cameroon Republic with some American Catholic Sisters. To get there from Nigeria is an adventure in itself because the road is incredibly steep and winding but it was worth it. The Bamenda area is a beautiful grassy hill country with an almost temperate climate. We positively enjoyed putting on sweaters and stockings with our long skirts on Christmas Eve

Vining Centre
30th December 1974
From Buea

Dear Ma and Daddy,

I can't quite remember where I finished the last letter. I think that it must have been in Bamenda - on Christmas Day.

Now we have been to Mount Cameroon. Golly! I have never climbed so high. I went up to Hut 2 which is at 9,100 feet which is where we spent the night. You start at 3,700 feet and then go up the first 2,000 feet through forest and the rest up steep grassy slopes with volcanic stones which are really like coke. The path just goes straight up, with no zig zags and is very steep. I found it quite exhausting and wondered if I would make it. Also, I only had old plimsolls so I was not as comfortable as I would have been in walking shoes. We took about 7 hours to reach Hut 2 which was slow going. The hut was just 3 rooms with a metal roof and a shelf with hay on it for sleeping. 10 of us slept on the shelf - us 3, 2 French girls, 1 English boy and 4 French men including 2 Catholic Fathers!

Ruth and Mary started off at 5am and went up again to the summit, 13,000 feet. They came down again about 12.30 and had found it stiff. I was disappointed in a way not to go up and see the volcanic cones etc. at the top but I know that I wasn't fit enough - and that I should have held them back - or had to return. Anyway, I enjoyed watching the sunrise from Hut 2 and then one of our 2 porters, Matthias, took me up a bit more and I collected flowers from that area - very interesting. Our Guide and 2 porters were very kind to us and extra-ordinarily patient when we didn't go as fast as they could.

We all started down again at about 1.30 and were coming down until 6.30pm! Ruth's legs ceased to function reliably in the last part -

and I was pretty jelly legged too, so we were rather slow. I think that if I had attempted the summit I would have been carried down!!

When we got back, we all had baths and then went and had a delicious supper with a Swiss woman called Lotti - of the Presbyterian Church office in Buea. She was a delightful person and had taken a lot of trouble to look after Thankanma our Indian teacher (from Ughelli) when we were up on the mountain. She took her to visit a Cameroonian family and to the local Church on Sunday.

January 2nd:

I have now arrived back in Akure. My legs still ache! and my nose and face has peeled and so too has one arm - and my lips have swollen - all a result of the sunshine at 9,000 feet. Our return journey was uneventful except for one near skid off the road because a stick got under the car and jammed the hand brake on. It took me 2 days with 6 hours driving, one day with 4 and one day with 12 hours driving to get back (to Akure that is). We stayed in Iyi Enu Hospital with Elizabeth, Mary, and Marie. Marie hasn't been very well. Elizabeth said that she had a note from Dorothy Dykes saying that Maureen Olphin is to be married - but no-one knows if it's true or who she is marrying. Have you any light on this?? I should be very interested to hear.

With love to you both

Elizabeth

Vining Centre

5th January 1975

Dear Ma and Daddy,

The post is not very kind. The last letter I have from you is written on Dec 16th, so I haven't yet heard how you spent Christmas. I hope you got my letter from Cameroon.

The last few days -i.e., Fri and Sat I have just rested and done a 1000-piece jigsaw. My stiff leg is getting better, but it still aches if I walk a lot. Then my right shoulder has peeled in a big chunk – much to the amazement of Nigerian friends. The sun at 9000 feet also got my lips and they have swollen up and produced a nasty crop of cold sores. Really it was an 'experience' rather than a 'holiday' going to the Cameroons.! It is just as well that I have another week to recover before the term starts again. I must go to Ibadan during the week and get all our materials and book stock for the New Year.

While I was away Richard called to greet me. He came down from Gusau for Christmas. It was a pity that I wasn't in because I understand from Tokunbo that he came from Ilesha by taxi because he was so tired after driving from the North.

John Fabuyi came yesterday. He is now in Owo. They have changed the Educational Administration in the Western State and now have Divisional Education Officers in 25 places. Doug Evans will be in Ibadan at the centre with all these 25 officers under him to deal with Secondary Schools. He is still here in Akure although this change was to take place on Jan 1st. He has no house to go to in Ibadan and they say he might have to go to the Catering Rest House which isn't much fun at all. He was here last night to supper – and Sheila and Grace Webster who is down from Ado for the weekend.

The main topic of conversation now is UDOJI. This is a Commission set up to alter salaries in Gov't posts especially, but it is going to affect everyone. It means that all salaries for Civil Servants, doctors, nurses, teachers etc have gone up – and the minimum wage for a labourer has doubled. So that a cook for example in a Gov't school will now get N60 a month …. but at present most cooks get about N20. Nurses are to increase in Gov't hospitals so how are the Missions going to pay for their nurses without them going to the Gov't. Unless something happens, the Mission Hospitals will be threatened with closure. I pay Tokunbo N22 now. I can't possibly pay N60 out of N150 a month!

In fact, I am not required to because he is not a Gov't employee but nevertheless, he has got to live, and prices are shooting up. Sheila has kindly said that she would like to use her Udoji money to raise his salary to N30 or so. People in high places have gone up a lot. E.g, State Commissioners at present earning N6,800 p.a. have gone up to N14,00!! AND everything is going to be back dated to last April. Sheila says it will be about N20,000 for her teachers in Fiwasaiye I suppose all the money is coming out of oil. It will hit the Churches. How are graduates going to become clergy when they can earn so much more in the Civil Service?

Much love,

Elizabeth

Vining Centre
12th January 1975

Dear Ma and Daddy,

It was good to get your letters this week describing your Christmas activities. I am sorry that my letter from Lagos took such a long time. I hoped it would reach you before Christmas because post from Lagos is usually quick.

This week the great problem has been ' no petrol'. The reason for this was that the tanker drivers went on strike because the police in Kwara State had begun a new scheme of 'mobile courts' – which empowered them to fine drivers accused of dangerous driving or with something the matter with their vehicle on the spot. They had put 6 drivers in prison for refusing to pay – and the drivers were irate because they claimed that they would have to pay for things that were the owner's fault. So, they didn't drive their tankers .... so, no-one could get any petrol...... except if you fought for the little that there was at the petrol stations and then it could cost N1 or N1.50 per gallon instead of 45k.

This meant that I couldn't go to Ibadan on Mon as I had thought. It was probably a good thing because I was still tired after the Cameroon journey, so I was happy to stay put. On Tuesday however I discovered that Sister Martinian was going to Lagos, via Ibadan while taking 2 Ghanaian sisters to the airport and that she had enough petrol to go and come back. So, I took the petrol that I possessed – 3 gallons in a can and went with her. I was able to do part of my shopping with them on Tuesday and I went and stayed the night with Sam and Jose. Then I offered Sam 2 gallons of petrol in return for the use of his car. This he was happy to do, and he gave me a driver from Oxford University Press where he works to take me around. So, I was able to do everything that I would have been able to do in my own car despite the petrol shortage. On Thursday morning the tanker drivers made some agreement and so petrol began to come into Ibadan petrol stations again. The queues at the petrol stations were fantastic so the police and the army were out to deal with the distribution. In Akure we are not yet so fortunate. There is some petrol in a few garages but there is a great fight to get it. I understand that there was a fire in one station because someone was smoking! Everyone fled in great panic.

Term here at the Vining Centre started on Friday. We had a staff meeting in the morning which lasted from 12 till 2 pm. About 14 out of the 22 women expected have shown up so far. Some of the others are sick and no doubt others are held up for lack of petrol. Tomorrow, Monday, we have a visit from the Commissioner of Economic Development. He is coming to look at our 'Martin House' which is now almost completed. We are going to ask him for a grant towards its building! So far, we have 2 couples living in this new house. There is no bathroom and no kitchen yet. These don't seem to be a priority in Cornelius' mind. He is content to build them from metal pan and 'manage'. I think that we should try and get decent ones built because it seems nonsense to have a smart house but no-where to wash or cook decently.

Today we had a very good Communion Service. Cornelius took as his theme – Unity – and spoke about Eph 2. It was a very relevant theme because of the large number of students from different parts of the country. He went on to say that we were all united in Christ. He was the foundation stone and that United we stand. Divided we fall. He brought a broom and asked one woman to pick out one piece of the palm and try to sweep a table with it! Then he asked a second woman to come and do it with the whole broom. Then he asked one man to come and break one piece of the palm – which is easy … but a second man was asked to break it all - and that is impossible.

Yesterday (Sat) we went to a very nice concert by the girls of Queen's School Ibadan. They sang in a choir and there were a few solos too as well as a recorder group. Some piano players and a clarinet player. These were not superb geniuses, but they tried, and the singing was very enjoyable.

One student arrived with 2 children with measles! I was not amused and packed them off to the hospital. I have forbidden them from coming out of their room until the measles has gone. Today a first-year fellow fell out of his top bunk and gashed his leg – so I took him to the hospital for stitches before Chapel at 9 am.

I think you made a mistake on what I intended for the Christmas presents. I thought of the tie and dye serviettes for Ruth and Trevor – and the mats for Stuart and Jutka. The curtain material was a separate thing. Anyway, it doesn't matter – but Ruth may wonder what happened to their 'Christmas' present.

We have Leper Settlement Open Air today – for the first Sunday afternoon. The men are just drumming off so I must get ready. Still no petrol so the women can't go except for 3 in my car.

With much love, Elizabeth

Appendix Operation

Vining Centre
16th January 1975

Dear Ma and Daddy,

I received your letter on Monday from Edinburgh. I am very sorry to hear of Auntie Chrissie's death – but it does sound as though she was fortunate only to be in hospital for a week if she had inoperable cancer.

This has been a very busy week because it is the first week of term. On Monday we had a visit from the State Social Development and Reconstruction officer. He was an extremely pleasant gentleman and spoke as a real Christian of how our work at Vining Centre and their work is really the same.

I was beginning to get to know the new students yesterday and today .... but it now looks as though I shall have to take some time off! Maddening really. Today at lunch time I had a funny pain in the lower abdomen .... a different pain such as I hadn't had before. So, I went to bed in the afternoon.... but I was still uncomfortable in the early evening (6.30), so I decided to go and ask the doctor's advice. I went to Dr Wilde whose father is English and Mother Yoruba. His wife is on the staff of Fiwasaiye and is a super person. He has a clinic just down the road from Vining Centre. Anyway, he asked all sorts of questions and then examined my abdomen very carefully and announced that I have appendicitis and it should be removed tonight!! He says it is too far to go to Wesley Guild Hospital, Ilesha – and too bumpy. I could go to the Catholic Hospital in Ado.......but he has a very good reputation as a surgeon and said that he would do it here. So, I have agreed. It seems foolish to go jumping over the roads when he can do it here.

It is a bit of a blow .... because I guess I shall have to convalesce for some time – but it is easier here among friends – and it is a specialist hospital here in Akure.

Anyway, I am now waiting in Fiwasaiye with Sheila. The doctor will phone when he has got the Theatre organised. I haven't got a fearful pain – just oddly uncomfortable.

The women will just have to manage at Vining. Cornelius and Co are all very concerned and will be praying – so I am not afraid. Our lives are in God's hands.

With love to you both,

Elizabeth

Sheila wrote:

Good Morning: Peace. All is well. The operation was finished before 1 am and she was put on a drip. I have just come from seeing her now and she is relaxed and smiling. Marvellous girl. We will take every care. She is very dear to us, and to me especially. Love Sheila

Vining Centre
26th January 1975

Dear Ma and Daddy,

I had your letter from Joppa. It is good that you were able to spend some time in Edinburgh and so meet some of the folk like Auntie Marjorie and Kath and so on.

It is funny that you will have just heard about my appendix. I wonder whether to try and phone in case you are worried............but if it is not clear it could be worse. There is nothing to worry about anyway. Everyone has been so kind, and I have been surrounded by praying and caring friends.

On Friday (8th day) they took out my stitches and I was announced discharged immediately. It has healed completely and beautifully. Only. I am a bit afraid of unzipping. It seemed safer before because it was laced together with stitches and reinforced with plaster. Now there is nothing.

I started roaming around the hospital towards the end of the week and visitors abated so I was able to rest in the afternoons. It is good to be out and on a more comfortable bed – in Sheila's at Fiwasaiye. But I still need to rest and relax completely and this I don't find so easy. I am not yet sleeping right through the night even though I take Mogadon. Also, I can easily get tired.... but I think this is just to be managed until I have had time to recuperate. Dr Wilde says I must rest for 2 weeks then we shall see.

They are very good at Vining Centre and have managed to organise themselves in my absence remarkably well so I can forget them and enjoy my resting.

I have a super book which Martinian has loaned me. It is called 'The City Boy' by Herman Wonk, an American writer. It is hilariously funny in parts so is very good for exercising my abdominal muscles. Then there are more nice books to read, my knitting to finish and perhaps I will get my paints out.

My plan is to stay here with Sheila this week and then on Fri 31st Jan to go to Ife University to stay with Prof and Mrs. Rodgers. He is the Irish surgeon that I stayed with before. It seems the most ideal place to go – quiet and homely, and Mrs. Rodgers is in all day to keep me company. I will stay a week but if they advise me to stay longer then I will agree. I have no intention of going back to the Vining Centre too soon.

Please give my love to Ruth and Trevor and Stuart and Jutka. I meant to write to Stuart to welcome him into his new house, but it has not been possible, but I will be writing.

With much love,

Elizabeth

I suggest you continue to write to V. Centre, and they will forward letters.

Vining Centre
2nd February 1975

Dear Ma and Daddy,

I am still in Sheila's house – planning, all being well – to go to Ife this afternoon. Thank you so much for your super letters received on Friday and Saturday this week. I was beginning to wonder where your first letter had got to on Thurs. night because Sheila had her mother's reaction to my appendix on Tuesday. So, I tried to phone you on Thurs evening. We got Lagos after a lot of trouble and booked your number – but it never come through. Anyway, it didn't matter when I got your letter in the morning – and it was so helpful especially your thought about humility Ma, and yours Daddy that since you were praying anyway it didn't matter that you didn't know the exact need at that very moment.

I am much better – but it is true that convalescence is not easy. On Friday I felt very well – and so did quite a lot – i.e. I went to V.C. to pack my bag and went to town (by mistake in fact because I had forgotten my house key) and found it very noisy. Also, there is a dispute about the naming of the new Deji of Akure and the riot police were practising with tear gas. It is a horrible stuff. We got a whiff right into the car when we passed the Police Station. Then there was a dance here at Fiwasaiye so we were kept awake late.

The result was that yesterday I felt very weak and tired and did nothing much at all. So, it was a good thing that Doug Evans didn't want to go to Ibadan yesterday after all because he had fever. So, I am going today – in fact, with Bro Tom the Principal of St Peter's and not with Doug because he is transporting his cook's wife and family as well.

Anyway, I will be with Prof and Mrs. Rodgers – and I suspect that it is most likely that I will stay there for 2 weeks so that I have a complete month away from V.C. - that is until Feb 15th-- but I will leave the decision to them and Yomi.

Sheila has been so good and looked after me very well this week – but it has been a busy week in the school. I went to Dr Wilde on Friday, and he was very pleased with the healing of the wound so that is encouraging.

Today Cornelius brought Communion again. It was super. I have never really appreciated the importance of Communion for the sick before --- although I know Daddy always has. It is lovely because you can be quiet and really prepare for it. Do you have Diary of Private Prayer by Bailie? Look at Day 2. I read it as my prayer before the Communion this morning.

With much love to you both,

Elizabeth

4th February 1975

Dear Ma and Daddy,

It is 4.30 am! I am convalescing - on Prof Rodgers 'non-medicine' which I think you would really approve of – Daddy especially. Since I had the operation, I hadn't slept properly and was taking Mogadon and then waking at 2am and taking another half a tablet and generally getting stewed up that if I didn't sleep all the old 1971 troubles might recur. I had a bad night the first night I was here, so I asked Prof Rodgers for advice .... but in fact, didn't get the advice because there was a surgeons meeting here in the house which lasted till 11 pm and

I slept off at 10 pm without anything. Then at 11 I was woken by the doctors going away and I stewed then till 12 when I decided to take 2 Mogadon – which I did and slept till 7 am but woke up with a headache. At breakfast I told Prof Rodgers what I had done – thinking that it was rather good that I had managed to sleep. His reply was that he didn't think that I should be taking sleeping tablets at all – it would be better to be awake – relax and decide that you enjoyed being awake and resting – and that it didn't matter if you didn't sleep all night - even if you didn't sleep for a week you would sleep in the end. This was a bit of a bash on the nose…. but he is such an eminent surgeon and such a sincere Christian gentleman … and it sounded just like Daddy! So, I decided to try it. He also said that it was good to do as much as you were able during the day so that you would feel tired at night. (This is in fact the snag of his theory I think in the tropics – especially if you are in a sedentary teaching job.)

So, I got up yesterday after elevenses and began a puzzle. Then I went out with Mrs. Rodgers in the car before lunch. Then I slept in the afternoon for about 40 minutes (my usual). Then I had tea and went for a walk – and looked at where they were burning the bush. Then we went to Yomi and Kelu's and I washed my hair there – because they have hot and cold water, and we have no water at all at this top Professorial end of the compound. After supper I finished my puzzle, and I did feel tired and very relaxed. I went to sleep soon after 10 and slept with a few dozy breaks till 4.30and I feel quite refreshed. Maybe I shall become like Daddy and have my Quiet time before 6 am. We shall see …. but I have certainly begun to lose my fear of ' it all is happening again' and feeling that I <u>must</u> sleep at all costs.

Yomi and Kelu are well and send you greetings. Prof Rodgers and an Irish anaesthetist here both speak very highly of Yomi. The Irish lady is a Prof Kelly from Dublin (aged about 65) who has only been here 2 weeks and she said that Yomi's behaviour in the theatre was outstanding. She knew he was a Christian by his specialness and the way he dealt with the situation.

Mrs. Rodgers is a dear.... it is just like being at home here so I am sure that I shall get better in double quick time.

With much love,

Elizabeth

10th February 1975

Dear Ma and Daddy,

It is now Monday morning, and I am sitting in Inga's house in Ondo waiting for transport to come and take me to Akure. I was supposed to be going there yesterday. Inga kindly picked me up from the Rodgers in the morning and brought me to her house for lunch. Then Sheila was to come in the afternoon to take me back to my house but there was a shortage of petrol in Akure, and Sheila was too tired to wait a couple of hours in a queue so she phoned to say that she couldn't come. She had not remembered that my car is sitting there with a full tank of petrol and Ezekiel, the V.C driver could come. By the time we got through on the phone from here it was too late for him to come yesterday........... so, I am hoping that he is on his way now. I am ready to get back to my own house ….and I want to see what is in the post!

The rest of my time at the Rodgers was nice and restful. It was a bit like when you are on holiday. The more you rest the more you feel like being lazy.

Back here in Akure:

Thank you for your letter which was here on my arrival. What a swindle about the telephone call because we also got a man in Lagos very clearly and he said he would ring back when he got through.

I have written to C.M.S London about my leave and said that I would like to be free from Aug 8th and have the first week in Sept. free. So, we shall have to see when they fix the Deputations. The Missionary's Conference is the first week in July so that only leaves 3 weeks after that. Maybe they can fit everything into those 3 weeks.

I am not going to teach today, and maybe not tomorrow. Wed is Ash Wednesday so we may not have many lessons. I am not very hot on the Commination Service! So, I shall be happy to be 'sick' till after that!

In fact, I am feeling very much better – just a bit strange to be back in my own house on the compound.... with the sound of the Women's Classes going on without my assistance! They have managed very well. The health Office have sent a Nursing Sister this week and last to speak to the women on Health. I am sure they are better at it than me. So, I have no need to rush to get back to work. I can relax and do what I feel like this week- and maybe start again next week.

With much love to you both,

Elizabeth

Vining Centre
15th February 1975

Dear Ma and Daddy,

Thank you for the letter of Feb 5th telling of your visit to Stuart and Jutka. I am interested that Daddy produced his ideas on a wedding service. I wrote a very long screed on the same subject. I wonder if they received it. I am sorry that Lance gets so drunk and beats Jenny.

I have met the new Rector at the Priory – and his wife.... at Foxbury in 1971. I think that I brought them from Chislehurst Station. Certainly, I remember them helping me to push Jacqui Henry's old car down the hill.

No, you didn't tell me about Trevor. Pity, because Ruth did but her letter was so contradictory that I thought it was someone else who had a breakdown. I have just read a book about changing a remand home to a therapeutic community in the Cotswolds. The book is called 'Spare the Child' it brings out how demanding such a set up can be especially on the staff …. and in that case, they were mostly trained social workers. I can imagine that it could be a great strain, especially working with untrained people. Perhaps Kilworthy was a bit too 'way out' for Trevor and Ruth. I am sorry. But it is good that they can go back to Pilsdon. That Percy man sounded a very understanding fellow - older too. The Kilworthy set up is very much run by young people Isn't it?

I must write to Ruth again. She will think my last letter was right round the bend. How is Trevor? Is he depressed and withdrawn and uninterested in work or people.......or what? It will not be easy for Ruth. What do you mean - “They need more time for each other” ....was that the trouble at Kilworthy?

I came back here on Monday morning and did nothing much the rest of the day except wonder how I was going to settle down in my own house, on my own, eating meals by myself after 3 weeks of 'company' or staying with other people. I taught one lesson on Tuesday. Wednesday was Ash Wednesday. I was told our service was at 9 am but it started by 8.30 and I was still in bed, so I didn't go. It was just as well because Sheila came in great distress from Fiwasaiye because she had just had a telegram to say her father has died …. probably on Sunday – but no date was clear, and you have no way of knowing how long cables take. He was ill before Christmas with bronchitis, but no-one had taken it very seriously, so it was a real shock to her. I got out of bed and helped her go round the town getting money, health cards stamped, and a re-entry permit in her passport. We phoned Ibadan and booked a ticket, packed her bag, and set her off with a driver and a teacher at 12.15 - They were in Ibadan soon after 3 pm. She got a plane' to Lagos at 4.30 and then went to Myrtle and Pat's for the night and flew home on Thursday. I will miss her here, but Sister Martinian at the Noviciate has been very good at visiting me this week and we have been out to the Agric for walks on 2 afternoons. Then yesterday, Sat, I went over to Ondo for the St Monica's Old Girls Dance. Only about 20 old girls there so I don't think it was a great financial achievement, but the schoolgirls did some local dances and that was very lively.

I hope to start teaching full time this coming week. I feel much better and am sleeping well.

With much love to you both,
Elizabeth

23rd February 1975

Dear Ma and Daddy,

Thank you for the letter written on Ash Wednesday which arrived here on Thurs. this week. I am hoping to leave here around June 15th and then maybe going to Athens for a few days if I can fix that. I shall certainly be home before June 26th. Missionaries Conference is at Swanwick from June 30th -July 6th. I have heard from C.M.S and they have put down July 8-24 for Medicals and Links and reserved Sept 8 -12 for any additional deputations.

This week I have been back on Full time teaching, and all has been well. The week was only 4 days long! Because we now have half Term Weekend. Joe and Brenda Batt are here from Ibadan with Catherine. They came on Friday afternoon. Yesterday we all went together to Ado to see Grace and Shelagh and we went to the pool in Ado in the afternoon. This morning the Batts have gone off climbing rocks and so I have stayed at home to write letters.

We had our first Lent Fellowship on Tuesday at Sandra's house. We are taking 'The Fruits of the Spirit' as our theme this year.... and taking them one at a time and having thoughts and meditations on each one and then prayer at the end. I started last week with 'Love' and read from Quoist ' There are 2 loves only' and from a book I was reading called 'Spare the Child'. Afterwards Sandra and I stayed behind to drink coffee and Sandra came out with the fact that she hasn't been feeling well and has no energy since Christmas, and she is wondering if she shouldn't go home earlier than July so that she can have a good medical checkup at home and more advice on how to deal with her diabetes. Anyway, she has gone to Ife to see the Rodgers this W/E and I hope she will discuss the matter with them.

We are going ahead with our idea of having a 'retreat' weekend at Easter – Myrtle, Pat, Sheila and I and Grace and probably Jane Pelly with Richard Childerstone to be our 'Chaplain'. We hope to go to the Baptist compound at Oshogbo.

Thinking of you often, especially Daddy on hospital visits.

With love from,

Elizabeth

2nd March 1975

Dear Ma and Daddy,

Thank you for your letters of 17th and 20th February. I got them both this week....in the wrong order!

I am sorry that Daddy's undercarriage needs more repairs, but as you say it is probably better to get it fixed as soon as possible. I hope that you don't have to wait too long. I see in the Guardian that the hospital waiting lists are getting longer because the consultants are not happy about their conditions of service.

As I am writing this, I am thinking of you at St Julians. Very nice too! I am reading your book 'A Mind at Ease' and finding it very practical. I am finding a balance between 'rest' and 'work'. Still need extra rest now. Sandra and I have been going out walks at the Agric and we are finding that it does us both good. Sandra has now been told by an American doctor at Ife that she doesn't have diabetes at all! … and the reason why she was feeling so tired was because she wasn't taking enough energy giving foods! So, she is experimenting to see if he is right …... and maybe he is for she is eating sweet things and not suffering.

I am glad that Anne may come with us to Iona. I think that she will enjoy it and she will be a nice person to have with us.

We have had a busy week in the Vining Centre, and I have 2 children in hospital with measles and bronchi-pneumonia. They are both improving I am glad to say. I hate to see them gasping and hot. One had a temperature of 104.2 when he was admitted.

We had our Lent Fellowship on Tuesday at the Noviciate and the Leper Settlement Committee on Wednesday at Dr Sijuade's house. This week's Lent Fellowship will be at St Peters- the Catholic Teacher Training College. We are taking ' the fruit of the Spirit is PEACE' Sheila will be back on Tuesday.

It will be sensible to alter your will. I don't mind being named 'executor' – except I haven't a clue what it means! We can discuss that when I am at home. And remind me to give you some hints on what to write in a telegram if someone dies. The one Sheila got saying that her father had died was a bit unsatisfactory because it said that he died 'Today' and there was no way of knowing which day it was sent ......nor was there a clue as to when the funeral was. In fact, it all worked out because she got home on Thursday and the funeral was on Friday. She didn't receive her telegram till Wed but her brother in Uganda was already home by Tuesday!! so he got his much quicker.

This week one of the Leprosy Settlement people was admitted in the hospital.... and has had a Caesar today ...the first time since I have been here, thanks to Dr Wilde, so things are moving, praise God.

Thank you for your prayers. I continue to pray that you may know God's peace and His power.... even in times of operations.

With much love,

Elizabeth

9th March 1975

Dear Ma and Daddy,

Bother! It's Mothering Sunday and I forgot! Sorry. Thank you for your letter and news of Stuart's Concert. It sounds very inspiring. But I hope that you are not 'pushing yourselves' to travel about the countryside too much and so getting too tired. Maybe by now you have the date of Daddies 'op'. I hope that you don't have too long to wait- but perhaps it's not so bad – you can get used to the idea. I just had 3 hours' notice!

I got your letter sent by Sheila – and the Arne record. That's super. I have played it almost every day since Tuesday – and I have it on now. It is nice and soothing. I am now feeling completely normal health wise.... but it is incredibly hot and sticky and refuses to rain properly. Everyone is finding the weather a bit desperate – but I am lucky because I have water in the house most of the day.... and it must rain soon now.

Sandra and I went to Ondo yesterday afternoon and stayed the night with Inga. We went to see the play 'The gods are not to blame' by Ola Rotimi. It was superb – very dramatic and worth going to see. I saw it once before, but it was well worth a second seeing.

I think that having given our ideas we shall just sit back and let Stuart and Jutka organise their own marriage ' service' or whatever they want to have. We can pray for them. Also, it is really the parents of the bride who should have most 'say' in what goes on. You have 2 daughters and have had the joy of joining in one marriage in a Church. It is Jutka's parents' 'day' as well as our families and they might feel stranger in a Church set up than we shall in a registry office and a Hall. It is a creative relationship and a happy marriage for Stuart and Jutka that we are praying for. If you can rake up an eligible husband for me, I promise you I shall have a Christian marriage!! Then we can arrange it just how we like.

We had a good evening on Tuesday – thinking about 'Peace'. We have readings – some thoughts and discussion on the readings and then singing of hymns or choruses or psalms on the same theme. Sister Mildred of St Louis has a lovely voice, and she usually leads the singing. This week it is to be 'Patience' It seems to have been a week when patience has been tested a good deal! I got thoroughly annoyed at a couple of my women on Friday who hadn't done as they were asked about going to the hospital!

Cornelius hasn't been very well – but is 'managing'. Sheila is back – and very busy because there are things to catch up with and the end of the term is only 3 weeks away. We are planning to go to Oshogbo over Easter for a couple of days of 'Retreat'. Richard Childerstone in going to be our Chaplain.

With much love,

Elizabeth

14th March 1975

Dear Ma and Daddy,

I hope that this may reach you by Easter Day and that this Easter time may be a time a great blessing.

I am preaching at Communion tomorrow here in the Vining Centre. It is my E. Deeks version of Archbishop Coggan's sermon at his consecration as Archbishop in Canterbury – based on ' In the world you will have tribulation, but be of good cheer, I have overcome the world!! 'A good Easter time message.

With much love and prayers,

Elizabeth

16th March 1975

Dear Ma and Daddy,

No letter from you this week – but a Woman and Home. I gather from Eyesorun who had a letter from Anne that you went there for a meal. I hope that you are not too tired after your journeyings. I wonder if you have news yet of Daddies operation date.

Yesterday I went up to Ado at teatime and found Shelagh Jebb packing up her house because she is going on leave this week. I sent a book called ' Strength in Weakness' with her. I hope you may get it by Easter Day. We are hoping to be in Oshogbo on 'retreat' over that weekend. We plan to keep silence from Good Friday at 12 noon until before lunch on Easter Sunday. I think that we shall be 7 – Myrtle and Pat, Sheila and Jane Pelly, Grace and I and Richard Childerstone who is going to be our Chaplain.

I have had a notice about the Fountain Trust gathering in Westminster from July 28 to Aug 2nd. It looks as though they are expecting plenty of people and it looks like a very inspiring set up.... the Fisherfolk and Fr. McNutt and Rev Watson and Rev Pilkington are all to be there. Anyway, I have sent in my name to book. I think that I will be able to find some accommodation where I can stay.

By Friday this week I really felt very tired and weary. But there is only one full week to go before Easter time so I think I shall manage. I felt better yesterday and today. I think that it is time for leave! It is not long now.

Cornelius hasn't been so well this last 2 weeks. He is resting a good deal. The doctor has put him on Librium and sleeping tablets. In my opinion he won't feel 'well' until he comes off those.

We had a good session on 'Patience' on Tuesday. This week we are looking at 'Humility' It is a good exercise looking at the Fruits of the Spirit because you see you haven't got more than 'buds'. I am much more inclined to self-pity, depression, panic, impatience, and pride than to love, joy, peace, patience, and humility!! Still, I suppose even buds can grow if you just let them have water and sunlight.

We shall be having exams in the coming week starting with the Practical Exam on Tuesday. I think that there are only 4 women who cannot write this time so that is a help. It has been extremely hot in the past few weeks so the women have been falling asleep in class. Everyone has been complaining. It seems that all the surrounding towns have had some rain, but Akure has been left out. Fortunately, today it is a bit cooler and there is a breeze so maybe we shall soon get our turn.

I was talking to our men on Monday night about the persecution of Christians in Eastern Europe. I read Sabina Wurmbrand's book called 'The Pastor's Wife.' It is a very moving book telling of her sufferings. Now I am reading ' On the Beach' by Neville Shute!

Sandra had a nasty shock on Wed evening. She found a man hiding under her bed!! a thief. He was so intent on getting away out of the house when she discovered him that he left his shirt and his knife behind and didn't have the chance to steal anything. So, she was lucky and lost nothing but it was a nasty scare! Now I lock my door when I go out in the evenings!!

Much love,

Elizabeth.

22nd March 1975

Dear Ma and Daddy,

Thank you for your letter of 10th March. I am sorry to hear that Joyce Gell is now so muddled – no wonder you felt completely exhausted after her visit. I am glad to hear that Eric is still going strong in his student hostel work. It is good that you were able to go and see Anne. I am sure she must have been glad to see you. Certainly, I don't mind her having my slides. I am going to use some of hers for my deputation.

This week we have been doing some exams with the women. We did the practical exam on Tues and so all the women were busy cooking or cleaning and Mama, and I went 'up and down' to see how they were getting on. Then on Wed and Thurs we had other written exams. On Fri we prepared in the morning for the visit of Bishop Falope of Ilesha. He was supposed to get here by 12 noon.... the women pounded yam and the man practised their drill to make a guard of honour. We waited till after 1p.m. Then we ate the pounded yam, and the students went for lunch. The bishop arrived by 4 pm!! The trouble was petrol. There is an acute shortage again – something to do with the refinery and there is a hold up in Lagos docks so no diesel oil has been shipped in and this means that the oil tankers can't run on the roads. My petrol has just run out – I may be lucky and get some – but often you must wait in a hot sticky queue for 2 or more hours.

The men students did 2 plays this week – real spontaneous efforts-but excellent. The first was the story of Nebuchadnezzar and Shadrach, Meschach and Abednego. The second was done by the army students – they did the Trial of Jesus in front of Pilate. It was very dramatic and moving.

There has been no light at Fiwasaiye and so Sandra and Sheila have been here each night to do their marking of exam papers. Today I am going to speak at Fiwasaiye in the evening service. We are having a special service to pray for students in connection with their S.C. M week. Then on Wed our term will finish – the students go home on Thursday morning. On Friday morning we shall go off to Oshogbo for our weekend 'retreat'. I think that we shall all be needing a good rest by then. I have found that I have very little energy for anything extra and feel very tired in the evenings. It has rained a little which is good, but it is still very hot in the middle of the day. I wonder if you have your operation date yet Daddy.

My continued prayers are with you,

With love,

Elizabeth

Easter Retreat in Oshogbo

Vining Centre
1st April 1975

Dear Ma and Daddy,

Thank you very much for both your letters, the lovely Easter card, and the book 'Enough is Enough' which you sent with Sheila. I will enjoy reading it.

I have just returned to Akure after a very helpful retreat at the Baptist Compound at Oshogbo. It was a beautiful place, and the Americans there gave us a super welcome. We were 7. Myrtle, Pat, and I each had a bedroom in their 'Round House' Guest House.

Then Sheila and Jane were each given rooms in the house of Barbara (a Baptist missionary) and Grace Webster and Richard Childerstone were given rooms each in the house of Mr. and Mrs. Congdon. We used the round house as our base.

On Good Friday we arrived in Oshogbo about 11am and sorted ourselves out before starting our retreat at 1pm. We had a '2 hour' meditation with Richard giving readings about 'Who killed Jesus' from a book called Jesus of Galilee. It was very good indeed. In the evening we listened to 'St Matthew Passion'

We did our own cooking and serving of the food sharing it 2 by 2 and preparing (almost!) in silence and then having silent meals with music in the background rather than reading books St Julian's style or 'being read to'. This was a lovely way to have our meals – and the kitchen was so convenient and had just everything that we needed so it was no trouble to get the food ready – in fact, it was a valuable part of the retreat.

On Saturday morning we had a morning worship and then a Quiet Day til the evening when we had a time of prayer together followed by some more records. I enjoyed Saturday best; I think. I made a tomb on the table in the front hall and started to paint a picture of the garden. This is the first time that I have got my paints out so that was a great triumph. The only snag was that the time was too short really to get the picture finished.

On Sunday morning I was awake very early and we rolled back our stone and put the linen cloths inside the tomb. Myrtle came and scattered frangipani flowers all over the 'tomb garden' and it looked gorgeous and bright. Then we prepared our living room for Communion service – and we had a lovely simple Communion – 1662. Richard reads very slowly and meaningfully, and it was super. I read the Epistle from the Living Bible. Altogether it was a very moving experience.

Afterwards we had breakfast with red painted eggs and Easter cards given and received and each person had an apple and a tube of Smarties! It was amazing how much longer breakfast took when everyone was talking! We then listened to Donald Coggan on the radio preaching an Easter message from Canterbury Cathedral. It was good to join in with the Church at home. Then Mr and Mrs. Congdon invited us all to the most enormous and gorgeous lunch in their super house – carpeted sitting room and beautifully polished furniture etc. The Congdon's have been in Nigeria for 37 years – that is since 1937! They were very kind to us.

You asked about Richard Childerstone. He is now retired but he still teaches in Ibadan in a private school that is owned by Bishop Okunsanya's sister. He is not happy there now and may go to Jos to the school from which Elizabeth Newton is retiring.

Fancy you're getting snow on the Malvern's! We have had some rain here, but my garden is still jumping with locusts like grasshoppers who consume all the plants and bushes.

Pat Akinbadewa's mother and sister are here – staying in their partly finished new house in Alade on the road to Idanre. They came here on Thursday morning, and I showed them round Vining Centre and round Akure and then to see the Eyesorun. We finished our term on Wednesday night. Cornelius has not been well and was confined to bed in the hospital for 3 days to rest properly. They are having the Ondo Diocesan Retreat here at the Vining Centre this coming week so there is a large notice board at each of our entrances saying 'Come into the dessert and rest awhile!! 'When I told Cornelius in the hospital that this was written he said he thought they were going to write 'wilderness'!! That I thought was an even better joke.

On getting back from Oshogbo yesterday – Easter Monday: Grace, Sheila and Jane came here for lunch. Then Grace stayed on, and I took her back to Ado later in the afternoon. We still have terrible petrol troubles with queues and fights at the petrol stations when the tankers come.

We waited last week from Monday till Thursday with promises from Texaco and never got it – in fact, we lost our container there. We only got enough to go to Oshogbo and back because Sheila got a 'note' from the garage owner. There is petrol. It is just very difficult to come by because it is in such short supply. Before I could take Grace back to Ado yesterday Ezekiel kindly sucked and spat with a rubber tube and syphoned out half a bucket of the precious liquid to give me some in my tank. Today with a bit of long leg with a Mrs. Dada who owns the BP petrol station I managed to get almost 4 gallons in a container- but you couldn't get near the place with a car.

Anyway, I was glad that I went with Grace because it meant that we had a chance for a good natter and I had a nice early night and came back this morning in time for the Baptism in our chapel of the Wilde's 3 sons aged 6, 4 and 2. It was a lovely ceremony.

Now this afternoon we are hoping to have a feast at the Leper Settlement – prepared by the girls at Fiwasaiye school. It was supposed to be at 2 pm. Now it is at 5 pm because the schoolgirls disappeared into the market and the Eyesorun's van driver disappeared into the Petrol Station looking for petrol until it became obvious that no food would be ready by 2 pm at all.

Anyway, all was well in the end. I took 4 of our students to help in leading the sing- song and in the distribution of the bowls of rice and goat and a gang of Sheila's girls were there to dish out. Everyone sat down on their benches and all their bowls were submitted and put on the floor(!) and then rice put in them. There was a good deal of noise when the bowls were then reclaimed by their rightful owners.

I think I shall be here this week. I have the leader of the retreat staying in my spare bedroom. We have 3 weeks holiday – but I want to get ahead with clearing up papers and so on so that I can pack up quickly when I come home on leave. Also, I want to find out if Greece is possible.

With much love to you both and thank you for your regular letters,

Elizabeth

Vining Centre
6th April 1975.

Dear Ma and Daddy,

No letters this week – and no petrol again! Rather a 'low week' overall – but triumphant in the end. I am now at Ado with Grace because I was asked to take the evening service here at Ile Abiye. I decided to talk about the resurrection appearances – and I see that Jesus is with us especially when we feel low – as He was beside Mary when she was weeping in the garden – as He came to Thomas when he was doubting - as He walked with the men on the road to Emmaus as they were perplexed and depressed thinking that Jesus was dead - and as He helped Peter when he felt useless and couldn't catch any fish in the Sea of Galilee.

Anyway, these stories helped me this week. It is stupid really …. but I am very bad at coping with holiday times on my own and this week I read the book ' Who walk alone' by Margaret Evening. It is a very penetrating book and helpful in that it pinpoints the fact that a lot of single people have a lot of problems to face – but that many have managed to win through with GOD's help.

At Akure there was the Ondo Diocesan Clergy School this week on the Vining Centre Compound so there were about 80 clergymen having lectures and so on together. I was not included – but maybe that was my fault. I am sure if I had asked, I could have gone – but it was 'all men' and the women were cooking pots in the kitchen – and I wasn't needed for that either.

Sheila has been very busy marking her exam papers. We spent most evenings together so that was good. I helped to add up some of her mark sheets. Grace had invited her to come to Ado, but she felt she must stay and mark her papers which was disappointing. However, Grace and I went yesterday and sat and chatted in the swimming pool here in Ado – in about 2 feet of water because it was just filling up. Then in the evening we went down to Ikerre to see the Krol's – a Dutch couple who are working with Ekiti Diocese and setting up a new mechanical workshop and training centre. It was a nice change – and they gave us a gorgeous supper.... a bit late …. after 9pm. Marianne made pork cutlets and served them with carrots served in sour cream!! They are both 'characters' and need lots of prayer. A great deal of money has gone into this 'project' and in the end it will help the work in Ekiti Diocese, but all depends on Mr.

Krol. He is an experienced engineer and does most of the work himself now. If anything went wrong and he suddenly left it would be disastrous.

I hope that you both had a happy Easter, and that Jesus gave you joy, faith, hope and a feeling of usefulness.

With much love,

Elizabeth

Vining Centre
13th April 1975

Dear Ma and Daddy,

It was good to hear your news of Easter week. Fancy having snow on Easter Monday! I wish we had some here. It is still hot – but the rains have started. Yesterday Sheila and I went to Owo and spent the day with Joan and on the road coming back we had a terrific storm with incredible black clouds and lashing rain. Fiwasaiye are not likely to have electricity for some time because some trees fell and cut their main electric wires.

Inga phoned yesterday to tell me that she was going home to Bristol because she had just had a telegram to say that her father had died the previous weekend. Dear Inga – it was very hard for her that the message should take a whole week because obviously she would be too late to get there for the funeral. Also, because it arrived on a Saturday, she had to beg the Bank Manager to give her money – and she can't possibly do the necessary Immigration formalities quickly. Anyway, she has gone (17 Belluton Road, Knowle, Bristol 4 if you want to write to her)

I am enclosing a letter to my friends for duplication if you can bear it. I thought it was better to let them know our new address in Malvern and that I shall be home. Last time half of my pals didn't know until September.

I had hoped to go to Ibadan this week to see about my idea of going via Greece – but we have NO petrol. Whenever I join a hopeful queue, they stop selling! I will try and find out somehow – at present I have written to the Harborn's asking if they will be there in Athens during the week June 16 - 21st and if so, I should like to go there on Monday June 16th and travel to London on Thursday June 19th …. but of course this plan is not possible if there are no flights on those days. That would give me 2 full days in Athens which I think would be worthwhile. The only alternative is to go in September on the way back, but I think that end will be more rushed anyway.

I am enclosing 2 Postal Orders. Please can you put them in my bank a/c – or cash them and use the money for postage of my letters – as you like.

I am glad that Daddy is enjoying the book about Vanier. I have just been reading a book called 'Healing' by Father McNutt, a Dominican priest who is one of the speakers at the Fountain Trust meeting. One of the people he most often quotes from in his book is Agnes Sanford and 'The Healing Light' and 'Sealed Orders'.

This week I helped Sheila to write her reports from Monday to Thursday. There were only 2 weeks for the school holidays so really, she didn't get a holiday at all which is a shame because she is very tired. I am lucky because I have another week to go.

We are going to the Convent this evening to have supper with the sisters. One of them is going home to Ireland on Tuesday so I will ask her to take this letter and post it. Our post has been very slow here recently because of the petrol problem, I think. I hope it improves soon.

Much love – and looking forward to seeing you both,

Elizabeth.

Vining Centre
20th April 1975

Dear Ma and Daddy,

Yesterday I got 2 letters from you Ma. The first written on 7th April and the second on 14th April. I think that the petrol shortage here has affected the postal deliveries. I heard that no post left Akure at all for one complete week after Easter.

I am sorry to hear that Judith is still not well. It must be very worrying for Marguerita. How will Judith manage when she is married and must manage her own food? What are they going to Cliff College for? Isn't it a Methodist lay training College? In Newcastle? It is the place where John and Christine Job are going to be on the staff as from September. They are Methodists at present on the staff of Emmanuel College, Ibadan.

You certainly had a fair family reunion with Rod and Olive, Geoff, and Marguerita and co and then Joe on the phone. I am sorry that you have no news from Ronkswood and that you are still waiting to hear the date of the operation. It is difficult when you know it must be done and you want to enjoy the summer.

How much does Ruth weigh now? The last I heard about her weight she was 14 stone and now you say she has gained another stone! But I am glad to hear that she had a good Easter and is writing home cheerfully about life.

Prices are still rising here and Mama 'doesn't know where we are going'! I looked at my market book from a year ago and see that the price of meat has doubled in one year. 50K to N1.00 now. Eggs have gone from 70K to N1.00 per dozen. The latest in Akure is no tinned or powdered milk. I am OK for this because I get my pint in a plastic bag each other day from the Agric, but it is not so good when you want milk to put in the student's tea.

We started our continuation of the Lent Fellowship on Tuesday at the Noviciate. We studied the story of Jesus appearing to the disciples by the Sea of Galilee and then had a time of prayer together. It was a good beginning but a little disturbed by the mosquitoes which were nipping our legs and feet. The prayers were interspersed with the Novices shuffling their feet or slapping their legs! We hope to meet every 2 weeks. The next one will be at Mrs. Wilde's house.

This week we have our Leper Settlement Committee meeting on Wednesday.

The petrol crisis has continued, and I was running in the reserve on Monday and Tuesday. Before we went to the Fellowship meeting on Tuesday, I ran over a hoe with a spike which entered my back tyre, so I had a large puncture. I took it to be mended in Esso on Wednesday morning and left it there. In the afternoon a tanker came to Esso so there was a very long queue. Sheila and I joined the back of the queue and Sheila walked down to the front to see what the situation was. She came back and said, 'You are number 39 and its not moving'! So, we decided to go. But I drove down to collect my mended tyre and parked outside the petrol station. I went and got my tyre and while I was gone a soldier on duty saw us and said ' Come, Bring your container'! So, we did – and got 4 gallons from the middle of a chaotic crowd without even asking.

We have just finished our Communion service – 1 ¾ hours long! I have back ache! I shall be very happy to have 3 months at home with services of about 1 hour. This afternoon we go to the Leper

Settlement for an Open Air. We usually have 3 sermons at that!! In Yoruba. But it is not so bad because it is interspersed with choruses.

Last night Sheila invited Mr. and Mrs. Sambasivam and their daughter to supper together with Sandra and me and Dennis the C.U.S.O French teacher at Aquinas college. The Sambasivam's are Hindus from Ceylon. He is a Water Engineer for Akure and district. The wife is very friendly and cheerful, and the daughter is beautiful.

This evening we are going to the Eyesorun's for supper.

Yesterday afternoon I went to visit Mrs. Bali the wife of the Army Commander in Akure. She comes from near Jos. I met her husband for the first time. He is incredibly young for the Commander. He has been in England for training and seemed very pleasant and friendly. They live in a big house on the reservation with an Alsatian dog and an army guard on the gate. Mrs. Bali wants to come to our 'prayer' meeting.

I am going to have snails for lunch! Tokunbo is not so good at cooking them as Mrs. Fabuyi was. They are rather rubbery. One of my students brought them as a gift at the beginning of the term.

I have no new information about coming home – but plan to be coming in the week of June 16 -21st Goodee!

With much love,

Elizabeth

Vining Centre
27th April 1975

Dear Ma and Daddy,

Thank you both for your letters this week. I am sorry to hear you are still waiting for news about the hernias. Perhaps GOD's plan is to let the bud of the fruit of the Spirit - patience – a chance to grow!

This past week has been uneventful. Ezekiel was able to get 16 gallons of petrol so I have 4 gallons out of it and therefore can go around the town. We had a good Leper Settlement committee on Wed. evening, and we had the Board of Governors here on Tues. Arch. Opalami and Arch. Banjo were both here and sent their greetings to you.

I have been engrossed in a Taylor Caldwell novel called ' The Dynasty of Death'. It is an amazingly detailed story of the building up of the armaments industry in U.S.A beginning in the 19th century. It has 3 volumes – and goes on to the 20th century but I must get some other things done before I get involved in that!

It looks as though we may get a 3rd member of staff from Ibadan. This is good news – providing he fits in well here and is not being asked to transfer because he doesn't fit elsewhere. I will have to ask the Batts opinion because at present I do not know him.

I preached the sermon in Communion this morning. I should think that I have put them off asking me again for I must have spoken for 25 – 30 mins. The whole service didn't finish till 8.45. It begins at 7am! I talked about the difference that the Resurrection makes – in our experience of life, in our belief about life, in our belief about death and in our experience of death. I read the story of the death of Pastor Yoma in Rwanda.

I am glad you wrote to Inga Ma. I don't know when she will be back.

I have decided not to go to Greece after all. The time is too short, and the excess money is too great. If my information is correct C.M.S can go on a special cheap flight for N400 return instead of the usual N513. To go to Greece would be N594. At the best the excess would be N81 but at the most it would be N194 and really it is quite 'out' to be considering paying almost N140 to spend 2 days with the Harborne's in Athens!! Apart from the fact that I don't have that money to spare!

Please tell Dr MacDonald that I have written to C.M.S – some weeks ago to agree to add Malvern Priory to my Links.

Fiwasaiye have had more trouble with the thief-man. He came to Sandra's house again on Friday night. She was sleeping at Sheila's. He stole her crash helmet and some bread and butter from her fridge as well as some diabetic jellies! The policemen were on the compound – but they were down beside the dormitories and heard nothing. So now at Vining Centre we have 'emergency whistles' …. but we are safe really because we are behind the police station. So far, our whistles have only been used once – to call the men out to catch a goat!

Thank you for helping with the duplicating and addressing of letters etc. I am looking forward to my leave. I plan to fly on Mon 16th or Tues. 17th.

With love,

Elizabeth

Vining Centre
4th May 1975

Dear Ma and Daddy,

Thank you for your letter of 29th received today. I went to Ibadan on Friday and came back yesterday so I didn't have time to write to you on Sunday as usual. I am tired after the journey and tramping around Ibadan doing the shopping.

We were fortunate on Friday to get some petrol. Mrs. Dada, the wife of the Principal of the C.A.C School opened her petrol pump specially to give us a full tank, and some extra so that we should have enough to go and come back.

I stayed on Friday night at the Picard's in Immanuel College and saw Grace that evening. She was well and seems to be enjoying her university course. Then on Saturday I stayed with the Batts, and I went to see Joy Fletcher at Wesley College. On Sunday morning I visited Richard Childerstone who was in bed after a bout of malaria. He is now saying that he would love to come to the Vining Centre to teach!! It would be a good idea in many ways, but the Board of Governors have just approved the appointment of the Bishop of Ibadan's chaplain to come and teach here – so it will be difficult to accommodate both, and to find the salary for 2 people.

We dropped in on Yomi and Kelu on the way back – but they were out. Then we called to see Inga who had just come back from leave of absence – and was a bit shattered at the idea of going back to school today. She has a very uncooperative staff – who don't go to classes regularly etc and she doesn't know how to cope with them, 5 of the women are pregnant which doesn't help.

You seem to be having plenty of visitors – that's nice.

Some of our children have got whooping cough here – one has it badly …. it is bad for the children – and bad for all of us in class – because – cough, cough, cough - whoop …. vomit etc. repeating somewhat disturbs the class!

We had our Fellowship Group on Tuesday in Mrs. Wilde's house. We studied the appearance to Thomas. It was very good and a thoughtful meeting together. The next one is in my house on 13th May. I don't know what I shall do yet.

I shall be glad to get home. I feel like staying in bed for a week! How super that Janice is at home. It will be good to see her again.

With much love, Elizabeth.

Vining Centre
11th May 1975

Dear Ma and Daddy,

I have been thinking of you a lot this week because it was Ma's Birthday and Daddy's operation. I hope that I shall hear good news of the operation in the next letter. It is good that you have been able to share the Mission to Worcester before going into the hospital.

When did you say that Judith was getting married?

Please can you help me to make an appointment with the dentist – 2 or 3 doors up from Alison's house. If possible, in the time between coming home and the 26th of June visit to London.

I have 3 fillings which have holes in them. I went to the Dentist in Ado yesterday and he said that he wouldn't do them because it meant removing the whole filling and that the reason, I have been having a bit of toothache is that food has got up under the gums. Maybe he is right – but I should still like to see the dentist at home at the beginning of my leave.

Sandra and I went to see Inga on Tuesday evening and enjoyed watching the rest of the film about the singer in the Empty Quarter. Then we saw a film of 'Civilisation' by Kenneth Clark. It was part of the Television series. Very good.

On Friday we went to look round the new Army site here in Akure. It is an amazing place - a whole housing estate of houses for officers of different ranks – then blocks of flats for the Privates – offices – the Mess. A Catholic Church, a Protestant Church, and a mosque - a health centre …fantastic. The buildings are almost complete but there is no electricity and water yet.

Yesterday we went to Ado and had lunch with Grace. The Picard's came from Ibadan to see Sheila. They are all coming here today for lunch – so I shall have to do something about getting some food ready.

Vining Centre plods on. Did I mention last week that Richard Childerstone is now saying that he would like to teach here? This week we hear that he is in hospital with infective hepatitis. Not so good – and it is not easy for him to rest when he is discharged because he lives on his own. He is 63 and so has 2 more years to go before he can retire with a clergy pension.

I had a good long letter today from Stuart. He seems very concerned about feeling part of the family and so on, and still a bit stewed up about deciding where they should be married. Maybe the simple registry office ceremony will be the answer after all. Di seems to think it was sincere and dignified. I also hear from Ruth – that she hopes to see me at Stuart's wedding – I hope to see her before that!

I hope all is well operation wise.

With much love,

Elizabeth

Vining Centre
18th May 1975

Dear Ma and Daddy,

Stuart and Jutka will be with you today – Whitsun day- collecting their furniture. I wonder when Daddy will be out of hospital. It is good news that he is walking so soon after the op. I hope that the wound has mended well and that there is no trouble with the stitches. I am glad that there are interesting people in the Ward with Daddy. You remember Janet Olodumila who took us to the Club in Ondo? I met her in the next bed when I was in hospital in Ife!

It has been a normal week here …. except that I am tired and find everything a bit of an effort. I am OK when someone comes and needs something …. or I have a class in front of me to teach – but when I get back to my house on my own, I tend to flop and only feel like doing nothing. However, it's only another month till I came home.

On Monday evening I taught the men in my weekly lecture about the Sudan and traced the history of C.M.S work there and read some extracts from 'Yes' and from Ken and Betty Ogden's last letter.

On Tuesday evening we had our Fellowship here in my house. We took parts of 1 Cor 15. My record player conked out suddenly so we couldn't have 'I know that my Redeemer Liveth' and 'The Trumpets shall sound' as I had planned. I think something has gone wrong with the motor. It was a refreshing evening.

On Wednesday evening Sheila, Sandra and I were invited to the Noviciate to the Farewell for Sister Martinian. The novices did dance and a play – very good and amusing. We had Vespers together, then supper, then entertainment, then Compline …. all very nice.

The Epton's – V.S.O's from Ode, came on Friday and I went round to Fiwasaiye for coffee with them. Yesterday they all come to me for supper. I made a meat loaf because Tokunbo had gone to Ado for the day. Today we had a 2-hour Communion service. The students have gone now on a procession of witness. I have stayed behind.

On Thursday evening I was out between 11 and 12 midnight getting one of our babies admitted in the hospital with pneumonia. I saw the baby at 5pm and thought it would do till the morning – but no luck. The hospital had no ampicillin, so you must buy it yourself and of course no shops are open at 12 midnight, so we had to wait till morning for that.

I have just read ' Topaz' a novel about the Cuban crisis by Leon Uris. His books are very readable and compelling. Thank you very much for sending out the Circulars. I have heard from Di wanting me to go and see them in their Kentish Cottage. It is not far from my Kent village links.

No news yet of the flight time etc.

With much love to you both,

Elizabeth

Vining Centre
23rd May 1975

Dear Ma and Daddy,

It is great to hear that Daddy was discharged on May 14th. May and June are a good time for convalescence too. I hope that all is still going well. It is good that you retired before having these operations. Then there is no rush to do things again – you can just relax and accept the healing God gives in His own time.

It is Trinity Sunday today – and I am at Ado. I came over yesterday at lunch time - and will go back today for lunch at Sandra's. Grace has a weekend off but she has no transport, and it was pouring with rain yesterday morning, so I decided to come over and see her. Also, I find it 'renewing' to get right out of Vining for 24 hours or so. I was reading the Epistle for today this morning – Ephesians 1 and was very struck by the fact that on Trinity Sunday the main note is PRAISE – I think that I have heard too many sermons on the 'Trinity' talking all about the mathematics of 3 in 1 or about the development of the doctrine of the Trinity and so I have always thought Trinity Sunday a rather uninspiring day – but it is a super Epistle, and the Gospel is Nicodemus.

We have our prayer group on Tuesday at Sheila's. She is taking 'The Holy Spirit' as the theme of meditation

Martinian has gone home this week. I shall miss her. We often have long talks on the books we have read.

It is great to hear from Marguerita this week that Judith is so much better. I must write to her and congratulate her on her engagement.

This last week I did my lecture with the men as usual on Monday evening and read the story of a woman who was from a Moslem family and became a Christian in the 1930's in Khartoum and was baptised. It is from Oliver Allison's book – The Pilgrim Church.

On Tuesday Sandra and Sheila and I went to the Ceylon Water Engineers home, and we all had a very interesting supper and an evening's 'conversation' with them.

On Wed. evening we had the Leprosy Settlement Cmttee at Dr Sijuade's house. On Wed morning I sent 19 men to the hospital to donate blood – an achievement – because they are not very willing to go. The rest of the students are not very encouraging – their main thought is 'What do you get in exchange for giving your blood?' or they pour scorn on the whole set up and say:' Of course they will sell your blood to someone'!!

I was leaving this space to let you know my flight date and time - I thought I would phone Lagos tonight and try to find out – but the line to Lagos is 'bad' they say so there is no chance. I will let you know as soon as I find out.

With much love to you both,
Elizabeth

28th May 1975

Dear Ma and Daddy,

The flight that I am coming on is on Monday June 16th. Flight BR 368 leaving Lagos at 9.30am and arriving in London at 17.25pm I presume it is Heathrow because I asked to go to Heathrow, it will be super to see you then,

With much love,
Elizabeth.

Vining Centre
1st June 1975

Dear Ma and Daddy,

I hope that you will have received my letter about the flight time on Mon. June 16. I am in Ife today so I don't have the numbers with me, but I shall look forward to seeing you between 5-6pm on that day.

It is Half Term just now and I have come to Ife with Sandra, and we are staying in Prof Rodger's house. Unfortunately, Yomi and Kelu have gone off to Lagos, so we have not been able to see them – but we have had a very nice restful weekend, and we were able to buy some cheese and some cucumbers yesterday. Then in the evening we went to a 'Potluck supper'. Everyone brought their own food – Indian or American, Nigerian, or Japanese, or English – and then we ate out of it all. There were between 60 and 80 people there. It was all a bit of a squash. The main object of the business seemed to be eating. There was some delicious food.

Earlier in the week I think I had bilious attack- I don't know whether it was malaria or what. I just felt sick. However, it went off by Thursday. We had Board of Governors on Thursday, so I didn't have much to do.

On Tues. we had our Fellowship, and it was the Eyesorun's birthday, so we had special refreshments for that. Now there are only 2weeks left and I shall be home. People are beginning to think of their 'shopping lists'!! We have exams this week and then the Commissioning on June11th and the organisation of what the women should do when I go away.

I am writing this quickly before we leave Ife and move on to Ondo to stay tonight with Inga. Then Prof Rodgers will post it in Ibadan tomorrow. No letters from you for some time. Post is bad here now.

I hope Daddy's convalescence is going well. It will be good to see you both and the rest of the family.

With love

Elizabeth

Home on leave July to August 1976

This was a good leave. I felt invigorated and strengthened by all the happy meetings and experiences of my time at home. The highlights included my brother, Stuart's wedding to Jutka Fischer and a very happy holiday in Scotland with my parents and Anne Harris and a lovely uplifting week in Iona

Vining Centre
29th September 1975

Dear Ma and Daddy,

Really, I am so much blessed by loving parents and family in England and then more friends and people to care for me here in Nigeria. The flights were good – only held up waiting for all the baggage to get put on both in London and Amsterdam. Some Nigerians bring so much .... for selling here I imagine. The woman next to me spent £237 in excess luggage!! Just about my allowance for 3 months. I read 'Green Dolphin Country' most of the way – between snacks and meals and drinks and chatted a bit to the people next to me. Then when I got to Lagos Myrtle and Pat and Tokunbo and Ezekiel were all there to meet me. Wasn't that super? So, we came here together. Tokunbo and Ezekiel have gone next door to be with Mr Iwuchukwu who is an old student of is V.C. who was ordained yesterday? So, I am really feeling that I am beginning to be back in Nigeria. Of course, we have had a good natter and talked all about Iona and people we have met etc. Then Sheila phoned from Akure. She sounds a bit strained. A girl died suddenly in the hospital last week and they are all very upset about that. Martinian is not yet back – so I hope that she is well. Tomorrow I shall be going back to Akure – probably going <u>into</u> Lagos in the morning because Shelagh Jebb has sent an assignment to buy some drugs.

Tues am:

Lagos is hot as usual! And I didn't sleep particularly well with the air conditioner humming so I am looking forward to getting back to Akure.

Thank you both for the super leave. There are so many happy things to remember and so much generosity that I feel rich. Now you will be able to do all the various things that people phone up about and you say: 'Well, my daughter from Nigeria..............!!

With much love,
Elizabeth

Vining Centre
5th October 1975

Dear Ma and Daddy,

Thank you for the 'Welcome letter' which I received when I got back. It is true - there are so many happy memories of the time at home, and it was lovely to see so many friends. It was almost too good! And makes me a bit home sick, but I think I will be alright when I get adjusted to being back here.

Our journey back from Lagos on Tuesday was not entirely uneventful. Tokunbo and Ezekiel and I went into Lagos to look for some B.C.G vaccine for Shelagh Jebb. This took some time because I went into CMS and saw Rev Faji there and then walked to various wholesale chemists who didn't have B.C.G. The new Gov't have tried in Lagos to relieve some traffic congestion. There were a lot of police and soldiers directing the traffic. So that is hopeful. They are also busy 'retiring' people – particularly if the person became very rich in his post or was doing it inefficiently. This is also a good thing if it is done justly.......which is not so easy.

On the road back to Ibadan we had a puncture and took a long time to get the hub cap off. Then we had to spend more time in Ibadan waiting while the spare tyre was mended. The net result was that we arrived in Akure about 9 pm rather tired, hungry, and dirty.

On Wednesday I spent some time unpacking and then went with Sheila to Ondo to have lunch with Inga, and to visit Bro. Fred and Sister Mildred who were both in Ondo sick. Then Thurs. Fri and Sat have been busy days preparing for the beginning of term. Grace and Shelagh came over from Ado yesterday and had lunch with me, so it was good to see them.

Today we had our first service of the term. It started at 9 am and finished by 11.15! Cornelius spoke about 'Prayer' and how the most important thing for the students to learn from here was how to pray. It was a good message for us all. We have no 3rd member of staff after all. The fellow who was to come in the holidays has gone to university and the one promised from Lagos isn't coming after all. The Bishop of Ondo is now trying to find someone. Cornelius is very disappointed and everyone is very disgusted at the Bishop of Ibadan sending us someone who he must have known wanted to go to university, except that it sounds as though he didn't want the fellow to go.

Today I have had a good 'Scottish' morning because the service on the Radio was from Foyers and now I am listening to a record of Scottish songs and music which Dr Salama gave me to give to Dr Sijuade. It is 'Step with my crummock to the Isles' now. There is no water in the taps. I can't think why at this time of the year. I will have to try and wash my hair using a bucket of hot and a kettle of cold water. Prices have shot up a bit in my absence. Martinian is back from Ireland so that's good. Sheila is here too. I will soon get used to getting back I expect.

Thank you for all your love and prayers.

Elizabeth.

Vining Centre
12th October 1975

Dear Ma and Daddy,

It was very good to get your letters this week. There was a Public Holiday here on Mon and Tues. for the end of Ramadan, so no post came through before that. I expect yours from me was late too for the same reason. We didn't keep the holiday here in the Vining Centre but continued with the work of the beginning of the term as usual. It seems more than a week since I came back, and we are settling into the routine with the women. The men still only have 2 members of staff and there are now 18 ordinands from different dioceses, so the task is almost impossible. The Bishop of Ondo is very sympathetic, and he is trying to help us to find another person, but really it isn't very fair when our 2 present members of staff are from Ondo Diocese.

I discovered today that Tokunbo has sold the bicycle that I helped him to buy 3 years ago. Presumably he needed the money to give to his new 'Wife'. I don't know and I am bad at finding these things out – and questions like that would get stonewalled. Then, sometime in September he had the nerve to apply to the Vining Centre for a loan of N80 to buy a new bicycle.!! Then he will be wanting a rise from me to pay it off!! Cornelius hasn't given him the loan and I don’t support it. As Mama Ademoye says – 'he doesn't know how to cut his coat according to his measurement'.......and the biggest snag is that his mother has never liked his wife and has always said that he should take another woman.

So it is difficult to know what to do. I don't see why I should pay him more to cover his sins, but inflation is still on here and prices are going up and up in the market so that he is going to find it difficult to make ends meet. It would be better if he could find an afternoon job and do my chores in the morning – or get a more highly paid cook's job for a family or a company rather than just for a single missionary. Then I could get a girl to come and help me with washing and cleaning and do my own cooking. That's what Inga is doing now.

I was over in Ondo yesterday and saw Inga and had lunch with her there. She is going on leave this coming Tuesday for 4 months. First, she is going to Germany and then she is going back to her mother in Bristol. I think she would like to do a course while she is at home. She liked the sound of Iona for a holiday, but I told her that Bishop's House was closed in the winter. Is that true of the Abbey?

While I was in Ondo, I met the new VSO girl at St Monica's. She is called Christine – rather a scruffy modern English graduate with black eye paint around her eyes – a long skirt, platform shoes and no bra under her singlet type top. I hope she will be happy at St Monica's and not get herself all tied up with Nigerian men who have no good intentions. I am sorry, I brought the VC photos back here. I had intended to leave them with you. On the other hand, the people who are in them are very happy to see them.

It is good that you got your tyre mended on the AA. No AA here! And not much petrol either. We are back to the situation before I left of queuing for petrol. I don't know what has gone wrong now. The papers report more than 400 ships now waiting at Lagos ....so there's no improvement on the 300! Today there is a photo of General Gowon in the Daily Times taking his food in Warwick University cafeteria. It says he used to be surrounded with servants and now he is having to serve himself. But he looks happy enough. I am glad that you have contacted Ada Chukwura at Lawnside. I knew one Mrs. Cole who was at UMC. She helped us with one SU Camp here in Akure in 1996. Her daughter, Taiye Cole taught history at Fiwasaiye. Maybe she is Ada's grandmother, or she is related somehow.

Shelagh Jebb was here yesterday and left a note for me asking me if I would consider being the CMS Rep when/if she goes to Yemen. I guess I shall be about the only CMS person left!! I am not sure who I shall be representing. Anyway, I shall have to discuss it with Shelagh when I next see her. I hope to go to Ado before Grace goes on leave at the beginning of November.

Thank you for tying up of my ends like the Building Society and Will and Pax house affairs. I think Eric is due to come on November 1 or there-abouts so the time for Pax things is not so long.

We are going to have the meeting of our Fellowship on Tuesday. It will be at the Noviciate. I was there on Friday together with Sheila and Christine (the Canadian Volunteer now at Fiwasaiye) I showed them my slides and talked to them about Iona. I enjoyed seeing the slides again anyway. It was like going back to Iona. I think I am going to talk to our men this week on 'Christian Communities'.

This evening I went up to see Dr and Mrs. Sijuade and had quite a long chat with Mrs. S. She is not happy in Akure. Her husband doesn't take his holidays because of all the work involved in being head of the hospital and that means that she doesn't get any proper break either. Janet Olowoyo is now at Ife University doing a Proficiency course. I think it is for one year.

Apparently, it has been cold here this wet season but today is quite sticky and hot. I have finished the white dress with roses and am wearing it today. It seems to be quite successful. Eyesorun took Mrs. Bali's hat and dress down to Lagos last week. She should be back at the end of this week so I will hear if it was OK.

Thank you for your letters, and your love.

With much love to you both

Elizabeth

Vining Centre
18th October 1975

Dear Ma and Daddy,

I have received your letter of 9th Oct Daddy during this week. It is good to know that Skiddy has renewed the Guardian, because I was wondering when it ran-out and the papers kept coming. Today's service on the Radio was from a Dominican school in Northern Ireland. The girls are singing with guitars. They sang 'How great thou are' very beautifully and then ' Rejoice in the Lord always....'We had our Fellowship on Tuesday evening at the Noviciate. It was a good time of quiet and prayer with the Catholic Sisters and Brother Fred from St Peter's.

I talked to our men on Monday about 'Communities' and showed them slides of Iona. Then I asked them to write up what they had learnt. One fellow reported that we remember the first missionary to our land was Christopher Columbus! This after my explaining that Columba was the first missionary to Scotland. On Wednesday I again looked at my slides of Iona with Pat and Francis Akinbadewa. Pat had been there long ago, so she was very interested to see how the buildings have changed etc.

We had a new baby on Tuesday. We went to the hospital and left the Mum about 1 am and she 'put to bed' and delivered a female child by the next morning. I think I may have caught a cold going out in the night – or maybe it was getting my feet wet after a great rainstorm on Tues. Anyway, I got a rotten headachy feverish cold on Wed and Thursday, so I didn't enjoy teaching on those days. But by Friday it had cleared off and I felt much better. It is amazing how easily you can catch a cold here. I think it must have something to do with the humidity.

Yesterday I went up to Ado to see Shelagh and Grace. Grace is busy packing up ready to go home at the beginning of November. Today I am going to speak in the evening service at Fiwasaiye

I took Veronica, one of the Leprosy patients to the hospital yesterday to see Dr Wilde, because she is pregnant. It is great that Dr Wilde will now see them for Ante- Natal care. The building of the new doctor's room at the settlement is almost complete. We shall now need to furnish it.

The new government seem to be choosing good people for some of their 'cabinet' posts so that's hopeful. The Eyesorun has been asked to be the Commissioner for Trade and Cooperatives! So, she will have to be based in Ibadan as part of the Western State Government. It is a pity for us in Akure because we shall miss her here very much indeed, but it is good for the government.

Thank you for your letters and prayers,

With much love,

Elizabeth

Vining Centre
26th October 1975

Dear Ma and Daddy,

Thank you for your letters and all the news therein of Lois 's visit and of Lorraine's championship. That's great, isn't it? I will write her a card of congratulation – but I may have to send it via Malvern if I don't have the Motherwell address here. I am sorry you didn't think much of Harry Blech. I remember the last time I heard him in London I thought he had passed his best. I hope you had a good time with the Bennetts.

We have a 'boy' on the staff now to help the students in Years 1 and 2 with their English and Yoruba. He is a W.A.S.C fellow (school cert) and is better than nothing but doesn't really solve the overall question of shortage of staff.

It has been a good week this week. I talked about 'High Church' and 'Low Church' with the men on Monday and changes that are taking place in the Church at home. This week I am going to describe Series 3 – and introductions into the communion Service like Kiss of Peace and people joining in the Intercessions etc. I hope then to go on to look at Prayer Book revisions in general and then at the Reformation.

I went to see Martinian on Monday and we had a long discussion about prayer and how we are so often inattentive in chapel etc. She loaned me some books, one of which I have read called ' He touched me' by a Jesuit - John Powells. I have also been reading Donald Swann's book 'The Spaces between the Bars'. It is very thought provoking. Sisters Macnoase, Martinian and Agnes Mary came to supper on Wednesday, and we had a very happy time together.

I have been thinking especially of the chorus ' Father, I adore You, lay my life before You. How I love You' from Sounds of Living Water. It is very helpful in one's Quiet Time I find. I taught it to the men the other day and they sang it in 3 parts and liked it too, I think.

Ebun is here this morning – on a visit. She has been through all my photos and can identify the whole family accurately. She seems very well – although, she has gone 'piss' twice in just over an hour!

Yesterday I went with Cornelius to the wedding of our Archdeacon's son. It was in Ondo Cathedral with great pomp and circumstance and thousands of naira worth of brocade and lace. They say that Ondo women buy lace for such occasions and then sell it in

Akure market! I think that there were 40 clergy officiating and there were about 20 attendants – Pages, flower girls, junior bridesmaids and senior bridesmaids and maids of honour etc etc!

One of our students – Ekpo, has asthma. He had an attack last night and didn't sleep at all, I think. The other students were all frightened out of their wits. Please pray for him. He has seen umpteen doctors and has medicine – but I am sure that he needs to be able to relax in his mind and not be so worried about his condition. He is a soldier – but in the Education Corp so he is not a 'fighter' soldier.

We have our Fellowship this coming Tuesday. We are taking the theme 'Enlightenment' It is in Sheila's house.

The sun is shining here. With much love,

Elizabeth

Vining Centre
2nd November 1975

Dear Ma and Daddy,

2 letters this week from you – very nice. It is good that you had the Bennetts to stay and that you went to see Jose Spurgeon. I am glad that you liked Malcolm Bole. It will be interesting to see what happens to the Bennett's idea of retiring to Malvern. Perhaps they should bring some of their friends with them? What about the Thorpe's? I am sure they would like to be nearer Barbara.

I have had Titi Okotun to stay this weekend. She came on Saturday afternoon loaded with onions, carrots, cucumbers, tins of milk and dried fish from Ibadan – and shampoo, soap powder, a nighty, and a towel – all for my birthday. Wasn't that sweet of her?

I shall be interested to see how Eric arranges for my Pax things to get here. The most sensible thing would be to leave them with someone so that Jesse Hillman can bring them. He and Rev Faji from Lagos are coming here on Nov 28th. Thank you for all the phoning and so on involved in getting the things.

If Ada has Grade 9 in any subject that is a failure and not a pass in W.A.S.C – but you can still get your certificate if the aggregate of the best 6 subjects passes muster. Probably It is just as well if she repeats at O level stage.

Last night I was at a real Nigerian 'Do' – organised by the Women's Christian League of St David's Church to raise money for their

Society to give to the Church. You invited all the big wigs and business tycoons you can think of and blast their ears drums with an amplified band, feed them with chicken and coke and beer and ask for their donations. It said 7pm but nothing happened till after 9pm and we couldn't escape till 09.30 when the donations were taken. I was sitting near Adeniran, an old Andrian, who was a friend of Talabi J and said he visited us in Kilburn. I didn't discover this until 9.25 – mainly that the band was so noisy that you couldn't hear your neighbour speak.

This morning I went to the Salvation Army School Harvest Thanksgiving. I was the speaker! A bit daft because everything had to be translated. I told the story of the Sower with pictures. That part was OK and the whole thing was well organised until towards the end when everyone came forward in groups to bring their offerings. Then things became a bit chaotic.

The most extraordinary piece of news is that Jane Pelly has been told to transfer from Kazaure Gov't G.S to Benin Gov't G.S and the Indian woman at Benin has been told to go to Kazaure. No one knows the reason, but neither are happy. It is a big blow to Jane – she is good at starting schools and that's what she was doing in the North, but Benin is already an established school. These frequent transfers are one of the great plagues of the Education system here. Sheila has just lost her Yoruba graduate – transferred to the Teacher Training College in Ado. Maddening.

Mrs. Bali liked her dress and hat. I have not seen her, but the Eyesorun took them to Lagos

The headlines in the Daily Times this week were 'Conspiracy of Sabotage' accusing overseas countries of flooding the market with cement!......which they admitted the previous regime had ordered – 20 million tons of it.

I am reading about Luther and the Reformation now. I am enjoying it.

Praise God from whom all blessings flow.

With my love,

Elizabeth

Vining Centre
9th November 1975

Dear Ma and Daddy,

Thank you very much for the super card of Jubilee Drive that came for my birthday. It is a lovely reminder of home.

I had a good day yesterday with a very successful and happy party in the evening. There were just over a dozen guests – Mama and Adeoba and Sobukunola – Sheila and the Whittals from Ondo Fred from St Peter's, Sisters Martinian and Mildred. Susan -a V.S.O at St Monica's and Dennis and Heidi – 2 C.U.S.O (Canadian) volunteers. Cornelius and Victoria didn't come because Cornelius is 'resting in the hospital' again although if you ask Victoria after him, she says 'He has travelled'. I do hate this kind of unnecessary lie. It seems to me that it is because they are not facing up to the problem of Cornelius' ill health which I am sure relates to drinking too much. I really fear that he is becoming alcoholic - but they won't admit it. Very sad.

Mama Ademoye hasn't been well this week either, but her sickness is more straightforward. I think she was just exhausted after supervising the cutting up of cows and goats for the feast following the marriage of the Archdeacon's son in Ondo!! So, she was ordered a week's rest. Anyway, she improved after the week in bed.

Susan the V.S.O stayed the night with me last night. I like having visitors. This morning we went and had a walk around the Agric. We will go and have lunch with the Whittles and Sheila at Fiwasaiye. Next week I am going away for our Half Term holiday. I am going to Ibadan on Thurs/Fri and then on to Ife on Sat/Sun to stay with Prof and Mrs. Rodgers so I shall be able to see the Bamgboye's there.

I am listening to the Cenotaph Service on the radio – the same ceremony for the last 55 years – I should think the British Legion fellows are getting a bit old. They are just on the Last Post. I am still reading up about the Reformation and finding it very interesting. I have a Catholic History book as well as several Protestant ones. It is fascinating reading about the same people in the 2 books.

Jesse Hillman will be around at the end of the month. It will be good to see him and see if he has any suggestions towards solving the staffing problem of Vining Centre.

I wore the white blouse you gave me last night – it is light and comfortable. It is now becoming hotter – we are starting the dry season. 84 degrees F in my sitting room this afternoon at 5pm.

With my love to you both,

Elizabeth

Vining Centre
16th November 1975

Dear Ma and Daddy,

Thank you, Daddy, for the bank statements and your letter. No letter from Ma last week – maybe it is still in the post.

I am now on Half Term and staying with the Rodgers in Ife. It is good to get away for a break and think about completely different things. I had a happy time in Ibadan yesterday and stayed with Jose but also saw the Nightingales and Grace and Titi as well as some of the husbands of my women. I also spent a lot of money in Kingsway – partly because I wanted to stock up a bit before Christmas and to buy some Christmas presents. If you don't do this now in November it becomes increasingly difficult nearer Christmas.

I have just finished reading a book called 'Corrymeela' – the search for Peace by Alf McCreary. It is about a Christian Community in N. Ireland where they seek to provide a meeting place for Catholics and Protestants. During the crisis times they have taken groups of children out of Belfast and given them a country holiday as well as the opportunity to get to know children from 'the other side'

I hear from Odd Down that Frank Northcott has had a heart attack and he has been told to do nothing for some months.

This last week in Akure has been much as usual. I talked to the men about Luther on Monday night. On Tuesday we had our Fellowship meeting -only 4 of us- but a time of quiet prayer fellowship. On Tues and Wed nights Doug Evans was with us – he stayed with me because Sheila already had other visitors. Daphne is coming in 2 weeks' time. Cornelius was away in the hospital all the week, but several of the men had their G.C.E papers so they had plenty to do.

I went to see the Eyesorun in her office in Ibadan on Friday – a great large, air-conditioned office with fitted carpet and a giant-sized desk. She has a great task – but I am sure she will do something worthwhile. Her main aim is to help the ordinary people, and to get some control into the prices of foodstuffs and other consumer goods.

Sunday: I was at the service in the University this morning. It was a good service. Afterwards I went with the Rodgers to a Christening Service of one of the steward's children and then we went to the Staff Club for a very lovely lunch. Yomi and Kelu were also there having a lunch party with one of the Methodist ministers who is now to go to Immanuel College on the staff. Dear Yomi was very welcoming. Then up comes Kelu – also welcoming but obviously 'offended' that I hadn't written to her from home! Isn't it sickening that I always seem to be in her black books? Especially as I am sure that I wrote them a postcard (maybe I forgot) Anyway I will go down and see them this afternoon. I have forgotten to bring the photos of Stuart's wedding – another clang! Anyway, I will never greet anyone with 'You promised to write, and you never wrote!!' Later: In fact Kelu was very friendly when I went to see them.

Thank you very much for the cheque of £5. I wore 'your' blouse for my birthday party, and it was very comfortable. I am glad you are enjoying 'Power in Praise' How nice of them to give it to you.

With much love to you both.

Elizabeth

Vining Centre
23rd November 1975

Dear Ma and Daddy,

Thank you for letters. It is great to be in touch with you. I received 2 letters from Ma this week- written on Nov. 1st and 9th. The boys in our sorting office were doing G.C.E I was told! Maybe that's what held up your letters. I also received the Pax parcel from Eric – all very satisfactory BUT there is no bill? I assume you paid that with my blank cheque. Please could you let me know the amounts for each thing because the women are giving some of the things to the Centre and I need to know how much they cost.

I haven't finished the film in my camera. I will do so and maybe send it with Jesse Hillman. Please tell Mr Iliffe that I have seen his 'Theatre' – It is still there – but it is not used for anything now. I will try and take its photo.

Rev S.O. Komolafe is not I think and old Andrian of your day. Your Akomolafe is a Chief and lives in Ibadan, I think. When are the Bennetts going to move into their new bungalow? I wonder why Dr McD was after 'news' -Did they not get my Link Letter which I wrote in October? Please be careful about giving out my weekly letters for magazine materials! It could sometimes be disastrous- either if a comment on politics was printed without explanation – or if a personal criticism or comment on the situation in V.C got back to the source. I shall be interested to hear of your visit to Stuart and Jutka, and Anne. I hope the latter is not down the drain – she doesn't write recently. I shall also be interested to hear how your family pow wow gets on.

This week has been a rather higgledy -piggledy week. Cornelius returned from the Hospital on Monday and seems perfectly well – but continues to run the compound without informing the rest of the staff what is going on or what is going to happen next. This I find most aggravating. Maybe I am at fault too because I find it so difficult to forget the niggle of annoyance that he didn't feel that he should tell us when he was in hospital. Then on Thursday afternoon – without any warning - the men had a Sunday School course run by 2 outside clergymen – so the women had to rush up and down and cook food. On Friday morning I discovered that all our tables from the classrooms had disappeared to the hall – and had to be recovered. On Saturday morning we went to the Leper Settlement Harvest – which I knew about- but while we were away there was an enormous tree cutting campaign on the compound which upsets me because we keep cutting down beautiful trees (which may be necessary for the safety of houses), but we never replace them. Also, the trees help to shade the houses and make them cooler. We were supposed to have a staff meeting on Thursday, but it was cancelled at the last minute because of the Sunday School teachers' course. Cornelius always says he thinks the staff meeting is important – but he always needs to be reminded to have one.

Today I preached the sermon at the Communion Service and read about the Dry Bones in Ezekiel – saying that God has the power to revive us, and to revive our Church. We sang 'O breath of life come sweeping through us' which the men enjoyed and learnt quickly. Did I tell you they didn't catch on to 'Holy Holy' at all?

I am still reading about the Reformation. We are going to look at Henry VIII, Edward VI, Mary, Elizabeth 1, and Archbishop Cranmer tomorrow!

I have forgotten if I left anything for you for Christmas!! I thought of giving Daddy McNutts ' Healing' book, but I think you said you were going to get that somehow. Was that so??

Sheila has had all the Anglican Sports at Fiwasaiye this week, so she came here today to try and sleep it off. She did well and slept 2 hrs. in the morning and 1 hr. in the afternoon – but she is still very over tired. Jesse Hillman and Rev Faji from Lagos come here this weekend.

With much love,

Elizabeth

Vining Centre
30th November 1975

Dear Ma and Daddy,

It was super to have your letter telling of your visit to Stuart and Jutka and Uncle Joe. Sorry you had such a nasty journey getting there. It is always amazing how people turn out to help when you are in a fix. I am glad you are enjoying reading 'Healing' by McNutt. I have still to listen to his tape with Sheila and Martinian and others. We had a very thought-provoking meeting last Tuesday on the subject of 'Dialogue' between people and between us and God.

Jesse Hillman came on Friday with Rev Faji, and we had a useful time together. Jesse has suggested that we try to arrange for a C.M.S Area Secretary to come to Vining Centre for one term – so that they can teach the men and get some insight into the Church in Nigeria. Then he promised that C.M.S will look out for someone in the future. So that is good. It seems that the Bp of Ondo doesn't favour Richard Childerstone coming here because they seem to have the idea that he doesn't get on with people – presumably a garbled version of the fact that he had a disagreement with Mrs. Ogunlesi about his financial affairs. So, he may well go home finally.

Jesse also told me that Willoughby Carey has died. Maybe you have heard this already. I will write to Jenny – thro' you -because I don't have their home address. I have sent the film that I almost finished at home with Jesse – and some Christmas cards for a few of my friends so that they can be sent with my Christmas letter. Jesse gets home on Dec 13th so they should arrive after that. I am sending my letter today so that it can be duplicated and sent out. Please DO

NOT send a copy to C.M.S for Link Parishes because I have sent a different letter to C.M.S this time.

I had a letter from Anne. She is obviously very down and depressed and lonely. She asks if I can suggest any helpful books. Maybe 'Beyond ourselves' by Catherine Marshall. What do you think? Can you get it and send to her?

Christine our C.U.S.O volunteer at Fiwasaiye is pretty upset now. She has a fiancé in Canada – and parents and family- but there is a postal strike so that she has only heard once or twice since she came in September. She tried to phone- and has been trying for 3 days without success. The worst thing was that Lagos was through to her fiancé yesterday morning, but they didn't get through to Akure. Poor kid – it is miserable for her.

Ruth Howard will be coming to stay with me for Christmas – probably with her mother. Joy Fletcher from Ibadan may come too. It is nice that you met Ruth and her mother in Moffat because you will be able to imagine us better at Christmas. I am glad that you have decided to go to Stuart and Jutka. I am sure you will have a very happy Christmas there although you will miss your friends at St Matthias. Gemma is not coming to Nigeria just now. She wrote a very cheerful letter. Her house church in Hampstead seems to have done her a power of good. It is good that she went to see Stuart and Jutka and that she saw Ruth there too.

We have just had our Harvest today. It was a very enjoyable service although we were at it from 10am to 1.20pm. I then went off to Sheila's for lunch and a rest and came back to my house before 4 pm. The students were still drumming in the Hall at the Auction Sales! They stopped about 5 o'clock. They say they have raised around N400 so that's a real record. We are hoping to extend the chapel and make it bigger, so this is a good start to the fund.

The next 2 1/2 weeks will be busy with exams and the end of term events. There will be 42 certificates to write for the men and 14 for the women. You should get another letter before Christmas – maybe two – but post is taking its time now.

Often thinking of you – and so glad to get your cheerful letters.

With much love,

Elizabeth

Vining Centre
7th December 1975

Dear Ma and Daddy,

Good to get your 2 letters earlier this week, and the Pax House Receipts. Sorry to hear of the corrosion under the car needing £110 but I agree it is best to do it rather than thinking of a replacement.

I had a very good letter from John Riddout telling of some of the happenings in the Priory particularly the time when they had Robin McGlashin to lead a kind of 'meeting point' I am glad that you are enjoying McNutts book on 'Healing' and that your cell is stimulating. I gave the men a lecture on Monday night on how after Vatican 2, there was so much more hope of working together with the Catholic Churches. Then I asked the men to write 'Suggestions for improvements and changes needed in the Anglican Church of Nigeria in 1975' I have found their answers fascinating. Many of them feel very strongly against the Book of Common Prayer and keeping rigidly to liturgical worship without any participation by the people. They also want more music with drums and dancing in the services...... and many other points. So, there is hope amongst the younger men I feel if the bishops and oldies allow them to have a look in.

Today I am with Shelagh Jebb at Ado – and enjoying being in a different atmosphere. I am to take the service tonight in their hospital chapel. This morning I went with Shelagh to the Cathedral communion service and afterwards got talking to the Bishop of Ekiti about staffing at the Vining Centre and mentioned Richard Childerstone. The bishop had not heard of his being mooted before and he thinks it would be a good idea – so was going to phone Cornelius about it! We shall see what happens because I think Cornelius has just written to Richard refusing him.

One leprosy patient – Veronica – was admitted in the hospital on Thursday and she delivered twins – one boy and one girl. So that was great. The Health Sister, Mrs. Omigbodun made all the arrangements. I only went to visit and then on Sat. morning to take them back to the settlement. They are 5lbs 2 and 4lbs 9 so that's not bad – but I still fear that they may get an infection or something at the settlement. They are so small, and the place is by no means ideal for bringing up infants.

One of my students – Mrs. Ogunbiade- has had a lot of abdominal pain and been generally sickly all this year. I sent her to Dr Wilde, and he thinks she may have grumbling appendix so he sent her to the Surgeon – Dr Atalabi – who didn't even bother to examine her himself but said he would operate. The snag is that I just hope this fellow knows what to do. He apparently studied for surgery in Edinburgh but didn't pass anything, but he is not an impressive caring doctor at all. Dr Wilde can't easily do it because he is not the surgeon anymore and because he is on holiday until Dec 26th. So please pray that we may make the right decision so that she may be healed.

Here at Ado, I have met Lily Stott who has come to Ile Abiye. She is a lady in her 60's – a Sister Tutor and a Quaker- who came out to Rivers State in 1968 to help with Relief work. She is going to come and stay with me for the weekend of 19th -20th so that will be nice. Shelagh has loaned me the tape of the Sound of living Waters so I shall be able to share some of it with our group. Sister Martinian was away in the North all last week. She came back on Thursday night – so it was good to see her again on Friday.

With much love,

Elizabeth

Vining Centre

14th December 1975

Dear Ma and Daddy,

I am sending this to Hackney with a tape in the same post. I hope that you get the tape if not before Christmas, then during the time you are with Stuart and Jutka. It comes with lots of love – and really takes the place of my letter this week so I won't write all that I said. I am hoping to send it off with Jane Pelly tomorrow, so I ought to go round to Fiwasaiye soon to give it to her.

We had a very enjoyable carol service this afternoon as you will gather from the tape. Most of the singing is from St Louis Carol Service which I went to on Wed. At our own service I kept forgetting to put the tape recorder on – and our singing wasn't very remarkable till the end when I was diverted from the tape recorder because I went off to get some refreshments. The students were then singing lyrics in different languages. Anyway, it was fun.

Thank you for Daddy's letter and his quotes from Philippians. It is good that you are going to help in Westminster Abbey – rather an interesting experience I should think. Thank you too for the parcel via Eric which I have not yet opened – according to instructions- and thank you for the nice Christmas card. I had a great heavy parcel from Ruth this week. She is a dear. She has hardly any money and then sends me mighty parcels costing over £1 in postage. I have saved that too for Christmas Day.

I do hope you have a lovely time – of fun and laughter – and sharing and understanding with Stuart and Jutka. PS You might just phone Hackney Hospital and ask for Dr Salama and greet him for Christmas for me.

With much love to you all at Hackney,

Elizabeth

Vining Centre

20th December 1975

Dear Ma and Daddy,

Mon. Tues. Wed - no post at all in our box. Wed. night – all the students departed – Thursday all the post was released .... I had 36 letters or cards!! including yours of Dec 2nd, 6th, and 9th so I hope you receive my tape sent last weekend.

We had a good week with our various events. The plays on Monday night were a hoot. The year 2 men did 2 plays and the women 3! so it was quite a long do till after 11pm. Martinian came with one of her novices and they enjoyed it all. I did a good deal of writing of names in books – and writing of certificates on Tues and Wednesday and got everything ready in time for the Commissioning service on Wed. afternoon. Then the students departed. I shall miss some of them. You just begin to get to know the women after a year, and some of the men were great characters, and very lively.

On Friday Lily Stott come from Ado. She is replacing Grace at Ile Abiye. She is a retired nurse from Yorkshire who came to Nigeria with a Friends Relief Team in 1968 and worked then in the S.E State. She is a great character, and it was good to have her to stay. Yesterday I took her to Idanre and Ondo. We had a picnic at Idanre on the Akinbadewa's verandah looking over their gorgeous view. The we went on to Ondo and met the Medical Missionaries of Mary (M.M.M) sisters there. Lily had worked with Sister Leone in S.E State so there was a great reunion. Lily has just gone this morning (Sunday). We will go to Ado on Wed evening to have a Christmas Eve meal together. Sheila's Carol Party is to be on Tuesday night -

she seems to have invited about 50 people. I hope that it's not too many for any meaningful fellowship.

I received your parcel with the Pax materials, but I haven't opened it yet. I forgot about the gloves …. but of course, I remembered as soon as you said. I am glad we got them together. Maybe Jutka and Stuart got you something else as well.

Thank you for your concern for Cornelius. He has been ever so much better since he came out of the hospital, and I haven't seen any signs of drinking at all. Maybe the Doctor warned him, and he took it seriously.

I didn't hear of Peggy Harpers play about Ogun Festival, but I know she does that type of thing. Janice Hobday told me that she met Peggy Harper at the Fisherfolk place–and that she was a 'Charismatic'.... but I don't know. I met Doreen Wren once at Iyi Enu – rather domineering was my impression, but maybe I was wrong.

Thank you for getting the letter duplicated.... let me know the amount for postage etc so I can send a cheque.

I hope you may get this while still at Hackney. Love to Stuart and Jutka ….and Andy too.

With love for the New Year.

Elizabeth

Vining Centre
28th December 1975

Dear Ma and Daddy,

I was thinking of you all in Hackney on Christmas Day and hoping that you received my tape in time. I had a very happy week with Ruth and her mother coming on Monday and staying till Saturday. On Tuesday Ruth made a lovely 'mobile' with coloured ribbons in the shape of a fish and I made about 90 mince pies which we ate in the evening at Sheila's house where we had a carol Party. There were about 50 people gathered. I should think the majority were Catholics! It was an enjoyable evening – but I think that I prefer to sing carols in a hushed worshipful atmosphere rather than a 'Party' atmosphere.

On Wednesday we finished our decorating, and I got a lovely piece of casuarina tree from St Louis. Ruth and Mrs. Howard made lovely silver stars to put on it and another mobile of stars. In the afternoon we had the Leper Settlement Christmas Feast. I distributed plastic balls to each of the 30 children. Then in the evening we went to Ado

Ekiti and spent a happy evening with Shelagh and Lily. We had pork and apple sauce made from pawpaw and mince pies for seconds.

On Christmas Day we went to the Communion Service at St David's and returned here for breakfast when we opened our presents. Thank you very much for the 2-super drying up cloths. Everyone admired them especially the one with the pictures of birds. I will stick them on my kitchen door until I need them more urgently. Thank you too for the earrings which I will enjoy wearing. We had lunch on Christmas day at Sheila's house – and a light supper.

Then on Boxing Day we took a picnic to the Akinbadewa's house at Idanre and Ruth, Lily, Shelagh, Mrs. Howard, and I climbed up the steps at Idanre to the Rest house. It was superb, although it was midday and therefore quite hot. It was a pity we hadn't gone a bit earlier, but Sheila and Joan were having a lie in, and we waited for them before leaving. However, we were able to finish a lovely puzzle of a Swiss mountain scene before we set off. In the evening all these 7 people came back to my house, and we ate chicken, stuffing, bread sauce, roast potatoes, beans, peas, and plantain followed by trifle and ice cream.

On Saturday Ruth and her mother left in the morning and returned to Ughelli. I am thinking of going down there to stay with Ruth during January – and take the opportunity of visiting some of our old students in that area at the same time. Yesterday afternoon the Evans came with their 3 children and had supper and stayed the night here. This morning they have gone off with a C.U.S.O girl to climb Idanre.

The only blot on the landscape is that Tokunbo has driven away his wife and taken the other woman to stay with him here. Cornelius and Mama feel he shouldn't stay on the compound for his new wife's husband may come and fight. I shall be thankful not to have his problems on my hands- and if I am to give him the sack – I dread the showdown...... but it would be better for him to get a better paid job if he can. Anyway, it is a nasty mess, and I am not very good at dealing with these kinds of situations.

I shall be thinking of you in Westminster Abbey Daddy.

Much love,

Elizabeth

Vining Centre
4th January 1976

Dear Ma and Daddy,

I received 2 nice long letters when I returned from Ibadan on Friday - and am now looking forward to the next instalment telling of how you got on over Christmas. Thank you for all the hard work in getting off the Christmas letters. Please thank Miss Court and Mrs. Lees for their help in sending out the letters.

It seems very unlikely that Richard Childerstone will come to Vining Centre. He is very 'touchy '- and took offence because Cornelius wrote to him and asked him to apply 'to the bishop'. He'd felt Cornelius's letter was cold - and he now says he wouldn't come to the V.C. even if he was asked. It is a pity...... but he is very set in his ways - and sentimental and easily upset so one wonders if he would manage being here. On the other hand, we are still going to be short staffed next term as far as I can see - the C.M.S. Area Sec. plan is not likely to materialise until the Second Term ... and it is visa-providing anyway.

I went to Ondo on Monday and stayed with the Whittles for the night before going on to Ibadan on Tuesday. In fact, I spent Tuesday getting to Ibadan because I chatted to Olowoyo's in Ondo and then had lunch with the Rodgers at Ife University and then tea with Daphne Evans in Ibadan. It was almost 7p.m. by the time I reached Wesley College which is where Joy Fletcher is. She has moved into a new house and so now has a spare room and therefore is able to have friends to stay much more easily than before. She is lecturing in Maths at Wesley College and has been writing some textbooks for the teaching of Maths in Primary Schools (Modern Maths).

I saw Janet and John Nightingale - who now have a new baby girl called Mary. They are going to return home in June this year. Then I went and had lunch with Grace on New Year's Day - and I returned to Akure on Friday bringing Rev. Owadayo as far as Ondo because he wanted to see the bishop. I stopped in Ife and saw Kelu who said she was expecting me to stay the night! I always seem to put my foot in it as far as she is concerned. Yomi had gone to Lagos with the children. Anyway, I couldn't stay on account of Owadayo and, I wanted to be at the Profession Ceremony at St. Louis on Sat. morning. This was a lovely simple Ceremony. We had the 'Peace' in the Communion Service which was nice because you felt that there was something to join in, when you don't take the Communion it's a bit bleak. There were two sisters who made their first profession vows - Winifred and Virginia.

Jane Pelly showed up at Shola's house in the afternoon - there was a strike of Nigerian Airways, so she was on her way to Benin by road, instead of by air as she had planned.

Today I listened to the Service from Portree, Skye with the Moderator of the Church of Scotland taking it - and I mended a dress and wrote some letters. I heard from Richard last week. He is still in Gusau in the Northwest - and is now Vice Principal of the Teacher Training College there. He is not coming South to visit his relations in Ilesha this Christmas because he fractured his ankle in Kano. He was knocked down by a motorcycle. So, he won't be coming this way just now. Then when I returned from Ibadan, I discovered that, Eliz. Leicester and her mother are not coming from P.H. after all - Rather a disappointment because that's why I had planned to come back here just now. Anyway Prof. Rodgers said they may come to Akure on Tues. But I don't enjoy being on my own in the house during the holidays. It is much nicer to have someone to stay...... or failing that to go and stay with someone else. So, I may go down to Ughelli at the end of this week and spend 10 days or more there.

I heard from lots of friends over Christmas. Sheila is now busy with the beginning of the new term. Mrs. Wilde is transferred to the Commercial School. So, Sheila is a bit anxious to know what the new Vice Principal is going to be like. It is a man who says he will come tomorrow. The Ministry is crazy in its transfer policy.

With much love to you all

Elizabeth

Vining Centre
9th January 1976

Dear Ma and Daddy,

O-ho! So, you went to see Dr. Salama. What a hoot! I told you he lived in chaos.... now you can imagine what a trouble I had trying to help him pack up his things. It was funny - as I was reading the first part of your letter where you said you had no tape-recorder - I thought that Nabil would gladly loan you one - and he is so near .... and then I read on and found that that was exactly what happened on Boxing Day! Anyway, I am glad you went to see him.

I don't get National Geographic Mag - that's the American one, isn't it? I used to get the British one - Geographical Magazine which I prefer but it hasn't come recently. Don't bother to send the N.G.M unless you think a particular article is of great interest - it will be heavy on postage, I guess.

I had a letter from Anne this week - she is obviously very "down" again, and said she hadn't been sleeping well, but had been weeping a lot and had gone to consult the doctor. It is a pity that she can't find a friend nearby or that she can't share her flat with someone to keep her company and take her out of herself. Anyway, it was good that you were able to take the tape to her, and that you were able to go and see her.

At the beginning of this week, I was a bit dismal - no visitors from P.H and everyone else madly busy with the beginning of term. I am getting fat - sitting down without enough exercise or activities. I don't like going walking on my own much. I had started a bit of dressmaking … but fear it won't fit…. and I read 'Gentian Hill' by Eliz Goudge. On Tuesday we had our fellowship and we read the story of the Other Wise Man because it was Epiphany. It was a good evening. On Wed. Yemi Wilde (aged 9) came here in the afternoon and I showed her how to make stars and 'lilies' to hold candles - by folding paper. She was very intrigued and went home to teach her mother and brother how to do it. In the evening we had the Leper Settlement Committee with a good turnout. Mr. Onalaja the Leprosy Officer told us that he had found one man to have taken N30 from a newcomer to the Settlement and wanted the Committee to go and warn the people against such evil practices. This we did on Thurs. afternoon i.e. yesterday. In the morning I went round to St Louis and had a good long chat to Sister Martinian who I hadn't seen for some time. She has been having a big palaver about one of her young Nigerian Sisters who she feels is not suitable to be renewing her vows` and should leave the sisters.

Sheila has been very busy with the first week of the term at Fiwasaiye. Her new Vice Principal turned cup on Tuesday (Term was supposed to start the previous Friday). He is a man of 45+ - a NBK Graduate. I am not sure how he is going to settle down to work under a younger woman Principal. The biggest snag is that there is no Vice-Principal's house on the Compound and so there was no house ready for him on arrival and he is having to look in the town for accommodation. It would have been easier if he had come in time.

Pat and Francis Akinbadewa came to supper last night which was nice. Tomorrow, Saturday I hope to go to Ughelli, and I plan to stay for a week with Ruth and return on 19th Jan. We have a Board of Govs on Jan 20th and our next fellowship. I hope to visit some of our ex-students in their villages while I am down there.

Wish much love to you both

Elizabeth

Vining Centre

19th January 1976

Dear Ma and Daddy,

I have had a lovely week here in Ughelli - real holidayish and relaxing. I find Ruth very easy to stay with, although of course she is out in the school most of the day. We played tennis at 6.30 a.m. on three days and then sent swimming in their portable pool almost every evening around 9 at night. Very nice too - my tennis has improved quite a lot in a week - and the aches and pains began to wear off. I must try to find someone in Akure who would like to play tennis - or go walking in the Agric so that I can get some more exercise - because really, I get very sedentary there.

On Monday I went with Mary Griffin to Warri. It is amazing how that town has boomed since the oil came to this area. The big stores there are better stocked than those in Ibadan, and there is a fine new road through the town.

On Wednesday I went to Oreokpe and then to Eku where I visited one old student called Eyitemi. It was his wife who had twins and one died. The little boy seems fine now. They are an older couple and rather illiterate, but his Church looked in good order and they have built a new pulpit out of formica.

On Friday I went back to Oreokpe because Kaku who is the Catechist there wasn't in on Wed, so I went again. He came with me, and we went together to greet Mr and Mrs. Okotie who are now at Abraka. Okotie and Eyitemi both have small mud houses in the Church compound - Kaku and his wife are managing in a room and a parlour which they rent in the village until they can raise enough money to build a house. They gave me a very nice lunch of yam and stew before I came back to Ughelli.

On Sunday, yesterday, I took the Service at 8 a.m. at Ruth's School in Ughelli and talked to them about Ebun. Then I went to Oreokpe again and talked to the people during their Service at 10 - 12. It was a small congregation - but all in very good order. It was Matins with Te Deum and Jubilate. I am still not convinced that Liturgical worship was a useful import. The people were very welcoming and friendly, and I think Kaku was happy that I went. I showed them the flannel graph of the good Samaritan which I think they enjoyed.

After the Service I went back to Ughelli for lunch - and then in the afternoon I drove on to Benin where I am now - staying with Jane Pelly. Her School are in temporary buildings now - rather horrid in a long line - like an Army camp. It is next to the University Teaching Hospital so I should think Jane will be able to make friends in Benin.

With much love to you both

Elizabeth

Vining Centre
26th January 1976

Dear Ma and Daddy,

When I arrived back from Ughelli last Monday there were several letters piled up from you, so I was able to catch up on all the news from Jan 5 - 18th. I also heard from John, Ruth, and Stuart all in the same post!! A great haul. I have also received the free film in the post this week - and the photos. I have written to thank Mrs. Young and Anna for their kind Christmas presents. I still have Tokunbo. I think his father talked him into it. Anyway, Mama Ronke is back with the 3 children and the other girl has presumably gone back to her former husband. Inga's home address is 17 Belinton Road, Knowle, BRISTOL. Yomi and Kelu live on the University campus now. I am sorry to hear of the Bennett's robbery. Where is their new bungalow? You told me all about the one they didn't get but I don't know anything about the one they did. Ruth and Trevor will be with you this week. I hope that you have a good time together. What did Madge Braby die of? It must have been sudden. Isla Williams is the woman in Colwell who Angela and I went to see. She is a retired schoolteacher who taught Angela at Wycombe High and was on the staff there with Dorothy Browning who I went to see down near Shaftesbury. I shall be very interested to hear what happens next in your 'Cell.'

It is amazing how these X-rays can tell what is going wrong before you get any trouble. I am sorry to hear about Daddy's blocked up tubes - but at least they know and can presumably do something about it…… but it is disappointing that hospital visits are still on the agenda. On the other hand, I feel that I had more real contact with people last January when I was getting my appendix fixed than I have this January when I have been pottering around here doing very little and seeing relatively few people …… and just getting lazy.

On Tuesday we had the Board of Governors meeting and there was quite a good turnout. The Staffing situation is much the same - but I think the Board took it seriously. They say that we must have more local people helping - including the Army Chaplain - and then that in June they will be able to send us someone when the ordinands come out of Emmanuel College. Rev. Faji came from Lagos and stayed the night in my house. We had our fellowship meeting on Tues. evening at St Louis Convent. Mr. Sobukunola took it and talked about Songs and Hymns that were used in Christian worship. We learnt a nice new Song on the Holy Spirit that Sheila found - and I taught them Holy, Holy, Holy.

On Wednesday Martinian came round in the afternoon and we went for a walk at the Agric. She has now gone off to Ikare for a few days rest and holiday. I asked her if she would like to come here……. but I think that she wanted to get out of town, and it is easier for the sisters to stay in a Convent as they are used to. I don't know what their 'rule' is about it.

On Wed. and Thurs. I noodled about - read a Georgette Heyer and started to think about the lists that need to be made for the new term. Also, I started to write an Annual Report for the Leper Settlement Committee. On Friday I went to Owo and sat all day on the Board of Governors of St John/ Mary College. It started at 10.30 and ended about 3.30. It was to investigate a disturbance caused by Year 3 students which had led to them being sent away. The palaver had been because the students wanted to wear coloured clothes (their own) on Sat and Sun and not the 'Uniform 'and had put their own clothes on as a demonstration and refused to take them off when requested by the principal. It had caused such an uproar because the new Principal was obviously trying to be over strict with his students…and to run it like St Andrews Oyo in the old days. He was trying to tell them to have dances only up to 9.30 at night and to have lights out at 10, when previously they had been allowed up till 10.30.

On Saturday I went in the afternoon to see Marianne Krol - the Dutch woman whose husband is setting up the Motor Mechanics Workshop etc. in Ikerre for Ekiti Diocese. She invited me to stay to supper and I did and enjoyed pork steaks with pineapple. She is a very good cook. I was glad that I went to see her. Yesterday I preached at Fiwasaiye in the evening.

With much love from

Elizabeth

Vining Centre
1st February 1976

Dear Ma & Daddy,

We have started the term. I can't tell you yet how many men students we have… it is a mystery yet to be fully revealed. I have found beds for 108 of them. The women are easier to count because there are so far 10 of them. Two are yet to come, but are sick and 2 have called off, in one case because she paid N100 for her father's hernia operation in Eku Baptist Hospital and so is trading in Port Harcourt to find the money. This I think is a great pity, especially since she came from Ughelli area where they do need wives with training. If she had come and asked, we might have loaned her the N100…but now she has paid N60 for the rent of her stall in P.H. so she has committed herself to trading for the first half of the year. The second one who hasn't showed up was not married to the student! - only engaged, and the parents won't release her until the man pays N50.!!

We had a good Communion Service this morning with Cornelius preaching on" How small is your God?" and saying that we must aim to get a bigger idea of God this term. He took 7 points about God from the Lord's prayer…. that He is a Great Father, A King, A Judge, A Provider, A Forgiver, A Leader, and A Deliverer. It was a good start to the term. In the afternoon we shall go to the Leper Settlement for the Open-Air Service.

Last Wed. I went to Ibadan with Mama Ademoye in the College Van. It was quite an exhausting business particularly for Mama. We couldn't leave Akure till after 9 a.m. for Cornelius had forgotten to get the money out of the bank so we reached Ibadan in the heat of midday. They let me out at C.S.S. Bookshop to go and get my shopping on foot…… which was O.K. because Sam Aighbokai has his office nearby and I was able to use it for a dumping ground for my loads…. but it is not as straightforward as when you have your own car. Mama & Co got in hot water down in the market streets because there is a new law about parking and the soldiers were trying to drive them away. It is a good law from the point of view of traffic congestion in Ibadan, but it would be better if more parking places were made…. because there just is nowhere to park near to the wholesale shops in that part of Ibadan. On our way back we stopped to buy fish at Asejire and when we started again our gear jammed in 3rd. So, we crawled to Ife, drifting down the hill slopes and going up the other side in 3rd gear. We got to Ife after dark where some mechanics were able to fix it… but it meant we didn't arrive here till 9.30 p.m.

Martinian has a new dog called Bilbo Baggins (from Hobbit) and she wants to exercise it so it looks as though we shall be able to go for more walks in the Agric…. which will please me greatly. I shall be thinking of you especially Daddy on Feb 10 when you go into Ronkswood again. I hope all goes well and they can sort out the trouble.

I was interested that you noticed that Ananias ought to be the one honoured for Paul's conversion…I was struck by that from B.R.F. too. In fact, the readings with their comments have been good in the last few weeks. Oreokpe is on the road between Warri and Eku (Nr Sapele.)

I hope that you had a good time with Ruth and Trevor…. and that Ma's journey with Joyce Gell was successful. Shelagh Jebb and Lily Stott are here today for lunch and Eyesorun is also in town. I hope she will come today to see us. Last night she phoned about 5 and I said Sheila and I would go and see her later in the evening …. which we did, to Dr Sijuade's house……. and met no one there so we went away, and only discovered later at about 10 p.m. that she was in her own house at the other end of town. Then Sister Martinian and Sister Agnes Mary are coming for supper in the evening, so it is quite a busy day.

With much love to you both

Elizabeth

Vining Centre
7th February 1976

Dear Ma and Daddy,

I received the photographs this week. Thank you very much for them. I like the one of Anne beside Loch Fyne and the one of Jutka and Stuart by the Festival Hall. Also, Sundri has come out well. Mrs. Kohl will be pleased if I send it to her.

We have had the first week of the term at V.C. The women are a responsive set - 16 of them now. One is yet to come. The men are yet a 'mob' .... it was only at the end of the week that we got the list of the names of Year one sorted out. There are 54 newcomers so there is a fair crush in some dormitories - and they are constantly carrying chairs and benches about because when they are using them in the dining hall there are none in the Hall. However, they seem to have settled down peacefully and several "lecturers" (Alias local clergy) are coming in to help to fill up spaces in the Timetable.

One baby is already in hospital with measles. Two soldiers claim to have peptic ulcers and one fellow came to tell me that he had been taking Ephedrine since 1962 because he has "sleeping sickness" - if he doesn't take the medicine, he will fall asleep. I went and asked the Chemist who told me that the drug is a stimulant and if one has been taking it so long, he must be addicted to it by now. Also, he said that Ephedrine is no longer imported into the country and can only be given on a doctor's prescription. So, we shall have to see what the doctor says about him. I am sending our Leper Settlement Annual, Report - so I shall write the rest of this letter in with that.

Much love
Elizabeth

Vining Centre
8th February 1976

Dear Ma and Daddy,

The great event of this week is that 7 new States have been created in Nigeria and Akure is to be the Capital of Ondo State! They have been talking about this for some time, but it has suddenly become a reality. We have a new State Governor - Major Ekpeme. He will live in the old residency...... but no one knows where his Commissioners and Permanent Secretaries will live - presumably the doctors and heads of departments will have to move out of the bigger houses on the reservation to make room for the incoming big-wigs. But where they will go to is another problem. There will be a tremendous upheaval in the next 6 weeks or so - and they will need to plan to build a lot of houses and offices quickly.

The Western State has been divided into 3 parts which are now called Ogun, Oyo and Ondo States with Abeokuta, Ibadan, and Akure as their State capitals respectively. Civil servants will have the possibility of going back to their own State of origin……… and many will go - and exchange with others. It looks as though we may lose Dr Sijuade to Oyo, but Eyesorun is coming back to be a Commissioner in Ondo State…. so that's one good thing…. but we shall miss many good friends.

The people of Ondo are apparently not very happy about the making of Akure the State Capital. They wanted it to be in Ondo and I heard that when some Akure's living in Ondo were rejoicing that the Ondo's beat them up and the police had to go and settle it. The Ondo's have a chip on their shoulder that none of their Ondo people are present Commissioners or Permanent Secretaries and that they have been cheated. I should have thought they should be thankful for the Creation of the State and produce some men willing to work for its good who will be soon made Commissioners etc. Anyway, we hope they settle down soon. The new States are supposed to be in working order by April 1st!!

We had our Leprosy Committee meeting on Wednesday - and people were speculating what would happen to the Leprosy Settlement - because if the town expands along the Owo road it will quickly reach their place and their land may easily be required for something else. (The land is not owned by the Ministry of Health even - the patients are there as well-established squatters.)

On Tues. we had our Fellowship meeting - at the Noviciate, and one of the novices led us in a meditation on the Gifts of God - seeing, hearing, touch, smell, and taste. It was thought provoking - because you had time to think of the great variety of colours and sounds etc.

On Sat. night I went to Ikerre to see Marianne Kroll. She had made special Austrian dumplings out of potato flour with plums inside…. very filling. Anyway, it was a peaceful evening. We had a real good rainstorm in the afternoon - the first of the Season. This means that the rains are likely to be early this year, so I guess that we shall not have a hot spell in Feb/ Mar as we do when the rains come late.

John and Janet Nightingale and their 2 children are staying with Sheila this weekend - and coming here to lunch today. They are on their way to the East (or at least Asaba) for some Conference.

I shall start my lectures with the men again tomorrow night - and am now taking a Singing period on Tuesday - with the aim of teaching some new Songs and Choruses in English. I plan to do 'Creation 'in the Mon. night talks at the beginning of term.

With much love

Elizabeth

Murtala assassinated in Coup

Vining Centre
15th February 1976

Dear Ma and Daddy,

Two letters this week ... of Feb 4th - telling of Mother's adventures trying to pack Joyce up… and Daddy looking after himself at home.

I expect that you will have heard our news…. probably more quickly than we heard - although in fact news flies here faster than any radio announcements. We heard on Friday morning that the head of State had been killed and that there was a change of Government. Then in the evening we heard that the Coup had been thwarted - and it wasn't till Sat. midday that it was announced that Murtala Mohammed had been shot in the trouble in Lagos and taken for burial to Kano. None of it makes much sense here because there are so many gaps in the information given. One doesn't know for example what these young revolutionaries headed by Lt. Col. Dimka were angry about. Was it only the Head of State they were after? Or did they want to topple the whole Govt.? Did they plan to kill all the State Governors? If so, they were apparently not very successful - although the Military Gov. of Kwara State was killed in Ilorin. We don't know if the lives of the others were threatened. It seems a great pity - because in the Western State for instance everyone respects Jemibewon because he is such a dynamic hardworking fellow who really wants to get things moving…. and although the new creation of States is going to be inconvenient for those who must move house etc. - overall the decision to create the new States is supported by everyone. Maybe it is something about this creation of States that made Mohammed unpopular…but I don't know what. It sounds as though it is "politics" within the Army and maybe personal rivalries. This week is to be a week of National Mourning and Friday is to be a Public Holiday to pray for peace.

Sheila is with me this weekend. She had a cold on Monday - but it didn't clear off and she felt rotten at the end of the week - so I took her to Dr Sijuade on Thursday, and he put her on Tetracycline. She came here on Friday night and will certainly stay over till Monday. She is in bed most of the time and sleeps a lot. I think she is just generally run down and maybe anaemic so hasn't been able to throw the cold off…. also, she has a swollen gland in her neck and lost her voice, so she probably has another infection too. It is nice for me to have her to look after and to nurse.

St John/ Mary is a T.T. College, and the present Principal is an old Andrian - Rev. Ojo - but I think since your time. It is soon going to be Daddy's 70th birthday. I wonder what he would like. Are you going to do something special on that day? I think I will have to send some money. It is safer than going through the mail order firms when you don't quite know what it is going to be like. Would you like a wood plaque? You can ask them to be made in any subject you like. I have seen cocoa farming or dying and weaving cloth - or a Bible story - or nativity scene. If you like the idea I could order one and ask Sheila to bring it home in July.

I have started my Monday lectures again - and have taken 'Creation 'as the topic. I started with the Earth and how we get day and night. Then I asked the students to write a prayer or a litany of prayer in 'Praise of Creation'. It was very interesting to read what they all said. Most of them were just long involved prayers but one or two I felt were poetic.

Marianne Kroll came here on Tuesday and had supper while she waited to try to phone her husband in Holland. She was not successful. Our new State Governor was in Akure Stadium. Some of our students went to welcome him - but it was really for Chiefs of all the local areas. I was teaching that morning. I should have liked to have gone if I had been free.

I hope that you are both well. I shall be looking forward to hearing the results from Ronkswood.

Much love

Elizabeth

Vining Centre
22nd February 1976

Dear Ma and Daddy,

I hope all is well with you - and that Daddy is O.K. after his investigation in Ronkswood. The 'failed 'Coup and the closure of the airport has meant that no letters have come through, but someone said that they may open the airport soon - so we shall be able to communicate regularly again. I hope that this may reach you by Mar.

4th; but if it doesn't, I know that you will know that I am thinking of you very much on that day - Daddy's 70th birthday.

It has been a very quiet week here - everyone is very sad at the death of the Head of State, Gen. Murtala Muhammed particularly because he seemed really to be getting things moving in the country and trying to make a stand against corruption. We have had Curfew at night from 8p.m. till 6a.m. the next day. I don't like this much because it means I can't go and drink coffee with Sheila around 9 p.m.... But I guess it is to prevent the 'wanted soldiers' from travelling round at night. They say that Lt. Col. Dinka has not yet been found. He was the man who announced the overthrowing of Government over the radio and then apparently went to the British High Commissioner to ask them to contact Gowon in England. It appears some in the Army wanted to return the former Government to power. A lot of the former leaders have been probed and their 'assets' have been confiscated. Some of them had acquired millions of Naira, and hotels and cinemas and farms and all sorts of property while in office.... and it looks as though some of them were behind the assassination of Murtalla. It looks as though Gowon must have a been in the know of it, and because he didn't warn anyone - must have approved. If this is true it is <u>very</u> disappointing that he should revenge in this way when he himself was treated so reasonably by the Government. Anyway, it's all a nasty ugly situation and we can only pray that the present leaders will be able to maintain stability in the Army and investigate the whole episode fairly. We had a Public Holiday on Friday - as a special day of prayer for Peace in the country. We went from V.C. to St David's Church. The new Governor of Ondo State was present - and several new Commissioners for the State, including the Eyesorun. There were soldiers on guard around the Church and police escorts too. No doubt we shall be seeing more of this kind of thing when Akure becomes the State Capital. It was a great pity that this attempted Coup should come at this time, because it is not a good start for the new States. It is going to be difficult enough anyway to work out the details of making a new Ondo State without the added difficulty of everyone being suspicious of one another and afraid that they may be being plotted against.

The doctors and others living on the reservation have mostly moved house into the town - although it is not easy to find flats etc. there. So, the new Civil Servants will move in.

Last Sunday a filling came out of one of my teeth - so I went to the dentist in Akure on Monday to have it removed. Unfortunately, there were only stumps left and so it had to be removed bit by bit…… and I am not sure if it all came out. I should think there are some bits left inside. Anyway, I had to go and have Seclopen injections each day this week and I hope no abscess will form. It seems O.K. so far. I have been reading the 'Healing Lights 'and trying to apply it to my teeth…… but I am not very successful at driving `away the notion that it might form an abscess!!

I do hope that you get this before March 4th because otherwise you may be wondering how we are here. The answer is that Akure is quieter than usual!

I do hope that you are able to do something special to celebrate Daddy's birthday. I wish I was able to be there too!

With much love to you both

Elizabeth

Vining Centre

29th February 1976

Dear Ma and Daddy,

No post yet. I thought that there might be something filtering through by Saturday because the airport was open on Monday - but no luck. Maybe they are censoring the mail, or maybe they have a big backlog and are taking a long time to clear it. Anyway, I hope that you are all well. By the time you receive this you will have celebrated Daddy's Birthday.

It has been a normal week up till Saturday. The Curfew was lifted on Monday so we were able to have our fellowship meeting on Tuesday. We listened to the Mc Nutt tape…… and people found it interesting and stimulating to a lot of discussion. It is amazing how he concentrates so much on Jesus - and what he would do if he were on the earth - and that our main motive should be love and that this will develop with prayer.

We have measles on the Compound and some of the children have been sick. They get pneumonia so quickly and then have a great high temperature and panting breathing. It is amazing what penicillin does to get it under control so quickly.

Yesterday, Saturday, was the day when then new Deji of Akure was given his rod of office by the new Military Governor. We went to the Stadium for the event but unfortunately, we were late and so didn't get a seat but had to stand. However, we saw glimpses of all the dignitaries and heard all the Speeches. I went with Sheila because Cornelius and Victoria didn't understand me when I said I would go with them. Afterwards I had a frustrating time looking for gas - my gas had run out, so I decided that I would go to Ondo and get more and have lunch with the Whittles at the same time. So, I phoned them and made the arrangement. Then I set off - but I had a puncture about 2 miles out of Akure and decided that I had better come back and get it mended because my spare tyre is rather bald. So, I came back and cancelled my lunch arrangement and phoned the gas place in Ondo to check that I could get it in Akure at their new branch at 27 Adesida St. So, I went to look and couldn't find the place at all. I also discovered that my tyre was 'condemned' because the metal was sticking outside - so I had to buy a new tyre - costing N25! After all this I got off to Ondo - a nice drive now along the new road. It only takes about 30 mins. When I got to the gas man in Ondo, he told me that his new branch is not at 27 Adesida but at 27 Oyemekan Rd. and the fellow on the phone had told me wrongly!!! So, I needn't have gone at all!! Anyway, I went to see the Whittles and had tea with them which was nice. Then came back in the evening and Sheila came round for supper.

Our new State Commissioner and permanent Secretaries should be coming here this week. It will be interesting to see how they manage to accommodate them all. It will be good to have the Eyesorun back amongst us. I hope to hear your news during the coming week. I still don't know how Daddy got on in Ronkswood on Feb. 11th.

With much love

Elizabeth

Vining Centre
3rd March 1976

Dear Ma & Daddy,

What a dreadful shock to hear that Geoff died in a car accident. I am so very sorry; I have tried to write to Marguerita. I am now anxiously looking each day at the post and hoping that your letter will come out of the pile… but still no luck. Yesterday was my first post from the U.K. and it included a letter from Dorothy Dykes saying that she had just heard of it - on Feb. 13th and then one from Colin Judd saying he was at the funeral. So, I suppose the accident must have happened around about the 12th which was the time Daddy was in Ronkswood. I wonder if you were able to go to Huddersfield. Poor Marguerita. She must be very cut up…and all the family. It must have been a great shock to you too…. because Geoff was the last of the brothers - and an accident is so much more sudden than a sickness.

It is Ash Wednesday today and we are having a quiet day, with 3 Services - at 8.30, 12 noon - Litany and 6 p.m. - Evening Service. I have found it a peaceful day - but challenging too. Martinian loaned me a book about Ash Wed. and the Stations of the Cross, and it explained how when they put ashes on people's heads they say "From dust you come and to dust you return" - so we should be humble…because really our lives are very short. Then it goes on to say that the message of Lent - suffering and confrontation with the facts of Sin and death - leads on to the message of Easter - Joy and resurrection.

I tried to think today about these verses:

When you draw close to God
God will draw close to you.
Wash your hands you sinners, and let your hearts be filled with God alone to make them pure and true. James 4
Create in me a clean heart, O God - filled with clean thoughts and right desires. Isaiah 51

Then when we come to the evening Service the preacher started off with "Create a clean heart in me…" so, it all fitted together. I painted a picture - or started to - of 3 flowers - a hibiscus, a harmattan lily and a white frangipani - each one has a pure clean centre - and from the centre comes the new life - the stamens and so on. Also, the hibiscus only lives one day - tomorrow is like a new birth. Maybe we should learn to live a day at a time like the hibiscus flower. I am going to Ado this Sunday to take their Service there.

I hope to hear news from you tomorrow.

With much love

Elizabeth

Vining Centre
7th March 1976

Dear Ma and Daddy,

I got your letters on Thursday and the tape on Friday - so I was very glad. It was good to hear that Daddy's hospital visit was clear of serious trouble, and that Ruth and Trevor were able to take you up to Huddersfield for Geoff's funeral. I am sorry that I was not there to share it all with you, as I said in my Ash Wednesday letter.

It was super to get the tape and to hear your voices on it. It is true that it makes people seem much nearer. I was most interested to hear of all Daddy's contacts in Westminster Abbey - and to hear the voices of the 2 Nigerian girls at Lawnside. I will take their greetings to Yomi and Kelu. The tape gave me a great boost on Friday and cheered me up a lot. I especially appreciated hearing Grannie playing the Spinning Wheel. It took me right back to 24 - and it was especially fitting that she should have played it for G. & M. when they were going to Nigeria in 1955 - and that it should have been dear Geoff with all his interest in tapes etc. who had the wisdom and foresight to record it and keep it - so that I could listen to it in Nigeria in 1976. Amazing! It just drew me back into the family when I had been feeling far away.

I haven't yet listened to Basil F and the Contemplative Prayer for there wasn't time before coming to Ado on Sat. to take over as the C.M.S. Rep. to see Sheila - and to prepare a Service for the nurses there.

Isn't it great to hear that Ruth and Trevor are expecting a baby at the end of the year? It will be fun for you to have a new baby grandchild resident in England - especially when John and Pat & Co go back to New Zealand. Really, your family was planned well for providing grandchildren of different ages.

Mon. 8th March: I returned from Ado to Akure this morning - leaving there at 6.30a.m. and getting here in time for breakfast. Shelagh Jebb was very happy because Randy Carson the nurse (male) who used to help her…but left because the pay wasn't worked out according to him - has now agreed to come back on the Ilera De Team so she will have someone to hand her work over to properly. She will probably leave Ado at the end of this month - go home to U.K. and then on to Yemen.

The news over the W/E is that the police have caught 'Dimka' the fellow who assassinated the Head of State and announced himself over the radio as taking over the Government - then went to the British High Commission to phone Gowon. He is to be tried this week for Murder and Treason, both of which carry the death penalty.

Our new Ondo State is to start functioning from April 1st.

Much love to you both

Elizabeth

Vining Centre
14th March 1976

Dear Ma and Daddy,

It is nice to be back to the old pattern and to have letters coming in the post. Last week I was writing from Ado. This week I am in Ibadan - staying with Joy Fletcher at Wesley College. She is busy packing - because she is transferred to Oshogbo to be the Principal of the Baptist Girls School in Oshogbo. It is a bit daft in my opinion to move someone experienced in teaching Maths in a Teacher Training College to be the Principal of a Secondary School. Anyway, she seems very organised with her packing up.

We have Half Term this week - which is the reason why I am gadding about again! I went and spent Thursday night with Inga who seems to me very tired despite her 4 months leave. She says that she has not been sleeping very well since she came back. Also, she has no car, and she has been rather compound bound. She is staying with Jose over the weekend. Jose hasn't been home to England since 1960 and really, she needs a complete change and a holiday. She is very on edge - especially if Sam is away touring with the book publishers, as he is now.

I saw Grace Ohikhena in Ibadan and discovered that Tokunbo had her appendix out 4 weeks ago - and really was very sick at the time because the appendix wasn't recognised as the trouble until late in the day. However, she is O.K. now.

On Sat. I went to see Sister Jean at the Catholic Hospital about my tooth.... which I think I told you was only partially removed in Akure. I went to see the Akure man again last Wednesday and he was on leave, so I felt free to go and get sorted in Ibadan when I was on Half Term. Sister Jean took an X-ray, and this revealed that all the roots were still in situ. So, she took them out...... not a very long business. Then she put in 2 stitches. I felt a bit groggy the rest of Sat. morning but since then there has been no trouble at all - and I was really relieved to be rid of it.

I shall continue to pray for Daddy's valveless ureter. Does it mean the valve has got lost - or worn out - or that he never had one? I like Basil Farncombes' "The Lord is my healer." Today I was reading the Monday Meditation in Seed Thoughts for Daily Meditation - particularly the part at the end of Page 6 about health and harmony and peace of mind.

I am looking forward to getting back to Akure to see Eyesorun - you know she is our new Commissioner of Health in the Ondo State. She should be coming to Akure sometime over the weekend. There is so much to be done in developing Health facilities and she will be able to do a lot provided there is a time of peace and no more upsets in the Government. On Saturday we read in the paper that 32 of those involved in the abortive Coup of Feb. 13th were executed by Firing Squad on Bar Beach in Lagos. One was a Major General Bisalla. Most of the others were from the Plateau Area - which is Gowon's area. The papers say that he was in support of the Coup which was aimed at putting him back in power. They have asked the British Govt. to send him home for Trial.

I was very encouraged after my Monday lecture last week. I told the men about the size of the Universe - distance of planets from the Sun etc. and the way of calculating light years to the nearest Star. Afterwards one of the oldest men from the delta Rivers area came and thanked me for how the lecture had helped him. He said that every night he thought of the greatness of the Universe - and he had had a problem that was "biting" him in the chest - and he was very worried about it - and couldn't put it out of his mind - but then remembered that GOD the Creator was able to take control of the Planets and the Stars - and therefore He could manage to control this problem....... so, since then his problem has been relieved, and it doesn't worry him as before! Isn't that great?

With much love from

Elizabeth

Vining Centre
1st March 1976

Dear Ma and Daddy,

Thank you for the letters this week - they seem to have been coming more quickly - i.e., in 5 or 6 days. So, here's hoping that this might reach you by next Sunday to greet you on Mothering Sunday. Shelagh Jebb goes on Friday so I will send a card with her so that it can be posted in England. I went to see her yesterday and found her in good form. I gave her the silver brooch yesterday when I went up to Ado to say goodbye. I think that she was pleased because it has a hut and a palm tree on it and so will be a good reminder of Nigeria.

This week I taught the students the Hymn, "How Great Thou Art" … and they learnt it very well and sang it in the morning at the Holy Communion Service with real meaning. I preached the Sermon about Forgiveness - and brought in a few points that had been brought out in our Fellowship last Tuesday when we thought about "Father forgive them - they don't know what they are doing." It was a good Fellowship. The sermon was a bit long. It is difficult to cut down what you want to say…. Daddy will appreciate this especially! You need to be very concise in a sermon…. but then there is the temptation to rush……. and I feel if you talk too fast no-one takes in what you are saying.

It has been a normal week, in fact a bit less busy than usual because I didn't have any of the men's books to mark since we were on Half Term last Monday. I went to see the Eyesorun on Thursday evening. It is good to have her back in Akure. Martinian came on Friday, and we went for a walk on the Reservation. There is a lot of new building and renovation of offices etc. going on so that the new State can "take off "on April 1st. The Evans were here - staying with Sheila so I had supper and spent the evening with them on Wed. Yesterday when I went to Ado, Shelagh Jebb kindly removed the stitches out of my gum so now my tooth is better! A great relief. One of the women students was confirmed yesterday so I went to the Confirmation Service in the morning at Fiwasaiye.

Today Sheila Davis has gone off to Benin - en route for the All-Nigeria Principals Conference which is this week in Enugu. I shall miss her. Also, Martinian is going to Ghana on Wednesday so both of my buddies will be away. Maybe I shall go to Idanre next Saturday and see Pat and Francis. I am glad to hear that Marguerita has got a job at least part time - and that Martin is in for the apprentice training. I hope that Judy sorts herself out and applies for the Domestic Science Course - and that this helps her to become a bit more stable.

I am sorry to hear that Daddy wasn't well over the 70th birthday - and that he has been getting so tired easily since then. But it is amazing how you are both able to fit in so many Services and meetings and to keep contact with so many folks. It will be interesting having the Bennetts nearby. We shall continue to pray for the right decision about Daddy's bladder valve.

I heard this morning that 2 boys at St Joseph's Ondo - opposite St Monica's were killed on the road by the round-a-bout into Ondo.... and that the rest of the schoolboys took their revenge and burnt the car....... and that they were still out of hand late in the evening. This kind of mob-action always makes me think of the Crucifixion. I don't know what happened to the car driver. I expect he ran away. The message of forgiveness hasn't gone very deep.... but then nor has it in Northern Ireland. We can only do our own little bit to sow seeds of love and forgiveness.

With love to you both
Elizabeth

Vining Centre
24th March 1976

Dear Ma and Daddy,

I hope that this will be a quickie because I am sending it with Shelagh Jebb. Sheila is away this week in Enugu, and I thought that I might be lonely - but yesterday afternoon I discovered that Christine the C.U.S.O. at Fiwasaiye was sick - nausea and vomiting... so I spent the evening finding a doctor and then brought her back here. She is better today and eating a bit this evening.... so has drunk gallons of fluids today. Consequently, I haven't even got my marking done - because I have been making soup and so forth and then talking to her visitors. An Irish girl from Ikerre who I had not met before came for supper and went after 9 p.m. It was nice to meet her for I think she likes to play tennis.

With much love to you both
Elizabeth

Vining Centre
4th April 1976

Dear Ma and Daddy,

Thank you both for your letters. I am glad that you have reached a decision about going ahead with the operation. It does seem wiser to get it done if these big experts reckon that it is advisable and necessary. I shall be waiting to hear when the date is fixed - and hope we don't have another 'Coup 'so that I must wait such a long time to hear the result this time!!

I am sorry about the Priory's photo. I think that I am just not photogenic. It is partly the fault of specs because `always when a photographer is going to take the picture, he says you must look up or down so that the light doesn't reflect on the glasses. Anyway, I'll try. I think a good colour snap is better than a bad portrait type.

I do hope that you have a happy Easter. We shall be in term time until Easter Monday. We have our final Commissioning Service on Easter Sunday at 4 p.m. Three of the women are to be commissioned. Before that there is a lot to be done. We shall have exams starting this Wednesday - and on Palm Sunday I am hoping that the Ordinands are going to do the special Palm Sunday Service that we did in 1968 at St Monica's. I have started to practise it with them. I think they will do it well because they approach the rehearsals with a very mature and sensitive attitude.

Christine went home on Tuesday. She seems to be much better and has gone off with some friends to Dahomey for the holidays so that will give her a real break.

We had our Lent Fellowship on Tuesday night only about 8 of us this week because Martinian is away in Ghana and Mildred was not well so none of the Noviciate Sisters were there. Anyway, some interesting points came out of the meeting. Yesterday Sheila and I went to Ado in the afternoon to visit Mildred who is in the Catholic Hospital there. She has had tests etc. - and is on a Course of Vitamin injections because she was very listless and anaemic.

It is hot now - especially in the afternoons. It is the sort of weather when you are really waiting for the rains. We had rain earlier, but it seems to have stopped and now we are ready for it. We have no water this weekend. I have some in my outside tank, but the students have run out and are roaming around looking for water.

The new State Capital “took off” on Thurs. - April 1st. It didn’t affect us much here except that we saw the military Governor’s helicopter arriving overhead. There was a cocktail party in the evening for all local big wigs. I am not a big wig. Sheila was there and said it was a polite conversation affair. There has been a good deal of turnover of personnel, and it will take some time for the new Government officials to find out their new jobs and to settle down. Dr. Wilde has left the hospital. He is posted to Shagamu. Several other staff have also gone from the hospital, and so far, I haven’t seen any new doctors. We just hope and pray that we get some hard-working fellows who are doctoring to serve the people and not to line their own pockets. The Leprosy officers have gone - so I must go and try and meet the new ones. Our craft teacher from the Min. of Economic Development is also transferred so we shall have someone else next term. The last lady was exceptionally good so we shall miss her.

They have cleared the garden around one bungalow house and made a car park and put a flagpole and a flag in the middle of it – that is the Military Governor’s office!! There is a lot of new building going on around the Secretariat and air conditioners and carpets have been installed for the Commissioners and Permanent Secretaries Offices. The number of cars in Akure main street has increased fantastically and I see now that a whole crop of advertisement hoardings has appeared.

I talked to the men on Monday about 'man’s mis-use of God’s Creation' - Specially talking about ‘soil erosion, cutting of trees and air and water pollution.’ I just hope that in the development of the State Capital here that the expansion is planned thoughtfully, and that valuable farmland is not used up indiscriminately, and that they don’t cut down all the trees without thinking of which ones they can replant for beauty and shade.

I am writing this letter now to wish you a very Happy Easter time - because letters written next week may not reach you in time. I must write Ruth and Stuart too some time. When are John and Pat and co travelling? I may go to Aba to see Jane Backhouse after Easter - but nothing is yet planned. There is plenty to fit into the next 2 weeks.

With much love to you both

Elizabeth

Vining Centre
11th April 1976

Dear Ma & Daddy,

Thank you for your letter of 29th March. Thank you for dealing with the S.H.H.S. letter. Quite an Enfield Clan in Malvern now - with Mrs. Munns and the Bennetts. What about the Thorpe's moving nearer to Barbara!!? Talking about retiring - I have one American lady here staying the weekend - called Elsie Clitheroe (Mrs.). She is 84 and has glaucoma and cataracts and deformed feet and arthritis … but when she was 70, she offered herself as a Peace Corps Volunteer and came to Nigeria and taught at Fiwasaiye. She is now on what she reckons will be her last visit to Nigeria to see Jane Pelly. She was staying with Jane and the 2 of them were coming to stay with Sheila over Easter - but Jane's father died last week so Jane went home on Friday and sent Elsie to Akure to stay with Sheila. Sheila has gone to Ibadan – so Elsie is staying the weekend with me instead. She is a great old character…. but was a bit put out because she fainted for the first time in her life in Lagos Airport and obviously caused quite a commotion.

This evening we have our Palm Sunday special Meditation Service. The men have been practicing each day this week… so it has been quite busy. On Wednesday the women did their practical exam…… and Mama and I were so tired that we declared a holiday on Thursday before we started our other exams on Friday. Inga came on Thursday with Fanny and Charlie the Aigbokhai's children and we went to look at the animals at the Agric - and to have a picnic lunch there. Then we collected Sheila's baby antelope (duiker) at Fiwasaiye and brought it back here where I am looking after it for the weekend. It is rather a pet. It likes to eat hibiscus flowers and so Tokunbo's children come and feed it and it gobbles up the lovely red flowers.

Thank you very much for your Easter message. It is a lovely one. Thank you too for the card with the beautiful fresh flowers on it. We had a new baby born on Saturday. The woman was cleaning her house at 9 p.m. Then just before mid night they came to call me to take them to the hospital - so we went and found that they were extremely busy. The 3 beds in the labour rooms were all occupied - and in the pre-labour room there were women in labour on every bed. In fact, while we were there one of them had her baby on the bed. Our student was told to manage to sit on a chair because there was no free bed until someone else delivered! Fortunately, she got a bed space before the baby was born about 1 a.m. but they were 2 on a bed in the post-natal ward so she was asked to come home next morning!! Fortunately, everything is O.K.... this is just as well because Dr. Wilde has gone and no one else has come to replace him so there is no doctor qualified for gynaecology now in our hospital. This is all because of the changeover to new States.

Sun. Night:

The meditation Service is over - they did it very well and thoughtfully. Martinian and 4 Nigerian novice Sisters came and so did Sheila and Brother Alfonse. It was good to have them. Martinian is back from Ghana - and she brought a dear little wooden antelope as a present. It is good to have her back. The Evans are hoping to come and stay on Easter Saturday - so it will be good to see them. Special thoughts and prayers for the operation.

With much love

Elizabeth

Vining Centre

19th April 1976

Dear Ma and Daddy,

Thank you for your letter of 6th April with the Account of your "fast" weekend with Dorothy Dykes. She is supposed to be coming to Nigeria in Oct. - Nov. so I shall have to be ready for her. She won't find V.C. very fast. I am glad that the confirmation Service was so inspiring.

I am writing this in the evening on my verandah with the dark still night all around and am thinking of you at home with Stuart and Jutka arriving for the week. I feel very weary and ready for an early bed - because we finished the term yesterday - on Easter Sunday- and today Christine and I went for a picnic to the Akinbadewa's and trekked with them up onto the rocks at the back of their house, and then on up another rocky viewpoint.

We had a good end of term, although it was busy. We finished our exams on Tuesday and on Wed. and Thursday the women were cleaning up and cooking fish stew and rice for the Leper Settlement feast on Thursday. On Friday we had a morning Service at 9 a.m. when Cornelius gave a very moving message. He took 7 things that were given to Jesus in Holy Week - a donkey, a box of ointment, a room, a shoulder, a request, a drink, and a tomb. He brought out a message from each saying that we should be ready to give such things to each other - and to Jesus e.g., humble service - donkey, our most costly possession - Joseph's own tomb. Sharing burdens with others etc. He finished up with the story of the boy who stood on the collection plate and gave his life to missionary service. I remember Daddy used to tell that story. We also had Meditation from 12 - 3 led by the ordinands. This too was good.

On Easter Sunday we had a great Thanksgiving Communion Service 9 to 11.15. Then the women cooked jollof rice and goat which obviously was not ready in time. At 3.30 it was just about cooked so there was a great hiatus to be ready for the 4 p.m. Commissioning Service. We started by 4.15 and it was blessedly short - 1 hour with Mrs. Akintemi being the Speaker. The students were up at 3.45 a.m. to go out singing in the town on Easter morning. Then the next morning they were up at 4am to go home on the buses home for the holidays

Martinian has gone home - she went yesterday to have a lump on her breast seen to in Dublin. We hope it is a benign thing, but she is a bit afraid because her father died of cancer - and, she has been very weary and not very well this year. I shall miss her a lot if by any chance she isn't able to come back. We shall just have to wait on the result of the biopsy. I gave her my Ash Wednesday painting of the flowers as an Easter present.

I am planning to go away for a week. April 21 - 28 to go via Onitsha to Aba to see Jane Backhouse and maybe to reach Port Harcourt and meet Eliz. Leicester.

Much love to you both
Elizabeth

Vining Centre
25th April 1976

Dear Ma and Daddy,

I was fortunate to be able to extract your letter from the post office before I travelled last Wednesday. On Monday I went to the

Akinbadewa's with Christine. On Tuesday I rested at home and went to the Leper Settlement with the Eyesorun in the afternoon. Then I set out on Wed. a.m. and drove to Ondo where I had coffee and a natter with Inga. Then I drove straight to Onitsha and stayed the night with Anne and John Philips. They seem well. Anne Philips is always bright and cheerful. On Thursday morning I continued my way and stopped by at Iyi Enu to greet Eliz. Edmunds and Sue Lumley, the other doctor now there. Then I went down to Owerri and had lunch with Jennifer Carey before proceeding on a nasty road from Owerri to Aba. It was tar in the middle and then eroded sides and you must keep getting 2 wheels up and 2 wheels down to avoid the lorries lumbering in the other direction.

At Aba I was warmly welcomed by Jane. It was good to see her again. She took me to Uhmahia on Friday because she had a meeting of Church Leaders and Sunday School leaders and suggested that I should spend the morning with Ann Goodchild. When we got to the meeting place, we were met by 2 rather gloomy looking clergymen who said, "Everyone came yesterday!" Only Jane and the speaker were there on Friday. All the other people had come for the meeting on Thursday because Jane had written the notice about it and told them to come on Thursday 23rd (Friday was the day she meant). Dear Jane, she does make muddles with dates and meetings because she is in such a tearing hurry.

Anyway, we had a very pleasant morning with the Goodchilds and then returned to Aba in the afternoon. On Sat. I went to Port Harcourt and found Elizabeth Leicester at home. She has worked for 10 years in Edinburgh as a medical social worker and finds P.H. rather a contrast. She is not a very relaxed person, but I got on quite well with her. Her cat is called Scallion She was very impressed that I knew that it was a mountain! She has a very 'towny 'house - very clean floor - stair up to the bedroom above. While I was there, she took me round to see one of my Vining Centre students who is a Catechist in P.H. He was very happy to see me, and we arranged that if Colin Judd came, he would take us down to Bonny to stay the night there - that means a nice 'creaky 'boat journey. So, we shall see. We have another student who will be in Bonny by then.

I went to Kingsway - Leventis in P.H. and was impressed by their stock. Port Harcourt has some nice places in it - although I gather that the old town is pretty grotty. Aba is a horrid town - dirty, noisy, and full of traffic. It took me 45 mins to get through it and apparently sometimes it can be worse.

Last Monday at Pat's I stubbed my toe when walking and put a plaster on it. The wretched thing began to go septic, so I have been soaking it in salt and hot water - but on Sat. night my leg began to ache, so Jane took me on Sunday to a Church of Christ mission hospital with an Englishman as the doctor - a young chap, Bob Whittaker, who comes from Knighton. He and Jane's friend - an American girl, Nancy were very helpful and gave me Tetanus Toxoid injection and Tetracycline. Since then, it has improved. It is amazing what a nuisance a minute wound can be.

On my way back to Akure I am stopping at Owerri with Jenny Carey and then in Benin with Jane P. At present I am with Jenny who is in the process of writing a speech for the bishop (Ben Nwankiti) on the inauguration of the Imo State Prisoners Welfare Association. What jobs one must do!

Greetings from Jane Backhouse, from Ann Goodchild and Jenny.

With much love to you both

Elizabeth

Vining Centre
2nd May 1976

Dear Ma and Daddy,

Next Sunday will be our first Sunday of term and your birthday Ma. I hope that it is a very happy day. Inga's mother's birthday was last Sunday and she phoned her and got through in 1/2 hr. - so I may try. It might be that Sunday afternoon is a good time - but don't be too hopeful. I am enclosing a cheque for £8. - which is for Ann's wedding present - £4 something I think you said - and the rest to buy something for your birthday. I hope the freesia bulbs do well. I thought that your sheltered garden might be O.K. for them.

I posted my last letter to you in Benin on Wed. I think. I stayed Tues. night with Jane Pelly. She was back from 10 days in England - for her father's funeral. He had a very good write-up in the Trowbridge local newspaper. I drove from Benin to Ondo on Wed. morning and had lunch at Inga's. Her car is not working again so she was bit low. I stayed there to rest and then came on to Akure before dark. I was thinking of going to Lagos with Pat and Francis

Akinbadewa on Thurs., but I gave up the notion when I heard that they were coming back on Friday. It seemed daft to go all that way for one night - so I think I will go to see Myrtle and Pat when we have our next Half Term holiday.

I heard from the St Louis Sisters that Martinian's lump is not serious - so that is a relief.

On Thursday morning I delivered my Leper Settlement minutes and met some of the new people in the health Office. They seemed very friendly, and I hope they will start to come to our Leper Settlement Committee.

On Friday I took Mama Ademoye to Ondo to see if the needed new spectacles and while she was waiting, I went to see Inga and then Cynthia Whittle. Sheila came to my house for supper with Lily Stott who is staying with her this weekend. Then yesterday morning I went back to Ondo to go to a Home Economics Exhibition at Adeyemi College with Inga. I only discovered that it was on around 9 a.m. and the opening was at 10 a.m. so I had to hurry to get over there in time. The Eyesorun was the Opener. I was very glad that I went because I missed it last year - and it is a new department in the Teacher Training College. Their aims and objectives are very much the same as ours in teaching the women here - except that ours is on a more 'village' level.

We were very intrigued to see some of the things that they had done with local materials - like making dye out of teak leaves and guinea corn stalks. They also had made some very good-looking baby oil out of coconut oil.

I am sorry to hear that your friend Fred Fish had died. Jane Pelly's mother is still going strong in Salisbury. I am glad to hear that Stuart is getting music work, and that Andy is doing some art. Is he still at Monica Huggett's place? How interesting to hear of George Ripley again? It will be good if Ruth and Trevor go to visit Findhorn. Someone was telling me about the book about the Yorkshire vet so I shall be very intrigued to read it. Thank you for sending it.

I shall be trying to fit new students into rooms this week. I fear I may have admitted too many women for comfort - but I expect we shall manage.

With much love to you both,

Elizabeth

Vining Centre
9th May 1976

Dear Ma and Daddy,

I was very interested in Daddy's account of the people "flying" off the Malvern Hills - and the visit of Stuart and Jukka. It sounds as though they had an active holiday.

I am thinking of you especially today because it is Mother's birthday and because Daddy will be in the hospital. I tried to phone on Thursday and booked the call in Lagos around 6 p.m. and the line was very clear, so I was hopeful. They said they would phone back around 8 p.m. but when I tried them again after 8, they said they couldn't hear Lagos anymore. Wasn't that disappointing? I wished I had asked them to put me through at 6. Anyway, I just wanted to wish you well in the hospital.

I hope that you had an enjoyable visit to Pilsdon and found Ruth and Trevor in good form.

Last Saturday night 5 of Fiwasaiye Form 5 took themselves off to a dance without permission and returned to the compound at 2 a.m. so you can imagine there were ructions which occupied Sheila on Sunday and Monday morning. She was very tired by it all but wanted to take 2 of them to Benin and deliver them by hand - so I offered to drive her there in my car. On the road between Ore and Benin my steering wheel started to violently dance every time we went over any bumps - which was most of the time. So, we had to slow down and drive carefully all the way to Benin. We arrived on the outskirts of the town at about 6.45 and decided to deposit the schoolgirls before going to stay with Jane. But mother lived at one end of town and Papa at the other so by the time we had sorted them out and negotiated a terrible traffic jam where no-one would budge in any direction - it was 9.15 p.m. Anyway, we had a nice night with Jane and the next morning I took the car to Mandilas, and they fitted a new steering damper and had it ready before 12 noon - so that was good, and we were able to be back in Akure before dark.

Then on Wed. and Thurs. I was able to prepare for the students who arrived on Friday. Our room list is even tighter than before, and we really are using all nooks and crannies of space. I have 23 women - if they all show up. One has had a threatened miscarriage so she's not likely to be here very soon.

I have felt a bit off colour at the end of this week - like neuralgia pains around the neck and generally weary. Maybe I have a bit of fever. It's a bit stupid after 3 weeks holiday. However, I feel better tonight so perhaps it's just a passing phase. We were at the Leper Settlement this evening for our Termly Open-Air Service.

By the way, Elsie Clitheroe was not here for 14 years - but only for 2 years. Since then, she has visited Nigeria again twice.

The Eyesorun and Mrs. Sijuade were with me yesterday evening, which was nice. We have started the new term properly today with cleaning of the compound - the men cutting grass outside and the women cleaning the hall and the classrooms. Tomorrow we shall start lessons. This morning in the first half hour 2 men had cut themselves with their cutlasses - one badly enough to go to the hospital for A.T.S.

Looking forward to hearing the result of your operation.

Much love
Elizabeth

Vining Centre
16th May 1976

Dear Ma & Daddy,

Your joint letters, posted on 5th May reached Akure on 14th - so post seems to be taking 10 - 11 days now. I hope to hear news of Daddy's operation in the coming week - and do pray continually that it will be successful, but also that Ma doesn't get too tired running back and forth, nor too lonely sitting at home… although the numbers of meetings and activities reported in your last letter don't allow much time for turning round, far less sitting down. I am glad that you were able to see Trevor and Ruth - but I agree - visiting people in a community set up is not nearly as satisfactory as staying in someone's home where you have their full attention - particularly at mealtimes. I always felt that when they were at Lee Abbey. You would have thought that Pilsdon could be made elastic enough so that if relatives came to stay, they could have separate meals with their folk - but maybe as you say Percy is not very elastic.

Rain has been coming sheeting down this afternoon and has made everything cooler - but it looks damp outside - just the weather for sitting inside and writing letters. At the beginning of the week, I felt weak and was full of aches and pains especially neck ache, so I went to see Dr Sijuade on Tuesday and he said that there was nothing the matter with me except for tiredness due to driving so far in the holidays! So, he gave some tonic called Orepthal and Novalgin tablets… and I took them and recovered my energy by Thursday when I went and bashed a tennis ball to and from with Christine. Then on Thursday night Richard and Jane Smith from Wusasa turned up to stay 2 nights. It was very nice to meet them particularly because they had known Ruth at Lee Abbey. On Friday after classes I took them up to Idanre and we climbed up to the Rest house and sat and looked at the view. They went away on Sat. a.m. and in the afternoon, I had another go at the tennis, and we had a knock up with 2 fellows at the Agric. So now I feel heaps better - and all my aches and pains have departed - except for the calf muscles which are aching from the unaccustomed exercises.

One sad thing happened and that was that a man at the Leper Settlement died. I felt bad about it because I saw him last Sunday - when he was 1st sick, and I gave him 2 largactil because he was vomiting and reported to Dr. Sijuade and then to the Leprosy office on Monday. Then no-one came to tell me he was still sick, so I thought he'd be better, and I didn't go back to the Settlement again. The Leprosy Officer went 3 times I was told but either he didn't call the Doctor - or Dr. S was too busy to go .... Anyway, no doctor went, and he died on Friday - pain in the abdomen. It was particularly upsetting because he was one of the strongest men who did a lot of farming.

I am interested that you found Clarke's Second Shops in Street. Rather good, aren't they? The shoes that I have had from there have always done very well.

Thank you for the verses from Basil Farncombe's Retreat Day. We had a peaceful Fellowship gathering last Tuesday - one of the novice sisters led it on Peace. I was very struck by a verse in Peter's sermon on the day of Pentecost which I had not noticed before - Acts 3 v 19 - 'Now change your mind and your attitude to GOD and turn to him so he can cleanse away your sins <u>and send you wonderful times of refreshment from the presence of the Lord'</u> This I pray for you both during the time of Daddy's convalescence.

I was at St Louis for lunch today – super lunch! Sister Mildred is going home in 2 weeks' time. Brother Fred is also going – to cross the Sahara and stay in Pere de Foucould's hermitage for a 2-week retreat.

Looking forward to your next letter,
Much love
Elizabeth

Vining Centre
23rd May 1976

Dear Ma and Daddy,

It seems that letters are taking the best part of 2 weeks to get to you these days. I am sorry that I was therefore late for your birthday.

I am very happy to hear that Daddy seems so well after the Op. - and that there is no great scar to heal up. It is amazing what they can do nowadays. How do they manage to repair a valve but working up such a little hole?? I shall be thinking of you both during the time of convalescence…. and hope that Daddy will be well by the time John and Pat & co come from New Zealand. It is nice to have the Bennetts so near - to go on outings together. How are they enjoying life in Malvern after Enfield? I wonder if the Cullingford who is coming to Malvern College is any relation of Rev. Cecil Cullingford, whose son Antony taught in Nigeria in 1965-6 or so.

This week has been a normal week. I talked to the men on Monday night about Health - and gave them doses of Nivaquin etc. for Malaria and ideas of what to take for common complaints. I set them an essay on 'building a Healthy Nation' - but got rather bored reading their accounts and haven't yet got through the 120 exercise books.

Today I gave the talk in the Communion Service and spoke about Rogation Sunday - and the 'Theology of Enough' from John Taylor's book. We are talking about planting more fruit trees on the compound. The Government has launched a "Feed the Nation" Campaign as, "Operation Feed Yourself" to encourage everyone to grow more food, because there is not enough produced by the farmers, many of whom are old - and young people are not going to work on the farms. Have you ever read Isaiah 56 v10 -11 in the Living Bible? It is a priceless warning on how not to be a leader.

The phone to Fiwasaiye has been out of order for the past 2 weeks so I have wasted a good deal of petrol hopping up and down to discover if Sheila is in for coffee or if Christine wants to play tennis. We don't really play yet - but we are practicing. On Friday I went with the Eyesorun to the Agric, and we sat on a rock and looked at the view. On Thur. in the evening, I went round to the Sijuade's for an hour or so and had a very pleasant evening drinking their wine and coffee.

This coming week is going to be full of visitors - Susan Lumley, the doctor at Iyi End is coming from Mon - Friday, Lily Stott from Ado is coming on Friday for the weekend - and so too is Ruth Howard, I think. Jane Pelly will be with Sheila. So that will be rather nice. I am going over to Ondo today to have lunch with Inga. Joseph's 'wife' at Ife University had her baby last week so she is staying with Inga now. She is just about to do her final exams - when the Exam week comes, she will have to rush up and down the road to Ife and fit in feeds between the exams!!

I have been reading part of "Christian Response" by Quoist this week - particularly about doing one thing at a time - and concentrating on it… and thanking GOD that He gives us 'time '- and gives us enough work to do - but not too much.

We will be having our Fellowship this Tuesday - I think we are going to read parts from this Quoist to direct our thinking. It will be the last time that we see Bro. Fred and Sr. Mildred before they each go on 3 months leave.

I am still trying to write a link letter. I hope to get it in the post this week because it is 6 months since I wrote to either the Parishes or my friends. Any news of Anne Harris? I hope she is O.K.

With much love to you both

Elizabeth

Vining Centre
30th May 1976

Dear Ma and Daddy,

Thank you for your letters - telling the good news of Daddy's recovery, and the happy time that you had in Bristol over Jutka's birthday and Stuart's Concert. All the Malvern friends seem to have come up trumps in providing meals for Ma, when Daddy was in the hospital.

This has been a good week here - for visitors! Sue Lumley - the doctor at `Iyi Enu came from Monday till Friday. She was a very easy guest. I took her to the Agric, and to Idanre, on Wed. afternoon but she was very happy to potter around on her own or just read or knit. She told me that it was very normal for there to be some blood in the urine after Daddy's type of Op. She also described how they use a telescope type of thing to do the Op…so that was reassuring and interesting. She is Tricia Davies 'cousin - so she went off to Ado on Thursday to visit Ile Abiye and Christ's School.

On Friday Lily Stott from Ado came here to stay for the weekend. It is good to have her…. but she does 'talk' a lot about her theories of Nursing training and you can't really get on with your own things when she is around. Anyway, it's the weekend so it doesn't matter. Jane Pelly is here too - staying with Sheila, with a very nice Pakistani lady teacher. Jane has brought 40- of her girls in a bus, on an Excursion to Idanre and the Agric. etc. All very well, but it has meant that Sheila hasn't had any half term holiday to talk of which I think she needed.

All these folk - and Eyesorun and Joan Steward came round to supper here last night so that was very nice. Ruth Howard was also supposed to be here - but she didn't come. She has decided not to leave Nigeria now after all -but has taken on the job of Head of Idia College - the Govt. Girls College in Benin - with H.S.C. Now she is running the 2 schools!

I have also been playing tennis - three times I think at the Agric - and I get very hot and red, but I am improving with practice. The men who play there are very friendly and don't mind if you boggle up their game.

On Thursday it was Children's Day - and all the schools and colleges went and marched around the Stadium and saluted the Military Governor. Our men marched as Boys Brigade officers - and looked very good. I took the women and managed to get them a seat in the Stand. I had a ticket which was remarkable because I am not usually on anyone's list!

I have an idea now that I might come home for the month of August! What do you think? I would like to see John and the family - I don't know what I need to be doing here - Are you going to be in Malvern in Aug? What are Stuart and Jutka going to be doing I wonder? I guess Ruth and Trevor may be in Scotland.

The thing is that I have discovered that there is a summer flight programme that goes at the cost of N270, and you can go on July 27th and return on Aug. 31st. Dear Sheila says she will give me N100, and my Aug. Allowance is N150 so if I spend that I could come home. I don't think C.M.S. will object - after all most of the people in schools go home each year. It would be good to see you all - and to be on ‘holiday ’without worrying about Links or such like at all. What do you think?

Anyway, I am going to investigate further. I phoned the woman in Lagos who organises this - Inga has been twice with her, and Eyesorun last year. It sounds as though I can get a ticket if I book now. So, here’s hoping!

With much love

Elizabeth

Vining Centre
6th June 1976

Dear Ma and Daddy,

So good to hear that Daddy is out of hospital and that all seems very well. It doesn’t sound as though Daddy is very bed-ridden in his convalescence if he is walking up the Happy Valley, studying the swallows. I also had a letter from Marguerita this week. It was good to hear from her - but sad to hear about Judy.

I have sent my N270.00 off for my ticket this week.... so, I am likely to be coming. On Friday I had a letter from the lady in Lagos who organises these, Charter Flights. She said that I had already introduced 6 people to her and if I introduced 8 more - I could get a free ticket. What a pity that I didn’t know this earlier for I might have found more people. Now I think it’s a bit late, because if anyone wants to go, they will have already made their arrangements. Anyway, I am going to try and Eyesorun is going to put notices in Ministries etc. All rather a hoot.

Anyway, the more I think about the notion of my 5 weeks holiday in England - the more I like it. This week I gathered that our Bishop wrote to cancel Colin Judd’s visit at the end of April…and never told me a sausage and nor did Cornelius. They are the end. I think it is particularly disappointing because it was a chance for the Nigerian Church to entertain an English Clergyman and give him some experience of life overseas...... as a return to the many Nigerian Clergy who have spent time in Parishes in England. But they don’t seem to have looked at it like that - and only think that now we have a 3rd Clergyman here, so we don’t need an Englishman.

As far as I am concerned it makes September free as well as August - but I will still return on August 31st. We planned a special Leprosy

Campaign Week at our meeting last Wednesday - and it will be good to be free during Sept. to help to organise it.

Sheila is here this afternoon - having a long sleep. She has been very tired this week and not very well - had a spot of running tummy. She has just 3 more weeks before she goes so there is a lot to do in that time, especially as School Cert is on. The only condition of her gift of N100 is that I will go and visit her and her mother sometime in August. So, I shall hope to go and spend some days with Stuart and Jutka - and see Sheila at the same time - she lives in Brixton. Apart from that there is John and Pat & co… my main reason for coming home - and I would like to see Marguerita if possible. I just mention this for your thoughts as you think of August. I really will be very happy to spend most of the time sitting down in Malvern doing dress making … and having good chats and visits to Midsummer Common etc. It will be very nice to come home and have no deputation to worry about… although I may go and see Dorothy Dykes if she is planning to come here in October on a visit.

I am thinking of you especially this week as you welcome Pat and John and the children. I expect they will have changed a good deal.

Much love to you both

Elizabeth

Vining Centre
13th June 1976

Dear Ma and Daddy,

Thank you for your letter of June 1st which reached here on June 10th. I am now waiting for your next letter with your reactions to my coming home in August. I hope you will think it's a good idea - because I can't get my money back now! The more I think about it the more I think it is an excellent idea. I am sorry to hear that John was so sick - but I should think that Vancouver would be a good place to recover.

I think that if the Iliffs want to send something to the Leper Settlement - it is best if they send me a cheque - or give me when I come. Then, depending on the amount I can either pay in Naira myself - or ask Sheila to do so, and then I would pay her in English money.

I am sorry that Daddy's legs are so stiff and that he can't read happily. It is difficult not to be "doing" something. I suppose it is part of our upbringing and education. Perhaps we need to learn from the Africans who seem content and happy just to 'sit 'and 'be 'for hours on end. After all everyone up till the 15th Century had to manage without any books to read, or the radio or Tele. It is good that you are in Malvern where you can so easily get out into the beauties and quiet of the countryside.

I am glad that the Panters are returning at last. I should think that Peter Dunlop is very well able to cope with the whole Parish, especially if they combine more with the Priory.

Have you read John's book yet? It sounds a bit off track!! Yesterday I had 8 men helping me to compile some Song books for the Chapel - 16 sheets of Songs and a cardboard cover - threaded together with a piece of string like a loose-leaf file. We had quite an interesting time discussing 'Division of Labour '- i.e., one man compiling the sheets in order, one trimming, one punching holes and 3 threading. We calculated that our efficiency increased with practice - we made 23 in the 1st half hour but 35 in the second half an hour - so we reckoned up the time that was needed to complete the job when we meet again! This is the level of my Industrial management!!

This last week Ebun was in the hospital - she was discovered to be very anaemic - -about 36% and on Monday they announced that she was to have blood, so we were to find 6 men willing to donate. So, I came back and appealed to our men - and 6 of them went on Tuesday. They said that she has hookworm, that might be the cause of her anaemia.

I am going on Half Term on Thursday, and may well take Ebun to Abeokuta, for her check up on Friday. Then I am hoping to go on to stay with Myrtle and Pat for the weekend. I am not sure if I will take Ebun along, or if I shall let her return to Akure on public transport.

Our Ordinand students are leaving at half term to prepare for their Ordination in July, so it will mean that there is a little more space for the men students.

Sheila is very tired - she goes home in 2 weeks' time. Just as well. She needs to have a good rest. I have her duiker here now, in an enclosure near my back door. Patrick and Cynthia Whittle are coming tomorrow, and they say that they will bring their young male to join her - so then I shall have two. They are very easy to feed because they like hibiscus flowers and jasmine flowers and the skins of mangoes, plantain, and pineapple - so you can use them as a dustbin.

I am hoping to write a Link Letter and send it off soon so maybe you would like to start an envelope. It has been raining the last few evenings - which I like because you always feel much wider awake, and you can sleep cozily under blankets .... so, I may get round to the Link Letter!!

I am taking our Service this evening with some of the women helping to do readings. I will enclose the Order of Service. The 3rd reading is to be acted (Pharisee & Publicans) The theme of what I want to put across is "A Greater Understanding of GOD's holiness leads to an increase in man's humility." It is a special Service for Trinity Sunday, as well as being a farewell to the ordinand students. I hope that the 2 times of Prayer will be times of Open Prayer.

The enclosed cheque for £10 was sent to me by Anne for the Leper Settlement. I will give the Naira to our Treasurer here. Please can you help me to pay it into the bank? I had Sheila, Christine, and Dennis here to supper last night - Tokunbo had gone to Owo, so I made a Sponge with eggs, sugar, and flour only - most successful, and much appreciated.

Much love to you both
Elizabeth

Vining Centre
20th June 1976

Dear Ma & Daddy,

It was good to get your enthusiastic letter this week. I have now got my ticket. It is for the 27th of July leaving Lagos at 8 a.m. - called SNB 238. I don't know the time of Arrival yet - but it is Heathrow. I think sometimes these Charters can be subject to delays and come in later than scheduled. The return flight is on Aug. 26th and not 31st. But that still gives a clear 4 weeks at home, which will be marvellous.

I am now sitting in Myrtle's living room listening to a record of Faure's Requiem from King's College Cambridge - beautiful. Myrtle and Pat have gone out to Church, but I decided to stay in and write some letters... including my Link Letter, if possible.

I came to Lagos on Friday. It is our Half Term so in fact I left Akure on Thursday afternoon and went with Ebun to Ibadan where we stayed the night with the Nightingales. Ebun is now very good and has no trouble at all staying in European houses. She had even had the wisdom to cook her own rice, fish and pepper stew and bring it along with her! The Nightingales are in the process of packing up for their return home in July. On Friday morning Ebun and I left early and reached Abeokuta soon after 9 a.m. The Doctor at Aro was very good and let us jump the queue very quickly. Ebun was given 3 months more tablets. She just takes one at night and we were out of the hospital around 10.30. So, then I took Ebun back into Abeokuta town where she had beans and rice in a 'hauf 'and I had dodo in the street. Then I took Ebun to the lorry park to get transport to Ibadan where Sheila was meeting her to take her back to Akure.

Then I continued on the road from Abeokuta to Lagos which has greatly improved on how it used to be, but it is still being constructed in parts and it is wet season so parts of it were very muddy. My car was filthy by the time I got into Lagos. I had a horrid headache by the time that I arrived - a touch of malaria, I think. It is lovely to be with Myrtle and Pat. They have just both got the MBE, so it is a great joke, and rather a thrill. Yesterday we all went into Lagos to see Rev. Faji and then to sit and relax at the Federal Palace pool and brown our noses. There wasn't a lot of sun, but it was lovely, and the traffic to and fro wasn't bad at all. It is quite amazing what they have done in the building line in Lagos. They seem to have gone mad with Concrete and have got fly-overs all over the place. They have also been doing a lot of Sand-Filling in of swampy ground - but somehow, they haven't calculated very well for wet season because they have blocked some places where the water used to drain away - and so last Friday there was a cloud burst of rainfall - 23cms they said and high tide - and flooding in all the low-lying parts of Lagos. Myrtle's school was in a 2-foot lake! Horrible mess because you can imagine all of Lagos drains overflowing with the flood water - and soakaways overflowing!!

I was very happy to hear that Susanne came to see you. She wrote me a nice letter to tell me the same things. She is a nice girl, isn't she? She is the one I used to play tennis with. Sheila goes home next Friday so then I shall have the month of July on my own - but Eyesorun is there - and Mrs. Sijuade is always happy to have someone to talk to.

My Service last Sunday night went well - all the ordinands were most appreciative.

Much love to you both

Elizabeth

Vining Centre
27th June 1976

Dear Ma and Daddy,

How nice that you were able to go to N. Wales for a break. I am sure that the change did you both a great deal of good. It sounds like a lovely spot. How awkward to find that the last people hadn't gone away - but I am glad that it all worked out in the end.

I was in Lagos when I wrote to you last week. It was so nice to see Pat and Myrtle again. On Monday morning I went round the school. It's amazing how it has grown and how the school has developed. They will miss Myrtle, but she really has put the place on its feet.

After going to the School, I went to see Mrs. David - who has the travel agency that organises the Charter business that I am coming on. She was in her inner Sanctum - little cubby hole place above the travel agent in the new shopping precincts in Surulere. Very smart. She gave me a cup of coffee and we had a chat while her daughter wrote out the tickets for the Eyesorun. She is an enormous woman, and a great character. She is from Ife and related to Dr Sijuade.

On my way home between Lagos and Ibadan I decided to drop in at the Nigerian Youth Camp and see Kath Dick and Co. I was very glad that I went because Kath has had Shingles for the past 8 weeks and was still recovering and not looking very well. Next year she will have been 45 years in Nigeria!! Mary produced a lovely lunch which fortified me on my way home. I then continued via Ibadan and Ondo and reached home about 8 pm.

The rest of this week has been centred round Sheila going away for leave - on Friday. We had our Fellowship on Tuesday at the Eyesorun's house - and made it a sort of farewell meeting for Sheila. On Tuesday evening I went over to Fiwasaiye to help to write Sheila's reports. I shall miss her company very much.... because there is not a day when we don't either drink coffee together or at least phone each other up. Anyway, it's only a month till I come home too so I shall survive.

Yesterday – Friday, I went to Aquinas College - the Catholic Boys 'School to say farewell to Father Evans. He has been there for 9 years but wants to step down and let a Nigerian be the principal. On Friday they had a Cultural Dance Display at which all the local schools performed. Some of them were extremely lively.

Then last night they had a Dinner in honour of Fr. Evans. I went with Pat Akinbadewa and sat beside Sister Macnoase. The Deji of Akure was in the Chair. Eyesorun was there and a lot of other Akure dignitaries - especially leading Catholics and Old Boys of the School etc.

Myrtle gave me an old copy of a book written by Anna Hinderer about their coming to Ibadan. Inside was a letter written in 1933 by a lady in Bedford who said that she remembered the Hinderers coming to her house when she was a child - and Bp Crowther and Bp Phillips. It makes the "history" of the 18th Century seem very nearby.

With much love to you both and prayers especially that Daddy may be stronger each day - Thank you very much for the Vet book- Great fun - came at just the right time.

Elizabeth

Vining Centre
2nd July 1976

Dear Ma and Daddy,

Great to hear that John and Pat & co are home, and that you were able to meet them all happily at the airport. I am not surprised that you were tired after all that. I hope that it is all working out well with them in Malvern. You will just have to learn when to say No to activities and expeditions and let them go off on their own so that you don't get too exhausted.

I am now at Ado staying with Lily Stott. She has always got plenty to say...... and tends a bit to "go on" ...but thinks it is just a complaint of people who are often on their own. I do the same. If I suddenly have someone to talk to then the flood gates open!!

Yesterday morning Janet and Bose Olowoyo came to Akure, and Janet stayed with me while Bose went to a meeting. Then they both came to lunch. It was good to see them again. I was over in Ondo on Wednesday talking to St Monica's girls about 'Pollution 'and then staying with Inga in the evening to see some very good films about Reclaiming the Desert. Inga came over on Tues. and we went round some of the Ministries together.

On Monday night I lectured the men about Bp. Crowther I went to see Mrs. Sijuade, on Wed I went to see Eyesorun - Thurs -to Ondo and on Friday I went to say goodbye to Dennis the C.U.S.O. fellow at Aquinas College. He and his girlfriend Heidi are going home across the Sahara. They were setting off on Friday morning. So, I haven't had a chance to be lonely with Sheila away!

This coming week looks as though it is going to be equally busy.

We have Leper Settlement Committee, Blood Donors Committee, and our Fellowship meeting, and we shall probably start our women's exams with the practical exam on Thursday. It is only 3 weeks on Tuesday, and I shall be coming home. Tally ho! I need to get my re-entry permit but apart from that I am all set, I think.

With much love to all the family - especially John and Pat

With love

Elizabeth

Vining Centre

10th July 1976

Dear Ma and Daddy,

Thank you for your letter of June 28th. It is good to hear that John and Pat & Co are now in Malvern. It does sound hot there! It is perishingly cold here! - wet and drizzly and cold especially at night. I am glad of my 3 blankets on the bed, and some days we have been wearing cardigans or sweaters right through the day. When I came back from Ado last Sunday my feet were so cold that I had to boil a kettle and soak them in warm water to heat up. So, it sounds as though I may find sunshine if I come home during August. The flight is scheduled to leave Lagos at 8 a.m. and reach Heathrow at 2.10 p.m.… But I understand that these Charters can be delayed. Anyway, we can just hope for the best.… It will be great to see you.

For Mr. Illif's information. My Bank is Barclays Bank, Akure. Maybe I can see him about it when I come. This week has been quite full. On Monday night a fellow from the Min of Agric. came to talk to the men about the 'Feed the Nation' Campaign which is the thing of the moment. All students are to do some farming - i.e., School pupils and University students - to increase food production and to try to reverse the trend of people leaving the farms and going to towns for jobs.

On Tues. evening we had our Fellowship at the Noviciate. I went with Eyesorun. We shall not meet again till Sept. because so many members are away on leave. On Wed. evening we had the Leprosy Committee here - about a dozen people. We are planning to have a special leprosy week in Sept. I went to Ife on Wed. afternoon and bought some books to give to Myrtle and Pat and the Nightingales as leaving presents. I went to Bamgboye's house, but they were either out or asleep. On the way back I went into St Monica's for 1 hour of the farewell they had arranged for Provost and Mrs. Akintemi who is going to be the new Bp. of Ijebu. He has just returned from UK where he went to buy his robes, so I was a bit narked when the first thing Mrs. A says on discovering I am coming home in Aug was - please will you get me 2 dresses!! I am afraid I refused point blank. I am determined that this is a holiday - and I am not going to do anyone's shopping.

On Thursday morning we had our Practical exams - and Christine left to go to Lagos on her way home. In the evening I finished reading Anna Hinderer's Journals - incredible life the missionaries lead in the 1860's. There was a war between the Ibadans and Ijayes - and the road to the coast was blocked by the Ijebu's. Sometimes they waited for 6 months for any post!

I thought we saw Anna Hinderer's Grave in St Anne's Churchyard. But this book says she died at home and was buried in Norfolk. On Friday evening I went to St Louis and had supper with the sisters there. They are only 2 in residence, but Fr. Evans was there and an Irish family who teach in Ifarki. The Sisters now have Tele...... but I haven't yet found any programme that is worth watching, except maybe the News.... but last week I was mad because the Matron at Ile Abiye watched the Wimbledon finals and I didn't know it was on.

This morning 3 of our couples (students) got themselves properly married - and gained rings and certificates - not before time. One of them has a son in Sec. Sch. It was a tedious Service - 10-12. 1st 1/2 hr. - waiting, 2nd 1/2 hr. - Service, 3rd 1/2 hr. Sermon in Yoruba, 4th 1/2 hr. - writing 3 sets of Certificates and photos.

Much love and looking forward to a good chat

Elizabeth

Vining Centre
18th July 1976

Dear Ma & Daddy,

Not much to say, except that I am counting the days! I have marked my exam papers and only have the reports of the term to write, and other end-of-term activities. We finish on Wednesday. I think I have had some fever around, so I took Nivaquin yesterday and therefore feel very heavy headed today and distinctly like doing nothing.

I was in Ondo last night watching an old film of Great Expectations in Inga's house, with all the Olowoyo family. It was a good film, although as I say 'old'. John Mills was Pip.

I am going to lunch with the sisters today…. which is nice because I was just wondering if I could be bothered to cook much here - and Sr Macnoase rang up to say come and eat there.

All news when I come. I think I told you the proposed time of arrival is 2.10.

It's still cold here and drizzly rain almost every day. We have seen the sun for about 1/2 hour this week. I Shall be glad to get away.

Much love

Elizabeth

HOME ON LEAVE FOR FOUR WEEKS

The main reason for this was that John and Pat and their 3 children had come to England on holiday in August and so we were able to meet in Malvern.

Vining Centre
28th August 1976

Dear Ma and Daddy,

This is just a quickie from Lagos to let you know that I arrived safely this morning. The flight was late - and left London about 8 p.m. so we didn't reach Lagos until 2.30 a.m. and then all those suitcases had to be sorted out so that I reached Sola's place about 4.30 a.m. Natasha's mother and Nigerian father kindly took me to Sola's house. Then I had a sleep for an hour or so. I was originally thinking of going up to Ibadan today but decided to sleep this morning and then stay tonight at the C.M.S. Guest House so that I feel more like going up to Ibadan tomorrow. So, this journey has developed into one rest day after another! Then I discovered that my car only came out of servicing yesterday afternoon so I couldn't have driven it to Ibadan anyway.

Thank you very much for coming to the airport to see me off and thank you for everything during the past month. It was a great experience in every way.

It is cool here in Lagos with a good breeze off the Lagoon. The Akinbadewa's were lucky enough to get a morning flight instead - because there were 12 places in a normal flight. I was worried when they were not on the plane, but all was explained when I saw Mrs. David in Lagos.

I hope you have a happy time in the coming week with the children and John and Pat and that you are not too exhausted after all the activities. Don't forget to ask Dr Harcup about your mouth Ma if it is still causing a lot of pain. There may be some simple remedy that you don't know!

Sola is well, and was happy to have all her nappies etc.

I am just experiencing Lagos traffic hooting and jostling for position on the roads! Only 10 months to go.

With much love to everyone

Elizabeth

Vining Centre

4th September 1976

Dear Ma and Daddy,

I am now back in Akure - sitting on my verandah in my long dress. It is cool with a breeze and rain in the air. I am just about to prepare the lunch for Sheila and the new C.U.S.O. teacher who is called Corrine Lamire. She is aged 52 and has 4 grown up children. She is divorced from her husband. I think she will be a great help at Fiwasaiye because she has taught before, so she should be able to cope with teaching French without a lot of trouble. I have taken her down to the town shopping a few times this week and yesterday we went together to see Pat and Francis at Idanre, we had a very happy afternoon with the family there.

This morning has been quite busy. Last night Bola Asafa and his wife came to sleep the night here while attending a friend's wedding party. They came about 10 p.m. went to the party at about 10.45 and returned around 2 a.m. They got up by 6 a.m. and I gave them breakfast about 7 a.m. Then one fellow from the Leper Settlement came to say that a woman there wanted to deliver. So, I told them to go to the hospital in a taxi. I then went to Mrs. Sijuade to tell her that they would be coming to the hospital, and I went to Communion at 7.30 a.m. at St David's Church.

After my own breakfast I went to the Settlement to see what had happened and discovered that the woman had delivered at the Settlement because she had left it too late to go to the hospital. The baby girl looked fine except that she had a long bit of cord dangling and they had already put her on an old granny's back. I advised that they lie the baby in a clean place and cover the cord with a clean cloth! Then I discovered that the child was born with a 6th finger - a tiny growth out of the little finger which you should tie with cotton so that it falls off. Unfortunately, the granny midwife had already cut it off!! So, it was bleeding under a piece of cloth.

So, I went back to Mrs. Sijuade and got more advice and went back to the Settlement with bandages, Streptomycin powder, ergometrine and Aspirin tablets. All this took me to coffee time. I had coffee at Fiwasaiye. Dear Sheila has a horrible head cold - and all sorts of major problems to sort out at the beginning of the new term.

I then went round to St Peters where I saw Brother Alfonse who was asking after you both. After that I came back and cooked the lunch for Sheila and Corrine. Then I read some of my Hawaii book and had a very pleasant afternoon snooze.

I am enjoying being here with 4 weeks holiday before the beginning of the term because I have an extra supply of energy after being at home and I can get on with making dresses and reorganising things in my house. Thank you for all your love and prayers. I thought that I might be depressed as a reaction against all the activities of August - but I am not at all. So that's great. Hope you are not too tired.

With much love

Elizabeth

Vining Centre
11th September 1976

Dear Ma and Daddy,

It is good to get your letters again - and to hear about the Binnings and getting back into the swing of things in Malvern. I am so happy that I was able to come home - it made my Summer too! And it has made such a difference to this September. I have really enjoyed being here in Akure without working .... and I have been busy going up and down as they say here so that I don't think I shall ever dread staying on the Compound in the holidays again. It is nice to have time to go to meetings and to visit friends without having all the routine College work to do. On Wed. I went to 3 functions! In the morning it was the International Literacy Day Celebrations, and I met the Deji and shook his hand.... and I sat in the front row so appeared on the Television - so I am told. I haven't seen it. In the afternoon I went to a Red Cross meeting which was a shambles really. They spent 1/2 hour+ waiting for people to arrive. Then 1/2 hour making corrections to the Minutes. Then about 50 mins debating the subscription for different types of members of the Red Cross - and at what time of year they should pay their annual dues. I had to give up before we ever got to any business in the meeting! We had our Leper Settlement Committee at 7.30. That finished about 10 p.m. - but it was a good meeting I felt, and a lot of useful points were raised.

The Government has started on its plans to improve the buildings at the Settlement. They are now talking of a nurse visiting the Settlement once or twice a week - so we pray that they will find one who is willing to go there. We are not having our Leprosy week until we have heard if we can get a film or posters to show. It will probably be in Oct. or Nov. now.

There is a young boy who may be mental, we don't know, but he has appeared as a beggar in the middle of Akure. It is thought he was dumped there by people who don't want him - like Ebun. So, I spent some time making contacts with the Social Welfare people to see how they could help him. The upshot is that we made an appointment for Dr Sijuade to examine him tomorrow and if he says he is mental then I will take him to Ayo when I go with Ebun on Thursday.

On Saturday afternoon I went to Ado with Eyesorun and Corrine. We went to see the Matron at Ile Abiye and then the sisters at St Louis. Today I went to Idanre with Eyesorun and saw Pat Akinbadewa. Eyesorun was trying to check up that a 'Youth Corps 'doctor was settling down in Idanre. We discovered that the girl was in Akure!

Please can you send me a copy of Series III Communion Service? Our Clergyman is asking for it here. Please give my love to all the New Zealanders. I hope they have a good journey back.

With much love to you both

Elizabeth

Vining Centre

19th September 1976

Dear Ma and Daddy,

It is great to be getting your letters. Thank you for writing to the Leprosy Mission person. It would be good if he came here on a visit. On Monday evening I went to the Settlement, and they told me that they had all been weeping because that morning a caterpillar (bulldozer) had come to part of their farm and cleared the land - mashing up their precious yams in the process. Terrible calamity! It appears about 8 families are affected. Since then, we have been trying to find out who is the caterpillar owner - and trying to press the Ministry of Health to take steps to see that the land ownership is investigated. But can you credit that someone can be so heartless as to bulldoze yams when if he had given them one day's notice the yams could have been collected out of the ground because they are ready for harvesting?

Then I also discovered that the patients at the Settlement still haven't been given their allowance of N6.00 per month for the month of August. They say in the office that it is pressure of work in the Accounts Section. On the same day I heard that there are 6 doctors staying in a hotel in Akure because there is no room for them elsewhere - and the Government is paying N20.00 a night for the hotel. Then food is N2.50 a meal. (£1 = N1.15K). Incredible. The hotel is owned by one of the richest men in town.

One very good thing happened on Wednesday and that was that the Welfare people acted and removed the boy who was destitute in the centre of town. They were very happy to find that he is not violent, nor is he apparently mentally sick but has been thrown out of his home in Ado Ekiti by a senior wife, after his own mother died. It was marvelous how pleased the welfare people were when they had taken him in, washed him and taken him to the hospital for treatment. I pray that this case may give them the courage to take up others in future.

On Thursday I went to Ibadan and then on to Abeokuta on Friday to take Ebun for a checkup and to fetch Vero who was admitted in Aro for the past 4 weeks. The Doctor there is very good to us and allows us to jump the queue because we came all the way from Akure. Ebun and I stayed with Doug Evans on Thursday night. Then I left Ebun, and Vero on Friday at St Louis and I went to stay with Jose. I found them just about to go out for supper and they asked me to go with them - so I did - -to the Premier Hotel! It was to meet an English businessman who is in Cocoa business. It was a very interesting evening.

I saw Grace in Ibadan. She is busy going up and down between Ibadan and Ogotun - because her father died about 2 weeks ago. I called in Ife, but Kelu was in Lagos and Yomi is in U.K. for a Conference. I saw Prof. Rodgers. In Ondo I saw Inga who was not at all well - with fever and a nasty sore throat.

Guess who is back in Akure State Hospital? Dr Kumuyi! Do you remember he came for the day in 1972 Jan - and I took him to Dr Sinclair? He came here to greet me last Monday and seemed very well and very relaxed. Apparently, he didn't pass his Part 2 Fellowship Exam, but he is here now in charge of the Chest Clinic. Another person who has come to Akure in this new State set up is Tola,

Grace's sister. I haven't yet seen her, but I have found her house. I was at Fiwasaiye this evening taking their Service.

With much love to you both

Elizabeth

Vining Centre
26th September 1976

Dear Ma and Daddy,

Thank you for your letter from Sherborne. I wonder if Ruthie's baby has come yet. How exciting. I hope that everything is O.K. and that she has a normal delivery and doesn't have to have any Caesar. You have been gadding about - what with Yeovil and then Hackney. It is just well that you had the car serviced. Have you heard anything about the Expository Times bill? Because I promised Daddy that I would send him £50 when I heard about that…. i.e., providing it wasn't too much. I hope that Pat and the children got off happily and that they were not too overloaded with plastic bags!! Do they take apples or toothbrushes on the plane?

Nothing very world shaking happened last week. Nothing at all happened to help the Leper Settlement troubles. I will have to go the rounds again this week. I went to see Inga on Tuesday because she wasn't at all well and was staying at home and not teaching. She had a dreadful sore throat. Then on Tues. evening we had our first prayer fellowship - here. There were 6 of us but it was a helpful evening with very open discussion. Mrs. Sijuade is on sick leave after a prolapse op I think, so I went to visit her twice - and Eyesorun once. The Ministry of Health have been having big personality clashes at the top it seems and the Director of Medical Services and the Director of Nursing Services have both been transferred by the Permanent Secretary who seems to want to be the big boss. It's very sad.

On Friday afternoon I went to Ado to stay with Lily Stott. While we were there, we went to see the Hicks who are right out in Ekiti. I think that I have probably described them before. They have a rhesus problem and instead of doing anything about it - as you can these days to stop the antibodies developing - they did nothing, and their 2nd baby was induced at 6 weeks prem. It is a little girl, who is now 1 year - but she doesn't yet sit up and has very cross eyes. They have just been to U.C.H. Ibadan and found out that she has extensive nerve damage - which has affected the Optic nerves and the ears amongst other things. She doesn't seem to hear at all. Very, very tragic - especially when it could have been avoided if they had listened to people's advice.

Lily and I also went to greet an Egyptian Doctor and his wife in Ado - and there we met the Egyptian Gynaecologist and his wife who are here in Akure. I haven't met them before. We also met some Pakistani teachers and their wives. They were all congregating together on Friday because it was the end of Ramadan festival.

The School Cert. results are out this week. On the whole they are not very good. St Monica's results were very bad. Less than 50% passed but Mama's twins have both failed, so has Eyesorun's son.

Janet Olowoyo's mother has died this last week in Benin Teaching Hospital. That's Archdeacon Ajomo's wife - the one you gave the little bag to ……. or was it 6 pence? at Akinmorin. When we hear the date for the memorial service, Inga and I will go together.

We start our term this coming Wednesday. Victoria Olowomeye is going to Ife University to do the Associateship Course for 1 year. I am not quite sure how Cornelius will manage the house in her absence.

With much love to you both

Elizabeth

Vining Centre

3rd October 1976

Dear Ma and Daddy,

A lovely long letter last week telling of your visit to Yeovil and then on to Hackney. I am glad that you were able to see Pat and the children off. I must write to them more regularly now that I feel I know them better. Please write down their birthdays again for me!! I am very sorry to hear about the nasty way in which John G. is writing to Stuart and Jutka. Some people really are very strange, aren't they? You'd think that they would be overjoyed that someone is improving their house. No news yet of Ruth's baby. I hope to hear in the coming week.

The new term has now started here. The students came on Wednesday, so we cleaned on Thursday. Then Friday was a Public Holiday for October 1st (Independence Day) and there was the usual Parade of School Children and the Army and Police at the Stadium. I went to it with Corrine Lamire the C.U.S.O. lady. Unfortunately, on our way out some wretch picked her wallet from her bag. It contained N80 and 250 dollars of Travellers cheques. Maddening, and very upsetting for her because she has only just arrived. On Friday evening she was pestered by some Form 5 girls who are repeating and are looking for a place to stay in the compound. They have their eyes on her spare room, but she doesn't want schoolgirls always around. Then on Saturday morning she discovered that all her gas was leaking out, so Tokunbo and I went up to help her to get it fixed - to buy her more gas and to get a gas man to fix her stove. Sheila asked Brother Tom to invite her to lunch - which he did - so she was more cheerful in the afternoon.

Lily Stott came to lunch with a friend called Wally Dentex from Oyo. I have heard of this Wally for a long time but have never met her. We all went to Idanre together and visited the Akinbadewas. Before we went, we had a hilarious half an hour with 2 fellows who came to campaign about Life Insurance. I can't describe the conversation, but it was extremely funny. The bit that put Lily into hysterics was the fellow asking me if I was committed to be celibate!!

We were at the Leprosy Settlement this afternoon - still no doctor or nurse visiting the place - and still the poor people suffering from not enough attention. The newborn baby has a horrible boil-like thing right across the chest. Pathetic. It's like banging your head against a brick wall to get anything practical done to improve the situation. Money is useless if there are no people willing to go and care for them. We have a committee again this coming Wednesday. Several extra people have promised to come to see if we can do something about the land situation so that the Ministry of Health reserve an area properly for their farms. We can only press on and pray that people will take an interest.

Sheila is tired and over worked at Fiwasaiye. This evening there was a palaver about food - and all the girls screaming in protest 3 pieces of dodo instead of 5. Really, these schools become more impossible to run as they get bigger.

Dr Kumuyi came to supper on Tuesday - Sheila came too. He was full of talk - much chattier since he came from England. He used to be rather silent. He is still in the hotel.

I got a new baby duiker from the bush this week so have bought it (N3) and am feeding it with milk from a bottle 4 times a day. Its rather a pet. I hope it doesn't die.

Janet's mother died - did I tell you that? The funeral is next week Saturday. I will go with Inga. Bose has borrowed N1, 2000 from the school for the expenses!! Incredible.

I cut and bruised my toe this morning by dropping a tin of milk on it. Maddening because I was hoping to play tennis this week.

Much love

Elizabeth

Vining Centre
10th October 1976

Dear Ma and Daddy,

I am still waiting to see what the news of Ruthie is. Hopefully it will be in next week's letter. I can imagine you sitting at home glued to the phone waiting for Trevor to ring. It's raining here now - pouring. My baby duiker got wet and dirty outside today so it's just as well I have a place for him to stay on the verandah at night so that he is dry.

I have been away this weekend - Sat & Sun morning. Inga and I went to the funeral of Janet Olowoyo's mother. It was at Archdeacon Ajomo's home village - Okpe, about 40 miles from Auchi. We set off about 10.30 a.m. on Sat. and drove up through Owo and then on to Oka where the road climbs through the hills...... a lovely run although not a particularly lovely road surface. We reached Okpe about 1.30 and so were in good time for the Service at 2.30. All the 7 children were there - dressed in navy blue - the daughters all looking amazingly alike with the same uniform floppy hats. The older son who is a doctor had come especially from England. The village is tiny and the Church minute - but all in a beautiful setting.... and the whole village was involved in the funeral. There must have been 40 or more Clergy - so many that when the procession with the bishop at the front were going to the door to meet the coffin the back of the procession wasn't yet out of the vestry. Then they all turned round and there weren't enough seats for all of them, so I think some in the tail had to retreat and stand in the Vestry or in the Chancel. Certainly, there wasn't room for the Choir. They are a lovely family, and I was very glad that we went to join in the Service.

Afterwards Inga and I went back to the house for some refreshments and then we went on to Ikare for the night and stayed there with the sisters at the Convent. They were very hospitable and welcoming, but I had a slightly unsettled night because there were troublesome mosquitoes and no net on the bed. Then I woke up at about 11.30 p.m. and felt something wriggling under the sheet at the bottom of the bed. I leapt out very fast and dismantled the whole bed by candlelight and discovered that I was sharing it with a lizard that had got between the mattress cover and the mattress!!

Jane Pelly was here this weekend staying with Sheila, so I saw her briefly when we got back to Akure for lunch. My bambi is still doing O.K. I phoned Cynthia Whittle for advice On Friday night, and she told me that when they are sucking the mother usually licks their bottom (!) so she advised me to rub its anus to encourage it to stool. So last night I did so! - and immediately it obliged!! Very funny.

We had Leper Settlement Committee on Wed. evening - I felt we talked a lot and achieved very little - but a new person came called Mrs. Adepoju who came out with the amazing information that she is a C.M.S. member, is ordained as a Deaconess and had read about Ebun in Yes!! I must see more of her.

Greetings from Tola - Grace's sister now in Akure

Much, much love to you both

Elizabeth

Vining Centre
17th October 1976

Dear Ma and Daddy,

No letters very recently. I am waiting to hear your reports on the new grandchild. This week I spent 2 days in bed - Tues. and Wednesday. I suddenly got a streaming cold on Monday - it had been raining a lot - but on Tuesday it had developed into a splitting headache, and I think it was malaria. Anyway, it was only bad for one day and I was back teaching on Thursday. My only trouble then was a sort of bilious feeling - with nasty taste in your mouth and no appetite. I think that this is a result of the nivaquin.

Mrs. Sijuade is on holiday now, so she came to see me both on Tuesday and Wednesday and was full of chat about all the goings on in the hospital. Inga was here on Thursday at lunch time - thoroughly fed up with the Ministry of Education's attitude to the principals. They treat them as though they were all naughty children who need to be disciplined.

On Friday evening Sheila and I went to a birthday party at Mrs. Kolawole's house - she is Sheila's Vice Principal now. The food was good, and Mrs. Kolawole was very welcoming, but the event was a complete wash out as far as meeting anybody was concerned. Most of the talk was in Yoruba - but no one introduced us to anyone, so we hadn't the faintest clue who they were.

On Saturday morning I went with Mrs. Sijuade to St Louis, and we had coffee there with the sisters. Sister Martinian comes back on Tuesday this week - so that will be good. In the evening I went to Ondo with Dr Kumuyi and had a meal in a new motel there. It was a well-cooked meal, and everything was very clean and pleasant. I think he was happy to be out of his hotel for a change. He is very fed up with having no accommodation given to him yet - He has been here 2 months now.

Today has been a normal Sunday - with morning Communion - letter writing - visit to Eyesorun for 11'ses, Sheila here to lunch, Evensong, me to Sheila for supper.

I discovered today that one of our students is sick at home. I thought that she was in hospital - but apparently, she is psychologically sick - she just sits and says nothing. When they ask her to take food, she says she has eaten - but she hasn't. They are giving her native medicine I expect. Unfortunately, the place is 12 miles off the main road past Ikole - and the road is bad - but Mama and I may try to go and see her this week and see if we can persuade her to come to Akure and see the doctor here.

Next weekend I have said I will go up to Omu Aran in Kwara State and take a kind of Ruth Martin weekend. We shall see how it goes. I wish in some ways I'd refused to do it but if it's a wash out then I'll know not to do such again, especially in term time. I hope that you are not too tired running up and down to Yeovil.

With much love

Elizabeth

Vining Centre
24th October 1976

Dear Ma and Daddy,

I returned this afternoon to Akure from Omu-Aran in Kwara State. I went there yesterday morning and enjoyed my visit to Rev & Mrs. Alieu. It was their Women's Guild Anniversary, and I was one of their 2 speakers - talking about 'The Bible and Women in the Church 'All went well - except that there was no afternoon rest for 2 days, and I am ready for bed tonight. I slept last night in a 'hotel 'in Omu-Aran - very nice comfortable and clean bedrooms - and good breakfast - except that their corn flakes were stale. But I wish somewhere in the development of Nigeria there had been a recruitment of plumbers and lavatory cleaners! In fact, this place was clean, and water came out of the tap - but it could be so much better if there was a little more care to detail - no loo paper, no plug in the sink for example.

Then this morning I talked to the English Service.... it was a small Congregation of Training College students - I talked to them about Ebun...... On Friday I went to a committee organised by the Social Welfare people to decide how to look after the Destitutes and Beggars in this State. The Federal Government have decreed that all beggars and destitute are to be removed from the streets by Nov 15th! So, they are planning to put them in a disused school in Ado Ekiti.... but they say that they don't want lepers there or 'Lunatics.' It's not yet clear where these 2 groups will go.

This morning was a marathon of Services - 7 a.m. Communion, 8.30 to 9.30 English Service; 10 to 12 Morning Service including M.U. Enrolment and Thanksgiving of 'Women's Guild. 'Then I drove back from Omu-Aran, and we had Evensong here at 6 p.m. followed by Plays for the outgoing Ordinand at 8 p.m. - so you can see why I am ready for bed.

It has been a normal week - I can't think of much to report. We had our Prayer Fellowship on Tues at Eyesorun's - a good group. Ah! Martinian is back - I have so far only seen her briefly when she had just arrived. Sunday mechanic took my car on Friday morning and said he was just going to fix a small jet in the carburetor...... he brought it back at 10.30 at night! Goodness knows what he had been doing all day with it.

I had letter from Gemma saying that she will come for Christmas - also saying that she has sent you the photos. I hope some are good.

With much love to you both

Elizabeth

Vining Centre
31st October 1976

Dear Ma and Daddy,

So sorry to hear about Dahosa. Eunice must be dreadfully upset. It sounds as though you had 'quite a day 'Ma on your visit to London, with missing your train and then not being allowed on the bus. It's just as well Stuart and Jutka live in London.

I think that I wrote last week when I arrived back from Omu-Aran. Since then, I have had an active week. I talked to the men on Monday about Visual Aids. On Tuesday we had our Board of Governors meeting, but my car was in the mechanics, so I stayed most of the time in my house getting some correspondence up to date. On Wednesday I went to Ondo in the afternoon with Mrs. Sijuade to visit Cynthia Whittle who has been in bed with bronchitis for over 10 days now. On Friday I went and had supper at Fiwasaiye with Corrine and Sheila and distributed my Leper Settlement Committee Minutes and attended the second meeting of the Beggars and Destitute's meeting. It seems to me that the Committee is in 2 parts - those who feel that the exercise is only a temporary thing, while there are a lot of visitors in Nigeria for the Festival of Arts in Jan, and those who really have a concern that these people should be rehabilitated. I think those who are going to be the biggest problem are the mentally sick - because so few people believe that they can be cured or improved.

Yesterday I came to Ado to stay the night with Lily Stott - and to prepare to take the Service in their Chapel this evening. Lily is doing a good job here in teaching the midwives, but she will probably leave Nigeria finally next March. Those in the Ministry of Health in Akure are so slow with the paperwork of contracts and salaries etc. - but also the Hospital Secretary here at Ile Abiye seems to be thoroughly incompetent. It is a very sad thing that the examples laid down by the missionaries in the running of a hospital like this aren't being carried on. It seems that there are a whole lot of financial peculiarities about the running of the hospital. Very sad when the last manager had to be dismissed for embezzlement. Perhaps one of the snags was that the missionaries were not worldly minded enough so didn't train anyone to understand contracts and salary scales in detail.

Chief Ojo came round the other day with Chief Adeniran - both send greetings to you. I am thinking of having a birthday party next week and inviting all sorts of folk - like them and Tola and her husband. I made a list about 60 people, but whether it gets launched remains to be seen

Monday.

I have just received your letter telling of Stella Macdonald's Memorial Service and John coming to stay for the weekend. It is good that you were able to get down to see Ruth. I hope that she feels stronger soon. I expect that it's the loss of blood and weight that are making her feel so weary. I get a bit blasé about babies being born here. We had a new addition on Sat. night - when I was at Ado. I was happy I missed it this time because it was at 3 a.m. and they hadn't done any shopping. I hate banging up shop keepers at 3 a.m. for sanitary pads and razor blades and bandages. Anyway, the baby and his mother are back this morning, and I went and told the mother to rest - I found her hanging her washing on the line

Much love

Elizabeth

Vining Centre

7th November 1976

Dear Ma and Daddy,

Thank you for your nice birthday cards and for both your letters. thank you too for the Cotswold mats - they are greatly admired + Gemma's photo.

I am going ahead tomorrow to have a party - in the Vining Centre Hall! I have invited between 60 & 70 people!! - including Prof. Ojo and Chief Adeniran. I hope they will come because they are both very busy touring around and organising the local election campaign for Ondo State.

The highlight of this week was some progress in the Leprosy Settlement affairs. We had our Committee on Wed. night and decided to go ahead with a Special Leprosy Week at the end of November. Then on Thursday I met the man in charge of the Health Education Unit who was very nice indeed - and very ready to help to organise an educational campaign to try to break down some of the prejudice against leprosy. On Friday I went with him to the Ministry of Information who said that they would help us too. Then I also saw the Physiotherapist at the hospital and asked if we could borrow some crutches for one woman whose leg is amputated. The Physiotherapist said that he would come to the Settlement with me next Tuesday to see what could be done there.

Altogether it was a very busy week, I was out every night! Mon - lecture. Tues. - prayer group. Wed - Leper Settlement Committee. Thurs - Sheila's for supper because it was Fred's birthday. Friday - St Louis. Then on Sat. evening I baked biscuits for my 'party' - today I have done 3 cakes, I hope they are O.K. One is at the top of the oven and looks to me as though it's going to get burnt on top. I will have to ice it!! Tokunbo made 80 rolls yesterday. I hope to make pancakes, sausage rolls and fish balls tomorrow.

Next weekend I hope to go to Benin to see Ruth Howard. It is our Half Term holiday W/E. I shall be happy to get away for a few days and get a bit of energy stored up for the rest of the term, which is going to be well occupied as far as I can see. Dorothy Dykes is coming on 28th - then on 20th we have the Leper Settlement Harvest in the morning, 21st. - I am speaking at our Communion Service, 28th - is our Harvest and around then we are going to have this Leprosy Week. On Dec. 5th I am taking Evensong here. Dec. 12th - will be our last Sunday.

One Deputy Permanent Secretary in the Ministry of Health has taken to coming here to visit - a lacy gentleman in a 504 Peugeot car. He keeps on about some 'Outing' and I keep on about being "too busy." He's an Oba's son and I am sure has a wife at home - he is not very good at taking the hint - and I don't want to be rude and bad mannered because he is one of those planning the future Health Services, including the future of the Leprosy Settlement.

Sorry, Daddy's legs are stiff, and he feels he can't go to Westminster. Perhaps they can give him a stint in the summer months. Thank you for writing to Janet. She received your letter. She is not at all well herself now and has come to Akure for a barium meal. Duodenal ulcer?

Much love to all

Elizabeth

Vining Centre
15th November 1976

Dear Ma and Daddy,

Thank you for your letters. I had a very happy birthday on Monday. About 40 people turned up and we had heaps of food. It entailed a good deal of preparation during the day, but the students helped to butter things and carry chairs and it was all very peaceful. The only sad thing was that the Eyesorun couldn't come because she had to go to Lagos. Mrs. Sijuade forgot! And Mrs. Adinlewa had no transport so didn't come. So, some of my close buddies weren't there. Anyway, it was worth doing occasionally. I have reached the end of the 30's!!

On Wednesday we had our Leper Settlement Committee meeting and we started to plan details about our Leprosy "Week" which is to be from 24th to 28th November. We have sent to the North to borrow the Lepra film called Leprosy which was recommended to us. So, I have had quite a busy time going to the Ministry of Health people and the Ministry of Information people to get their help and projectors etc. Our meeting on Wednesday finished around 10 p.m. and there were so many things hopping round in my head that I didn't sleep very well. One of the things was that I saw Joseph Kumuyi that afternoon who suggested that we become 'special friends.' Exactly his intentions not now crystal clear. I enjoy his company but find him somewhat of a mystery. He is sometimes apparently aloof and standoff-ish - and then his lovely smile breaks through and he is quite different. Anyway, please pray that we may have a joyful friendship and that it may not be spoilt by tension.

I have just been away for our Half Term W/E. I went and stayed with Ruth in Benin and had a very enjoyable and relaxing time. On Sunday, we went together with 2 of her schoolgirls to Ossiomo - the Leprosy Hospital.... do you remember the mud!? We visited Dr Odegbe the Leprologist there and had an interesting talk with him and saw round the hospital, which is not very well cared for we felt. While I was in Benin, we also visited Dr Thomas and his wife who used to be in Ile Abiye hospital. He has written to a friend of his in India who is at present working in Vellore in Leprosy to ask him if he would like to apply to Ondo State. Ruth's School is very big - she has 900 girls and is trying to lick them into shape. It's quite a task because the school was not very well organised before she got there. I took 3 students on the journey to and from Benin. It was good to have their company in case the car packed up - which it didn't. That road is rather pot holey. One of the men students discovered when we reached Benin that his son aged 7 had just died! It was a great shock because the letter telling him this news was in the post. So, he had to come back and tell his wife here. Very sad.

I hope that you are both well - and managing your legs and shoulder. How is the lamp helping?

With much love

Elizabeth

Vining Centre

21st November1976

Dear Ma and Daddy,

Golly! It's been a busy week. I have been preparing for 'Leprosy Week 'in Akure which is supposed to be launched next Wednesday. I am enclosing the programme so that you can see what we are about.

We got the film from the North last Tuesday. I sent a soldier student to Jos! and back. I hope that we are going to be able to use it effectively because there is some hitch about the uses of the Min. of Information Projectors - and then the people in Ibadan refused to loan out some supporting films to go with the main film. Anyway, I shall be rather glad now when it is all over and done with - the main event is the 'Launching 'on Wednesday when they have promised us full coverage on the Tele, Radio and Press locally!! We shall see. I hope some of the guests show up. Anyway, it's worth a try and I personally will feel more confident at launching something another time when I have learnt from the mistakes of this time.

Because of all these activities I completely forgot that today was Sheila's birthday. This morning she phoned to say she was fed up and could I come to coffee and only when I got there did I suddenly fall in that I had clean forgotten that it was her birthday. So, then I was really fed up with forgetting because I bought her a book for her birthday when I was in England. Anyway, I am going there for supper tonight.

Joseph (Kumuyi) came on Friday evening and drank coffee here, but he was very tired after working hard at the estimates for the new T. B Complex for the hospital and not particularly communicative. He was remembering his first Sunday in England in

1972 when he came to Malvern. I had forgotten that we went together to see Ewan on that day. I will see him again next Tuesday I hope - but it is really a bit difficult to meet at all without the whole place being aware of it. If he comes here the whole Vining Centre is all eyes - and there is no point in their speculating if there is nothing to speculate about. On the other hand, his place is worse - because he only has the one rather pokey room in the hotel. Probably we'd better get out of the town and climb Idanre together or something, but that all takes time, and you can't do that in the evening when we are free, but only in the afternoon when it's hot.

Anyway, please pray so that we may find the solution to all the practical problems. I have a great calm that whatever happens it will work out for the best. Now I am just astonished that he should trouble to come and visit me after such a long time in England. I always remember him as my 'miracle doctor 'after he came and listened to my woes at the time of the abortion in Ondo - but I didn't know I meant anything much to him - except of course that he took the trouble to travel from Exeter to Malvern and froze on British Railways to come and see us that time. Please - this is for your prayers now, and not for distribution around the family. I know I can rely on your love and understanding.

We had the Harvest at the Leper Settlement yesterday morning - it lasted till 2.30 in the afternoon - but I departed around 12.30 a.m. This morning I preached the sermon and took the theme of being thankful for our hands after seeing some of the leprosy patients who have none.

I have been going to several friends telling them about the Leprosy Week. One lawyer and his wife are very enthusiastic to join us. I spent about an hour this morning telling them the saga of Ebun.

We had Destitute's and Beggars meeting at Ado on Wednesday. They have done a lot of work there in the short period of time that they have had. Soon they are going to do a rounding up campaign. One very keen Pentecostal fellow is on the Committee. He has founded an organisation in Ibadan called Good Samaritan International which has a home for handicapped children in Ibadan. He came here and spoke to our students on Wed. after the meeting in Ado. So, it was a very long day because he didn't go till 6 p.m.

I hope all are well at home. I can hardly believe that it is cold there. It has suddenly become very hot here especially in the afternoons. Dorothy Dykes should be here next weekend - and we have our Harvest Festival on Sunday. That will just about finish me off after this Leprosy Week's activities.

Much love

Elizabeth

P.S. I am still teaching at Vining Centre between all the other activities!! But I have forgotten to tell you the other great news of the week and that is that Cornelius is leaving at the end of term. He was made the Archdeacon of Owo on Friday, much to his great delight. Great rejoicings. He has done a good stint here. My great delight is that Jeremiah Fabuluje who I knew well in Ondo is to be our new Principal. He is the only fellow whose name came into my head when Cornelius originally talked of going elsewhere. So that's great. If you have a chance, you might tell Ruth Martin this piece of news - and the Howards. Both will be interested.

Much love,

Elizabeth

Leprosy Week

Vining Centre
28th November 1976

Dear Ma and Daddy,

Our Leprosy Week is now over - and I think it was quite successful. We had about 150 people at the launching ceremony when we looked at the film from the North. Everything seemed to go reasonably well, and we raised over N400 by just taking the hat round. So that wasn't bad. All the Committee members were greatly encouraged by it all and I think it gave some of them a real boost.

On Thursday the 'Jumble Sale 'wasn't much of a go. I took my women - 20 of them which was just as well because the gathering was rather sparse. I don't think enough explanation had been given to explain to women the meaning of' Jumble Sale.' If we do it again, we shall have to publicise it more thoroughly, and invite groups of women especially to the event.

On Friday we had our Film Show in the town and it drew a very large crowd of young men. I was a bit afraid that someone would get knocked down because the crowd extended to some standing in the middle of the road on an island.

Then on Sunday we went to the Settlement, and they were very pleased to have a film show there. Eyesorun came with us and talked to the patients. So, all in all I think we achieved something. At least we made a start and discovered some of the hazards of dealing with the Government Ministries.

The Leprosy film was shown in Schools on Mon and Tues nights, but the electricity failed on Thursday, and we couldn't get a generator on Friday, so we haven't been able to show the film to every school as we had hoped. However, I think that it has been worthwhile. It is an interesting film that has taught us quite a lot. We still have the film for the coming week and hope to show it here and in some other schools. The only snag is that there is going to be a Moslem holiday on Thurs and Friday so we may have to cancel on those days.

Apart from this Leprosy week - which has taken most of my attention and energy I have had Dorothy Dykes and Canon Faji to stay here this weekend. I went to Owo on Friday to buy some rather nice thorn Carvings for Dorothy. Then on Saturday night Dorothy and Canon Faji came with me to Owo to Joan Steward's birthday party. We got back here at 11.30 p.m. Then today we had the Harvest Festival Service in Vining Centre which lasted from 10 to 1 p.m. in Church and then 1 - 5 p.m. in the hall for the Auction Sales. We dodged the latter! Apart from this we have had one Naming Ceremony and one Baptism Service during the week. And I spent part of the evening on Tuesday with Kayode Kumuyi in his hotel chatting to a couple of his friends and visiting a National Youth Service Corp doctor who I have discovered is the daughter of Canon Saba at Kafanchan. Just pray on about Kayode and me - I hope to see him this coming Wednesday …… last week was so busy that it wasn't possible to meet again. Anyway, he was going to Ibadan. He goes often to see his mother who is staying in Ife with his married brother. She is diabetic. Grace Ohikhena came here and stayed the night on Friday night.

Cornelius's mind is set on the buying of his Cope to be the Archdeacon of Owo. He wants to import from Whipple's or some such for about N400! Nuts. Makes you feel like giving up the organised Church with its hierarchy system.

Much love

Elizabeth

Vining Centre
5th December 1976

Dear Ma and Daddy,

Thank you for your letter and for your prayers which are always there behind the written words. I have tried today to write a circular letter for Christmas. I will now type it and send it to you, and to C.M.S. I am sorry that I am always a bit last minute about it and it gives you a lot of extra work just before Christmas as you write my envelopes as well as your own. I don't think that I shall be sending any cards this year. I will try to write some personal letters around Christmas time, but I don't see much chance in the next two weeks.

We started our Practical exam on Thursday morning and the women will be doing exams next week too. Next Sunday will be Carol Service and then we shall have our Farewell for Cornelius on Monday 13th and the Commissioning Service on Wed. 15th.

I played tennis on Friday with Taiwo at the Agric - and enjoyed it, although it is very hot now during the day. There is heavy harmattan with dust in the air, and then it is suddenly quite cold in the night. I saw Joseph on Thursday. He was away to Lagos until Wednesday. He was not very relaxed, and I still find him somewhat of a mystery. I can't make out if he is seriously interested in me or just looking for a temporary girlfriend.

Today I am taking the evening Service and have chosen the theme 'Called to Care.' 8 of the men are going to read about the 'Call' of different people in the Bible ... e.g., I am Abraham who was called.... I am Moses who was called... I hope that it will go over well. After that there is the Carol Service at Fiwasaiye to which I hope to go.

We have petrol shortage here already which is not a good sign. It is usually difficult during December, but I think it is going to be worse this year in Akure because there are so many more cars in the town since we became the State Capital. I seem to have had a bit of malaria this weekend - so I took Nivaquin but still feel a bit "off" in the head. No doubt it is partly just end of term feeling - but it is a nuisance to feel under par when the exams are coming up and all the other end of term activities must be attended to.

I have just had a long letter from Sasha. Really, she does write extraordinary 'adult-type' Letters. I will write to them all before Christmas.

Much love

Elizabeth

Vining Centre

12th December 1976

Dear Ma and Daddy,

I hope that you got my circular letter and that it was not <u>too</u> late to join yours in some of the envelopes. I am afraid that I am not really organised about Christmas this year. I haven't done anything interesting like tape recordings or sending through a mail order firm. The tape recorder isn't working at present - I must try and get it mended. So, I am sending you this cheque with which I hope you will be able to buy something from me.

This week we have had Exams with the women. It was supposed to be Tuesday - Thursday but we had to cancel Thursday's exams because Cornelius said that we should all come out to welcome a big shot from the Army in Lagos. So, all the women put on their white and we waited from10, the appointed time until after 11. He never appeared!! By then the babies were fretful and it was too hot to start exams. Very annoying. The fellow then turned up on Friday! But the women were released after introductions in Chapel and so we were able to finish our exams.

Now I must finish the marking - write the reports - write the Certificates in fancy writing and deal with all the other end of term activities - Carol Service and Play this afternoon, Farewell for Cornelius on Monday night - farewell to the Archdeacon of Akure who is retiring on Monday morning and Commissioning Service for all our outgoing students on Wednesday afternoon.

Petrol has become short again and there have been queues in the town this week. I was fortunate to pass a petrol station just as they started to sell a new supply, so I got in before the queue formed, but Inga was not so lucky earlier in the week and had to wait 2 hours. I hope that it is not so short over Christmas time that it makes travelling with Gemma difficult. Other shortages this week are butter and flour and there is no dried fruit around. They say that there is a world shortage.

Joseph came for supper on Thursday evening. He has no car now because it is being serviced in Ibadan. He was hopeful of getting a flat last week but when he went to the Ministry about it there seemed to have been no progress at all so it is likely that he will have to stay in the same nasty hotel for a bit longer.

I shall be going off to Benin around 20th. I think and shall stay with Ruth. I am going up to a place near Auchi with them or with Jane and Sheila and Joan. I will meet Gemma in Onitsha on 27th I hope.

With much love to you both
Elizabeth

Vining Centre
19th December 1976

Dear Ma and Daddy,

I got your letter of Dec. 6th talking about John and Pat's decision to get divorced. I received it on Friday - but haven't yet seen any sign of their letters sent through Yemi. I will be going off to Benin tomorrow so I may not get them until the New year. I was very sad to hear that they have decided to be divorced - but at the same time not entirely surprised. I admire them for sticking it out for so long if there was really no harmony or love in their relationship. No wonder we all thought something was lacking in the summer. As you say perhaps it will be a case of the new wine and they will both get a new release of life in the future. What is their plan for the children? What's Pat going to do? I hope she will also find someone else to marry or I think she may become harder and brittle. Who is John's Mary ? In fact, it is very annoying not to have their letter because I expect some of these questions will be answered in them.

I am happy that you have the Cooks and others to discuss the whole matter with I think you are marvellous to be able to look on the positive side of it so much. I am sure that's the only way to help them - and I don't think you should be thinking that you have failed as parents in any way. Rather the reverse. I don't know of any other parents who can continually love and support their children in such a real way - as you have been able to do for Stuart and Jutka, for Ruth and Trevor and for me, and for John and Pat and looking after all of them for the Summer. I just continually marvel at GOD's Love as seen through you both.

Martinian was telling me yesterday of an upset in their family when a young cousin who became a Priest in his 20's went to Korea. His mother was proud of him as a Priest. Then he came home when he was 40 or so and told them he was giving up the priesthood - and then it was discovered he had a Korean wife and baby...... but through all this stress he had a break down and it was a long time before his mother reconciled to him at all.

I am sure that the Bible is telling us that the most important thing to do is to build relationships of love and caring - and this may well be achieved more by giving each other freedom to start again as in Pat and John's case. Who is to say how much children suffer from being brought up between a father and mother who don't really love each other? That I think is the cause of many tragedies and couples continue to live together only to be respectable and everyone suffer from the tension and bickering.

I go to Benin tomorrow - 20th and then I hope to go with Ruth and her Mum to Auchi on Tues/Wed. We will spend Christmas in Benin and then go to Onitsha on 27th to pick up Gemma. What are you doing for Christmas? Jane Pelly is here this weekend with Sheila. I baked yesterday - a Christmas cake and biscuits and some rather sunken buns.

Much love to you both
Elizabeth

Vining Centre
27th December 1976

Dear Ma and Daddy,

One bad thing about going away for Christmas is that you don't get any post, but there are other compensations, like not worrying about the shopping and the food supplies as you do when you are the hostess.

Everything has worked out well so far - I came to Benin on Monday and then went with Ruth and her mother to Auchi on Tuesday night. We stayed at the Catering Rest house there and had a good few laughs. They always seem to leave these places in charge of some rather clueless boys without adequate supervision so that things like bath plugs are nonexistent and anyway the bath is not cleaned. At supper time I was given a bowl of soup with a fly floating in it - so I said I would take the fly out, but the boy insisted on taking it back to the kitchen for a refill. So, when he returned and put the new plate in front of me, we were all astonished and surprised to see another fly in the new soup. "But I changed it" he spoke. We couldn't make out if he had changed the fly as well as the soup.

Then in our house we opened all the shutters to let the air in and I was very astonished and annoyed to be woken up at 2.30 a.m. by a night watchman shining his torch on my bed and telling me in a very loud voice "Why you open the windows?" Thief man will come. He then went round the house and noisily closed all the shutters, even though everyone had thief wire across the windows. On Wednesday we went to Ososo which is a Rest House right up in the rocky hills north of Igarra. Jane Pelly and Sheila Everard from Owerri were there for a couple of days. A gorgeous hide out. We had a picnic there and climbed one rocky hill then we came back to Benin for the night.

On Friday, Ruth and her mother and I went round to see Eunice's sister Margaret and we had tea there together. I told her sister about Dahosa being in Scrubs because they didn't know the result of the Court

Case and were disappointed that Eunice wasn't coming for Christmas after all. In the evening Thankanma made an enormous Indian meal with Spicy meat, peppery cabbage, yogurt and pourri which are those puffy things made like small pancakes and fried in deep fat. I did the frying and was fascinated by the way they puffed up. The afters were a milk pudding like Ambrosia rice but made with vermicelli and nuts and raisins and spices like Cinnamon. Thankanma made so much that we have been eating it for breakfast for the past 3 days. Saturday, Christmas Day we went to Church for Communion in the morning, then we made a puzzle and some coloured stars to stick in the window. Jane and Sheila and Joan and Sheila Everard all came for Christmas dinner in the evening. Mrs. Howard had made Christmas pudding, so it was very authentic. Yesterday, Boxing Day we all went to Jane Pelly's for supper. In the afternoon we took a picnic to NIFOR - the Palm Oil Research place - a lovely park like compound - ideal for picnics and walking. Today we are going to Onitsha to pick up Gemma and I will take her back to Akure on Wednesday - when I hope to receive your letters.

Much love

Elizabeth

Christmas Letter - 1976

Vining Centre
December 1976

Dear Friends,

Today I am trying to prepare a sermon for the finalist students who will be leaving us before Christmas. Some will take up work in remote villages in the bush, some will be in busy crowded urban areas, some will be down in the delta creeks and others will be assisting the Chaplains in the Nigerian Army.

My theme for the service is that we are 'Called to Care'. My thoughts on this subject have been inspired by a book called "Out of Solitude" by Henri Nouwen. He says that "the word 'care' finds its roots in the Gothic 'kara' which means lament. The basic meaning of care is to grieve, to experience sorrow, to cry out with. I am very much struck with this background of the word care because we tend to look at caring as an attitude of the strong to the weak, of the powerful towards the powerless, of the haves towards the have nots. But the one who cares is the one who can share our thoughts, who can listen, who can be present with us in trouble. Every human being has a great, yet often unknown gift to care, to be compassionate, to become present to the other, to listen, to hear and to receive. If that gift could be set free and made available miracles could take place".

I have struggled to put this into practice recently in Akure in trying to enter the suffering of one of our students who went to Benin at Half Term where he discovered that his 7-year-old son who was being looked after by his sister had just died of convulsions. He then returned to the Vining Centre to tell his wife who had just had a new baby. The couple wept all night. I prayed and wept with them in the morning. What else can we do as Christians?

I have also been very much occupied in the last few weeks with organising a "Leprosy week in Akure". The aim of this was twofold. Firstly, we wanted to make a start in breaking down some of the prejudice and fear that people have of lepers in this part of Nigeria. Secondly, we wanted to raise some funds to help at the Akure Leper Settlement. We showed a film produced by Lepra which I think made many people start to think. The film emphasised that leprosy is a disease that can be cured if treated early and that if properly cared for leprosy patients should not develop any deformities of hands or feet. Another fact which struck me particularly was that it said in this film that only 20% of those having leprosy in the world are receiving treatment and that one reason for this is that there is a shortage of people working in this area of medicine. Certainly, that's true round here. We have no doctor or qualified nurse working in leprosy in this State where there are about 1000 known cases of the disease. The distribution of dapsone is done by rural health inspectors. Our new Ondo State government has money ready to pay the salaries of more qualified personnel but so far there are no people to fill the posts. If any of you know of any doctor who worked in leprosy and would like to come to Nigeria; Please let me know!

The other thing that I have become involved with recently is the Ondo State Government's committee for the Rehabilitation of Destitute's and Beggars. This committee has been set up following instructions from the Federal Government that all destitutes and beggars should be cleared off the streets. This is partly because there is to be a big Black Arts Festival called Festac in January and so there will be many visitors coming to Nigeria for that, and therefore the government wants to clear away the beggars, much as we did in England at the time of the Coronation. At the same time there is a genuine desire to do something to care for and rehabilitate these unfortunate people within the community. So far, the Committee has prepared a place in Ado Ekiti where they hope to house about 100 destitute people. They are going to collect "normal" beggars to go there, those who are "lunatics" or "lepers" are not going to be admitted with the others. The care of these 2 groups is going to come to us in Akure. It is suggested that extra buildings should be put up at the leper settlement for destitute lepers who are probably discharged patients and that extra buildings should be put up at the Herbal Healing Home for those who are mentally sick. This Herbal Healing Home is the place of mediaeval treatment that I described when we took Ebun there. It is still the only place in Akure which takes in mentally sick people. We hope that both these schemes will be temporary because there are plans to have a proper Rehabilitation centre for the disabled and destitute and a psychiatric unit attached to the State hospital in the future.

Here at the Vining Centre, we have a lot of celebrations at the end of this term because in addition to the usual carol service and Commissioning Service we shall be having Farewell functions for our Principal. Cornelius has been here for 8 years, and he is now going on to be the Archdeacon of Owo. He will be replaced by Jeremiah Fabuluje who I knew in Ondo when I was there. He is a younger man and a graduate, who I always remember in St. Monica's as someone who really had something to say in school services. I think he will do well here and is a very good choice for the new Principal. We shall miss Cornelius and all his gifts of understanding the men and being a master hand at settling problems. We shall also miss his carefully thought-out sermons and his special gift of bringing a real atmosphere of worship into our weekly Holy Communion service, but he is happy to be going back into the Parish and will do well in Owo.

This letter comes to wish you a very happy Christmas and Peace and Joy continuing in 1977. Our latest Hymn here is:

God is love, He is the care
Tending each, everywhere
God is love - all is there!
Jesus came to show Him
That mankind might know Him.

Sing aloud, loud, loud
Sing aloud, loud, loud!
God is good, God is truth
God is beauty, Praise Him!

With my love and prayerful best wishes,
Elizabeth

Vining Centre
1st January 1977

Dear Ma and Daddy,

A new year - 1977! I hope it will be one of many new blessings and experiences that bring us nearer to God. It is good to have Gemma here in Akure. Ruth and Mrs. Howard and I went to Onitsha on Monday and picked Gemma up and brought her back to Benin on Tuesday. Then we had a great time in Benin because on Tuesday evening we went to supper with Eunice's sister, Margaret, and her other sister, Lydia - a gorgeous English type supper with meat and chicken and kidneys and potatoes and vegetables with soup to start with and jelly and ice cream afterwards. While we were there, we phoned up the Ukpomas who we discovered were in Benin with ALL the family. The parents were celebrating their 25th anniversary and so had paid for the 5 children studying in Europe to come home. So, on Wednesday morning Gemma and I went to see them in their Benin mansion - marble floors and stairs .... Gemma will give you her impressions. Ewan was there painted in the face and balancing on spiky high heels - all incredible. Ewan and a friend of hers who is the granddaughter of the Oba of Benin took us to look at the Palace in Benin. Then the Ukpomas invited us to their home in Lagos when we go down for Gemma's flight - so that's good.

Gemma and I came back here on Wednesday – and stayed that night with Inga who had Joseph's baby on her own for the past week. Joseph's wife, Henrietta, is now with him in Sapele so really, they would be better to have the baby with them.... but Inga still has her – not a very good idea really.

I discovered from the Bishop of Ondo that he has already transferred Rev Adeoba from Vining Centre to a parish in Akoko – so we are very 'new' on the staff with a new Principal and a new Men's Warden starting here at the same time. Rev Fabuluje has arrived and is settling into his house. He will start to do something about Vining Centre on Monday – tomorrow. It is not going to be very easy to tell the newcomers all the habits of the Centre. On the other hand, it gives us the freedom to think for ourselves how we want the place to be.

Since we have been in Akure we have been up to Ado where we saw Lily Stott and the folk at Ile Abiye - and then we went today to see Pat and Francis in Idanre, and this afternoon went to the Noviciate where Martinian had arranged a party for the children at the settlement. We hope to go to Bida on Thursday and stay with Gwen Hall and then go on to Ibadan and Lagos from there.

I don't quite understand from your letters exactly what the doctors think is the matter with Daddy's ear. First you say, 'tests and biopsy' - then you say, 'ray treatment'. I haven't yet had the things from Yemi. How did she reckon she was coming to Akure.?? Maybe she has left the letters etc. in Ife. Anyway, I will get them in the long run.

Much love
Elizabeth

Note from Gemma:

HAPPY NEW YEAR. Marvellous here and I'm loving it all. Meeting masses of Elizabeth's friends and always an enormous WELCOME. Have taken 4 rolls of film since arriving in Akure 3 days ago! You'll see all soon. Travel is hair raising but the East much worse, the telephone is Elizabeth's lifeline! I just praise the Lord that let me come back to Africa. See you soon.
Much love G.

Vining Centre
9th January 1977

Dear Ma and Daddy,

I am having a very happy time with Gemma, and we are at present in Bida staying with Gwen Hall. It is a lovely compound and so very different from anything in Akure. I feel as though I am in a foreign country.

It has been a good week. I was able to get the main preparations for the beginning of the term done at the Vining Centre on Monday -> Wednesday and at the same time to show Gemma round Akure - mainly meeting friends. We had a very good fellowship group on Tuesday evening, at St. Peters. Fred led it and took the Epiphany Story and led us in thinking especially about the 'gifts'. Gemma was very taken with the sisters, especially Martinian and Mildred. Really, I am very fortunate with all my good friends in Akure.

Jeremiah Fabuluje has lots of new ideas about Vining Centre and we had a very good staff meeting on Wednesday. He and Rev.

Ayodele are both educationalists and hope to make some sense out of the timetable and the schemes of work. The new men's warden is Rev. Adeyelu who is very quiet - rather a shy little man who at present doesn't really know what he is to do because Rev. Adeoba has handed over nothing - but I think that when we get sorted out things will be changing for the better.

Rev. Ayodele took Gemma and I out to supper on Wednesday night at the Catering Rest House and there we met an old student of St. Andrew's Oyo - called Mr. J. Olatoregun, who sent special greetings to Daddy. During our supper I found out that Rev. Ayodele's daughter, Nike, has been staying at the Sacred Heart Hostel, which is that Convent place that you pass between the Tiger and Stuart's place in Hackney. Isn't that amazing? She may be moving to live with someone in Leyton. I will send Stuart the address because he may be able to look her up.

I took Gemma to the settlement, and she took some black and white photos which we may be able to use to make cards for selling in the future. We set off for Bida on Thursday morning - and I had planned to leave Akure around 9am but we went over to say goodbye to the Eyesorun in her office and she told me that Dr. Alade, the Senior Consultant Surgeon had a packet from the Bamgboyes in Ife. So, we phoned him, and he came over to the health Office to tell me to come up to his house to collect it. He also said that he was Yomi's best man at the wedding!! I knew him in Akure, but he hadn't made this connection and nor had I. So, Gemma and I went and sat in his sitting room for about 20 minutes while he went upstairs and banged around opening cupboards and drawers and came down to say he couldn't put his hands on them!! His house boy took his things out of his car, so the packets were somewhere in the house <u>OR</u> they had got unloaded in Ondo where he had dropped some schoolgirl. Was I mad!! And we didn't set off for Bida till 10.30 and so had to finish the journey in the dark. So, I am still waiting to read the letters from New Zealand. We go to Ibadan tomorrow and then Lagos on Monday and I return to Akure on Wednesday.

Much love to you both

Elizabeth.

Vining Centre
16th January 1977

Dear Ma and Daddy,

Thank you for your letters telling me all about your Christmas and New Year. I am sorry that the post was so disappointing over the holiday period, and I hope my letters have reached you by now. I posted them in Benin and Ibadan purposely so that you would get them as quickly as possible. I expect that by now you will have heard from Gemma. She promised to phone you when she got back so no doubt, she will give you all the low down on Akure.

We went to Lagos on Monday and stayed that night at the CMS Guest House. I don't enjoy staying there as much as I used to because it has become a small hotel for people on business in Lagos and has no longer the atmosphere of a CMS family house which it used to have when there was a resident missionary there. But I expect that it is making some money for the Lagos Diocese. I saw Rev. Faji while I was there. He upset me by saying that he had 'heard' when he was in Akure in November (presumably from Cornelius) that I was entertaining men, staying out till midnight, and meeting Catholic Fathers!! I felt that these were unfair comments on my activities and friends but also annoyed at Cornelius for gossiping to Faji rather than coming to talk to me directly. After this discussion with Faji Gemma and I went along to the Federal Palace Hotel to swim but were not allowed in because the Head of State had taken it over for the Festac visitors. So, we had to go on to Bar Beach instead, where we had a good lie in the sun.

On Tuesday evening we went to the Ukpomas and were given a very warm welcome and I left Gemma there on Wednesday morning because I needed to get back to Akure. I stopped in Shagamu and saw Mrs. Wilde. She took me to their house and gave me a cold drink which was very welcome. Then I proceeded to Ibadan where I called on Richard Childerstone around lunch time. He was in bed with a cold but gave me cheese sandwiches and fruit salad. He is still not quite settled about when he will finally retire and come home to UK. I was very tired on the road back, but I was in time to go to the Leper Settlement Committee in the evening.

We have started our new term this weekend. We had a very good Communion Service this morning and I think that Jeremiah Fabuluje will have good ideas as a principal. The new women are a blank so far - very few of them seem to hear any English. It is a pity that my Yoruba is not better. Anyway, we shall see - sometimes they know more English than they appear at first sight.

Last night I went to a party given by Dr. Sijuade in honour of Mrs. Sijuade being promoted to being a 'Sister' in the hospital. It was a very pleasant evening. I talked most of the time to Mr. Solanke and Mrs. Olowo who are both in the Leper Settlement Committee. Mrs. Olowo and her husband have lived in England for a long time and have recently come to Akure. They both came to our service this morning and they hope to come regularly when we have an English-Speaking Matins Service.

We go to the Leper Settlement for an Open-Air Service this afternoon. Then we shall be starting the term on Monday.

Sheila has gone down with malaria this morning, so she is in bed.

I met the wife of the Bulgarian doctor - Mrs. Velev - yesterday at the party and they have invited Corrine and I to go and watch part of the Black Arts Festival on their Television set. Tele is coming here in a big way. Both Fabuluje and Adeyelu, the men's warden have it.

Good to get all your news. I have written to New Zealand. Maybe you have heard back by now. Thank you for the photos and the hankies and the address book.

Much love

Elizabeth.

Vining Centre
23rd January 1977

Dear Ma and Daddy,

I think you must have snow - something has held up the post so that nothing has reached here this week. I hope to hear early in the coming week.

Sheila had malaria last weekend and so she came here and stayed Sunday night and Monday night. She was better by Tuesday and went home again. We had our Fellowship Group in her house on Tuesday evening. We took the theme of 'Unity' because it was the first day in the week of Prayer. It was very interesting to hear people share about their old prejudices about Catholics and Protestants .... rejoicing that now there was a chance of breaking down some of these barriers. But there is still a long way to go in the officialdom of the Churches.

We have had a good start to the term. I was afraid at first that very few of the newcomers could understand English but in fact they divide evenly between Mama and me. I discovered on Thursday that very few of the new children had been injected for anything and so I sent them all off to the health office to get B.C.G. and D.P.T. injections. One wife from the rivers has never held a pencil before - so we are getting her started. I think she is quite bright so I hope that she will make progress and learn to read and write.

Jeremiah has been away at the end of this week - touring around the bishops to get some money to run the Centre. He seems to have been quite successful and came back with several cheques. He also says that we have been given N12,000 from an American body which is to be used to build a new dormitory or staff house. So that is encouraging. We had a visit from the Principal Army Chaplain in Ibadan on Friday - and today Fabuluje and I have been asked to help entertain him with our Army Chaplain. They have invited us to go out for lunch in a hotel in the town.

Mrs. Olowo - the health Sister - has begun to take a real interest in the health of the people at the Leper Settlement. She is keen that things will improve. One old lady, Mary, has a terrible foot - a sore that has not improved in several years. It looks as though she will have to have the leg amputated. So, we hope we can find someone who will be willing to do it.

Sister Martinian is going ahead with the idea of doing Leprosy work full time. It will be great if she can get to Ethiopia.

I went to see the Ministry of Education People about Myrtle and they said she should write to them directly. They are planning 3 Special Schools - Deaf in Akure - Blind in Ondo and handicapped in Ikare. It's a pity that Handicapped is not in Akure.

I should be home sometime around June 20th. Ann Forgan is going to let me know what is happening at Orthona in August. I am really very happy in Malvern. Do you have any plans?

With much love to you both,

Elizabeth.

Vining Centre
30th January 1977

Dear Ma and Daddy,

Thank you for your letters - and writing out Pat and John and Mary's letters a second time!! Thank you too for getting the Circulars out. I was glad to hear that you had such a happy time with Robert and got a chance to bathe and feed him. How are Stuart and Jutka getting on baby wise?

I expect that you will have heard from Gemma about her mother. What a homecoming for Gemma. I hope that you have a happy weekend with her in Malvern. She has plenty to talk about Nigeria. I am especially happy in that she says that this visit has helped to heal some of her bitterness against CMS. Her coming was certainly a boost for me. The only snag is adjusting to living on your own again when you have had company for some time.

This week, on Thursday, Mama and I went to the launching of the National Council of Women's Societies in Nigeria when the State Governor spoke to them. We got there at 9.30 and met chaos and bedlam - women shouting at the tops of their voices trying to get order - the main snag was that there were hardly any chairs!! Someone went off to get 150 chairs in a last-minute effort before the Governor came. Fortunately, he was about 20 minutes late (-10.20) and so there was peace and quiet before he got there.

Yesterday all the staff from here, and a van load of students went up to Ikare to the Induction of Cornelius as the new Archdeacon of Ikare. I took Mama and Mrs. Fabuluje and Mrs. Adeyelu in the car so had loud Yoruba for the journey which was along a bumpy road anyway. Then there was a long service. Cornelius looked terrible - sick and thin and according to Mama's diagnosis had been drinking too much. Certainly, he was not himself and behaved in a very odd fashion. It is very sad if he has started to drink again because he can be so super when he is at his best - but it is often for a big occasion that he disgraces himself.

Jeremiah Fabuluje has started to make some changes in the College timetable - this is excellent - and has long been needed. He has also started to improve the menu of the students .... but the snag all the time is 'no money' because it seems that we must have overspent a lot on our budget last year.

Yesterday we received a gift of N175 which was given apparently in memory of Brownie so I assume that she must have died recently. I don't quite know why we get the money when she was at St. Annes and St. John/Mary, but I guess we are the only surviving CMS institution in the area of Owo and St. John/Mary is now a Federal Government T.C. so they have plenty money.

I have had no phone this week which has proved very annoying. One young English graduate called David Lewis stayed here on Tuesday night because he got stuck while negotiating about a car. He has been posted to a T.T.C. near Ikare where there is no running water. At present he is staying in a guest house waiting for his own accommodation to be ready - and waiting for his wife who is to join him in April.

I have written to Faji to say that I hope to fly on June 20th or 21st. That will be good. Only four and a half months.

With much love to you both,

Elizabeth.

Vining Centre
6th February 1977

Dear Ma and Daddy,

Thank you for your letters. The New Zealand folk seem to be OK. It is good that John can keep such a close link with the children and encouraging to hear that Stuart has become so sensible.

Thank you too for putting Anna Hendrie's £10 in my bank. I want to buy a portable typewriter I think - when I am at home this time.

I have had some papers from CMS this week giving the usual gen. The Swanwick Conference starts on June 27th so if I travel on 20th or 21st there will only be a few days at home before that. Then I expect that there will be deputations in July as usual. The Fountain Trust Conference is at Westminster from August 1st - 7th and Agnes Sanford is apparently going to be there. I should like to go to that - and will ask Gemma if I can stay with her then. What about a Quiet Place to go? Would you like a week at St. Julians in August - or do you have any other suggestions in Wales or nearer home? Ann Forgan said she would let me know about the Orthona Community - and I would like to visit/or stay a little in Crowther Hall's set up organised by Maureen Olphin.

Today we have 2 new baby boys! - both born yesterday - one in the morning and one in the evening. Both arrived with very little bother.

It has been an active week - Monday night lecture, Tuesday night fellowship, and Wednesday night Leper Settlement Committee. The Fellowship was especially refreshing. It was at St. Louis and Mildred took the theme of "Thanksgiving". We were quite a crowd with some new folk joining us - 2 Sri Lankan Teachers - a new Catholic priest, just ordained last December - a real radiant Christian- and Rev. Ayodele from Vining Centre. Eyesorun was there too .... I suppose about 20 of us. I gave thanks that Daddy's ear is very much better - I received your letter that morning. That's great!

Today I preached the morning sermon at the Communion Service - and talked about Colin Urquart's example of the kettle - we need to take the 'lid off' .... I said that the Churches main characteristic should be a "Receiving Church" and that we as Christians should be "Receiving People". Rev. Ayodele translated into Yoruba - and, I felt, improved on what I had said!

I am thinking of going to Ondo today to have lunch with Inga. She is planning (so she says) to do a course in Bristol starting in September. I hope she goes off on it. It will do her a lot of good to leave St. Monicas.

The big Black Arts Festival is still going on in Lagos. Every day the papers are full of pictures of dancers and singers - the theme is mostly on 'Freedom from Colonialists' as far as I can see. Someone told me that there were 400 Mercedes cars bought by Festac to be used by important visitors .... Drivers were employed in a hurry to drive them - and all 400 disappeared!! Stolen. Incredible.

Martinian had her Peugeot car stolen from outside their bedroom windows - pushed out down the drive. That was 10 days ago. Then this week they had a coffee table stolen from inside their sitting room. A very nasty feeling - and a lot of trouble with the police.

I think that you will have Gemma with you this weekend - or next. I am sure she will have plenty to tell. I wonder how her mother is.

With much love to you both

Elizabeth.

Vining Centre
13th February 1977

Dear Ma and Daddy,

Thank you for the letter on the back of S.H.H.S. letter, and my own circular. Thank you too for the Geographical Magazine and the Priory Newsletter Mag. which I also received this week. I was glad to hear all the news of Robert's christening. What a hoot using the old christening robe. I am glad that Lynette was with you to enjoy it all.

This week has been a normal week of teaching - with a few extras! I asked my students to write an essay on 'difficulties of sufferings' they had known in their lives. The result was shattering. A collection of incredible stories of hardships - no money to pay for school fees - looking for jobs in Lagos and finding none - one in prison, accused of poisoning someone! - another turned out of his home for preaching about Sodom and Gomorrah - sickness and death of children and wives - managing in faraway villages with no water, electricity, shops etc. etc. I found that I learnt a great deal through reading them.

I had Victoria Saba to supper on Tuesday - together with one teacher from Fiwasaiye G.S. Vic is the doctor working with Nigerian Youth Corps here for a year. She is the daughter of Canon Saba in Kafanchan, and she is very frustrated with the work she is doing here - and lonely in a Guest House Room at night.

Yesterday we had the naming ceremony of Rev. Adeyelu (Men's warden's) new son. That was in the morning. In the afternoon one student was knocked off his bike by a car and was admitted in the hospital with, I think, a bruised spine - I hope it is not more serious. He will have to wait till Monday for X-rays etc. In the evening I went to Corrine's for a small party - it's her birthday next week. Dr. and Mrs. Velev were there and then the Pakistani teachers at Fiwasaiye, the brothers from St. P and Sheila.

Sheila wasn't well on Friday - she came out in a very itchy rash which Dr. Sijuade said was caused by A.T.S. injection the week before. He told her that she must never take A.T.S. again or it would be very dangerous. Then he gave her some antihistamine tablets that made her sleep all day. I have been bothered by an intermittent rash for the past 2 weeks, so I have started on a course of my old friend Banocide!! So far there are no ill effects .... but I only started yesterday.

Did I tell you about the Good Samaritan International fellow who came and asked me to find a British woman social worker to come and organise his movement on a state level? - and he would be willing to marry her!? Yesterday I received a letter from him saying well that it's me he has in mind - and can I give him an appointment to discuss the matter further! I think he belongs to some C.A.C. Pentecostal Church - or his own church. I don't know and he has visions of being a social reformer, and helping handicapped people etc. I agree with his aims in life! - but that's a far cry from marriage! Really these men are incredible. I hear that Dr. Kumuyi came back from leave yesterday and that he went to England. He is a dark horse. Perhaps he has an English girlfriend there. I don't know. He ought to settle down and marry but he certainly doesn't have me in mind.

We have started to have a 10am service on Sunday mornings, but I don't think I shall be going regularly to 10am as well as 7am H.C. Grace Webster is back at Iyi Enu.

Much love to you both

Elizabeth

Vining Centre

20th February 1977

Dear Ma and Daddy,

No letter this week so far from you. I shall be expecting to hear early next week how you got on with Gemma for the weekend. She wrote and told me that she was carrying her mighty album of photographs up to Malvern for you to look at.

This week Lily Stott is here from Ado. She is leaving there in 2 weeks' time and retiring from nursing finally. She says that it is 40 years since she qualified and so she feels she has done her bit. She is going to be in Birmingham for a term, April - June, staying in the Quaker set up there.

I have been taking Banocide this week - without any real ill effects except that I still find it makes me feel a bit forgetful and not quite "with it". I think the itchy places are reducing.

I had a letter from Ruth Martin saying that her father has had a slight stroke and that the doctor says that he should not be left in the house alone so that poses some problems for her. She herself has had a fall and cracked her knee cap.

Cornelius has now been discharged from the hospital and gone back to rest in Ikare. He seemed a lot better before he went away.

We have a Board of Governors meeting here on Thursday. It will be Fabuluje's first meeting with them. I know he wants to increase some things on the Budget, including the salaries of some of the Compound workers and I guess this may lead to some resistance from the bishops who will have to find the money. I hope all goes well because Fabuluje does have some very good ideas about really training and educating the men. I had my second batch of essays in this week - again an incredible set - several stories of suffering during the war .... but also, it seems that a lot of our men came from the unemployed - or the too poor to continue paying school fees section of the Community.

We have Half Term next weekend and I have planned to go to Ife and stay with the Rodgers. I haven't seen them for ages. I expect I shall also see Yomi and Kelu then although they are going off to a Funeral on Saturday.

Corinne has had a blow up of her arthritis this last week. It was her birthday on Wednesday, so Sheila had a small dinner party for her. Then that night Corinne's knee began to swell and to be extremely painful. She looked very old and worn out on Friday.

Joseph Kumuyi is back. He came round last Sunday evening - he had been in England for almost 4 weeks .... but no satisfactory explanation as to what he had been there for!! I think he may be wanting to complete some exams or even to get appointments in some hospitals, but I am not sure.

Jane Pelly and Joan Steward are here for the weekend. It is their Half Term this week, and so they are both staying with Sheila. They are all coming here for supper this evening.

I hope Daddy's ear is still improving.

Much love to you both

Elizabeth.

Vining Centre
28th February 1977

Dear Ma and Daddy,

I have just written to Daddy for his birthday, and I am not sure exactly what I included in that letter, so I hope this one is not terribly repetitive. I am staying now with the Rodgers in Ife. It is our Half Term weekend, and it is a great delight to me just to rest in an English home - and at the same time to listen to all the talk about the Medical School here - and to hear folks reminiscences of the old days. University people have a great complex of relationships all over the world .... Did you know that so-so-so is now the Professor of Surgery at -----? I met him when I was in Dublin or Belfast etc. etc. .... I have met several people over this weekend - mostly Scots! There is a doctor called Christabel(!) with her husband, Seamus, at Wesley Guild now. She has promised to come over to Akure sometime. She has 3 children so I suggested we went up to Idanre so that will be nice sometime.

I had a letter this week from Freddy Mayes. A very nice letter. He says that he will probably be in an open prison somewhere near Bristol around April, and that he is waiting for the date of his release. I wonder how he will get on finding a job - very difficult I should think in these days of unemployment.

I haven't heard from John - I shall be very interested to read his poems .... maybe when I come home. Perhaps you could send me a photo of Mary so that I can see how she looks. I also had a letter from Stuart (N.Z.) which I must reply to.

I have been taking Banocide this week and it seems to have aggravated the reaction so that I get more itchy spells rather than less, which has not happened before after I started to take the medicine.

I hope Daddy's radium therapy treatment was successful. How soon does one know?

We had a Board of Governors meeting last Thursday. It was a long do - 11am till about 3pm. It was rather disappointing in that not very many of the Board were there - only the Bishop of Ondo among the Bishops. It seems that the Accounts for 1976 are not really very clear. A lot of sections were wildly overspent with no very satisfactory explanation. It is going to take some time to sort out. It seems that the deficit is something like N15,000. That includes students' deposits for 1977 which have already been spent in 1976 - thus making it extremely difficult for Fabuluje to start the new year and buy books etc. for students.

We celebrated Ash Wednesday this past week by having a quiet day. It was not particularly successful as far as I was concerned because I couldn't seem to settle on anything. I think it was partly the Banocide.

I hope to go to Ibadan tomorrow morning to get some books and provisions and then I will return to Akure in the afternoon.

This morning I went to the Ife University Chapel service - about 800 students present and a sermon by a Baptist Minister. I haven't seen Yomi and Kelu since I came here because they have been away at a Funeral in Ekiti somewhere.

With much love to you both,

Elizabeth.

Vining Centre
6th March 1977

Dear Ma and Daddy,

I hope you have received my letters - for Daddy's birthday etc. I shall be looking forward to your next letter to find out how Daddy got on with his radio therapy.

I have heard again from CMS, and it looks as though my leave will follow a similar pattern to 1975 - Swanwick June 27th to July 1st. Home from July 2nd - 11th. Then Missionaries Day and Links July 12th - 31st. Fountain Trust August 1st - 5th. Bruges 6th - 8th. Holiday from August 9th - 31st. Links September 1st - 8th. Then I hope to go to Selly Oak sometime in September to see the new CMS set up there.

Please could you help me to make an appointment with the dentist, between June 21st - 25th? I haven't any trouble, but I might as well get the teeth checked up early. I think there are some chipped fillings.

I had a very nice letter this week from the Indian Doctor who has applied to come here to do leprosy work. He is obviously a real Christian who says that because I wrote to him and told them that there was a real need here, he is thinking of coming? That is very encouraging because I wrote to tell him that there was no hospital and that he would have to start from scratch, because I didn't want someone to come here with false expectations. But goodness knows how long it will take for his papers to be processed.

We had a good 'Fellowship' on Tuesday at St. Louis. We are taking the Beatitudes as the starting point for our meditation and prayer. Eyesorun was at the meeting and Dr. Ijose the Commissioner for Finance.

On Wednesday evening we had a Leper Settlement Committee - but there were not very many of us there. However, it is good to keep them going once every month.

Yesterday, Saturday, I went up to Ado to see Lily Stott. She leaves Ado on Monday and will be reaching Birmingham around the end of April. She is spending the intervening time with friends in Lagos and in the North. I shall miss having her as a place to go and stay.

Martinian and I went and sat on the top of the rock at Agric on Friday evening and had a long chin wag. She is going ahead with the Leprosy work plans. I must check up when she is going to be in England in June and July and see if she can come to Malvern.

I have started taking Banocide again this weekend. I gave it up for a week! I have bought some new tablets - and think it is possible that the reason for the others not working was that they were very old. So, I am hopeful about clearing off the rash with these ones.

We have the most extraordinary weather for March - Heavy dusty harmattan - everything is very dry, and the dust is incredible. Also, it is still very hot. We badly need rain - there is no water. They say that the river Owena which supplies us is almost dried up. They say that there is only one tanker for Akure!

Roll on June 20th!

With much love to you both

Elizabeth

Vining Centre
13th March 1977

Dear Ma and Daddy,

I am sorry that one of my letters was so late in arriving and hope that you have had subsequent letters more promptly. I am glad that Daddy has started on his treatment and hope that it does the trick. There are amazing services in England aren't there - with people willing to drive folk into hospital. I am sorry to hear that Marjorie Bennett is not so well and hope that she is feeling better. Please give her my love.

It seems to have been a busy week - lecture on Northern Ireland on Monday; Lent Fellowship on Tuesday on "Blessed are they that mourn" - talking about mourning for our sins, and the wrong things in the Church and nation. On Wednesday evening Omodara from the Ministry of Health came and chatted and told me that the Indian doctor's applications have come to his office. On Thursday evening Vic Saba, the Nigerian Youth Service Corps doctor from Kafenchan came for supper and stayed to chat. On Friday evening I helped to entertain a young businesswoman called Sylvia Jupp who was in Akure for the weekend staying with the Adesidas. An incredible character - lives near Guildford and is a partner in a firm that makes fire extinguishers and things like bullet proof personnel carriers. She is 29 and has been married twice. Her present husband is of Rhodesian parents, but he has left Rhodesia because he refused to join the army. She came here on Friday evening and then I went with her to Corrines. Yesterday Sheila and Corrine and I went with her to the hot springs at Ikogosi. She was decked up in high heeled shoes - very red toenails - blue eye make-up and bikini! With long flowing blond hair and chain smoking .... a bushy valley with a hot water pool with leaves and insects floating on it and 3 women wasn't exactly her scene!! She had been staying at the Ikoyi Hotel in Lagos - comes to Nigeria for a 'trip' of about 3 weeks costing about £3,000!! Anyway, it was interesting to have her and to hear all her talk - friends of Lord Hesketh etc. ...! She couldn't credit that we had survived for 10 years here without any MEN .... she said that 3 weeks is enough for her away from her husband. She does her business with the Nigerian Army and the Government departments in Lagos and was supposed to go to a party of Brig. Adebayo's in Ekiti on Saturday night - to meet people for business contracts - but unfortunately there was a death in the Adesida family and so all the big wigs she came with from Lagos were in mourning so going to the party was cancelled.

On Thursday and Friday, I took one of the men from the Leper Settlement to the hospital for X-ray and tests and it was discovered (as we had suspected) that he has T.B. So, he has gone on treatment for it. As soon as I got back to the Settlement with him another fellow showed up saying that he thought he had T.B. too. So, I expect I will take him next week.

We have NO water - no rain but dusty harmattan weather. It is like 1973 again. I am OK on my own, but families are hard hit, and the schools are finding it very difficult.

Much love – Elizabeth

Vining Centre
20th March 1977

Dear Ma and Daddy,

I got your 2 letters on Tuesday which brightened up a particularly dreary week. It has been SO hot .... and no sign of rain .... and everyone hunting for water. I am fortunate really because our students carry water for me, and I have never been 'out' - but when it is very hot and sticky it would be just gorgeous to be able to have enough water for a bath. It is hot at night and sticky and so you must sleep with the fan on all the time and still you don't feel refreshed in the morning. Then I have been taking 9 Banocide a day towards the end of the week and I don't think that has helped.

However, this afternoon there is the first sign of rain - a few drops just wetting the roof - but there is also a bit of a breeze which is a great relief. We only have 2 more weeks of term so apart from the fact that we will have the exams to set and mark - at least there will be a break at Easter time.

Yesterday I spent part of the morning running up and down to the hospital with one of our women who has chickenpox - and a 5-day old baby. Her husband is in Benin, and it would really be better if she went home - but I couldn't face the idea of a journey to Benin today. While I was in the hospital, I saw Kayode Kumuyi who had said that he would come and see me on Saturday evening but he called off because he had visitors - fair enough but it upset me thoroughly - and was just about the last straw in a tiring week. Anyway, I am just stupid to let it bother me.

On Thursday I went with Corrine to visit Linda and Fred, a couple working with Taylor Woodrow. They were talking about all their food being sent up from Lagos in Ice Boxes and that they now had permission to build an airstrip so that they would be able to fly down to Lagos in future! They also told us that they have had experts drilling for water all around between Akure and Ondo and so far, have found no underground water supplies so it looks as though the Government had better get a move on and build some dams, or we shall suffer badly in future. Now the Water Corporation people are saying that if we don't have rain in the next 2 weeks we are going to be in serious trouble because all the streams and rivers are drying up. Now it takes a tanker 3 - 5 hours to fill up at Owena because the pressure of water flow is so low.

I am very sorry to hear that Mary has had to go into hospital. I am glad John is writing to you - he hasn't penned any words in this direction. I hope to hear good news of Daddy's ear in the next letter. It seems odd to me that Jutka's gall bladder should be giving her pain in the chest. Janet Olowoyo had gall stones, but she had ghastly pains in the abdomen.

Mothering Sunday today. Sorry you didn't get any card or flowers from me this year. I have been thinking of you today - and looking forward to June. Great about St. Julians. I should think that is the best time to go there. Goody! It will be a good rest after the Fountain Trust and Bruges!

Much love
Elizabeth

Vining Centre
27th March 1977

Dear Ma and Daddy,

Thank you for your letters - 2 this week, one written on 15th with a photo of Mary in it and the second written on 21st. I am happy to hear that Daddy's ear is improving - but very sad to hear that Mary has cancer inside her. However, it is amazing what can be done these days with the deep X-ray treatment. I thought that they usually did a hysterectomy if you had cancer in your womb. I do hope and pray that she will be completely healed. It seems very hard to accept when she and John have only just found each other and obviously have so much to give each other. Anyway, I am happy that they are both writing to you in such detail so that you can share with them in a deep way and know what to be praying about.

I also had a letter from Gemma about her mother's death and how she, Gemma, had to face up to all her "hurt" feelings about the bad relationships in the family. There are so many things in the world that need healing.

This week we have had exams at the V.C. for the women. I find sitting with the exams gives me backache and I was very tired by Friday. We have 7 women this term who are not able to write their answers and it is quite a labour getting the answers orally.

We had a very good Fellowship meeting on Tuesday evening at the Catholic Mission in the house of Father Joseph Akinjo, the newly ordained Catholic priest. He is a super Christian and led us in thinking about "Blessed are the Pure in Heart". The only thought I had was how frequently we need water to wash ourselves and how easy it is to get dirty! The thought coming from the continuation of the hot weather here with not enough water - but if you look in the bible how often God provides water - and it is used as an illustration of his abundant provision of forgiveness and his being able to make us pure.

Our Friday it rained at mid-day and so we had a blessed 24 hours of coolness. It was amazing what a difference it made. The temperature went down to 10 degrees and suddenly you felt like being active again. We are hoping it will rain again soon because it is hot again today.

Sheila has been practising Jerusalem Joy with her choir and they are going to sing it tonight at Fiwasaiye and then tomorrow at Vining Centre. I went to the Rehearsal last night and tried to help with some of the actions that they are doing. I wished I had been before to help them.

On Friday evening Sheila and Fred and I went to the Christian Wake Keeping - Hymn singing and readings - at the house of Mrs. Dada. Her husband was a Principal in Akure till recently, but he died 2 weeks ago after being knocked down by a motor bike in Akure. He was only 50, and very well liked so everyone was very sad.

We end our term next Thursday. Eyesorun is going to come and speak at the Commissioning Service.

Much love to you both

Elizabeth.

Vining Centre

3rd April 1977

Dear Ma and Daddy,

I think that I have answered your latest letters re John and Mary etc. I received the book of poems this week - took 3 months to reach here. I am sorry that nothing has got off to you in time for Easter, and

I don't suppose this letter will reach you until the week following Easter. I do hope that you have a happy time. I shall be thinking of you with all the lovely white and yellow spring flowers all around. I hope to be at Ikogosi with Sheila and Jane. Sheila wants to be quiet and have a complete 'retreat' then - but I am happy for Good Friday - to retreat then - but I am not sure that I am in the mood for 'silence' for the whole weekend - especially with Jane and Sheila. I haven't heard yet if Ruth Howard is coming. I had hoped that she would come too so that I have my own buddy.

We have finished the term this week - with the Commissioning Service for 3 of the women on Thursday. Eyesorun was our commissioner and she spoke to the women. This meant that the week was very pleasantly busy - in fact by Friday morning I was tired enough to stay in bed till 9am. On Friday there was a meeting of Expatriate teachers in the State here in Akure, so Inga came for lunch and then the Hick's family also came. I think I have told you about them before. John Hicks talks all the time and Sue says nothing until he is out of the way. I think that she is afraid of him. It is really very, very sad. She is so desperately lonely but doesn't really have any real understanding from him which makes it worse. Sue would like to go home but he wants to stay and teach in Nigeria. They have a baby who was premature and has some nerve damage. She is deaf and has not complete sight. Sue wants to be in UK to get all the help she can for the baby, but John seems to think that they will be able to manage just as well in the back of beyond in Ekiti! It is very difficult to help her - one feels like advising her to leave him if he is so stupid but on the other hand, she is completely dependent on him - that's the main trouble she is so dominated that she doesn't have a voice to say what is in her own mind. It seems that they don't share the same Christian faith either. She said, for example, that she would like to listen to a Christian programme on a Sunday - but she was afraid to put it on because it might annoy John!! They stayed here from 2 - 6 and their 2 1/2-year-old had wet both my cushion and my mat before they went!

Inga came and stayed Saturday and Sunday nights - and it was good to have her company. We went to Oka on Sunday after the morning service here. It is very beautiful - and I hope we can go again when the view is clearer. Although we have had a little rain. It is still very hot and there was a lot of haze. At Oka the Catholics have made a shrine to Mary - with a statue of Mary right up on the hill. It was rather a lovely place. We met a Catholic Father who has been in the country for 34 years. He seemed to have learnt to drink a good deal of beer in the time - but was a very hospitable Irish man.

Inga and I have both been reading John's poems - and found them interesting in seeing some of John's feelings. I think some of them are very expressive. Others I am not quite sure what he is getting at .... I am not very good at poetry.

I am not sure if I will travel out of Akure during these holidays. Probably I will go to Ibadan and see Grace - maybe next week. As you know I am not very good at managing here during the holidays - no problem next holidays!!

With much love to you both,

Elizabeth

Vining Centre
11th April 1977

Dear Ma and Daddy,

I received Daddy's letter of March 28th when I got home yesterday from Ikogosi. It is good to hear that the radium treatment has finished and that the skin behind his ear is looking healthier. I hope that this has done the trick.

We have had some rain here, but the rains haven't really started yet, so it is still hot but it was very pleasant at Ikogosi because there was often a breeze in the trees.

Jane and Sheila and I went off to Ikogosi on Thursday afternoon and stayed there till Sunday afternoon. We had 2 quiet days - Saturday and Friday and a programme of Morning Intercessions and mid-day meditation with Trevor Huddleston on Friday and Michael Baughan on Sunday from All Souls. Then we also listened to the Easter Cantata 'Jerusalem Joy' which Ruth gave me on a record - and a play called 'On the Hill' written by Frank Topping who used to be at Sussex University. Was he at St. J at one time? In the evening we had another session from 8-9. We each led one session a day and prepared one meal, so it worked out very well. Jane only got me down once when she decided to go and paint on Saturday morning, so we had to change the programme! She is taking Banocide so was feeling a bit groggy as well as being very tired from school.

The chalets at Ikogosi are very well equipped and easy to stay in. I did some dabbling with paint - more by way of experiment than painting a picture - but I enjoyed it.

On Thursday, before we went to Ikogosi, I had quite a busy morning running around the Leper Settlement Committee members to tell them that the Governor's wife was going to the Settlement on Good Friday to distribute clothes for the children and that as many as possible should turn up. Then I went to Eyesorun's office to help receive a donation of N50.00 and a whole load of clothes given by the different Churches at the time of the Week of Prayer for Christian Unity. Then I went with Eyesorun to Ado to visit Mrs. Sijuade who is in hospital there after a small operation on her bladder on Wednesday. She was feeling a bit 'shocked' as you do after an 'op' and especially because she felt that something had gone wrong at the beginning of the anaesthetic and she thought she was going to die. So, she was just thanking God that she was still alive on Thursday morning. I hope to go and see her again today with Sister Martinian. I was not at the Settlement on Friday - because of going to Ikogosi - I should have liked to have met Mrs. Ikpeme, the Governor's wife - but by all accounts, the visit went off as planned. The Ministry of Health Officials turned out in full force which is a bit of a hoot since I don't think some of them had been to the Settlement before.

We went to Communion on Easter Sunday morning at Igbara - Odo where Canon Awosusi is the Vicar. He was an Andrian of your time. After the service he and his wife gave us breakfast of coffee and sardines with bread. It was a very happy morning. What news of John and Mary? I look forward to hearing the latest.

With much love to you both

Elizabeth.

Vining Centre
20th April 1977

Dear Ma and Daddy,

Post here seems to have seized up. I suppose it it is still a result of the back log after Easter. Then I didn't write as usual on Sunday because I was seized up with a cold in the head and felt like doing nothing at all - which I did! On Wednesday last week I went to Ibadan together with Corrine and Ebun and Vero. We had lunch at Ingas and then went on to Ibadan where I dropped Ebun and Vero at St. Louis

Convent where they were to stay the night. Then we went on to the University and found Grace in her new house on the Campus. It was good to see her again also Tokunbo and Bim. We stayed the night there.

On Thursday I took Corrine first to the CUSO Headquarters and then we went on to the shops. We had a rather tiring, hot trail around and then went to the Coco Dome where I hoped to swim but that idea was thwarted because there was no medicine in the water - till tomorrow!

There was also no soft drinks - only beer and a malt drink called Maltina which I had tried but didn't like. We waited there until about 3.30 and Vero and Ebun didn't come back from Abeokuta, so we decided to wait a second night in Ibadan and travel to Akure on Friday. So, we went to see Jose and her 4 children. Sam had gone off to Sokoto on book business. Corrine and I stayed in Jose's spare room and found it extremely hot.

It is amazing how long the hot weather has continued this year.

So, we returned on Friday and Corrine was back to school directly. I offered to help Sheila to process the results of the Common Entrance Exam - so I did that over the weekend. It means writing about 450 envelopes after working out the addresses from a code of numbers.

It rained heavily on Friday night, which was good, but I think the sudden fall in temperature gave me the cold, which, as I say, was a nuisance on Sunday. I felt better by Monday but still have a slight cough and sound odd. On Sunday night Michael and Ruth Beaver and their 2 children came to stay the night. They arrived late because they took the Ilesha Road which is very slow. Then they set off to Onitsha the next morning. Their 2 children - Anna and Julian - were very sweet until it came to eating their breakfast and then there were all the horror scenes of 'eat up dear' - tears and screams - and Daddy taking son outside to talk to him quietly to be more sensible etc. etc. I don't know how it is that Nigerian children always seem to eat everything without fuss.

Last Monday I discovered that Sarah at the Settlement, who is mentally sick, and I had taken to the psychiatrist, had run away! - so I thought that there wasn't anything else we could do for her. Now, yesterday, I discover that she has returned and is shouting in the night and disturbing everyone so we shall have to start again. I am going to the Palace this morning with the Taylor Woodrow people's children.

Very much love to you both

Elizabeth

Vining Centre
24th April 1977

Dear Ma and Daddy,

You will be at Pilsdon this weekend. I hope you found them all well there and that you also enjoy your visit to Barbara Waterman and others.

I have been in Ife during the weekend - at the celebration of Yomi Bamgboye's 50th Birthday. I went on Saturday afternoon and helped to stir the pots to make some moin moin. Then I went to look for a bed with Professor Sheila Kenny, an Irish Anaesthetist. She is a widow of about 60+ who came to Ife 2 years ago very shortly after her husband died! She is sometimes 'up' and sometimes 'down'. I met her very down and wondering if she could manage the next 3 months before she leaves. She was feeling that she couldn't cope with her work - and she couldn't face people. She nearly didn't come to the party in the evening. She needs a lot of prayer because she is very afraid of what she will do when she goes home. She says she couldn't bear to be on her own and she fears that she may have to go into mental institution for treatment. She is at present under a psychiatrist and on one of these MAO type drugs that you can't eat cheese with. Anyway, I was very thankful that I went to see her because although at first, she didn't want to see anyone she kindly put me up for the night and we had quite a long chat about her troubles, and this morning prayed together. I hope she will come over to Akure for a weekend in 3 weeks' time.

The party was supposed to be starting at 7.30 but it rained cats and dogs and washed out all their chairs arranged in the garden with coloured lights around the trees. Everything had to be quickly shifted to the hall of the staff school and we ate there at about 9.30pm. I suppose there must have been about 200 people present. Then this morning they had a Communion Service at 7am in the Methodist Church and they invited their friends back for breakfast in the garden. This was really a family occasion and they cut the birthday cake which we ate with our breakfast of omelette, bread and sausage with tea. The children are now very tall and thin - especially the 1st 3 - Ayo, Ebun and Yinka.

I came back this afternoon and went straight to the Leper Settlement Open Air Service which always marks the beginning of our terms here. The students came back on Friday. Sheila has had no electricity at Fiwasaiye this last week, so she and Corrine came round here on Thursday night and we did the Guardian Crossword together - or most of it.

My cold that worried me last weekend is now better - although I didn't have a lot of energy during the week. I took Vit. C and that helped, I think.

Now I need to get geared into the new term's work. So far, I feel disjointed .... but that is often the case at the beginning of the term. As soon as you start teaching then I find that you get into the routine. I must write to Lagos about my ticket.

With much love to you both

Elizabeth

Vining Centre

1st May 1977

Dear Ma and Daddy,

May 1st already! This year seems to be going very quickly. I hope perhaps that this letter will get to you in time for May 9th. Thank you for your lovely tulip card at Easter. It reached here in good time, and it helped in the decoration of our 'tomb' at Ikogosi (a sort of Easter Garden that we made between us).

This week has been active - there are always several things to be seen to at the beginning of term. Then it has rained a few times towards the end of the week - so at last I have begun to come out of my general lethargy. Joseph Kumuyi came to visit on Monday evening - a very 'polite' visit I felt, like John's poem "deep fish", but the ice was not broken. On Tuesday Sheila and Corrine came round because they had no electricity at Fiwasaiye that evening, so we did the Guardian Crossword together - or part of it. Sheila is very good at them, so she is teaching Corrine and I to do it. On Wednesday I went with Corrine to see Dr. and Mrs. Velev - the Bulgarian doctor and his wife. Corrine is supposed to have gold injections and unfortunately, she didn't bring enough to last her 2 years, so she has been trying to get them. It seems the stuff is not available in Nigeria and so she sent to her chemist at home to send some to her, but the parcel never arrived either so now we are afraid that the medicine has been seized in the customs in Lagos. She is desperate as to what to do next and she hoped that Dr. Velev would write her a referral letter to UCH Ibadan so that she could see the Specialist there and get some heat and physiotherapy treatment. In fact, he didn't write any letter, he gave her some different tablets to try - so she wasn't very satisfied because she had had this arthritis for 12 years and she tried all sorts of tablets before it was discovered that the gold was successful.

There was a film on Wednesday night at Taylor Woodrows - but I didn't go. It doesn't start till 8.30 so it makes rather a late night. Corrine went so that was good. She misses films and entertainment a lot. On Thursday evening there was no light again at Fiwasaiye, so Sheila and Corrine came again. Corrine had made up a Crazy Crossword, so Sheila and I had to try and solve it.

One of our students cut his leg quite deeply this week while cutting in the bush with a cutlass so I had to take him to the hospital for stitches. It is a very deep cut just below the knee and seems to be exceptionally painful so I think he may have cut through the tendon. The students were cutting the bush at the back of the principal's house because on Wednesday evening there was a scare that a thief was trying to get into their house through the back door.

I had a letter from John this week saying that Mary is to have 72 hours of isolation with radium inside her. It sounds dreadful. I do hope and pray that it does some real good in healing her. It is great to hear that Daddy's ear is better. Praise God for that.

Sheila is here this afternoon, having a sleep after a rather harassing day yesterday when there was a major palaver in the school with Form 5. The usual school-girl trouble in this country - friction between juniors and seniors - the junior reports to the staff and then the senior is punished and then everyone is angry. Sheila is in the middle trying to mediate between senior and junior girls on the one hand and between staff and senior girls on the other hand - and of course everyone has their own points of view and probably the trouble is 50 - 50 anyway. The result is that Sheila is completely exhausted by trying to hold them all together. The result is that she slept from 1.30 to 4.30pm! I offered to help her by taking the service at Fiwasaiye so produced a rather scratch effort on Romans 12 9-12 picking out 2 things - being constant in prayer and serving the Lord. I described 3 people they could pray about - the girl who needs calipers - I forget if I told you about her - the mental woman at the Settlement - and Professor Kenny at Ife. It is amazing how students listen when you tell them about people - and they shut off when you start to preach in theory.

I do hope that you have a happy birthday Ma, and that you can do something special on the day. I am just enclosing a very small cheque - because I would like to get something to bring home for your birthday. Maybe sometimes I should come home for March/April/May so that I can be there for your birthdays - but I don't see that fitting very well at this end.

With much love to you both

Elizabeth

Vining Centre
8th May 1977

Dear Ma and Daddy,

Thank you for the week's news - telling of your visit to Ruth and Trevor and other folks in Dorset area, and then to Freddy at Leyhill Open Prison. It sounds as though he will be happier there and that it will help him a lot to adjust to 'coming out' altogether.

I was the preacher at this morning's Communion Service, and I talked about "Serving the Lord with gladness". At the beginning I played a song from a tape that Gemma has just sent - it is called "Worship with the Fisher folk" and has some lovely songs from Sounds of Living Waters etc. on it. Father Joseph - the young Catholic priest here is very interested in the charismatic movement so I loaned him the other tape yesterday, and I think he will enjoy this one too.

Yesterday I went to Ado with Corrine. Her arthritis is bad - because she hasn't been having her gold injections - now they have come at last through the post, but she doesn't want to take them again without specialist help. So, we went to get advice from Sister Carmel at Ado. She told Corrine to go to UCH in Ibadan. I also consulted Sister Carmel because I seem to have had some urinary infection for the past 3 weeks that hasn't cleared up with penicillin - so she gave me another antibiotic and told me to come on Wednesday for urine test etc. It seems to be better already .... but I was very uncomfortable on Thursday and Friday because I kept wanting to go to the loo. Anyway, I was much happier after I had seen her.

I went to supper with Linda and Fred Roberts of Taylor Woodrow on Thursday night. We had sausage, egg, and chips with spaghetti rings! They told me that the firm had arranged for a load of frozen meat to be brought up from Lagos for the 20 of them here in Akure. There was N1,000 worth of meat in it - ducks, chickens, legs of lamb, lamb chops, ham, sausages etc. etc. - But something went wrong with the van - it didn't keep cold properly - so <u>all</u> the meat had to be buried!! Isn't that awful?

I went over to Ondo for lunch with Inga and then went to see the Whittles at teatime. Inga has had a rotten time recently because she has had a horrible inspection report. It seems to have been a 'put up job' to pull the principal to pieces and was started by a letter from some of the Old Girls to the Ministry of Education accusing Inga of bad discipline in the school. It all sounds very miserable to me. I just hope that she will go home on her course to Bristol in October.

We had our Prayer Fellowship on Tuesday night at St. Peters - the last one on the Beatitudes - Blessed are the Persecuted for Righteousness sake. Then on Wednesday night we had the Leper Settlement Committee meeting at Lawyer Fesobi's house. There was a good turn out and we said goodbye to Mr. Ojo, the Leprosy Officer who has been replacing Mr. Akinbulumo while the latter has been in Ethiopia. Mr. Ojo has been very popular at the Settlement and has worked very hard indeed for the patients. I hope Mr. Akinbulumo has returned with a lot of useful knowledge from his course.

Sister Martinian goes home at the end of May and then she will return in October to start her work with leprosy.

Not long till June 20th. I will let you know times as soon as I get the information. I hoped to get the ticket from Lagos last week, but nothing materialized.

With much love

Elizabeth

Vining Centre
15th May 1977

Dear Ma and Daddy,

Thank you for your letters. It's Sunday again - so time to write to you. Sheila Kenny and Winnie Stafford from Ife University are here staying for the weekend. It is good to have them. Sheila Kenny is much brighter than when I saw her in Ife, when she was so depressed. Sheila Davis and Corrine came and joined us for supper last night and then this morning after chapel we went up to Idanre and climbed up part of the way to see the view. Then we went on to see the Akinbadewas and had a nice chat with them, before coming back here for lunch.

This evening I went round to see Eyesorun and spent the rest of the evening there and ate her stew and fish and rice. Mrs. Sijuade was also there pouring out her woes to Eyesorun, most of the time in Yoruba. Really Nigerian men are quite incredibly selfish and thoughtless - or at least her husband is. You will remember that I told you that he has Tokunbo's sister as his 'junior wife' but that he lives all the time with his proper wife. Anyway, last week Florence had a baby in Ibadan - her second. The first baby was also born in Ibadan, and they had the naming ceremony also in Ibadan. But today they had the naming ceremony in Akure. Dr. Sijuade rents a home here for Florence when she comes to Akure from Owo, where she works. So, several Sijuade relatives from Ife came for the naming and went to stay in the Doctor's house - so Bisi had a rotten day cooking food for all these relatives who had come to celebrate the other woman's baby by her husband! And they tried to persuade her to go to the Ceremony which she didn't want to go to avoid embarrassment. Terrible! Then in addition to that Bisi has wanted to go on holiday for the past 2 years to see her daughter in Canada - but her husband puts up obstacles in her way and says, 'Who will look after me?' But he won't take a holiday himself. He seems to think that the hospital would fall apart if he took a holiday, (probably it would of course!) but nevertheless he ought to take a holiday.

I went to Ado on Wednesday and had Lab tests for my urine infection. The results came on Thursday saying that nothing was seen so the antibiotic must have done the trick - but there was one test to go. They hadn't been able to do that test because the amount of urine wasn't enough! So, I went into Ado again on Saturday to provide another sample and because I was still worried by some of the symptoms. Sister Carmel gave me some pessaries and said that the only thing that had come out in the tests is that I might have sub-clinical filariasis and that could be causing the irritation. That filaria is a troublemaker! However, I am feeling alright.

I now have my ticket! 20th June. Nigerian Airways to Heathrow. WT902. leaving Lagos at 10.30am arriving 18.35.

Much love

Elizabeth

Vining Centre
21st May 1977

Dear Ma and Daddy,

I am glad that my birthday card reached you on the right day. I have done rather well this year as far as you are concerned - O dear! as I write this, I see that it's May 21st and Stuart's birthday on 24th! Clang!! You seem to have been very busy lately. Don't overdo it will you? I don't think I shall be able to keep up with your pace when I come back.

At lasts my infection seems to be on the mend and I can go to the loo in comfort. The last test showed some infection that was still there so Sister Carmel sent me some more tablets called Flagyl which are to clear up parasites. I am to go for another urine test when I finish these tablets - so then I hope it will be clear.

Yesterday I went to Ado, together with Eyesorun and David and Jane Lewis from Ikare who were staying with me for the weekend. It was for the ceremony of installing the same Dr. Carmel - a St. Louis Sister, as a Chief in Ado. She is the doctor who started the Catholic Hospital there which is a very well organised place and Sister Carmel is a very devoted and efficient doctor. The Ewi of Ado celebrates being on the throne for 40 years this week. He was in great form and looked very young I thought. He mentioned that the last European who he made a chief was Archdeacon Dallimore and made a very nice speech about the contribution of the missionaries in Ado. Sister Carmel looked super in Yoruba costume, and she was marvellous at the dancing!! It was a very happy occasion.

Then this morning I went with David and Jane to Idanre, and we climbed the steps up to the old village where we went to visit the new Owa of Idanre. He is in the old palace on the top of the hill most of the time. So far, they haven't changed anything so really it is very tatty looking. The houses on the road to the Palace which used to have some ancient inhabitants are now derelict and tumbledown so really it is depressing. However, we saw beds in the rest house up on the hill so maybe that will soon be opened. The Owa said that there was a plan to build an escalator up the hill!! I can't imagine an escalator outside - I should have thought a chairlift or cable car was more practical.

Yesterday evening we had a good time with Sheila and I, Jane and David combining to try to solve the Guardian Crossword which was one without any numbers. We made it - except for one clue which we couldn't think of so that was a triumph.

It has been raining more frequently in the past week, so it has been cooler in the evenings particularly. This is a great blessing I must say because it means you can sleep without being too hot. However, by Friday evening I was very tired because on Wednesday and Thursday I was woken in the night and had to go to the hospital. On Wednesday it was for a delivery around 2am and on Thursday it was for one of the women who had asthma. That was around 4am.

Sheila has Half Term next weekend so she and Corrine will probably go to Benin. I may go up to Idanre on Friday night and spend the night with the Akinbadewas and then go walking with them on Saturday - and go up to see the waterfall which I have never yet seen up there.

I also started to play table tennis this last week with Mr. Taiwo at the Agric. It was a good bit of exercise and I enjoyed it.

With much love to you both

Elizabeth.

Vining Centre
29th May 1977

Dear Ma and Daddy,

Good to hear all your news as written on 18th May. You sound very busy with visiting and visitors. I hope that you are keeping John and Mary's letters. Yes, I have got 2 out of 3 of John's letters and I have now replied. I do hope that Mary now goes from strength to strength. I also had a happy letter from Stuart. It will be great to see you all, and Ruth, Trevor, and Robbie when I get back home.

Martinian goes today or tomorrow. She came round here for supper on Wednesday, and we had a good walk at the Agric before supper. I will miss her - but may have a chance to see her in London in August. Sheila and Corrine have gone off to Benin for the school Half Term holiday - they should be back today. I had a good day yesterday with the Akinbadewas. I went up to Idanre on Friday evening and then went with Francis and Paul and Anike (their 2 eldest children) up to Idanre to go and see the waterfall there. It was quite a long walk - along paths and over rocks and down a valley slope and then we got to a place where we were above the waterfall, but we couldn't see it because it was going away below us - so we then waded across a stream and cut our way through the bush on the other side of the river and eventually got ourselves out at a place where we could see the waterfall clearly. My legs ached afterwards, but it was worth it! We left the house soon after 7am so it was nice and cool most of the time. I suppose we walked for about 3 hours and then we met Pat and the 2 younger children at the Rest House, and we had elevenses before going down for pounded yam. I was happy that I went to stay, because it was a good chance to chat with them and it also saved me from being lonely when Sheila and Corrine were away.

I finished my tablets on Wednesday and went up to Ado on Friday morning to get the urine test checked. I hope everything has cleared off. Certainly, I don't feel any more trouble. I don't want to come home with some complaint that means visits to a doctor. It wastes too much time on my precious leave!

I am taking the service in the Chapel this evening - Whitsunday. I am doing it like a short Carol Service with 4 lessons interspersed with Hymns and Prayers. There are 4 points - the Spirit brings New Life - Unity - Power - Fruit. In fact, I am grinding down to a halt and feel ready for a break. I haven't got many new ideas to put over, and find that I am just managing to get along with classes etc.

After the service: Most encouraging! The students afterwards said "We liked your programme. Please can it be cyclostyled?" I will preach that sermon in my first service when I go home! "It was more or less (!) a revival service"!!!

Anyway, it is good to be encouraged at this stage - it will help me through the next 3 weeks of getting ready to come home. I am sure that the students here need to be given more inspiration in services - there is so much emphasis on practising their sermons in good English - all written out and read with a great struggle - and it <u>must</u> last 10 minutes, and it is stuck in the middle of Evensong or Matins so that there is no elasticity of structure. I just pray that some of them go out and allow the Spirit to lead their services sometimes rather than the Prayer Book.

Sheila is back from Benin where she had a happy time with Jane. Corrine had a bad night with her arthritis and certainly looked groggy when she got back. Only 3 weeks more till June 20th.

With much love

Elizabeth.

Vining Centre

5th June 1977

Dear Ma and Daddy,

I guess that this will be the last letter before I get home. I will be looking forward to seeing you at Heathrow - W.T. 902 arr. 18.35.

I am on Half Term now and for the first time in History I am staying on the compound mainly because I want to get a bit organised for our exams and so on in the next 2 weeks so that I don't have a horrible rush at the end. On Friday evening Inga and Susan from Ondo came over and we went to a "Western" film at the Taylor Woodrow club house - the goodies and the baddies and most people dead was the gist of it.

I went to the Tax Office on Friday morning and met a notice on the door "No entry. Peep through the window"! So, you look through the windows (louvre ones) and see curtains and the backs of a line of clerks. One girl said, "Good morning, Miss Davis" and came out to help me but then another clerk locked the door so she was locked out - then he wouldn't let me in because he said the man that I needed to see was busy - "Come back by 12". I went back by 12. They said - "Go away and put your request in writing! - and come back by 3pm." So, I went back by 3pm and they found the tax card which I now need to get photocopied to take it to the bank - but I still must go back on Tuesday for what I was looking for.

We had the Family Planning Film on Monday night and a Dr. Adetunji, from the School of Health Technology came to answer questions. It was a useful evening.

On Tuesday we had our Fellowship group at Eyesorun's house. Numbers were smaller than usual, but it was a helpful evening. On Wednesday we had the Leper Settlement Committee meeting and heard something of how Mr. Akinbulumo, the Leprosy Officer, got on in Ethiopia. Also, I went up to the Public Service Commission to find out what they had done with the Indian leprosy doctor's papers -

and discovered that they have done precisely nothing. I was very annoyed that I hadn't gone there to stir them up before.

You will be having a holiday weekend to celebrate the Queen's Jubilee I understand this weekend. Sheila is going to have a supper party on Tuesday to celebrate in Akure.

Monday: Today I took 4 of the men from the Leper Settlement to Ondo to see the Eye Specialist because their eyes were bad. Two of them were blind or blind in one eye so nothing can be done about them. Another one had his eyelashes growing in onto the eyeball because I think the leprosy affects the muscles of the eyelids and makes them slack. Anyway, it was a worthwhile journey - but I am sorry we didn't go before for one of them. Two weeks today!

With much love

Elizabeth

Home on leave June to September 1977

During this leave times to be at home and times to be on holiday are fitted in between CMS commitments. The CMS time included the CMS Conference in Swanwick, a Missionaries Day in London and then my Link Parish visits in July and September. In August I attended meetings of the Fountain Trust in Westminster Hall and stayed with Gemma in London. In August I went by train to Bruges with Stuart and Jutka where Stuart was playing the violin with the Academy of Ancient Music conducted by Christopher Hopwood. Then I spent 2 weeks having a quiet holiday with my parents at St Julians. In September I went to Selly Oak to visit the new CMS Training College named Crowther Hall, where I worked as a Tutor when I came home to England in the 1990's.

Vining Centre
29th September 1977

Dear Gemma/Ma and Daddy,

It was an incredible and most frustrating 3 days. I thought of you and your 55 hours saga and feel that I can rival it. I have never known so many things go wrong in such a short time and yet I have at last arrived. The events were these:

Monday 7am: Marjorie who was taking me to the airport came rushing into Marion's to say that her car battery was flat - she had borrowed her husband's van but its clutch had gone and stuck at the corner of the road! We phoned 4 mini cabs, but none answered. We phoned the curate and woke him, and he came round in a rush and took me to the airport.

7.40am: Met Stuart and Jutka at Heathrow and went to KLM weighing in. Strike of loaders on KLM only since the night before - no luggage accepted. Advised to go and see KLM desk upstairs. Struggled there with bag - and told no booking available for Lagos on any flight for another week! Went and had breakfast and mull over the situation.

8.45am: KLM agreed to weigh in luggage and promised to send it later by freight when the strike was over. Thankfully got rid of case.

9.10 - 5.30pm: Smooth flight to Lagos via Amsterdam! Sat next to a Dutchman building a new airport at Ilorin.

5.30 + **:** Usual hassle through immigration queues etc. Filled out forms about the suitcase.
6pm: Got out to be met by Sunday the CMS driver with my car and a note from Faji with money in as requested. Great! (Except he had given me N17.00 short because he reckoned, I had over claimed (which I hadn't). BUT the car had not been serviced or mended in the 3 months that it sat in the garage! Rev. Faji said he had tried to book it 2 weeks back, but M & K would not accept it till Wednesday 28th September, so it hadn't been done. The driver said that it was not good and not safe to drive!! It gave up at every junction and stopped in traffic.
7pm: Arrived at Sholas with the driver and the car and my hand luggage - i.e., books, your jug, tin of marmalade, chocs, your tape and seeds - no change of clothes and no toilet things. I sent the driver with the car into Marina - because I couldn't use it on Tuesday, and I decided it would have to be mended before I took it back.

Ate and slept at Sholas - who hadn't received either my P.C. written at beginning of leave or letter telling her I was returning. Borrowed her night dress and towel etc. Booked a phone call to Akure and tried to get through at 8, 9, 10 & 11. Failed. Told they would ring me.
Tuesday 6am: Booked phone call again.
8.30am: Told "Didn't they tell you that the lines to Akure are bad?"
9am: Set out to get a taxi to go into Lagos to see Faji re: car, case and transport. I couldn't get to him on the phone - nor to the Convent at Maryland to discover if Martinian was still on Tarkwa beach.

Continued next letter ....

Tuesday 9am: Shola met a friend of her husbands in the road who said that he could loan me his driver and his car to take me into Lagos. He would only be a few minutes and then he was going to his office, and I could have the car. Super! - but snags. half an hour in the bank, half an hour at John Holte at the Airport, half an hour shopping in Kingsway, half an hour trailing miles to his office to a place that I didn't recognise. Then coke and a polite chat.
11.30am: Set off into Lagos. Met long go slow on the Eko bridge - usual hazards - lane swapping etc. Reached Marina about 1.30. Saw Faji and he agreed to send the car with the driver when it was ready, and to go to the airport and (hopefully) collect my suitcase when it arrived! I gave him papers, ticket, letter of authority and key. No "apologies" for doing nothing about the car. He was sick. Myrtle told

me that he had a sort of breakdown - so I said nothing. No offer of help with transport to Akure. Agreed he still owed me N17 and would add it to future allowance. No food.
2pm: Hungry and miserable - went to P.O. and got air letter to send home. Went to Olu's office to see if he was there - just gone home! Tears as walked down the 5 flights of stairs - no lifts working. Washed face in loo in CMS - dirty unkempt flooding loo.
3pm: Told that bad time for taxies to Ikeja and would have to pay N12. Too late to go to Tarkwa on the boat to see if Martinian was there. Took taxi to Ikoyi - N1.
3.30pm: Found Olu and Marie in and eating their lunch. Marvellous. They saved me. Ate dirty lettuce and hoped I wouldn't get a runny tummy for public transport. Olu only back from UK for 1 week and full of tales of Lagos traffic and other problems. Their 2 cars were of the same starting numbers - so what did they do in January last year? .... bought a 3rd car with the other type of number plate!! Many Lagos people have done that so increasing the number of cars.
5pm: Set off with Olu and Marie to go to Yaba and try and book a Mid-West line bus for the next day. Met solid go slow near the racecourse - sat in it for half an hour and didn't get nearly as far as CMS. We gave up and went back to the house where the electricity had failed .... because of the size of the deep freeze, I guess. Olu went for NEPA men.
7.30pm: Went to Ikoyi Club for supper - me in grubby non-white blouse and blue skirt (only clothes for 3 and a half days). Ate kebabs or steak at N4.50 a time.
8.30pm: Started journey towards Ikeja again and met Go-slow where we had left previously but it was moving. More go slow in Yaba
9.30pm: Transferred to taxi in Yaba and went at great rate up new highway and then rattled round muddy back streets. N4.00.
10pm: Arrived Sholas! Washed shirt and pants. Phone not working.
Wednesday 7am: Taxi to Maryland - on road to Ibadan N1.00; Met Catholic sister to ask for news of Martinian. Thought she was coming from Tarkwa on Thursday or Friday.
8am: Got on to a V.W. van transport to Ibadan after discussion with the driver about his speed of operation.

I was comfortable in the back seat with 3 women and babies alongside - and the driver was good. No tension about that. We got on well for about 60 miles. The baby opposite peed down my leg but nothing else unusual happened. Then the bus began to chug and object to going up hills - so it was stop - tinker - manage - free-wheel downhill - start engine - roar up - chug - stop - tinker and so on .... I should think repeated about 10 times.

Around the 4th time one young man got out - paid his money and went to flag down something more hopeful. About the 7th time of stopping at the side of the road there was a half empty mammy wagon in front and one man, and 4 women evacuated to try that. Haggle about money - sorted quickly. We were only 6 who remained faithful to the original transport, which maybe because it was lighter managed a lot better. So, we limped into Ibadan around 12. Cost N1.50.

I then went with 2 schoolgirls, and we caught a similar taxi bus in Ibadan, 10k a go - this took us to the centre, by Dugbe market and the second of the same sort took me near to Mokola where St. Louis convent is. I walked the last half mile across the valley along a path and arrived hot and sweaty and tired. Asked about Martinian's time of going back to Akure - no news - probably Thursday or Friday. Felt couldn't face any more public transport .... wept over coffee and sister 'saved' me - showed me to a clean room to lie down in and provided soap, towel, and talc to have a shower and help me to book a phone call to Akure. Real caring provided great relief - and the phone call came through loud and clear - dear Sheila at the other end - very sympathetic - would send car or Vining van immediately. I was just to wait in Ibadan at Immanuel College. Read Water Ship Down on St. Louis bed.

2.15pm: Had a nice lunch.

3pm: Took taxi to Immanuel College and walked over to the Institute to discuss about the letter needed for the visa of a couple at Crowther.

4pm: Sat and waited for transport to Akure in Emmanuel Gbonigi's house - lovely smiley wife.

8pm: No sign of transport. No phone working in either the Institute or Immanuel College - Emmanuel took me to SU house to phone - got through after 30 mins and Sheila said that Vining Centre driver had left around 2pm but had gone to town to buy a spare tyre so hadn't left Akure till 4pm

Discovered that Owadayos were going to Akure the next morning at 6am. Arranged to go with them. Then met Vining bus and driver and a student but decided to go with Owadayos in car anyway.

Had supper with Gbonigis. Then Emmanuel took me over to the Institute where he had booked a room downstairs for N5.00. Spent the night killing their mosquitoes. No towel. No nightdress - only toothbrush and paste which I had bought at Kingsway.

Thursday 6am: Left Ibadan with Owadayos - good smooth journey arriving about 9am. Great welcome by all on Compound. Went into my house and discovered streaky yellow distemper in the living room and battleship grey paint on the kitchen walls making it look like the black hole of Calcutta!! Horrible. Went to Sheila's for breakfast - road a sea of mud. It's great to be back. Great relief to have arrived.

Much love

Elizabeth

Vining Centre

2nd October 1977

Dear Ma and Daddy,

You will be glad to know that I am now in Akure - after the most eventful arrival so far. I spent Tuesday getting into Lagos and out again to Ikeja - and gave all the papers about the suitcase to Canon Faji. I just hope that he can get it for me and send it up, and that I don't have to go to Lagos again. Lagos is just horrible. I went to Olu and Marie's place on Tuesday afternoon, and they saved my bacon - gave me lunch and later took me out to the Ikoyi Club for supper in my dirty shirt.

On Wednesday I went on by public transport to Ibadan and the sisters of St. Louis saved me by giving me a shower, and lunch and the chance to phone Akure, and to contact Sheila. They sent transport from Vining Centre, but it was so late in coming that I had already arranged to stay the night in Ibadan and to come to Akure by car on Thursday morning with the Owadayos. I have written a detailed diary of the upsets of the journey to Gemma and asked her to send it on to you for the archives! - and so that I don't need to write all the details out again. The main thing is that I have arrived and Tokunbo had my house ready with all the household things unpacked and flowers to welcome me. The painting work done in my absence was mostly disastrous - the living room walls are streaky and there are speckles of paint over the floor but at least it is distemper. The kitchen is the worst because it is battleship grey and very dark - and spots of gloss paint are not so easy to deal with. I suppose it's all a lesson to me not to be independent and let someone meet me in

Lagos - and secondly to supervise my own car repairs and the painting of my house in future - but this country does not become easier to cope with. There is water sometimes - there is no gas in the town and food supplies are in short supply (i.e., no coffee they say) - or very expensive, and the road is becoming a sea of mud - and very congested because of the rebuilding of the main road through the town. Yesterday I heard that the American/German/Nigerian company called Lastra are not able to pay their salaries at the end of September - so the building of all the side roads in Akure is likely to come to a halt. Then phones are almost impossible. Most of them are out of order - or disrupted by road building.

I realised when I got back that I took the needle out of my record player to get another one. How I forgot I don't know but I think the old needle must be somewhere in the top right-hand drawer in my bedroom - maybe inside a little box. If you can get a new one like that, I should be happy - the cartridge No is: EPC 40TT8 112. I have also written to Stuart - if you can't get another send the old one in a letter if you find it.

Much love

Elizabeth.

Vining Centre
5th October 1977

Dear Ma and Daddy,

Thank you for your letters. I haven't yet got any written since I left - but the others are very welcome. I have not found this past week very easy because so far, I have no car. There is the van, and the 2 other staff with cars are very good at letting me use theirs - but everything is just one extra effort without a car of your own. I hope that my car will come this week.

I was very happy on Wednesday morning when my suitcase arrived just as I was eating my breakfast. Fabuluje went to Lagos on Tuesday, and he was able to bring it back with him so that was very good

Martinian started in the health Office this last Monday - so I saw a good deal of her. She came to report what had happened on most days. She was here for supper last night and today goes off to Ossiomo. We had a meeting of the Committee on Wednesday - there are several new members since I was away so that's very encouraging. One of them is the young doctor who came to talk to our men last term on

Family Planning. He has now said that he would be willing to go to the Settlement every Friday to do a general clinic - so that's a great step in the right direction.

There is an American gentleman of about 55-60 who is working on the Radio - T.V. Satellite station which has been set up about 7 miles outside Akure. He is called 'Ed' and is a member of the Full-Gospel-Businessmen's Fellowship. He is a very one-track charismatic type. Very off-putting I find. He has come to our prayer group for the past 3 times and last time apparently said we needed a 'prayer chair' so that people could sit there and be prayed upon. He seems to have decided that our group is not ready for the Baptism of the Spirit. Maybe not! - but we were learning to love one another - and I believe that the Spirit works in different ways - not only one. Please pray for Ed that he may want to get to know us as people and not just want to push his own thing onto the group.

I think I may need my glasses changed - or need reading glasses. I am not sure - but something isn't quite right with my eyes. I went to Ondo on Tuesday and saw the eye doctor there - and Inga. The doctor gave me an ointment which caused a lot of irritation and itching! - so I went again yesterday, and he changed it. I am happy that it has improved the situation.

A sad thing happened last week - that was the death in a motor accident of Emmanuel Alieu from Omu-Aran who I stayed with last year. Didn't he write to Daddy? There was a very sad funeral yesterday. I didn't go but Mama and others went.

With much love

Elizabeth

Vining Centre

16th October 1977

Dear Ma and Daddy,

Thank you for your letter and the ones from Sheila and Fabuluje which are now answered - and for the message "Even there .... I hope that the CMS Association meeting went well. I expect that I shall hear about it the next letter from home. How typical of Dr. Salama!!

This week has been much better than last, and I feel that I am beginning to settle down to being back. Sheila has had a nasty cold and no voice so she has been in bed or in her house since Tuesday so she very kindly loaned me her car - then I can visit her! This has meant that I have been a bit more mobile and so have been able to visit some of my friends - like Eyesorun.

On Tuesday we had a very good fellowship group - very quiet and prayerful - and then Sister Mildred shared with us her conviction that we should meet every week in future and that we should consider following a course of study that had been very helpful to Charismatic Renewal Groups in the Catholic Church. It goes for 7 weeks, and we all felt that we should give it a try because we wanted to grow in fellowship and "In the Spirit" - although everyone there said that they had 'fears' of being "charismatic". I felt we had a great unity and the beginnings of real honesty within the group.

On Thursday I took part in a symposium on Preventive Health - and I was a bit put out because I was asked to take part in a panel discussion and to be ready to answer questions about the Lepers Welfare Committee. So - Eyesorun the Commissioner read a speech of introduction at the beginning and then the Chairman said, "Now Miss Deeks will speak on the 'Role of the Voluntary Agencies in Preventive Health'" and I was given a microphone in front of my nose!! Golly gosh! I managed - but it was a rotten speech.

Today, Sunday, I took the morning service of Matins - and I wasn't very well organised because Martinian came yesterday afternoon to tell me about her first week in Ossiomo and then Linda and Fred Roberts from Taylor-Woodrow came in the evening, together with Sheila for supper. Anyway, I talked on the Quoist prayer "Lord I have time ...." saying we need to find time for quiet inside if we are to remain human in the rush of modern urban life - e.g., Lagos. A High Court Judge was there, and it really rang bells for him - he and his wife came and chatted afterwards for about 1 hour. So, it was a good week.

With much love to you both

Elizabeth

Vining Centre

25th October 1977

Dear Ma and Daddy,

I am writing a mid-week "quicky" - partly because there may not be time on Sunday I hope to be in Benin with Sheila - Jane, Ruth and co and maybe (petrol permitting) to go and see Martinian at Ossiomo on Sunday. It is good to get your long letters again which keep me in touch with the activities (Ma) and thoughts (Daddy) of 64 Church Road.

I hope that my car will come tomorrow (Friday). Canon Faji promised to send it up with the driver - so then I shall be mobile which is especially nice for visiting friends. The town in fact is not very enticing because everything is mud and road works and lines of cars and there is nothing much in the shops when you manage to get there.

On Tuesday we had our Prayer Fellowship and there were 24 of us there. We are going ahead with our special series of Seminars and will start next week. Four of us are to be sort of group leaders - i.e., me, Fred, Sister Anna, and a newcomer called Akin. We shall meet on Sunday evening in preparation for Tuesday.

Yesterday I went to Ondo in the afternoon and saw Inga and the Eye Doctor. My eyes seem to be better, but I wanted to ask if I should continue with the drops. While I was there, he was asking about my dark glasses. You will remember that I went to the Optician in Malvern Link - is it Tromans? and got my old glasses "sprayed" - or treated in some new way to make them dark. Please can you help me to find out about the process. Do they do it there - or send the spectacles away? If so, where? What is the machine like? Who sells it? Can they send details? Dr. Akinyosoye is very interested because he would consider buying such a machine and bringing it to Nigeria because lots of people are wanting dark glasses.

I am glad that you found a bus up to the Wyche. Anna's arthritis can't be so bad if she managed to walk all the way up to the Beacon and down to St. Ann's Well.

Monday:

I thought that I would get this posted before I went away for the weekend - but it didn't get away. My car is back! So that's great. We had a good weekend in Benin. I stayed with Ruth and Sheila stayed with Jane. On Saturday Ruth and I went to Agbor and met Martinian there. We got back around 6.30 and then I had the meeting in preparation for Tuesday in my house around 8pm. I expect that the next 7 weeks will work out OK but now I am reacting badly towards the prospect - I think because it is all "organised" - 15 minutes talk then group discussions etc. I valued our group so much for its relaxing atmosphere and suddenly I am afraid that we are going to get pushed into spiritual sausage machine.

Much love

Elizabeth.

Vining Centre

30th October 1977

Dear Ma and Daddy,

Thank you for your letters with all the news of Max Warren's Memorial Service. It sounds as though it was a great occasion. Sorry to hear that Stuart has his foot in plaster. Dear Tosca - she really is a very special dog. I am glad that you had a good time with Moira.

This week: On Monday night Brother Peter - a Nigerian brother came and talked to our men about "Communities in the Catholic Church". He started off by saying that we were all meant to live in Communities - see Adam and Eve!! and went on to talk about a celibate set-up and to say that it would be difficult for married people to live in a community. Apart from this blind spot what he said was very interesting.

On Tuesday I went to the Radio Station to read the Quoist poem on the Womens Hour programme. I was asked to be there at 3.45 - and so I was. I was not such a keen broadcaster when it was 5.30 before we were called into the studio. We shall see. I will give up after a few programmes if I must waste 2 hours each time - specially as my subject is 'Using your time well!!'

On the evening of Tuesday, we had the first of our series of 'New Life in Christ' studies. Father Joseph gave the talk - not very special - rather going over ground that we knew inside out - but then we had a small group discussion - 5 in my group and I felt that that had more depth. Sister Mildred was in my group.

The Head of State of Nigeria visited Ondo State from Thursday to Saturday, so all the Government Departments were smartened up and there was a good deal of clearing of rubbish in the town. He went to the Hospital and St. Peters TTC. I didn't see him - I just heard the sirens in the town. Bola was around and came and saw me yesterday evening with a Forestry friend.

Yesterday I went to Ondo for lunch with Inga and we went together to Ife in the afternoon where I delivered Kelu's Hair Dye and Pants - but I didn't see either Yomi or Kelu. Yomi had gone to Ijebu and Kelu was somewhere getting her hair plaited. It was good to see something of Inga. She is going to get some paint for me in Ibadan so that I can do something about my streaky walls. This is especially good because she can get 20% discount if she gets it with the school paint.

Tonight, we have our meeting to discuss the Prayer Group next Tuesday. It's in my house.

Much love to all

Elizabeth

Vining Centre

6th November 1977

Dear Ma and Daddy,

No post so far this week so I am living in hope. It has been a good week and I have felt well although at this precise moment I feel very hot and sticky. The weather has changed, and the dry season is starting so it is much hotter in the afternoons.

I had a good lecture on Monday evening - I am talking to the men about the encouragements of the 20th Century through the Ecumenical Movement. I have been reading them some sections out of "When the Spirit Comes".

November 9th:

Sorry - this hasn't got finished on Sunday as usual. I had rather a busy weekend. I was taking the Service at Fiwasaiye on Sunday and then we have our team meeting on Sunday for Tuesday night, so Sunday was full up. Then I was preparing for Tuesday night when I was giving a talk about New Life - and it was my birthday.

I am enjoying the tapestry and have now got it rigged up on a proper frame which Joan very kindly got made for me in Owo.

Our Group meetings are going well, I think. The small group discussions help the more reticent people to talk .... and we are beginning to get to know each other in our groups

An amazing thing happened on Saturday. Richard suddenly turned up to greet me for my birthday with a gorgeous big card and 3 super pouffes from the North. He came all this way! He is now the Principal of a Teacher TC near Yelwa which is on River Niger to the North of Kainji Lake. I haven't seen him since 1974 so it was a real joyful reunion. He stayed here for lunch and then we talked and prayed together before he went back. He has a terrible job with a big college of 580 students of 16 classes but only 15 teachers. They have no water, so all water supplies must come from Yelwa 20km away. It was very good to see him, and very nice of him to remember my birthday - so it made my 40th birthday rather special. I am having a small party on Friday. I have invited 24 people of whom maybe 4 will not be able to come.

I did my second effort on the radio last week - on Keeping a Flower Garden. I am now asked to prepare something on the meaning of Christmas to families. So that's very interesting.

I have spent a good deal of time in the past week going up and down to the hospital about a boy, Abiodun, aged 12 whose mother is at the Leper Settlement and only has one leg. The boy is very undernourished but seems to have some big abscess inside his abdomen. Some of this was drained off today and he is having 2 pints of blood tonight and tomorrow. The nurse told me that he may be sent to UCH Ibadan. He is in a very poor condition - so we are all praying that he will be healed and get well again. His father is a polio case who farms in Ondo. He has a stick and one good leg. We have been trying to visit Abiodun pretty frequently, but it is not easy. No one from the Settlement is allowed to go to the ward. I received your card and letters on Monday - thank you for them and all your continued love.

With love Elizabeth

Vining Centre
13th November 1977

Dear Ma and Daddy,

Thank you for your birthday card, and letters. I think I told you in the last letter that I didn't really celebrate my birthday on the 8th - but I had a party on the 11th - Friday. It was a nice, relaxed event - the staff of VC and a few close friends - Fred, Sheila, Pat, and Francis - the Taylor-Woodrow Fred and Linda - Dr. and Mrs. Adu (she is German), Inga and Eyesorun for a short time. Several invited couldn't come for one reason or another. We had curry and bits with birthday cake (made by Sheila) and sponge (made by Fred) and small cakes (made by me) afterwards. On Wednesday afternoon I played tennis with Mr. Taiwo and beat him 6 - 1 much to both our surprise since he usually beats me. He said it must be because of my birthday!

Most of this week has been taken up with worrying about Abiodun and trying our best to help him. He began to get very weak as from last weekend and on Wednesday when the doctors saw him, they suggested that he should be transferred to UCH Ibadan, because they were unsure of the diagnosis and felt more tests were needed. So, we made elaborate arrangements for him to go on Saturday morning. Two VC students were to accompany the ambulance and the staff nurse, and I were to go in my car to Ibadan with Inga so that I could arrange for people to visit him while he is in UCH. His mother has an amputated leg and is a leper and his father has a polio leg and walks on one leg and a stick - and is sick on his farm so can't come to Akure to help. Everything was set and I left Akure at 8am and reached UCH about 12 and then sat in the emergency room till 1.20. I then phoned to Akure (a miracle that I got through to the Hospital and that Sheila was there in the ward!) - to hear that they had never left because Abiodun had gone into convulsions and had been put on oxygen and so was not fit to move. So, I then went to Immanuel. College and arranged with Emmanuel Gbonigi that if Abiodun came to Ibadan on Monday that they would visit him from there.

So, we returned to Akure in the evening, and I found Abiodun sedated and on a drip, but more peaceful. We are praying hard. He is very sick. My main job seems to be going to inform the mother the latest - which is not very easy.

On Sunday morning I came from Akure to Ikare to stay the night with Jane and David Lewis. It is our Half Term, so I had planned to come on Saturday am but went to Ibadan instead. It is nice to have a break in Ikare even if it's a bit short.

With much love

Elizabeth

Vining Centre
20th November 1977

Dear Ma and Daddy,

Thank you for your letters, including my bank statement. Please Daddy, don't worry about the 9p a debit. I am perfectly happy to pay it. I use the account so seldom that it really doesn't matter. I only pay out of it for birthdays and so on. I am just happy that there is £48 in it. Thank you for the £3 balancing it.

I think that I wrote to you from Ikare last weekend. On Monday morning I returned and found that Abiodun had died during the morning. Sheila had stayed up all night with him in the hospital. Everyone was very upset as you can imagine - but the people in the hospital were marvellous. A deputation from there went to tell Abiodun's mother at the Settlement. I think in fact God was especially good to me and I was out of Akure when the crises about Abiodun took place - and so other people coped. Then when I came back, I was able to take my own share. I went with the father to the hospital and collected the corpse and we then returned to the Settlement for a very moving funeral and burial service. About 40 of Fiwasaiye were there - some VC students - the sisters and Father Joseph who led the service. So many people were concerned. The schoolgirls collected N100 and gave it to the parents. I think it brought some measure of comfort to them.

On Wednesday there was another crisis at the Settlement because an old man was in great pain with 'hernia' trouble. The Leprosy Officer and I took him to see Dr. Sijuade at the hospital. We had to wait for an hour and a half and eventually saw the doctor at 3.45 to be told that it was "strangulated" BUT that he wasn't prepared to admit the man because since he has leprosy people would 'talk' and the good name of the hospital would be spoilt!! So, he gave the man an injection and sent us back to the Settlement and told us to pray!! I was very upset. The only good thing was that Sijuade said he would speak to the Surgeon to see if he could help. Anyway, I went away and hoped that the man wouldn't die in the night and arranged through Sister Mildred that he could be taken to Owo the next day to the Catholic Hospital. But at 9.30 that night our prayers were answered because Sijuade phoned to say that the Surgeon - from UCH would operate then and that they would fetch the man from the Settlement in their car. This they did - he was operated - and admitted on the veranda - and is OK. Amazing.

With much love

Elizabeth.

Vining Centre
27th November 1977

Dear Ma and Daddy,

Good to get the letter of 16th November - received 26th. I think post is slow because we had 2 Public Holidays because of a Moslem Festival last week. This week has been busy and hot, but I am lucky to have had water - usually in the night - but so far, no great shortage. They are saying that there is drought again and that the rains this year were very poor on the Sahara fringes. This means that the Niger is so low that the electricity people are already worried that there may not be enough force of water to make electricity, so we are having a system of cuts to try and save us from having a complete black out next February. In fact, it's not bad here - State Capital I suppose. We have no light from 5.30 - 7.30 each morning.

On Monday it was Sheila's birthday - it was a Public Holiday, so she was away with Joan in Owo over the weekend and then came back for a 'party' in the evening in her house.

On Tuesday we had our special prayer session. A man from the Catholic Charismatic group in Ibadan came to lead the prayers. He was a very fine person. Each person came out to one side of the circle and was 'prayed with' by 2 others laying their hands on them. It was an inspiring experience. I felt very moved by the prayers and since then have had a new joy and freedom - and a sense of 'release'.

On Thursday I went on an outing to Ogbomosho with the Lepers Welfare Committee. We were 9 of us in a bus from the Military Governor's Office. We set off about 8am and got back around 8.30pm. The road from Ede to Ogbomosho was terrible and everyone agreed that we would not return on it, so we took the main road to Oyo and Ibadan then Ife-Ondo-Akure. We went round the Baptist clinic for leprosy patients and the Baptist Hospital. It was an enjoyable outing because everyone got on well and we had a lot of laughs together - especially about people's inbuilt fears of leprosy. The Health Sister from Akure wouldn't open her flask of tea on the premises of the clinic and when we got back to the hospital, she washed every visible bit of her body. Mrs. Adinlewa wouldn't touch a fan that I had bought from a discharged patient. She wanted to fan herself, so she solemnly wrapped the handle in newspaper before holding it. We all hooted at her. She is a great character.

I hope that your plans for Christmas work out. I am not quite sure what I shall do. Ruth and her mother may come here. If they do, I shall stay put - but if they don't then I shall go to Onitsha and see Grace and others there.

The man with the strangulated hernia is doing fine and they are all looking after him in the hospital on the veranda. The girl Chike has had her operation in Ife - a Cystectomy. We sent 6 men in our bus to Ife on Wednesday and 3 of them donated blood for her. I went to see her on Saturday after the Harvest at the Settlement which was in the morning.

I am now to talk about Boxing Day and then New Year Resolutions on the Womens Hour. I haven't heard the programme yet! - although other people say - I heard your voice on the radio.

It is getting hotter - and the electricity is off this afternoon so there is no fan. It makes me feel very lethargic and disinclined to do anything.

With much love to you both

Elizabeth

Vining Centre

30th November 1977

Dear Ma and Daddy,

One point in your last letter I didn't answer - please can you ask Dr. Iliff to write and tell me exactly how much he has sent to Sheila's account. She won't know for ages from the bank. Then I can check up with Sheila if that's OK. It may be better in future to transfer the money directly through the Bank to my account in Akure - because there is a lot of trouble about foreign exchange deals here now. Some people have been sending millions of Naira overseas and there are big tribunals going on. Sheila is allowed to send half her salary home and she doesn't so I think she is covered, but it is not worth risking 5 years in prison - the food is not very nice apart from anything else!

We had a good group discussion meeting on Tuesday. The 6 of us in our group have got to know each other quite well over the past 6 weeks and this has been very valuable. We are - Sister Mildred from St. Louis - a music and BK teacher, Sister Catherine from St. Louis, Owo - a nurse, Olu Komolafe who is on the staff at St. Peter Teacher Training College, Taiwo from Agric who I play tennis with and Sister Veronica, a young and very shy novice sister at the Noviciate and Olu Olofintuade who is a graduate English Teacher at Fiwasaiye. We are 3 Anglicans, 3 Catholics and 1 Baptist.

The man with the strangulated hernia op was discharged on Wednesday. His wound is not quite healed up, so he must go for dressings to the hospital every 2 or 3 days. I went to Ife on Saturday and saw Chike the girl who has had cystectomy operation. She seems much better. I also tried to see Yomi and Kelu, but they were out - at a funeral in Ekiti! according to Jide. I went with Inga and did some shopping at Leventis on the University campus. The shop was very crowded - but prices are terrible and there are shortages of a lot of essentials. Last week we were short of petrol, gas, and flour. There is no coffee and no imported tinned foods. 1lb pot of jam cost N1.50. One large onion in the market in Akure costs N1 (that's 80p for a decent onion!!) Crazy! It looks as though Ruth, and her mother will be coming here for Christmas. I got through to Benin on the phone the other night which was a miracle.

One of our ex-students is in hospital in Ife. He was involved in an accident where all the passengers except himself died. He has had one leg amputated and the second one is in traction. He is very cheerful despite this disaster. Yomi is the doctor who amputated his leg.

We now have 2 weeks left of this term - we break up on December 16th so there is plenty to do. It is the end of the academic year so most of the women are leaving, together with the 3rd year men. So now we are preparing for exams. It's hot in the afternoons and this makes me weary.

With much love to you both

Elizabeth

Vining Centre
12th December 1977

Dear Ma and Daddy,

Thank you for letters - and for the information about the tinting of spectacles. I will pass it on to Doctor Akinyosoye in Ondo. I am happy to hear that you were able to hear Ian Petit in Hereford, and that you liked him too. It is also good to hear that Robert Barbour is such a good line, and that you have been able to link up with him.

I think that there have been some hold ups in the postal system. All letters are taking a long time. There was a near air crash at Lagos which I think disrupted the airport for a bit, then we had a couple of public holidays. All this apart from the fact that there are no extra facilities here for the 'Christmas rush'. In fact, we are already experiencing the December shortage of petrol. The queues in Akure are incredible. You can see 30 cars lining up for petrol at a time. It makes you want to stay at home rather than travel anywhere. You just must keep your eyes skinned for a lull in the lines or go out looking for petrol about 11 at night or very early in the morning. I was lucky on Friday because the mechanic, Sunday, took my car to mend it and he very decently spent about 2 hours on the line and brought the car back with a full tank. Wasn't that kind of him?

I will certainly be here in Akure for Christmas and Ruth and her mother will be coming here.

A very sad thing happened on Wednesday. I went to the hospital around 12 to discuss the Leper Settlement meeting with Mrs. Sijuade. She told me that Cornelius Olowomeye had been rushed down in the night from Ikare and that he was admitted in the hospital. I was just about to go to the ward to see how he was when a nurse came to say that he had just died! So, I went to the ward and found Victoria there weeping beside Cornelius who was dead in the bed. A real shock and a great tragedy. He must have had some internal haemorrhage because he was vomiting blood during the night. He had not been looking well for some time, and he had all those bouts in hospital before. Maybe it was the result of too much alcohol. He was not yet 50 and his dying is a great loss to the Diocese as well as to his family. As you can imagine Victoria was very upset. She came here to Mama Ademoye's house for the rest of Wednesday while messages were sent to their people in Ilawe and to the Church people in Ikare. I went to Fiwasaiye and collected Bolanle and then to Oyemekan school to get Gboyega.

They have 6 children, the eldest is training at Ile Abiye. The bishop came over from Ondo and they arranged for the funeral to be in Ilawe on Christmas Eve (not the brightest choice of day as far as I am concerned but there we are).

I was out at the Taylor Woodrow camp this morning and they were talking there about how some of their young men seem to be alcoholics and get drunk and then go off sick or have breakdowns. All very sad indeed.

We are having our Carol Service this afternoon, with the usual Christmas play. The principal is off at his home village doing the Harvest there so I expect he will be late. I don't think I have ever met someone who you can rely on so completely to be late for every event! I can't think of one thing that he has been in time for - except for services - since the beginning of the year.

In our group we are going to have a Carol Service on December 20th so our next meeting, this coming Tuesday is going to be a preparation for that. Last week we had our final meeting of the series so we are now thinking what can come next in the New Year.

On Thursday Inga came over with her projector and we looked at a film of the 1975 Expedition to Mount Everest - with Chris Bonnington the leader. It was rather sad because of the fellow who died.

On Monday Joseph Akinjo, the Catholic priest came to talk to our men about the changes that had taken place in the Catholic Church since Vatican II. It was very interesting and very worthwhile in opening a few windows for our somewhat ignorant Anglicans here. I felt that there was a real spirit of understanding and readiness to listen.

On Wednesday we had our Leprosy Settlement committee. Dr. Sijuade was in good form and very encouraged by our visit to Ogbomosho. Chike, the girl in hospital at Ife, was discharged on Thursday and Sister Mildred went to get her back. They said the bill would be N85! but when Archdeacon Olupona in Ife explained the circumstances of her being there - they cancelled the bill and gave her everything for free!! So that was very good.

On Wednesday, Thursday, and Friday we did our end of the year exams so as you can see it was a full week. I spent yesterday at home all day, marking books, and resting. Sheila came in the evening and rubbed my back for it ached. Also, I was weary because some young men who came as guests to the Archdeacon of Akure's daughter's wedding on Saturday came and stayed in our dormitory on Friday night - and they disturbed us all with a great lot of noise about 2.30am and so I didn't sleep at all well. Today I feel much better.

I am enclosing a cheque for £30 to be put in my account please. I am sorry that I haven't sent anything to you for Christmas - but I don't know what to send from here - and the Mail order people are a bit disappointing. Therefore, I am sending a cheque for some Christmas goodies - or to buy a small present from me. I feel that when I come home on leave is really my "Christmas" - both for giving and receiving presents. I have done about 6 inches of the tapestry, and I will enjoy doing more over the holiday period.

I haven't written my Christmas letter, as usual I reckon it will be a New Year letter. It would be good to synchronise one year I agree, but if I don't write that letter at half term then the beginning of December is just hopeless.

I am glad that Stuart and Jutka have decided to come to Malvern for Christmas. I'm sorry that I can't come too. Maybe it can be wangled next year. There is a Christmas Charter Flight for N230, and if John and Mary are coming, I shall be very tempted to come too. Inga is talking of going this year.

Martinian is back from Ossiomo this weekend, so it is very nice to have her around again. We have our final Commissioning Service on Thursday. Then the students will be away on Friday.

I shall be thinking about you all very much over the Christmas weekend. You can be thinking of us all at the funeral on Christmas Eve! I recorded a 'Christmas message' for the Radio Womens Hour - not quite up to the Queen. It wasn't particularly inspired either because I wrote it while I was sitting in the doctor's waiting room waiting for him to see the strangulated hernia man.

With much, much love - Elizabeth

P.S. I hope you get the letter of November 6th weekend eventually because it told all about Richard coming with pouffes all the way from Yelwa - Apply to Gemma if you have no letter.

Vining Centre
18th December 1977

Dear Ma and Daddy,

Thank you for your letter of November 30th. Post seems to be taking ages now. I hope that Lagos is not seizing up. They say that the Government has a deficit - a mixture of over-spending and a slump in the oil business. Two military governors have been "redeployed" in the past two weeks and a permanent secretary and 7 others in the Ministry of Works and Housing in Ondo State have been dismissed this last week, for malpractices.

This letter might reach you by Christmas Day because I hope to send it with some Taylor Woodrow men who are going home for Christmas. I went and had supper there last night - roast beef, beans, potatoes, parsnips and tinned fruit and cream. Very nice too.

Joan Steward from Owo heard on Friday that her father has died. He was a farmer in Yorkshire. The telegram took 6 days and arrived here on the day of the funeral which was a bit miserable. However, she got things organised and went down to Lagos hoping that there would be a night flight on Friday. She came back last night! All flights are fully booked until next Wednesday. Isn't that rotten?! She will stay with Sheila till then.

Last night during the night there was a horrible noise of an animal in pain. I thought a cat had been bitten by a snake or something. I shone my torch outside; but didn't go out. This morning I found that one of my duikers had been attacked, presumably by a dog and it was half eaten away at the back - and dead. Very sad. I may fatten the others and eat them.

On Friday Inga and I went to Ilawe with the Fabulujes - to greet Victoria Olowomeye. I think the whole town are sad about Cornelius dying. He was the first pastor ordained among their children. His father was one of the first baptised Christians there. There is a lot of 'talk' about Victoria - and why she didn't tell them that Cornelius was sick earlier, and other nasty rumours.

Last week was very busy up till Thursday when we had our Commissioning by the Bishop of Benin. I was kept at it - marking exams, writing reports and certificates, and checking all our cupboards etc. The students went off home on Thursday night/Friday morning.

Today, Sunday, I am going over to Ondo for the Ordination of 8 of our students.

Later: Isn't the ordination service long - especially in Yoruba with every hymn having about 6 verses. Today's service lasted from 11am to 1.30pm Then I went and had lunch with Inga and a snooze in her house before going up to Idanre to see Pat and Francis. I am trying to plan towards going up to the Rest House at Idanre for a night or two in the week between Christmas and New Year, and to persuade Pat and Francis and the children to come as well, with Ruth and her mother and me. It looks as though it might be a possible plan. I think it would be super to wake up in the morning and look out at the view across the Idanre Rocks.

Tokunbo reckons that it wasn't a dog that got my duiker but a bush animal like a hyena or wolf! He says that he was woken in the night because something was disturbing his rabbits and that the animal cut a hole in his rabbit cage. So, although I am sorry not to have saved my duiker, I am rather glad that I didn't go out for I might have been attacked by a hyena!! If it was. Maybe it was just a bush dog.

Next Tuesday we hope to have a carol singing session with our group. It will be at Fiwasaiye probably in their chapel.

On Thursday 22nd we will have a nice goat feast at the Settlement.

Ruth and her mother came on Friday and Jane Pelly will come to Sheilas - and Jane's nephew, Andrew, who is teaching near Ikare for a year.

On Saturday is Cornelius' funeral at Ilawe at 3. Sunday is Christmas day. HC here at 7am and Matins at 10. Probably Christmas Dinner at Sheilas on Sunday - she has a turkey. I have a duck and a chicken which I expect we shall have on Boxing Day. Mrs. Howard has brought a Christmas pudding.

I expect we shall have a Christmas party for the Settlement children on Boxing Day. Then Tuesday? to Idanre and maybe Wednesday or Wednesday/Thursday to Ikare and then on to Auchi and Benin with Ruth for the New Year.

I shall be thinking of you at home with Stuart and Jutka. It's cold here at nights - harmattan - 3 light blankets - 70 degrees F!!

With much love to you all, Elizabeth

Vining Centre
29th December 1977

Dear Ma and Daddy,

I am sending this letter with a Taylor Woodrow person who is travelling home, so I hope that you will get it quickly.

Today I am going off with Ruth and her mother. We are going to Ikare for 2 nights and then to Auchi and Benin. Ruth tells me that Eunice Russell is in Benin, so I hope to be able to see her while I am there.

We have had a happy Christmas. The funeral on Saturday was smooth. The only rather embarrassing thing was that I was asked to make some 'notes' about Cornelius at the VC - and I made notes - which I thought someone would use as a fact sheet for the 'appreciation' - but lo and behold the bishop read it all out 1.2.3. and some of it wasn't suitable.

Ruth and her mother came on Friday. On Christmas Day we had breakfast here with Jane and Sheila as well after the Communion Service - then we went to Sheila's house for Christmas Dinner - turkey and roast potatoes and cabbage and carrots with Christmas pudding from Moffat and ice cream. I made mince pies in the morning after listening to the Queen and with a background of the Service of 9 Lessons and Carols from King's College, Cambridge. We ate my mince pies in the evening at Sheila's house - very good too. I kept the mincemeat from last Christmas.

On Boxing Day, we went to Pat Akinbadewa's for lunch - she made turkey and rice. I had a duck and a chicken for the evening but after we had eaten so much in the afternoon, we decided to have cold food in the evening - so I had 9 people here for cold duck and chicken, potato salad, cabbage (cold) and some cold jollof rice followed by Christmas pudding made by Fred and trifle made by me. The nine people were Sheila, Jane, Ruth, her mum, Andrew (Jane's nephew), Ed and Fred and Guy and me. After supper some played scrabble, some mastermind and some did a jigsaw. We ate by candlelight on the veranda.

On Tuesday Ruth and her mother and I went up to Idanre and stayed the night in the Guest House up on the mountain together with Pat and Francis and their 4 children. It was a great adventure - sitting round a fire in the dark and cooking a pot of yams. We thought that it would be very cold in the night, and we carried up a lot of blankets but in fact it was warm. In the night there was a full moon and the place looked eerie. The guest houses are fully furnished but not yet opened and so everything was rather dusty and there were smelly dead lizards in the bathroom and the loo, so we didn't use those. Really a great deal of money has been spent on them so that it is ridiculous that they aren't officially opened because everything is ready. There is even a generator which works and gave us electric light - and a pump for water which worked on the next day when we had already left.

On Wednesday morning we went quite a long trek around the rocks with the son of the Oba in the old palace at Idanre. Then we came down. I went to a party in the afternoon at the local remand home. Now today Thursday we are going off for a few days.

I do hope that you had a very good Christmas. There was a fire in the General Post Office in Lagos on Christmas Eve so some people say that letters may be delayed as a result, so I took the chance to write this and send it with someone.

With much love to all

Elizabeth

Vining Centre,
6th January 1978
Epiphany Day.

Dear Ma and Daddy,

The post seems to have ceased up here over the Christmas and New Year holiday, so I am sending this again with someone going home by air. The reason for lack of post at this end may be the shortage of petrol, or due to a fire in the G.P.O in Lagos or just that everyone has had a good holiday.

I am sending my New Year letter along with this as you will see. I have not sent any copy to C.M.S so please can you do that when you have it duplicated.

I came back yesterday from my holiday with Ruth and her Mum. Everything went smoothly on our journey, and I enjoyed their company. We always sat round on our beds to drink tea both early in the morning and after afternoon siesta, which was very chummy.

We went to Ikare on Thurs. and Fri. nights and stayed with Jane and David Lewis. Then on Fri. we all went together to Guy's school at Okeagbe and walked around his farm and forestry plantation and lake which the boys dammed themselves. Guy is very neurotic and is always saying everything is 'too much’, but they have achieved a lot in his school.

On Sat. we set off for Auchi and stopped for a picnic up a little road we saw on the map North of Igarra. It was the road to Samonika – a small town in the hills. Much to our surprise the road was not quite as we had thought but full of cars, lorries and taxis from all over the Western and Mid-West States – hooting and honking and rushing up a very steep sandy road which we didn't attempt in our car. When we asked them what it was all for, we were told that you could get a very strong juju up there – to protect you from all troubles – and to solve all your problems. Amazing that so many people should be rushing up there.

We went to Auchi where we found Mary and Thankanma in the Teacher Training College. They have put the staff houses and the new college buildings in a bulldozed desert. They have been there for 3 months with no electricity or regular water supply and only a bed, a chair, and a table each – and a gas stove. Everything was very bare. Mary had been sick of fever and looked rather thin.

On Sunday we went to the New Year service and Archdeacon Ajomo was the preacher. He really ought to retire I felt – but at least his sermon was short and to the point. In the afternoon we returned to Benin.

On Monday Eunice Russell came to supper with us! She is on a 4 week's holiday in Nigeria -the first visit since 1958!! Her conclusion was that the roads and buildings had changed a lot – but the people and the confusion was just the same as ever. It was good to see her. She didn't really have a chance to see different places because petrol was such a headache over the holidays.

On Tues. I went to Onitsha with Jane Pelly in her van. I didn't enjoy the journey because the road was very full of traffic and Jane kept telling the driver what to do and what not to do and I had no confidence in his skill as a driver – but it was good to see Grace at Iyi Enu- and the Williams, the Beavers, Ann and John Phillips and Barbara Breeze who was up from Aba where she took over from Jane Backhouse. She will probably leave in April after only one tour because she found the church 'dead' and has felt that they had people capable of doing what she was doing if they put their mind to it. Grace is in Iyi Enu teaching. She is waiting for a van before she can go to her riverine area. It seems that she has lost all her main belongings because she left them in Ikerre with the Krols and they say they don't know what has happened to her barrels – rather a nasty blow.

I came back to Akure yesterday – Jane Pelly very kindly loaned me her car and her driver, so I had a comfortable journey. He was a good driver.

I was at Sheila's last night for supper. Martinian should come here this evening. I hope to go to Ibadan on Sunday to do some shopping for the beginning of term on Monday and to go and see the Failings at the Institute.

Tues., we have our Prayer Fellowship.

Wednesday is the evening for Leper Settlement Committee.

And so, the term will start again on Friday Jan 13th, and we shall be back in the routine.

I hope that you had a Happy Christmas in Malvern. I expect I will get your letters in due course when everything is sorted out.

With much love,

Elizabeth

P.S. I have no other copy of my 'letter' so I should be glad if you can send me one. I hope it's not too much trouble for you.

Vining Centre,
16th January 1978.

Dear Ma and Daddy,

Lots of letters this week – a sort of Christmas clear out in the New Year. It is good to hear all your news of Christmas time. I am glad to hear that the record from Sheila arrived. Don't send it in the post. It is almost bound to get warped. If I think of anyone who can carry it here, I will let you know, otherwise keep it. I have written to Anna Young to thank her for the £10. Isn't that good of her?

I am sorry to hear that Daddy's legs are stiffer. Maybe you should seriously ask doctors to advise about hip operations. Thank you for the Geographical Magazine. I haven't had it for some time, but I expect it will come one day. The same is true of some book parcels that I sent myself in September.

Martinian is not a nurse - but a teacher -but she learnt enough at Ossiomo to be able to help to organise the dressings of the leper's sores etc. The surgeon who did the hernia op is from U.C.H but working in the meantime in Akure Hospital. I haven't written to the

Cowan's for their £2. Is it your circular or mine? I think it is yours. I am glad you got over to Symonds Yat. Wasn't that very thoughtful of Mary Jenkins? Really, we are very lucky with our kind friends. Dear Sheila gave me £50 for Christmas to buy new curtains for my bedroom. She also gave me a new fridge – by swapping my small fridge with a bigger one which is not only brand new but it has a bigger freezer compartment so I can keep more meat in it if I want to.

Last Sunday I went to Ibadan – and had lunch with Inga on the way and then a chat with Yomi and Kelu in Ife. I stayed with Lynn and Elaine Failing who have just come out to the Institute in Ibadan from Crowther Hall. It was good to see them. They were camping rather because they are waiting for their loads to arrive. Their baby, Aaron, has not been v.well and had diarrhoea for 17 days. He was being tested at U.C.H to see if he had coeliac disease.

I managed to get in and out of Ibadan on both Mon. and Tuesday without getting stuck in any traffic jam so that was a real achievement. I also got several useful books and materials – but spent a lot of money on very little. Prices of so many things have doubled – or more!

I returned on Tues. We had our prayer group that night – I wasn't in a very prayerful mood! On Wed. we had Leper Settlement Committee and decided to have another Leprosy Week – Mar 13th – but that we should divide up the responsibility for different parts of the organisation. On Thursday Sheila and I went to a Cocktail party at Taylor Woodrow to meet their Director from UK. It was rather dull really- and a few of the men were getting drunk towards the end. I was very upset on getting home to discover a note from Joseph Kumuyi saying that he was just off to U.S.A and had called to say goodbye! I saw him briefly in the hospital last Friday and he never said a word about it then. He is a 'surprising' fellow...... On Thursday we had a staff meeting lasting from 9 -12.15am.

On Friday I spent the morning nursing my 'hurt' about Joseph's departure by keeping company with Martinian at the Settlement, Sheila for coffee and Bisi Sijuade who had the day off so was at home. On Saturday Sheila and I went to Owo to see Joan and then Sheila, Marion – the new CUSO girl at Fiwasaiye and Bisi Sijuade all came here for supper which was very nice. Today I was at Sheila's for lunch, and we have the Settlement Open Air this afternoon – then I am going to St Louis for supper. I find the best medicine for low spirits is to go and see your friends.

I had a nice letter from Jane Backhouse. I think she is finding retirement rather tough. Maybe you could contact her. It's not so far away. I will try to write to her.

The new women students seemed very quiet when I met them for the first time yesterday A few can understand English but there are several blanks in that direction. I expect I shall get more enthusiastic about the term when it gets started properly. I need to have a good sort out of papers and things. I don't know how some people contrive to be neat!

I hope you have received the Link letter.

With much love to you both,

Elizabeth

Vining Centre,
22nd January 1978

Dear Ma and Daddy,

I received your letter of Jan 7th earlier this week with news of the New Year and the Dunlop's farewell.

We have just completed the first week of the term now, so things are back into the College routine. We have found beds for all the existing students and have turned a garage into another bedroom. We are working on the completion of the chapel extension – which has been standing in a half-built fashion for the past year ….it is shown in Gemma's album as Cornelius Folly!

The new women are not as illiterate as their husbands made out. Several of them can cope with English. There are 4 who are Yorubas who have never been to school and are a blank wall as far as I am concerned and 1 Urhobo who never went to school. I started her on Laubach's literacy book …. and I followed the Teacher's manual exactly as it says you should …. and it seemed to work. She could read a page by the end of the week!! much to my surprise and joy. We have a nice smiley 'Christian' Senior Student for the men this term so that is good too. My woman Senior Student is a capable woman too so I feel that the term has started well.

On Tuesday evening we had our Prayer Group. Sheila and I decided that we have got a bit stuck on praying these days and so we would try and meet each evening and do a Meditation together from a book by Jim Wilson. We have done it 3 times so far.

On Wednesday afternoon I went up to Ikare with Mama and Eyesorun to sympathise with a clergyman there – Canon Jaiyeoba- whose son aged 27 had been killed in a road accident in Maiduguri. He was with the National Youth Service Corps. Very sad. He was their first son and they had struggled to educate him through to university and all their hopes were in him. It was a sad day, but I am glad we went.

On Saturday I went up to Ikerre to see if I could find out anything about Grace's loads – but I drew a blank. The barrels she left with the Krols seem to have disappeared. Then I went on the see Mrs. Oriola – an American negress married to a Nigerian. She made doughnuts in her new doughnut maker that she had just brought from the States.

Today I went for a nice peaceful walk with Sister Martinian in the Agric.

It seems that the high up people in the Ondo State Government are being questioned this week about what happened to the money given to a company called Lastra who were supposed to be building roads but obviously were lining their own pockets.

Much love,

Elizabeth

Vining Centre

28th January 1978

Dear Ma and Daddy,

Thank you for your nice long letter of Jan 14th. It is good that you are enjoying your St Matt. Group. Does that mean that you aren't going to the cell anymore? Maybe it is good that one changes a 'group' every so often. I feel that our prayer group is in the doldrums now. I feel that we are not being real with each other – and nor are we getting to know each other as human beings. We need to do a real course of study during Lent.

Sheila and I have been doing a short meditation each evening – following Jim Wilson – growth in prayer. It is the ideas of contemplative prayer, and I am finding that very helpful.

I am sorry to hear that Daddy is still having a hernia trouble and that his walking has not been so easy this winter. I hope that Dr Sinclair has been able to help. I have been feeling especially well in the past few weeks I am happy to say. I decided to take my malaria tablet only once a week, as prescribed. Then our meditation has been

' I AM with you always – and that means NOW' and I think that has made me feel better.

Very good news reached us on Tuesday – Mrs. Kohli is coming at last- she should arrive this coming Friday. It will be nice to have her around again.......but I think she will need some 'caring for' as she settles down here without her husband and family.

We had a bit of an upset on Monday because the Provost of Ondo sent his brother's wife here expecting her to be admitted .... when she is not expected until Jan 1979. I think he expected Fabuluje to overrule everything and let his relative come here for 3 years. I sent her away. Fabuluje wrote him a rather hasty note. The provost referred it all to the bishop! So, then I had to waste a lot of time putting all the facts on paper and trying to smooth it all out. It was alright in the end.

Yesterday I had a day out with Mama Ademoye. We went to Ile Oluji first for a wedding. Mama knew the bridegroom's family. The bride was in my class at St Monica's. It was a very nice wedding. Afterwards we went to greet Archdeacon and Mrs. Okunfulure – the retired Archdeacon of Akure who lives in Ile Oluji. Then we went on to St Monica's and we went together with Inga to Okeigbo to visit Mrs. Ojo whose husband died suddenly last week of a heart attack. Mrs. Ojo is a great character who has a shop in Akure and is a member of St David's Church. She was very grateful that we went to see her. We then returned to Ondo and went to greet the bishop. He and his wife were sitting comfortably in their sitting room watching wrestling from Manchester or Blackpool or some place on the colour Tele! It is an incredible world. Mrs. Ojo was keeping the tradition of Okeigbo until her husband is buried (probably Feb 28th) she will not eat any food cooked in her own house. She will only eat food cooked and prepared by friends and relatives in other houses.

Today I am having a quiet day at home. I am reading a book on the life of Lenin!

Much love to you both,

Elizabeth

Vining Centre
5th February 1978

Dear Ma and Daddy,

Thank you for your letter which enclosed the circular letter. I don't think the latter reads very smoothly – and it's rather depressing. However, I will have to write another better one.

I am writing this letter on ordinary notepaper because Linda Roberts is going home on Wednesday for a couple of weeks and so I shall ask her to take the letter. I am afraid this method makes letters come in fits and starts but it is nice to have a quicky.

This week has been HOT – then on Friday and Saturday there was no electricity till evening-so no cold water – and no petrol. My fridge defrosted so that my butter was runny, and my meat was bleeding and the fish ponging, so I cooked the meat and fish and took them together with the butter to the Taylor Woodrow fridge (they have their own generator and are fully air conditioned) When I went there yesterday with my 'hot' food – they were sitting round their 'bar' in the living room eating tinned mussels, cod roe and cheese! So, I joined on! How the other half lives.

On Friday afternoon Mrs Kohli arrived. I spent – or rather wasted- a good deal of time on Wed and Thursday trying to check up that the Ministry of Health were sending transport to Lagos to fetch her. It all worked out well in the end. I suggested that she stayed the W/E with me here, but she is very determined that the Ministry should take responsibility for her accommodation, so she has a room in the Oyemekan Hotel. It is a rather dreary room on the ground floor with 2 beds occupying most of the space – and then 2 metal upright chairs -so you are forced to sit on the bed.

I had a good lecture on Monday night – on Series 3 Communion Service. But I was very tired on Tuesday – partly because Monday was a busy day but also because some retched Revivalists were shouting through a loudspeaker - Alleluia and Praise the Lord and so on …. until 2.30am. The result was that I felt very unrevived the next morning!

The group on Tuesday was quiet and prayerful. We still haven't decided what to do for Lent. We shall have to have inspiration quick!

I am going to do the Lent Services at Fiwasaiye this year. I hope to make out a form of service that will be the same each week and then I want to take the 10 Commandments as the basis of what to say.

Mrs. Kohli is sleeping in the hotel, but she had supper with me on Friday – then I fetched her on Sat afternoon, and we spent the afternoon and evening at Sheila's. Today I fetched her here in the morning and Sheila came for lunch. Now we have had a rest and I will take Mrs. Kohli our to see Eyesorun and look around the other hotels in the place to see if she fancies any of them more than her present one. She will probably find out tomorrow how long she will be in a hotel before she gets a house. I hope it is not too long- and I hope too that she gets transport soon so that she is mobile. Otherwise, I shall be continually worrying about her being bored and lonely. She is really very easy – but wants to sit and chat all day – she doesn't read much. And Lent is not a very good time for entertaining people to supper -

Mon. night – teach 7.30 – 9
Tues. night - pray 8.00 – 9.30
Wed. night – Lent service at V.C 6-7
followed by
Fiwasaiye at 8 or 8.30
Thurs night Lep Settlement committee every 4th week.

One fellow in the Ministry of Health – called Joshua Omodara is on a course in Birmingham. I may have mentioned him to you – I can't remember. He was a bit of a pain in the neck at one time coming round here 'visiting' and inviting me out which I constantly refused because he is married, and I have no wish to be 'involved' with him. On the other hand, he is always very friendly and helpful when I go to the Ministry about the Lepers, and he helped Martinian to get her post. He is the 2nd to the Permanent Secretary. He sent me a post card yesterday from the Bull Ring so I thought I would reply and give him your address and phone number. He might like to come over to Malvern for a day out – and talk about the old days in Nigeria and look at your photo albums. Anyway, if he phones or contacts you, you will know who it is.

I am sending a Daily Times with Linda for Annette and the Priory people.

There is a great lot of activity in the town now with Taylor Woodrow bulldozing part of the market. This means that the people are moving to another place – so you can see them struggling along the roads carrying chairs or benches or whole market stalls on their heads or pushing them in hand trucks.

Ash Wed tomorrow – I don't know yet if we are having a Quiet Day as usual. The principal disappeared to Ibadan yesterday! (As usual)

I must go and do some shopping with Dr Kohli and then take these letters to the post.

It is a bit worrying to have the hernia come out again …. but at least it's not an unknown sickness! I shall be looking forward to news of the visit to Mr Nicholas.

With my love and prayers,
Elizabeth

Vining Centre
12th February 1978

Dear Ma and Daddy,

I hope you will have got last week's letter quickly through Linda - and that you won't have to wait too long for this one.

Lent has started this week – it seems rather 'busy' so far because although we had a Quiet Day on Wed. with no lessons, I was taking the service at Fiwasaiye in the evening. I decided to get 3 men to help to dramatise Cain and Abel so by the time we had practised it here and at Fiwasaiye – and rearranged the benches in Fiwasaiye chapel the performance took up a good deal of time. I think it was worthwhile because the girls listened well even though there was no electricity, and everything happened by flickering candlelight.

It means that during Lent I am busy on Mon. Tues. Wed. evenings and, I have something on most Sundays. This last Sunday I went to the village Church at Iju and talked about a mirror – we are supposed to be made in the image of GOD …. and we need to look and see how we are doing during Lent.

Our Tuesday fellowship is going to be studying the I AM sayings in John's Gospel starting here this Tues with I AM the Bread of Life.

On Monday evening I am doing something about the Reformation – Wycliffe and Luther. Then Wesley and the Missionary Movement so I did a good deal of browsing in books to prepare for that at the weekend.

Dr Kohli is still in her hotel. I guess she will be there for a few weeks. She has met up with the Jahns and some other Indians so that is good. She is always wanting Sheila or I to go and eat with her in her hotel – but it is not so easy to find the time. Apart from the fact that I am not very comfortable eating N4 a meal very frequently.

The weather here just now is extremely hot and tiring. I sleep with the fan blowing but wake up in the morning feeling only like staying longer in bed! It may rain in the next few days – that will be a mercy because it will clear the air a bit.

Sheila is going to Benin for her Half Term this W/E and Mrs. Kohli may come and stay with me on Sat/ Sun. The following W/E is our Half Term as I hope to go to Ibadan and spend some time with Grace and see the Failings and Titi Ikotun and maybe Bishop and Mrs. Okunsanya.

Mrs Adu – the German wife of a doctor here has had her 7th baby this week – so I went with Eyesorun to visit her in Ijare (about 6 miles away) on Sunday afternoon. Mrs. Adu is a very cheerful pleasant person- I must try to get to know her better. She is also a doctor.

What news of the hernia?

With much love and prayers,

Elizabeth

Vining Centre
19th February 1978

Dear Ma and Daddy,

Very good this week – 2 letters from you – one of Jan 31 and one of Feb 6th from Daddy.

Thank you for paying for my postage. You seem to be busy as usual. I am glad that you were able to get to London to Jutka's exhibition. I am sure that they would be very grateful that you went. It is good that Jutka is getting orders. She will have plenty of work to do at home afterwards.

This week has been much as last week – we did Naboth's Vineyard story at Fiwasaiye on Wed. and had a good gathering here at the Prayer Fellowship on Tuesday. We took I AM the Bread of Life as the theme. I was interested in Eyesorun's thought that it was amazing that everyone sat down in rows so there was organisation and order and so everyone got a fair share. She thought this was a very important message for the Ministries – and people organising petrol queues!

On Friday evening I was very tired. I hadn't slept well on some nights – either it was too hot, or my mind was too busy. But Martinian came and we had a good natter on Friday night, and she invited me to the Convent for lunch on Saturday. I went there around 11am and did my tapestry on their veranda and then I had lunch with them and slept for nearly 2 hrs. I felt much better afterwards. It was like a day off in a different environment. Yesterday evening I went to collect Mrs. Kohli and brought her here to stay the night. She is staying on tonight too because it is a Public Holiday tomorrow, so she won't be at work. She invited me to lunch in her hotel- prawn curry! So that was rather nice. I met a Scotsman there from St Andrews who is fixing up the refrigeration plant in the mortuary in the hospital.

I have been reading about the Reformation and hope to tell our men something tomorrow about Wycliffe, Huss, and Luther. I found a very interesting book about the writing of the Prayer Book- it's an old book from our Library. There are lots of things about Church History that I don't know.

Mrs. Kohli has been allocated a house in a new housing estate for Junior staff. She is happy to think of moving out of the hotel – but she sees all sorts of snags in the house.... it is all rather amusing to me – she is a bit of a snob and has always had a real Colonial type house. As for this one it has no veranda – no garage – no servants quarters and would you credit it? Only ONE ceiling fan. She is fan mad and has my fan going day and night whereas I only use it if it is very hot in the afternoon. Now I am sitting in my cardigan because I find the fan cold!!

With much love to you both,

Elizabeth.

Vining Centre
25th February1978.

Dear Daddy,

This is to wish you a very Happy Birthday on March 4th. I hope that you can do something special on the day. I am at present in Ibadan staying in the house of Grace Ohikhena for my half term holiday. It is good to be with Grace, but it is much hotter here in Ibadan and I feel very sweaty. Also, they keep the windows closed in their living room at night which I think means that it is very stuffy in the morning. I hope to post this letter to you in Ibadan so hopefully it will reach you a bit sooner. I hope to go and see Bishop Okunsanya and Mrs.

Okunsanya sometime today or tomorrow. It is a very long time since I saw them. The traffic in Ibadan can be very bad so I hope I don't waste too much time in Go-Slow.

I will go back to Akure on Sunday – and have lunch with Yomi and Kelu on the way – and stay with Inga on Sun. night. We start our term again on Tuesday – so it's a nice break. I hope I shall also get a swim while I am here. Tonight, I shall go with Grace to a cousin of Titus and have dinner with them. They are entertaining a Director of Heinemann Books (who he works for), The Director is an Englishman, I think.

I am sending a card in a separate envelope – but I have left my cheque book behind so can't enclose anything in it- but will do so later.

With much love – I shall be thinking of you especially on March 4th.

Elizabeth

Vining Centre
5th March 1978

Dear Ma and Daddy,

A great day on Wednesday! Linda Roberts came back with 2 records, letters, and chocolates. Super! It is good to hear more quickly sometimes. I have put the chocolates in Sheila's fridge to save them for Easter. I am afraid I will open them if I keep them here. The records are lovely. I have not yet had a chance to listen to them completely but hope to do so this evening at Sheila's. I still haven't solved my own needle problem despite everyone's efforts.

Yesterday was Daddy's Birthday. I hope you got the letter I wrote in Ibadan. I am afraid the card is still here! I will still send it together with a card for Mothering Sunday – today. I was hoping to get a quick Taylor Woodrow postage but haven't succeeded yet. I have been thinking of you both!

My Lenten commitments are coming to an end which is a great relief. This past week I was out on Tues. Wed and Thurs. evenings with Prayer Fellowship, Fiwasaiye Lent Service and Leper Settlement Committee. On Fri afternoon I went to take Dr Kohli out shopping and my clutch cable snapped so the expedition came to an abrupt halt. We pushed the car to the side of the road. Dr Kohli got a lift back to her hotel and I trekked round to find the mechanic -Sunday. He came and pushed the car back to his workshop and fixed it by Sat. midday.

Dr Kohli is the mother of Rajan who came to our house when he was at Bloxham College. He is now at Rugby doing a University Course. Mrs Kohli is an eye specialist and the whole family were here before. She has now come back for 2 years to earn the money to pay for Rajan's fees in UK. Because of inflation the money they saved in England is not enough- and they can't send money from India to U.K for fees. She is in a room in a hotel in Akure – but she comes to Sheila or me for the weekends. She is here now – reading an Agatha Christie while I am writing to you. Her husband is a Pathologist, and he has stayed in Delhi because he has a laboratory there. It is a real sacrifice to educate their son – but it is not easy for her in the hotel because you are couped up in a small room by yourself for so much of the time.

I am sorry that Ma had 2 days in bed – perhaps you caught cold going up to London?

Today I went to take the morning service at St Thomas' Church in the town. It is a special service that the Vicar there is arranging for students. I talked to them about Ebun .... it always goes down well with students, and I think gives them 'hope' about helping mentally sick people.

Sheila came for lunch. I had a giant piece of pork (Mrs. Kohli only eats pork and chicken – not beef) and carrots, yam, and dodo (plantain) followed by jelly and instant whip which I got in Ibadan last week.

I had a letter from John telling me about their plans for building a house and that they may not come for Christmas after all – but they still may. I'll save up ....but I am not banking on coming till June 1979. I am thinking of helping Martinian for part of the holidays this year.

With much love to you both – Elizabeth

Vining Centre
12th March 1978.

Dear Ma and Daddy,

A great long screed from you this week – very nice. I am afraid my letters are rather 'shorties' just now – maybe in the holidays you will have a better 'go'. This week on Monday there were riots in some of the schools in Ekiti. Children went out on supposedly ' Peaceful Demonstration' but ended up stoning cars and blocking roads. It was somehow instigated by teachers who were on strike the previous week on account of salary levels and loans which the Govt had not given.

The result was that the Military Govt closed all the schools and Training Colleges in Ondo State. So, all the pupils went home on Tues. This doesn't affect us here, but it means that Sheila and others are not working, and no one knows when they will start schools again. The 'negotiations' about the matter seem to be in deadlock.

The road building in the centre of the town is making the place into a place you want to avoid. You take ages getting to and fro to the Bank – and I spent 40 minutes going over to see Mrs. Adinlewa one day. However, the work is due to be finished by July so it's not so long. The T.W people say that it should be finished in time provided the Govt pay them. They say they are owed N6million now – and that some other companies have stopped work on the road they are building because they are owed so much money. The economy of the country is I think going to go through a difficult time in 1978 because according to the newspapers the Development Plans presumed a high revenue from oil which is not working out in practise. I heard on the radio this week that there are going to be further cuts in imported foods.

On Wed. Pat Akinbadewa brought me a kitten which she has allowed to go partly wild. It is to be handed on to the Oriola's at Ikere. It has led me a dance because it refuses to be picked up – so if you want to handle it you have to catch it. I have spent a long time calling 'Kitty Kitty – come'.... and it has run away. Yesterday I thought it had disappeared completely, but it is back today. It cries in the night too!

The Failings from Ibadan came on Saturday and stayed the night and went back on Sun. It was good to have them. They brought news.......which I hope is true that Myrtle <u>is</u> coming to Ikare after all and hopes to come in Sept/Oct. That's a miracle! Because we had given up hoping for anything at this end, but it has happened at the London interview end I gather. Isn't that good?

On Sun. Mrs. Kohli wade a gorgeous meal at Sheila's house and I went with the Failings, and the Roberts were there, Ed is back, and Joan was over from Owo. We have done well with Indian food this week because on Friday we went to the Jahns. They are vegetarian Hindus of some sort, and we had a lovely meal there. On Thurs. we had supper at Eyesorun's house!

Now there are 3 weeks left of our term so I must start preparing exams. We are also celebrating Easter here. I am hoping to prepare a

Palm Sunday dramatised reading with the men ....but I am not quite sure when we are going to fit in the rehearsals.

Our rains have started early this year, so it is already quite cool – that's great.

I am glad that Joshua Omodara was able to come over. He sent me a PC from Winchester Cathedral with a promise of sending me your pictures.

I had a letter from Sister Gemmel this week. She is in the Drapers Wing of St Christopher's Hospice and sounds in great form. She had some ops last year and was in hospital for a lot of the time. She says it was the most 'marvellous time'. She had 'Hallelujah Anyway' pasted on her locker.

With much love to you both,

Elizabeth.

Vining Centre,
19th March 1978

Dear Ma and Daddy,

Great to have your 2 letters this week telling of your visit to Crowther Hall. It sounds as though it was quite a day. I am sorry to hear that Mr Nicholas has died. Somehow you don't expect your doctors to die before you! I shall look forward to hearing news of how the plans for going to St Luke's progress.

I do hope it's true that Myrtle is coming to Ondo State. We shall have to wait and see for further developments.

Today it is very hot and there has been no electricity since during the night last night. Sheila and Mrs. Kohli and Guy came here for lunch – rather chewy chicken! We are having our special Palm Sunday service this evening – with acting out Peter's denial and Pilate washing his hands etc. I have been busy all week rehearsing it. It is a moving service if it is well done. The students in Year 3 are taking it ......so that means about 36 people to cope with – and give them all something to do. We have invited several friends. I hope some of them can come.

We start exams tomorrow – for 3 days – Mon. Tues. Wed. Then we shall be celebrating Easter here on the compound together.

The schools in Ondo State are still closed and no announcement has yet been given about opening them again. They won't be open now till after Easter. 16 Principals or teachers have been taken to court and are to be accused of inciting riots on Mar 4th.

Our Budget Day is April 1st and all the talk in the newspapers indicate that it is going to be a stringent budget. There are already cuts announced in the things people can buy from overseas. It appears there has been big overspending and now loans from overseas on a large scale. All these building contracts are frightfully expensive, and I think that prices are made very high by the overseas firms. Everyone wants to make a good fat profit and if there isn't enough oil money to pay for it there is going to be a big 'gap' somewhere.

Later, Sun. Night 10.15

I have light and water- it just came. We had our special service, but it would have been better if we had had it a bit earlier because it was getting dark towards the end which meant we didn't see very clearly. Also, I was a bit disappointed that only a few 'visitors' came – and we had invited about 50. Sheila was coming – but she slept till6.30 so missed it – that was disappointing. Fred and Ed came and afterwards we went and ate ham sandwiches in his 'caravan'. He lives among the electronic machines – but it means he always has electricity which is a bonus.

Next Sunday will be Easter Day. Jane will be here from Benin I expect. I shall be thinking of you both at home, and the good folk at St Matthias.

With much love,
Elizabeth.

Vining Centre
27th March 1978

Dear Ma and Daddy,

Thank you for the Easter card – and for the chocolates. I am keeping them in Sheila's fridge so they will spin out. We all had one after our Easter Sunday lunch yesterday. Super.

On Saturday I went for a picnic with Sr Martinian.We went together to Idanre and climbed up the hill. Then returned to the Akinbadewa's house for a picnic lunch up on their rocks. It was good. In the afternoon I went to an engagement ceremony of Mrs. Adinlewa's niece to Dr Adetunji who is the doctor who is now helping at the leper settlement on a weekly clinic basis. It was an enjoyable affair – although the women who take the main part do enjoy spinning everything out to the maximum. I sat next to Chief Adeniran. He sends greetings to you.

We kept Holy Week thoroughly with a service each day. Rev Adeyelu took the service from Mon. to Wed., and I found it a bit of a penance. His delivery is very bad, and he is difficult to listen to. Rev Ayodele took Thurs. HC and Fri am. This I enjoyed. On Thursday he talked about the Last Supper and the meaning of Communion in an interesting fashion and on Friday he took Rev 4 as the theme – 'Worthy is the Lamb that was slain'. He brought out very strongly the Triumph of Good Friday. We had a 3-hour service 12 – 3 which Fabuluje took – but I felt that he filled it with words which was a pity. There were no silences or times for meditation or prayer.

Jane came from Benin late on Thursday evening and she has been staying with Sheila. Ed has joined us for most of the meals. They came to me on Saturday night, and we ate antelope. I decided to kill one of them because they don't do very well in wet season. I gave some of the meat to Mama and to Tokunbo, for Easter, but in fact there wasn't a lot of meat on it.

We finished our Women's exams on Wednesday, so I spent some time marking them. I declared a holiday on Thursday for the women so that Mama and I could have a rest! We break up for the holidays on the 30th and I plan to go off to Port Harcourt the next day to see some old students who live in Bonny. I hope also to manage to see Ann Goodchild in Umuahia. She is expecting a baby and has been in bed most of the time since Christmas.

Inga was here the other day. Bunmi has had measles – badly it seems. Really it is a ghastly responsibility to take on looking after someone else's child. I went to see the Taylor Woodrow people on Friday afternoon. They are becoming quite angry with the Ondo State Govt for not paying them the money they owe them. They say they may stop work on some sections as an effort to squeeze the money out of the Govt. So, relationships are not good there. The Federal Govt has just pulled all its money out of Barclay's Bank as a protest at their having shares in South Africa. There is a lot of talk in the papers of not dealing with anyone who has South African investments. If they take this to its conclusion it would mean that all the big construction firms at present working in Nigeria would get pushed out. We shall see. Our budget comes out on April 1. Everyone says it will be tight because oil money is less than expected.

With much love to you both,

Elizabeth

Vining Centre,
2nd April 1978.

Dear Ma and Daddy,

I am sitting on Grace's veranda at Iyi Enu Hospital where there is a gorgeous view right across the valley. Grace and Sheila and Eliz. Edmunds have just gone to the evening service in the chapel, and Ruth and Jane and I have stayed at home. I had not planned to come to Iyi Enu at all, but it has worked out very well so far.

The last week of our term was very busy, and I worked hard at reports and all the end of term arrangements. I worked flat out till Thursday evening and then scurried around to get ready to leave the next morning with Joan Steward to go to Port Harcourt. But Joan never arrived and so I decided to go with Sheila who was going to Onitsha, and then onto P.H on Monday. There is a principal's conference at Port Harcourt starting on Tuesday – and my aim is to go to visit some old students at Bonny while they are conferring.

In Benin Sheila and I picked up Ruth and then came on with her to Grace's place. We met Grace rather tired because she was just recovering from a fever and tummy upset and had been in bed for the past few days. We were very tired too. The plan had been to go up the Anambra River and stay a night in Grace's village. She is starting a health centre there – and has an idea that Sheila and I might like to start a Secondary School in the place!! We decided to only go for the day – to rest on Sunday....and I was very relieved. In fact, I nearly didn't go. I was just weary after the end of term and not sleeping well on Fri night because of all the taxis coming to collect the students. Anyway, I went.... we set out around 8am and drove to Oku Ocha on the River Anambra. We then waited about for some time and ate breakfast before climbing onto a boat that held about 30 people – we were only about 15 on it. You sat on planks at the side of the boat – all rather uncomfortable ......for 4 hours. We reached the village around 2 pm and walked along the sandy paths to the house where Grace has her clinic where we started to cook rice and tinned chicken over the oil stove while a whole heap of children gawped at us through the door and windows. It then transpired that the elders in the town wanted to welcome us – so we went to the sandy market square in the middle of the town and sat on benches with about 20-30 very ancient gentlemen squatting on stools wearing red hats. Some of the old men looked just like the pictures of the elders in ancient missionary days. Some had white paint round their eyes. The whole town was riddled with shrines – little covered shelters with odd tins and bottles underneath and a bamboo pole with a long white flag on it. Grace spoke to them all about her idea of community development there and they presented us with 4 giant sized yams and a goat on a string which only wanted to eat the yams! It was all rather incredible and like something out of a book. We then returned in the boat and the last hour and a half or so was in the dark going down the river shining torches at the bank when it came near. We got back to Iyi Enu around 10 pm at night – whacked out. But I was glad that I went to see Grace's project. I was also very glad of a lovely restful day here today to recover before we set off to Port Harcourt tomorrow. I still hope to get to Bonny!

With much love to you both,

Elizabeth

First visit to Bonny

Vining Centre
9th April 1978

Dear Ma and Daddy,

I think I last wrote to you from Onitsha after going up Grace's River. Now I am back in Akure and have just received your letter talking about Sr Gemmel on the T.V on Maundy Thursday. How super. I must write to her.

On Monday last week we spent the morning in Onitsha – I went to see the Beavers for a natter and did some shopping. Then in the afternoon we drove down to Port Harcourt, arriving there just as it was getting dark. We went first to a big hotel where Sheila and Ruth thought they might be booked in – but they weren't.... you had to pay N100 to secure a place! Full board cost something like N55 a day. Frightful. Then we went to Elizabeth Leicester's place because I had written to her and had planned to be there on Friday night. Now it was Monday. She is a funny somebody.... she was most off putting and said that the spare bedroom wasn't very clean – and wouldn't dream of Sheila and Ruth putting camp beds on the floor. She told us that she had a guest for supper and didn't offer us anything except a drink. The 'guest' would you believe it turned out to be her mother! In the end we all decided that maybe the mother had had a nervous breakdown or something because she didn't even greet us – but went off upstairs with a book. I never saw her smile. Very sad. Elizabeth did in fact help us to find accommodation and eventually about 10.30 we were organised to stay in the P.H Christian Council Project Guest Rooms – at N3.00 per night! The hotel where the others were in fact booked in had given out their rooms to someone else.

On Tuesday morning we had breakfast in the Presidential Hotel. Sheila treated me. It was N3 so I asked for sausage with egg - but none. Rather a swizz. I then went down to Bonny Waterside and found out that you can get a 'flyboat' to Bonny. There was one standing out in the creek. To get to it you had to first walk on foot across the mud and then get into a canoe for 10k to be paddled out to the waiting motorboat. Then we had to wait for passengers and the driver. I was there by 10. The boat was full (12 people) by 11....but no driver. So, then some got out and others got in and at 1pm the driver arrived, and we were 13. Then we had to wait again until No 13 was persuaded to get off. Then the engines were not as good as they should have been.... (According to the rather bad-tempered driver – we had too many loads) and the journey which should have taken 1 1/4 hrs took 2 ½ hrs. I arrived in Bonny about 3.30 in the afternoon. An amazing journey – all through miles and miles of waterways through mangrove swamps.

Of course, I was not expected on Tuesday – and was now 3 days late – but I had such a warm welcome from Mr and Mrs. Pepple and their family of 6 children. The next 2 days were marvelous and very enjoyable as well as interesting. I didn't know it before, but Mr Pepple previously worked as a cook for European company people – Dutch, Italian and English. He had been to Port Harcourt on Friday and his brother had given him money to entertain me properly. So, I had the most super food. On Tues night I had sausages and chips with soup before and fruit afterwards. On Wed. it was chicken and roast potatoes. On Thurs. evening the biggest omelette I have ever seen. It was a lovely surprise, and everything was so carefully thought out and prepared. I was thoroughly spoilt. It was just as well that I had gone because if I hadn't shown up Pepple would have had all that expense for food etc. for nothing. I was very touched.

Then on Saturday they had had a reception for me........but I wasn't there. On Sunday I was billed to preach the sermon in the Cathedral – but hadn't shown up! I was rather glad about that. So, on Wednesday morning it rained and Pepple went off to tell everyone that I had arrived and there would be a 'repeat' reception in the afternoon. I stayed in and read all the history of Bonny – very interesting. The Church was started there by Crowther in 1864 and their king – George Pepple went to school in England for 8 years and came back very Anglicised and keen to promote Christianity and education in Bonny. It says in the book that he used to read the Times regularly, that he wore a London -tailored suit, scented his handkerchiefs with the newest essence, criticised the comic operas of Gilbert and Sullivan and gummed his moustaches to a fine point!!

The amazing thing is that the people of Bonny are still incredibly 'English'. They talk English most of the time and have European sounding names – like Freeman, Jumbo and Baningo. Their cathedral is like a beautifully kept English parish church – with stained glass windows, lovely, polished wood pews, a brass eagle lectern and an imported marble altar and pulpit as well as a pipe organ. At the back is a tower in which you climb up ladders and it has a clock which chimes each hour. The original, if you please, was imported by ship. It has a wooden structure and was sent in pieces over 100 years ago. The wooden roof and pillars are still there. The walls have been replaced by cement blocks.

The reception in the Vicarage on Wed. at 4 was another amazing thing. About 20 people came. It was very informal......but there was a programme with 17 items on it! This is the programme:

Order of Miss E.C.J. Deeks' Reception at Bonny 5th April 1978

1. Opening Prayer by Mrs. E.V. Dimieari.
2. Formal self-introductions.
3. Short introductory speech by the host.
4. Songs and Solos if any.
5. What does God require of us by Miss Deeks.
6. Songs by host family.
7. My Cathedral by Dr. Dan Jumbo.
8. My Town by Mr. M.B. Freeman.
9. Songs and Solos free.
10. Shell B.P. in Bonny by Mr. Gentle A. Okoro.
11. Life in England now – by Miss Deeks.
12. Free speeches.
13. Chorus by Hosts Family.
14. Short speech by Guest of Honour.
15. Vote of thanks by the host.
16. Closing Prayer by Mrs. Oruama.
17. Grace by all.

Please note that each speech should take not more than 6 minutes
G. H. Pepple

Dr Jumbo was the first doctor in Bonny – now retired. He had lived 12 years in England and wanted to know what had happened to the Church in U.K because he said the after the War, he found full churches and now they were empty! He was an incredible character and made a very dramatic speech. His son is schooling in England. The refreshments at this gathering were sausage rolls, pieces of cake, fish cakes and pieces of chicken all set out on trays covered with tinfoil. Just like an English garden party.

On Thursday morning I went on a sightseeing tour with Mr. Pepple. Bonny is a long narrow town on a sandbank with one tarmacked road going along for about 3 miles. There are 8 taxis and some private cars. The 'Mission' – i.e., Cathedral + pastors house + catechist's house + school is on an open green grassy place between this road and the beach. There are oil tankers standing in the sea channel offshore – a beautiful sight at night with their lights shining over the water.

Because I was supposed to be getting a boat to go back to P.H on Thursday afternoon Mr. Pepple 'took me out' to lunch in a very nice Guest House down beside the sea water. There I was served with another 3-course meal! Noodle soup + steak and chips and rice with vegetables + fruit salad and coffee. Then Mr. and Mrs. Pepple followed me down to the boat place where we waited from 2.30 to 5 pm hoping for the boat that we were told was coming. But it disappointed so we returned to the house and visited some people in the town in the evening. I then set off at 6 am for the boat the next morning and was lucky enough to get the fastest speedboat (carries 8 people) and so reached P.H around 8 am. I then took a taxi to Elizabeth Leicester's house. She greeted me with 'I thought we might see you for breakfast' - and I thought 'Good'. She then proceeded to forget about breakfast and gave me coffee and a bit of shortbread! I then went with her and her unsmiling frozen mother to Kingsway Stores. Port Harcourt is the one place in Nigeria that I have been to lately where you can buy things in the shops – effect of oil people I imagine. The shops in Warri are equally well stocked.

I was a bit anxious to find Sheila and Joan and not sure how to go about it because we hadn't made any arrangement to meet that a.m. Eliz said she wanted to take me to Eloikoia – the Conference place but first we went to queue up for petrol – about 15 cars in the line. As we were waiting Sheila and Joan came and joined the line in the same petrol station. Wasn't that marvelous? So, I was able to transport myself and my bags into their car. We then went back to the big stores because they still wanted to shop. Later we had a picnic lunch and set off for Onitsha about 3.30 and arrived there around 7.30 pm and had a drink. I should have been happy to stay the night, but the others felt we should continue to Benin. We arrived at Ruth's at 10.45. I stayed there. The other 2 with Jane. Then on Sat. I returned to Akure with Sheila in her car. Joan to Owo in her own car. A great week!

Much love,
Elizabeth

Vining Centre
16th April 1978

Dear Ma and Daddy,

I have had a very restful week – I have written several letters, including a Link Letter which I hope to send with the Taylor Woodrow daughters who go back at the end of this week. Angela Roberts had to have her appendix out suddenly which was a bit of a shock to them all. She had it done in Ado Ekiti by Sister Carmel. I have also been reading the autobiography of Hilary called 'Nothing Venture, Nothing Win' I found this interesting because it gives you a whole picture of his life with the Everest climb being only a small part of it all.

On Friday I went to see Inga and to go to the funeral of Dr Akinsete who was a well-known and much-loved doctor in Ondo. I didn't know him really, but Inga relied on him a lot. His wife used to teach at St Helen's T.T.C in Ondo and is now at St Ann's Ibadan. We went to the Christian Wake Keeping Ceremony – hymns and readings – on Friday evening 8-10 pm. The atmosphere was very subdued and quiet, although several hundred people there. A similar wake keeping was held in Ibadan at the same time. On Saturday morning I helped the schoolgirls at St Monica's to make wreaths. We made 5. 2 for the hospital, 2 for the school and one for Janet Olowoyo's school. Then the St M girls lined the road, and we watched the procession of cars coming from Ibadan. The service was at 3 pm in the Catholic Church. It was Mass and Funeral service- quite a lot sung in Latin, but the English was printed alongside. Grace Ohikhena and her husband were there from Ibadan. Yomi and Kelu from Ife – and many others – thousands, I guess. The coffin was carried by doctors – Sijuade, Agidi, Akinyosoye + Egyptians and Indians too. Mrs. Kohli was there because she was a contemporary in Ibadan. He was a Catholic, but he was also a friend of all and was Medical Advisor for Ondo Anglican Diocese. There were 2 Catholic Bishops taking the service – and 5 Anglican Bishops attended – Ondo. Ilesha, Ekiti, Ibadan and Ijebu. An amazing event. I think there were more Anglican clergy in the procession than Catholics.

After the service Inga and I went and had cold drinks with the sisters of St Louis. Sister Mildred and another sister sang a lovely solo song in the service. Then I returned to Akure with Dr Kohli whose car broke down on going there. This morning I took the service at St

Thomas Church Akure – it is a student service in English. I talked about Leprosy.

With much love to you both, Elizabeth

22nd April 1978

Dear Ma and Daddy,

I have been thinking about you a lot in the last week since hearing that Daddy was to go into St Luke's for his hernia op., I do hope that all has gone well, and that you have been able to stay with Stuart and Jutka, and that all worked out happily. What has happened about the arthritis? Are you asking about this in London?

I have had a good week overall. Now the students are back, and we are starting the new term at Vining Centre. Mrs. Kohli is here this weekend and so she is with me now. Her son Uppi has just heard that he has an immigration visa for Canada, so he is proposing to go off there. She is a good deal upset by the prospect especially as he is 26 and is not yet married. I think she must have spent a good deal of time last year trying to find a suitable wife for him, but he turned them all down – and now he is going off to Canada, probably for 5 years in the first instance.

On Tuesday I went to Ikare and stayed the night with David and Jane Lewis. They were very welcoming, and I had a good evening chatting to them. On Wednesday I went to greet the Jaiyeoba's whose son died in Maiduguri. I am not very good at such visits. Mrs. Jaiyeoba is still very upset. As Mama would say -'She has tied her face'! I then went to see the sisters at Ikare and found Sr Catherine there – she is the sister from Owo who came to our Prayer Group last year. She is a dear. She was recuperating after fever in Ikare. Really the Catholic Sisters are very lucky to have so many houses to go and rest if they have been sick.

On Thursday we had our Staff meeting here in the morning and got set for the beginning of the term. I have 4 new women expected of whom 2 have come so far.

On Friday I went out for the day with Sister Martinian. It rained heavily on Thursday evening and in the rain Martinian bashed her car bonnet and smashed her headlights into the back of a kit car which suddenly turned left with no warning. So, on Friday Martinian wanted 'to get away' and go to look for a wood carver in Ekiti called Bankole. She was told that he came from Usi, so we went there and discovered that it was a wild goose chase. But it didn't matter because we had an enjoyable ride round the roads of Ekiti and we went to visit Rev Olugasa who is the principal of a school up at Ulogbo. He used to be the Treasurer of the Leper Settlement Committee here in Akure. He is an exceptionally nice person – and a hard-working Principal. It was good to see him. After rain it's like a crazy skating rink.

The worst news this week is that there have been riots in the Universities. This was caused by the increase of university fees to something like £500 per year from Sept. The students set out to demonstrate in the streets on this subject, but the police barricaded them, and they were prevented from going. Then the battle began. Students with sticks and stones and Police with tear gas and later guns. About 8 students in the different Universities have been killed in the trouble so most of the Universities have been closed – till May 1st to cool off. But it is all very unsettled and there is a lot of criticism in the paper of how the government handles the Universities.

We went to the settlement for our Open-Air service today. It was a happy service. Mama Ademoye is not very well. She has a cold but also blood pressure. I hope she is going to cope with the term.

Dr Kohli is really fed up with her hotel. I think she may come here as paying guest for part of the week - until her house is ready.

It is lovely and cool today after the heavy rain of yesterday. It is much better for working in than when it is oppressively hot.

You should get a small parcel for your birthday, Ma. I hope it is a happy day.

With much love to you both,
Elizabeth

Vining Centre,
30th April 1978

Dear Ma and Daddy,

I received the letter of Apl 3rd and the BRF notes and your letter of Apl 16th this week- but I am still waiting to hear news of Daddy's operation. Our post seems to be very erratic now. To answer your questions – No, I didn't tape the service on Palm Sunday although maybe Fabuluje did – I will ask him (he has travelled – as usual!) As you say the oil boom everywhere is being exploited by profiteers....

but I think we are going to suffer for it here...because the oil markets have reduced – and because of overspending and bad planning as well as extravagant political promises which they are now unable to carry out – it seems to me that the present Nigerian Government is in a fix which it is struggling to get out of. The Budget was a 'pull in your belts' one. Imported foodstuffs are restricted more than before – resulting in even greater increases in the market prices. Customs duties have gone up a lot. Then the Govt is not subsidizing food and lodging in Universities or Secondary schools as much as before, so fees have increased from £150 to £490 a year so there is a great outcry. There have been protests this week by secondary sch pupils.

The Universities were mostly closed last week. The demonstrations this week were violent in Ife and Lagos – burning vehicles. In Ife the prison was burnt, and 58 inmates let out! Yesterday the Ondo State Governor called all the Sec. Sch Principals to ask them to keep their pupils in control.

It seems that there are anti-Government people behind all these upsets, deliberately trying to make trouble and maybe overthrow the Government. No one is happy at the present situation. We can only pray that money maybe more carefully spent and that there may be an overwhelming desire for peace and fairness.

Jimmy Carter and co stayed in Lagos- I didn't see them! Guy is the principal of a school near Ikare. He is a neurotic Italian/Englishman bordering on genius who has a school where they have a big farm, + printers' workshop and so on. Ed is the Full Gospel Businessman's Fellowship chap who is working on the radio satellite station at Oba-about 4 miles away. Brother Fred is the Catholic brother.

We had our Prayer Group on Tues. at Eyesorun's. I was late at the beginning and felt out of gear throughout. I have been rather depressed all week. I felt I was pushed into being the host of next week's group which I didn't want to be and let down by Sheila who did the pushing. Then as I say the state of the country is depressing. However, I got some preparation done for my Monday lectures. I hope to do something about the founding of the Church in Nigeria. I read a book ' The Romance of the Black River' written in 1930. Amazing. I hadn't realised how the church in Nigeria was always basically Nigerian run and that the first missionaries in the Niger and Abeokuta were all Nigerians returned from Sierra Leone.

Looking forward to hearing news of the operation. I hope you got my birthday parcel safely.

With much love,

Elizabeth

Vining Centre
4th May 1978

Dear Ma and Daddy,

No letter yet since Daddy's operation. Our post is all topsy-turvy now. The student demonstrations have quietened down but some post offices in Ibadan and Lagos were stoned so maybe that explains the dearth of letters.

Anyway, I would like to hear how Daddy is! I expect that your letters will get here in the long run – but Linda Roberts suggested that you could send a 'quicky' through Taylor Woodrow. The Roberts may not be here anymore after June or July, and I don't think we should use this method too much – but it is a good idea if post has been held up.

All is well here – but no water in the taps! - only in the sky. It has been raining heavily.

I hope all in going well with Daddy's convalescence. No phone here either -since January. They say they have broken a cable and have no replacement.

With much love,

Elizabeth

Vining Centre.
7th May 1978

Dear Ma and Daddy,

Still no news from your end. The last letter I received was on the night before Daddy's operation. They say that there are heaps of mail bags in Akure Post Office – unsorted! This week the news hasn't been so bad. I think everyone was shocked by the result of so called 'peaceful student demonstration'.... which ended in hooligans joining them and burning cars and even houses in Lagos so that, whereas before people were sympathetic to the students, now they are much more hostile.

The doctors have now decided to go on a 40-hour week and work civil servant times as a protest against a decree banning private practice and because they say they should have better pay scales than other Civil Servants.

On Monday night I started my term's lectures on the history of Christianity in Nigeria. We started with Bonny! - then I asked those from Delta Diocese to tell us some of the difficulties facing the Church in that area so that we could all pray better for them there. Then I asked the students to write down what they knew about the start of Christianity in their home village or area. The essays are all most interesting- Jebb and Dallimore feature in some of them. Then some students come from villages where there is yet no church. One from a strong Moslem village - in the Mid-West near Auchi. He himself became a Christian through the witness of one of our old students in 1973. His family rejected him, and his wife too so he had to start again with a new wife, a Christian.

On Tuesday we had the Fellowship Group here in my house – about 16 people. We took the Prodigal Son and thought about how we all need to repent of our selfishness – but that Nigeria also needs to repent of reckless extravagant living and pray that the present time of 'no money' may not lead us all to famine and eating anything we caught!! I preached the same message this morning to the students in the Communion service.

On Wed. Mrs. Kohli and Dr and Mrs. Karim from Bangladesh came to supper. Dr Kohli and Mrs. Karim played Master Mind. The Karims are Moslems.

Yesterday, Saturday, I went to Ondo to attend the marriage of one of our students but got to the church to meet no-body - so I went away. I went to see Inga – who wasn't in- gone to Ibadan – so I went up to Idanre and found Pat and Francis at home. I stayed there for the afternoon and had lunch with them. It was good to see them all.

May 9th

Happy Birthday Ma. Yesterday I received your letter of 20th April and the letters sent through Omodara. Very good to be more up to date and very glad that Daddy is doing well, and that you have been given definite advice about the hips. Great.

With much love to you both,

Elizabeth.

Vining Centre
14th May 1978

Dear Ma and Daddy,

It was very good to hear all your news at the beginning of this week, and to see your photos – brought by Omodara. I am very glad that you now have some definite instructions on the hip operations and that the surgeon has agreed to do it so soon. It looks as though 1978 will go down on Daddy's record as operation year!

People here i.e., Fred and Sheila are getting keyed up about going on leave and I have been thinking about what the right thing is to do with this long vac – July and Aug. All indications at this end seem to be to stay here. Martinian will be here so I thought I could spend some time at the Settlement. Dr Kohli will be here. The Lewis's at Ikare will be here. We are planning to have Leprosy week in September so I can spend time preparing for that. Then there are just so many things that need doing – mending or making dresses etc here that it will be good to settle down and do it. I also thought that it would be fun to go through some of the old records of A.T.C and try to compile history. For this I would want to write to some of the old timers and get them to write some reminiscences. I may also go and see some old students in Kwara State – Kabba area. So, I think all in all the guidance is not to think of any Charter flight scheme this year (probably too late anyway – I haven't investigated it all) – and then, as you say, to look forward to coming home in 1979. I hope this is Ok by you. I am sorry not to share in the hip affair at first hand but unless you have some very definite thoughts in the opposite direction, I am not going to make any plans to take extra leave.

Last night I went with Mrs. Kohli to a 'Dance' to raise funds for the Nigerian Red Cross. All rather a hoot – not much interest in dancing really – it was just an excuse to get people to sit down and donate to towards the Red Cross Funds. It was the final event in a Red Cross Week. I went to a lecture on Wed on Indian Hemp Smoking and its dangers – some of our students were there. It seems to be a problem that is just coming into Nigeria.

Martinian has had this week off to rest. She went to Ikare. It will be good to have her back next week. Post is still erratic here, but other things seem to be more settled.

With much love, Elizabeth

Vining Centre,
21st May 1978.

Dear Ma and Daddy,

A good week for letters! I received your postcards sent through Taylor Woodrow and your letter of May 7th. I am glad to hear that Daddy is doing well and able to be out in the garden despite his stiff legs. It sounds as though all your Malvern friends have been keeping a good eye on you.

This last week has been much as usual – but I was very tired and head achy on Wed. Thurs. and Fri. and I think maybe I had a bit of malaria. I took Nivaquin....and it made me feel a bit sick so yesterday I had a day of rest at St Louis with Martinian, and that sorted me out so that I feel much better today. I taught the men on Monday night – but it was a rather messy lecture because I was wanting to fill in some maps that hadn't duplicated very clearly and there was no electricity, so everything had to be done by bush lamp.

On Tuesday afternoon I escaped to the Taylor Woodrow swimming pool and had a dip and a read. Very nice and refreshing-especially welcome because we have had no water in our taps for the last 3 weeks. That was another thing I did at St Louis – washed my hair and had a hot bath. We had our prayer group on Tues. night at St Peter's – a good time of prayer, but then we went on discussing up till about 10 pm. I would have been much happier if it finished by 9.30 pm. We start soon after 8.

Mrs. Kohli invited me to supper at her hotel on Wed. and then she came here for supper on Thurs. She hates any day that doesn't have 'a programme' – and someone to keep her company. I find this a bit wearing because I am looking out for a free evening with 'no programme'! and last week there was none. She was here last night with Sheila too and went off with 2 Arthur Haley books that should keep her amused for a bit.

On Friday evening Sheila and I went to the Robert's at Taylor Woodrow for supper. Really gorgeous. We had prawn cocktail followed by roast beef and Yorkshire puddings, carrots, peas, roast potatoes, and corn pie with egg custard afterwards. All served with Rose wine! We had a good natter with the Roberts. I will miss them. They are going home in the middle of June.

I have started reading the book called 'Roots' and am enjoying it. It is very well written. I have pasted your post cards of Malvern and

Worcestershire on the back of my bathroom door. I am glad you got the Circular letter and are processing it. Thank you for all your efforts in getting it posted.

I had lunch with Sheila today – and Dr Kohli and Ed, the Full Gospel American. I still felt a bit bilious in the stomach and found I couldn't cope with Ed's continual talk about people with a 'wonderful ministry'. He usually greets people with 'Alleluia' 'What has the Holy Spirit done for you today? What miracles have you seen this week?' - or something. It turns me off. I think I can't be a 'proper' Christian. I am much happier with the greeting 'How are you'? I am just basically self-centered I suppose.

With much love to you both and hoping that you are well.

Elizabeth.

Vining Centre
28th May 1978.

Dear Ma and Daddy,

Thank you very much for your letter including the copy of my circular letter. Meg Bishop is now at home I think but I have rather lost touch.

This week I met a young Ibo boy called Humphrey who is from Asaba. He knew all the Asaba 'lot' – i.e., Jane Backhouse, Eric and the Inmans. He was asking after the Inmans especially. Is their address still Broadwater etc Woodbridge, Suffolk? Or did something happen to one of them? I have a feeling that somebody died.......but I am not sure. Please bring me up to date.

Fabuluje goes travelling to various committees and meetings – like Diocesan Committees and Boys Brigade and to his home village where he has a farm and is building a house and is encouraging the start of a Sec School and a Health Centre. Ann Travis is going home to Liverpool to have her baby – expected at the end of July.

This week here ended with the students of U.I in Ibadan being sent home again on Friday. Their leader is in detention. It seems that he is involved with 'Socialists' and that they are using the student's unrest to stir up trouble against the Government. All the students refuse to go to classes until he is released from detention. There is a complete boycott arranged on classes and doing exams. Any students who try to go to lectures or departments who try to organise exams are prevented from doing so by the 'militant lot' I hope to go to Ibadan next weekend so I expect that I shall get more up to date news then.

At the same time the Doctors are up in arms and are protesting the Govt decree banning Private Practise by Govt doctors. Many of them do P.P in the afternoons when they have finished in the hospital. The snag is that if it is banned all the good doctors will leave and open Private Hospitals and only the young and less qualified men will be running the hospital – and they will be fewer in number.

Yesterday one of our children had a convulsion ......caused great panic .... especially to the parents. The father was trembling and the mother shouting. Fortunately, we were seen quickly at the hospital and the baby recovered quite soon. It obviously had a good strong attack of malaria. I seem to have a very full week – out every night!

Mon – lecture. Tues. - Prayer Group.

Wed – looking at slides of leprosy. Thurs. to Mrs. Kohli for supper.

Fri. to Sheilas. I also managed to get to Taylor Woodrow twice to swim in their pool. Very necessary for we still have no running water – the 4th week.

Today, Sun, I went to the Federal Govt Girls College to take their morning service. We have been asked to do this. There are about 60 little girls – all in one class!

Bro Fred goes on leave tomorrow. He is hoping to visit the Hermitage in Tamanrasset again (middle of the Sahara Desert!)

I hope all is well with you – I think of you often.

With much love,

Elizabeth

Vining Centre,
5th June 1978

Dear Ma and Daddy,

I have just got back from an interesting holiday weekend in Ibadan. I went there on Thursday and stayed with the Failings who are the C.M.S couple at the Institute of Church and Society. While I was there, I was able to see Grace and Titi and a few other old friends at an S.C.M meeting on Sunday. I also had a chance to get further on in reading the book 'Roots'. It is a terrible book – but very gripping. I was just breathing a sigh of relief that the horrors of the Atlantic Crossing were over – only to find the next part was worse! Just dreadful. It is not surprising that the Southern States still have a name for violence after all that ghastly history.

The highlights of the weekend away were the service at Immanuel on Sunday, the S.C.M group meeting, and a superb meal out in a place called The Cavern in Ibadan. Lynn and I had steaks and Elaine had 3 lamb chops! Next time I go there (when I have saved up!) I will try the lamb chops.

In the Immanuel College service Rev Adegbola who is the Director of the Institute took a Bible Study Service: Hymn – Prayer – Hymn and then Bible Study for the best part of an hour. It was led in a very stimulating way by Ade. He said a bit and then paused for comment from the congregation – and people gave their comments. He had us sitting on the edges of our seats wanting to contribute. The passage was from 1 Peter 2 verses 13-17 so there were a lot of topical comments – like: Do we believe in the divine right of Kings anymore?- Does that mean the Oba's ? What about the Government? Do we believe they are appointed by GOD? Some Government officials or politicians even say over a loudspeaker that there is no GOD. How then can they be appointed by GOD? He went on to question who has the right to punish and to praise others. Are we not all doing this whereas we should be concentrating on the work that GOD has given us – whether we are teachers or doctors or civil servants? He was very funny about civil servants.

In the afternoon we had a very happy meeting of the S.C.M Senior Friends group. Titi Ikotun was there and Bisi and Segun Sowunmi who I hadn't seen for a very long time – also, the Pearsons who used to be at Wesley Guild Hospital. This group has been studying Ezekiel in the past year and decided they wanted to study Schumacher's book 'Small is Beautiful' in the coming year. They were talking about how they could help in some of the villages where the Institute have co-operative activities and projects. Anyway, it was all most interesting and stimulating. I am sorry not to be nearer Ibadan to attend their gatherings.

I discovered on Sunday afternoon that a nut was missing in my car engine, which is supposed to hold the carburetor together, so I got that fixed on Monday before I returned to Akure. It was very good that I discovered that it was gone before I left Ibadan because I think it would have conked out on the way home if I hadn't had it fixed.

Now we are back for the second half of the term. I heard from Myrtle at last – she is hoping to come to Ikare in September – but the red tape is not yet buttoned up. I hope it works out because it would be great to have Myrtle around here.

Thank you for the form for the licence. I have filled it up and am sending it back with the cheque for £5. The old licence is at home. It may either be with my P.O Book in Mother's desk or in my drawer or suitcase. I think you should be able to find it without much trouble. I hope so. Thank you for sending it on. I am also enclosing the paper for a new cheque book. Please can you get it for me and then sometime in August, I suggest you send it to Sheila so that she can bring it back. I will give her address nearer the time.

With much love to you both,

Elizabeth

Vining Centre,
11th June 1978

Dear Ma and Daddy.

I just got your quickie letter yesterday. You must now be in North Wales – Gorgeous.

I hope it doesn't rain too much. It is very wet here these days – but I like it so long as you have plenty to do in your house.......one's brain works more quickly. But if you venture out then it's a muddy business.

I finished reading 'Roots' this week. The end of it is amazing. In fact, altogether it's a very well written book – and one that you will always remember.

I am glad that you found my driving licence – I expect you will have got the form and the cheque by now.

There has not been much time for standing and staring this last week. Tues. night – fellowship. Wed. night, I drove the Men's Warden to Iju because someone had died, and he wanted to collect a child from school there. Thurs. night – Lep Sett Cmttee. Fri. night – Scrabble with Mrs. Kohli – then cake and coffee with Penny, the American girl. Her fridge has gone wrong, and her car has broken down, so she is just 'managing'.

Today, Sunday I am taking Matins here at V.C and then the evening service in a school. I am going to Dr Kohli for lunch.

This week I heard from Myrtle and when I went to the State Board, I met Lady Jibowu the Chairman who said that she was going to

London to interview next week Tues. and Wednesday, and that she hoped to see Myrtle there. So, I sent messages to Myrtle to make sure she shows up …... and I do hope it works out so that she can came here.

Martinian was here to lunch this week and she suggests we go away for a week together when she has holidays. We may go to Tarkwa, or we may go to Ososso Rest House, that's between Auchi and Ikare. That seems a good idea to me.

Today is St Barnabas Day – and so I did a kind of Bible Study about him in the place of a sermon. I found it interesting to prepare – but I am getting like my father …. it takes so long to say all that is in your head! Barnabas was a very loving person – and a man of action with a vision for missions. He gave his field. He believed in Saul and encouraged him. He brought Saul to Antioch – a key city. He went out as a missionary, and he was humble enough to play second fiddle to Paul. He was involved with giving money to Jerusalem when there was threat of famine. He gave John Mark a second chance.

On Friday my phone rang for the first time in 6 months. They were testing from the Post Office. I was very happy. By Fri. evening it had ceased to function! But there is hope.

With much love,

Elizabeth.

Vining Centre,
19th June 1978

Dear Ma and Daddy,

I do hope you have had a super time in North Wales and that Daddy is feeling fit and ready for the next spell in hospital. I hope that the car played up well and allowed you to get out and about to see the countryside. I was very glad to hear that you had such a happy time with Marguerita and the boys, and I am glad that Judith is happier – and continue to pray for her and for Pam.

On Fri/Saturday/Sun Jane and David came from Ikare and we had a great time on Saturday painting my living room – walls: Magnolia, doors, and windows: White Gloss. We had a roller each, so we finished the main work in about 2 hours. I was very pleased with my wall – it really looks good. David was a bit slapdash and hasty and got rather fed up with his section but all in all it was a very successful event. The only snag is that I have felt very weary since then, particularly as on Sunday we had a commissioning service in the afternoon + photos at 3pm.....therefore no rest.

We went to see Penny on Saturday and found that she had no fridge because hers has gone wrong. So, on Sunday midday I borrowed our Volkswagen van to go to Fiwasaiye and try to borrow my old fridge which is now in their classroom. On the road David was sitting in the back and suddenly shouted "Stop! Stop! The door has fallen off." Sure enough, the sliding door clonked onto the ground – just dragged along by one part which was still attached to the van. Calamity! Such could only happen in Nigeria. So, we had to stop and struggle to get the door off and yank it into the bus. When I got back, I was all apologetic in going to the principal ...... but he said. 'Ah Yes' – the same thing happened to him! - No one had told me that the door was faulty! In the end we didn't take the fridge either because it wasn't in very good shape.

We have now 3 weeks of the term left. The men are going on a one week's mission in Ondo area for the last week July 1-7, but the women are staying behind. We shall be doing our exams. I have yet to get round to setting mine.

Mama Ademoye celebrated her 60th birthday yesterday. So, on Sunday she sent around great bowls of jollof rice for everyone. I think that I will be eating jollof rice all week.

I had a letter this last week from a clergyman in Lagos called E.O. Oyebajo who said that he was at St Andrew's Oyo and wished to be remembered to you both.

We had a very happy Prayer Group last week at Humphrey and Patricia's home. She was an old girl at St Monica's, and he is from Asaba and knew the Inmans. Ed has gone on leave – and it looks as though he may not be asked to come back to Nigeria by his firm. The Robert's of Taylor Woodrow are transferred to Lagos – I will miss them.

Much love to you both,

Elizabeth

Vining Centre,
26th June 1978.

Dear Ma and Daddy,

It's your wedding anniversary! 43 years ago. I hope that you can celebrate it somehow. It's nice to have celebrations on a Sunday.

It is 5.30 pm here – I didn't have space this morning to write to you because I preached at 8am to students at St Thomas Church and then took the service at 9.30 am at Federal Gov Girls Coll. I was home by 11 am. Then I went to see Mama Ademoye who went to Benin yesterday to the Funeral of Archdeacon Akinluyi. I think he must have been at Oyo in your time. He was very well known in Benin – I think related to Eunice somehow. Mrs. Kohli and Sheila came to lunch – corn and avocado pears and tomatoes and rolls and cheese. They went about 2.40. Then I had a rest till 4 and after that washed up and washed my hair. Then I hope to go and say goodbye to an Indian family called Jahn around 6 and to Sheila's for supper with Sr Martinian and Sr Philomena. I am not quite sure when I am going to get my exam papers set – I should have them ready by tomorrow!

Yesterday I went to lunch to St Louis and had an afternoon rest there – I slept for ages and felt much refreshed. Earlier in the week I was wilting and feeling weary ….so much so that I didn't go to the Prayer Fellowship on Tuesday but went to bed instead. I think it was just the aftermath of painting on Sat. + period time.

Sheila goes on leave in 2 weeks' time. I will miss her. Dr Kohli is talking of moving into Sheila's house because she may not be able to stay in the hotel much longer. I hope her son Rajan comes in August because otherwise I can see that I will be a very frequent port of call – which is OK- but I do find her rather domineering sometimes.

I am so glad you had a good time in N. Wales with good weather and the chance to get about by car.

Have you heard from John recently? I haven't written for his birthday. I will still do so. Have they said anything about Christmas? How is their new house building? We can only pray about the marriage – and patiently wait as you say. I feel that I shall probably stay here till next June – then take the maximum leave that C.M.S can manage …... especially if Gemma is wanting to come to Nigeria again at Christmas.

I had a nice letter from Richard this week. His college is a Federal T.T Coll and is suffering as most of Nigeria is by cut backs since the last budget. He must go over 300km to Sokoto to beg for money to pay his salaries. In the North many things are given to the students free to encourage them to be educated …. but it is more difficult to be economical after you have had such a lot 'given' before.

Maybe the next letter will have news of the hip operation. I remember Mrs. Welsh saying that the pain was terrible when she started to use it just after the operation – but that it was well worth it in the long run. My thoughts and prayers are with you both.

With much love,

Elizabeth.

P.S Please thank Iliffs for letter.

Vining Centre
2nd July 1978.

Dear Ma and Daddy,

Good to get your letter of 19th June and the picture book of North Wales. So many gorgeous pictures of places that I remember well. How very nice too to have the Mc Cann's from Belfast coming to see you. They must know the Rodgers who were at Ife – because Prof Rodgers was for many years Prof at Queen's Belfast. Angela Joynson is also in Corfe Mullen.

We are now at the end of the term. Only the Women Students are here this weekend because all the men have gone off to the Ondo area on a Mission. I spent Wednesday and Thursday struggling to read 6 sermons each for 15 men – on the theme 'Jesus is the Answer'. The women have been having exams since Thursday – also managing the compound on their own which is rather fun because they are not used to ringing the bells and organising the Chapel and so on which the men generally do.

Sheila is preparing to go on leave – on July 10th. I may take her down to Lagos because her driver has gone off to the North on an excursion.

There is a new Post and Telecommunications engineer in Akure. - from India. He is staying in Dr Kohli's hotel. He came to our Chapel this morning and told me that his grandfather used to oversee Vellore Hospital and that his younger brother is working with the Leprosy Mission in India. His wife has just gone home to have their 2nd baby. He said he would come to our Prayer Fellowship on Tuesday evening – so that was – an interesting contact.

I am looking forward to the holidays and thinking up all sorts of things to be doing. I want to do some more painting in my house – and to make some clothes – and do some mending......then there are a few people who I have intended to visit for some time, and I rarely get round to it. We shall see if all the schemes work out.

Sheila and I went to Dr Kohli's hotel last night for supper. It was rather a hoot. I think Mrs. Kohli better get out of that hotel soon because she gets very ratty with the staff. She raps on the table with her spoon in a very irate fashion and shouts on the stewards to come. The 'service' is clueless and bush but really, she doesn't bring out the best in them.

After supper we went to her room and played Chinese Chequers. She is always happy to have occupied her spare time.

Sheila and I find this quite hard to cope with because we are usually on the lookout for some 'space' between activities. She is looking for activities to fill the spaces. It looks as though she may at last get into her house and so may move this week. She is looking for pots and pans and plates etc. and hoping to borrow out of Sheila's house while she is away. She seemed to reckon last week that Sheila would like to bring her back a toaster and an electric iron! Sheila was busy putting her right on that. She also wants enough knitting wool to knit Rajan a sweater. I am rather glad that I am not coming home this year and therefore don't have to worry about everybody's requests.

Looking forward to your next letter with news of Stanmore.

With much love, Elizabeth

Vining Centre.
9th July 1978.

Dear Ma and Daddy

I received your letter this week saying that you had had the green light from Stanmore, so I am now thinking of Daddy learning to manage a metal bone. I am a bit sad that I am not coming to visit him – but I am sure it's the right decision to stay here. I will be looking forward to the next letter telling how the operation went off. How long will Daddy be in Stanmore and how long in St Lukes?.........Then does he stay there until the 2nd hip, or do you get a break in Malvern in between?

I am sending this letter with Sheila, who is flying tomorrow night. I will take her down to Lagos by car and then come back on Tues. or

Wed. I hope that you were able to watch the Borg v Conners match yesterday. Incredible that he should be only 22 and to have won Wimbledon 3 times in a row. I listened to the 2nd half of the match…....and, to the Women's Final. I found that my radio reception was very good. I think it is better in the morning and the afternoons than in the evenings. I must experiment during the holidays.

I am enclosing my photo in the Daily Times – you can hardly recognise me because it is so dark. I was very amused by the misspelling of my name – Miss Deeds indeed!

Our women went away on Friday morning, so I was kept busy until then writing reports and completing the marking of their exam papers. On Thursday I went to the Launching of the Ondo State Committee for organising activities for the Year of the Child 1979. I am not quite sure why they should invite me to be involved in that, but still. It was a rather chaotic meeting in my opinion but was just to elect their officers for future meetings. In the evening we had a Leprosy Welfare Committee -with some new members coming. We fixed the last week in September for our 'Leprosy Week' so we shall see.

We don't know what will happen next about the doctors here in Nigeria. The Government is trying to tighten up regulations about Private Practise and has prohibited Government doctors from doing any P.P. in their spare time. This means that many of them are thinking of resigning and doing Private Practise full-time but the Government is now regulating the standards of clinics etc. that you can set up.......this is good of course – but they have said that each private hospital should have a lab and a qualified pharmacist and an X-ray unit and rooms of certain sizes etc. …...stipulations which make the setting up of private practise almost impossible without a lot of capital. The result is that the doctors in Lagos have all gone on 'strike'- and people are dying as a result or running to the hospitals in Abeokuta. Terrible!

The snag is that doctors can get more money in Private Practise than in Government service particularly if they are a well-known doctor. Dr Sijuade is in a fix because he was doing both before and he doesn't want to give up the hospital where he has worked so hard to build it to a better standard ……. but he has got used to the money from the P.P that he was doing in his spare time. I think he will resign. Money, money, money …....rules the lives of many here.

I had a letter from Mr. Pepple this week and he said he would pray for Daddy and his operation. This is what he says 'The world's greatest Physician is our dear Lord and Saviour, and I am sure He will supervise your father's operation. So let not your heart be troubled.' I am thankful that it is London anyway and not Lagos where Daddy is having his operation!

Jane Pelly came here this weekend to stay with Sheila. Her sister, Robena has just come out to spend a month with Jane and to see her son, Andrew who is teaching near Ikare with Guy. So, we were 6 for lunch- me, Mrs. Kohli + Jane, Robena, Andrew, and Sheila. The only snag is that I now have some food left over and I am going off tomorrow. We had steak and kidney pie + beans, plantain, macaroni, and egg curry for Mrs. Kohli who doesn't eat beef – and then fruit salad and sponge followed by coffee. Mrs. Kohli is still here. The weather here is cool now – it rains on and off.

I hope to see Sola in Lagos and then to come back to Akure via Ibadan. I will then return here on Wednesday I expect. Then on Thurs I will probably go to St Louis and spend a long weekend with Martinian. She is on her own in the Convent next week. Later – the last week in July to Aug 5th Martinian and I hope to go to Tarkwa together and stay in the Dominican's house there.

With lots of love to you both – looking forward to hearing news. I hope the steel hip isn't too painful. I guess it will get better every day. Hallelujah anyway!

Elizabeth

Vining Centre
16th July 1978

Dear Ma and Daddy,

I am at St Louis this weekend staying with Martinian and I will send this letter off via Dublin because another sister is going home tomorrow. I haven't heard anything yet since the operation on July 4th. I do hope that all went well. No doubt it is this week and next when you will begin to know if the legs are better or not. Here's hoping!

I think that my last letter will have ended on Sunday. I set off with Sheila on Monday and we went to Lagos. There was no trouble on the road. We stopped for a picnic at the Nigerian Youth Camp. Kath Dick was there – just the same as ever- and Mary looked after us and gave us plates to put our picnic on.

We reached Shola's place around 6 pm and she kindly gave us coffee followed by supper and we sat and watched colour Tele. Then we went to the airport and discovered that Sheila's plane wasn't going because of engine trouble. Wait till tomorrow. So, we returned to Shola's. Sheila slept on a camp bed and was cold. I was cold too and didn't get off to sleep till after midnight because the Tele was blaring next door. It was amazingly cold in Lagos – wet season. The next morning, we returned to the airport and I left Sheila there around 9 am. I then went on to return to Ijebu-Ode. There is a new four lane highway from Lagos to Ibadan which you can only go on if you have a pass –that is very quick- but since we had no pass, we had to use the old road. It is better since I suffered on it last year but there is still a hold up for about 1 hour because you go along in 4 lanes and then it narrows to one lane and consequently, there is a bottle neck where you are likely to be squeezed between a tanker and a bus if you are not careful.

In Ijebu-Ode I stopped to see Mrs. Wilde who is now the Principal of the Ang. Gram. School there. It was good to see her. She is not very settled because her children and husband are still in Shagamu, so they are separated except at the weekends. After that I went on to see Dr Olasimbo. He has just retired and is now running his own private hospital. Dr Olasimbo was well and has built himself a beautiful bungalow on the outskirts of Ijebu.

I then went on to Ibadan and stayed the night with the Failings. They still haven't got a car although C.M.S have sent the money. I don't know what Faji is doing in Lagos. He is going to work in N.B.C on Religious broadcasts and a Bishop Akintayo who was to be the bishop of Warri but was rejected, is going to look after us – as part of the job as Secretary to the new Provincial Synod. I hope we get a look in.

I tried to see Yomi and Kelu on the way back from Ibadan – but they had gone to a funeral in Ondo, so I didn't see them. I saw Inga in Ondo. I bought some flowering bushes in Ibadan which I hope to grow in my garden, so I went and bought some wire to keep the goats out. I hope it is successful.

On Thursday evening I came over to St Louis and have had 3 very peaceful days – especially today. I went back for our service at 10 am this morning and found Mrs. Kohli there with some other Indians. She is anxious for me to return from St Louis! Yesterday I was visited by a new Taylor Woodrow couple who have just been in Akure for a week. They have 2 children and they had met Brenda Batt in a sweet shop in Horsham and she had told them to look me up – so they did. It was rather funny because Martinian was in her pyjamas, and I was in my yellow house coat. We were just having a cuppa – and in these people trooped - to see me! At St Louis Convent. I couldn't think who they could be, and I thought for a ghastly moment that they wanted to stay for the weekend. Anyway, we soon sorted ourselves out.

On Friday one of the most pathetic fellows at the Leper Settlement was admitted at the hospital with vomiting and diarrhoea. He is blind in both eyes – but the eyes ooze! He is really a poor old man and not very cheerful at the best of times. The doctor at the hospital put him on a drip – but he dragged it out of his arm so there was blood all over his cloth. Frightful. Martinian is marvellous – she has been going 3 times a day to check him up and yesterday morning helped to clean him up – he'd wet the bed. Afterwards she went to Fr Joseph's house and was sick. Then last night it was cold, and we prayed for Folarin. Then we went to bed. Martinian got undressed and then decided she couldn't sleep thinking of the poor fellow without a blanket, so she got up and dressed again and went off to the hospital around 19.30 pm to give him a blanket.

There has been a complete change in the Military Governors this week. They have all been replaced by other men who are called Administrators. I am not sure of the significance of this move. It is a step forward towards civilian rule and maybe a chance for some of the ex-Govs to leave the armed forces and go into politics. I don't know if Daddy will still be in Stanmore this week – or if he will be in St Lukes now. I am sending this letter to Barnet, so I hope you get it in time. I hope you get lots of letters written this holiday – but I haven't made much progress so far. I bought some cloth to make a dress yesterday. I am reading Mrs. Rose Kennedy's book about her family very interesting. I also did a jigsaw yesterday and today which was satisfying – quite a difficult one with a lot of colour all the same – but a beautiful picture of a Swiss lake in the end.

I hope you got the 'messages' that I sent last week with Sheila. I am thinking of you lots and looking forward to having your next letter.

With much love to you both,

Elizabeth

Vining Centre
23rd July 1978

Dear Ma and Daddy,

I have Mother's letters this week written just after the op. I am thankful to hear that everything has gone according to plan so far. I imagine that by now you must be in St Luke's. It is a great blessing to have such provisions for looking after you when you are sick. I hope that Daddy is not in too much pain. I wonder how much he can move now – when you wrote it was flat on your back. One thing about being in hospital is that you have time to think and to meditate and to pray.

I seem to have had rather a 'going up and down' week. I haven't really settled peacefully to anything – but on the other hand, I have made some interesting contacts with the new Taylor Woodrow people. One couple came for supper on Friday, another woman and her 2 children come to our chapel service today.

Dr Kohli is hoping to be able to move into her new house early in the coming week. Her whole mind is on the move and getting her house clean and buying the things she needs to be able to set up house. She has the furniture she needs now but she still needs a fridge and a cooker before she can live there.

The old man who was sick last weekend from the settlement died on Wednesday, so we had a funeral in the afternoon. It was a mercy really that he died because he had gone completely blind. He died very peacefully back at the settlement among his friends – so that was better than being in hospital.

On Tuesday afternoon Eyesorun had a party to say goodbye to Mrs. Ekpeme the wife of the Governor. All the State Governors are to be replaced by Administrators starting from tomorrow. It is a step towards civilian rule they say. I helped Eyesorun with the flower decorations at the party. There are 7 Taylor Woodrow wives now and they were all invited so that was a chance to meet them. It was a 'ladies only do' organised by Eyesorun and Lady Jibowu who are both widows. Mrs. Kohli was there and Penny Lana, the American negress woman.

Last week a bulldozer came in onto the Leper Settlement farms and finished about 2000 heaps of cassava so Martinian has been running up and down this week trying to see what can be done about compensation, and more importantly moving the Ministry of Health into moving the place to a new piece of land – which must include enough land to farm – or they will all be beggars.

Then on Friday Martinian was told that she is not due for any leave except for 2 days at a time- so that cancels our going to Tarkwa. Martinian was very upset because she needs a break and is completely exhausted now. She doesn't think that she will be able to continue working at the settlement if she doesn't get any decent holidays. It is just too much – there is no doctor or nurse or driver or clerk to help her so she is really taking on what should be about 6 peoples work.

I am sorry about not going to Tarkwa because I had been banking on that week as a real break getting right away from Akure etc. I don't want to go there by myself – but I am not sure now where else I can go......... or who to go with. Anyway, I expect something will get sorted out.

I am very sorry for Martinian, and I think that they should bend the Ministry Rules in her case and give her a week off 2 or 3 times a year.

I think that I mentioned before that I would like you to send my cheque book to me via Sheila. Her address is Miss S.H. Davis, 55 Trinity Rise, Tulse Hill, London S.W.2 2 Q.P. She is already. overburdened with other people's luggage so please don't send anything else to her unless it is small. Greetings from Joshua Omodara – He has just called here this afternoon. I've not seen him for ages.

I made a dress yesterday afternoon and almost completed it – it remains the sleeves. I took ages about the zip which is down the front. After I did it once it was wrong and so I had to unpick it again.

It is wet here. Rain almost every day. I have been reading Mrs. Rose Kennedy's book – 'Times to Remember'. Have you read it? It is very well worth reading. An amazing family – and she has a great faith. Through all the tragedies she is not bitter at all. After reading 'Dr Ida' and then this book - it makes me feel very small.

I must hurry, because I want to take this letter to Ondo for posting with a sister.

With lots of love and hugs and kisses

Elizabeth.

Vining Centre
30th July 1978

Dear Ma and Daddy,

Good to get a letter from Daddy this week and to hear that he has graduated to sticks. I hope that this good progress has continued. I am happy that the chocolates got to you. I hope that by the time you get this you will be back in Malvern.

What a houseful with all the Scotties at Chimney Tops. They always do well on their holidays, don't they? I think I must save up and do something ambitious next year – like going to Gemma's caravan in Italy. I am disappointed that our proposed week at Tarkwa hasn't worked out. On Saturday, I found out that I could still go with some other sisters who were leaving Ibadan today. BUT I wasn't ready to down tools and go just like that – no money- a punctured tyre – Mrs. Kohli coming for lunch today – it was too late to sort myself out and anyway I don't want to go with some strangers and leave Martinian here working. I expect there is some 'reason' for it. I had a busy week and made some interesting contacts at the Committee for the International Year of the Child and at the Destitute and Beggars Committee. Then today Ebun turned up. She has left Akure and gone home to trade. She saved N900 while cooking at Fiwasaiye and spent N700 on provisions to sell in a shop. She is with her mother in her home village. She is to go to the psychiatrist for an injection on Tuesday, so she has come for that visit. She is staying here. It is good that she is wanting to branch out on her own and be independent, but she is likely to blow all her money. I have her Passbook with the remainder in it.

Dr Kohli moved into her own house last Monday, so she is now getting herself organised there. We had a Celebration supper in Fairmont Hotel on Monday – to celebrate her departure. She has no running water in her house which is a bit of a nuisance because she is having to carry water in containers in her car.

I spent most of the morning on Friday at the Leper Settlement and started to rule out a stock book for the store cupboard.

Yesterday – Saturday, I had the Bond family with their 2 children to lunch and Martinian and Sister Davnet for supper, Eyesorun and Mrs. Sijuade came for tea! Today it is Mrs. Kohli for lunch and Ebun and her brother for breakfast. This evening Ebun is preparing her own fish stew and pounded yam – the smell is everywhere and there is palm oil all over the stove.

On Thursday I was in Ado for the Destitute's and Beggars meeting. We were to meet at 9 am but didn't take off from Akure till 10.30. We arrived in Ado about 12 for a 10 o'clock meeting. The meeting finished around 2 and we reached Akure again about 3. 45 – stopping at every yam pile on the roadside and pricing them all but buying none. In the meeting the Minutes read that the 'Minutes was unanimously passed'. I said that it should be were, but my judgement was queried, and I was told in no uncertain terms that was, was correct because it was the Queen's English!! I was so flabbergasted that I kept my mouth shut after that!

Much love and many prayers,

Elizabeth.

Vining Centre,
6th August 1978.

Dear Ma and Daddy

I have just received your letter from Malvern. Great to hear that you are home again, and that Daddy has made such good progress and is using sticks now. I am sorry that I missed your wedding anniversary. I seem to get worse and not better at remembering dates. I can quite see that Ma must have been exhausted after staying with Anna Young. I can remember my head was already going round after one evening of her talking. I am reading the book Poustinia now – saying that everyone needs a quiet place of withdrawal. I was sorry I missed going to Tarkwa because I felt that would get me right away from Akure. However maybe it has worked out for the best.

Ebun was here till Wednesday – she ate an enormous lot of rice and yams. Martinian and I took her back to Ado on Wed and visited the Destitutes and Beggars Home while we were there. On Thursday Martinian and I went to Ibadan and carried 2 rabbits for the Failings. We stayed the night in the Convent at Mokola. There were 5 Sisters, 1 priest and me and I felt a bit overwhelmed and not very relaxed. 4 of the sisters were going to Tarkwa and really, I began to be thankful that I hadn't gone there with a gang of Sisters. I love Martinian, but it is much nicer to have her on her own. I went shopping in Ibadan – mainly for Mrs. Kohli who wanted several things that she couldn't find in Akure. We came back on Saturday evening.

On Sunday afternoon Richard come to visit Akure. He is on leave for 14 days. It was good to see him. He seems to be involved in many things in Sokoto State. He is busy looking for teachers for next term. He is still 16 short.

I am starting a vegetable garden – or at least that is my plan. Martinian has grown seedlings in her place, and I am going to plant them out here. So far, I have tomato, lettuce, cabbage, turnip plants and seeds for parsley and beans. I will have to keep an eye on the watering and see what can be done. Our soil is not very rich, and it is stoney but we have cleared a new piece of bush, so we hope for the best.

I think I prefer to keep on the Geographical because it is of a more worldwide interest than the Illustrated London News – which I agree is good.

I went out on Monday afternoon to deliver my Leper Settlement Minutes and afterwards went to see Penny and talked with her till about 8.30. When I returned home, I found David and Jane Lewis and Andrew (Jane Pelly's nephew) all sitting in my house. They had had supper provided by Tokunbo! It was very nice to see them all. David and Jane are staying till Thursday. Then on 21-24th they are going to come again with Jane's parents....... so, I can see that I am going to have plenty of company during August.

I shall be thinking of you on Aug 16th as you go for a visit to Dr Kemp. How soon will he do the second leg? I expect you will get to know then. Alleluia anyway! I hope that you are both keeping a good siesta in the afternoons!

My love to all friends in Malvern, Elizabeth

Vining Centre.
13th August 1978.

Dear Ma and Daddy,

I am glad to have heard that the 2nd op. may be tomorrow or Tuesday. It sounds as though the first leg is doing well, so I believe the 2nd one will be good as we all surround it in prayer. There is a nice verse in Proverbs 3v26 which says: 'The Lord shall be my confidence'

Aren't people kind? How nice of Moira and co to pick fruit for you so that you could make jam. I am sorry to hear that Kathleen G. has left her home to go and live with a jobless man. I will pray for her and the Griffins.

Dr Olasimbo was the doctor who came to St George's on Easter Sunday. Yes, he was in Ondo. Dr Kumuyi is in U.S.A doing a course in New Orleans. I thought I told you that before.

I heard Arch, Scot on the Radio service last Sunday. Then I heard another comment about the Lambeth Conference saying they couldn't finish all the things on the agenda and that the 3rd world bishops weren't getting a look-in. Pity.

The Govt here is to change to Civilian rule in October 1979 – but the ban on Political parties is to be lifted in Oct 1978. That's what everyone is excited about now. This morning I went to the service in the Army Brigade chapel – the chaplain is one of our old students- and they invited the new Administrator for Ondo State and his wife. It was rather a joke because they sat in the front row – place of honour – and I was in the same pew. Brig. Tuoyo's wife left during the sermon – she had a sniffy nose, or maybe she found the pew too uncomfortable. She fidgeted a lot- rather big build.......so then there was me on the right side of the pew – and the Administrator on the left. Afterwards he asked: 'Who is this European?' - so I was introduced. Rather a hoot!

On Friday I went up to Idanre with Penny Lana and her 2 children. I stayed overnight with Pat and Francis Akinbadewa. Fanny and Charlie Aigbokhai were also there – they are Jose's eldest children from Ibadan. So, on Friday we were 8 children + 4 adults for lunch. Pat is amazing. She seems so vague and yet she can cater for an army and produce gorgeous food. Inga came on Saturday with Bunmi who she is 'looking after' for Joseph. It was nice to be with them all, but I don't think I could cope with so many children. I am used to a quiet life! Penny Lana seems more depressed than ever about living in Nigeria. She keeps talking about going back to the States. She needs really to settle her mind on staying here and getting down to getting used to it.

Canon Faji is coming here tomorrow. I hope to be able to farm him out to the other staff for some meals etc. I expect it will work out alright. Myrtle has written to say that she will come on Sept 7th so that will be good. Sheila will be back in the first week of Sept – suddenly the holidays are almost over. I had a good meal with T.W people on Wed – pork and stuffing and peas and potatoes. Splendid. We had a good leprosy committee on Thursday evening – 14 people there.

With much love to you both,

Elizabeth

Vining Centre.
21st August 1978

Dear Ma and Daddy,

You must both be in London again this week. I am hoping to hear soon how the second operation went. I hope that everything goes smoothly as the first leg. How good of the Carters to offer to take you back to Malvern. Please give my love to Lynette. What a good thing that she has her home in such a convenient place.

The Expository times doesn't need to be renewed. I used to order it for Cornelius. Sorry to hear that Robbie had measles. I must write to Ruth. We seem to have got rather out of touch.

The past week seem to have been full of comings and goings. Canon Faji came on Monday and stayed till Saturday. I farmed him out to the Principals on Wed and Friday nights. Then Rev Ayodele took us to the Catering Rest House on Thursday. Grace came to stay on Thursday and is still here. I was also expecting David and Jane and Jane's parents but they haven't arrived – the Charter flight is delayed till next Tuesday.

I found Faji a bit of a trial as a visitor but I 'managed'. He is a bit of a 'weed'. He had never driven as far from Lagos as Akure on his own before and he was congratulating himself all the time for his courage in doing so! He was afraid to drive into Akure to the Post Office because he didn't like driving in strange places. I found that conversation flagged........everything was much better when Grace came on Thursday. On Friday Inga come through Akure on her way to Ado and dropped off Charlie and Fanny (Jose's children) and Bunmi (Joseph's child) for me to look after for the morning.

On Friday evening Grace and I went out and visited some mutual friends where we had supper – Nigerian food. On Saturday we went to Mrs. Kohli's for lunch and on Saturday evening we went together to supper to Sue and Doug Stevenson at Taylor Woodrow. Sue made sweet and sour sauce and rice – with dark chocolate cake and ice cream and cream and guava sauce. Quite an international range of foods for one weekend.!

Yesterday, Sunday, I went to the Catholic Cathedral for the Final Profession Ceremonies for 2 of the sisters – Isobel and Monica. It was billed for 9.30am with lunch after. We sat in the Cathedral until 1 pm and on wooden chairs in the Noviciate until 4 pm! I was exhausted. Their Bishop gave a very long-winded homily and then translated it all into Yoruba. In the afternoon there were long speeches too, so it was rather an endurance test.

Martinian was sick last week but she is better now. Tokunbo may be getting another job. I am not certain yet. I go to Kabba on 25th for the W/E.

Much love from.
Elizabeth

Vining Centre
27th August 1978.

Dear Ma and Daddy.

Today I am in Iyamoye, near to Kabba in Kwara State. I am with Rev and Mrs. Atibioke who are both old students of mine from Vining Centre. I preached in their beautiful church this morning and talked about Ebun to bring out the fact that the most important thing we should be doing is to love our neighbour – but also, that this is how God judges us – not the outward appearance of the Church building – but on whether the congregation are alive – see 1Sam 16 v7, Luke 10 v 27, and 1 Peter 2 v 5. I was happy for the way that they listened despite it being through interpretation.

Mrs. Atibioke has 7 children. 1 boy and 6 daughters. The house is tiny, but beautifully kept- clean and orderly. My stomach is like a football with pounded yam and rice. The hole in the floor in the loo is only about 6 ins in diameter. I find I am not a very good shot! I have had a hot bucket bath morning and afternoon since being here – which is better than Akure where there has been no water for the last few weeks because of the road construction.

Grace stayed with me last week up till Wednesday. I was expecting Jane and David and Jane's parents – but they didn't come....... very miserable – somehow the Charter has got out of order. Jane and David went on Friday to meet them – nothing- they phoned home from Lagos. Again, on Tuesday midnight they returned to Lagos – no plane from U.K – phoned home again and they say next Monday. Very disappointing – and expensive. They have spent £150 on hotels and phone calls.

Tokunbo got a new job on Monday – with the Government to cook for the new Administrator. I am relieved really – although it will take some time to organise myself. I intend to do most of my own cooking – but I hope that a schoolgirl -Abigail- will help with the housework, washing and ironing. She came on Wed and Thursday and did all my washing and ironing in 2 mornings. Her parents are at the leprosy settlement and living in a tiny room. She will come here and have a room on the compound. She will go to school – she is going to class 3 Secondary then she will do my chores for about 1 hour each evening – and work on Saturday morning. I think it will work out all right.

I came up to Kabba on Friday and stayed the night there with Canon now Archdeacon Kato who I stayed with before with Anne Harris. He knew Skiddy in York. On Saturday morning I went to the Women's Guild Conference for Kabba area. About 10 of our old Vining students were there so it was quite a reunion. In the afternoon I came here with Mrs. Atibioke.

I hope to hear news of Daddy's 2nd op when I get back to Akure tomorrow.

My love and many prayers,

Elizabeth

Vining Centre

31st August to 2 Sept 1978

Dear Ma and Daddy,

Thank you for your letters. It is super to hear that Daddy is so bright and cheerful after the second op. I do hope that everything goes well and that you are able to manage OK when you get home – with Daddy having '2 pinned' legs. Amazing what they can do these days. I am sorry to hear about the man whose ball jumped out of the socket. I hope he is getting better now.

Last Sunday I was in Iyamoye via Kabba. I wrote to you from there. I came away on Monday – loaded with an embarrassing lot of gifts: N15, 2 framed photographs taken with the congregation, 2 doz eggs, and a bag of oranges and bananas. Then on my way home I collected another N5, a chicken, more eggs and yams and a pot! Not bad for a weekend out! On the journey Home I stopped at the home of another old student who gave me lunch – rather tough fried chicken and some meat that I couldn't chew and so had to smuggle it into my handbag for disposal later.

I was at Dr Kohli's on Tues and Fri evenings. She came here on Tues. hoping that I would like to go to Ondo to buy some curtain material. I didn't! I stayed Monday night in Owo with Sister Catherine who was on her own. One of the St Louis Sisters in Jos was sadly killed in a road accident so the rest of the Owo house had gone to the north leaving Catherine by herself.

On Thursday we had our leprosy committee. We had a good meeting and were nearly finished when Dr Sijuade arrived and changed a few decisions. Really, he is very pig headed and annoying. He only thinks along his own track. It is not surprising that the doctors in the hospital resent his dictatorship. He has now resigned as P.M.O in the hospital and is going to do his own private practice. We are planning to have a special leprosy week at the end of September. There is a good deal to be done in preparation for it – but I think we are further ahead than in 1976.

David and Jane's parents arrived – at last! In fact, D and J went to Ikeja and asked about the flight and were told that it would be in by 2.30 am. So, they went to their hotel and 'slept off' – till 5 am!! and went back to the airport to find that Mum and Dad had arrived by 1 am after all. They all came here for lunch on Thursday. My cooking is going quite well – I tried bread today. Not perfect but reasonable. Abigail does the washing, ironing, and cleaning. I think it may work out quite well when I get organised.

With much love,

Elizabeth

Vining Centre.
10th September 1978.

Dear Ma and Daddy,

Very good to get your letters through Sheila so that I know what you were doing last W/E. Thank you too for the photos from 64 Church Road and from New Zealand. John and Mary's plot of land looks a gorgeous site. Thank you also for the books about Uganda which I have almost finished reading already AND for the chocolates which I have finished!

I had a most frustrating week. I was told about 3 weeks back by the Central Schools Board that they had sent the money for Myrtle's ticket and that she would be receiving it. I was assured the same thing around August 31st, so I was expecting to go and meet Myrtle on Thursday. Sheila was to bring the message of what flight she was on. So, I waited for Sheila who had a rotten journey – delayed over Mon. night in Heathrow – reached Lagos on Tues. evening – the driver had left the airport so wasn't there to meet her – she and Joan spent the night with the sisters at Maryland and came to Akure by taxi on Wednesday. So, I didn't discover till then that Myrtle had no ticket on Monday.

On Thursday I went to investigate in the C.S.B. The man in charge of travel arrangements was on casual leave. Who is doing his job? Nobody. I went to the Travel Agents office which is a new 'branch' in Akure. It just takes messages to Ibadan. The boy there said he was new. His predecessor had left without notice. He told me that if I wanted to know anything about the booking, I must go to Ibadan with the date that the letter was written from Akure. Back to the School Board. Can I see the file? No. You are not an officer in this Ministry. Then went to look for Lady Jibowu the Chairman.' on leave till Sept 15th – and the Secretary – 'busy'. Eventually one man helped me to look in the file – and said that they had written for the ticket on August 22nd. So, I went to the Post Office to try to phone Ibadan. All the telephone numbers in the country have changed so first we had to find out the new number. We got through – wrong number. We tried Leventis where the Travel Agent is and got the store which is in the same building – but they couldn't put us through. So, I went to Ibadan in the Vining Centre van because oil is leaking out of my car and it needs to be fixed. When I got to Ibadan they said: 'Yes, we received the letter of Aug 22 and sent a form to Akure which they must fill up. They have not sent it back to us!!! so no action has yet been taken on the ticket. After we get the form back it must go to the Central Bank, Lagos and then to British Caledonian, Lagos and then Brit. Cal. London who send your friend her ticket' Can you believe it!! So, I came back with the form – but the man is still on casual leave until Monday so we are waiting to see what he says next. Incredibly maddening. Poor Myrtle. After leaving the Travel Agent, I went to the Post Office and spent 1 ½ hours standing in a sweaty line before I was able to get a cable and a letter written to Myrtle. After tomorrow if I can see the man in the C.S.B I may try and phone Myrtle and if necessary, tell her to ask C.M.S to buy the ticket from that end. I don't think I will be able to get through from here. I shall have to go either to Lagos or Lanlate which is between Lagos and Abeokuta.

Please excuse the 'stamp' on the 1st letter. Ian got at my table. Ian is the Bond's 3-year-old son.

It is very annoying about Myrtle because the school was supposed to start on Friday and 50 or 60 children with all manner of handicaps were told to arrive in Ikare on that day. I don't know what has happened to them – and Myrtle won't know what has happened at this end – nor do we of course! Maybe the C.S.B man filled the form and gave it to the Tess Travel man who has left. Who knows? Communication is really very difficult here. My phone hasn't worked properly all this year -and to try to phone to England would mean spending a very long time sitting in the telephone exchange.

We are busy trying to organise our 'Leprosy Week' which is from 25th -29th. A good deal of the organisation falls on me – to get printing done etc. Dr Odeghe is coming from Ossiomo to talk about leprosy. The Radio have co-operated. The Director of Programmes went to the settlement, and they are planning to help us in 2 or 3 programmes in that week so that is excellent. Then we are having a Sale – Bring and Buy Sale and a Cultural Show and a Film Show. We hope to raise some funds during the week. We are going to have membership cards -N10- life Members N1.00 Annual Members and 50k – Student Members.

September 11th.

Back to the Central Schools Board. The man says that he had filled up the form about 3 weeks ago so that Tess Travel, Ibadan are at fault – or their messenger. So, he will go to Ibadan tomorrow. On Friday the children did turn up in Ikare and parents were furious to discover nothing ready for them. Mr. Adeyemo who went there said it was 'chaos' – but he was the one who asked them to come.......so really it serves him right! I am glad that Myrtle wasn't there. Maybe they will be wiser now and get things ready. He said that the parents were going to send a delegation to the Ministry on Wednesday to complain. It is a great country this....so long as you don't want anything done quickly!

With much love,
Elizabeth

Vining Centre.
18th September 1978

Dear Ma and Daddy,

Thank you for your letters. I am very glad to hear that you are back at home again. I hope all the gadgets are doing well and helping Daddy to get better daily.

On Tuesday this week an amazing thing happened about Myrtle. I met a man in the Ministry of Education who brought a consignment of wheelchairs and equipment for the handicapped school. We got talking and he knew Myrtle from Lagos. He said he would help about her ticket. On Thursday he came back from Ibadan to say that he had seen the head of Tess Travel in Ibadan – a relation of his, and he had got Myrtle's ticket by telling the Tess Travel lady that her reputation in Akure was terrible and she should issue the ticket and wait for the approval of the Central Bank afterwards. So, she did this and the man-who is also related to Grace Ohikhena's husband's cousins – said he would take the ticket to London and deliver it to Myrtle. So, if he does so that would be tremendous. Mr. Adeyemo in the Ministry said that there was chaos on Friday at Ikare when they gathered the handicapped children. Their mothers and fathers were so annoyed at finding nothing ready that they threatened to come in a delegation to Akure to protest. I hope Myrtle gets here this week sometime, but they say that there are delays in the European airports.

On Thursday Jane and David came with Jane's parents from Saltash in Cornwall. Delightful people. We went to visit the Deji's palace on Friday morning and then to Idanre on Saturday after arranging the flowers for the reception of a marriage. Mrs. Deacon was an expert, so they looked rather good. They were all super at helping with the washing up etc. but it was still quite a lot of work cooking food for 5 for 4 days. Anyway, everything went well – the meat was not tough, and the ice cream was just frozen. Shortages of water and electricity are the biggest hazard.

Penny Lana is the American Negress wife of an Idanre man. She is not very well settled in Nigeria.

I had a letter from Richard this week saying that some of his relatives were now telling him that he should have married me. Please pray for him. He gets so little spiritual help in the North, and it is easy to be lonely and depressed when you are separated so long from your wife and children – and he can't get a transfer to the South. Life is not straightforward.

With love to you both,

Elizabeth

Vining Centre,
24th September 1978.

Dear Ma and Daddy,

I have been busy all the week with the organising of our Leprosy Week which. is next week 25 – 29th. We have something on every day:

Mon – Launching of the Week and talk.
Tues – Film Show and talk
Wed – Sale.
Thurs - Cultural Show.
Fri - Opening of a shop at the settlement.

There are 4 programmes on the radio - then there will be press coverage etc. etc. at the Launching, when we hope that important personalities will be present. I was on the radio panel discussion – we recorded it on Thursday afternoon. Some members were better than others. I felt a bit nervous and not very well prepared. However, Dr Adetunji did very well, and I think some good points will come over. Martinian has been working very hard for the week. She goes on leave on Oct 1st. She is setting up an exhibition of the work of a carver at the settlement.

Our students come back on Friday so we are now into the new term – or at least we shall be from Monday onwards. We go to the settlement today for our Open-Air service.

Yesterday, Saturday at lunch time I came back from the Market and who should I find had just arrived but Myrtle!! Super. Incredible really. She flew on Friday from London to Lagos and then got a taxi up to Ibadan and stayed with the Failings – and met the Lewis's from Ikare, and Jane's parents too. Then on Saturday she got another taxi from Ibadan to Akure – and so arrived here. It is lovely to see her ……and great that she got her ticket through Mr. Ilebode. I think if we had waited for the 'machinery' to grind along she might not have been here before Nov or Dec. Myrtle says that she phoned you and that all is well – and Daddy's legs are improving so that's good news. Myrtle will go to the Ministry tomorrow and then we shall see how it will all develop. It is quite exciting because the children are ready to start the school and it just needs all the pieces of the jigsaw to be put together for it to take off.

My car was taken to Ikerre this week to be mended – oil leaking out and a 'clonk' at the back. It cost N80 to fix it, but I think it is better. At least those complaints are fixed – although it still seems to have some other noises. Dear Sheila loaned me her car to use while mine was away, so I was able to go to and fro with the arrangements for the week.

Abigail, my new house girl is getting into her stride a bit better. She should move into a women's dormitory today so that she will be going from here to her school in future.

With much love,

Elizabeth

Vining Centre,
1st October 1978

Dear Ma and Daddy,

We have now finished both the first week and Leprosy Week. The latter nearly finished me! But in fact, everything really worked out fine. I guess we may have raised about N2000 but at the same time gained a good deal of publicity and several new supporters. I hope to write a Link letter about it and have sent our pamphlets home with Martinian. When I get round to the Link letter, I will ask you to include the Information pamphlets. A lot of the big wigs who we invited for our launching didn't turn up – but that is inevitable I reckon. At least if they don't come then you can follow them up for a donation if you have sent them an invitation card. Some of our Committee members really came out trumps in our 'week' and turned up every day. It rained for the Sale and the opening of the shop at the settlement, but we managed to get N400 at the Sale and the opening of the shop happened very happily with umbrellas up.

Myrtle is still here with me – and likely to be for another week, but many things have developed during the past week. Nothing is ready for the school – just 4 derelict classrooms, but she has a flat, without any furniture so far and she has also begun to get to know the people in the Ministry and is busy on getting a car loan and a car. Not much choice really – only Beetles are available quickly in Akure. It looks as though Myrtle will be able to start the school around October 20th with a few children and then build on that.

Martinian has gone on leave. In fact, she is having a week at Tarkwa Bay before going to Ireland. She will be staying at home till

Christmas or the New Year. I will miss her here a lot. What a shock that the nice new Pope should die so soon. Very difficult to understand.

I am glad that the C.M.S Association seems to be waking up. I am not quite sure what is required of me on the tape. Do you want something about Vining Centre – or the work of a missionary today? I will try to rig up something and hope to get it off in time for Nov. 16th. Your rent is a bit shattering. How are you going to pay £600? I hope the Pension has gone up accordingly.

Myrtle and I went over to see Bishop Idowu this afternoon in Ondo – and we also saw Inga. We had lunch with Dr Kohli yesterday and with Sheila today. Sheila and Martinian came here on Friday evening – after we finished our leprosy week.

From Myrtle:

Oh- it is good to be with Liz and I shall never be able to say thank you enough to her for all she has done and is – she just listens and advises and does – and I am very grateful indeed – she's made this new appointment possible – lots of friends all around and now in the Ministry as well. I do hope that you are getting stronger everyday Mr. Deeks and that you are well Mrs. Deeks. Thank you again for Liz. Love Myrtle.

I am now to teach one class of the men's English – so I am glad about that. I got stung by a bee yesterday and have a sore arm today, but it is not too bad.

Much love, Elizabeth.

Vining Centre,
11th October 1978.

Dear Ma and Daddy,

Thank you for your letter of 17th Sept which I received this week. Post seems to be a long time getting through these days. I am sorry this one will be late because it is going to be posted on Wed. instead of Monday. There was no time to sit down and write to you this last weekend. It was partly due to Myrtle being here. We went shopping on Saturday afternoon and Sunday, after preaching at St Thomas at 8 am and then trying to organise the Sunday School at 10. We went to Dr Kohli's for lunch which lasted till 4 pm. Then Myrtle preached at

Fiwasaiye and we had supper at Sheila's. All in all, I got very tired and in fact went to complain to Dr Sijuade yesterday that all my joints were aching. He gave me some 'Magic' pills – iron, I think! And I feel much better now.

Abigail is now living here at V.C. This means that she can do a good clean or wash each evening – and she is doing it very well. I bought some Lino for the kitchen and the bathroom floors, and they really look super, and are much easier to clean.

Myrtle had quite 'a week'. She applied for her car loan on Monday and got the cheque on Wednesday. She had to go to the Accountant General for the State before the money could be released. Then she got the cash from the Bank. The car arrived on Thursday evening – all number plated etc. and on Friday Myrtle set off to go to Ikare for the day.......the car didn't reach Owo before it conked out!! So, Myrtle had quite a day – mechanic in Owo and Taylor Woodrow helpers in Ikare – but they couldn't fix the car and she had to come back to Akure in a taxi – leaving the car in Owo. Can you believe it- on the first day out!? So, on Saturday she had to go back to Owo to get the car with a mechanic. They fixed it on Monday, and she set off again on Monday afternoon to Ikare. I hope it is O.K now. It was lovely having Myrtle to stay for 2 weeks - but not very surprising that I was tired out yesterday.

Jane and David are the Lewis's who live at Ikare. Myrtle is now staying with them until her flat is furnished. They are the couple who came and helped me to paint my living room last term.

I hope the apples don't overdo it this year and none come next year! I am glad you are getting some decorations done through the Clergy Pensions. I am glad to hear that Daddy is progressing with his walking die die.......slowly does it. (That could be the national slogan here!)

With much love to you both,

Elizabeth

Vining Centre,
14th October 1978.

Dear Ma and Daddy,

I got 2 letters from you this week – the second one reporting Daddy's first visit out to St Matthias, and Sue Stevenson's telephone call. I must write to her. She is a very nice person. It will be good if she and her mother are able to come over to Malvern. Her stepson

Peter is at Loretto. I think I told you that. This morning I had a visit from a man in a big agbada who came to see me after Church with his nice round lacy wife. He said that he had just had a letter from Dougan Mayes. He used to be one of the 'Mayes Boys' in Owo and Dougan had told him that he should look me up.

Myrtle has been up in Ikare this week, but I am expecting to see her tomorrow. She is now waiting for some furniture before she can get into her flat. I was able to go to the Taylor Woodrow swimming pool twice and I had Thursday night in as well as this afternoon and evening (Sun) On Wed I had supper with Sheila. On Friday Sheila, Mrs. Kohli and Marion (Canadian girl) came here. On Sat. Sheila and I went to Ondo in the morning and then to Dr Kohli in the evening. This afternoon I stayed in bed and read a 'vet' book – but not the Herriot one. A bit rubbishy but quite fun.

I have been trying to get the Sunday School into better shape – and felt that we have made a little progress today because the children all got divided up into smaller groups for their lessons - but our men really haven't got a clue – and they shout at the top of their voices in front of a lot of small children.

The weather has changed this last week and become a lot hotter. It's the changeover of the seasons and so rather thundery and headachy. Margaret Bond has decided to go to the Leper Settlement 2 or 3 times a week to help them there. She is a nurse, so that's good. The only snag is that she doesn't have transport and she doesn't drive herself, so it is quite difficult getting her fetched to and fro.

Myrtle came on Monday morning and returned to Ikare on Tuesday afternoon. I am sorry this letter didn't get off earlier – but on Monday we had a Staff Meeting 4-6 pm and then I invited Lawyer Ogedengbe to talk to the students about the New Constitution. He talked about all sorts of things. He started at 7.30pm and finished around 10.30 pm!! Myrtle and I staggered home and went straight to bed!

For Christmas – I haven't really thought.... but I do need deodorant. Arrid seems to last a good time and it is in a plastic container – and talc is always a special treat – or perfume spray. Then I could do with a W.H Smith loose leaf pad- narrow Feint and Margin ruling 10"x 8"(Quarto size).

With much love to you both, Elizabeth

Vining Centre,
21st October 1978

Dear Ma and Daddy,

I am writing this from the Akinbadewa's house in Idanre – very relieved that I have finished the 2 assignments of the morning – to talk at the Communion Service at V.C. at 7 am and then to talk at the Anniversary service at Idanre – in Francis Akinbadewa's school. My theme in the H.C was on 'Be still and know that I am God' – and 'listening' to God's voice ......it's just as well that neither of you were there because you have heard a good deal of it before! At the Idanre school service I talked about 'choosing' – and choosing to be wise – like a 4-legged chair – all legs are necessary.

W = Wisdom from God. I = interest from ourselves. S = Sociability – being friendly with others. E = Education. To be balanced people we all need all 4 legs – if our whole aim is only to get a certificate then we shall be one legged when we come out of school.

On Tuesday we had our Prayer Fellowship Group – I read out part of Daddy's letter about 'Our Father'. It fitted very well with the theme of the evening which was praising God for Creation. Thank you for your contribution.

I am delighted to hear that Daddy's walking is so much better. Die die... little by little. God's slow miracles are just as exciting as sudden miracles.

Myrtle's plans for her school seem to be taking some shape. They will probably start in January. Before then Myrtle is going to go round the State visiting the children who have applied in their homes so that they can be properly assessed. Now they are all just 'handicapped' – no one knows 'how'. All being well Myrtle should get her furniture in the coming week so then she will be able to move into her flat. I hope to go there and spent the Half Term weekend with her. That's Nov 4-5th

I haven't yet done anything about your tape for Nov 16th. I must try and do something <u>soon</u> or you won't get anything.

Thursday: So sorry this letter is going to be late. I received your letter about your visit to London on Tuesday. Great News. It really sounds as though Daddy's legs are doing very well. Thank you too for the information about the tape. I am in the middle of preparing some Prayer Requests. I may only have time to send that – rather a waste of tape but never mind. I hope it will reach you in time. Maybe I will copy out the script and send it by letter as well as the tape - so that at least you will have one of them. I hope all goes well. I had a super letter from Elaine Seager the other day – and from Percy Walton – churchwarden at the Priory. Please thank them.

Much love,

Elizabeth.

Vining Centre,
5th November 1978.

Dear Ma and Daddy,

I sent off a tape last week through Taylor Woodrow post. I hope it reaches you in time. It's rather an odd tape because I only found time to do the Prayer Requests – and I did them twice. The second shorter version is the better of the 2. The other one might be usable in a Prayer Group context. Perhaps when you have finished with it you could send it to Odd Down and ask them to send it on to Miss Rosalie Smith – 13 Ladbrooke Gardens, Notting Hill, W11 2PT.

I am now thoroughly enjoying being on Half Term holiday - staying with Myrtle in her new flat in Ikare. She moved in last Monday and has already made the place very homely. It is an upstairs flat with a beautiful view across to some hills. Gwen is here too from Bida and Meg Merrifield - a new C.M.S person in Bida. Meg and I went and climbed Oke Oka this afternoon- a beautiful panoramic view. I was feeling very tired before coming here – but I now feel completely refreshed and ready for the 2nd half of the term.

This is the prayer Myrtle wrote about her experience of waiting:

'O Lord I am just waiting'.

Waiting for the moving of the waters -
Waiting for your hand to move and point
In the direction you want me to go.
Lord, I have tried – tried so hard to plan the next move,
And somewhere inside me Lord, I am still trying,
And yet Lord my life is as clay in the hands of the potter.
I cannot make myself; I cannot use myself,
I can but wait and if you want – go on waiting knowing that -
You can take even this deeply marred vessel and use it,
Fashioning it continually for the purpose you have for it.
O Lord, give me patience, and humility and vitality

Help me to be content, dear Lord, to wait and rest on you
For this speck of time is eternity.

Thank you very much for the birthday card and the £5 which arrived this week for my birthday. I think I shall probably be celebrating it on Sat 11th because Jane and Ruth are coming from Benin.

We had a good Prayer Group on Tuesday about waiting for God's time. On Thursday evening we had our leprosy committee at which we discovered that we had received around N2000 during the Week and that at least 10 people had come to ask for checkup and 4 new patients were discovered. So that was good.

I am glad that Daddy was well enough to give Ma a day in bed – and that her pain went after prayer from Basil Farncombe. You must both learn to do what you can and know when to stop. That seems to me the secret. Resting frequently enough to regain your strength and give you enough thinking space. I am very thankful to hear of all Daddy's progress with his legs. Super.

I am trying to organise something for the Christmas holiday time with Gemma. I hope we can go to the North and then maybe Bonny for Christmas.

Later:

I arrived back safely from Ikare – except that I had a puncture about 2 miles out of Akure and I couldn't shift the nuts on the wheel. But a Taylor Woodrow driver helped me, and I was OK. I then went to see Mrs. Kohli and met a man from UNICEF who is going to come here to see how they can help us.

It was good to be with Myrtle. I will go there again when I need a break.

With much love to you both,
Elizabeth.

Vining Centre,
16th November 1978.

Dear Ma and Daddy.

Thank you for your letter. It is good to hear how well Daddy is getting on with his walking. It sounds as though you had a great dose of nostalgia at the Waters Golden Wedding. I have Sue Stephenson's address somewhere! - but I can't lay my hands on it. I will let you have it. I fact I must write to her too – I understand they will not be coming back to Akure after all – a pity

Last week my birthday was on Wednesday. Eyesorun very kindly brought a cake, so I invited all the Vining Centre staff for 'tea'. In the evening Sheila and I had supper with Dr Kohli – and a very happy evening there. On Saturday I had Sheila and Jane Pelly and Ruth Howard and Eyesorun for supper and cooked chicken with a rather special salad. Eyesorun brought me a rather nasty looking large fish which I spent a long time struggling to clean. It had a fin along the back with spikes on it like a porcupine. Ruth stayed with me for Fri and Sat nights. It was good to see her. Jane stayed with Sheila, and I felt she was very strained and tired and needed a good rest. I think she hadn't really accepted the idea of going home. She feels she 'ought' to go and be with her mother, but she doesn't know how it will work out. She doesn't really 'want' to leave but the Federal Govt have left her with no choice because they say they won't renew her contract. All a bit rough when you have been here 20 yrs.

Guess what! A leprosy doctor has come!! I met him the other day.... he speaks mostly Arabic and very little English – but I hope he will pick up more English soon. As the headman at the settlement said, "If he can help, we don't mind what language he speaks" He hasn't been to the settlement yet. I hope he gets settled down to work soon – there is plenty to be done.

Myrtle came here on Tuesday this week and went back to Ikare today. It was good to have her here – but all these visitors have prevented me from getting round to write to you this week. Sorry that this will be late. I heard from Stuart and Ruth for my birthday so that was nice. I must write to them both. We are trying to plan an 'International Supper Party' – all nations in Akure invited – bring your own food! It is getting hot in the afternoons – so I am glad to escape to the Taylor Woodrow pool,

Thank you for the photo of the Mayes boys. I will find out that gentleman's name and show him the photo. Chief Adeniran is having a Thanksgiving this Saturday. He was made the Baba Ijo in St David's Church.

With much love to you both,

Elizabeth

Vining Centre,
20th November 1978.

Dear Ma and Daddy,

I received your letter today. Praise God for Daddy's great strides. It is super that he is really 'on his feet' before the winter sets in. I shall be thinking of you next week with Ruth and Trevor and Robert coming to stay. I hope that they find a job that suits them all for next year.

On Thurs 30th we are planning to have an 'International Supper' here at the Vining Centre – organised by Eyesorun and myself. The idea is for each nationality to come and bring some food cooked in their own way. Then we will share it. So far, I have contacted Philippines, Pakistanis, Indians, Sri Lankans, Canadians, American negroes, Sierra Leonians and British! -there are also Egyptians, Greek Cypriots, Polish, Bulgarians and Irish ….so we could be quite a large party. I hope it will work out as a happy meeting point.

We had a lot of activities last weekend – especially on Saturday when we had the naming ceremony of the principal's new baby. That was at 7 am and it was followed by the Baptism at 8-9. Then at 11am till 3 pm our students went to the Leprosy Settlement for their harvest. Also, at 11 am was the Thanksgiving of Chief Adeniran who has been made the Baba Ijo of St David's Church. Sheila and I decided that we should go to the service …. so, I left the harvest and went to the Church. Then I regretted it …. because we had missed the sermon (which was in Yoruba anyway) and they spent a whole hour 'doing' the thanksgiving …. i.e., different groups went to the front with their money and singing a song.

On Sunday morning I preached the sermon at the morning Matins. I talked about the 'spirit of service'....and played the song 'I want to give you this day'. It seemed to go down quite well, but I was a bit upset because I was only asked to do the sermon when I much prefer to take the whole service and follow the theme through.

On Sunday evening I went with Dr Kohli to visit the Sijuade's. Dr Sijuade has a new 'Private Hospital' so we went and looked round it all – very smart......but it is a pity that all the good Nigerian doctors are leaving the State service and going private. It then means that the hospitals are staffed mostly by expatriates who may or may not care about the patients.

Inga is going on leave next week – she needs a good rest, so I hope she gets it at home and isn't too stressed with her family problems.

Much love,

Elizabeth.

Vining Centre,
26th November 1978

Dear Ma and Daddy,

I think that my last week's letter was posted rather late and therefore contained most of the week's news. I stayed Wed night with Inga and finished your letter there if I remember rightly. Inga is going home on leave today. On Friday we had our women's practical exams. On Saturday I went to Ibadan for the day with the Bond family. I went to visit Lynn and Elaine Failing – to see their new baby – and to see how they are getting on. A Taylor Woodrow driver drove us to Ibadan …. too fast for my liking. I am not good with drivers – I prefer to potter along at my own pace.

Our proposed International Supper is going to happen on Thursday. There could be over 100 people. I hope we shall be able to cope with them all and make it an enjoyable evening out.

The next 2 weeks are going to be very busy; I think. I hope that Gemma and Shirley come wanting to rest a bit before we start off on any travels. I am still not sure where exactly we shall be for Christmas because I have not heard back from several people who I wrote to.

On Friday I went with the Leprosy Officer to collect about 30 small dried up looking yams which had been given from the Governor's farm. Then it was announced for the benefit of the Press that 80 FAT yams were being given to the settlement, the deaf school, and the remand home and that these institutions should learn from the good example of the Governor to grow foodstuffs!! The irony of it is that the settlement produces heaps of gorgeous fat yams, but the 'Government' is allowing people to take away their land to build housing estates.

December 3rd

Deary me! I thought that this letter had gone to the post. Really, I am in an end of term muddle. All my papers need a good sort out. I have now heard about the meeting of Nov 16th. Sorry the tape wasn't played. I had a nice letter from John Ridout about the meeting. Please thank him for it.

Our International Supper was a great success – at least 100 were there and they all ate well. I only heard of one who had tummy palaver the next day! I met several new people, and several expressed the hope that we would form an International Club in Akure.

I now have exam papers to mark - before writing reports. Today is our 'Harvest' Sunday. Great Jamboree. I am going with Gemma and Shirley to stay with Myrtle in Ikare 11-13th or so.

With much love to you both,

Elizabeth

Vining Centre,
10th December 1978.

Dear Ma and Daddy

Gemma and Shirley got here on Thursday and brought so many goodies. I don't know where to start to say thank you. Listening to the tape you sent made you all seem very close, and I have enjoyed eating your apples. Then there is jam to make me sweet – also, the long blue housecoat suits me fine, the calendar will be on my wall, and I will be writing notes on the pads. The bowls which Jutka made are on the sideboard on display – they are beautiful......and the chocolates are still wrapped up inside the fridge. I will keep them for a New Year party. Thank you very much. I feel thoroughly spoilt.

Gemma brought me a typewriter – and some photos of you both and the Malvern hills – as well as up to date news. Gemma and Shirley have gone off this afternoon to the Taylor Woodrow pool to sunbathe. I went to Ilawe in the morning to a short memorial service for Cornelius who died a year ago.

Our plan is to go to Ikare and stay with Myrtle tomorrow – and then to go to the North ….Yelwa – Zaria – Jos and back to Umuahia to stay with Ann Goodchild from 18th – 22nd. Then we hope to be in Bonny for Christmas and to return to Akure for the New Year. It will be a bit of a marathon, but it will be good to see folk in the North.

I had thought that Gemma and Shirley wouldn't reach here until Friday. Dr Kohli had gone to Ibadan on Thurs and was going to bring them back on Friday, but they got a taxi before she reached there. So, when they arrived, I was not prepared – in fact, I was out at a leprosy committee... the beds were not made and there were papers all over the living room. They had unpacked and gone off to the college chapel to take photos of the students and listen to their music.

I hope you have had a happy Christmas. We have made a cake. Gemma brought some mincemeat. I am not sure how much we should carry with us.

With much love, Elizabeth.

Travel with Gemma and Shirley to Bonny

Vining Centre
17th December 1978

Dear Ma and Daddy,

I am not quite sure if you will get this letter before Gemma and Shirley get back to England because there are so many public holidays between now and the New Year.

We are 'on tour' – Gemma and Shirley and I – and it's quite a tour! It goes Akure – Ikare – Yelwa – Zaria – Jos – Umuahia – Port Harcourt – Bonny – Umuahia – Benin – Akure !!!

We spent last Mon and Tues with Myrtle in Ikare and saw around her school in the morning. Then we went to Oka in the afternoon and climbed up the hill there. On Wednesday we drove via Kabba and

Ilorin to Yelwa where Richard has his T.T College. He wasn't there because he had gone to Jos for a Principal's Conf so that was disappointing, but we stayed in his house and went on to Zaria the next day. Jane and Richard Smith gave us a great welcome. They live in 2-storey mud house 50 years old. Their baby, Jonathan, is now 7 months and doing very well.

We went to a very 'cold' concert – mostly rather wishy-washy looking Europeans from the University. It was like going to a 'formal' Church service where everyone sits on their own seat and doesn't talk to anybody. Very odd and very un-Nigerian. The choir sang a Mass by Charpentier. The best thing about the whole evening was Gail Scott – a C.M.S missionary at Wusasa who sang contralto beautifully. Gemma and Shirley and I - and Jane Smith got rather giggly at it all.

On Sat. we left Zaria and took a rough road up to Jos. The road rattled us, and car was not happy. We had to stop at a roadside mechanic who decided that we needed 2 new spare parts – a coil and a contact breaker. He they fixed us, and we limped on to Jos. I think that the mechanic was wrong, and we only had a loose wire. There was certainly a loose wire when we continued the road – we had to keep getting out and fixing it. In the end I tied it together with some tape. We reached Jos and then Bukuru where I had written to the bishops (C.M.S new folk on the staff of the Theological College at Bukuru) They had booked us into the S.U.M guest house in Jos. This was very clean and tidy with good food all at a reasonable cost. We stayed there Sat and Sun nights. The amazing thing was that Janet Dominy, the S.U.M missionary who oversaw the Guest House was at Henrietta Barnet with Gemma! So, there was a great reunion. Also, Janet was a close friend of Catherine Galpin.

On Monday morning we set off at 5 am and drove all day to Umuahia. The road near Makurdi was potholed and slow so we took a long time over it. Then we drove on and on …... It was quite a day. We arrived at Umuahia at 8 pm at night – very thankful to be there because it is not good to travel after dark in the East. Also, we hadn't any petrol left in the tank (although 4 gals in a container)

We are now here with Ann Goodchild and her amazing big baby – Colum ….called after Columba really. He looks like a 1-year-old but is only 4 months. He has 2 teeth and sits up. He is gorgeous. Anne Bent is also here. She talks a lot. She has come on a visit for the first time since the War.

We are expecting Ruth tomorrow and then we hope to all go to Bonny together for Christmas.

With much love,

Elizabeth.

Vining Centre
26th December 1978

Dear Ma and Daddy,

Gemma and Shirley and I have had an amazing Christmas – at Bonny with the Pepples. We came back by boat on Saturday and will go back to Umuahia on Wednesday. We had a tremendous welcome when we came off the boat and were taken to the Chief Jack Wilson Pepple compound to drink a glass of wine in celebration of our arrival. After that we were brought back to the Parsonage where we are sleeping. Gabriel and Lucy have looked after us beautifully and fed us royally. It is hot and steamy here – with mosquitoes at night. We have had a fair do as far as services are concerned – 10 am and 7 pm Carols on Sunday, 10 am on Christmas Day and 7 am HC + Baptism the following day (St Stephen's Day) Amazing services – all in English and lasting a good long time. On special Sundays like Christmas, they have a 'Thanksgiving' for different things – sparing life in an accident or for a daughter returned from U.S.A, we liked the thanksgiving by the pipe organ committee for preserving the new parts for the organ from fire when the vehicle carrying them from Lagos caught fire! For each item the congregation gets up and dances forward to give their donation of thanks to the cathedral for that blessing. I have become the godmother of Gabriel Pepple Junior – 2 months old who was baptised today together with 32 other children. It was quite a baptismal jamboree.

Here in Bonny, there is a custom of having groups dancing through the streets of the town on Christmas Day. It is a bit like a Rag Day with everyone involved. All the streets are full of people dancing and drinking and celebrating. An incredible sight, some of the dancing is done by masqueraders and I guess there is a good deal of traditional juju involved. It is quite difficult for the church members to be single minded about following Christ. Everyone has been very welcoming and friendly especially Gabriel Pepple's older brother – Adonis and his family.

Before crossing over in the boat to Bonny we stayed on Friday night in Port Harcourt. Everything worked out very well. It was the first time our letters telling of our coming has reached the people before us. Everywhere else, except Jos, we were unexpected. We took the local boat to Bonny and not the fast-flying boat. Our boat took about 3 hours and really was more comfortable than the speed boat. As I am writing this now, we are returning in the same boat to Port Harcourt.

Everyone agreed that it was a 'Christmas with a difference'. I expect that Gemma and Shirley will tell you all about it when they get back. Yesterday we went visiting several fascinating people in Bonny. One Chief Jumbo was a timber contractor and exporter who had a sawmill in Fulham! Then we visited Dr Stephen Jumbo who was at King's College Cambridge in the 1940's at the same time as the Kabaka of Uganda. We also went to see Mrs. Dimieri with her photo of Ledbury Parish Church. She told us a very dramatic story about how the army came to their house during the war and they were saved from harm. The night before the bishop had a dream of a man in white saying 'Don't be afraid. I am with you.' Then we also went to visit some old people who were sick at home – some of them very poor. It was a great time – you would have enjoyed it all – except for the heat and the sweat. Poor Gemma was dripping!

With much love to you both,

Elizabeth

Vining Centre

New Year's Day 1979

Dear Ma and Daddy,

We are now back in Akure after our travels. I posted the last letter in Port Harcourt but maybe this one will get to you first - via Gemma.

We did some shopping in P.H. and then drove to Umuahia where we spent the night with the Goodchild's again. Their baby Colum is very big and keeps Ann very much on the go. John Goodchild is a rather anti-social fellow and goes off to his office to read or "work". I found him rather like cardboard. Gemma got very upset because she felt that Ann was not happy.

On Wednesday we left Umuahia and travelled to Onitsha in the morning via Owerri. We went there to see the Kybird's who are a new CMS couple who have taken over after the Kirkpatrick's as the Diocesan Missioner for Bishop Nwankiti. They were not in but we drank coffee in their house and read some of their children's books about Mr. Noisy and Mr. Chatterbox - very nice books in the series about 'Mr. Man'. I am sure

Stuart would like them when he is a bit bigger. Gemma got fever that morning, so we dosed her with Nivaquin. She really felt rotten. At Iyi Enu we saw Doctor Anne Phillips and Sue Williams busy in their consulting rooms and then we went on to the Bevers where we also met the Kybirds. The Bevers are leaving after another year in Onitsha. The Kybirds are a very nice young couple with a baby called Seth and another on the way. They were at Crowther Hall with Myrtle, so they hope to come over this way sometime.

After a picnic lunch in the Bever's house we crossed the Niger and went to see the Bishop of Asaba - who was out - we left a message about Dorothy Dyke's visit in February. Then we found Grace Webster with Mary Griffin and Thankanma staying in Asaba, so we had a chat with them before continuing the road to Benin where we stayed the night with Ruth.

Ruth hadn't been able to join us in Bonny partly because of pressure of schoolwork and partly because a friend of hers, Irene, who used to teach at St. Ann's was bereaved of her husband very suddenly. He was a Nigerian aged about 40 who suddenly died of a heart attack. Ruth came to Akure for Christmas and then went to see Irene from here.

Jane Pelly was also in Benin. I do find her a funny fish. She is now packing up and getting ready to go home in January. I am not quite sure how it's going to be when she gets home. I thought she was going to live with her mother but now she says that her mother doesn't want her to share the house and she keeps sending her adverts of jobs in places like the Cayman Islands!! So, it's a bit rough.

Gemma really collapsed at Ruths and had proper Malaria, including nasty nightmares .... but she quickly recovered after a day more - and is OK now. We had a puncture on the road from Benin to Akure and so we wasted a good deal of time getting the tyre changed and then getting a man to put in a new inner tube.

When we got back to Akure we discovered that Rajan Kohli had never come for Christmas - and Mrs. Kohli was very depressed because of that, and because she had heard that her younger brother had had a heart attack in India. She was depressed especially because there was no post to say what had happened to Rajan's flight - or to the brother after the heart attack.

It is good to be back - it's a good deal cooler here than in Bonny, especially at night. Then Gemma and Shirley enjoy going to swim at the Taylor-Woodrow pool.

We have had a quiet weekend and done a jigsaw and had meals with Sheila and Dr. Kohli .... and yesterday we had Sheila and Jane here for a 'Christmas lunch' - chicken, sausages, cabbage, carrots, potatoes, bread sauce and gravy followed by Christmas pudding with ice cream and jelly. Sheila and Myrtle very kindly gave me a liquidizer for Christmas, so I have been trying it out. Afterwards we ate some of your chocolates with our coffee - super! I had toffee and mallow.

January 2nd:

We spent yesterday, New Year's Day, at Idanre with the Akinbadewas. Their road is bad, but it was good to see them - we went together with the Bond family. Gemma has a rash all over and a headache. Shirley felt sick yesterday - I am the only one who had been healthy throughout our trip. Maybe we travelled a bit far!

I am sending a thorn carving with Gemma - really for a birthday present I think - in advance. I hope you got the Christmas presents - brooch and paper opener.

Thank you again for all the super things that you sent through Gemma - and thank you for the birthday money - yes, I did get it.

Ruth Howard gave me an Iona tea towel so that is now on the wall. I think Malvern will get used.

My plan in the summer is to fly to Rome and meet Gemma in Italy and then we shall go together to her caravan for 10 days or so before coming home. I hope to take the full 4 months leave that I am due - and to start it in the beginning of June, so I should be home by mid-June; Where would you like to go together? I am happy with any idea you like - during August will probably be the best.

It is very interesting that the Keiths are going to be in Jerusalem at the hospice there. I thought that they were not likely to retire so easily!

I am sending you back John's photographs of his house, and of the children. I am sending a tape - about Bonny - this is for family use <u>only</u>. It is mostly chat from Gemma and me. We did it quickly last night when we returned from supper with Eyesorun.

With much love to you both

Elizabeth

Two cheques are also included for depositing in the bank for me - thank you. £25 and £5.00

Vining Centre
14th January 1979

Dear Ma and Daddy,

So far only one letter since Christmas – but it is very good to have that and to know that Stuart and Jutka came to Malvern over the Christmas weekend – and that you had such inspiring Church Services at St. Matthias Daddy is obviously enjoying his new legs. Super.

This has been a preparation week – although as usual I have got to the end of it and the students are already here before I really feel ready. Anyway, I needed some time to readjust to life without Gemma and Shirley. I read 2 rubbishy novels and did a jigsaw!

We had a good staff meeting I felt on Monday – but we have let ourselves in for more work. We decided to have a tutorial group system for Year 3 men – to go over their sermons and to get to know their problems better. It's a good idea and I thoroughly supported it – but it means giving up Wednesday evening to do it – and being present during evening chapel on Wednesdays and Saturdays and Sundays.

We have 28 new women so far – 5 of them are Hausa! 4 can't speak much English but mercifully no. 5 can. One Mid-West woman can't come because she is looking after her mother .... terrible story: she had a whitlow last September – her finger swelled: her brother – a quack medicine seller – injected her and infected her vein. Her hand became gangrenous and 'fell off' at the wrist (!)

Our student went home in December and he and his family tried to persuade her to go to a doctor – but she refused because she didn't want her brother to be implicated. She said she preferred to die, and she threatened to commit suicide rather than go to the hospital. So, the daughter is looking after her – the hand smells so much no one else will go near her. Terrible. The husband is also upset because he wanted his wife to benefit from this year at the Vining Centre.

Myrtle came and spent Thursday night in Akure – here – she has started her school and the children are doing fine. The main snag is no money from the Ministry except for food.

Dr. Kohli left to go on leave – early – on Friday so I now have a Peugeot 404 to look after.

I hope you got our tape.

With much love to you both
Elizabeth

Vining Centre
21st January 1979

Dear Ma and Daddy,

No letters this week. I think that you are snow bound and strike bound, and we have a petrol shortage, so communications are likely to be delayed. I hope that you haven't suffered too much in Malvern

This week was the first of the New Year. Some weeks too! I have been trying to sort out the new set of women and get them divided into manageable groups. Some are Hausa and can't talk much English, 3 are Ibo - one with no English; 2 Yorubas are illiterate, so I am not quite sure how we are going to cope with it all. I thought that Dupe Oshin would be able to come and help this term, but she says she can't yet.

Then I have spent a good deal of time trying to sort out the Sunday schools for the new year. Dividing the 150 men into umpteen places for Sundays and then selecting the lessons that they are to teach. There is a lot to do to get things going at the beginning of the year.

We had a good seminar on Wednesday with all the staff attending the discussion on the sermons and then dividing into groups afterwards. My house is covered in dust - we have harmattan dust in the air. Abigail has a septic finger that was lanced on Friday, so she hasn't functioned very efficiently. I really must get round to some dusting! It is getting bad. I preached the sermon in the chapel this morning - but felt "rushed" and I don't think what I had to say went over very well. I talked about today's Gospel - healing of the lepers and the centurion's servant and brought out Jesus' response to the requests of these two was "I will ...... do something to help". I then mentioned a girl at the settlement who needs a job as a house girl - and 2 people came and asked me afterwards for more details so at least that bit of the message sunk in.

I have Dr. Kohli's car now - to look after while she is on leave. My own car really needs several mechanical repairs which I hope to get fixed while I have Mrs. Kohli's Peugeot.

In between all the other activities this week I went for a pre-leave medical check and blood and urine and stool tests and discovered I have round worm .... eggs at least - so I took worm medicine (not Mintessol!) and hope that they are no longer!

22nd January received your letter of 6th today and one from Gemma - staying she has spots. Glad you like the tape.

With much love

Elizabeth

Vining Centre
26th January 1979

Dear Ma and Daddy,

Two letters this week January 6th and January 9th. I am glad that you got the tape .... and so were able to hear something about our Christmas at first hand. I hope that you will edit it before letting other friends hear parts of it. Gemma got very upset at the Goodchilds and so it was all on her mind a lot. I hope she has got over her rashes now and they didn't turn out to be some nasty disease.

I am glad to hear that you have got new wallpaper. I am looking forward to seeing it as well as the newly covered Edwardian chair. I am also glad to hear that my tape is being used - and only sorry it wasn't a bit more carefully prepared.

I have written to CMS about my dates of leave - 1st week in June -> 3rd or 4th in September. I will have been here 20 months and I am due 6 days leave per month = 100 days. I hope to take most of it this time. So, we must plan for August. I would like to spend as much time as possible in Malvern. But Scotland would be lovely - or North Wales. I would like to go on a 'Retreat' sometime. Do you have any programmes? What's going on at Iona? or the Worcester Diocesan Retreat Place? I am staying with Myrtle, and she goes to a place near Cambridge called St. Francis House, Hemingford Grey, near Cambridge. It sounds lovely but Cambridge is a bit off my beat. I think not St. Julians and probably not the Fountain Trust Conference this year - although I see that all my favourite speakers are there .... but it is so big, and you don't get to know people very well - except those you knew before. It is July 30th - August 6th. I will write to Ruth Howard and ask if she is going to Iona - but I think it is a bit far for all of us without a car. (Ruth says she does hope to go 11th - 18th August or 18th - 25th and has written for the programme.)

We are expecting Dorothy Dykes to come to Ikare - Akure - Ondo - Ibadan - February 19th - 22nd. I hope she is not too tired by then after all her journeying around the country. She is to be at the Inauguration of the Province of Nigeria on February 25th.

Jeremiah Fabulije is going to be in England with Interchange for 3 months - March 6th -> June. I don't know how tight his programme will be - it is organised by John Ward. It would be nice if he was able to come and see you in Malvern. I hope that his visit works out well. I pray that he will have contacts with places which have lively spiritual worship. I have some reservations about how suitable a person he is to represent Nigeria to the English Church. He has so much to learn about being a Principal of a College and spends so little time sitting down actually doing it here that I fear that 3 - 4 months absence overseas will just add to his "going up and down" as Mama Ademoye says. He wants to go to Rome and Jerusalem on his way home! I will write to the Keiths because I should have thought that that would be a good place to stay.

It is good to have Myrtle nearby. Coming to Ikare is like a rest cure. Then Martinian is also back - this week - so that's good too.

With love

Elizabeth

Vining Centre
4th February 1979

Dear Ma and Daddy,

A very nice long letter from you both written on January 18th. There are some advantages of a cold snowy spell - you can write letters! But it sounds as though the strikes have taken some time to settle and schools and hospitals have been disrupted - as well as cemeteries. I guess the answer to grave diggers strike is to get cremated!

It has been a busy week here and I was very tired by Friday. I think I must take some vitamin pills. Yesterday - Saturday - was a complete 'non-day'. I was just tired and depressed. But things brightened up in the afternoon when I went out to the Agric with Martinian and the 2 Bond children. We collected palm nuts and cocoa pods etc. and took them home. Their parents had gone to a cocktail party in Ife .... so Martinian and I continued the baby sitting till they returned around 10pm. It was good to have a chance to catch up on Martinian's news from her leave.

Today I took the service at the Federal Government Girls College and told them the story of the snake who stole eggs and crept out through a hole in the wall but that he was caught when the farmer hard boiled the egg. The text is Numbers 32.23.!

I am sorry to hear that Tony Cooke is still sick. Bronchial asthma is a distressing business. I didn't get to the Prayer Group last Tuesday because there was just too much marking to do. We had a good Tutorial Group on Wednesday evening and discussed our whole system of sermon preparation and criticism - and preparation of sermons in general. On Thursday evening we had the leprosy committee meeting - here. Myrtle is coming tonight to stay here before going to the Ministry tomorrow. Next week Dorothy Dykes should reach Ikare on Sunday night and they will come here on Monday and Tuesday.

I am looking forward to coming home. It's hot here just now - although it has rained once - amazingly early really. That cooled us off a bit but it is still sticky. Anyway, there are only 12 more working weeks before I come - so that's good.

Today I have a punctured back tyre - it just went down at my front door fortunately. When I go to jack it up - no jack - old Sunday Mechanic must have removed it .... maddening. I must go and track it down.

With much love to all

Elizabeth

Vining Centre,
11th February 1979

Dear Ma and Daddy,

I am sorry that I am missing your snow - but not sorry to be missing all the strikes. Our main problem this past week has been that it is too hot in the afternoons! So hot that my brain ceases to work - or even have any desire to work! I was tired on Thursday - but then we had a 'surprise' holiday for Mohammed's birthday - so I took myself to bed and had some extra sleep .... so, on Friday I felt much better. I marked my books in record time and then read quite a lot of the book about the Findhorn Garden - the big book that was for sale in Malvern. That book gives you much more insight into what they are thinking and doing there than the smaller paperback which is written by an outsider. We could do with a gang of compost minded, tree minded people here in Akure. It is quite frightening how people destroy all the growing things of nature in the name of development and urban growth.

Myrtle was down on Monday, and again on Friday. On Monday she had a very good interview with the Commissioners and others, and they made several sensible decisions e.g., to buy a school typewriter! and to have a Youth Corp Physiotherapist full time there. But she has no money to run the day-to-day things of the school and she is using her own salary for all sorts of things. She has now said that she will have to ask the parents to keep the children at home after half term if there is no money from the Ministry. So, we shall see. The snag is that there is no money in the Government purse now.

I had a letter from Pat Hooker. I gather that Roger had an unsuccessful operation on his pituitary glands in December and is to have another one on March 6th. Apparently, his extremities are still growing. She asks for prayers. I hope that the next operation will be successful. Myrtle says that he has a very long nose, and that that is part of the problem.

Dorothy Dykes is to be here next week. I will take her to Ibadan, and from there she will go to the Inauguration of the new Province of Nigeria in Lagos on 24th February. I can't say anything about the new Archbishop - Olufosoye .... on account of Daddy's rule! I preached at St. Thomas' this morning - rather badly I felt.

Titi Ikotun came rushing out of Ibadan yesterday - very unsettled in her school and with the people in her house and the fact she is not married. Please pray for her.

With much love to you both

Elizabeth

Vining Centre

19th February 1979

Dear Ma and Daddy,

I am returning these two papers as requested via Dorothy Dykes. I am writing this week's news in the usual blue air letter .... so, I won't be duplicating it here. The two should reach you about the same time.

Titi has gone off for a week - she will be back on Tuesday 27th. Then she should get a job in Ondo and hopefully will find accommodation there and so will move out from here. Please pray that she may settle down. She seems to think that she can rely on me to find her a husband and solve all her problems for her! Not easy.

Dorothy has suggested that I think about having an extended leave and doing some course - maybe in Teaching of English as a second language or something of the sort - but mainly as a break from teaching the women here .... with the possibility of coming back to Vining Centre and teaching more to the men. So, the matter is to be investigated. She asked how my parents would react. I said I thought they would be delighted!

Anyway, don't let's count chickens before they are conceived far less than hatched .... but I thought you would like to share the idea.

I hope to see Ruth in Benin on Friday - for our Half Term Holiday - then I may hear more about Iona.

Anyway, if you think of any suitable courses for me for September .... in Birmingham or somewhere near - let me know - ! and we shall see what works out.

With love
Elizabeth

Vining Centre
19th February 1979

Dear Ma and Daddy,

Very sorry indeed to hear of Tony Cooke's death .... although maybe the main thought should be thanksgiving that he was given the strength to live so long and do such a good job. I have never seen "Come, ye thankful people, come" for a funeral before - but it is very appropriate. I will try and write to his wife.

Titi came here on Tuesday - bringing all her clothes and sewing machine and Tele and countless other bits and pieces which are now "occupying" my spare room. She hasn't really been a demanding visitor because she has slept most of the time, but I have discovered that I am very intolerant and am just praying that I keep my hair on till tomorrow when she is going away to Ife. Then I shall pray like mad that she finds accommodation in Ondo quickly. She has left her job in Ibadan and has been offered another in Ondo as from March 1st. I think it was just as well that she did leave because she was at the end of her tether and feared that she might have to go back to the Doctor at Aro - Mental Hospital if she didn't find peace of mind. So, I am glad that she was able to come here to 'sleep' and she says she feels heaps better. But I find her very annoying and know that I couldn't cope with her in the house for long - my house is much too small for 2 unless you are close friends. I just feel 'put upon'. She eats twice as much as I do - she has turned my spare room into a slum and Dorothy Dykes is coming tomorrow! - she washes her clothes in the bathroom and then you must mop the floor - she puts hot food in the fridge - she finishes the bread and doesn't tell you - she takes 'purgative' and doesn't flush away the frequent results!! Bah! She makes me very bad tempered and then I feel bad that I am so unchristian and unloving!!

Then my bread didn't rise well and I went all the way to Ondo to fetch Dr. Kohli's car - only to find that it wasn't ready .... and I could have saved my time if the telephone worked between Akure and Ondo, but the line is bad. So, all in all a thoroughly frustrating week .... the only good thing was that I went to Myrtles on Friday evening and had a nice restful morning on Saturday when I did my tapestry.

With much love - sorry it's not a very interesting letter! Looking forward to leave.

Elizabeth

Vining Centre
25th February 1979

Dear Ma and Daddy,

You will probably get the letter that I wrote via Dorothy Dykes before you get this one. Since then, I have been thinking over what she said about doing a course, and I have discussed it with Myrtle and Sheila. I have written to Stuart to ask him to send me a booklet containing the list of all the courses available - and I have thought that it may not be possible to get on a course this September and if that were so maybe I should organise it this year and then come back to Vining Centre for one more year and then come home for a break. I just want to find the right time - for V.C., for other commitments in Akure and for myself. To leave here in 3 months' time seems very soon, especially as there is no one to hand over the women's work to. Then it depends on what courses are available and seem right - and whether the aim is to do something to come back to teach V.C. men more; or if it is to have a complete break - to pack up and then see what opens again in the future - either here or somewhere else. So, you see there is a lot to pray about. Certainly, I feel that Dorothy is right that I should have a break at home - but the timing is not yet clear to me - maybe this September or maybe next September.

Are there any short or long courses that happen in Worcester in Teaching of English as a second language? Alison might know.

I decided not to go to Benin for the Half Term Holiday as I had thought - but to stay in Akure with Sheila and have a rest here. We went to swim at T.W. pool on Friday and I have done a good bit of my tapestry. Joan is also staying here. So, it has been a good thing. I feel more rested - although it is still very hot in the afternoons; 95° F or so. It has given me a chance to get used to the idea that I might even be leaving V.C. in 3 months without getting panicky and upset about it and I am sure that the Plan will unfold gradually. Last night we played scrabble and I got "inquires" and therefore got 50 bonuses so I was well away and was a clear winner at the end which was fun. Today Sheila and I went to the V.C. Chapel Communion Service and Sheila gave the sermon on 'God the Father'. It was very challenging - particularly to parents because she talked about what being a good father meant. Myrtle spent the weekend with Gwen in Ibadan. I hope they enjoyed the break because there is curfew in Ibadan - since there was a nasty wave of armed robberies. Myrtle is having the Opening of her school in Ikare on March 10th. I hope to be able to go. Martinian is on retreat this weekend, but I hope she will come today or tomorrow to go a walk in the Agric together. That will be good.

Happy Birthday Daddy. Card coming.

With much love

Elizabeth

Vining Centre

1st March 1979

Dear Ma and Daddy,

I am at Myrtles again today and as usual enjoying her nice flat and lovely view. I will return to Akure this afternoon. Yesterday was the official opening of Myrtle's school by Eyesorun. It was a very impressive occasion with everything very well organised and an interesting programme. The children sang some songs and recited some poems and then 'ran' two races. One a wheelchair race with 4 contenders and the other 2 flat races with the children running as best they could. One girl won her race by going along on her seat - swinging on her arms. Amazing.

Afterwards we came back to Myrtle's flat with Eyesorun and the Ministry of Education officials from Akure and had jollof rice for lunch with lots of cold cokes. Then everyone went away, and I stayed overnight with Myrtle. I was very happy to have a nice rest here today because I had fever (malaria) last week and at one time I was a bit afraid that I might not be able to come to "Myrtle's Opening".

Fabuluje left on Monday. I hope you got my letters sent by him. He has a head like a bucket with a hole in it.

On Tuesday I didn't feel like getting up and making lunch for Martinian was an effort. I had backache and began to ache all over. Then I took some women to a meeting and began to feel worse so I went to see Dr. Sijuade and he said I should take the usual - Nivaquin and Aspirin - because my temperature was 102°. So, I then had 'fever proper' Tuesday night and all-day Wednesday and it was still 102° on Wednesday night. However, I had cooled down by Thursday although I was still in bed and on Friday I stayed in again, although by then I was feeling much better. I still feel a bit worn out by the event but have benefited from coming here to be with Myrtle, despite the drive and the potholes between us.

I was so 'out' most of the week, so I had no energy to get upset by anything Titi was doing in my kitchen. In fact, she was a great help and looked after me - getting water and so. Then Sheila and Martinian were both in and out a good deal, so I was very well cared for. My women came in a troupe daily and prayed for my recovery and the men students sent their delegates.

The Archdeacon took over as Acting Principal on Monday and we had a very good staff meeting together. Unfortunately, he was rushed to the hospital on Tuesday night with diarrhoea and vomiting -? cholera so our staff was rather reduced for the second half of the week.

Myrtle sends much love - and so do I.

Elizabeth

Vining Centre
3rd March 1979

Dear Ma and Daddy,

I am sending this letter with Jeremiah Fabuluje. John Ward seems to have him well organised. I only hope that he is not a disappointment as an Interchange Visitor. I think the experience will help him to have a larger view of the Church. I hope he won't be frozen in UK March.

I have now discussed with the bishop the possibility of my going to do a course - maybe this September if I can get accepted for such. If not, maybe I shall have to postpone till September 1980. The bishop was very understanding and agreed that I needed a change from the women's teaching. Everything depends on 2 things:

(1) if another woman teacher can be found.

(2) if I can get organised in time to

a) choose a course
b) be accepted for September 1979.

I am sending 2 more "little people" with Fabuluje - I hope you like them. They are 'Birthday Presents' for March 4th and May 9th. I have given Fabuluje your address and telephone number. I don't know his programme and if he will be in Birmingham or not during his visit. Please can you send the enclosed thank you letters - you will see the names inside. Was Mrs. Sainsbury's and Anna Hendre's money for letters or lepers? I have assumed that it is for letters.

Disaster! The wind blew the curtain and knocked down the man digging so he is broken - but I think he could be stuck with a good gum and you would never know - the snag is that I have no Araldite or such so I am sending it broken - Sorry Oh!

Titi has been here all this week from Tuesday. She has now got a job in Ondo so I hope that she will settle down there. She is to go tomorrow and see about the accommodation. I do hope she can move quickly because I don't mind having her as a temporary visitor, but I can't cope with her as a semi-resident.

I find that I am just like my mother! I really get upset with someone sharing my kitchen - or worse still taking it over. Yesterday Titi put on some beans on the stove and then went out and they burnt. I found the burnt saucepan on the floor in the evening under the sink. Then she brought some beans with jumping bugs in and mixed them in a tin with mine which were good whole beans. Then she occupied my whole kitchen cooking snails and vegetable stew and dripping the blood from the fish down the back step - so I went out and had lunch with Sheila! I came back to prepare the meat that I had defrosted for a stew for the lunch on Sunday. Would you believe it? - she had cut it in small pieces and made it into a peppery stew!! Without any by your leave. I was hopping mad! She did apologise for that and went off to the market to buy some more meat! I think she got the message that I liked to cook in my own kitchen.

Fabuluje has just been here with his 3 pieces of winter clothes - one balaclava like hat, one thick sweater and one woolly looking woman's jacket. All are quite sensible and warm - but he put on the coat and had a good laugh about a human being looking like an animal - it is rather a bear like coat. He will need gloves or mittens. He has some boot like shoes which look OK.

I hope you get this letter OK, and that it is not lost en route.

It rained yesterday - lovely. I slept like a top and suddenly felt much more lively and able to get on with things that had been stagnant for weeks. We really needed it - the weather was getting oppressive and heavy.

With much love to you both, Elizabeth

Vining Centre
17th March 1979

Dear Ma,

So sorry to hear that you have a broken wrist. The typed letter reached here on Tuesday 13th and Daddy's letter saying that you fell on Wednesday 14th. I will write properly tomorrow but I wanted to try and send a quickie with Titi who is going to Ibadan today. She is still here!

I do hope that the wrist is mending well and not too painful now.

E pele oh! Please buy some chocs or flowers or any nice thing that you think will make your arm feel better.

With much love
Elizabeth.

Vining Centre
18th March 1979

Dear Ma and Daddy,

Two letters this week - Tuesday and Wednesday - telling me in the wrong order that Ma had a broken wrist. But it was good to get the typed one first and to know that you were being well cared for by all the neighbours. What a lovely lot of different foods you were given! People are really very kind. I hope that the wrist is mending well. You should take extra calcium. Do you know the fizzy tablets? - calcium and vitamin C made by Sandoz. Ca C1000. They are nice.

This week has continued to be HOT. The temperature in my living room is often 90° or 92° F even in the evening. It's OK at night so long as the electricity doesn't fail, and the fan goes off .... but it is still sticky with the fan. We just pray that it will rain soon and clear the air.

Ebun came back this week in a great state from her village - thieves had stolen all the goods from her store - very little is left of her N900. But worse than this she went to the house of her proposed husband

and was feeding one of his children by his 1st wife - force feeding - and the baby died! Terrible. But a double tragedy that it should happen to Ebun with her history. So, she is at Sheila's house - eating her out of house and home .... so really, I can't complain about Titi - who is still with me. We don't quite know what Ebun can do next. Titi has a job - at Okeigbo Grammar School between Ondo and Ife .... but no accommodation. She wants to live in Ondo but seems content to sit down and wait to see what Inga can find for her. Certainly, it is not satisfactory for her to commute from Akure to Okeigbo as she has done this past week. It is about 40 miles. Also, I want her out of my hair.

On Wednesday at Fiwasaiye one of their blind girls was knocked down by a car in the compound. She mercifully didn't break any bones but has been in the hospital since.

The best week for Ruth to go to Iona is August 11th - 18th so she has provisionally booked for that. The most interesting one is I think August 25th - September 1st 'Paths from Poverty' but that is too late for Ruth, and it would be nice if we went together and maybe I could meet her before - or stay longer after so that we could walk together in Scotland. What are your ideas? I am willing to come to any of your hideouts for a nice quiet week. Maybe North Wales? or somewhere in Herefordshire - or did you fancy Scotland too?

With much love to you both

Elizabeth

Vining Centre
25th March 1979

Dear Ma and Daddy,

I have decided that I don't like Mothering Sunday! All the children of our chapel congregation come and invade my garden and swipe my flowers! and make me hopping mad. It's time I came home - I am tired and scratchy. This past week we have had 2 days of exams for the women, and I was completely exhausted afterwards. There are about 14 of them who want to do the exam orally so if you give them 15 minutes each that adds up to 3½ hours! On Friday I sat from 9 to 1pm and then again from 3 to 6pm trying to see if they know anything. It gave me backache!

You will be glad to hear that Titi has moved out today to her new house in Ondo. She has a 3 bedroomed house on an estate there - <u>with</u>

running water! She says she will come here on Tuesdays, Fridays, and Sundays!! But I must say I find it a relief to be on my own again and to be able to go to the fridge and find what you left there, still there. I think she will be OK in Ondo. She is very enthusiastic about her new house and getting it organised, and an Indian teacher at St. Monica's is in the next house so they will be able to keep each other company.

We have just one week of the term to go and then 3 weeks holiday March 31st - April 20th. I may have to go to Lagos to see about my ticket home, and whether to sell my car. It is now 6 years old, and it looks as though it is going to be expensive in repair bills soon - although it is running well in the town. Then Sheila and I hope to go to Myrtle's for the Easter weekend - for a "Retreat". I also want to go and see some friends during the holidays - to say 'goodbye' - Grace, Bamgboyes, and maybe Richard. I haven't heard anything from home or from CMS in the past 10 days and I am waiting for some information. Now the future is 'blank' - with an increasing feeling of the relief it would be <u>not</u> to come back in September! but I don't want to leave the women teacherless. Looking forward to hearing news of 'the arm' and Fabuluje's visit.

Much love

Elizabeth

Vining Centre

31st March /1st April 1979

Dear Ma and Daddy,

The last week of the term was exhausting, and I was very thankful when the Commissioning Service on Tuesday was over so that I could look forward to the beginning of the holidays.

On Friday morning we had a naming ceremony of our latest new baby. In the afternoon I had a surprise visit from Richard. He came to Akure with a friend from Ilesha. He came to tell me about his commitments for the holidays - and so I cancelled the idea of going to the North. He will probably come to Akure again before Easter. He is hoping to transfer to Oyo State and to be Principal of an Advanced Teachers College in Oyo, as from September. I am glad about that because he will be nearer to his family in Ibadan.

On Friday night I went to St. Louis and stayed in the Convent. I then had a complete 'rest' day on Saturday and began to feel more normal and rested. I came back to my house and found that the Failings had come from Ibadan - for lunch, and to stay the night.

Fortunately, they had brought some food with them because I was going to Sheila's for lunch - and we all went together taking our contribution with us. Then about 4pm Dr. Kohli arrived back from her leave full of talk about her son's marriage etc. I was to take the service at Fiwasaiye at 6pm and I had intended to prepare in the afternoon .... so, it was a bit of a scratch affair.

On Monday (yesterday now) I spent most of the day helping Dr. Kohli to get organised in her house - and to report for duty in the hospital. 3 of our students went to help her to clean the 2 months dust away. Also, Inga came over to sit in my house and mark her exams and I had a swim at the Taylor Woodrow pool, and I went to the shops with Inga. Sheila and Myrtle are coming to stay here for next weekend.

I hear from Gemma that your plaster is off. That's good. No letter yet about Fabuluje's visit. Looking forward to hearing.

According to the Failings Dorothy Dykes reckons I have been 'long enough' in Akure. It sounds a bit as though she didn't approve of my house, which I agree has defects - the loo seat is broken - and Dorothy couldn't understand why I didn't get a new one .... I never got round to it!

With much love to you both

Elizabeth

Vining Centre

8th April 1979

Dear Ma and Daddy,

I hope this may reach you for Easter and that you will have a joyful time. I can imagine all the lovely spring flowers in the Church. Please use the enclosed cheque to buy some Easter chocolates - with my love .... I hope that Mother's arm is now out of plaster and that it is not too stiff. I expect you will need physiotherapy to get it going again. The second cheque is to go into my bank account in England.

Today is Palm Sunday and Myrtle and Sheila and I went to the Early Communion at 7am. The weather is still very hot, and we are hoping very much for rain. There was a great wind this evening but someone else got the rain.

Margaret and John Bond of Taylor Woodrow have just come in with N290 which was raised at a snooker tournament at Taylor Woodrow this week. Great! It's to buy mattresses for the patients at the settlement. Myrtle has just gone to their house for a bath - hot and cold water there. Sheila and I are at home writing letters.

Mama Ademoye has just returned from the Thanksgiving Service following Ayodele's father's funeral. She said it lasted till 1.30pm and everybody was called to go up and dance and give their thank offering - she said, "all except the ducks and chickens were called!"

We shall be here over the Easter Weekend and hope to be joined by Ruth Howard and maybe Grace Webster. We hope to keep silence on Friday and Saturday - and maybe listen to the St. John Passion. No-one seems very clear what services will be held here over Good Friday and Easter.

Please give my love to Ruth and Trevor and Stuart and Jutka - maybe you will be on the phone to them. I haven't written any other Easter letters except this one! I still haven't heard anything from Dorothy Dykes or CMS but am beginning to think in my own mind that it would be better to wait till 1980 and get something properly organised. I don't want to just 'do' a course and find it dull - and there will be more chance to sort it out at home. Please tell Stuart that I received 'the book' of courses.

Much love
Elizabeth

Vining Centre
8th April 1979

Dear Ma and Daddy,

I am writing a blue air letter because I think they get through faster.

It has been a good week and I have relaxed after the end of the term. Now this weekend Myrtle and Sheila are both staying here to have their rest. Sheila is completely exhausted and was very strung up at the end of the week.

On Monday I helped Dr. Kohli get settled with her house. On Tuesday I spent a good part of the day delivering the Leprosy Committee minutes for the meeting on Thursday. It was a good meeting too - there were 16 of us present including 4 doctors. The future of the leprosy patients is still in the balance because of the building development all round - and because there is no money in the new budget for future development of the plans for hospital and rehabilitation centre. So, there is nowhere for them to move to if they must go from the present site.

I have begun to do a bit of clearing up in my house. I want to get my books and papers straight to that there is not too much chaos in June. I haven't made a lot of headway yet, but some things are more organised. Ruth and Myrtle and Sheila and maybe Grace are going to all come here for Easter. We decided to 'retreat' at Vining Centre rather than Ikare because there is Communion and services in English here whereas at Ikare it is a long Yoruba event.

I was happy to get your letter telling of Fabuluje's visit. It sounds as though a good deal was packed into his days in Malvern.

Yesterday was the funeral of Rev. Ayodele's father - he died at aged 95 so was born in 1884. Amazing thought to have lived through almost all the 20th century so far, and to have seen all the changes that have taken place in Ikare. The Bishop of Ekiti was there - and a good number of clergy as well as a church full of people. The burial ground was 3km way from the Church and so everyone trekked in procession - at least a lot of people did. 8 of our students carried the coffin. I went by car with the Commissioner of Finance! He is the chairman of our Chapel Committee at Vining Centre. Afterwards we went back to the Archdeacon's house and ate a gigantic plateful of jollof rice and moyin moyin and goat. The bishop said that his moyin moyin looked like the Alumo Rock it was so big. All in all, it was quite a jolly funeral - but Ayodele looked completely exhausted by it all .... and they were going to have an all-night party and a thanksgiving service today. I do hope you have a very happy Easter.

With much love to you both

Elizabeth

Vining Centre
16th April 1979

Dear Ma and Daddy,

I hope you had a happy Easter. We had 2 Quiet Day's Retreat - Good Friday and Easter Saturday. It worked out very happily. Sheila and Myrtle slept in Mars House, and we had our prayer sessions down there. We prepared the meals and ate them in my house where Ruth and I had a bedroom each. I spent a good deal of time down at Mars House because it is not easy to meditate and retreat in your own house with all your 'things' around. It is easier to be uncluttered. We had 3 sessions each day like this:

Good Friday	9am	Meditation - Myrtle
	12.30 - 3pm	St. John Passion (record)
	8pm	Intercession for people in prison and persecuted Christians.
Saturday	9am	Meditation - Ruth
	5pm	Intercession for friends and families especially people who have gone home from Nigeria
	9pm	Compline
Sunday	7am	Holy Communion.

After this service Myrtle made her promise of wanting to join the 'Companions of Brother Lawrence'. I don't quite know why she wants to join this as well as CMS, but I think she feels that their prayer fellowship will help her in Ikare.

Myrtle painted a beautiful watercolour. I did a rather garish oil painting in a bit of a hurry - it is quite effective from a long distance!! I read 3 chapters of a book called 'Friday Afternoon' by Neville Ward. Very thought provoking - on 'Forgiving', 'Hoping' and 'Belonging'. I also read about half of Sheila Cassidy's book - 'Audacity to Believe'. I haven't yet got to the torture bit. She writes very honestly.

It was good having Myrtle here again and seeing Ruth - the first time since Christmas. We have booked Iona from 11-18th August .... I may go up to Moffat either before - or more likely after this - depending on other plans both of Ruth's and yours.

I still haven't heard any word from Dorothy Dykes - so I don't know what they are thinking that end. I haven't yet been to Lagos about my ticket home. I ought to go this week, but I keep putting it off. It is so <u>hot</u> still. 90°F most of the day - but even 82 or so at <u>6</u>am .... and over 80°F all night. It still hasn't rained properly.

I didn't go away in the week before Easter because I was expecting Richard to come to Akure. He never showed up, which was disappointing. I hope he is OK. I had a very vivid dream last night that he had died in a road accident. I don't often dream so it alarmed me and made me quite anxious. I expect he was just too busy.

I am not sure how to organise going to Italy. I may come to London and go off the next day with Gemma on an excursion ticket. This way the money will be about equal to stopping over - and it might be simpler - although a bit tantalising not to see you till 10 days later.

Much love

Elizabeth

Vining Centre
20th April 1979

Dear Ma and Daddy,

I have just returned from Lagos where I went to see about my ticket. I had a very pleasant journey, because I went with Eyesorun in the Commissioner's Peugeot 504, Air-Conditioned Car. It made everything much more comfortable as you can imagine, and her driver is good and knows the roads. I enjoyed it all. Lagos has really improved. If you take the flyover routes it is quite an impressive city.

I stayed the night in the Guest House at the Marina and had a nice hot bath there. Everything was very nice and comfortable. There were 3 men staying there - one Philippino UNICEF worker and one Ghanaan with WHO.

Now we are back - and the students have arrived today. We shall start the term tomorrow morning by welcoming the newcomers. We still have no new teacher, and I still have heard nothing from Dorothy Dykes - but I did discover in Lagos that it will save on money if I get off at Rome and go to Gemma's place en route rather than coming to London and going back again.

The probable flight is on Wednesday June 6th at night so that I will meet Gemma in Rome on Thursday June 7th. Then we shall come together to London on Saturday June 16th if all goes according to plan. Gemma should be able to tell you when we shall come to London. She will probably know before I do.

I hope it all works out well. It will be good to see you both in mid-June.

Much love to you both,

Elizabeth

Vining Centre
22nd April 1979

Dear Ma and Daddy

No letter for some time - but perhaps they are coming. I heard from Ruth today - written on 11th April, and I had your nice Easter card with the lambs on it.

I think you will get my 'card' and note before this - I sent it off the day before yesterday - and it has information about my going to Lagos.

This is the beginning of the new term - and there are only 6 weeks before I come home on leave.

We had a 'terrible' Communion Service this morning, taken by Rev. Adeyelu. First, he gave a long sermon; about 30 minutes; in which he traced the whole history of the O.T. up to the time of Nehemiah. Then his main point seemed to be that we were all to work hard at the new term - just as Nehemiah worked hard at the building of the walls of Jerusalem. It was an exhausting sermon. Rev. Ayodele is already off sick after the efforts of last term and the arranging of his father's funeral. Then I think Rev. Adeyelu realised that we were running late and so he 'raced' through the communion section in a most undignified fashion. It was incredible - and shattered any thought of worship as far as I was concerned. I really wish I was a man, and a clergyman and so could do something about our services here.

We have a new electric organ - given to us by the Army .... but it is rather loud and piping with too much tremolo .... and when it is not very well played it is not so easy to drown as the old harmonium. It all makes me sad because I seem to be powerless to do anything about it. Perhaps I should come home and do a course on how to play an organ!

Sheila and I were at Dr. Kohlis last night for supper, Sheila will come here for lunch and maybe Dr. Kohli .... and we will all go to Sheila's this evening. Before that I shall go with our students to the Leper Settlement for our beginning of term open air service.

We still have no signs of another teacher to help with the teaching of the women. Please pray about this because we need someone, whether I return in September or not.

Titi has just turned up - for the 10 o'clock service, I guess. Maybe she will stay for lunch .... it's a pity that it's just going to be soup and sandwiches and jelly for afters because we are eating at Sheilas today.

Joseph Kumuyi is back from America. He is busy building a house on a plot of land in the housing corporation. He seems well and cheerful. I hope Mother's arm is steadily getting better and is less stiff and painful.

With much love

Elizabeth

Vining Centre
29th April 1979

Dear Ma and Daddy,

Mummy's written "Mummy" is improving - not so squiggly so that's a good sign. I like your thought "I will go before you and make the crooked places straight". I hope that He will go before me and make the blanket of fog clear off!

I haven't heard from Dorothy Dykes, so I don't know if I am coming or going .... or rather 'staying or going'. I assume that I will be staying (i.e., returning in September) and then doing my 'course' in September 1980 .... because there is nothing definite about this year. I just don't know what is right to do. Now I feel that I should probably come back for 1 year and then pack out of Vining Centre altogether and do something different.

I feel I need a change from the Yoruba Church. Certainly, working with 3 of their clergy at present on the staff here I find increasingly depressing. It seems to me if CMS wants to help the Yoruba Church, we need to be about 10 .... and not just one. Maybe they need Graduate Geography teachers in Uganda?!

Titi has settled in Ondo, you will be glad to hear. Also, Ebun, who was staying with Sheila and making her spare room stink of gari has a job as a cook in another school - so that's a real answer to prayer. It was good you had Moira to stay for a few days. She is getting about, isn't she?

It looks as though I shall get home on Saturday June 16th, I think. I told you that in my last letter. Then I shall have a week or so at home before the Swanwick CMS Conference which is I think in the last week in June.

I was just wondering what I should do this term in my Monday night lectures when Justice Orojo, the Chief Judge of the State, offered to come and speak to the men - so I jumped at it and have now got him to come and talk about Civics and Government on Monday evenings. This means that I will be free of that preparation. Then when he can't come, I can fill in the spaces with some Prayer Topics from the Newspapers.

I had lunch yesterday at St. Louis and so I saw Sister Martinian and had a good chat. In the evening I ate at Dr. Kohlis and today for lunch I was at Sheilas - now I am back to scrambled egg on toast in my own house. Next Saturday 16 of our students are going to be married in Church! In batches I understand. It sounds as though we may be spending all day in the chapel. I have just vetoed the idea of the women going out to buy white material to make themselves wedding dresses. Nuts! We are really celebrating the legalization of their marriages which happened long ago.

Much love

Elizabeth

Vining Centre
7th May 1979

Dear Ma and Daddy,

Two letters from you this week - on Tuesday from Easter Monday and 24th March. I am glad to hear that the arm is getting better - the writing is looking more like normal now.

I am at this moment sitting in Myrtle's flat at Ikare. Myrtle is 'chopping' in the kitchen and Dr. Kohli is here with us - sitting in the chair reading now. We came here yesterday afternoon - I drove Dr. Kohli's car - a nice Peugeot 404 .... the one I looked after when she was on leave. Now it's flapjacks and coffee! We have just been out visiting - first the school, then a Pakistani couple with a tiny 1st baby, then a Nigerian family who were having the naming ceremony of their baby today - we ate pounded yam and peppery stew there.

I think I mentioned in last week's letter that Justice Orojo was coming to speak to the men on Government. He came on Monday and gave a very interesting talk on the Nigerian Constitution. I am looking forward to the next instalment this week. All in all, it was quite a good week. It is much easier in the 2nd term than in the first when you are trying to settle everyone in.

On Saturday we had a mammoth 'marriage' - or as I called it a celebration of making your marriage legal. 17 students were doing this. Quite an event. I signed all the Certificates in Advance as a witness - stayed for the 1st hymn and the beginning of the service and then I skived off to Ikare to Myrtles.

Sunday evening 9.30pm

We are now back from Ikare. I have gained 2lbs on my scales since Friday! After lunch a) pounded yam- we had lunch b) Myrtles - yam, salad, and ham then tea and flapjack at 4; Fanta to drink in Owo en route then Indian supper including egg less Birthday cake at 7pm and Sheila's supper of roast chicken, yam, beans and cabbage and jelly at 8pm. I don't think I need to eat at all for the rest of this week.

We had our Prayer Group at Dr. Ijomos on Tuesday. Then I took the men for sermon discussion on Wednesday and on Thursday I went to supper with Martinian. On Friday night I hoped to get some books marked but Omodara came and chatted for an hour and then Sheila came for coffee. Everyone discussing Mrs. Thatcher's move into No. 10. I shall be interested to hear the news of this from your end.

I had a letter from Richard explaining how he couldn't get away before Easter - and he thought we were in Ikare over Easter so didn't come over from Ilesha then. If the telephones worked in this country, it would be much easier to keep contact with your friends. He may be able to visit Akure before I come home. He is hoping to be transferred to Oyo in September.

I also had a telegram from Gemma, so it looks as though Italy is on. But I have had nothing from Dorothy Dykes. Odd.

With much love to you both

Elizabeth.

Vining Centre
13th May 1979

Dear Ma and Daddy,

Quite a good week for letters - but nothing yet from Dorothy Dykes. I had fully made up my mind that I would be back in September and so had ceased to worry about 'leaving' for the time being - but then on Tuesday I heard from Fabuluje and Gemma inferring that it was still on the cards that I was coming home this year and saying that Dorothy was waiting to hear 'confirmation' about something - if it's a course they mean then she must have applied, on my behalf - but I don't know for what! I hope it's not something dull in London. You might be able to find out for me. I have no idea what is being organised for me - and it's becoming late to know nothing because I must go and tell the bishop if I am really going this year .... apart from telling all my friends!

Myrtle was down from Ikare this week for a meeting, and she stayed on Thursday night. Then I had a letter from Jumoke to say that she would come and stay for the weekend with her husband and 3 children. They were supposed to come on Friday; but in fact, didn't come till Saturday - a blessing really because I found 24 hours was exhausting. My house is not really geared for 2-year-old twins and a 3-year-old - they bang the glass doors and pull the books out of the bookcase. And Jumoke has a loud Yoruba voice.

We had a very good discussion on Tuesday evening at Dr. Kohli's house - on 'Forgiveness'. We have had several follow up discussions since then, particularly on how the healing of forgiving love fits into keeping God's law, and punishment and judgement.

We are planning to have another International Supper - on May 31st at Fiwasaiye School. I went round to collect the people to represent their different countries for a committee meeting at my house. All but 2 turned up so that was good. I hope that I won't have the responsibility of organising a lot of it this time - because I shall be busy packing up at that time.

It is really very difficult not knowing if I shall be here in September or not. It is a very awkward time to leave Vining Centre women - and very difficult to think how there will be any continuity if I am only able to hand-over on paper.

May 15th:

Would you believe it? Last night I got an application form for the Diploma in Teaching of English as a 2nd language course in London Institute of Education and a note to say that I should hurry up and apply - but the course was very full, and I might not get in. No letter from Dorothy Dykes answering mine suggesting 1980 would be better! I really don't know if I can face the thought of the impersonality of London University. I am very reluctant to fill the thing up - with no further discussion about the whole matter. Very difficult.

Thank you for your love and support in prayer.

Elizabeth

Vining Centre
17th May 1979

Dear Ma and Daddy,

I went to see the Bishop of Ondo yesterday to discuss the forms for the London University Course which CMS have sent me. Inga tells me that the Teaching of English as a Foreign Language is not relevant to teaching in West Africa where it is teaching English as a second language. Also, that course is very specialised and I was thinking of doing something more general.

I have never had a reply from Dorothy Dykes about my suggestion that it would be better to plan this year and start in September 1980 - so I am still betwixt and between. The bishop suggests that it would be better if they can find a Nigerian woman by September to help me with the women's teaching - then that person can take over in September 1980 but he told me to fill up the forms and send a covering letter explaining my doubts about that course - then hope to return this September. If CMS insist, I do the course this year, then Vining Centre will have to manage somehow - but this would be less satisfactory. So, you can see my packing is going to be difficult.

I will go to Lagos in the coming week to check up about my ticket. My plan is to fly to Rome on Wednesday 6th June arriving early on Thursday 7th. Then to wait for Gemma till evening - she has already sent me 30,000 Lira for taxi money etc.

We should then get to Luton on June 17th. I think she will have told you details. I would like to come to Malvern directly (unless of course we arrive in the middle of the night) - but not to stay in London.

I want to see you first and unpack, and there is the Missionaries Conference at Swanwick in the last week in June. I will have to arrange to see Fabuluje between 17th - 21st but that's the only thing I need to organise then. Medicals etc. can surely wait.

Looking forward to seeing you both and all the folks in Malvern.

With love

Elizabeth.

Vining Centre

20th May 1979

Dear Ma and Daddy,

I got your letter via Kaduna this week - about 1 week after the duplicate sent by post! I have just written one letter to you - talking about the application forms for London. I have filled them and will send them off tomorrow. It took 4 days to get a Passport Photo processed because the Government is not importing films and so photographers are reluctant to waste any and because there was no NEPA for 2 days.

Now yesterday we had a staff meeting which gave us something else to think about. Archdeacon Oyinlade, the Acting Principal, told us that the Army wanted their Year 3 students to stop their course this July and then he would send us a new Year 1 in September (the course normally starts in January). So, he proposed that all of Year 3 should be commissioned in July and we should start the new Year in September! This means that a new set of women will be coming in, and the present ones (most of them) will be leaving. So that means quite a lot of extra work now - preparing their Certificates, finishing their Accounts etc. and taking in the Applications for Year 2 wives. It ought to mean doing exams - but Mama and I have decided that it's too late to do that before I go, and we will have to rely on the exams we did last term. This change is another indication to me that it would be much better if I came back here in September 1979. The staff is already inadequate to deal with the men and women students. It will be much better if we can have another woman teacher to help next year - and then I can hand over to her in 1980.

Lagos: May 22nd Tuesday

I have come to Lagos and now have my ticket in my hand! Very good. I came down in Dr. Kohli's car - very good of her to loan it to me, and I brought a soldier student as a companion/bodyguard!

I stayed in Ibadan with the Failings last night - and hope to go back this afternoon.

June really is round the corner! Looking forward very much to seeing you - all being well at Luton.

With much love
Elizabeth

Vining Centre
27th May 1979

Dear Ma and Daddy,

I think that I have written about my journey to Lagos on Tuesday - so there is not a lot to say about the latter part of the week.

On Friday I received a telegram from Dorothy which reads "Course still not definite may have to wait till 1980". So, I am interpreting that as a go ahead that I will be coming back in September 1979. The course can't be definite anyway because I still have the application forms here!! Everyone said I was a nut case to think of filling them in when the course was most likely irrelevant in London and that I didn't want to go till 1980. So, I have kept them. Anyway, they would take 3 weeks to reach England and I will be there as soon as that.

Everything seems to be hotting up for take-off. The women are to be Commissioned on Wednesday 30th so I need to write reports and certificates etc. We are having the International Supper on Thursday 31st May. Dr. Kohli has a farewell supper on Saturday June 2nd. Vining Centre staff have invited me and 6 friends for supper on June 5th. Myrtle is coming to drive me to Lagos on June 6th.

Myrtle came last Wednesday with Gwen, and we went out together for lunch in the new Chellerams "Prestigious Snack Bar". Rice and Chicken cost N3.00! and they have sandwiches for sale.

On Thursday Joshua Omodara came and took Sheila and I out to the Catering Rest House for a meal. It cost N9.00 each! Ridiculous price. But it was nice of Omodara to treat us and take us out. All these events are really because of the possibility of my "leaving"! So, it's a special bonus considering they will all see me again in September by the looks of it.

It will be great to see you both again. I hope you have had a good time in the Lakes.

With much love
Elizabeth.

Home on Leave 7th June to 24th September 1979

I flew from Lagos to Rome on June 7th where I was met by Gemma Blech. We stayed for a couple of nights in a Guest House run by some nuns and we visited the Sistine Chapel in the Vatican and saw the Pieta in St Peter's Basilica and then joined other tourists at the famous Trevi Fountain and climbed the Spanish Steps. Then we went south to Maratea in Calabria and stayed in Gemma's caravan which was halfway up a road which had 26 hairpin bends ending at the top of Monte San Biagio with a statue of Christ the Redeemer. We spent a good deal of time on the beach reading and sunbathing and evenings eating pizza in the village of Santa Catarina where you chose what should go on top before the bread was put into the oven. I continued my journey to London by air from Rome on June 16th.

Lagos
24th September1979

Dear Ma and Daddy,

The flight was very smooth - no hitches - good food - we got refreshments 3 times - once before we reached Amsterdam - then lunch around 1.30 and then another snack around 4pm. There was a rather weedy film about Dracula - not very frightening - just a bit crazy - police chasing Dracula around New York before he could suck people's blood and turn them into vampires!

At Lagos airport everything was very smooth in the new and fancy airport. All quite different from the old scrum. I was met both by Jeremiah and the CMS Driver, Sunday! The latter brought me back through Lagos traffic to the Guest House and I will go to Akure tomorrow with Jeremiah. I will ask Sunday to drive me out of Lagos and then drive the rest myself with Fabuluje nearby. It was good of Jeremiah to come down - but really, he should be in Akure for the first night of the term.

The Guest House is really getting very tatty. Everything looks as though it needs a good wash - carpets and cushions and things. I don't think the accommodation is fully used and the stewards become slack. It really used to be a much livelier place when there was a CMS Missionary in charge. It just looks run down. I am here on my own tonight so I can have a bath and an early night. I thought I would see

Bishop Akintayo but he has gone to Ibadan until Monday. I could have stayed with Shola if it hadn't been for getting my car.

It is hot and Lagos traffic is still incredible, but I am beginning to feel "back". You must be in Worcester now at the CMS Rally. It was good that we were together at Gemma's last night. I hope the rest of your day went well. Thank the Lord for Sister Gemmel!

With much love

Elizabeth

Vining Centre
30th September 1979

Dear Ma and Daddy,

I am writing this today from Sheila's house at Ado. It is looking over towards Christ's School - on the opposite hill. Dr. Kohli and I came here together yesterday, and we will return to Akure tomorrow. October 1st is a public holiday - the new Government is taking over as from this week.

Sheila's house is needing a lot of things doing to it. It has grey gloss paint over all the walls and darker grey paint on the window frames. The floor needs a coat of paint of some kind. The kitchen and the store are dark and grimy. Then Sheila moved her junk from Fiwasaiye and she hasn't really sorted out most of it. She has too much to do in the school and she is less domesticated than me. I have spent this morning trying to bring a little order into her kitchen. Her cook, Albert, left yesterday so she has no-one to look after her.

My own house seemed terrible when I arrived last week. I think after 3 months in England you get used to the 'standards' of cleanliness and neatness at home and when you get back everything 'hits' you again. Like cockroaches scuttling in my kitchen cupboard and a dead rat in Sheila's water bucket this morning. Then I tried to get water out of Sheila's well/tank with a bucket on a string and I dropped the whole thing into the tank! We had to ask some schoolgirls to come and fish it out with a long bamboo pole. Lack of water in your taps really is a great nuisance.

When I got back to my house, I found Myrtle there. She had got the worst of the dirt of 3 months removed and had unpacked some of my plates - bed linen etc. Also, she and Sheila had brought all the main food stores that I needed. I was really spoilt, and it was a lovely welcome.

Abigail was nowhere to be seen - I haven't seen her yet but am told that she has got herself pregnant by a driver with whom she is now living in the town. She has left school. It is a great disappointment to her father. I have 2 men to clean my house and 2 women to wash my clothes now, so I am doing well.

Arrested by the Traffic Police ! 30th September 1979

The great drama of my arrival was that on Saturday when Jeremiah Fabuluje and I were driving up to Akure from Lagos we both got arrested by the Oyo State Road Safety Corps! I was in front and drove round a wide bend and when I could see nothing was coming in front, I overtook a very slow truck. Fabuluje followed me. Just up the road we were stopped and told that we had crossed a white line on the bend. They took our licences and insurances and told us to come to court in Ibadan on Monday. Misery! I was very upset because neither of us were driving dangerously but they wouldn't listen to "begging". So, on Monday morning when we were expecting to start the Vining Centre term both Fabuluje and I had to start off at 6am - reach Ibadan by 9 - find the court - down an incredible muddy road, and then sit on a ½ broken bench listening to a long rigmarole. One UPN man was quarrelling with an NPN man at a polling station because he said the NPN man had brought juju charms to frighten the voters away from voting. The charms were all displayed as Exhibit A and the agbada under which he had hidden the charms as Exhibit B. The magistrate wrote everything down verbatim in an enormous book. The NPN man said that the UPN man had fought him and torn his 'trouser' - Exhibit C was the pair of torn trousers. Two witnesses took 2 hours, and the case was then adjourned for 2 weeks. Our cases came up at about 1.15, by which time I had a headache. There were 4 people who had overtaken on a bend. The 1st man was fined N50.00, the second man the same, then Fabuluje was fined N25.00 and then it was my turn. We were allowed to give our "explanation". I told them that I had just arrived from UK and that I was watching the traffic and hadn't looked at the white line! I was let off with a warning and nothing to pay. I was sorry for Fabuluje because he hadn't done anything bad either. Also, the other people who were stopped on the road at the same time as we were not in the court. Presumably they had paid their donation to the Oyo State Road Safety Corp on the road and avoided being brought to the court.

It is a good story afterwards - but it didn't help the 1st week of the term at Vining Centre. However, by Friday I had my first lessons, and things are sorting themselves out. We have 2 Nigerian Youth Corp men teachers to help us - but no woman, so we have still to 'manage' as before. Mercifully, there are only 30 women and all but 5 Yorubas can understand English. I shall not teach the men's English this term so I shall have time to concentrate on the women.

Myrtle has a physiotherapist! Isn't that great? She is a Canadian volunteer - CUSO - called Irene. She and Myrtle came to lunch on Wednesday. Please tell Betty Sinclair this bit of good news, because I may not get round to writing to her very soon.

There is no butter any more in the shops and prices are very high. Four rather nasty tomatoes in the market were offered to me for N1.00. I declined.

Thank you for all your love and care during my leave. I will let you know if I hear from Plymouth.

With much love
Elizabeth

Vining Centre
1st October 1979

Dear Ma and Daddy,

I am writing this as a "quicky" because the longer letter may take some time to reach you. I think that air letters are often quicker in the post.

Today the Military Government have given over power to the new Civilian Government. All the Government were sworn in at ceremonies this morning. Alhaji Shagari was finally declared the correctly elected President last week. His Vice President is an Ibo - a son of a clergyman. The Western States are all UPN. They <u>say</u> that they will put their own policies into action in those States - but I hope that they are not too rigid in their opposition to Shagari and the NPN or there could be a split like that in 1966.

We are all waiting to see who will be appointed as the new Ministers and State Officials here in Ondo State.

I have described my first week back more fully in the other letter. Thank you for your two letters. It was super to hear from you all - including Ruth and Trevor. Thank you too for the chocolates - they were shared with Sheila and Myrtle and Fred and Martinian and others and certainly helped to brighten up the first week.

I regret not getting my hair permed. It's so greasy and rat taily and it would have been much more comfortable if it had been dried out by a perm. There have been very heavy rains this year so the roads in parts of the town and between some towns have broken up in places. Myrtle says that the Ikare road is terrible and the road to Ado has some nasty patches.

Greetings from the Fabuluje's especially to you, and to the Carters. All the students and other members of staff have been asking after you.

I miss being able to go and see Sheila in the evenings. Dr. Kohli is not quite the same. But I have been having a regime of early nights to get readjusted to getting up at 6am. Also, our timetable has been altered by ½ hour - so Dispensary is now at 7.30am.

Sundri, my cat is back sitting on my armchair.

With much love to you both

Elizabeth

Vining Centre

7th October 1979

Dear Ma and Daddy,

It was great to get your letter of September 23rd. I have sent the cheque for £63.37 to Watts. I thought they wouldn't agree to take the materials back. I will have to leave it at home until I find someone who is willing to bring it. Maybe someone from Taylor-Woodrow who is going home for Christmas would oblige.

I will have to ask Joseph Kumuyi what he wants to do about the "Medicine". I have not seen him since I got your letter.

This week has really been the 1st week of the term. Most of my lessons have got off the ground and so I feel that I am "back". I have baked bread and I have been to the market. I couldn't face Akure market last week - so much MUD and puddles of dirty water.

On Thursday evening we had a meeting of the Leprosy Committee and Sheila was 'sent off'. There were about 20 members there - at Eyesorun's house, and it was a very happy evening. All those people are good friends - so that too helped me to feel back in harness. Sheila stayed the night so that was super. I miss her a lot, especially at the weekend and in the evenings. I expect that I will go up to Ado quite often. I don't have any services to take so far - so I am free at the weekends now.

On Wednesday we had our light disconnected because we hadn't settled our bill. We paid the money + N30 reconnection fee but the light was not reconnected. Fabuluje decided that the men wanted a bribe and he became annoyed and wrote a nasty letter to this effect. By Saturday morning I was tired of this quarrel - and I wanted to put meat and fish in my fridge so I went myself and after about 2 hours - getting our receipts - watching a man write the official reconnection papers and going to the other end of town to get the fuses - we were successful. I was very thankful because no running water plus no fridge, no electric kettle, no iron, and no light in the evenings is a bit gloomy.

I went to Federal Girls College this morning to take their service. I talked about 'putting on other people's shoes'! They listened well. After the morning service I went to see Tola and took her the blouse and bra from Marion. She paid me in naira and gave me some plantain. She sent greetings to you. Then I went to Dr. Kohlis for lunch and had very good Indian food - she is very clever with her use of spices, and we had nice Yoghurt too. I spent the afternoon and evening at home trying to get used to my own company, and getting letters written.

With much love to you both

Elizabeth.

Vining Centre

10th October 1979

Dear Ma,

Thank you for your letter and all the enclosures. I am sending the £10 cheque to be put into Midland Bank please. Thank you for the letter about the wafer machines. I am delighted they cost so much because now maybe the Archdeacon will stop worrying me about them!

I am enclosing a letter to the Medicine magazine, with a cheque for £6. Please send this letter + the paper for ordering + the 2 cheques - making £18 in total. I am asking them to send the magazines to you. Then if you can post them by sea-mail and tell me the postage I will reimburse you.

I am glad you have finished your dress. I will pay for the tapestry - but want to get a bank statement from Malvern Link first.

Much love

Elizabeth.

Vining Centre
13th October 1979

Dear Ma and Daddy,

I am just now sitting in Sheila's house at Ado Ekiti. I came yesterday and plan to go back to Akure via Myrtle at Ikare. They say that the road is bad from Ado to Ikare. Horrible potholes I imagine. The main road from Lagos-> Benin via Ore is closed so all traffic to the East is coming through Akure, and even to Ikare - then Auchi -> Benin. This means that heavy trucks are chewing up or blocking the Owo -> Ikare road. Myrtle met such a block on Thursday and had to go round by Idoani. The journey took her 4 hours!

Sheila seems to be coping very well at Ado. Both she and Myrtle are coming to spend the weekend with me next week. So that will be lovely. Sheila now has a girl to do her cleaning and washing and marketing, so her household arrangements are a bit better.

I was at Dr. Kohlis for supper on Friday evening - it was vegetarian Indian food because the Jain family were there.

This has been my first complete week of teaching and I have been happy with the way my women have settled down. They are an easier group than those we had in January to June because there are no non-Yoruba and non-English speakers. I am not teaching English to the men and so I am not over pressed with work! I will therefore be able to spend more time on Leper's Welfare Committee and going to see Sheila and Myrtle at the weekends. The Committee is to have a "presentation" to Eyesorun on Thursday 25th so there will be quite a lot to do to prepare for that.

Sunday evening - back at home again. I went to Myrtles for lunch - the road was pretty pot-holey, and I was lucky to get back on the Ikare -> Owo road because 4 enormous trucks were stuck parallel to each other on a steep hill. Only small cars could squeeze past at the side. Now Fabuluje tells me that they are announcing on the radio that the road is blocked! Somewhere on the road today I lost a tail pipe so now the car is making a noise like a tractor.

The new UPN Government in Ondo State are announcing that Education is now free, so parents are refusing to pay fees and Principals have no money with which to feed the children!! We hope there will not be serious troubles. It seems very unlikely that the Government will have enough money to pay adequately for food - books - uniforms etc. etc. for all the schools.

I have the 'sneezes' too - like Bishop Allison. I am glad your dress is OK.

With much love to you both

Elizabeth

Vining Centre
21st October 1979

Dear Ma and Daddy,

A lovely long letter from you both this week. It's good to hear that you were able to help Olufunmilayo James and Nike Ayodele about her lodgings.

I must finish my film quickly so that I can send it back to you before it gets ruined by the humidity here. Rajan Kohli arrived this week to stay with his mother for 2 weeks so maybe I can send it back with him.

Our New Government are trying to get themselves organised. One early suggestion that they should send a delegation to USA to see how a Senate should be conducted was squashed as a waste of public funds!

Here in Ondo State, we have a UPN State Government. Their watchword is 'Free Education'. So, they have announced that the Government is going to pay for all books, tuition, and school equipment BUT the parents are to oversee boarding houses. They plan for all schools to be day schools in the long run. OK in theory - but the transition is going to be quite difficult. Parents are expecting that everything will be free - but do not realise yet that if they want boarding schools for their children, they are going to have to pay for that - including building new boarding houses where necessary. We shall see. Sheila has been here this weekend. It has been good to have her. I made a cheesecake for supper last night - from the packet I bought. It was good and appreciated by both Fred and Sheila.

I am glad that you were able to see the Pope's visit to Ireland and USA. I didn't see him on the TV, but I did hear him speak on the BBC news. I have moved my record player/radio into the bedroom. Partly it's more secure there. I never close my doors during the day. Partly it's nice to be able to listen to the news when I am having my breakfast in bed at 7am. I have also been listening again to the record of the sisters singing. The words are lovely.

There seems to be a hold up in several imports - and shortages. Gas is one thing that is difficult to get. I am OK now but neither Sheila nor Myrtle have any and Sheila has very low voltage lights at night. She ought really to have a decent gas light - but that's difficult if there is no gas.

The Principal of the Federal Government Girls College died last weekend. She had cancer of the breast and because she belongs to the Apostolic Faith, she would take no medicines. She has been dying for the past 1 year. Very sad.

I must write to Worc. and Hereford about the possibility of grants. I suspect that there will be none. I had an official acknowledgement from Plymouth - but no other news.

I was invited to a party at the 'Motherite Club' on Thursday to honour Eyesorun because she was presented with a Nigerian Federal Decoration! The only big snag was that Eyesorun didn't get there - she was delayed in Lagos, so the speeches and the Presentation all happened without her. All a bit flat.

As I was writing this the Deji of Akure came to call! What a hoot!

Much love

Elizabeth

Vining Centre
25th October 1979

Dear Ma and Daddy,

Rajan Kohli is going back to England after spending 2 weeks here with his mother, so I am taking this opportunity of writing and sending this book about St. Andrew's Oyo - an early Christmas present! I haven't read it through, but it doesn't seem to cover your section in detail. I hope that you don't find it very disappointing - I am sure you will find it interesting.

Thank you for all your efforts to find digs for Nike through Ruth Wood. I hope something has been sorted out. Her parents are very grateful. I think they have now heard that her money has been sent from Lagos, so I hope that's OK as well.

Did you get my cheque for Watts and Co. and for Medicine magazine? I think I sent them together through you - but you don't mention it.

Your retreat sounds great. I played some of the songs from the sisters record at our Prayer Fellowship on Tuesday. They are very uplifting songs.

I am very sorry to hear that mother fell and damaged her spectacles. I hope the new ones are not too expensive, and that your bruises are better.

In my last airmail - written on Sunday - I was just finishing it when the Deji of Akure arrived on the compound to greet the principal and his wife - and then me! Very funny in my little house to have the Deji in his great damask agbada sitting in my chair - and his bare shouldered wife in the next chair. 3 henchmen - one with a trumpet sat on the verandah. In the middle of it the Bond's called to tell me that they had the film "Jesus Christ Superstar" at Taylor-Woodrow that night. Their faces were a picture!

Fabuluje has received the papers to fill up for references for Plymouth. He brought his draft over to me for comments. I feel quite strongly that confidential references should be confidential - so I feel that what he says - in his Nigerian way should be what goes to Plymouth BUT I felt I should ask him to subtract one phrase .... I thought it was just too funny .... He said, "She is healthy, clean and good looking"!! It has made me laugh all week.

Jesus Christ Superstar is set in a very strange desert place .... but some of the sections were very moving.

Yesterday I went to a meeting of the Society of Health, Nigeria - a planning committee in our Ministry of Health. I was representing Lepers Welfare Committee. There is to be the Annual Congress of this Society December 13th - 15th in Akure. I was amazed at how much was yet to be done - there seemed to have been very little progress since the previous meeting. They were to get an estimate of the cost - a committee was to be doing so .... not yet ready. This estimate must be presented for approval before they know if they have any money to fund the thing. Then someone was to make a list of hotels in Akure and their prices - this was not yet typed and it must be sent to Lagos and then circulated to all the Delegates all over the Federation. Joke! when letters take 4 weeks to reach some places. To crown all - at the end of the meeting the chairman pointed out that Ondo State has no branch of the Society of Health, Nigeria, and that something would have to be done to inaugurate the Society - have a meeting and elect officers before the National Congress!

Myrtle came down from Ikare last night. She is on her way to Ibadan to be with Gwen for the Half Term holiday. She seems very tired to me. I am sorry that she didn't come and stay last weekend. I will probably go to Ikare for my Half Term which is November 2nd - 5th. I just hope that Richard doesn't come here then. He sometimes comes to greet around my birthday - I don't even know if he is transferred or not.

It is Board of Governors meeting today so I am free. The women are all cooking with Mama - but I am not really needed - except to greet the people at lunch time.

I hope to go and see Sheila in the evening and stay till Sunday.

Thank you for John's new address - I must write to him. I have some stamps for Sacha.

With much love to you both

Elizabeth.

There is a film to be developed - also in the post with Rajan. It has mine of Nicola's christening.

Vining Centre

4th November 1979

Dear Ma and Daddy

On Tuesday we had our Prayer Fellowship as usual - we read 1 Cor.13. On Wednesday it was a Moslem holiday so there were no classes. I did some sewing - mostly mending of Sheila's and my dresses and then I had supper with Dr. Kohli.

Myrtle is well - but gets up at 5.30 which doesn't suit me! and the Nigerian downstairs plays his radio at full blast. I am always very thankful when he turns it off and there is peace and quiet. I think Myrtle is tired and getting older. It's not so easy to cope with this country in your 50's as it is in your 30's. It is great that she has a physiotherapist now. Two of her teachers are going off to do exams in the next few weeks so she will be short staffed. The night watchman didn't appear on Thursday night and had to be fished out of his house. He was suffering from too much drinking over the festival.

I must write to Ruth about the Christmas holidays. I think Mrs. Howard will be coming out. I wonder if you could phone her and find out when she is travelling. Maybe she would bring the cloth .... or at least the white. Her phone number is Moffat, 20132. Code 0683.

Also, can you get 'LAPUDRINE' - it's a malaria prophylactic. I need about 40 tablets - you take them once a week. I am sure Mrs. Howard would bring those. They seem to be "out of stock" here.

Did you get my letter with the cheque for Watts in it? Monday November 5th: arrived back this evening - and feel <u>much</u> better and rested from the weekend.

Much love

Elizabeth

Vining Centre
11th November 1979

Dear Ma and Daddy,

Thank you for your birthday card, received this week. Thursday was a good day. Sheila came from Ado and the staff, and a few other friends came in for coke and biscuits after supper in the evening. Dr. Kohli, Sheila and Martinian came for supper when we had chicken and yam and Surprise Peas and beans followed by milk jelly. On Wednesday I made a special 'loaf' which I found in a recipe book at Myrtles last weekend. It was like a giant Chelsea bun - with currants and sticky cinnamon paste. It was made in a ring with 36 rolls of bread which joined together to make the whole. It was fun to make and much appreciated. Brother Fred made a sponge, which looked superb - but he had put cloves in it so it had a funny taste.

On Friday the staff and girls of Fiwasaiye school gave a farewell party to Sheila. It was a very good evening with two plays and two dances and long appreciative speeches. Everyone agreed that Sheila was worth it. She has been at Fiwasaiye for 15 years.

We had several people sick this week - one man cut his leg with a cutlass and had to have 2 stitches. Another old man was stooling and vomiting at midnight last night, so we sent him to the hospital. Then another is asthmatic and it's touch and go how he is doing.

We are going to have a Presentation to Eyesorun on Wednesday this coming week - organised by the Leprosy Committee so Martinian and I are trotting round informing the members and inviting some guests and trying to organise the refreshments.

I have just listened to the tape of the Pope's visit to Ireland. It was very moving. He has a very distinctive, slow, and direct way of speaking and is obviously filled with the love of Christ. You could hear the singing and clapping of the people who obviously were very happy to see him and have him among them.

I also listened to the Cenotaph service on the radio this morning. Not much 'new' in that I felt .... but the work of supporting war sufferers goes on for a very long time. The news of the American hostages being kept in the Embassy in Iran is not very good. I agree with Sadat of Egypt that Khomeni is not a good advertisement for Islam.I spent last night with the sisters of St. Louis and did a bit of tapestry - in between power failures.

My love to you both

Elizabeth.

Vining Centre
18th November 1979

Dear Ma and Daddy,

Thank you for your letter and all the news. I have just driven back from Ibadan where I spent the night with Lynn and Elaine Failing. They are going on leave on December 5th and it's not certain if they will come back. Rev. Adegbola who they worked with has left the Institute of Church and Society because of various conflicts in the Methodist Church. He has virtually been removed by the Methodist Patriarch. Lynn and Elaine would like to follow Adegbola into his new set up - a sort of go-it-yourself Rural Development Project – but the archbishop and other Anglicans don't agree. So, they might not get back at all.

I went to Ibadan via Ondo and stayed Friday night with Inga. Then I went to see Grace in Ibadan. Her husband has been made the Commissioner for Education for Bendel State so Grace will be moving to Benin in December.

We had a good party at St. Louis on Wednesday when the Leprosy Committee 'honoured' Eyesorun by giving her a present of an extraordinary multicoloured glass fish. It was delivered with a suitable speech by Dr. Sijuade. Then we also 'honoured' Dr. S. This was a surprise which we managed to keep - he had no idea that he was going to get a present too. All in all, it was a good 'do'. Different people provided food and we invited some extra people who don't usually come to our committee meetings.

This evening Sheila is here - on Friday, Myrtle came for lunch with Irene her Physio. It is good that my house is in Akure - so near to the

Ministry of Education. It means that I have my friends coming to visit when they are here on business.

Does the building society money include the £500 that I put in this year? It looks as though I had better not send many Christmas cheques until someone gives me one! I am intending to send a Circular letter - but all my to-ing and fro-ing at weekends makes it difficult to get down to it. Next weekend 24th/25th I will be in Ado celebrating birthdays - Sheila, Joan, and Dr. Kohli are on 21st, 23rd and 25th. Dr. Kohli wants me to go with her to Ijero to have lunch with some Indians there. On Saturday it is the Harvest at the Leper Settlement so we shall all be at that. Our term ends on December 7th. I haven't heard from Ruth if she has any plans for Christmas. We may all go to Ado and spend Christmas with Sheila.

Joseph Kumuyi's mother has died - 2 weeks ago. I wondered why I hadn't seen him about. He has spent N900 on the 1st stages of the funeral celebrations!

Much love to you both

Elizabeth.

Vining Centre

25th November 1979

Dear Ma and Daddy,

I got your letter of the 18th posted 19th on 24th so that was a good effort. Thank you for all your efforts to send the Watts material via Mrs. Howard - and for sending off the Medical Journals.

I was going to Ado this weekend with Mrs. Kohli to celebrate Sheila and Joan's and Mrs. Kohli's birthdays on Saturday. But everything was changed because Sister Rose was killed in a road accident on Wednesday evening. It was on the Ife-Ondo Road and she was driven by the St. Louis Driver. Maybe he was overtaking - who knows; but they hit a taxi and Sister Rose must have died immediately. The 2 drivers are alive. Sister Rose was the head of the Nursery/Primary School and had been in Nigeria 25 years. She was very well known. All the sisters were very upset, as you can imagine. Yesterday there was a mighty funeral mass in the Catholic Cathedral. There must have been more than 50 Catholic Fathers and about 100 St. Louis Sisters there. It was a lovely service with Ps.23 Gelineau Holy, Holy, Holy, Holy, and other familiar songs. The thing that upset me most was not being able to participate in the Communion. The disunity of the Church over this is a great wickedness. Since Sheila and Myrtle and Joan and Mrs. Kohli all wanted to be at the Funeral - they all came to Akure. Myrtle returned to Ikare on Friday evening and Joan went to Owo this morning. Sheila has stayed 2 nights and will go back to Ado .... so that's nice.

We had the harvest at the Settlement yesterday morning. All our students trekked there to help them to celebrate. I have had a letter from Ruth saying that she and her mother are invited to Iyi Enu to Grace and Elizabeth .... so, we may all go there for Christmas. My term ends on December 7th but Sheila doesn't end until December 21st. I may go to Benin earlier.

I went to Ado on Wednesday afternoon because it was Sheila's birthday. Myrtle and I gave her a gas lamp so that she can work in the evenings when the Electricity fails or is dim. On Thursday we had our practical exam here. I always find that an exhausting event - and this time my mind was not really on it because I had just heard about Sister Rose.

One packet of books has come from home so that's encouraging. I don't know where the rest are. I wonder if Trevor and Ruth have any idea yet about jobs. It will be nice for you to have Ruth and the children for a short time - but I hope it's not too long from the financial point of view .... or will they collect the dole if Trevor has <u>no</u> job ?? Mrs. Kohli is worried about Rajan because he hasn't any job and he has now borrowed money from his brother's father-in-law because apparently Jane, his wife, needs money to spend for Christmas. I hope he gets a job soon and settles down.

Not much news here this week - usual routine. <u>Except</u> that Fabuluje says that there is a chance of Mrs. Alieu - a clergy widow - coming here to teach! That's great.

Much love

Elizabeth

Vining Centre
2nd December 1979

Dear Ma and Daddy,

No letters this week - I think because there were two last week.

Mrs. Kohli led us in a special prayer from her holy book in Sanskrit - it was sung and lasted about 10 minutes. It was very beautiful. It was a moving evening with lovely prayers also from Eyesorun - a Baptist and Sister Mildred.

I went to Ado yesterday to see Sheila, mainly because I was lonely in Akure. Dr. Kohli had visitors, Martinian was on a retreat, Margaret Bond had gone to Ibadan for a day's shopping. I came back today to attend our Harvest Service at 10am. It lasted to 11.45 - very short! Then afterwards we had an Auction and sales of foodstuffs etc. Mrs. Kohli came with her visitors - briefly - mainly to visit the cat, I think! I didn't get involved at the auction - somehow, I can't get any enthusiasm for it – Presbyterian upbringing coming out, I think. I like Peace and Quiet on a Sunday - whereas this Harvest meant that the women students started cooking at 4am - apart from being busy preparing all day yesterday .... by 5pm they were quarrelling! And most of them didn't participate in the Harvest Thanksgiving Service because they were still in the kitchen. I opted out and went to St. Louis for lunch and rest. Martinian is to go to Jos for a week's break to recover from Sister Rose's death. She needs a break. Joseph Kumuyi has hepatitis and looks very yellow. He is working in a half-hearted fashion. He really ought to rest completely.

With much love to you both

Elizabeth.

Vining Centre
8th December 1979

Dear Ma and Daddy,

I have just discovered that Eyesorun is going to London for her sister's wedding on 15th December so I can send a letter through her. This has prompted me to get a circular letter written. It seems a bit long. If you want to cut it do so - as you think. Mrs. Kohli is here now so I am finding it quite difficult to concentrate on what I want to say .... but it does seem a very good opportunity of sending the letter. She leaves tomorrow am.

I have got the cloth from Watts and the Lapudrine today from Benin .... so that's good. Thank you very much for sending them both. I am hoping to go to Benin on Saturday to see Ruth and her mother because they are having a launching of a 'Leprosy Committee' in Bendel State. Ruth is their secretary. They have the State Governor doing their launching so they will start with a big bang. I do hope you have a very happy Christmas at Hackney. I think the St. Andrew's book and the tapestry are from me this year - and the enclosed card.

Sheila and Joan and I are planning to go to Benin on 22nd or 23rd and then on to Onitsha on 24th to spend Christmas at Iyi Enu. Grace doesn't know that yet - I hope she will get my letter in time.

I will ask Eyesorun to telephone you if she can - to say hello from Nigeria. We have just had yet another party in her honour. Chief Adeniran sat next to me and sent greetings to you both.

I will put the rest of my weeks news in a blue air letter.

Happy Christmas!

With much love

Elizabeth.

Vining Centre
16th December 1979

Dear Ma and Daddy,

I think that your letter via Mrs. Howard can't have reached her in time - so there are 40 Lapudrine and a letter floating somewhere! Ruth sent me some Lapudrine which she had and Martinian now tells me that she has heaps of them at the settlement - so I am OK. But I am sorry to miss your letter.

I went to Benin on Friday to stay with Ruth, and her mother and to attend the Launching of the Association for Control and Relief of Leprosy in Benin. This was a most impressive 'do' organised by Ruth. The State Governor was the Guest of Honour and they had a very good turnout of people in a hall in the middle of the town. They collected N3,800 in donations to start the society. I went with Margaret Bond - who is the Taylor Woodrow wife who works at our settlement. Martinian was to have come but she has been in Jos this week - to have a break to recover from Sister Rose's death.

I have had a very lazy week really - except that I seem to have been occupied most days! Margaret has needed a break at the settlement so I usually fetch her around 10 - to bring her home for coffee and take her back at about 11am - so that has divided up the morning. Then I have no house help so I have been cleaning my own floors etc. This is a daily task because there is heavy harmattan and so a layer of dust covers everything each day. I have one woman doing the washing and ironing - a student who I thought needed some money .... but she isn't very keen.

On Monday night I had supper with Mrs. Kohli. On Tuesday we had our Prayer Fellowship. On Wednesday I went to Ado and spent the night with Sheila. On Thursday Joseph Kumuyi came and we had a good chin wag about the state of the world. He is always very up on world affairs and on Nigerian politics so it is interesting to talk to him. On Friday I was in Benin. On Saturday night Mrs. Kohli came here for supper. Tonight, I am expecting Myrtle. She was here on Thursday and we had shrimps fried in butter - gorgeous.

Most days I have managed a quick swim at TW and I have made a Christmas cake. I think it may be soggy in the middle. I have been expecting Jumoke's husband to come and collect my car. They say they want to buy it and that they would be here this week, but I have not seen them so I don't know what to think. I now have 2 cars - and I am beginning to get used to the new one. It is certainly more confident on long journeys. I will be glad when the old one is sold because it's not easy to keep 2 running. You tend to neglect one and then the battery runs down.

I was at Fiwasaiye Carols on Sunday night - and St. Louis on Monday - both good. The Fiwasaiye girls are 'livelier' about it - tend to shout their heads off but thoroughly enjoy it all. St. Louis are more Catholic and subdued.

I hope to get you a letter to Hackney before Christmas through Taylor Woodrow people. I hear on the radio that there are blizzards and storms in Scotland. I shall be thinking of you at Elaine and Robert's wedding.

Much love

Elizabeth.

Vining Centre
18th December 1979

Dear Ma and Daddy,

I received your "Mrs. Howard letter" this morning and hope that I can post these family cards with a Taylor Woodrow person going home for Christmas tomorrow.

We are planning a Carol Singing Party here on Saturday night. There could be anything between 30 and 50 people! I have got a bit confused with who I have asked and who has said 'Yes' and who 'No'. Myrtle and Sheila will be here. Then on Sunday we will go to Benin and on to Onitsha on Monday afternoon. It will be good to see Onitsha friends again. Then on Friday 28th we shall return and as far as I can see: Ruth, Mrs. Howard, Sheila and Joan may all be here for that weekend and up till after New Year's Day so I will be busy.

We are having a party for the Leper Settlement Children on January 4th and maybe having an International Children's party later in January. The latter is yet to be organised!

I hope you have a happy Christmas in Hackney.

With much love

Elizabeth.

P.S. Please phone Gemma and wish her a happy Christmas. Eyesorun may phone you sometime.

Vining Centre
27th December 1979

Dear Ma and Daddy,

I am at present sitting in Ruth Howard's house in Benin. Mrs. Howard is tapping out her letters on the typewriter. Ruth is in the office organising her school for the beginning of the new term. Sheila and Joan are on their way from Onitsha and we are expecting them for lunch. Grace Ohikhena is coming for supper.

We had a very quiet and pretty non-eventful Christmas Day. It started at 6.30 am with the Holy Communion service in Iyi Enu Chapel .... not many there at that early hour. We then had a lazy day - reading and doing 2 jigsaws and had our Christmas dinner in the evening - Grace and Elizabeth, Ruth and her mother, Joan, Sheila and me and Keith Williams, the pharmacist. Rather a female majority.

On Boxing Day Ruth and her mother and I went off first to Asaba and then on to Obiaruku. At Asaba we visited the bishop and looked over the house that he is getting ready for the new CMS people, the Mitchells, who are supposed to be going there in January. All the roads between main towns in that area are now very good so it was quite an easy journey down to Obiaruku. There we had lunch with Ron Howarth, Mary Eldridge and Joyce Dafy. Ron has a "cottage" there beside the river where you can swim. Mary is the Principal of Anglican G.S. - Asaba. Joyce Dafy is the wife of a Nigerian Chief in Obiaruku - her husband is a politician, I think.

When we came into Benin last night, we went to see Grace and Titus Ohikhena in their new mansion house - with large metal gate and uniformed gateman. Titus is now the Commissioner for Education for Bendel State. Grace will probably be working in Ruth's school next term.

On Saturday evening before setting off for the Mid-West on Sunday we had a Carol Singing Party in my house. About 30 people came and we sang carols by candlelight. Sheila and Myrtle were there and Sister Martinian and Mildred. Also, the Akinbadewa family and the Bonds. It was a very happy evening. Myrtle made mince pies in the morning with 3 of my women students. I iced the Christmas cake - rather a good one I thought. We took it to Iyi Enu.

I hope you got my letters by Christmas.

Much love from

Elizabeth.

Christmas Letter 1979

Vining Centre
December 1979

Dear Friends,

Someone somewhere must have been praying! When I was on leave in the summer and going around my Link parishes, I asked people to pray for four things: - a) for more staff at Vining Centre, b) for a physiotherapist for the Handicapped children's school at Ikare, c) for a bus for the Ikare children, d) for a boat for Grace Webster to use to reach her village clinic on the Anambra River.

When I arrived back in Akure at the end of September I discovered that we had two new members of staff to teach the men students. They are members of the Nigerian Youth Service Corps which means that they have just graduated from the University and are doing their compulsory one year 'service' to the country. I was disappointed to find that there was no new teacher for the women, but we have 31 students so Mama Ademoye and I are managing them between us, and it's great to have the two Youth Corpers.

The next thing I heard was that Myrtle has both a bus and a physiotherapist! The bus was provided by the Ministry of Education and the physiotherapist is a Canadian CVSO volunteer called Irene.

I can't yet report on Grace Webster and her need for a boat but I am sure your prayers are being answered for her too. The only thing I have heard about Grace is that she was invited to go to India to see some rural health projects there. We are so intrigued to find out how she got on in India that we are going to go to Onitsha for Christmas to hear all about it.

The last time that I returned from home leave was in 1977 and I had the most terrible journey; everything was very difficult - I was not met, my luggage didn't come with me and there was no car to bring me from Lagos to Akure. I took four days getting from Malvern to Vining Centre. This time dear Sister Gemmel promised to pray especially for a smooth journey back; and it was marvellous! The flight was on time, the food was delicious, the people on the 'plane were friendly and I was met by two people and my car was waiting in Lagos in good order. The only hitch was on the road between Ibadan and Ife where I crossed over the white line on the centre of the road to overtake a very slow-moving truck. It was on a wide bend where I could see that nothing was coming in the opposite direction. The principal followed behind me and overtook the same truck. About a quarter of a mile down the road we were both arrested by the Oyo State Road Safety Corps for overtaking on a bend and crossing the white line. We were told to come to the court in Ibadan on the following Monday. What a start to the new term! I was really very upset, especially as I felt we had both been driving safely and it seemed so unfair to catch us when there are so many crazy, fast dangerous drivers on the Nigerian roads. Our principal had to pay N25.00 fine but I was let off with a warning because I had just come back from UK. I was very thankful not to get my licence endorsed.

On October 1st the new civilian government took over from the Military regime. The President is Ahaji Shehu Shagari of the NPN party which has most of its supporters in the North. The five south western states of Lagos, Ogun, Oyo, Ondo and Bendel all support the rival party UPN headed by Chief Olalowo. This means that in Ondo State we have a UPN Governor and a UPN majority in our House of Assembly. We are also following the UPN programme of 'free-education' at all levels, so in Ondo State they are opening 125 new secondary schools in the coming year to accommodate <u>all</u> the children who come out of Primary 6 class in the primary schools. These children are to be placed in secondary schools without any selection exam next September. We shall see how it all works out. It looks as though teaching Form 1 in a secondary school next year will be no joke, unless the school's catchment area is in an elite housing estate.

I would ask you to continue to remember my plans for coming home in September 1980 to do a one-year course. I have applied to do a Diploma in Education (English Language teaching) at the college of St. Mark and St. John's Plymouth. I hope that this course will equip me better to either come back to Vining Centre, or to join one of the Ondo State secondary schools in 1981.

Please continue to pray for us at the Vining Centre and for our need of a Nigeria woman to take over from me next year. Also pray for our students. Two of the women are childless despite being married four or five years and they are very anxious about it. One man, Joshua Bar, has asthma and we have been struggling to get it under control.

Another student called Lisha has high blood pressure and gets giddy turns.

At the Leprosy settlement we now have a sewing machine for shoes so sandals are being produced, made to measure for each of the patients. They also have the job of making special boots to be fitted with callipers for Myrtle's handicapped children's school, so they are 'in business'.

Thank you for your prayers. I believe they are being answered, and I pray that 1980 may be a year of many blessings for you and your family.

With love

Elizabeth Deeks.

Vining Centre
6th January 1980

Dear Ma and Daddy,

I received your parcel for Christmas and your letter of Dec 16th, yesterday! It was a lovely surprise - sent up from Lagos by Eyesorun who hasn't yet appeared in Akure since she went to U.K. I expect she must have been delayed by something in Lagos. Sheila was here - so we were able to share some Black Magic immediately and then we did the Giles puzzle and Sheila began reading Prince Charles - and me the Vet book. Thank you too for the Lapudrine. I now have enough to take me to June.

I can't remember if I wrote to you last weekend - because the Howard's were here Friday to Tuesday, so I had my mind in the kitchen more than usual and Ruth brought a 2000 pieces jigsaw, which we were all involved in. We failed to finish it and Ruth took it back to Benin in sections - to be completed there.

Last Sunday we ate haggis from Moffat - so I thought of you. It was good haggis too. Sheila had some for the first time and enjoyed it. We all went to the sisters for lunch on Monday and ate their turkey and then Howards, Sheila, Dr Kohli, and I had a special new year supper here with chicken/stuffing, roast potatoes and beans followed by Christmas pudding and brandy butter. We didn't go to the midnight Service… mainly because Jeremiah announced that it started at 10pm and ended at 12.10. I felt that was a bit long. The Howards went on Tuesday and I had supper with Bonds. I had a low day on Wednesday - reaction from visitors. I read a Taylor Caldwell book - rather a dreary day. On Thursday I discovered that Martinian had been sick on Wednesday and stayed in bed. In the evening Sheila and I went to Owo for a party at Joan Steward's. It was a good party - delicious shrimps in batter made by a Sri Lankan teacher. I had a long talk with Maggie Brooks who is the rather eccentric wife of the carver who made those gorgeous carvings. He has about 6 wives - including Maggie who is English - aged about 55+ now. She was a great pal of Jane Backhouse's and used to live in Benin. I had not met her before. I also talked to Ali Kelly who is a young Irish Catholic Priest in Akure. We drove back from Owo around 11 p.m. The road is now lovely and smooth between Akure and Owo. On Friday we had a children's party for the children at the Settlement - it was organised by the Novice Sisters. In the evening Mrs Kohli, Shola and Joseph

Kumuyi all came for supper - we had chips! Then on Saturday Mrs Kohli went to Lagos to get her daughter-in-law from Canada. In her absence, she organised me into getting her a crate of drinks - baking 24 Queen cakes and making yoghurt and looking after her car. Sheila and I used the car to go to Idanre and see the Akinbadewa's. It was when we returned that we got your parcel.

With much love

Elizabeth

Vining Centre
13th January 1980

Dear Ma and Daddy,

Two letters - Dec 23 and Dec 30th came together this week. It was great to catch up on your Christmas activities. It is interesting to go away, but I expect you were glad to be at home in Malvern again after all the adventures on British Rail. I am glad that the Wedding was so inspiring. I wrote to Elaine, but I wasn't sure which address to put, so I sent it ℅ Worcester College for the Blind. Thank you very much for all your hard work over my Circular.

This week started with a tragedy on Monday. The daughter of a student staying here for the holidays was rushed to the hospital at 4 a.m with measles and died before 8. The sad thing was that she was sick since Thursday and had gone to the hospital on Friday where she was given the first of five injections. Then the mother thought that you couldn't get injections on Sat and Sun, so she stayed at home and never came out to report that the child was sick - to me, or to any other member of staff. The father was in Calabar - so the other men students here dealt with the burial while the women wept with the mother. I discovered that the 18-month-old baby boy also had measles, so I took him to the hospital and got him admitted and found the required crystalline penicillin injection in the Chemist's in the town. The alarming thing about sickness just now is that some drugs have run out in the hospital - not an unusual situation - but also, they are running out in the Chemists and they say they are not allowed to import more. Our new Government has a policy of free Medical Care ...... but it boils down to free Consultation and free Aspirin! (A slight exaggeration, but it's going that way)

On Tuesday and again on Wednesday two other children were admitted with measles - and so we had 3 of our women in the measles ward for most of the week. Two are still there. Several other children have died around them - all rather miserable.

The other thing that happened on Monday was that the Commissioner of Health visited the Leprosy Settlement. He paid a very detailed visit and poked his nose into every nook and corner. So, we hope he will now decide whether to preserve the present site of the Settlement - or, to make adequate provision elsewhere. Some big people in the town are pushing for the use of the land at the Settlement.

On Friday, I went to Ado and spent 24 hours in retreat with Myrtle and Sheila. I read a book about the beginning of the Post Green Community. Ken Ramsay is mentioned in it. I came back from Ado on Sat afternoon and Mary Griffin from Auchi is now here for a week. Myrtle and Irene and Martinian are coming for supper. Chicken and the last packet of apple flakes.

Much love

Elizabeth

Vining Centre
16th January 1980

Dear Ma and Daddy,

Thank you for the cutting from the Overseas Development magazine. I hope they will send me their application forms and then I can have a go and apply to them for a Grant. I have also written to Hereford and Worcester to ask if there is any hope there. I have not heard anything from Plymouth. Maybe I should write to them and ask what the chances are – because if I don't get a place there, I shall have to apply to somewhere else. I think Uncle Joe said he had friends in high places in the Ministry of Overseas Development. Perhaps I should write to him too!

Mary Griffin has been here all this last week while attending the All-Nigeria T.T.C Sports Festival. It has been good to have her company. She also introduced me to a Ugandan friend of hers who is now teaching in the Federal Polytechnic in Akure. She came to supper on Wednesday.

I spent a good deal of time on Tuesday with Martinian who was writing a 'paper' for the Commissioner of Health telling him all about the Leprosy Settlement. We want him to decide about the Leprosy Settlement – either to claim the present land for the Government so that it can continue to be used for the Settlement and be developed for that or to start work at a new site. I arranged a visit to the Commissioner by 5 of our committee members on Thursday but he had to go and see the Governor so we have postponed our visit til next Tuesday. It is all a bit of a game because some people on the Committee have bought some of the plots that have been sold at the Settlement site .... so, it is quite difficult for the Committee to speak with one voice on the subject.

It has been desperately hot this week – 86 degrees F last night when we were going to bed. It is 90 F now in my sitting room. I am sitting in the bedroom with the fan going. I don't like doing anything very active. One of the men at the Settlement -David -came this week to help with my washing, ironing, and cleaning. He is very slow and he is asthmatic but he is willing to help and gets it done in the end. I must say I am glad to have a helper in this heat.

I have not received any Medicine magazines yet. I expect they will come soon. The ones I ordered were supposed to come before I left – that's why they are coming to you. We had better carry on as it is. I will refund the postage if you keep a record. Joseph will pay me here. He had his British cheque stolen and hasn't received another one yet.

I talked to the Federal Girls this morning – on the search for God. I did the 'Lion Hunt' with them – a great laugh. They listened well.

So sorry you caught a chill over the New Year. Ma. I hope you have driven it off. Hard luck to lose the phone for 2 days!! They can't find the fault with our cable – or have no new one to put in. It must be 18 months since it rang.

With much love to you both,

Elizabeth

Vining Centre
27th January 1980

Dear Ma and Daddy,

I am now sitting in Sheila's sitting room at Ado on a hot Sunday afternoon. I was asleep until a loud noisy schoolgirl went howling by so I have got up. In fact, I am very tired with an aching back.... the result I think of 2 parties in the past week! The first was at Mrs. Kohli's on Wednesday, she invited about 80 people to her home to meet her daughter-in-law, Neeru. Most of the people were Indian, but Sheila and Fred and Martinian and Sister Philomena were all there too. We had no electricity from Monday until Thursday, so it was quite difficult to organise a party. I got the job of running around the town collecting ice trays and then trying to make lots of ice in the Taylor Woodrow freezer. In the end, Margaret, and John from T.W were so late that we didn't use the ice!

The second party was an International Party for children. This was noisy and hot and very tiring for those organising it, but I think the children enjoyed it. We had a Disney film of a football match between different animals, which they all enjoyed.

I was hoping to go to Auchi on Saturday - to meet Myrtle in Ikare and then to go on together to Mary Griffin's birthday party - but I couldn't face the long journey, so instead I sent to Ado to see Sheila. I was glad that I did go there because Sheila was very happy to have company.

I received the Form from the Overseas Development people this week - so, I will fill it up and return it to them. I am applying for a Bursary - not an Award - because I think my course is more in line with that. I hope so, anyway. It will be good if I can get the money because it will relieve any financial headaches. Thank you for getting the form so quickly. Thank you too for sending out my letters.

I had a great blitz on Thursday last week with my women - on rubbish and latrines on our Compound. Appalling flies jumping out of the latrines and, loads of rubbish decorating the bush around the dormitories. I think something may get done about it - on Saturday there seemed to be fires all over the Compound. I will have to go round and have a look at the progress. I hope that this coming week will be more routine than last - so that I can get dug into the term's classwork. Two parties in one week are too much! It looks as though there is a public holiday on Wednesday - for Mohammad's birthday. Sheila says she will come on Tuesday evening and spend Wednesday here - so that's good.

I had a letter from John this week. He received the letter written in October, after Christmas! I haven't yet written to him for Christmas. It looks as though we may miss each other in 1981. That will be a pity.

With much love to you both

Elizabeth

Vining Centre
30th January 1980

Dear Ma and Daddy,

Glad to hear in your last letter that Ma's cold is now better. How are Ruth and Trevor going to live in Derby and Trevor do a course in Hackney?

I am sending this as a quickie with Neeru - Mrs. Kohli's daughter-in-law. It is now 11.20 pm so it will be a quickie! I have spent this evening filling up the forms for a Bursary from Overseas Development. Sheila was here till 6 and Joseph came between 7& 8, so it was only after that, that I got the forms finished. It was a Public Holiday - so no classes - it was Mohammed's birthday.

Mrs. Kohli and Neeru came for lunch. Fred came for coffee. 6 Indian/ Pakistani/ Sri Lankan couples and 3 children came and drank squash around 12 noon. They were hoping to buy my car - but I have already promised it to Jumoke. I wish they would come and get it because its battery is now flat.

The first parcel of Medicine Magazine has arrived, so Joseph Kumuyi is delighted. He asked me specially to thank you for sending it on. Please keep a record of the postage - and I will pay you and claim it from him.

6.30 a.m. I have just had my breakfast, tea and toast and orange. I have scraped the last of the butter that I got in Benin at Christmas.... but, still have plenty of Ruth's marmalade so 'planta 'tomorrow will be o.k.

It's funny to have a holiday on Wednesday - today feels like Monday - but it is Thursday. I went with Sheila yesterday afternoon to see the Chairman of the Ondo State Central School's Board to ask if they would have a job for me in 1981 after my course. He said, 'Yes surely' - so, I don't think that bit would be difficult.

I want to listen to the 7 a.m. news and then get ready for Dispensary at 7.30. One rather neurotic student was taken to the hospital yesterday evening with "serious" stomach pains. Rev. Ayodele is the Men's Warden now, so he went with him in the van. I will go and see him this morning if I have time between classes. I think he is terrified of sickness and then does odd things like filling himself with someone else's tablets, which he doesn't know the name of - or dosing himself with some lethal "purge."

I hope you are both well - and it's not too cold at home.

With much love, Elizabeth

Vining Centre
3rd February 1980

Dear Ma and Daddy,

I hope you got my quickie sent on Wednesday. I received your letter posted 28th Jan on Friday 1st Feb, so that was an improvement on previous weeks. I am glad that your week of prayer for Christian Unity went well in Malvern. I don't think it went at all in Akure - at least, I heard nothing about it! Your Service in the Priory sounded an inspiring one - with symbols on a table in the middle. I wish that there could be some variety here and a bit of inspiration in the forms of Services. Our students were on the Ondo State T.V. programme tonight taking a Service - and it really seemed a washout to me - rather scratchy hymn singing with the harmonium accompaniment. The snag is that no-one has seen a high-class performance of anything on the Tele, so they don't realise how low the standard is. Anyway, it's a start and I expect that the standard will improve in time.

Not a lot to report since I wrote on Wed. I marked books on Thursday evening and typed some letters for the Leper Settlement Committee. On Friday I went to St Louis for supper - and had a chat to Martinian. Then after that went to see Mrs Sijuade. She had just returned from a family meeting in Lagos. They are 5 children - all adults.... but when their mother died their father married another woman who seems to have married him for his money and is taking more than 1/6th of the share of the property - rent on some land used by Contains company and rent on 3 houses that they own. She has even adopted a girl to whom she hopes to pass on her share .... the relatives are objecting.

The Bishop in Benin is Titus Akintayo - not Festus, but I expect that will be O.K. Thank you for writing to Mrs Harris. Joan Steward is the Principal of St Catherine's Owo. She is English and comes from Yorkshire. She came to Fiwasaiye at the same time as Sheila and is a close friend of Sheila's. She has been at Owo since about 1968.

I was the preacher at the Holy Communion Service today and I took Hebrews 12: 1-2 about the athlete on the Christian race. Parts of it went very smoothly I felt - but other sections I felt that I had not really worked them out carefully enough. After the Service, I went off to Ife to see what has happened to Jumoke and her husband who promised to come and pay for my old car last week and never showed up. It's now tomorrow, or next tomorrow! I think that they have the money now. I hope that they come soon because the battery is going flat.

I had lunch with Inga - very nice fried rice and a vegetable stew. Inga is very busy preparing for the 25th Anniversary of St Monica's, which starts next Sunday. They have a whole week of activities - plays, sports, lectures, and an Old Girls Dinner. I will go to that on the Saturday night I expect. I hope some of 'my' old girls will be there. Inga was in good form - busy making coloured bunting out of lots of pieces of cloth. It is hot now. It would be good if it would rain.

With much love to you both.

Elizabeth

Vining Centre
10th February 1980

Dear Ma and Daddy,

Thank you for your letter. I am glad that you are getting geared up for your June holidays and that you have heard from Meg Wilkes. I am trying to think how to organise my Half Term Holidays - Feb 29th to Mar 3…… one step at a time! The suggestion is that I go to Benin with Martinian who wants to go on to the Ossiomo Leprosy Settlement to see her friends there. I hope to get to Asaba to see the Mitchells and find out how they are getting on there.

I am at Ado today with Sheila - and I took their Service this morning - on "Putting on another person's shoes" (see Matt 7:12) I was happy because they listened well. It was quite an effort to get them all organised at the beginning. They are not in the habit of coming on time and bringing their bibles and song books, so Sheila and I stood at the 2 doors and refused to let anyone in until they had fetched the required books! It was worth it because it meant that they could attend better. When I was there before there was a lot of shuffling about borrowing books.

We didn't in fact ever see the Commissioner about the Leprosy land - we are going to try again. We had a good meeting on Thursday and hope to have a Leprosy Week in May. Thank you for your £1 - and that of Joan Lawrence. Please thank her for me. I will write to thank Skiddy's group in York.

Please send on the Norwich papers. I would like to see what is going on in their courses. It was the one of Development Studies that interested me most. Last week was the usual classes and evening activities - Monday lecture - Tuesday Prayer Group - Wednesday Sermon Clinic - Thursday - Leprosy Committee and Friday - Dr Kohlis for food after a 'party' to celebrate the birth of an Indian baby at St Louis. So, I had 2 suppers.

On Tuesday I sold the car for N1000 - to Jumoke.... so that was good - but I carried a can with 4 gallons of petrol in it and strained a muscle in my arm. It was very painful, and I could only drive with my left hand - and I couldn't do my hair. However, Dr Sijuade gave me some amazing tablets, which released the muscle pain very quickly - i.e., by Thursday a.m. ...... but made me feel very groggy, so I slept half the morning. I am now fine and drove to Ado without problem.

Much love,

Elizabeth

Vining Centre
17th February 1980

Dear Ma and Daddy,

Thank you for your letter of 10th Feb, which arrived on Saturday - that was good. I was happy to hear that Ruth and Co have begun to settle in Derby and that they have got most of the necessities of life in England already installed. I should think it was just as well that they left Pilsdon in January when Percy was in process of leaving too. I wonder what will happen to Pilsdon now...... It will be quite difficult to find someone to take over from Percy. I shall be interested to hear how Trevor gets on with his course interviews. Birmingham would be better than Hackney from the point of view of the family - and Trevor is not <u>that</u> good at coping without them, is he?

This week has been well occupied - on Monday night Mrs Kohli came to talk to the men of V.C. about 'Eyes' and stayed afterwards to chat about her family affairs - Rajan and Jane in particular - it seems that she and Dr Kohli pushed them to get married, because they were already living together and that the 2 of them have not been getting on very well since the marriage. This is added to by the fact that Rajan has no job and so they are living on Social Security.

On Tuesday evening we had our Prayer Fellowship in my house. I took the Subject of 'Guidance' and how to make decisions about the future. We had an interesting discussion. Taiwo is a strong believer in God speaking through dreams and Mr David felt that he was doing the right thing if he knocked his <u>left</u> foot against something when one was going out - but if it was the right foot then he would stay at home. So, we had quite a discussion on where Superstition ends, and Faith begins.

On Wednesday, I went to Ondo to the Sports held at St Monica's for the 25th Anniversary of the School. When I returned, I had supper at Mrs Kohli's house. Thursday was a day for visitors - As I was in the classroom the local clergyman drove up on his motorcycle with a scruffy note from the bishop: - To the Principal, or Miss Deeks - Prepare lunch for Rev Gordon - Cummings and Arch Olowokere. It was then 11.30 a.m. ...... a bit late notice. Mama was furious and so was I! So, I had to cut my lesson short and hurry around and make a meat loaf with yam cakes and cabbage and dodo - just about ready by 1.15 when they arrived. The English man was from Guildford Diocese - they have a special Link with Nigeria. Then at 3 p.m. Irene (Myrtle's Physiotherapist) came to stay the night - and Joseph came for supper, so we were still washing up at 10 p.m. On Friday, I was happy to be going out to St Louis for supper! Then, last night I came to Ondo and spent the night at St Monica's. It was their Old Girls Dinner followed by Traditional Dancing until 11.30 p.m. They did Nigerian dances interspersed by Dances from Sri Lanka, India, and Latvia. The archbishop was the Chairman of the whole event.

Now, today, we have the Thanksgiving Service at the end of the 25th Anniversary Celebrations. It is in Ondo Cathedral. Tod Langa the South African Principal here before Inga is here - in Nigeria on leave - she is really getting all the limelight - Inga who has served here for 17 years is rather put in the shade.

I got the C.M.S. Diaries - Thank you. I distributed them for Christmas presents.

Much love

Elizabeth

Vining Centre
24th February 1980

Dear Ma and Daddy,

The first news this week is that I have heard from Plymouth, and they have offered me a place there - and I have accepted it. So, it's all beginning to work out. The O.D.A. Bursary results will not come until May or early June, so I shall have to wait for that. I will probably stay here until August … but, haven't thought that out yet. The Term starts on Sept. 29th.

The second thing I seem to have spent a good deal of time on this past week has been sick students, or children of same. The first was a Rivers Man called Bibialaka who was constantly sick last year, and I felt that he was overanxious and psychologically sick - especially when he told me that he had been ill of this sickness since 1972, when he quarrelled with the choir master who threatened to poison him. So, I took him on Tuesday to the Psychiatric Unit. There they took a long-life history…. which helped me to see some of the problems. His first son got measles and went blind and then last year he died because there was no one to look after him properly when the father came here. His wife died in 1977 - she went fishing at night and in the morning, they brought the dead body. Nobody knows what happened - she didn't drown. So, now he has another wife who is looking after his children…. and I think he is all the time anxious about them and finding money for their feeding etc. The doctors gave him some sleeping tablets…. because he wasn't sleeping. Now he is sleeping like a block but is still not happy in himself and still talking of going home.

Then we had one child admitted who is a haemophiliac. This is unusual in Nigeria, so wasn't spotted before. When he falls, he bruises inside and must be given blood transfusions. So, I was busy appealing to our students for blood. He was given 3 pints during the week and is now discharged and much better.

On Friday, I went to Ibadan and stayed with Sam and Jose before going on to Abeokuta to the Enthronement of Bishop Akintayo. He is the one who has overseen our Lagos office for the past year. He was previously rejected at Warri. It was a grand ceremony - Awo was there in the front row. Afterwards, I tried to find Richard and his family, but failed to do so.,. I found his old house, but he has since moved - so, I was disappointed. He hasn't written for ages, so I wanted to know how he was getting on - I also wanted the loo and some food! But I went back to Ibadan instead. There, I went to Government House for a Dinner Party in honour of Tod Langa - a very nice informal evening - about 40 of us - good food - and me dressed up in one of Jose's dresses. All rather a hoot. I came back to Akure today.... and would you believe it? Found a letter from Richard in the post! One day, we shall meet again. I will write a separate card for Daddy's birthday and hope it reaches you in time.

Much love

Elizabeth

Vining Centre
2nd March 1980

Dear Ma and Daddy,

I am now sitting in the Mitchell's house in Asaba. It is in the Compound of the Bishop of Asaba - a very well-furnished house, in honour of the new C.M.S. missionaries. The people have really gone to town with lino on the floors and curtains on the windows etc.

I arrived here yesterday afternoon after spending Friday night and Saturday with Ruth in Benin. Mrs Howard is better - but still must go to the hospital for daily dressings. I don't know if I told you that she was admitted into the Teaching Hospital in Benin with a gangrenous leg - she fell at Christmas and grazed it and it seemed to have cleared up on the surface, but it suddenly flared up and had to be opened up under operation. She was lucky not to have had the leg amputated.... then she was in the hospital for 3 1/2 weeks. Ruth was busy going to and fro with food. Anyway, she now seems to be on the mend.... but yesterday fell and cut her hand in the hospital, so now has a bandaged right hand as well as a bandaged left leg.

I came to Benin with Martinian and we went together on Friday evening to the meeting of the Leprosy Relief and Control Association. They have a good enthusiastic group of people there - including Walter Ossai (this I have just discovered - I didn't meet him at the meeting.) They have a strong contingent of men - our group in Akure is rather more women. It was a good meeting. I think that I wrote to you last Sunday before I went to Fiwasaiye to take the Service. The girls listened well.... I did the Lion Hunt with them.

On Monday, Mrs Alieu came to observe the Women's classes for 2 days. I don't really think she will be able to take over as the

Women's Warden. She doesn't have enough confidence. So, it is a problem to know what will happen to the Women's training. In the afternoon I went to a "Fashion Parade" organised by the Business and Professional Women's Club in Akure but had to leave before the end to go and listen to Dr Thontteh speaking to our students about Family Planning. He was a bit disappointing I thought - didn't take the subject seriously enough. On Tuesday evening we had the first of our Lent Fellowships - at St Peters. We are taking the Theme of the Passover - the idea of release from bondage - and freedom. And that we are to daily pass-over from "The flesh" to the "spirit." On Wednesday morning at 7.30 a.m. I took the first in a series of Lent Talks on Searching for God's Power to Overcome...... (1) Temptation (2) Injustice (3) Despair (4) Fear (5) Suffering.

This last week was the 20th Anniversary of Fiwasaiye School, so there were Sports on Wednesday and 'Drama' on Thursday. I went to part of their Drama programme - from 5 to 9 p.m.! I came out halfway through and then went to see Martinian and took Joseph some bread. Sheila and Mrs Kohli came for drinks and talk - Sheila stayed the night.

The Mitchells seem to have settled down very contentedly at Asaba. The bishop is a lively character. The Mitchells have 2 foster boys - of African origin. They seem very well adjusted, but I think may get a bit 'bored' in the long run. They only plan to be here for 2 yrs. They are a very easy couple to stay with.

With much love
Elizabeth

Vining Centre
9th March 1980

Dear Ma and Daddy,

First, I want to say how sorry I am that I didn't send any birthday card for Daddy's birthday. I felt very bad on Tuesday when I realised this, because I had intended to send one the previous Sunday, and something diverted my attention. So, this one comes with my love.

In your last letter, you were with Ruth and Trevor in Derby. I am glad that they are settling in well. It will be very different from Pilsdon. I hope that Trevor manages to get a grant; maybe the TOPS thing will work out. Please thank Olive Goldsmith for the £1 given. I will put it in with the other money for the Settlement.

On Thursday we had a Leprosy Committee and planned our excursion to Ossiomo on 19th March and fixed the date for our Leprosy Week - the first week in March. It was quite a good meeting with more than 20 people there. Our Prayer Fellowship was on Tuesday - here we talked about the Last Supper and how the Church is supposed to be one family.

Mrs Kohli has been very agitated this week because she would like to go to see Rajan and Jane on her way home from Nigeria to India. She goes on April 3rd, or 6th. But there has been so much of a mix-up about the marriage, and the parents forcing them to be married - and Jane resenting this and wanting nothing to do with the Kohli's - that Mrs Kohli fears that she might upset the applecart further by visiting them. On the other hand, she has never met Jane and has such a bad opinion of her from afar that it might be better for her to know the truth by seeing them face to face. It seems to me that Jane must be a very odd person if she doesn't even want to meet her husband's mother.

Myrtle came for lunch on Saturday. She had been to Lagos to visit the Embassies there to collect some money for her School. She said that the American and British Embassies are now like fortresses in Lagos - walled around with spikes on top - metal framed doors and bars and what she suspected was bullet-proof glass. Sad……. She seemed to have had some success with the Embassy Wives groups who have promised to help them.

I preached in the Sunday Service today - on Moses and Dag Hammarskjold! How Moses was reluctant when God called him - but that God used him as a leader to take the people through the desert and to stand firm despite being surrounded by complainers and fearful people and disobedient and undisciplined people. So, we need leaders today, who say Yes to God. I was reading a book about Dag H., which is like a commentary on Markings. In 1953 when he became Secretary-General for the U.N. his book shows that he became much surer of his Christian faith and several of his 'Markings' are dwelling on the Word "Yes." The Sermon was very meaningful to me in the preparation, but I was a bit disappointed in the actual Service. I think I talked too loudly and too quickly - which can happen easily when you are half reading it. Anyway, I tried.

I must think out when I shall come home - August, I guess - but I don't know when, the beginning or end. So sorry about the birthday card. I will send a cheque, or a gift at the time of Mother's birthday.

With much love

Elizabeth

Vining Centre
16th March 1980

Dear Ma and Daddy,

Thank you for your letter of Mar 2nd and all your news - of Rod and Olive in their slippers etc. I am glad that you are enjoying the Morning-side book.

I heard this week of the sad end of Gemma's 'saga.' She must have been very upset. I also heard from Pat Hooker that Alan Galpin has died in Uganda after an operation. Dear Katie will need a lot of support in prayer. I must write to her.

I have just returned today from Ikare where I stayed last night with Myrtle. Yesterday she had the celebration of the 1st Anniversary of her School. It was a very successful event with about 30 people coming from Akure - including some of the senior officers of the Ministry of Education. I returned from Ikare via Ado where I had lunch with Sheila. I have the Reference to fill up about her proposed course in Birmingham next year - in Pastoral Studies. I am struggling to think what to say. It is difficult to confine a person to a few sentences on paper - and there are no guidelines for this.

March 23rd.

As I said in the note, which I sent via Taylor Woodrow this morning - this letter never got finished. I am so sorry! It doesn't often happen, even if it was Mothering Sunday!! I think it was arranging about going to Ossiomo Leprosarium on Wednesday that put me out. I got quite agitated about the arrangements for transport. Nothing is simple here and you can't rely on anything. Then, if you are the Secretary of an organisation you seem to get all the chores on your head. However, the visit was very successful in the end. We started off at 7.30 a.m. and reached Ossiomo by 11.30. Dr Odeghe and Sister Elizabeth showed us all round the hospital and then we had a giant lunch - provided mostly by Mrs Adinlewa's - rice and chicken - but with contributions from others too. We were about 20 people in the bus, so it was a good turn out for a weekday and the physiotherapist and the occupational therapist from the State Hospital both came with us. Dr George - our odd Egyptian Leprologist, nearly drove Martinian and I scatty because the day before he announced that he wouldn't go if his wife and 2 children didn't come too! No one wanted two squawking children, but he would not be put off. Then 2 people dropped out, so there was room for them, and we reluctantly agreed to let them come. When we were coming back to Benin, he announced - "I want to go to Mandilias and get a spare part for my car!!" No "would you mind", or "Is it far out of your way?" So, we had to waste 30 mins sitting in the hot sun while he went looking - and not finding any spare part. Very inconsiderate fellow....... continued on (2)

With much love

Elizabeth

(2) Letter continued

The trip to Ossiomo occupied the whole of Wednesday. We arrived back around 7.15 p.m. Then I went out to supper with Dr & Mrs Velev from Bulgaria - to say goodbye to Mrs Kohli. It was an entertaining evening with Dr V spinning the yarn about his times in Ethiopia, and Fred telling us about crossing the desert.

Yesterday - Saturday, Myrtle came in the afternoon, and we prepared together for my farewell party for Mrs Kohli. I invited 16 people and 14 came. Sheila didn't - she wrote a note to say she was too tired and Eyesorun didn't - I don't know why. Those who did come where Dr & Mrs Velev, Margaret & John Bond, Mr & Mrs Jain and Anita, Bro Fred & Bro Peter, Sister Martinian & Sister Philomena, Myrtle, Dr Kohli, and me. It was a happy evening and we had very good eats! Cold meat - chicken, ham, bush meat, stuffed eggs- salad - cabbage/carrot, tomato/ cucumber/onion, beans - yogurt and shrimps in white sauce, potato chips, bread, and butter. Followed by ice cream, jelly, fruit salad, and Drinks: Fruit punch, made by Fred; bottle of wine from Bonds and coffee.

Today, Mrs Kohli has given over her car to Dr Ogunleye the P.M.O. at the State Hospital. Tomorrow, she goes to Lagos to the Central bank. Next weekend she will probably move into my house until she goes on April 6th.

Myrtle and Sheila are coming here for the Easter weekend. We don't finish our term at Vining Centre until April 11th, then we have

3 weeks holiday. I hope to go to Myrtles in Ikare for part of that time. This week we had a major upset - and a disagreement in our Staff meeting over the discipline of a student who had stolen someone else's hymn book and torn 2 pages and put his own name inside. The Principal and Ayodele both decided that stealing meant expulsion - because we had expelled a soldier student last year for signing for another soldier's pay packet and taking his money. Mama and I both felt strongly that this punishment was too drastic, especially as the boy has no parents and was sent to us by the Church in Kwara. But no one would listen to us and the boy was driven out. I was so upset I couldn't teach on Friday morning. I still feel that it was wrong because it reflects a complete lack of interest in individuals among our students, by the staff.

I have not thought much about August. What about the Farncombe's cottage in late August, or early September? Richard is now in the Federal Advanced Teachers College at Abeokuta.

With much love

Elizabeth

Vining Centre
23rd March 1980

This is a "quickie" by Taylor Woodrow. It has been a busy week - and to my horror I discovered your letter - i.e., mine to you - 1/2 written last Sunday - still on my table yesterday. So, this quickie is to cover the gap! And, to send you my love and prayers for Easter. Myrtle is here today - last night we had a very happy party here to say goodbye to Mrs Kohli. Sheila didn't come - too tired, which was pity. I will write the week's news on the air letter - no time just now because the Taylor Woodrow people are leaving shortly.

With much love

Elizabeth

Vining Centre
30th March 1980

Dear Ma and Daddy,

Thank you for your letter and the Easter card received this week. Amazing to hear that it was posted in snow. We could do with a little here - it is sticky - although we have had some rain.

I have been in Akure this weekend - and some of the time has been spent helping Mrs Kohli to pack up. She is very well organised and so it has been easy. We had a special Leprosy Committee on Friday to say goodbye to her. She goes off to Lagos tomorrow but will still have to come back once more to remit her money through the bank in Akure. She is having to postpone her departure by about 2 weeks, because of getting her money cleared out of the country.

Sheila has heard that she is not successful in getting an O.D.A. Award, so maybe there is some chance of my getting a Bursary - at least I haven't been refused in the first batch. Sheila came on Thursday, briefly, and I was quite anxious for her - she was so "taut" and tense and very tired. I hope she will come here for a break over Easter and be able to sleep.

I am feeling pretty end-of-term now. We finish on 11th April, so this coming week is the Exam week for the women, as well as being Holy Week. I hoped to complete my exam papers over this weekend, but I haven't. However, I have made some progress and our typist is very quick. I got stuck into Forsyth's book called "The Devil's Alternative" - it's a novel based on the relationships between the super-powers.... and how hijackers can hold the whole world ransom.

Did I tell you that Archdeacon Banjo has died? I read it in the paper some time ago and meant to cut it out, but I don't think I did. Our Service today was supposed to be on the Radio - 'live' - so, a great van called Mobile Unit came at 8.30 a.m. and set itself up. The congregation was in good time and sang the first hymn with great gusto. Then the van drove off....... technical fault. So, we were not broadcast, after all. They must have put something else on at the last minute. Next year, I will be in England for Spring and Easter. All being well!

Much love

Elizabeth

Vining Centre

5th April 1980

Dear Ma and Daddy,

Thank you for your last letter – received on Easter Saturday – yesterday. Myrtle and Sheila are both here with me which is very nice – but it is a pity that we don't finish our term till next week because it is difficult to keep your mind on entertaining friends and at the same time to be marking exam papers and thinking about reports and the Commissioning Service. Mrs Kohli is also around – with her mind on her arrangements for going away – either today or tomorrow.

I have just read a book that you must get – buy it if you see it – I'll give it to you for your birthday. It is called 'Blessings' by Mary Craig. It is a very moving book but shows clearly how she overcomes her sufferings. She is also the writer of the book about the new Pope – 'Man from a far country'.

This morning at 4 am our students got up and went out singing in the town -the men went out and the women stayed behind and sang outside the Chapel where they have an 'empty tomb' – a large coffin shaped box covered in white cloths with 'a figure' in a white surplice beside it. The tomb is impressive but I was not quite so keen on the figure which looked a bit like a scarecrow.

The week has been uneventful really – exams on Mon. Tues. Wed. Then we had a Leprosy Settlement Committee to prepare for our Leprosy Week (May 5-9th) Please pray for that – now I am not 'feeling' like doing all the running about needed to get it going – but it is just the end of term feeling, I think.

April 14th.

Oh dear! I got diverted from finishing the letter – must have been the end of term – and visitors etc.......... Very sorry. I am now at Auchi staying the night with Thankanma and Mary – I came here yesterday with Myrtle. It is lovely to have a break and to be in a completely different environment. Mrs Kohli went on Wednesday and Myrtle too. Sheila stayed till Friday which was the first day of my holidays. I spent most of Friday and Saturday doing things for the Leprosy Week. Then on Sunday morning I preached at 8 am at St Thomas' Church before tidying up my house and getting off to Ikare to meet Myrtle.

I read Corrie ten Boom – 'The Hiding Place' this week. Here we are relaxing – reading and doing jigsaws. Now we are preparing to go on a picnic at Ososo before returning to Ikare.

Much love,

Elizabeth

Vining Centre
19th April 1980

Dear Ma and Daddy,

I think you may have had a long gap with no letters – sorry oh! This is a Taylor Woodrow quickie.

I came back from Ikare on Wednesday and have been planning for the Leprosy Week since then. I am enclosing some of our publicity for the week.

Today we had a visit from Donald Mason- he is here on a month's visit sponsored by his Old Students. He is going to preach tomorrow here at Vining Centre

It is hot in the afternoons now. 90 degrees F in my sitting room – so I am dying to go for a swim at the T.W. Pool!

Thank you for your letter about Easter Celebrations and the enclosed BRF. They have been good recently on the Psalms.

When I came back on Wednesday, I discovered that the principal had dumped several lorryloads of sand just behind my house and that 6 noisy students were to be there making cement blocks with a hand machine that goes Bang! Bang! I was really put out. The compound is so big. WHY choose my house to set up a racket in the holidays? When I complained Fabuluje said that the next sand would be put elsewhere – but they have 3 lorry loads to get through yet!

I am planning to go to Ibadan and Lagos tomorrow afternoon – (Lagos on Monday) – to meet the new man in our Lagos office – Rev Odukoya. I may go by Abeokuta and see Richard there.

All the schools end their holidays this weekend so most people are going back to work. I have 2 more weeks which is good because it means I have time to go up and down about our Leprosy Week. We have printed 500 invitations for the play so there is quite a lot of work getting them out.

Much love to you both,

Elizabeth

Vining Centre
21st April 1980

Dear Ma and Daddy,

I am now reading your Easter Air letter again in Bishop Akintayo's house in Abeokuta. I came here today en route for Lagos. It is a lovely comfortable house with all modern conveniences – e.g., plenty of fans and mosquito netted rooms. This morning I had breakfast with the archbishop – now in the evening I am staying with a Bishop!! In between I got hot and sweaty in Ibadan – going shopping and getting a driving licence and getting stuck in traffic jams. When I reached Abeokuta, I went to see Richard at his College and he took me home to his wife and family – loads of children all around. I had some lunch with them and then he brought me to the Bishop's Court. Abeokuta is a rambling town and it's very easy to get lost.

Donald Mason was in Akure last week – at the invitation of his Christ's School Old Boys Association. He preached at Vining Centre Chapel on Sunday morning – a very moving sermon – very well thought out. It was a good example of a sermon, but I think our students might not have understood how good it was.

I am sorry that you found the Good Friday > Easter celebrations druidic in parts. One certainly wonders what the Lord Jesus – Carpenter of Nazareth would say about His Church in the 20th century.

It is now Tuesday evening, and I am still in Lagos. I came this morning from from Abeokuta and got here around 9.15 am. I was then able to meet the new man in the Office – Rev Odukoya. He has been a Chartered Accountant before and seemed to me to be very efficient. Unfortunately, Mr. Oni the '2nd' who has always been there is not happy and feels that he hasn't had enough housing allowance etc and is now saying that he will resign. That would be a pity because he knows all the ropes here.

When I reached here, I found that Grace was staying here – so I decided not to go back straight away as I had planned but to stay the night and keep her company here. We went to the Ikoyi hotel pool and had a swim and then went to see Olu and Marie Ogunlami – the couple whose children stay with the Mayo's in the holidays – they are at school in England. Then we came back here for supper. I will have an early night tonight because I will have to get up about 5.30 am to escape out of Lagos before 6 am. My car is a Tuesday – Thursday car (according to the number plates). It's N100 fine if you are on the wrong days. Lagos has lots of flyovers and skyscrapers these days - and the cars drive very fast.

The Tele is on just now – snow stormy

Much love to you both,

Elizabeth

Vining Centre
27th April 1980

Dear Ma and Daddy

I seem to have finished my air letters and my notepaper - so will have to use this. Your letter of April 13th is my latest from you. I am glad that you got your spectacles replaced in the old frame very satisfactorily. Myrtle left hers in the 'Peacock Club' in the Eko Hotel in Lagos – and had to get a new pair. The cheapest ones here are 60 - 70 naira.

I think you will have received my air letter written in Lagos. I got up at the crack of dawn on Wednesday – alarm 5.30 – jumped out of bed – put on clothes – drank coffee – picked up bags and got into the car and hurried out of Lagos.... over the fly overs with others also running to get 'out' onto the Ikorodu Road before 6 am. My new car number starts with a 6 so it can only travel inside Lagos on Tuesdays and Thursdays! - or before 6 a.m! on other days. All was well, but I was anxious not to be late because the fine is N100! I reached Akure by 11 am after stopping for a short break with Inga in Ondo.

On Thursday I had a very frustrating morning chasing Martinian around the town because I needed the papers and invitations for Leprosy Week that she had, and she was busy delivering her own all over the place. On the same evening we had a rotten Leprosy Committee meeting because Dr Sijuade rushed everything through, hadn't read the Minutes, hurt people's feelings by changing who should do what and behaved like a spoilt schoolboy. His name was written on our proposed programme - and he wants all the limelight. Everyone felt disheartened afterwards and we didn't really make several detailed decisions that we should have. We are quite well ahead with our publicity – now we hope people will turn up to the events. I spent a good deal of time on Friday writing invitations and getting them distributed.

On Saturday I went to Ikare in the morning and went with Myrtle, Gwen, and Meg to Oka for a picnic lunch. We sat on the rocks at the top of the hill by the Oka Rest House and looked over the most glorious view. It was Myrtle's birthday, so this was our celebration. Some local boys came round to 'look at us' and help in raising 'cheers' for Myrtle's birthday. I came back to Akure in the evening.

Today, Sunday it has rained – a rain we have been waiting for for the past few days, so it is cool and overcast. I started to sort out some junk in a trunk – so that I can give some things for our Sale in Leprosy Week. Then I tried to sort some books- but the trouble is that you start to read them! Last night I drafted a reference for Fabuluje to send to the O.D.A for the Bursary Application so we are making progress. This time I am a 'kind lady'!

Much love to you both,

Elizabeth

Vining Centre
1st May 1980

Dear Ma & Daddy

What a pity that I can't come over for your birthday next Friday, especially as it's your 70th. We shall have to celebrate when I come home. I have said the last week in July - i.e., 28, 29, or 30th, so far for coming home, so we shall be able to celebrate in August. I am not sure if I should offer to do some Link Visits in September. I haven't done so yet, but I am thinking that it might be better to do a few Links this year so that I don't have an overdose next year. I have no plans, so far, for August - stay in Malvern will be item 1 - go and see Ruth and Trevor and a Co, must also be included. Have a lovely Birthday! Please spend the £10 on something you would like - as well as need.

Mama Ademoye says it's such a pity that England is so far, because otherwise I could roast a chicken and put some nice jollof rice inside! But she felt it would get bad before it reached you!

The enclosed letter is for distribution - when you can do it, including one for C.M.S. as usual. I have typed it myself. I hope it's good enough to go directly to the Duplicating lady.

We start term tomorrow. I have been having an almighty turn out today - tearing up papers etc. to be ready for the new term. Next week will be busy because it's 'Leprosy Week' as well as the first week of term. I am on a Radio Discussion Panel on Saturday morning!

With much love

Elizabeth

Vining Centre
4th May 1980

Dear Ma & Daddy,

Thank you for your letter telling of Mother's visit to Derby and that Trevor is suddenly off to Slough. It's good that he has got started on the Course. It will be lovely to see the children again, a year older. I can imagine that Robert will love school.

The N.C.W. is the organisation that Eyesorun belongs to, here in Nigeria. She is one of the big notches in it and has travelled overseas to represent Nigeria. I have been to one of their meetings here .... not quite up to the style of Malvern Theatre, I guess.

I wrote to you on Thursday with Ma's birthday card - so there is not a lot of news since then. One Filippino (American) Millionaire came here this afternoon talking about setting up a 'development group' of some sort. I think to do a kind of Community Development Project and bring in volunteers to man it. He seemed to think that I might like to be in on it .... and maybe become a full-time worker at N 15, 000 per annum! if I heard him right. All a bit mind boggling - the funny thing was that he talked to Martinian this morning after Mass, and he said she was interested in the whole thing. When I saw her later, she said she couldn't understand what he was on about! I think he really wants some introductions to people to discuss his ideas. He has big contacts with W.C.C. and organisations in America...... but is basically a businessman.

I went to speak this morning at the Federal Polytechnic. They have just started having their own service - an inter-denominational one. It was a group of about 40 students - all a bit late in starting and slow in singing, but nevertheless a worthwhile effort. This evening, we have been to the Settlement for our usual Open-Air Service at the beginning of the term.

We start our term tomorrow - a cleaning day. Lessons begin on Tuesday. There is only one new student, so far - there are supposed to be 3 from Immanuel College, so I don't know where the others have got to.

It is Leprosy Week starting tomorrow - I shall be glad when it's over! Four of us had a discussion on O.S.B.C. yesterday morning. It was rather impromptu, and we had to do it all ourselves. Last time they gave us a question master, and it was much better because he was an expert and took the lead. Anyway, we tried as they say.

I got forms this week for applying to Ondo State as a teacher in 1981. They can interview me before I come home, which will be useful. I shall be thinking of you especially, on May 9th.

Much love,

Elizabeth

Vining Centre
11th May 1980

Dear Ma and Daddy,

I was thinking of you a lot on Friday when it was your Birthday and I hope that you had an enjoyable Celebration with Stuart and Jutka in Hackney. Friday was the best day of the Leprosy week as far as I was concerned - we had what we called ‘presentation of Gifts’ at the Settlement and it was a great success. The Commissioner of Health came - which was a surprise to me because he was at the Play on Monday representing the Governor who didn’t come. So, it was super to have him at the Settlement too. Then there was a good turnout of the Committee members, representatives of C.U.S.O. and representatives from Oka, Owo and Ondo. It was very encouraging. They brought secondhand clothes, or gifts of soap, milk etc. etc or cash collected. Some N 20, some N50 and some N100. Then everyone went round the Settlement and looked at the Crafts etc. It was a real ‘open day’ and significant because it has never happened before - most people are happy to give donations - But, NOT to show up at the Settlement.

The Play on Monday was also a good Event. The invitees did not show up as we had hoped, but again Schools came in groups - different schools from Friday and we had a hall full of 500 - 600 people. The Play was about the boat of life and how all the handicapped people were kept off until everyone had argued a lot about it and then it was agreed that they had their part to play and so should be allowed on. The Commissioner of Health gave us N 800 in donations. During the week, including the money given on Friday, we collected another N1,600 and I think we shall get over N4,000 in the end. I went to the Mobil Petrol Station yesterday and the Manager there gave me N100!! So, it was all very encouraging - although at the beginning of the week, Martinian and I were praying for the end! The Sale and Funfair on Wed. was the least successful - the Jumble realised N 400, which was amazing, because there didn’t seem to be many people buying. The Funfair was disappointing because schools didn't come - there was a Careers Exhibition on at the same time, which hijacked them, I think.

The T.V. and Radio came up trumps in the end - after a good deal of palavering. The result was a T.V. discussion, 2 Radio discussions (one in English, one in Yoruba) and a radio 'Hospital Requests' - 1 hour programme, with the patients discussing and choosing the music they would like. Then on Thursday, I went to Fed. Girls Sch. with Dr Adetunji, to talk to them. He gave a brilliant lecture illustrated with slides and they asked lots of questions. So, all in all we felt that it was worthwhile. As you can see, it was a busy week - the first week of Vining Centre Term was going on at the same time, so all these extras were superimposed on the normal activities.

Martinian goes on leave in 2 weeks' time. I will miss her a lot. She came here for supper last night with Sister Philomena - to celebrate the end of Leprosy Week.

Much love

Elizabeth

Vining Centre
18th May 1980

Dear Ma & Daddy,

The last letter I have from you is written on May 4th. I am looking forward to getting the next one to hear how you got on, on your Birthday. I hope that you had a happy celebration in Hackney. Oh dear! I see from the bottom of your letter that I am too late to remember their birthdays this month. Perhaps, I can get a card off today and it won't be too late.

This week, I have been trying to get into the swing of the term at Vining Centre - and have succeeded well…. the women now have wool and materials for their handicrafts, so they can get cracking. Myrtle returned from Lagos on Wednesday. They had parked the car outside a Shopping Centre near Ikoyi and gone to get an ice-cream. When they returned, everything inside the car had gone - Irene's camera and N350 - all their clothes - bags - shoes - passport - papers - address book etc etc. They came back in other people's clothes. The police said they couldn't understand why the thieves had not taken the car as well - that at least was a mercy. Irene particularly was very angry/ upset - Myrtle was sad/ upset. Really rotten …. but they say that there are loads of thieves around - especially in Lagos.

Sheila came here yesterday. She has been accused of taking illegal fees from her girls, because their P.T.A. agreed to collect N40 each for development. Apparently, they did it wrong because Sheila was spending the money - not the P.T.A. and they collected it through the schoolgirls and it's against the Government's free education policy. Sheila collected about N16, 000. She was told this week that she is to pay it all back. So, now she will have to write 400 cheques for about N 40 each and return them - the money will come from the Govt. Grant for building a Library …. they will have to do without the library. Very upsetting - because she tried so hard to do it right and now, she is in trouble.

On Wednesday, I went with 3 others from the Leprosy Committee to the Town Planning Ministry to see if they could suggest any alternative site for the Leper Settlement - near to Akure. We discovered when we reached there that the Ministry of Health had already written asking for a piece of land 200 acres in area where they would not have to pay compensation - so, a piece has been suggested about 20m North of Ikare - right away in the bush, off a dirty road!! So much for all the progress in trying to get people to accept leprosy patients. Martinian and I want to try and meet the Commissioner on the matter before she goes on leave, to see what can be done.

With much love

Elizabeth

Vining Centre

25th May 1980

Dear Ma and Daddy,

I have your letter of 11th May - letters seem to be taking the best part of 2 weeks just now. I wonder if this one will reach you before you go off to Scotland on your holiday. Please greet all friends up there. Martinian has left Akure today and will be in London tomorrow night. She promised to phone you and wish you a happy birthday from me. I hope she does it. I think she will. I am going to miss her a lot in the next few months - especially after Myrtle goes too (June 11th). Myrtle was here Thur. Fri. and Sat. nights this week, so that was nice. She had a cold and was tired, so was able to recover. She came down from Ikare on Thursday after being summoned on Wed. by an official letter to attend a Presentation in the Permanent Secretary's office at 11 a.m. She had to miss her own Parent Teacher Meeting and last day of Term to come down and when she got there at 10.10, they had already done the presentation without her. It was N50 from some local Church group - so, she felt rather cheesed off by the whole aff I had a busy week, which was: Monday evening - Lecture on Iran to students; Tues -Prayer fellowship; Wed - Sermon clinic; Thursday - Leper Settlement Committee; Friday - Farewell to Deany Kemp from Taylor Woodrow. I got back from that about 10.30 p.m. (Myrtle didn't come because of her cold) and found that it was the S.U. prayer meeting night. They were singing, clapping, organ playing - they also had a Shouting man and a Screaming woman up till 12 midnight. I don't know if they were casting out the devil, or what - terrible noise. I didn't sleep at all. Around 1 a.m. I moved my mattress into the living room, drank some cocoa and took some aspirin and tried to sleep - not so near the noise.... but mosquitoes then came and bit my fingers - so, I then climbed up on my bedstead and got my mosquito net down and draped it over some chairs and tried again - not very successful. Around 2 a.m. I heard cars go out, so I returned all my things to the bed and lay down hopefully, but someone had waited behind and was practising all sorts of variations on the organ. At 2.30 a.m. I got out in my car and told them to shut up and clear off!! I really got very angry and felt thoroughly anti "Christian." And I felt dragged up all morning on Saturday. Only today do I feel back to normal again.

Last night, Myrtle and I went to St Louis for supper. Gorgeous chocolate cake with butter icing to say goodbye to Martinian.

Myrtle and I have written to St Julians to find out if they have any room for us for a long weekend - Aug 15th. Apart from that, I have nothing fixed. Sept 6 for a week sounds great.

Much love to you both
Elizabeth

Vining Centre
31st May 1980

Dear Ma and Daddy,

Nice to get your 'interrupted gardening' letter this week. I hope this reaches you before you go off to Scotland. I can't quite remember when you plan to go. Will you go near Moffat on the way up? Are you going by road, car, or train? Anyway, Mrs. Howard would be very happy to give you a cuppa en route, I'm sure. Please give my love to Meg in Edinburgh

I am staying with Sheila this W/E in Ado. She has had a lot of trouble, because the Parent Teachers Association agreed to levy themselves N 40 each and the Ministry of Education have declared it an illegal collection of fees and so, Sheila has had to pay it all back. Now the Commissioner of Education wants to interview representatives of the schoolgirls - All very troublesome. Sheila is going to Birmingham to do the Pastoral Studies Course. She wrote to Crowther to see if there was any room there - but there is none. Any ideas? She really wants to be in a hall, or a residence and not digs.

The most dramatic thing this week happened on Thursday afternoon, when one of the women misjudged her labour and came to me in the last stages. I had a ghastly drive to the hospital with a screaming woman and a bloody mess in my car. At the hospital, she was yanked onto the delivery table with the baby already coming out - legs first. Mercifully, the baby survived. The mother is O.K. too, but bled a lot and so, wasn't discharged the next day, as usual. I was really annoyed that she left it so late - it could have been disaster. She had been in labour since the previous evening but hadn't let on to anyone.

Margaret Bond is left at the Leprosy Settlement - with Dr George. She works at the patients' dressings and distributing rice, beans etc. He sleeps in his car! Sometimes, he attends to a few patients. He really is not an asset. We miss Martinian. I hope that she was able to phone you from London.

Myrtle went to Lagos for her concerts on Tuesday and came back on Wednesday, so it was good to see her on her way through each time. I will go to Ikare next weekend, June 8th - it is my Half Term and Myrtle's last weekend before going on leave. Margaret and I met the 6 Leprosy officers for Ondo State on Thursday and discussed with them the possibilities of having branches of the Leprosy Committee in each of their towns.

I have started to knit a sweater - or cardigan rather, it's fine wool - you can't get thick in Akure. I have tried to calculate the pattern, so that it fits despite the different wool. It is red.

Sunday night - I have just returned from Ado to discover that another woman delivered last night - 4 a.m....... so, am glad I was away in Ado. I have the job of planning the Sermon outlines for the Mission in Benin Diocese in July. This week I will be lecturing the men on that.

Much love to you both

Elizabeth

Vining Centre

10th June1980

Dear Ma and Daddy

A rotten week for post. I think something must be holding up the works. I can always tell if something is wrong if the Guardian doesn't come reasonably regularly. Except that I think there is something the matter with the newspaper people too - the Guardian is on ordinary paper and not on airmail paper. So, they must have a Strike, or something. (a lot of 'somethings' in this paragraph - I don't really think my English is up to doing a Course in teaching English to others!!)

I am sitting in Myrtle's flat at Ikare - it is cool and airy. So cool that I have my cardigan on. It rained cats and dogs last night and so today is quite chilly as a result. Myrtle is leaving here tomorrow so; she has been busy doing her last minute clearing up. She seems to be very well organised - but gets in a tizzy every now and then. I am sure that I shall be much worse in July. I must get something organised about a helper. I may ask Tokunbo if he can come and help me to pack. He is quiet and efficient.

It is our Half Term Holiday - Friday and Monday - so, I have been here at Ikare for 3 nights - Thurs > Sunday. I have really done nothing except knit and read Ngaio Marsh and potter into the town a couple of times. It has been very relaxing for me. Myrtle's Susanna is around to do most of the household chores and Gwen was here for a week last week and she helped Myrtle to pack up, so most of that is already done. We are both going out for lunch today with the St Louis Sisters - Francis and Agnes. Both were in Akure for a time, so I know them well, too.

I went to Ondo on Wednesday during the week and stayed the night with Inga. We had a good long chinwag. I came back to Akure in the morning before 7.30 a.m. in time for my Dispensary. Inga still has Bunmi with her, and she is still not happy in St Monica's. I think she could do with a break. It would be good if she could go to Canada and get a job there where she is near to her cousins. She has a lot of anxieties about her staff. One Sri Lankan man came about 2 years ago with his cousin - a woman - and they shared a house - but the "cousin" turns out to be a girlfriend! `Now, his wife and 2 boys have come from Ceylon and so he moved across the Compound into another house - but he still goes and 'visits' his "cousin" and his wife is miserable. To add to the complication, at Easter time the girlfriend was married secretly to another Sri Lankan - a friend of the man's who works in Bauchi, but she didn't go to the North with him - she is still carrying on with the husband. What a tangle!

Yesterday, Myrtle and I went to visit a man here in Ikare who is paralysed from the waist down. He was ordained at Immanuel College and 3 months later had a road accident in which his back was broken. He was then in Igbobi Hospital in Lagos for 3 years and Pat Green visited him there. Now, he has been on his bed 15 years. He is amazingly cheerful and Myrtle says very well adjusted to this handicap……. but he rarely gets out and he doesn't do anything. Myrtle is hoping that he may be able to get to her school in a wheelchair. His wife is a nurse, and they have 3 children, but she has just left him. Sad.

Monday evening: Myrtle is now with me in Akure, and we have just had supper. She is sorting letters and I am finishing this to you. I have started to sort out a cupboard today - took a long time with not much result. In the afternoon, I went to the Taylor Woodrow pool and had a nice swim; and then washed my hair afterwards in the Bond's hot water. Margaret had lost all the keys at the Settlement, so she was on a 'hunt the keys' campaign. Keys are a nuisance when they go astray.

I then went to the Velev's to get some yoghurt culture, because mine has died. Dr Velev was to have gone on leave to Bulgaria, but they have lost his file in the Health Management Board, so he can't make any progress with plans for going on leave! Sheila had to come and see the Commissioner of Education again today, so I saw her briefly - Two of her girls wrote very rude anonymous letters to the Commissioner, so the fat was really in the fire.

You must be in Scotland as I am writing this - or on your way. I hope that everything works out well and that you are all able to get a real holiday. I can just imagine you having a great time of nostalgia at Strachur and in Morningside.

My cat has got the fidgets and wants to sit on Myrtle's lap, which is covered in papers and letters. She is just like Sailor, if you are doing anything like writing, or knitting she is bound to want to get in the way.

No news yet of date of flight. I will let you know as soon as I hear anything. One baby is admitted today - a week old child who vomits everything she sucks and cries on stooling. I don't know what that can be.

I must go and wash up the dishes. We had a good supper - meat and kidney stew - potatoes - cabbage - okra in tomato followed by milk jelly and coffee. Very English, really.

With much love to you both.

Elizabeth

Vining Centre
15th June 1980

Dear Ma and Daddy,

I am imagining you all in Scotland, and hope that you are having a good time and that the weather is fine, so that you can get out and about. The C.M.S. Regional Conference at Derby Sept 12 - 14th sounds a good idea. Can you book me a place? Is Alison going, or anyone else I know, or are you thinking of going?

Myrtle left here on Tuesday. She said she would phone you - but I expect you will be in Scotland. I asked her to make a dentist appointment for me - early August, if possible, because I have broken about 4 fillings and I am just hoping that they will hold together until I get home! You can just walk into the dentist here and get seen on the same day.... but I hear that the machine with the drill that sprays water isn't working well and the water is not coming through, so it becomes like a red-hot poker! Mrs Thontteh went last week and got a badly burnt mouth.... so, I am not keen to go there unless I am forced.

This week, I saw Tokunbo and negotiated with him to come for a few hours each week to help me to prepare to clear up. I think that will solve my problems and get me moving on the packing before the last minute.

Concerning arrival - I agree that the Reading way sounds the best. If I come on a daylight flight (I hope to, because I get so tired after a night flight) then, I doubt if I can get to Reading by 6 p.m. It is more likely to be the last train at 20.50. Perhaps, you can organise for that to be met at Worcester. It is nice to be met at Heathrow - but, perhaps Stuart, or Gemma could do that and put me on the coach for Reading and then you would not have the expense, or the bother of journeying.... on the other hand, if you want to come, do.

Doesn't Aunt Marjorie have room for even one visitor? Funny set up. It's a great big house. I can take 2 visitors here and my house would fit into her sitting room, I guess. I have an interview next Thursday with the Ondo State School's Board. I also have the Board of Governors send-off here in the Vining Centre on the same day. I am not sure how the two are going to be fitted in together. I was in Ondo yesterday and Ado today, with Sheila - and hope to be in Benin with Ruth next weekend. I am lonely here without Martinian and Myrtle popping in.

Much love,

Elizabeth

Vining Centre
15th June 1980

Dear Ma and Daddy,

I am very sorry that no letter got written last weekend. I was going to write on Sunday a.m. in Benin and put it off to the evening when I was back in Akure - Then, just as I got home, I discovered that Margaret Bond was admitted in Sijuade's Private Hospital and John wants me to go and baby-sit.... while he took the supper to the hospital - and at the same time, Sheila arrived from Ado to stay the night - so, letter writing got pushed off the agenda.

Now, I have 3 letters from you in Scotland. This seems to have been the week for post - your 3 letters, one from Ruth Wood, one from Ruth Martin and one from Jutka - and 3 Manchester Guardians. I have also heard from the O.D.A that they have not awarded me any Bursary - rotten lot! So, C.M.S. will have to pay for everything. I must write and tell them so.

I tried to phone to Lagos this week to find out about my ticket. I was frustrated in the effort. My phone will ring out, so I can get the exchange in Akure - they then book the call, if they can - usually, the trunk lines are out of order - then if they ring me back, my phone doesn't ring - it only rings in the Principal's house - but, during the day he is usually out and the house empty and shut and in the evening his children are quite capable of sabotaging the phone by picking it up - saying they will come for you - and then putting the receiver down so that the Call is cut off!! The upshot is that I don't know yet on which day I am coming. I have a plan to travel with Sheila, if possible - we want to book on the same flight… but, until I hear from Lagos what they have booked, I can't get Sheila's ticket booked in the travel agent in Akure. If we come by K.L.M. - which is the one that has discount from Lagos- then we may arrive about 8 p.m. at night - either on Tues, or Fri. If that is so, it will not be possible to get to Malvern on the same day, so maybe I should go to Gemma's and come the next day - and you don't need to come up to London at all. I will let you know as soon as I know, so that you can organise it at your end.

It is good to hear all your news from Scotland - it sounds as though you have had a good time and seen a lot off old friends. I am glad that you were able to see your old haunts in Morningside while you were at Meg Wilkes flat.

Sunday evening - back in Akure. Margaret Bond is to go for a barium meal X-ray - she may have a duodenal Ulcer. I have also discovered that I am booked for 29th July (Tues) on KL 580 to Amsterdam leaving Lagos at 11.15 a.m. I'll find out when the connection arrives at Heathrow - but I think it is around 8 p.m. as I said earlier. Sheila is coming from Ado on Tuesday - then I will know if she thinks she can be ready by the Tuesday. But plan towards that day. I'll tell you if there is any change. Goody, Goody!!

With much love to you both

Elizabeth

Vining Centre
15th July 1980

Dear Ma & Daddy,

No letters this week - nothing from U.K. at all - whereas last week there was a lot. I should think that this will be my last letter to reach you at home before I do. The last few weeks seem to have flown past and there is a lot to do yet before I am sorted and ready to depart.

This past week has been 3 days of exams and then 2 days of hard work - sorting - cleaning - and chucking out from Vining Centre Women's stores. There are still some remnants of the 1930's! I have also given a lot of Christian books to the library - and I hope to reduce my books further by giving another lot to St Louis Sisters. I have 4 bookcases full of books! - and I don 't really need most of them. It will be relatively easy to pack up if I am lighter in books.

Some of my women did quite well in the exams - others don't seem to have learnt anything - very depressing. I am glad that I am going to have a break from them - I really get very scratchy at the end of term and my patience runs thin. I am sorry that there is no-one to hand over to because Mama Ademoye won't be able to cope on her own.

All the men staff and the students are away in Benin. So, the women have been taking the Services each day - they have done well - but, of course, congregations have been a bit thin. The men return tomorrow and then we have our Commissioning Service on Tues. It is going to be a rush for them - but I am further ahead with my reports and Certificates etc. than I have ever been.

I am looking forward to July 29th - especially seeing you and hearing all the crack. KL141 arr 20.00! It will be the European terminal - not the International. I haven't double checked that its Heathrow. I hope so! It should be.

With much love
Elizabeth

At College of St Mark and St John in Plymouth

Students on the course

I went to Plymouth in October 1980 to study for a Diploma in Education (English Language Teaching) This meant that I would be better qualified to teach our men students as well as the women at the Vining Centre. It was a very interesting and challenging course. There were 14 people on the course who were mostly Africans. There were 2 men and 2 women from Tanzania, a man and a woman from Togo and others from Malawi and Cameroons. The Europeans apart from myself were a fellow from Manchester who had taught in RAF schools in Cyprus and Malta and a Polish girl who had been teaching in a centre for Immigrants in Bradford.

I stayed in the student's hostel and my room looked out over Plymouth to the sea. I got involved a bit with the college chapel services and on Saturdays often went walking locally or along the Cornish cliff path.

The timetable included a variety of classes on things like – teaching oral and written English as well as teaching reading and phonetics and then psychology with much on Language and Linguistics and Language in Society. There were regular essays to write. For example:

1. The difficulties of knowing what is 'correct' in English.
2. The sociolinguistic factors that should be taken into account in preparing a syllabus for EFL teaching.
3. Teaching pronunciation of English – especially stress and intonation.

We also had to write a long essay of 10,000 words. My chosen topic was The Development of Pidgin English in Nigeria and some problems that this poses for the teacher of English as a Second Language. I still have a copy of this essay. It meant that I had to read widely on the subject and I was very pleased to be given 'A' for my effort. I was also pleased and astounded to receive a letter from the Principal of the College in July 1981which said:

Dear Elizabeth,

When the final list for the ELT marks came to Academic Board yours were all an A grade. This is the highest result we have ever had at the College and I would like to congratulate you on behalf of the Academic Board on your excellent work, and to thank you for the very valuable contribution to the life of the College during the past year.

Many thanks and our best wishes for the future.

Yours sincerely,

J.E. Anderson.

Principal

The other interesting thing that was part of that course was that we had to go on a teaching placement. I went for 2 weeks to teach English to Vietnamese Boat People who had come to UK as refugees and were in a camp on Thorney Island to learn English. There were about 700 of them but they were divided into small classes of different abilities. I taught one class of illiterate beginners when I was there. My work with the women in the Vining Centre helped with that.

My Closing Postscript

The whole Diploma course was important in preparing me for the next stage of my work in the Vining Centre when I returned to Akure in September 1981. I remained teaching in Vining Centre until December 1990 and you can read the letters covering my varied experiences during this period in Volume 3.

My Story in Photographs

Vining Centre

Signpost to Vining Centre

Outside my house with Yemi

The Principal's house Vining Centre

Women in Vining Centre

Children's Creche in Vining Centre

Students outside the Old Chapel

Leaving chapel on Sunday

The Oba's Palace

The Eyesorun of Akure

The Bamgboye Family in Ife

The Akure Leprosy Settlement

Leprosy Settlement

A typical house at the Leprosy Settlement

Leprosy Patients

The Head man outside the doctor's clinic

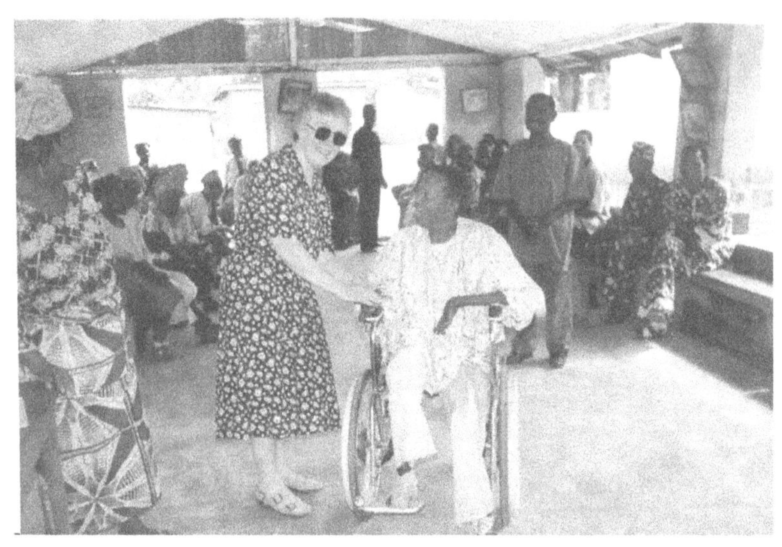

Sister Martinian at Settlement

Compiled by the WLTF Literary Agency
www.winstonfordebooks.com

Lightning Source UK Ltd.
Milton Keynes UK
UKHW020753031222
413248UK00011B/314